S0-ACK-702

WITHDRAWN

Aid to African Agriculture

A World Bank Book

Aid to African Agriculture

Lessons from Two Decades of Donors' Experience

Uma Lele
EDITOR

Published for the World Bank
The Johns Hopkins University Press
Baltimore and London

Manufactured in the United States of America
First printing April 1992

The Johns Hopkins University Press
Baltimore, Maryland 21211, U.S.A.

The complete backlist of publications from the World Bank is shown in the annual *Index of Publications,* which contains an alphabetical title list and indexes of subjects, authors, and countries and regions. The latest edition is available free of charge from Publication Sales Unit, Department F, The World Bank, 1818 H Street, N.W., Washington, D.C. 20433, U.S.A., or from Publications, The World Bank, 66 avenue d'Iéna, 75116 Paris, France.

Library of Congress Cataloging-in-Publication Data

Aid to African agriculture : lessons from two decades of donors' experience / Uma Lele, editor.
p. cm.
"Published for the World Bank."
Includes bibliographical references and index.
ISBN 0-8018-4366-9
1. Agricultural assistance—Africa, Sub-Saharan. 2. Economic assistance—Africa, Sub-Saharan. 3. Agriculture—Economic aspects—Africa, Sub-Saharan. I. Lele, Uma J.
HD2117.A37 1991 91-38842
338.1'8—dc20 CIP

Contents

Foreword

THIS VOLUME, *Aid to African Agriculture,* is the first full-length book to be published in a series of documents emanating from research into managing agricultural development in Africa (MADIA). Over the past five years, however, a large number of MADIA working papers have been widely disseminated and discussed. The MADIA study and the papers that have been published are important both for their content and for the process of diagnosis and analysis used in the conduct of the study. The MADIA research project has been consultative and nonideological; it has been based on the collection and analysis of much concrete information on specific topics that has been used to draw policy lessons. It represents a unique blend of country-oriented analysis with a cross-country perspective.

The conclusions of the studies emphasize the fundamental importance of a sound macroeconomic environment for ensuring the broadly based development of agriculture. At the same time they stress the need to achieve equilibrium in several difficult ways: among macroeconomic, sectoral, and location-specific factors that determine the growth of agricultural output; between the development of food and export crops; and between the short-run output increases and long-run development of human and institutional capital. The papers highlight the complementary nature of the private and public sectors, and the need to maintain a balance between them. They also promote recognition that both price and nonprice incentives are critical to achieving sustainable growth in output.

The findings of the MADIA study on aid effectiveness presented in this book were discussed in June, 1989, at a symposium in Annapolis, Maryland, funded by U.S. AID. The participants, senior policymakers and analysts from African and donor countries, recommended that donors and African governments should move expeditiously to implement many of the study's valuable lessons. The symposium also concluded that the MADIA research should continue in order to strengthen the consensus among donors and governments on ways to proceed in resuming broadly based growth in African agriculture.

Staff of the Africa Regional Office of the World Bank have participated actively in guiding the MADIA study and in reviewing and debating its conclusions at every stage in the research process. The World Bank is committed to assisting African countries in developing long-term strategies for agricultural development and to translating the MADIA findings into the Bank's operational programs.

Edward V. K. Jaycox
Vice-President, Africa Regional Office
World Bank

Preface

OVER THE PAST THREE DECADES billions of dollars have been transferred from developed countries to Africa. Yet there is a widespread view that much of this aid has done little to stimulate growth, alleviate poverty, or create human and institutional capacity. Poor performance in African countries is often blamed on their internal economic policies. But there is increasing recognition that aid is part of the problem. The volume of aid given to Africa is much too large in relation to the continent's absorptive capacity. The form in which aid is given makes its absorption more difficult than it needs to be. The large number of donors and the limited human and institutional capacity within Africa compounds the problem. There is much polemic about wastage of aid. Donors routinely carry out ex-post evaluations of their projects and (more recently the adjustment) programs, but they promote little well-documented analysis of factors in the political economy of aid—that is, the way donors operate, considerations that influence their aid allocations among countries and sectors and causes changes in these allocations over time, the types of lessons donors learn from their own experience, and the extent to which these lessons get reflected in their operations.

Lack of institutional memory in donor agencies is a pervasive problem. The macroeconomic difficulties of the 1980s have made this problem more acute by shifting attention away from concerns of long-term development to those of short-term crisis. Aid lobbies in developing countries have also grown in importance. This has led to a need for rapid and changing responses that are convincing to the supporters of aid.

The study initially focused on an analysis of macroeconomic and sectoral policies as they affected the performance of donor funded projects and agricultural sectors. But by the time the study was completed, the concern of the analysts had to shift to the excessive emphasis donors placed on short-term adjustments. This was often to the detriment of the myriad microlevel technological and institutional constraints that project assistance previously addressed. The World

Bank's long-term perspective study (LTPS), *From Crisis to Sustainable Growth,* which was being drafted at the time of the MADIA study's completion, was a refreshing departure from the earlier approach enshrined in the 1982 Berg Report, *Accelerated Development in Sub-Saharan Africa.* The LTPS acknowledged the fundamental importance of the many short- and long-term constraints that inhibit growth, including the problems posed by poor governance, the pervasive shortage of human and institutional capacity, and technological stagnation. It also placed a strong emphasis on equity and sustainability to balance the earlier concern with growth and efficiency. The conception of the LTPS led the World Bank to undertake many new joint initiatives, including the establishment of a fund for the Social Dimensions of Adjustment (SDA). Other initiatives included the establishment of units on food security and women in development, a thrust on the environment, a capacity building initiative (CBI), and a new initiative by the Special Program on African Agricultural Research (SPAAR) to develop regional approaches to agricultural research, to name only a few. In addition, the Bank recently collaborated with other donors and African governments in the establishment of the Global Coalition for Africa, a ministerial level North/South forum designed to mobilize political support for Africa's development efforts. These are all worthy initiatives.

Important problems nevertheless remain. First, most efforts tend to be top down, initiated by donor agencies. This is inevitable given that donors contribute too large a share of domestic investment and mobilize stronger intellectual (including African) power to bear on Africa's problems than do Africans.

Second, there is no sense of priority or a vision of long-term, country-specific strategies among donors who drive the African agenda.

Third, as this book shows, the internal technical know-how and capacity has declined considerably in most aid-giving agencies. At the same time, bilateral donors have tended increasingly to rely on the World Bank and the IMF to determine policy directions around which their aid is channeled. The World Bank does not, however, necessarily have a comparative advantage in all aspects of development. For instance, this study documents that the French, the British, and U.S. AID were able to make important contributions in the areas of technology, institutions, and human capital in ways that complemented what the World Bank had to offer. Now the capacity to help recipient countries in this manner has diminished in donor agencies, as has their determination to carve out a niche in areas in which they previously excelled. Instead, the bandwagon syndrome has become acute, with rapid and simultaneous shifts by all donors as to what is considered important for development. This can go from macropolicy reform to environment to governance, and on and on. Without a sense of priorities that donors and African governments agree on and implement consistently over the long term, little will change.

Underlying these shifts is the fundamental absence of an overall economic development strategy centered on Africa's own vision of its development and harnessing its own abundant physical and human resources. Nevertheless, as this book documents, there are important differences in this regard among African countries. Some have done better than others and laid more effective foundations for long-term development. Those who have succeeded have accorded central importance to the development of smallholder agriculture.

A fourth problem, as the history of aid to Africa presented in the book shows, is that donors' rhetoric of intentions tends to be stronger than their record of implementation. At the same time, African policymakers are not giving the necessary urgent emphasis to developing Africa's own internal capacity. Nor are they demanding the high quality of external input that will make this a reality. Rather the tendency of governments has been simply to maximize aid flows regardless of their quality.

The purpose of this book is to show that there are some important successes in Africa, to understand the reasons why, and to explore their implications for future actions by Africans and donors. These successes call for fundamental changes in the way donors and governments operate in Africa, changes that go beyond myriads of specific initiatives. They call for a redirection of the major portion of aid away from a quick balance of payments support to an emphasis on African capacity building, not just in macroeconomic management as currently envisaged, but in all facets of development with a view to achieving rapid productivity growth in the agricultural and rural sector. To build capacity will require thoughtful but massive investment in education and training and institution building in Africa. This should be done through long-term collaborative arrangements by African institutions with institutions in more developed parts of the world that have strong expertise on specific issues of concern to Africa and a commitment to contribute to Africa's development.

The changes called for also require selectivity in giving assistance to African countries that have shown a consistent track record on development. Without some genuine successes in Africa, the will to give aid will wane in Western countries. But without fundamental rethinking of aid and development strategy, there will be few successes.

Acknowledgments

In 1984, Anne Krueger, as vice-president of the then Economic Research Staff (ERS) in the World Bank, initiated a program of studies on aid effectiveness in the Development Economics Department (DED). She gave me the opportunity to head the Development Strategy Division in DED to develop the program. The MADIA study was a part of the program. The study turned out to be larger and more complex than initially envisaged. The number of participating donors increased. Rapid changes in the international economic environment and the nature of external aid to Africa were combined with major changes in the Bank's management and staffing following its radical reorganization in 1987. Given these many external shocks, the project would simply never have been completed without the exceptional support of a large number of agencies and individuals.

The World Bank's research committee contributed generously to the study's conduct. The seven participant donors (USAID, the UKODA, Sweden's SIDA, Denmark's DANIDA, the EC, France, and Germany) funded evaluations of their own programs. They also helped design a comparative framework of analysis to assess the effects of their programs, to the extent that their diverse approaches to aid allowed. They identified noted policy analysts from their own countries, shared confidential files, and discussed their own perspectives with researchers on numerous occasions. They also arranged many seminars in headquarters and field missions. As research results began to emerge, they became the study's strongest advocates, giving me the moral boost to continue. In particular, I would like to thank the following: Edward L. Saiers, Deputy Assistant Administrator, Africa Bureau, USAID; Patrick Fleuret, John Westley, Emmy Simmons, and Richard Cobb, also of USAID; Johan Holmberg of the Swedish International Development Authority (SIDA); Ole Moelgaard Andersen, head of the Technical Advisory Division (Agriculture) of the Danish International Development Agency (DANIDA) and Klaus Winkle, also of DANIDA; Andrew Bennett of the Overseas Development Administration (ODA); and Maria Novak, Chef de la Division, Caisse Centrale de Coopération Economique of France.

Gregory Ingram, director of the Development Economics Department at the Bank, offered a unique source of institutional memory and support even though, after the Bank's reorganization, he was no longer responsible for the economic research program. F. Stephen O'Brien, chief economist of the World Bank's Africa Regional Office and chairman of the internal steering committee, and Dunstan Wai and Vinod Dubey, the committee's members, were the study's strong supporters in the Bank's operational complex. Barber Conable, president of the World Bank, Stanley Fisher, chief economist and vice-president of Policy Planning and Research, and Edward E. K. (Kim) Jaycox, vice-president of the Africa Regional Office, ensured that the study was provided adequate resources and an administrative home for its successful completion after the reorganization. Numerous colleagues in the World Bank commented on the drafts of this and other work. Kim Jaycox also gave me the opportunity to manage a major program of regional studies in agriculture in the Bank's operational complex as a way of translating MADIA findings into Bank operations.

African governments provided invaluable cooperation, encouraged African analysts to work on the study, and organized formal and informal discussions throughout the course of the study, including, in particular, giving me the benefit of their perspectives. I particularly want to thank Harris Mule, then permanent secretary of the Ministry of Finance in Kenya and then vice-president of IFAD, and Ojetunji Aboyade, chairman of PAI Associates, for their strong and continued encouragement.

Ellen Hanak helped me to convince the skeptics in the World Bank and other donor agencies about the importance of doing the study. She also contributed in numerous ways to the study's design and conduct in its initial stages. To her I owe much intellectual and personal debt.

This book involves the work of many experienced researchers, but three research assistants, Maria Cancian, Stephen Stone, and Rahul Jain, call for special attention. Their freshness, enthusiasm, and hard work were a constant source of inspiration. My loyal secretary, Kim Tran, typed innumerable drafts; she also played a key role in the management of the program on aid effectiveness. My son, Abhijeet, quietly supported long hours of my time spent on this study by indicating his pride in my accomplishments.

Notwithstanding all this help, I alone must take responsibility for the shortcomings that exist in this work, which I offer to the women and men farmers of Africa, who are its inspiration.

Contributors

Claude Freud	*Ministère de la Coopération, Paris*
Ellen Hanak	*Special Studies Division, World Bank, Washington, D.C.*
Christian Heimpel	*Deutches Übersee-Institut, Hamburg*
Allan Hoben	*African Studies Center, Boston University*
John Howell	*Overseas Development Institute, London*
William K. Jaeger	*World Bank, Washington, D.C.*
Rahul Jain	*Special Studies Division, World Bank, Washington, D.C.*
Bruce F. Johnston	*Food Research Institute, Stanford University*
Walter Kennes	*Directorate General for Development, Commission of the European Communities*
Michael Loft	*Special Studies Division, World Bank, Washington, D.C.*
John W. Mellor	*International Food Policy Research Institute, Washington, D.C.*
Rajul Pandya-Lorch	*International Food Policy Research Institute, Washington, D.C.*
Marian Radetzki	*Institute for International Economic Studies, Stockholm*
Manfred Schulz	*Department of Sociology, Free University, Berlin*

Abbreviations and Acronyms

ADC	Agricultural Development Corporation
ADMARC	Agricultural Development and Marketing Corporation
ADP	Agricultural Development Project
AFC	Agricultural Finance Corporation
APMEPU	Agricultural Project Monitoring, Evaluation, and Planning Unit
ASAO	Agricultural Sector Adjustment Operation
ATP	Aid Trade Provision
BMWi	German Ministry of Economic Affairs
BMZ	German Federal Ministry for Economic Cooperation
CAMDEV	Cameroon Development Corporation
CAT	Coffee Authority of Tanzania
CBI	Capacity Building Initiative
CBK	Central Bank of Kenya
CCCE	Caisse Centrale de Coopération Economique
CCFOM	Caisse Centrale de la France d'Outre-Mer
CDC	Commonwealth Development Corporation
CEC	Commission of the European Communities
CFA	Communauté Financière Africaine
CFDT	Compagnie Française de Développement des Fibres Textiles
CGIAR	Consultative Group on International Agricultural Research
CIDA	Canadian International Development Agency
CIMMYT	Centro Internacional de Mejoramiento de Maiz y Trigo
CPCS	Cooperative Production Credit Scheme
CPSP	Caisse de Péréquation et Stabilization des Prix
CRC	Cotton Research Corporation

CRDB	Cooperative and Rural Development Bank
CRS	Catholic Relief Services
DAC	Development Assistance Committee
DANIDA	Danish International Development Agency
DRV	Disease resistant variety
EAAFRO	East African Agricultural and Forestry Research Organization
EAVRO	East African Veterinary Research Organization
EDF	European Development Fund
EIB	European Investment Bank
EMI	Embu-Meru-Isiolo districts
ESF	Economic Support Funds
FACU	Federal Agricultural Coordinating Unit
FAC	Fonds d'Aide et de Coopération
FAO	Food and Agriculture Organization
FCR	Fonds Commun de Revente
FIDES	Fonds d'Investissements pour le Développement Economique et Social des Territoires d'Outre Mer
FISS	Farm Inputs Supply Scheme
GAT	German Agricultural Team
GDP	Gross Domestic Product
GNP	Gross National Product
GTZ	German Agency for Technical Cooperation
HEVECAM	Société Hévéa Cameroun
HIID	Harvard Institute for International Development
IADP	Integrated Agricultural Development Project
IBRD	International Bank for Reconstruction and Development
IDA	International Development Association
IRAT	Institut de Réchèrche d'Agronomie Tropicale
IFAD	International Fund for Agricultural Development
IFPRI	International Food Policy Research Institute
IITA	International Institute for Tropical Agriculture
ILCA	International Livestock Centre for Africa
ILO	International Labor Organization
IMF	International Monetary Fund
IRCT	Institut de Recherche des Cotons et Textiles Exotiques

IRDP	Integrated Rural Development Project
IRHO	Institut de Recherche des Huiles et Oléagineux
ISRA	Institut Sénégalois de Recherches Agricoles
KARI	Kenya Agricultural Research Institute
KCC	Kenya Cooperative Creameries
KFA	Kenya Farmers Association
KFCTA	Kasungu Flue-cured Tobacco Authority
KMC	Kenya Meat Commission
KTDA	Kenya Tea Development Authority
LIDA	Livestock Development Authority
LLDP	Lilongwe Land Development Project
LTP	Land Transfer Programme
NPA	Nouvelle Politique Agricole
NCPB	National Cereals and Produce Board
NMC	National Milling Company
NRDP	National Rural Development Program
NSCM	National Seed Company of Malawi
ODA	Official Development Assistance
ODA	Overseas Development Authority (See UKODA)
ODNRI	Overseas Development Natural Resources Institute
OECD	Organisation for Economic Cooperation and Development
ONCAD	Office Nationale de Coopération et d'Assistance au Développement
PVO	Private voluntary organization
SAL	Structural Adjustment Loan
SAED	Société d'Aménagement et d'Exploitation des Terres du Delta
SATEC	Société d'Aide Technique et de Coopération
SCA	Smallholder Crop Authority
SCDA	Special Crops Development Authority
SCET	Société Centrale pour l'Equipement du Territoire
SEDES	Société d'Etudes du Développement Economique et Social
SEMRY	Société d'Expansion et de Modernization de la Riziculture de Yagoua
SIDA	Swedish International Development Authority
SPAAR	Special Program on African Agricultural Research

SOCAPALM	Société Camerounaise de Palmeraies
SODECOTON	Société de Développement du Coton du Cameroun
SODEFITEX	Société de Développement des Fibres Textiles
SONACO	Société Nationale de Commercialisation des Oléagineux de Senegal
SSA	Smallholder Sugar Authority
SSATP	Sub-Saharan Africa Transport Program
STABEX	System for Stabilization of Agricultural Export Earnings
SYSMIN	System for Stabilization of Mineral Export Earnings
TANSEED	Tanzania Seed Company Limited
TCMB	Tanzanian Coffee Marketing Board
TDL	Tanzania Dairy Limited
TDRI	Tropical Development and Research Institute
TFNC	Tanzanian Food and Nutrition Center
TIRDEP	Tanga Integrated Rural Development Project
TIRDP	Tabora Integrated Rural Development Project
TRN	Total receipts net
T&V	Training and Visit Extension
TWICO	Tanzania Wood Industries Corporation
UCCAO	Union Centrale des Coopératives Agricoles de l'Ouest
UKODA	United Kingdom Overseas Development Administration
UNDP	United Nations Development Programme
UNICEF	United Nations Children's Fund
USAID	United States Agency for International Development
USDA-ERS	United States Department of Agriculture, Economic Research Service

- All references to Germany are to the former Federal Republic of Germany.
- All references to dollars ($) are to U.S. dollars.

1 *Introduction*

Uma Lele

AGRICULTURE is the lifeblood of Sub-Saharan Africa. Not only is it a source of employment, income, exports, savings, government revenue, and raw materials for industry, but it also provides a market for the goods and services produced in other sectors. Many experts believe that the poor performance of agriculture is at the root of Sub-Saharan Africa's current economic crisis. Agriculture's problems stem in part from exogenous factors such as the deteriorating terms of trade and repeated droughts of recent years. But domestic policies, too, are to blame since they have favored rapid industrialization and thus have made the external shocks difficult to weather. To complicate matters, the population of the region has grown so rapidly in the past three decades that it has outpaced food production. The result is that almost all the countries of the region have come to depend on food imports while losing world market share in exports of agricultural commodities. Per capita incomes stagnated in the 1970s and declined in the 1980s in no small measure because of the slump in agriculture.

Although many general reports have been written about Africa's economic problems, there are few detailed country-by-country analyses of its agricultural problems and their implications for future policy.[1] The countries of Sub-Saharan Africa are so diverse in their physical, political, institutional, and economic circumstances that without in-depth, cross-country studies it is almost impossible to assess the relative importance of external and internal constraints on growth.

The MADIA Study

In response to these concerns, the World Bank in 1984 launched such a comparative study—"Managing Agricultural Development in Africa" (MADIA)—in collaboration with seven other donor agencies and six African governments. The purpose of the study was to determine the sources of agricultural growth in selected African countries in the period after independence; the extent to which domestic policies, the external economic environment, and donor assistance contributed to this growth; the effect of the growth on incomes, employment, and consumption; and the potential sources of future growth. Another topic explored was the nature of internal politics in these countries and its bearing on their agricultural policies.

The study focused on Kenya, Malawi, and Tanzania in East Africa and Cameroon, Nigeria, and Senegal in West Africa. In 1987 these six countries accounted for 40 percent of the population of Sub-Saharan Africa and for nearly half of its gross national product (GNP). They spread across almost all the ecological zones of Africa—the Sahel desert and the Guinea-Savannah in the north, the equatorial rain forest in the south, and the volcanic, humid, and subhumid highlands in the east and the west. And as a group they grow almost all the principal crops of Africa, including tea, coffee, cocoa, tobacco, cotton, groundnuts, cashews, sisal, sugar, maize, sorghum, millet, and rice. Cameroon and Nigeria are oil exporters and the rest are oil importers; Cameroon and Tanzania are land-surplus countries, whereas the others are land short; all have relatively stable political environments, apart from Nigeria, which has experienced considerable instability. Cameroon, Kenya, and Malawi have achieved relatively good rates of agricultural and overall economic growth, whereas the other three have not. Yet all six countries can boast agricultural success stories. In general, these countries have enough in common to permit a fruitful comparison that can help to explain how and why they vary in agricultural and overall economic growth and how economic benefits are distributed among crops, regions, and households.

Eight donors helped to assess the effectiveness of aid in these countries: the World Bank, the U.S. Agency for International Development (USAID), the Swedish International Development Authority (SIDA), the Danish International Development Agency (DANIDA), the United Kingdom Overseas Development Administration (UKODA), the Commission of the European Communities (CEC), and the governments of France and the Federal Republic of Germany. Together, these donors provide nearly 60 percent of the aid flowing to Africa. Although the level and content of their assistance has varied widely, in different combinations they have provided important financial and technical assistance as well as policy advice for each of the six recipients. In fact, aid to many African countries has been so large in per capita terms and as a share of government expenditure that it has significantly influenced the behavior and decisions of African governments. As a result, it has greatly affected the direction and outcomes of public investments, particularly in the countries with a poor internal capacity for planning and implementing policy.

Donors were drawn to the MADIA study largely because of their concern about the effectiveness of their assistance in Africa. Although donors have carried out many internal evaluations of individual projects and of sectoral and structural adjustment operations, they have conducted few in-depth analyses of the long-term effects of aid on growth and distribution. Little effort has been made to distinguish the effects of donor policies and intervention from the effects of country policies—perhaps because of the complex methodological problems outlined below. In any case, few such donor evaluations are available in the public domain other than those undertaken for the explicit purpose of mobilizing additional aid.[2]

Some assessments of foreign aid have been been made outside the donor organizations, but few are backed by a well-informed analysis of the content, causes, and consequences of donor actions.[3] These external reports allege that aid does not further the growth process, that it serves mainly the strategic and commercial interests of donors, and that it taxes the poor in donor countries but serves the political interests of the elite.[4] Donor bureaucracies either have been silent about this criticism or have ignored it. Clearly a great deal of aid is given for strategic, commercial, political, and humanitarian—as distinct from developmental—reasons. Thus various constituencies in aid-giving countries have a profound influence on the levels and kinds of assistance, as well as on the general direction of development concerns, which in turn affects the support given for achieving developmental goals. For this see a separate study carried out as part of the larger World Bank research program on aid effectiveness covering the experience of countries in Latin America, Asia, and Africa over the post–World War II period. In this study, Lele and Nabi have documented the instability of aid flows caused by strategic and political factors, and the problems of aid "booms and busts" caused for recipients in making effective use of aid.[5] That study also documents the many important ways in which external aid has contributed to the development of countries in Asia and Latin America. Assessment of aid in Africa will remain inadequate until the nature of this phenomenon and its implications for future donor assistance are fully explored.

Methodological Issues in Evaluating the Effectiveness of Aid

Admittedly, evaluating aid effectiveness is a challenging task. Quantitative indicators can give some insight into effectiveness, but they do not provide a complete picture. Also, many effects of aid are difficult to separate from the effects of other factors that influence agricultural growth—such as macroeconomic and sectoral policies, the availability of the necessary institutions and infrastracture, the organizational and management capacity of the government, and (not least important) the quality of natural resources. The effect of aid is therefore better evaluated in the broader context of macroeconomic and sectoral policies.

Another problem is that aid from an individual donor typically constitutes only a share of project (or nonproject) funds and comprises a set of activities within a wider framework of government and multidonor support. This makes it difficult to assess separately the success or failure of individual donors in achieving the objectives of a particular undertaking. Further problems arise in assessing the full effects of welfare services and the development of human and institutional capacity, which are difficult to measure quantitatively, and in determining the effects of technical assistance or structural adjustment loans given to economies in fundamental disequilibrium (a practice that gained considerable momentum in the 1980s). Even if the effects are measurable in principle, the data may be inconsistent, unreliable, or simply unavailable—as in the case of food crop production in Africa. Consequently, it is not always easy to apply systematic cost-benefit analysis or to develop objective indicators of effectiveness that can be reasonably compared across countries, crops, or time periods.

In any case, the unquantifiable benefits and externalities associated with activities such as institution building and learning by doing are part of a long and complex process and may not materialize within the time horizon of a single project or even a series of structural adjustment loans. Therefore the contribution of donors must be assessed by the recipient's achievement of broader and long-term goals of agricultural and overall economic development. This kind of assessment examines both macro-level and sectoral information, not merely the specific inputs and outputs envisaged in project design and objectives, and it is therefore that much more subjective.

Most of the donors responded positively to the MADIA study because they were searching for just such a holistic approach to analyzing aid effectiveness. They were particularly interested in (a) comparing their own experiences with those of other donors, hoping thereby to better understand long-term growth processes in Africa, and (b) exploring the implications of the study for their assistance programs. Donors helped define both the scope and the direction of the study by financing the aid component; by designating experienced professionals from the donor countries to undertake the analysis in consultation with African policymakers and researchers; by providing access to valuable internal documentation that was previously unavailable to researchers; and by participating in the discussion and dissemination of the study's findings.

Strong support also came from the African governments. They facilitated the recruitment of African scholars, provided access to data from government files, and offered substantive comments on the early drafts of the numerous papers produced by the researchers. All discussions held in African and donor capitals were followed by interviews with academics, farmers, and others having an interest in agriculture. This broad participation has given the study a progressive and positive outlook that has made it possible to draw lessons for long-term economic strategies and to avoid simply recapitulating the past.

In addition to this volume, the MADIA study has produced one other cross-country volume, two country-specific books, and fourteen discussion papers (see the appendix to this chapter). A number of journal articles, conference papers, and chapters in other books have also been completed. These works have been discussed at more than fifty seminars held in African and donor countries.

The findings of the study were presented at a symposium of senior African and donor policymakers in Annapolis, Maryland, in June 1989. The symposium was hosted by the World Bank and financed by USAID. The participants recommended that (a) donors and African governments expedite the implementation of many of the study's valuable lessons through country-specific strategies of agricultural development; (b) the study's consultative, nonideological approach to analysis be continued to ensure that donors and governments reach a consensus on the ways and means to spur broadly based agricultural growth in Africa; and (c) high priority be given to developing Africa's capacity for planning and implementing agricultural policy.

Conceptual Basis of the Study

Many analysts of long-term economic growth have pointed out that agriculture plays a crucial role in structural transformation during the early stages of development. They have also stressed that agricultural productivity must be raised and that small farmers must contribute to such growth in order to broaden the base of overall economic growth.[6] As has been widely demonstrated, broadly based agricultural production has an enormous impact on the pattern of consumption, saving, and investment. This in turn determines internal links between growth in the agricultural and nonagricultural markets, and external links between growth in the domestic and international markets.[7] These links govern the pace and robustness of growth.

Early growth theory stressed the role of physical capital in the growth process, but recent studies have demonstrated that growth depends more on technological change and the acquisition of knowledge than on the traditional factors of production (land, labor, and physical capital). Still other studies have pointed out that for sustained, broadly based growth, human, institutional, organizational, technological, and physical capital must complement each other.[8]

Some studies specifically concerned with the African context have identified adverse price incentives and excessive government intervention as the principal constraints on agricultural growth,[9] whereas others have criticized the recent emphasis on "getting prices right" as excessive.[10] Some analysts have argued that among the nonprice factors, technological constraints are the most binding.[11] Others have stressed the inadequacy of institutional, human, and physical infrastructure,[12] and still others have decried the bias toward large farms of the agricultural strategies pursued by many African governments.[13] The extent to which prices automatically induce the relaxation of various nonprice constraints and the ability of public policy to loosen technological, institutional, and organizational constraints are also matters of much debate in the literature.[14]

The basic engine of robust growth is, of course, the private initiative of a large number of men and women. A balanced accumulation of physical, technological, human, and organizational capital coupled with a price structure that minimizes distortions creates the conditions in which individual decisionmakers act to facilitate broadly based growth. These conditions can emerge only from a sound macroeconomic and sectoral policy framework that responds continuously to changes in the external environment (for example, changes in the terms of trade or new market opportunities), as well as to changes in the internal environment (for example, increased population pressure on land, droughts, soil degradation, and deforestation).

During the early stages of development, however, countries lack an adequate supply of public goods such as agricultural research, extension, feeder roads, and market information—all of which are vital to individual producers and determine the extent to which they can respond to price incentives. Public expenditures on agricultural research, extension, transportation and other infrastructure, market information, and the development of institutional and human resources furnish the incentives for farmers to mobilize conventional factors of production. In the absence of such incentives, the government is called upon to provide a variety of services that are normally offered by the market in more advanced economies. But African governments are hard pressed to provide even the most basic services and therefore need to establish clear priorities among activities so as not to overextend their resources. At the same time, they need to develop the capacity of both the public and the private sector to carry out a variety of developmental functions effectively.

Unfortunately, there are no theoretical criteria for judging the optimum allocation or balance of public expenditures. In any case, absolute levels will not reveal much about the effectiveness of such expenditures without some idea of quality. That is to say, effectiveness can only be gauged by the stability and predictability of capital and recurrent expenditures between sectors that contribute directly to development (for example, agriculture) and those that contribute indirectly (for example, education). Within the category of recurrent expenditure there is a need for balance between allocations made for wages and salaries as distinct from those for operations and maintenance.

Furthermore, if the emphasis in agricultural development is on mass participation and the viability of growth, patterns of public expenditure need to be viewed as part of a continuous and dynamic process. Since the late 1960s, there has been increasing recognition of the diversity of Africa's agriculture and the paucity of its resources relative to the extent of rural poverty.[15] In view of such conditions, public intervention must be selective and must be sequenced and phased in the context of a long-term strategy. Selectivity in rural expenditures depends, of course, on the extent to which governments allow other public expenditures on industry, defense, and public administration to compete with the business of transforming agriculture. Earlier studies have argued that a single blueprint for planning is not possible and that location-specific factors must guide the selection of interventions. In general, achieving the gradual but balanced accumulation of the different kinds of physical, human, and organizational capital essential for sustained growth requires the building of local human and institutional capacity while also providing more direct support for production.

Thus in the initial phases, rural development programs might be most effective if they were to concentrate on services that would stimulate private activity. Such service might include feeder roads, extension services, timely supply of inputs, and the development of a technology suited to the specific needs and resources of farmers. The early stages should also be devoted to collecting and analyzing detailed agronomic and socioeconomic data from specific locations. Such analysis is necessary to develop and implement a strategy for intensifying agricultural production in the subsequent phases of the program. Investment must also be directed toward social amenities such as health, education, and rural water supply if factor productivity is to be increased. The desired programs will be difficult to plan and implement unless resources are mobilized at the local and regional levels to meet the large recurrent costs of these services. Moreover, social choice and local participation at all stages will improve the quality of planning where economic and political power is equitably distributed. In general, earlier studies have shown that a phased, long-term program produces better firsthand knowledge of specific technical, administrative, and sociocultural constraints; facilitates the training of indigenous personnel; and ensures that development programs will expand more smoothly and effectively over time. In contrast, an integrated approach that promotes the simultaneous development of various parts of the economy makes untoward demands on the public sector's scarce administrative and financial resources.

Such criteria for evaluating public expenditures must also be applied to external assistance from bilateral and multilateral donors; this supports a large part of public expenditures in African countries. Donor assistance has enabled African countries to gain access not only to financial resources but also to considerable advice on development policy. The conclusion that emerges from the literature on external aid is that more benefits accrue from the marginal investments that financial aid allows governments to make (because of the fungibility of financial resources) than from specific projects supported by donors.[16] Although this statement is true of projects, it overlooks the effects of the size of official capital flows (in relation to the size of recipient economies) on the totality of recipient government expenditures, or on their overall quality. As this study will show, aid can have a profound influence on the level and pattern of public expenditures—and thus on the nature and rate of capital accumulation, public consumption, and the structure of price incentives. In fact, aid can have "Dutch disease" effects similar to those of a commodity boom. When spent on activities that produce nontraded goods, excessive donor assistance can exert upward pressure on the exchange rate, increase labor costs in the activities that produce traded goods, and suppress external competitiveness.[17] This decline in export performance can be reversed only through explicit policies designed to reduce the conflict between export promotion and the growth of nontraded goods.[18]

Guided by this broader vision of sustainable, long-term economic development, the MADIA study assessed the extent to which the selected countries, with the support of donors, pursued and achieved a pattern of broadly based capital accumulation and agricultural growth. So that their actual performance could be reviewed in the context of the conceptual framework outlined above, the variables affecting performance were divided into three categories: (a) the luck factors, which include the natural resource base and inheritance of physical, social, and institutional capital, as well as the subsequent impact on these factors of major external shocks; (b) macroeconomic policies, which include the exchange rate and price policies that determine explicit or implicit taxation of agriculture and the levels and quality of public expenditures; and (c) sectoral policies that affect the mobilization of land, labor, capital, and technology, as well as the development of physical, human, and institutional infrastructure. This distinction makes it possible to systematically analyze the interaction between a country's resources and the policy choices the government makes to manage and augment these resources. Such policies enable a government to motivate private individuals to take whatever action appears necessary in the face of numerous unforeseen shocks.

Outline of the Book

The book opens with an overview of the broad trends in donor assistance to the six countries under investigation and an analysis of country performance based on data from the records of governments and donors. This is the context in which the donor experiences related in the subsequent chapters should be reviewed. It also forms the basis for the assessment of aid effectiveness in chapter 12. Chapters 3–11 present the donors' reports on their experience. The discussions are organized around several topics (with varying degrees of emphasis):

- The policies donors adopted toward promoting agriculture; their changing perceptions of recipients' needs and goals; and their influence on recipients' agricultural or rural priorities and policies.
- How recipients' perceptions of their development needs and priorities influenced the amount and form of aid given.
- The context of assistance (that is, whether a viable and well-defined macroeconomic and sectoral policy framework existed in the recipient countries).
- How strategic, commercial, and humanitarian constituencies in donor countries, as well as various administrative, personnel, and financial constraints, influenced the level and content of assistance programs.
- The comparative advantage of donors with respect to their ability to provide agricultural or other specific kinds of assistance.

The donor studies are primarily concerned with agricultural production, the provision of welfare services, and institutional development, although chapter 11 examines food aid to the six countries and how such aid can alleviate poverty and improve agriculture without fostering dependency. The book does not cover livestock and forestry in any detail, although both play an important role in alleviating poverty in marginal areas and in ensuring environmental sustainability. Assistance to livestock diminished and became insignificant in the programs of most donors as a result of the many difficulties faced by early livestock projects. Similarly environmental and sustainability questions were on the backburner in the period covered in this book. Small-scale forestry components tended to be included as part of rural development projects, while most self-standing forestry projects dealt with large-scale public plantations. As a result, less information was available on livestock and forestry than on crops.[19] Nevertheless, some treatment of the livestock issues is covered in chapter 4 on Danish aid, and of forestry issues in chapter 5 on Swedish aid.

The book's final chapter assesses the donors' effect on country policies and performance and outlines the study's implications for future donor assistance.

Notes

1. Africa's poor agricultural and overall economic performance has been widely discussed for nearly a decade in the World Bank's various reports on Africa as well as in its World Development Reports. See, for example, World Bank, *Accelerated Development in Sub-Saharan Africa: An Agenda for Action*, (Washington, D.C., 1982); and World Bank, *Sub-Saharan Africa: From Crisis to Sustainable Growth. A Long-Term Perspective Study* (Washington, D.C., 1989).

2. See Robert Cassen and Associates, *Does Aid Work? Report to an Intergovernmental Task Force* (Oxford: Clarendon Press, 1986).

3. See Peter T. Bauer, *Reality and Rhetoric* (Cambridge, Mass.: Harvard University Press, 1984); and Graham Hancock, *Lords of Poverty: The Power, Prestige, and Corruption of the International Aid Business* (New York: Atlantic Monthly Press, 1989).

4. See, for example, Peter T. Bauer, *Equality, the Third World, and Economic Delusion* (Cambridge, Mass.: Harvard University Press, 1981); Peter T. Bauer, *Reality and Rhetoric* (Cambridge, Mass.: Harvard University Press, 1984); Theresa Hayton and Catherine Watson, *Aid: Rhetoric and Reality* (London: Pluto Press, 1985); Frances Moore Lappé, Joseph Collins, and Cary Fowler, *Food First: Beyond the Myth of Scarcity* (Boston: Houghton Mifflin, 1977).

5. See Uma Lele and Ijaz Nabi, eds., *Transitions in Development: The Role of Aid and Commercial Flows* (San Francisco: Institute of Contemporary Studies, 1990).

6. See Simon Kuznets, *Six Lectures in Economic Growth* (Glencoe, Ill.: Free Press, 1959); Kazushi Okhawa and Nabukiyo Takamatsu, *Capital Formation, Productivity and Employment: Japan's Historical Experience and Its Possible Relevance to LDCs* (International Development Center of Japan, 1973); Shigeru Ishikawa, *Economic Development in Asian Perspective* (Tokyo: Kinokuniya, 1967); Bruce Johnston and John Mellor, "The Role of Agriculture in Economic Development," *American Economic Review* 51(1961):566–93; Bruce Johnston and Peter Kilby, *Agriculture and Structural Transformation: Economic Strategies in Late Developing Countries* (New York: Oxford University Press, 1975); John Mellor and Bruce Johnston, "The World Food Equation: Interrelations among Development, Employment, and Consumption," *Journal of Economic Literature* 22(1984):531–74.

7. Jagdish Bhagwati has argued that a purely export-led growth that does not involve agriculture may be both necessary and desirable in some cases: for example, where agriculture is unimportant, as in the city-states of Singapore and Hong Kong, or where agriculture does not have a comparative advantage. See Jagdish Bhagwati, "Rethinking Trade Strategy," in John P. Lewis and Valeriana Kallab, eds., *Development Strategies Reconsidered* (Washington, D.C.: Overseas Development Council, 1986). The opposing case is made

by John Mellor in "Agriculture on the Road to Industrialization," in the same book.

8. See, for example, Bruce Johnston's elaboration of Harry Johnston's notion of capital in Bruce Johnston, Allan Hoben, William Jaeger, and Dirk Djikerman, "An Assessment of AID Activities to Promote Agricultural and Rural Development in Sub-Saharan Africa." Unpublished.

9. See, for example, World Bank, *Toward Sustained Development in Sub-Saharan Africa: A Joint Program of Action* (Washington, D.C., 1984).

10. See Michael Lipton, "Limits of Price Policy for Agriculture: Which Way for the World Bank?" *Development Policy Review* 5(1987):197–215.

11. See John Mellor and Christopher L. Delgado, "A Structural View of Policy Issues in African Agricultural Development," *American Journal of Agricultural Economics* 66(1984):665–70.

12. See Uma Lele, "Comparative Advantage and Structural Transformation: A Review of Africa's Economic Development Experience," in Gustav Ranis and T. Paul Shultz, eds., *The State of Development Economics: Progress and Perspectives* (New York: Blackwell, 1988).

13. See Bruce Johnston and Peter Kilby, *Agriculture and Structural Transformation: Economic Strategies in Large Developing Countries* (New York: Oxford University Press, 1975).

14. See Yujiro Hayami and Vernon W. Ruttan, *Agricultural Development: An International Perspective* (Baltimore, Md.: Johns Hopkins University Press, 1985); Yair Mundlak, "Capital Accumulation, the Choice of Techniques, and Agricultural Output," in John Mellor and Raisuddin Ahmed, eds., *Agricultural Price Policy for Developing Countries* (Baltimore, Md.: Johns Hopkins University Press, 1988); Uma Lele and John Mellor, "Agricultural Growth, Its Determinants, and Its Relationship to World Development: An Overview" (paper delivered at the Twentieth International Conference of Agricultural Economists, Buenos Aires, August 24–31, 1988).

15. See John C. deWilde, *Experiences with Agricultural Development in Tropical Africa*, vols. 1 and 2 (Baltimore, Md.: Johns Hopkins University Press, 1967); and Uma Lele, *The Design of Rural Development: Lessons from Africa* (Baltimore, Md.: Johns Hopkins University Press, 1975). A more recent treatment of this subject is found in Bruce F. Johnston and William C. Clark, *Redesigning Rural Development: A Strategic Perspective* (Baltimore, Md.: Johns Hopkins University Press, 1982).

16. See Hans W. Singer, "External Aid: For Plans or Projects?" in Jagdish Bhagwati and Richard Eckaus, eds., *Foreign Aid* (Harmondsworth, Middlesex, U.K.: Penguin Books, 1970).

17. The so-called Dutch disease refers to the contraction or stagnation of the market for traded goods in response to a favorable shock arising from either a discovery of resources or an increase in the price of a commodity export (for example, oil). This windfall causes a reallocation of productive factors: (a) factors of production move from other activities into the booming sector; and (b) because of increased spending on nontraded goods, factors of production move from traded goods to nontraded goods.

18. See Sweder van Wijnbergen, "Aid, Export Promotion, and the Real Exchange Rate: An African Dilemma," Development Research Department Report DRD199 (World Bank, Washington, D.C., October 1986).

19. Chapter 3 does cover DANIDA's assistance to the livestock sector in Kenya, however, and chapter 4 discusses SIDA's assistance to forestry in Tanzania. See Uma Lele and L. Richard Meyers, "Kenya's Agricultural Devel-

opment and the World Bank's Role in it," (Africa—Technical Department, Agriculture Division, World Bank, Washington, D.C., in preparation as a book).

Appendix

The following three book manuscripts arising from the MADIA study are in preparation.

Lele, Uma, and L. Richard Meyers. "Kenya's Agricultural Development and the World Bank's Role in it."

Lele, Uma, A. T. Oyejide, Balu Bumb, and Vishva Bindlish. "Nigeria's Economic Development, Agriculture's Role, and World Bank Assistance, 1961–1986: Lessons for the Future."

Lele, Uma, and Ellen Hanak, eds." The Politics of Agricultural Policy in Africa."

Eleven MADIA papers issued as World Bank discussion papers and three in preparation are listed below:

Gaviria, Juan, Vishva Bindlish, and Uma Lele. *The Rural Road Question and Nigeria's Agricultural Development*. MADIA Discussion Paper 10. Washington, D.C., 1989.

Idachaba, F. S. *State-Federal Relations in Nigerian Agriculture*. MADIA Discussion Paper 8. Washington, D.C., 1989.

Jammeh, Sidi, Mathurin Gbetibouo, and Uma Lele. "Building Agricultural Research Capacity in Senegal." MADIA Discussion Paper 12. Washington. D.C., in preparation.

Lele, Uma. *Agricultural Growth, Domestic Policies, the External Environment, and Assistance to Africa: Lessons of a Quarter Century*. MADIA Discussion Paper 1. Washington, D.C., 1989. Also published in Colleen Roberts, ed., *Trade, Aid, and Policy Reform: Proceedings of the Eighth Agriculture Sector Symposium*. Washington, D.C.: World Bank, 1988.

——. *Managing Agricultural Development in Africa: Three Articles on Lessons from Experience for Government and Aid Donors*. MADIA Discussion Paper 2. Washington, D.C., 1989.

——. *Structural Adjustment, Agricultural Development, and the Poor: Lessons from the Malawian Experience*. MADIA Discussion Paper 9. Washington, D.C., 1989. Also published in *World Development* 18, September 1990.

Lele, Uma, and Manmohan Agarwal. *Smallholder and Large-Scale Agriculture: Are There Tradeoffs in Growth and Equity?* MADIA Discussion Paper 6. Washington, D.C., 1989.

Lele, Uma, and Robert Christiansen. *Markets, Marketing Boards, and Cooperatives in the MADIA Countries: Issues in Adjustment Policy in Africa*. MADIA Discussion Paper 11. Washington D.C., 1989.

Lele, Uma, Robert Christiansen, and Kundhavi Kadiresan. *Fertilizer Policy in Africa: Lessons from Development Programs and Adjustment Lending, 1970–87*. MADIA Discussion Paper 5. Washington, D.C., 1989.

Lele, Uma, Mathurin Gbetibouo, and Paul Fishstein. "Planning for Food Security in Africa: Lessons and Policy Implications." MADIA Discussion Paper 13. Washington, D.C., in preparation.

Lele, Uma, Bill Kinsey, and Antonia Obeya. "Building Agricultural Research Capacity in Africa: Policy Lessons from the MADIA Countries." MADIA Discussion Paper 14. Washington, D.C., in preparation.

Lele, Uma, and L. Richard Meyers. *Growth and Structural Change in East Africa: Domestic Policies, Agricultural Performance, and World Bank Assistance, 1963–86.* MADIA Discussion Paper 3. Washington, D.C., 1989.

Lele, Uma, and Steven Stone. *Population Pressure, the Environment, and Agricultural Intensification: Variations on the Boserup Hypothesis.* MADIA Discussion Paper 4. Washington, D.C., 1989.

Lele, Uma, Nicolas van de Walle, and Mathurin Gbetibouo. *Cotton in Africa: An Analysis of Differences in Performance.* MADIA Discussion Paper 7. Washington, D.C., 1989.

2 *The* MADIA *Countries: Aid Inflows, Endowments, Policies, and Performance*

Uma Lele

AID FLOWS TO SUB-SAHARAN AFRICA can be divided into three groups: the small flows before 1973–74; those between 1973–74 and 1979–80, which were considerably larger but mainly in the form of project assistance; and those of the 1980s, which included a large amount of adjustment assistance related to macroeconomic difficulties in the countries of the region.[1] The vast change in the nature and level of external assistance after 1973–74 was precipitated by several factors, beginning with a severe drought in Africa and a coincidental decline in world food stocks caused by United States wheat sales to the Soviet Union. These events, together with the subsequent rise in the world market price of cereals, created widespread concern about the increasing vulnerability of the least developed countries to fluctuations in international food supplies. Donor concern about food security, poverty alleviation, and equity in Africa also reflected a consensus that the benefits of the green revolution in Asia had failed to "trickle down" to the poor majority and that exports of primary commodities were unlikely to generate much revenue.

When the internal price of food crops began to climb relative to the price of primary commodity exports, African governments resolved to achieve food self-sufficiency—an objective that they felt had been ignored by the colonial powers. They also decided to diversify out of colonial modes of production and export and to modernize through industrialization.

In response to these developments, the international community issued a call for a direct "assault on poverty."[2] World Bank President Robert McNamara, speaking in Nairobi in 1973, and numerous World Bank reports were among the first to elaborate on the theme and to discuss its implications for donor policies. The idea received the official support of other donors as well. For example, it was endorsed in a mandate of the United States Congress and in various White Papers in Britain, as noted in chapters 5 and 8.

Donors responded with a massive increase in total official development assistance (ODA) to Africa. During 1975–79, for example, Swedish, Danish, German, and World Bank assistance to Sub-Saharan Africa in real terms was almost double that of the 1970–74 period. Some of the sharpest increases showed up in aid to agriculture and rural development. The World Bank adopted an informal guideline recommending that these sectors should receive 25 percent of its total assistance. Bank commitments (in current dollars) to agriculture and rural development during 1975–79, compared with the period 1970–74, rose twelvefold in Nigeria, sevenfold in Cameroon, sixfold in Kenya, and twofold in Tanzania, Malawi, and Senegal (see chapter 2). Other donors were under similar pressure to disburse large sums to agriculture and rural development, although not all responded in the same manner. The U.S. Agency for International Development (USAID), for example, focused almost all its efforts on agriculture (see chapter 5) in any case, whereas the Swedish Development Authority (SIDA) channeled most of its aid to Kenya and Tanzania into the social sectors that did not go into the industrial sector (see chapter 4).

Within the agricultural and rural sectors, governments and donors shifted their support to food crops, began focusing on areas of low resource potential where poverty seemed intractable, and made equity a priority. The World Bank routinely compiled statistics showing the number of poor people that would benefit from its agricultural and rural development projects. Many of these projects contributed substantially to the expansion of public services in the MADIA countries. Because aid was allocated in response to top-down (and often constituency-driven) pressures, discussions about policy within donor agencies paid relatively little attention to the absorptive capacity of countries receiving such large amounts of assistance. This was a particularly serious omission on the part of donors, since earlier studies had documented conclusively that the recipient countries had little capacity for planning and implementing large development projects or for establishing clear long-term priorities.[3] Country-specific reports produced within donor agencies later in the 1970s also reflected these concerns. Nevertheless, no effort was made to design country-specific strategies that would take into account the problem of limited absorptive capacity.

By the late 1970s many African countries were experiencing serious macroeconomic problems because of a combination of factors. Most notable were the two oil price shocks of the 1970s, the decline in Africa's external terms of trade following the prolonged recession in the industrial countries,[4] the expansionary domestic policies in African countries, and the steep rise in official aid flows to countries without the necessary internal capacity for sound macroeconomic or sectoral management.

In 1981 the World Bank issued a report reflecting donor concern about the large size and inefficiency of the public sector in the poorer countries, the constrained role of the private sector, and the inadequacy of internal incentives for increasing agricultural production.[5] Despite its plea for increased external assistance to Africa, the report did not fully explore the effects of the large volumes of aid on the growing public sector or on technological and investment choices. It became increasingly difficult to manage the large portfolios of rural development projects, which had become financial and administrative liabilities for both governments and donors.[6] Donors had been slow to absorb the results of their own analyses of the infeasibility of large rural development projects in the mid-1970s. In the same way they were slow to recognize that project assistance would be difficult to continue in an adverse macroeconomic policy environment. As more and more donors came to agree that a sound macroeconomic and sectoral policy environment is essential for effective intervention in support of growth, the focus of development assistance shifted almost completely toward internal policy reform.

The primary concern of donors of aid to Africa was no longer to achieve equity and alleviate poverty, as it had been in the wake of the Sahelian drought, but to pursue macroeconomic balance. Thus during the 1980s structural adjustment loans and credits became important instruments of reform. Demand was to be managed through the devaluation of the exchange rate, the reduction of public expenditures and subsidies, the divestiture of and increased cost recovery by public services, and an increased role for the private sector. By the end of the 1980s, however, the single-minded focus on demand had begun to draw some criticism, as analysts pointed to the need for "adjustment with a human face." Thereupon attention turned to integrating macroeconomic management with longer-term development objectives.[7]

When the policy reforms of the 1980s began to challenge the vested interests connected with the previous aid strategy and to encourage greater aid coordination among various donors, recipient countries became disgruntled as they could no longer play donors off against one another to maximize their aid receipts. They also found externally imposed reforms less acceptable as donor assistance was growing more slowly than it had in the 1970s, when donor contributions had by and large moved forward the political, developmental, and welfare objectives of recipient governments. Toward the end of this period new initiatives emerged—for example, the Social Dimensions of Adjustment and the African Capacity Building Initiative—and food security, the role of women in development, and environmental sustainability returned to the top of the donors' agenda. At the end of the 1980s the World Bank prepared a major long-term perspective study, which took a broader and longer term view of Africa's development problems.

The challenge for the 1990s is to achieve equitable and sustainable growth within the framework of these new initiatives—and to avoid the swings in development fashions and the lack of internal capacity that have made it so difficult for the countries of Sub-Saharan Africa to adopt long-term development strategies.

Trends in Flows of Donor Assistance

As figure 2-1 shows, between 1970 and 1987 Tanzania received in real terms the highest levels of official development assistance, followed by Senegal, Kenya, Cameroon, and Nigeria (which received very little ODA in the 1970s).[8] Tanzania's aid peaked in 1987 at $684 million; Senegal's in 1987 at $498 million; Kenya's in 1982 at $470 million;

Figure 2-1. Total Official Development Assistance (ODA) Received by MADIA Countries, 1970–87.

Source: *Geographical Distribution of Financial Flows to Developing Countries* (Paris: OECD, various years).

Cameroon's in 1979 at $271 million; and Malawi's in 1987 at $218 million. During 1970–84, on an annual per capita basis, Senegal received the highest level of ODA (averaging $45 in 1983 dollars), followed by Tanzania ($24), Cameroon ($21), Malawi ($20), and Kenya ($19).

Total receipts net (TRN) reveal somewhat the same trends.[9] Senegal averaged as much as $58 per capita of TRN (at constant 1983 dollars) from 1970 to 1987, followed by Cameroon, Kenya, Tanzania, and Malawi, which averaged $39, $31, $29, and $23, respectively.

Although the per capita aid to these countries is quite high, the donor studies in this book make it clear that the figures overstate the real transfer. This is partly because the share of technical assistance is both large and frequently inappropriate. As these studies also point out, when aid is tied to either source or end-use, its real cost may rise and inappropriate technological choices may be made.

Data on the share of ODA in government expenditure can provide some indication of the extent to which a recipient depends directly on external resources and the degree to which donors exert a less tangible—but nevertheless real—influence on development strategy where the internal capacity for economic management and policy formulation is limited. In all the MADIA countries (except Nigeria), ODA has constituted a large percentage of government expenditures and thereby created the potential for Dutch disease effects. During 1970–87 the share averaged 44 percent and 42 percent in Malawi and Senegal, respectively, and 34 percent, 23 percent, and 21 percent in Tanzania, Kenya, and Cameroon, respectively. Given the growth in aid, the share was up to 70 percent in Malawi and Tanzania by the end of the 1980s (see figure 2-2).

Food aid was a significant component of aid flows and government revenue in Senegal, Tanzania, and Kenya. In Kenya it accounted for up to 10 percent of net ODA and 4 percent of government revenue. In Senegal and Tanzania, food aid accounted for 5.5 and 3 percent of net ODA, and 7 and 3.1 percent of government revenue, respectively. It was relatively unimportant in Nigeria, Cameroon, and Malawi.

Another feature of aid that should be considered is the number of donors. In Tanzania, for instance, thirty-two donors contributed a total of $8.1 billion in ODA during 1970–87.[10] In Kenya and Malawi, thirty-one donors provided $5.5 billion and $2.1 billion, respectively. In West Africa, Senegal received nearly $4.7 billion from thirty donors. Even though Cameroon and Nigeria, both oil-exporting countries, attracted relatively less ODA ($3.2 billion and $1.7 billion, respectively), they were supported by a total of twenty-eight and twenty-seven donors, respectively.

Figure 2-2. Share of Official Development Assistance (ODA) and Total Receipts Net (TRN) in Government Expenditure, 1970–86

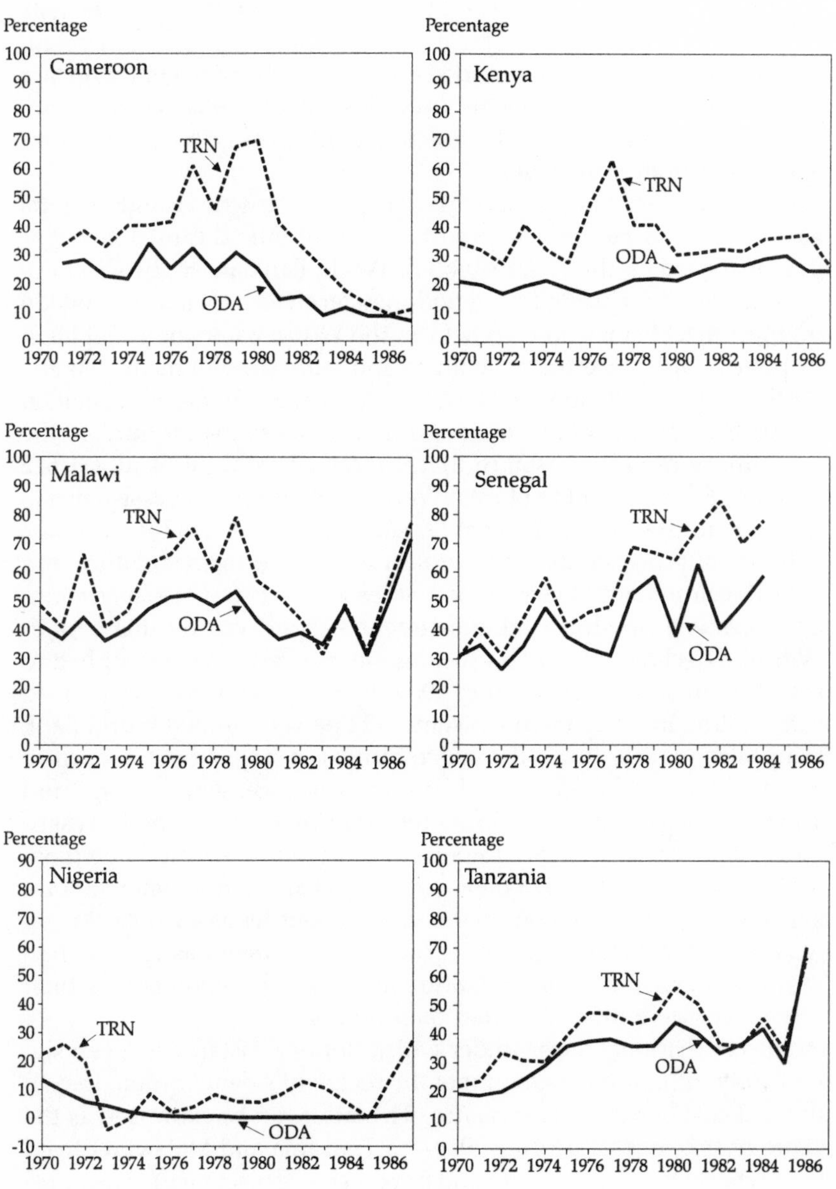

Source: See figure 2-1.

The effectiveness of donor assistance depends in large measure on how predictable, consistent, and stable it is. When aid is unstable—as in the case of United States assistance to the MADIA countries (see chapter 5) and to other parts of the world—governments heavily dependent on aid will have great difficulty planning and implementing development programs and keeping up with recurrent budgetary requirements.[11] Such problems are well known in Senegal, for example, where ODA levels usually fluctuated in excess of twenty percentage points from year to year.

Over the years nonproject assistance for structural and sectoral adjustment has become an important part of official capital flows, as demonstrated by the composition of World Bank aid to the six countries in 1965–88. During this period they received a total of $1.7 billion in nonproject loans and credits from the World Bank and $3.4 billion in project assistance for agriculture and rural development. Nigeria received more adjustment assistance than the others—$532 million (32 percent of the total)—although this was less than a third of the agricultural project assistance that it received from the Bank ($1,622 million). Senegal's share of total World Bank nonproject assistance to the six countries was 14 percent ($242 million), which in this case was substantially higher than the project assistance for agriculture and rural development ($168 million). Cameroon—a better managed country—received no structural adjustment support during this period. With the decline in oil prices (beginning in 1984), however, it had to resort to an adjustment loan in 1989. In East Africa, Kenya received $388 million in adjustment assistance (23 percent of total World Bank nonproject assistance to the six countries) in adjustment assistance and $518 million in agricultural project assistance, while Malawi and Tanzania each received approximately $250 million in nonproject assistance, each accounting for 15 percent of the total. At the same time, Malawi received only $178 million in project assistance, whereas Tanzania received $321 million. In the MADIA countries as a whole, Tanzania and Senegal relied more on structural adjustment assistance than on project assistance for agriculture and rural development, as their economies were more distorted than others.

The concessional terms under which donor assistance is given significantly influence the amount of the recipient's debt burden, that is, the real cost of external assistance. The latter can be expressed as the share of ODA in TRN. During 1970–87, Tanzania and Malawi received the highest shares (87 percent and 83 percent, respectively) of resource transfers on concessional terms (see figure 2-3). Senegal received 78 percent in the form of ODA, Kenya 62 percent, Cameroon 55 percent, and Nigeria only 12 percent.

Figure 2-3. Total Official Development Assistance (ODA) as Percent of Total Receipts Net (TRN) for MADIA Countries (1970–87)

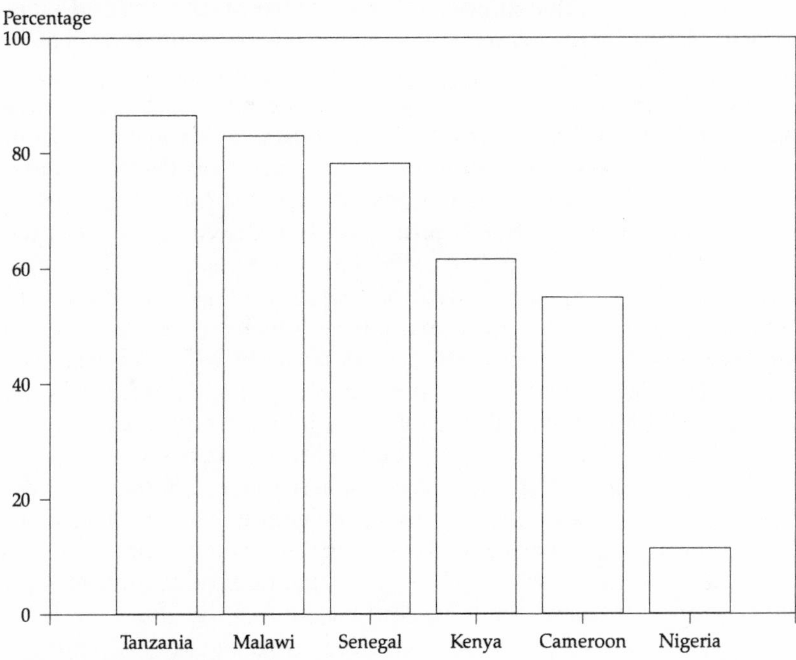

Source: See figure 2-1.

The terms of external assistance for Nigeria and Cameroon hardened when their per capita income increased with the rise in oil prices and currency overvaluation overstated their gross domestic product (GDP). Falling oil prices and a substantial devaluation of its currency (by about 800 percent) reduced Nigeria's per capita gross national product (GNP) from $800 in 1985 to $370 in 1987. As a result, Nigeria now qualifies for assistance from the International Development Association (IDA, the World Bank's concessional-lending affiliate). Other donors also began to offer Nigeria concessional assistance, although they remained concerned about how the country's large population might affect competing demands from smaller countries. This concern reflects the typical small-country bias of external assistance.

Among the bilateral donors, Denmark, Sweden, and the United States provided a higher percentage of their assistance on concessional terms than the others did. The percentage of TRN qualifying as ODA was smaller in the case of France (31–65 percent of TRN to all the MADIA countries except Nigeria) and the United Kingdom (40–66 percent of

TRN to the three East African recipients), as shown in table 2-1. Among the multilateral agencies, IDA provides only concessional assistance, although many of the countries it assisted also received World Bank loans in the 1970s for investment in relatively "harder" sectors such as infrastructure, industry, and agroprocessing for export crops. The European Communities (EC) also provided a high percentage of ODA (from 74 percent to 100 percent) to all the MADIA countries but Nigeria.

Colonial connections, commercial interests, and the recipients' political and ideological orientations account for the differences in donor support to individual countries and for the changes over time in a given donor's support for particular recipients.

Germany, the United Kingdom, the United States, and the World Bank have played large roles in Kenya—which obtained nearly 43 percent of total ODA from these donors between 1970 and 1987 (see figure 2-4). The most striking changes in Kenya are the decline in the United Kingdom's bilateral assistance (as it began contributing more aid through multilateral agencies such as the World Bank and the EC) and the diversification in the sources of assistance. Chapters 2 and 8 explore some of the issues relating to the change in U.K. assistance from a long-term presence aimed at establishing and managing important developmental institutions in the colonial period to shorter-term and task-specific assistance. This shift has limited the effectiveness of U.K. assistance, particularly in countries lacking the political commitment to sustain such institutions. Declining U.K. assistance is also evident in Malawi, where EC lending is in the lead (and where the World Bank's role has increased after a decline in the mid-1970s).

The studies of Danish assistance (chapter 3) and Swedish assistance (chapter 4) show how Tanzania's socialist ideology fitted into the internal sociopolitical philosophy of its donor countries. Denmark, Sweden, and the Netherlands together have accounted for more than a third of Tanzania's total receipts of ODA. As the process of democratization acquired momentum in Eastern Europe after November 1989, human rights issues in Kenya and the question of the freedom of its press moved to the center stage in Western media. But this was not a factor during the period covered. By 1987, SIDA had provided three times as much assistance to Tanzania as it had to Kenya, while the Danish International Development Agency (DANIDA) had provided twice as much. Moreover, as observed earlier, the much greater share of donor resources going to industry and social services in Tanzania than in other countries explains in part why Tanzania was able to continue favoring industrialization and to neglect agriculture. The support of these (and other) donors had enabled Tanzania to postpone until 1986 the reform measures promoted by the International Monetary Fund (IMF) and the World Bank. Since then, SIDA and DANIDA

Table 2-1. Official Development Assistance (ODA) and Total Receipts Net (TRN) to MADIA Countries, 1970–84
(millions of 1983 U.S. dollars)

	West Africa									East Africa								
	Cameroon			Nigeria			Senegal			Kenya			Malawi			Tanzania		
Donors	*Total ODA*	*Total TRN*	*ODA as share of TRN*	*Total ODA*	*Total TRN*	*ODA as share of TRN*	*Total ODA*	*Total TRN*	*ODA as share of TRN*	*Total ODA*	*Total TRN*	*ODA as share of TRN*	*Total ODA*	*Total TRN*	*ODA as share of TRN*	*Total ODA*	*Total TRN*	*ODA as share of TRN*
Bilateral																		
Denmark	22.5	41.8	54.0	7.8	250.2	3.1	30.6	32.0	95.8	205.5	207.5	98.8	56.0	56.1	99.8	433.3	448.1	96.7
France	908.4	2,439.6	37.2	20.8	2,108.5	1.0	1,159.9	1,854.4	62.5	59.2	186.4	31.8	10.9	17.2	63.1	31.6	102.2	30.9
Germany	298.6	336.7	88.7	188.0	2,066.7	9.1	142.5	165.3	86.2	444.9	614.5	72.4	177.5	198.6	89.4	590.5	632.0	93.4
Sweden	0.0	32.2	0.0	4.1	−13.6	−29.7	0.2	2.7	7.3	293.3	312.2	93.9	0.1	3.4	2.9	936.3	971.2	96.4
United Kingdom	48.4	159.5	30.4	192.4	3,944.0	4.9	9.7	43.1	22.4	643.3	1,646.3	39.1	424.5	647.3	65.6	361.7	608.0	59.5
United States	136.3	220.9	61.7	341.6	482.2	70.8	329.6	336.0	98.1	429.5	454.8	94.4	80.8	83.7	96.5	382.0	393.6	97.1
Multilateral																		
EC	304.5	343.8	88.6	16.6	41.6	39.8	570.3	596.5	95.6	169.5	228.7	74.1	91.9	103.8	88.5	242.5	243.2	99.7
IBRD	20.6	300.1	6.9	0.0	1,098.2	0.0	19.0	98.6	19.2	13.2	940.8	1.4	17.6	72.3	24.3	41.8	305.7	13.7
IDA	262.1	262.1	100.0	34.6	34.6	100.0	230.6	222.2	103.8	389.0	389.0	100.0	327.9	327.9	100.0	563.2	563.2	100.0
Total	2,683.5	5,125.5	52.4	1,580.4	12,794.8	12.4	3,381.7	4,598.3	73.5	4,225.5	6,852.9	61.7	1,585.7	1,968.4	80.6	6,310.8	7,477.5	84.4

Source: Maria Cancian, "Aid Allocations in Cameroon, Kenya, Malawi, Nigeria, Senegal, and Tanzania: A Review of the OECD Databases," MADIA Working Paper derived from *Geographical Distribution of Financial Flows to Developing Countries* (Paris: Organization for Economic Cooperation and Development).

Figure 2-4. Donor Shares of Total Official Development Assistance in the MADIA *Countries, 1970–87*

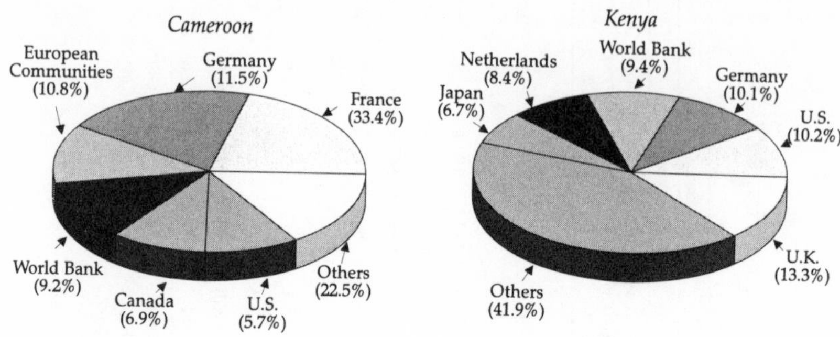

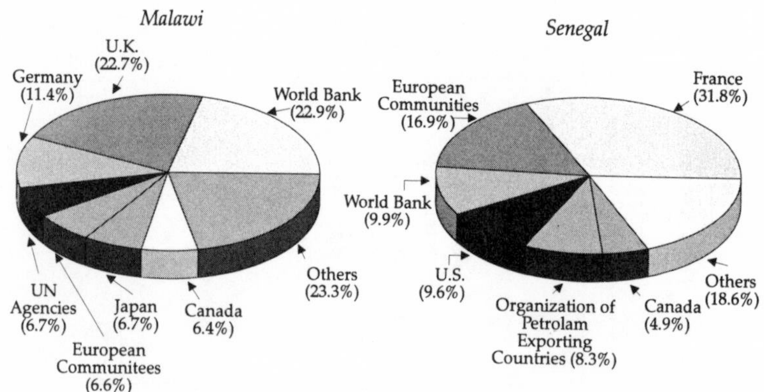

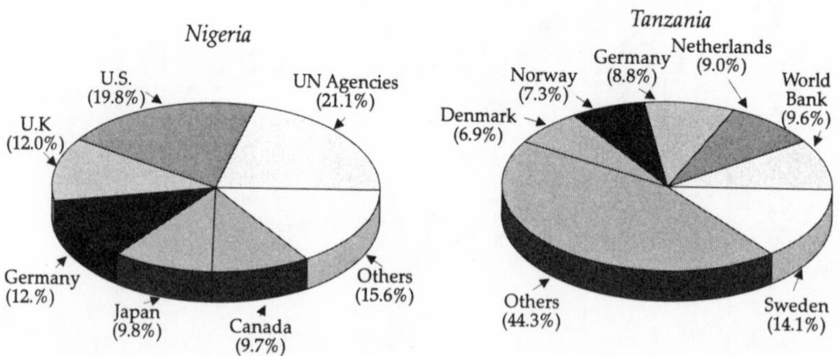

Source: See figure 2-1.

have shifted their position and have come to recognize the importance of sound policy management and strong recipient responsibility. The United Kingdom and Germany, both of which had colonial connections with Tanzania going back many years—terminated their assistance in the 1970s because of foreign policy differences over southern Africa, but subsequently both resumed their aid flows. A larger number of donors now contribute smaller amounts of assistance to Tanzania, but this trend, should it continue, will make it increasingly difficult to coordinate aid in small countries with limited planning and implementing capacity especially given the absence of a long-term development strategy. As the contributors to this volume demonstrate, the proliferation of donors and the large number of new initiatives originating in donor capitals has taxed rather than augmented recipient capacity to address this fundamental problem.

Donor-recipient relations in West Africa have also been affected by colonial ties (chapter 7). France has been the leading donor in Senegal and Cameroon and until 1987 provided nearly a third of their total ODA. It has sustained (and, in Senegal, further strengthened) its leading role—in contrast to the United Kingdom in East Africa. But because Senegal's per capita income has been declining for nearly a decade and a half despite substantial aid, France has moved toward some "burden sharing" with other bilateral and multilateral donors, including the World Bank and USAID. The share in ODA and TRN flows to Senegal and Cameroon of the EC (which France joined in the 1960s) have been reduced. Nigeria received nearly 27 percent of its total TRN transfers from the United Kingdom and 17 and 14 percent from France and Germany, respectively. In addition, the World Bank has been by far the most important external source of capital for Nigeria's agricultural sector since the departure of the United States in 1974 (after Nigeria joined the Organization of Petroleum Exporting Countries).

Overall, the World Bank's share in ODA flows in individual countries has seldom exceeded 20 percent of the total flows. IDA accounted for less than 10 percent of the total ODA received by Kenya, Tanzania, Cameroon, and Senegal during 1970–87. Only in Malawi has the Bank's share in ODA been as high as 22 percent. The share of Bank lending in total TRN was only 11 percent in Tanzania, 13 percent in Nigeria, 18 percent in Kenya, and 21 percent in Malawi. The Bank's influence in promoting important development ideas, however, has been greater than its financial share suggests.

The general acceptance of the Bank's leadership is explained by several factors. Apart from its financial clout, the Bank has a staff of experts (from close to 140 countries) and development experience that is widely recognized for its breadth and its depth. However, there has been substantial attrition in the Bank's technical expertise as experienced technical staff have been replaced by generalists to meet the new demands from the Bank's constituencies. Moreover, the personal commitment of past Bank presidents to various development goals—Robert McNamara to alleviating poverty and A. W. Clausen and Barber B. Conable to liberalization and structural adjustment—has played an important part. More recently, the Bank has shifted its emphasis from the broader, longer-term developmental concerns to more specific issues, such as debt relief, environmental conservation, and the participation of women. This new shift reflects the growing criticism and impatience expressed by various supporters and opponents of aid concerning the Bank's slow response to these issues. This response to constituency pressure is understandable and fully justified. But it raises questions as to whether the Bank and indeed the donor community at large can help Africa on the central issues of articulating and putting in place effective long-run economic development strategies.

At the regional and country level, much of the World Bank's influence has derived from the comprehensive and authoritative research of its country-specific economic and sectoral work, its role as the organizer of donor consortiums and consultative groups, and its contributions as a coordinator of cofinancing arrangements. In the 1970s the Bank's influence at the project level increased first in the Anglophone countries of Africa, where the Bank had begun to fill the vacuum left by the United Kingdom, whose role was declining. By the late 1970s, the Francophone countries, too, had become recipients of World Bank project assistance. When balance of payments problems and the need for policy reforms increased in the 1980s, the Bank took on an even more important role in the design of policy reform packages and the associated aid transfers.

Among the donors, the United States has been the most active supporter of the use of conditionality and lending for policy reform. The United Kingdom and Germany have, in general, aligned themselves with the United States position, although they have been less active in this regard. France recognizes that macroeconomic policy must be managed soundly but has been reluctant to accept the reforms in several specific areas because adjustment programs have tended to dismantle some of the long-standing institutions and policies that it established. These include the exchange rate management system maintained in countries of the Communauté Financière Africaine (CFA) and commodity-based agricultural research, extension, marketing, and development programs. The commodity-based programs have come under attack with the introduction of national agricultural extension and research systems under the World Bank's Training and Visit (T&V) extension and agricultural service initiatives. At the same time,

France's desire for greater burden sharing with the World Bank and the EC has led to a dialogue with the Bank on the specific measures proposed in policy reform packages. Similarly, the concern of the Scandinavian donors that the issues of poverty, the environment, and capacity building may not be addressed in short-term structural adjustment loans has encouraged them to establish a dialogue with the large donors, including the World Bank. That the donor community recognizes the need for a consensus on the substance of longer-term development issues is a positive sign. However, the primacy of donors in Africa cannot be reduced without strengthening the internal capacity of governments to plan and implement macroeconomic and sectoral policies for the broadly based development of smallholders. It is this challenge that the donor community will have to address in the 1990s. Whether it will be able to do so with the myriad of development ideas, interests, and donors remains to be seen. This will change only if African leaders are determined to be proactive.

The Domestic Context

This section presents an overview of the main trends in country performance in order to provide a broad domestic context for the detailed examination of agricultural performance and policies presented that follows.

Overall Country Performance

Given the importance of agriculture in the African economies, it is hardly surprising that the countries whose agricultural sectors have grown the fastest have also had the fastest growth in GDP. During 1960–87, agriculture in Cameroon, Kenya, and Malawi grew at the rate of 4.4 percent, 4.0 percent, and 2.8 percent a year, respectively, and GDP grew by 5.9 percent, 5.8 percent, and 4.4 percent, respectively (see table 2-2). Agricultural and GDP growth rates were significantly lower in Nigeria (0.6 percent and 3.1 percent), Senegal (1.2 percent and 2.2 percent), and Tanzania (1.4 percent and 3.3 percent).

In terms of resources, institutional development, and access to international markets, Kenya and Nigeria were the best-endowed countries, followed by Cameroon and Tanzania, with Senegal and Malawi having the least favorable initial conditions. But their resources and the external shocks are only part of the story. The performance of the MADIA countries was also closely tied to their macroeconomic and sectoral policies. Note, too, that even in the better-performing countries factor productivity showed little growth and much of the increase in production came from area expansion. Given the increasing demo-

Table 2-2. Comparative Macroeconomic Performance of MADIA Countries, 1960–87

	East Africa			West Africa		
Average annual growth rate	*Kenya*	*Tanzania*	*Malawi*	*Cameroon*	*Nigeria*	*Senegal*
1960–87						
GDP	5.8	3.3	4.4	5.9	3.1	2.2
Per capita GNP	2.1	0.2	1.5	2.8	−0.2	−0.9
Agriculture	4.0	1.4	2.8	4.4	0.6	1.2
Manufacturing	8.1	2.7	4.3	8.7	10.6	3.9
Mining	3.8	−4.0	—	29.8	8.4	—
Savings	10.5	−1.5	12.8	17.9	2.3	−1.7
Investment	4.5	5.4	5.0	10.0	6.5	1.9
Exports	3.4	1.2	4.9	6.9	3.1	2.7
Imports	1.1	6.2	1.9	5.1	7.8	2.8
Public consumption	7.3	14.9	4.9	5.7	8.5	2.8
Inflation	8.3	12.0	8.1	7.7	11.6	7.4
Population	3.7	3.1	2.9	3.1	3.3	3.1
1967–73						
Growth rate of real GDP	8.5	5.2	5.2	2.4	4.9	2.2
Growth rate of population	3.5	2.7	2.5	2.4	2.5	2.4
Growth rate of GDP per capita	5.0	2.5	2.7	0.0	2.3	−0.1
Ratio of investment to GDP	22.3	20.8	20.0	15.3	12.7	13.8
Ratio of savings to GDP	20.8	18.2	8.2	13.0	11.5	9.7
Ratio of net exports to GDP	−1.5	−2.6	−11.8	−2.2	−1.2	−4.1
Ratio of current account deficit to GDP	−3.0	−2.9	−11.7	−7.5	−4.1	−1.4
Ratio of debt to exports	61.4	120.6	148.7	61.1	29.0	39.0
Ratio of debt service to exports	4.7	5.6	7.1	4.8	2.8	3.8
Ratio of fiscal deficit to GDP	−3.4	−5.0	−2.4	—	−2.1	−0.9
Rate of inflation (CPI)	4.2	8.5	12.5	3.8	5.2	3.6
Rate of inflation (GDP deflator)	3.3	6.2	5.8	7.6	7.7	2.7
Growth rate of real output in agriculture	5.4	2.3	2.8	4.6	1.9	5.8
Growth rate of real output in manufacturing	14.2	7.8	5.5	6.5	13.9	6.9

Growth rate of real output in mining	12.8	−6.2	—	29.4	28.9	2.5
Growth rate of exports	3.1	3.6	5.9	3.8	16.6	2.2
Growth rate of imports	4.0	3.6	1.4	4.0	12.5	1.2
Central bank borrowing as percentage of GDP	1.0	3.6	1.4	0.5	3.3	0.0
Rural population as percentage of total population	89.7	92.8	93.6	78.7	83.6	74.7
1974–78						
Growth rate of real GDP	4.7	2.5	6.6	7.5	2.9	2.3
Growth rate of population	3.6	3.4	3.0	3.0	2.5	2.6
Growth rate of GDP per capita	1.1	−0.9	3.6	4.5	0.4	−0.3
Ratio of investment to GDP	23.5	20.6	29.6	19.8	23.0	18.3
Ratio of savings to GDP	20.0	11.0	18.3	17.4	25.4	10.5
Ratio of net exports to GDP	−3.5	−9.6	−11.3	−2.4	2.5	−7.8
Ratio of current account deficit to GDP	−6.2	−9.7	−8.9	−9.8	−0.3	−5.5
Ratio of debt to exports	74.6	187.1	181.7	72.1	11.7	54.3
Ratio of debt service to exports	6.4	6.6	12.5	5.9	1.7	7.7
Ratio of fiscal deficit to GDP	−3.6	−7.9	−0.9	−1.2	0.6	−1.1
Rate of inflation (CPI)	16.0	15.1	8.5	13.6	21.9	12.7
Rate of inflation (GDP deflator)	14.5	14.7	10.2	11.8	21.6	9.9
Growth rate of real output in agriculture	4.1	4.7	5.8	2.5	−0.7	2.3
Growth rate of real output in manufacturing	6.6	4.7	6.7	9.1	12.7	1.5
Growth rate of real output in mining	6.5	−2.7	—	24.1	3.9	2.5
Growth rate of exports	2.0	−6.8	−0.7	7.9	3.5	10.0
Growth rate of imports	7.8	2.8	6.1	7.1	28.6	11.3
Central bank borrowing as percentage of GDP	3.6	8.2	2.9	2.3	3.7	0.9
Rural population as percentage of total population	87.4	90.1	91.6	70.7	81.2	68.0
1979–81						
Growth rate of real GDP	4.2	2.1	2.0	13.9	0.9	1.9
Growth rate of population	4.0	3.2	2.6	3.2	2.8	2.9
Growth rate of GDP per capita	0.2	−1.1	−0.6	10.8	−1.9	−1.0
Ratio of investment to GDP	27.0	22.2	27.0	21.7	20.8	15.4

(Table continues on the following page.)

Table 2-2. (continued)

Average annual growth rate	*East Africa*			*West Africa*		
	Kenya	*Tanzania*	*Malawi*	*Cameroon*	*Nigeria*	*Senegal*
Ratio of savings to GDP	18.2	10.8	13.2	17.5	23.1	−0.3
Ratio of net exports to GDP	−8.8	−11.4	−13.8	−4.3	2.3	−15.8
Ratio of current account deficit to GDP	−10.5	−11.7	−12.7	−12.8	−1.4	−14.9
Ratio of debt to exports	120.2	261.1	211.4	101.5	19.5	136.8
Ratio of debt service to exports	14.3	9.4	24.8	9.3	2.6	17.5
Ratio of fiscal deficit to GDP	−4.6	−10.1	−1.0	−3.3	−13.9	−2.2
Rate of inflation (CPI)	11.2	23.2	4.0	8.9	13.1	8.1
Rate of inflation (GDP deflator)	9.0	21.9	9.1	8.4	14.2	8.8
Growth rate of real output in agriculture	1.5	−1.0	−3.9	12.1	−2.7	1.1
Growth rate of real output in manufacturing	5.5	−10.2	2.8	15.2	22.6	8.2
Growth rate of real output in mining	−8.3	2.7	—	185.2	−7.4	4.4
Growth rate of exports	−1.3	7.1	11.9	22.1	−5.3	5.7
Growth rate of imports	−9.9	14.3	−4.6	12.2	5.3	7.5
Central bank borrowing as percentage of GDP	6.0	18.6	9.3	1.5	13.9	5.9
Rural population as percentage of total population	85.8	88.2	90.5	65.5	79.6	66.6
1982–84						
Growth rate of real GDP	3.7	0.6	3.5	5.9	−4.7	4.4
Growth rate of population	4.1	3.5	3.8	3.2	3.3	2.9
Growth rate of GDP per capita	−0.3	−2.9	−0.3	2.7	−8.0	1.6
Ratio of investment to GDP	21.2	16.4	21.9	22.8	11.9	15.8
Ratio of savings to GDP	18.3	9.3	14.9	28.0	9.3	2.4
Ratio of net exports to GDP	−2.9	−7.1	−7.0	5.3	−2.6	−13.4
Ratio of current account deficit to GDP	−4.7	−7.4	−3.0	−1.2	−4.9	−12.8
Ratio of debt to exports	135.2	513.1	253.2	98.5	92.4	218.5
Ratio of debt service to exports	18.2	12.1	22.7	12.4	17.9	9.5
Ratio of fiscal deficit to GDP	−3.9	−3.9	−0.7	−0.6	−10.5	−9.4
Rate of inflation (CPI)	14.0	30.6	5.4	13.8	23.5	13.6

Rate of inflation (GDP deflator)	9.6	12.9	9.4	12.3	11.3	10.4
Growth rate of real output in agriculture	4.4	1.8	5.8	1.7	−1.1	3.6
Growth rate of real output in manufacturing	3.0	−9.9	3.4	13.3	−8.1	5.5
Growth rate of real output in mining	0.0	−2.7	—	22.4	−1.7	−0.8
Growth rate of exports	2.9	−16.7	−0.9	16.1	−3.5	2.4
Growth rate of imports	−6.4	−8.4	−0.4	−3.6	−19.5	−3.3
Central bank borrowing as percentage of GDP	10.4	21.9	19.3	1.8	20.3	13.8
Rural population as percentage of total population	82.0	85.0	88.0	59.0	70.0	65.0
1985–87						
Growth rate of real GDP	5.1	4.3	2.8	9.0	2.5	4.2
Growth rate of population	4.2	3.6	3.4	3.4	3.4	3.0
Growth rate of GDP per capita	0.9	0.7	−0.6	5.7	−0.9	1.2
Ratio of investment to GDP	24.0	17.2	13.5	19.8	8.9	13.7
Ratio of savings to GDP	21.7	4.8	11.6	25.3	9.7	3.6
Ratio of net exports to GDP	−2.3	−12.4	−1.9	5.5	0.7	−10.1
Ratio of current account deficit to GDP	−6.0	−12.7	−6.5	−0.2	−1.0	−13.4
Ratio of debt to exports	163.0	902.4	311.3	77.2	202.2	244.8
Ratio of debt service to exports	21.3	15.3	34.6	9.8	27.0	10.9
Ratio of fiscal deficit to GDP	−5.8	−4.3	−7.0	0.8	—	−1.6
Rate of inflation (CPI)	7.4	33.1	18.8	2.2	4.4	9.7
Rate of inflation (GDP deflator)	9.8	29.4	16.0	2.9	10.3	8.4
Growth rate of real output in agriculture	4.3	4.5	2.3	2.4	4.9	8.9
Growth rate of real output in manufacturing	5.0	−5.3	1.6	0.9	5.5	1.9
Growth rate of real output in mining	3.3	−4.6	—	1.3	−2.6	7.3
Growth rate of exports	4.5	6.0	9.2	6.6	−1.1	0.5
Growth rate of imports	5.6	13.8	−5.9	26.9	−22.6	−0.7
Central bank borrowing as percentage of GDP	10.4	22.1	16.7	2.1	18.7	10.0
Rural population as percentage of total population	80.0	86.0	—	58.0	70.0	64.0

— = Not available.

Note: The average growth rates for the period 1960–87 are calculated using the least squares method. They are all significant at the 5 percent level.

Source: World Bank Economic Database (BESD), 1989; IMF, *International Financial Statistics* (Washington, D.C.: 1987), for population figures.

graphic pressure on land, this demonstrates the importance of technological progress.

In general, the countries that relied on their comparative advantage in agricultural exports performed well and achieved rapid and sustained economic diversification, with a fall in agriculture's share in output, employment, and exports (see table 2-3). During 1967–85 the share of agriculture in GDP fell from 34 percent to 31 percent in Kenya and from 44 percent to 38 percent in Malawi. In Tanzania—which emphasized industrialization—the share of agriculture in GDP increased from 41 percent to 58 percent and in exports from 78 percent to 79 percent. The share of agriculture fell in all three West African countries, but most sharply in Cameroon. During 1960-87, manufacturing grew faster in Cameroon (8.7 percent) and Kenya (8.1 percent), the better agricultural performers, than in Tanzania (2.7 percent) and Senegal (3.9 percent) (see table 2-2).

Despite severe external shocks, Kenya capitalized on its favorable initial conditions to pursue a combination of macroeconomic and sectoral policies that led to broadly based agricultural growth. Cameroon, also capitalizing on its natural resources, increased its oil revenues but followed moderate policies (unlike neighboring Nigeria, where the oil boom created severe Dutch disease effects) and performed well with a large number of small farmers participating in the growth of food and export crops. Cameroon, however, did not grow as wide a range of crops as Kenya, and some of the Dutch disease effects caught up with Cameroon later, only as its oil revenues emerged at the end of the 1970s. Despite unfavorable initial conditions and adverse external shocks, Malawi also achieved a rapid increase in agricultural production. In Malawi's case, growth was skewed in favor of estates, and so the vast majority of smallholders did not benefit from that growth.

Following the oil boom, Nigeria's macroeconomic policies discriminated against agriculture and sparked a rapid migration of labor to the cities. At the same time, a series of military coups subjected the country to persistent political and institutional upheavals that prevented it from effectively using the vast agricultural and oil resources at its disposal. Agricultural exports plummeted, and food production could no longer keep pace with population growth. This led to a sharp rise in food prices and food imports.

In Tanzania and Senegal, agricultural exports declined and food imports increased. Although adverse macroeconomic and sectoral policies were partly to blame in both countries, Tanzania was endowed with far better natural resources than Malawi or Senegal and also enjoyed higher levels of donor support than Malawi or Kenya. The Tanzanian government made some progress toward its objectives of equity and social welfare but was unable to continue along this path

Table 2-3. Comparative Macroeconomic Structure of MADIA Countries, Selected Periods
(percent)

	Share of agriculture					
	In exports		*In employment*		*In GDP*	
Country	*1967–73*	*1985*	*1965*	*1985*	*1967–73*	*1985*
East Africa						
Kenya	75	57	84	78	34	31
Malawi	97	94	91	83	44	38
Tanzania	78	79	88	86	41	58
West Africa						
Cameroon	81	65	86	70	31	21
Nigeria	38	4	67	68	41	36
Senegal	71	46	82	81	24	19

	Share of GDP, 1960–87				
	Agriculture	*Mining*	*Manufacturing*	*Infrastructure*	*Other services*
East Africa					
Kenya	34.9	0.3	11.7	7.2	45.9
Malawi	42.6	—	10.1	5.8	41.5
Tanzania	47.3	1.4	9.1	4.5	37.7
West Africa					
Cameroon	29.2	6.1	10.1	8.8	45.8
Nigeria	41.5	12.3	7.0	4.2	35.0
Senegal	23.6	1.5	15.7	6.3	52.9

	Savings	*Investment*	*Exports*	*Imports*	*Public consumption*
East Africa					
Kenya	19.6	21.7	29.1	31.2	17.4
Malawi	9.1	20.0	24.3	35.2	16.4
Tanzania	13.5	19.2	19.1	24.9	19.9
West Africa					
Cameroon	18.0	18.8	24.4	25.1	9.9
Nigeria	15.0	15.1	15.2	15.3	9.0
Senegal	11.3	15.7	32.5	36.9	18.3

— = Not available
Source: World Bank Economic and Social Database (BESD), 1989.

because its import-substituting industrialization strategy had begun to undermine broadly based, agriculture-led growth. By pursuing an industry-based strategy, Senegal also attempted to diversify out of its traditional exports of groundnuts and related products, but agriculture was hard hit by variable and declining rainfall and soil degradation.

Agricultural Performance and Structural Adjustment

Table 2-4 presents more details on the growth rates of production and exports of major crops in the six countries during 1970–85. In Kenya the production of virtually all the leading crops increased, and the share of small farmers in the output of these crops rose substantially in relation to the output of large farms and estates. Smallholder tea hectarage increased almost tenfold and coffee hectarage doubled during 1970–85. Although the increase in smallholder production was due mainly to the expansion of areas under production and a shift to crops of higher value (with higher yields only in maize and coffee), estate production increased mainly as a result of higher yields. In contrast to most other African countries, Kenya increased its world market share of coffee from 1.8 percent in 1971–73 to 2.3 percent in 1983–85, and its share of tea from 6.5 percent to 10.7 percent over the same period (see table 2-5).

Despite a high rate of population growth (4 percent), Kenya was able to increase the production of hybrid maize and horticultural crops in areas of high potential and thus reduce the proportion of the population living in poverty. The absolute number of households living in poverty increased, however. The population growth in arid and semiarid areas exceeded that in areas of high potential. With the shift of hybrid maize production to smallholder households (which retain a large portion of their production for household consumption) and the shift of population and production to semiarid areas, the supplies of officially marketed maize became considerably more unstable than they had been in the colonial period. This, coupled with increasing urbanization and the growing dependence of rural households on the market for food, led to an increase in food imports and food aid.

In 1979, following the downturn in coffee prices, Kenya initiated a structural adjustment program. In the first half of the 1980s, the government devalued the currency, raised real interest rates substantially, reduced inflation rates (from 20 percent to 10 percent), reduced the budgetary deficit (from 10 percent to 6 percent of GNP), and held budgetary spending at about 27 percent of GNP.[12] In the latter half of the 1980s, however, the government made somewhat less progress in further reducing the budgetary deficit. Progress was also slow in other sectoral reforms, such as land registration, parastatal reform, and an increased role for the private sector.

Cameroon's achievements were less impressive than those of Kenya. Although the production of cotton, oil palm, and robusta coffee increased, the production and export of arabica coffee and cocoa—the country's two principal export crops—showed almost no

Table 2-4. Agricultural Performance in the MADIA *Countries, 1970–85*
(average annual percent growth rate, by volume)

	East Africa		
Crop	*Kenya*	*Malawi*	*Tanzania*
Major agricultural exports			
Coffee	3.8		0.8
Tea	7.5	5.2	1.9
Cotton	—	−12.5	−2.3
Tobacco	—	11.7	−4.7
Groundnut	—	−13.2	—
Horticulture	12.7	—	—
Major export crops			
Smallholder			
Coffee	6.0	—	2.3
Tea	13.5	—	13.7
Tobacco	—	3.0	−4.8
Cotton	4.9	1.1	1.6
Groundnut	—	−7.4	—
Sugar	16.9	—	—
Estates			
Coffee	1.0	—	−4.1
Tea	5.5	—	1.0
Tobacco	—	12.9	−7.5

	West Africa		
Crop	*Cameroon*	*Nigeria*	*Senegal*
Major agricultural exports			
Coffee	1.9	—	—
Cocoa	0.4	—	—
Cotton	4.6	—	—
Groundnut	—	—	−9.5
Rubber	−5.9	—	—
Palm oil	6.6	—	—
Major export crops			
Smallholders			
Coffee	1.0	—	—
Cocoa	2.0	—	—
Cotton	8.3	—	—
Estates			
Rubber	2.7	—	—
Palm oil	4.2	—	—
General			
Cotton	—	—	6.8
Groundnut	—	−3.2	—
Cocoa	—	−4.9	—

(Table continues on the following page.)

Table 2-4. (continued)

Crop	Kenya	Malawi	Tanzania
	East Africa		
Cotton	—	—	—
Sugar	—	14.7	0.8
Domestic food production			
Maize			
Production	3.9	1.5	2.1
Official purchases	2.4	19.1	1.1
Official sales	9.2	23.7	1.9
Food imports	6.4	3.1	3.0
Food aid	43.1	28.6	23.5

Crop	Cameroon	Nigeria	Senegal
	West Africa		
Domestic food production			
Rice	16.5	10.5	1.2
Maize	4.1	6.1	5.6
Millet/sorghum	1.3	0.2	0.2
Food imports			
Rice	—	46.7	7.3
Wheat	—	15.2	0.5
Sugar	—	20.0	−6.8
General	6.1	—	—
Food aid	4.1	—	—

— = Not available.

Note: Growth rates averaged for certain crops, e.g., burley and flue-cured tobacco. Growth rates for Nigeria production are calculated using FAO data.

Source: World Bank Economic and Social Database (BESD).

Table 2-5. *Export Volumes, Shares, and Growth Rates of Major Crops Grown by* MADIA *Countries and their Major Competitors: Average Values for Selected Periods, 1961–86*

	1961–63		*1971–73*		*1983–85*		*1961–86*
Crop	*Volume (thousand metric tons)*	*Share (percent)*	*Volume (thousand metric tons)*	*Share (percent)*	*Volume (thousand metric tons)*	*Share (percent)*	*Growth rate (percent)*
Cocoa beans							
World	1,043.2	100.0	1,185.1	100.0	1,319.5	100.0	0.74
Ghana	417.0	40.0	366.8	31.0	158.2	12.0	−4.05
Côte d'Ivoire	96.4	9.2	149.8	12.6	384.9	29.0	6.44
Brazil	76.1	7.3	101.4	8.5	144.1	11.0	2.65
Ecuador	33.2	3.2	42.9	3.6	40.5	3.0	−1.73
Malaysia	0.3	0.0	4.3	0.4	68.3	5.2	27.72
Cameroon	70.5	6.8	81.9	6.9	86.2	6.5	0.59
Nigeria	187.3	18.0	237.7	20.1	143.2	11.1	−2.75
Coffee							
World	2,910.3	100.0	3,559.9	100.0	4,220.6	100.0	1.54
Brazil	1,057.2	36.3	1,051.9	29.6	1,001.7	23.7	−1.39
Colombia	366.9	12.6	396.4	11.2	574.5	13.6	2.52
Côte d'Ivoire	160.6	5.5	195.5	5.5	216.3	5.1	1.71
Angola	140.1	4.8	192.4	5.4	22.7	0.5	−8.39
Mexico	85.1	2.9	111.5	3.1	196.6	4.7	3.71
Indonesia	64.5	2.2	94.0	2.6	273.7	6.5	6.54
Cameroon	39.2	1.3	70.6	2.0	90.8	2.2	3.49
Kenya	34.3	1.2	65.0	1.8	97.3	2.3	5.03
Tanzania	25.9	0.9	50.2	1.4	49.8	1.2	2.28
Cotton							
World	3,647.9	100.0	4,299.2	100.0	4,294.9	100.0	0.82

(Table continues on the following page.)

Table 2-5. (continued)

Crop	1961–63 Volume (thousand metric tons)	1961–63 Share (percent)	1971–73 Volume (thousand metric tons)	1971–73 Share (percent)	1983–85 Volume (thousand metric tons)	1983–85 Share (percent)	1961–86 Growth rate (percent)
United States	1,103.8	30.1	961.2	22.2	1,265.1	29.4	1.20
Mexico	366.8	10.1	182.9	4.3	85.7	2.0	−6.35
USSR	349.2	9.6	642.4	14.9	691.6	16.1	3.55
Egypt	278.5	7.6	304.4	7.1	175.7	4.1	−3.31
Brazil	214.5	5.9	264.6	6.2	99.7	2.3	−10.76
Pakistan	121.6	3.3	216.3	5.1	203.6	4.7	1.79
China	—	—	22.0	0.5	203.3	4.7	14.91
Nigeria	37.8	1.0	10.7	0.3	—	—	−8.85
Tanzania	37.3	1.0	60.0	1.4	33.1	0.8	−1.75
Groundnut							
World	1,385.0	100.0	917.4	100.0	785.5	100.0	−2.95
Sudan	105.5	7.6	120.9	13.2	17.1	2.2	−6.60
Niger	76.0	5.5	76.3	8.4	—	—	−29.65
South Africa	65.8	4.8	56.8	6.2	10.8	1.4	−4.96
The Gambia	50.4	3.7	34.0	3.7	31.0	4.0	−2.38
United States	14.8	1.1	163.4	17.7	266.8	33.9	12.54
China	2.6	0.2	32.1	3.5	154.0	19.6	13.50
Argentina	—	—	1.2	0.1	93.4	11.9	46.37
Cameroon	11.9	0.9	9.4	1.0	0.3	0.0	−20.62
Malawi	20.7	1.5	30.8	3.4	4.9	0.6	−4.78
Nigeria	554.7	40.0	147.1	16.0	—	—	−33.25
Senegal	249.9	18.1	17.2	1.9	13.7	1.8	−19.54
Groundnut cake							
World	1,426.6	102.6	1,630.8	100.0	591.1	100.0	−4.07

India	615.2	43.8	845.0	51.9	248.1	43.1	−4.07
Burma	152.3	11.0	51.3	3.1	4.2	0.7	−14.85
Argentina	127.3	9.2	73.5	4.6	30.6	5.5	−5.33
Brazil	101.5	7.4	150.5	9.2	28.9	5.4	−5.37
The Gambia	2.9	0.2	16.0	1.0	13.6	2.6	4.03
United States	—	—	—	—	16.5	3.1	1.80
Malawi	1.0	0.1	1.8	0.1	1.5	0.3	0.85
Nigeria	84.0	6.1	112.6	7.0	—	—	−25.41
Senegal	163.3	11.9	201.9	12.2	115.1	18.2	−2.70
Groundnut oil							
World	354.9	100.0	466.2	100.0	383.8	100.0	0.02
Argentina	55.2	15.2	53.0	11.5	35.6	9.3	1.95
India	37.7	9.8	0.1	0.0	—	—	−14.16
China	6.2	1.8	19.3	4.2	53.0	13.8	6.44
Brazil	5.6	1.5	59.8	13.1	54.3	14.7	6.19
Nigeria	60.1	16.9	64.5	13.7	—	—	−14.76
Senegal	116.0	33.7	126.4	26.2	109.1	26.7	−2.24
Palm oil							
World	601.7	100.0	1,378.2	100.0	4,513.7	100.0	10.73
Zaire	149.3	24.8	87.0	6.5	8.9	0.2	−14.48
Indonesia	109.1	18.1	236.0	17.1	435.2	9.5	6.64
Malaysia	106.4	17.7	689.4	49.8	3,029.1	67.6	17.36
Singapore	32.5	5.4	210.5	15.3	685.3	14.9	14.52
Cameroon	8.9	1.5	3.4	0.3	5.7	0.1	−0.29
Nigeria	138.5	22.9	7.4	0.6	—	—	−21.91
Tea							
World	611.4	100.0	778.0	100.0	1,049.2	100.0	2.46
India	213.5	34.9	196.9	25.3	216.1	20.6	0.16

(Table continues on the following page.)

Table 2-5. (continued)

Crop	1961–63		1971–73		1983–85		1961–86
	Volume (thousand metric tons)	Share (percent)	Volume (thousand metric tons)	Share (percent)	Volume (thousand metric tons)	Share (percent)	Growth rate (percent)
Sri Lanka	201.6	33.0	203.2	26.1	186.8	17.7	−0.47
China	30.2	5.0	43.7	5.6	135.7	12.9	7.26
Indonesia	29.6	4.9	40.0	5.1	81.5	7.7	4.74
Kenya	16.2	2.6	50.3	6.5	111.9	10.7	8.96
Malawi	12.0	2.0	20.4	2.6	36.8	3.5	5.47
Tanzania	3.8	0.6	9.0	1.2	13.4	1.3	5.73
Tobacco							
World	879.0	100.0	1,161.5	100.0	1,375.0	100.0	2.17
United States	223.1	25.4	260.1	22.3	247.1	18.0	0.49
Zimbabwe	76.9	8.7	60.0	5.1	90.7	6.6	2.21
Turkey	74.6	8.5	105.8	9.1	80.7	5.9	0.76
Bulgaria	68.7	7.8	64.6	5.6	61.7	4.5	−0.57
India	59.9	6.8	72.7	6.2	76.2	5.6	1.99
Greece	58.4	6.6	59.8	5.2	84.3	6.1	0.59
Brazil	45.0	5.1	63.5	5.5	187.6	13.6	7.12
Italy	15.6	1.8	22.8	1.9	87.3	6.3	12.63
Malawi	13.0	1.5	27.5	2.4	57.8	4.2	6.83

— = Not available.

Note: In cases where data for certain years were not available, interpolations based on averages were made to allow calculation of growth rates.

Source: World Bank Economic and Social Database (BESD).

growth. There was little change in Cameroon's world market shares in any of these crops: Its share in coffee rose marginally, from 2.0 percent in 1971–73 to 2.2 percent in 1983–85; in cocoa, it fell slightly, from 6.9 percent to 6.5 percent during the same period; and in oil palm, it fell from 0.3 percent to 0.1 percent. The production of traditional food crops kept pace with population growth. With abundant land, Cameroon continued to emphasize plantation agriculture well into the 1970s. Nevertheless, a large number of small farmers participated in the production of a wide range of food and export crops. An important development in Cameroon, as in other West African countries, has been the growth of maize production (albeit from a small base), which shows much long-term potential as a food and feed crop. Among the West African countries, Cameroon was also the least dependent on food imports—except rice, imports of which increased rapidly with the sharp rise in internal demand as a result of income growth and urbanization. Rice (and wheat) imports increased in Senegal and Nigeria as well.

In 1989, after two years of protracted negotiations, Cameroon received its first $150 million structural adjustment loan from the World Bank. Being a member of the CFA zone, however, Cameroon has had great difficulty in adjusting its exchange rate and producer prices, and therefore in restructuring the economy away from oil.

Malawi's inequitable performance is explained by the fact that the production of burley and flue-cured tobacco, the principal exports, has been reserved for estates (although the average size of estates declined over time). Estate crop production increased impressively, and Malawi's world market share in tobacco grew from 2.4 percent in 1971–73 to 4.2 percent in 1983–85. Its share in tea increased from 2.6 percent to 3.5 percent. In contrast to the stagnant yields in the smallholder sector, yields on estates registered strong increases (they were on average four times higher than yields on small holdings); in Kenya estate yields were only two times higher; table 2-15, discussed below, supplies additional details. Not only did the disparity between the living standards of estate owners and most small farm households increase, but the living standards of the latter worsened in real terms.

In contrast to Kenya, Malawi was able to prevent a significant rise in the effective demand for food because of the skewed distribution of income and the declining real wages of smallholder households there. Thus, although Malawi produced less maize per capita than Kenya, and although the Malawian diet is less diversified than the Kenyan, Malawi was a net exporter of food during much of the period under consideration. It was only in the latter half of the 1980s that pervasive malnutrition, high infant mortality, and other manifestations of the extreme poverty of most Malawians came to the attention of policymakers and donors.

Land-locked and trade-dependent Malawi embarked on a structural adjustment program in 1981, which has been hampered by the political problems in neighboring Mozambique. When its border with Mozambique was closed, transportation costs rose. With the influx of half a million refugees (or about 6 percent of Malawi's total population) by mid-1988, the government diverted some of its funds to support refugee-related operations. Nevertheless, most macroeconomic indicators improved by 1987. The budget deficit shrank from 12 percent of GDP in 1980 to about 7 percent in 1987, while the current account fell from 15 percent to about 5 percent of GDP in the same period. In contrast, the aggregate supply response of the agricultural sector was weak. As in Kenya, initial adjustment measures had been taken on short-term macroeconomic grounds and consisted of grain-marketing liberalization, the reduction of fertilizer subsidies, and a reduced role for the National Rural Development Program. The important nonprice factors constraining a supply response from smallholder agriculture—particularly the various legal restrictions on small farmers such as rights to grow export crops and sell them at international prices—received relatively little attention under the first three structural adjustment loans. More recently, the government and donors alike have recognized the importance of equity and some of these nonprice factors and are attempting to refocus reforms accordingly.[13]

In Tanzania, export agriculture on both large and small farms stagnated. As in Malawi, a strong shift from export crops to food crops occurred within the smallholder sector until the introduction of macroeconomic reforms in 1986. Tanzania's market share in cotton fell from 1.4 percent in 1971–73 to 0.8 percent in 1983–85, and its shares in both tea and coffee stagnated at around 1.3 percent during the same period. Despite surplus land and large amounts of donor assistance, the unfavorable policy environment had an adverse effect on agricultural production, and food imports rose rapidly. Informal markets became more active by the end of the 1970s, both internally and across national borders. Because of the growing overvaluation of the currency and severe shortage of consumer goods, maize offered flexibility in exchange for consumer goods across the border.

Tanzania reluctantly embarked on a program of macroeconomic reform in 1986. Aside from adjusting the exchange rate, it has established fiscal and monetary targets, improved foreign exchange allocation, achieved positive real interest rates, removed price controls from 388 categories of goods (out of 400), achieved real increases in producer prices for export crops, and reduced public sector involvement in the economy. After stagnating or declining in the first half of the 1980s, real GDP averaged 4.3 percent annual growth during 1985–87, exceeding population growth for the first time since 1980. Overall agricultural production responded well to these reforms, in part because of favorable weather, and grew about 4–5 percent a year in this period. Progress has been less impressive on some other fronts; inflation, for example, remains high at 20–30 percent, and the budget deficit, which was expected to fall to 1 percent of GDP by 1988, is still about 4–5 percent.

The data on Nigerian food production are by far the most inconsistent among those available for the six countries. Nevertheless, it is clear that palm oil, cocoa, cotton, and groundnut production declined between 1961 and 1986 and reduced Nigeria's share in the world market for these products, and that the production of rice and maize increased. Wheat imports increased sixfold during 1970–86, and rice and sugar imports rose eightfold during 1976–85. Imports of maize increased by a factor of 35 during 1976–82, albeit from a low base. In 1986 the government imposed a ban on food imports. The sharp rise in food prices suggests that the production of food could not match the rapidly growing urban demand, despite the increase in imports.

With the decline in the price of oil (beginning in 1984) and the fall in export earnings, Nigeria adopted drastic adjustment measures in 1986. These included a massive devaluation of the naira (by 800 percent), abolition of marketing boards, liberalization of cocoa producer prices, and budget rationing. To increase incentives for domestic producers Nigeria's new military government completely reversed previous trade policy and banned the import of rice, wheat, maize, barley, and edible oils in 1986–87. Numerous sector-specific constraints such as the poor state of technology, poor rural infrastructure, and weaknesses in the government's planning and implementing capacity, however, continued to hinder an aggregate supply response to the reforms.

Senegal had the lowest self-sufficiency ratio in food among the MADIA countries—with food imports accounting for nearly 35 percent of aggregate calorie availability (compared with 10 percent or less for the rest of the MADIA sample). Stagnant domestic production and expanding internal demand pushed rice imports up sharply until they peaked at more than 370,000 metric tons in 1984–85. Whereas in the 1960s groundnut exports alone could ensure as much as seven years of rice imports, by the mid-1980s they could cover only one year's supply. This was a result of the growing internal demand for rice and declining exports of groundnuts, groundnut cake, and groundnut oil (even though international groundnut prices had moved favorably with respect to rice prices through much of the period). Senegal's market share in groundnuts fell from 18.1 percent in 1961–63 to 1.8

percent in 1983–85, and that in groundnut oil from 33.7 percent to 26.7 percent. Although maize production did well in Senegal (albeit from a small base, with only a 3 percent share of cultivated area), overall agricultural production in Senegal fluctuated from year to year because of the weather.

Senegal embarked on structural adjustment as early as 1979, but severe droughts in the early 1980s dampened the adjustment and economic transition. Good weather and favorable terms of trade were the most important factors underlying the spurt in growth during 1984–88. GDP grew at an estimated 4.3 percent a year during this period (compared with a long-term performance of 2.2 percent), the overall fiscal deficit declined from 7.7 percent of GDP to 4.3 percent, and the current account deficit fell from 17.7 percent of GDP to 9.2 percent. However, the numerous and severe structural constraints in the country's agricultural (and industrial) sector have hindered a sustained supply response. Senegal is poor in natural resources and the possibilities for agricultural production are limited, the use of modern inputs has declined, the exchange rate has remained fixed within the West African Monetary Union, domestic costs are high, and there are no clear international markets for its traditional exports. A regional market with Nigeria needs to be developed actively for livestock and groundnuts. However, it is not an issue that has received the attention it deserves due to the colonially based anglophone and francophone division. Consequently, Senegal has been unable to achieve sustained growth, despite the prolonged effort at adjustment.

Several of the countries are correcting the larger, more obvious distortions such as the overvalued exchange rates and large budget deficits. But even if the reforms are sustained, it is too early to judge whether the growth rate will accelerate given the human, institutional, and technological problems these countries face. Such problems can be resolved only by detailed, practical strategies designed for individual countries and often specific locations. Even in the newer, more desirable macroeconomic circumstances, a sustained supply response will depend on whether institutions and the physical infrastructure can be rebuilt. As the remainder of this chapter makes clear, governments must be prepared to make an all-out political commitment and devote a considerable investment of time to such tasks if they expect to remove the longer-term structural constraints. An amorphous debate on governance has shifted attention from structural adjustment; yet the fundamental role of governments in the provision of public goods and the steps needed to ensure that provision remain unappreciated in the donor community.

Building on Different Bases: The Luck Factor

Macroeconomic and sectoral policies obviously influence a country's agricultural performance. No less important is "luck"—in the advantages it starts with (including its natural resources, physical and social infrastructure, and degree of institutional development) and the external shocks it experiences. In some respects, luck is a stochastic variable. An important question is the extent to which countries take advantage of their good luck and withstand the bad.

Resources. The population of most of the MADIA countries has doubled since independence and will double again shortly after the turn of the century. High rates of population growth—generally exceeding 3 percent per year and around 4 percent in Kenya—leave little room for doubt about the growing demographic pressure on the resource base of the countries under consideration.

Kenya, Malawi, Nigeria, and, to a lesser extent, Senegal are now experiencing substantial population pressure. By government definitions, these countries had no more than three-quarters of a hectare of cultivable land per person in 1985 (see table 2-6) According to definitions given by the Food and Agriculture Organization (FAO), the per person amounts are even smaller. Thus it appears that by the year 2000 per capita cultivable land will fall to less than half a hectare and to a minuscule 0.1 hectare in some parts of Kenya, Malawi, and Nigeria.

Note, however, that the countries differ greatly in the amount of land they classify as arable, and that the data are frequently unreliable. Estimates of arable land range from only 26 percent in Kenya to 75 percent in Cameroon and Nigeria. The proportion of arable land is 53 percent in Senegal and 56 percent in Malawi and Tanzania. Most government estimates include forests and permanent crops and tend to be more optimistic about the land available for cultivation on areas marginal for cropping than seems desirable from an environmental point of view. FAO estimates in some cases are significantly lower.

Furthermore, per capita land figures are deceptive in that they mask important differences in land quality and in the regional concentration of population. Among the six countries, only Kenya appears to have the high land potential to match its high population densities—together with relatively well-developed institutions bestowed by its European settler agriculture. Increasing population pressure and limited access to land due to land policies in the areas of high potential, however, are forcing the population to move toward marginal areas. Paradoxically, Kenya's areas of high potential face serious labor shortages.

Even in the land-surplus countries, population is concentrated on small amounts of land. In Cameroon, 70 to 80 percent of the rural population is concentrated on only 20 percent of the land. Millions of hectares of well-watered land in the eastern tropical rain forests go unused, while population pressure and declining rainfall in the semi-

Table 2-6. Per Capita Arable Land (Present and Projected) in MADIA Countries, 1965, 1985, 2000
(hectares per person)

	1965	*1985*		*2000*	
Country	*Total population*	*Rural population*	*Total population*	*Rural population*	*Total population*
East Africa					
Kenya	1.34	0.86	0.73	0.60	0.42
Malawi	0.86	0.81	0.73	0.60	0.45
Tanzania	3.99	2.59	2.30	1.68	1.44
West Africa					
Cameroon	5.99	5.23	3.34	4.76	2.09
Nigeria	1.22	1.01	0.71	0.88	0.48
Senegal	2.67	2.38	1.62	1.80	1.04

Note: Estimates and methodologies for calculating arable land vary. For Kenya, which conducted a detailed agroclimatic analysis in conjunction with the German Agency for Technical Cooperation (GTZ), the estimate is 26 percent. For other countries, such as Cameroon and Nigeria, where extensive soil analysis is lacking, the estimates reach 75 percent of total land area. Population figures are projected from most recent census in country to year 1985 and 2000. Rural population is calculated from government estimates of urban population and the percentage urbanized in year 2000.

Source: Ralph Jaetzold and Helmut Schmidt, *Farm Management Handbook of Kenya: Natural Conditions and Farm Management Information* (Government of Kenya, Ministry of Agriculture and German Agricultural Team of the German Agency for Technical Cooperation, 1982); Richard Mkandawiri and Chimimba Phiri, "Assessment of Land Transfer from Smallholders to Estates," paper written for World Bank; United Republic of Tanzania, *Statistical Abstract* (1973–79) (Bureau of Statistics, Ministry of Planning and Economic Affairs, 1983); Uma Lele, A. T. Oyejide, Balu Bumb, and Vishva Bindlish, "Nigeria's Economic Development, Agriculture's Role, and World Bank Assistance, 1961 to 1986: Lessons for the Future," MADIA Working Paper (Africa—Technical Department, Agriculture Division, World Bank, Washington, D.C., 1989); *République du Cameroon, Bilan Diagnotisque du Secteur Agricole au Cameroun* (Ministère de l'Agriculture, 1980); République du Sénégal, "Situation Economique du Sénégal" (Ministère du Développement Rural/Direction Statistique, 1982); and "Sixième Plan Quadriennal du Developpment Economique et Social, 1981–85" (Ministère du Plan et de la Coopération, 1982); Uma Lele and Steven Stone, *Population Pressure, the Environment, and Agricultural Intensification: Variations on the Boserup Hypothesis,* MADIA Discussion Paper 4 (Washington, D.C.: World Bank, 1989).

arid far north and northern provinces already have begun to threaten fragile ecologies. In Nigeria, Senegal, and Tanzania, the population has settled in the areas of highest potential, those with the best cropping possibilities or lowest risk of disease, but large tracts of fertile land remain sparsely populated. Population and land distribution raise important questions as to the extent to which physical potential is being taken into account in agricultural planning in Africa together with cultural, sociopolitical, and other institutional factors. The land population dynamics will need greater attention based on sound empirical analysis and armed with a broad macrosectoral policy/strategy perspective. Such a focus might help agriculture to prosper in the areas of greater agricultural potential, thus enabling this growth to be tapped for financing welfare activities in the more marginal areas.

Soils in East Africa are thin and low in nutrients, except in the subhumid highlands. Yields tend to be high initially, when chemical fertilizer is used, but they decline with repeated cultivation unless supplemented with organic matter. Regions that receive 400 to 800 millimeters of rainfall, including large parts of Kenya and Tanzania, produce mainly the hardy cereals like sorghum and millet, and, to a lesser extent, cotton, groundnuts, and tobacco. In regions with higher rainfall, between 800 and 1,200 millimeters, higher-value grains such as wheat and maize can be grown—along with tea, coffee, and pyrethrum in the higher altitudes of Kenya and Tanzania. The increasing frequency of cropping and shorter fallow periods are having an adverse effect on soil fertility and nutrient content. This degradation is accelerating now that more people are moving onto marginal land with long fallow requirements.

In the semiarid tropical regions of West Africa and parts of the humid and subhumid tropics farther south, soils are more susceptible to rapid degradation with continuous use than was previously thought: increasing applications of inorganic and organic fertilizers are required to maintain soil fertility.[14] In the semiarid tropics of West Africa, which receive 200 to 800 millimeters of rainfall a year, the emphasis is on lower-value crops and systems of mixed cropping: sorghum/millet, groundnuts, and cotton. Because of low and variable rainfall, fertilizer may go unused in a dry season or may be washed away in a sudden downpour, and it becomes risky to intensify fertilizer applications. Low level and variability in demand places decided restrictions on the extent to which the private sector can be counted on to meet the input needs of soils on small farms, given that returns to capital on alternate uses tends to be higher. The wetter climate of southern Senegal, the middle belt states of Nigeria, and northern Cameroon is more hospitable to cereals (such as wheat and maize) and a variety of tubers (such as yams and cassava). These regions receive between 800 and 1,000 millimeters of rainfall a year and have soil that is typically ferruginous, crusty, and prone to leaching. The clay content is generally below 20 percent. This kind of soil tends to be shallow and does not retain moisture, and therefore is not as fertile as soil with more clay or organic matter.

Although existing data appear to suggest that fertilizer response coefficients are low in comparison with similar areas of rainfall in South Asia, they are higher than in the drier regions farther north. The threat of trypanosomiasis and other diseases and pests, however, prevents the extensive use of draft animals and keeps population densities low, despite the potential for growing a wider range of crops than in the semiarid areas to the north. Eastward and to the south, in the lower parts of Nigeria and Cameroon, the soil is generally less stable and more vulnerable to acidification, and therefore susceptible to erosion when cultivated intensively. The problems of soil degradation and erosion are particularly acute in this zone because of dense population. The higher rainfall in this area, between 1,400 and 3,200 millimeters, is well suited to the production of tropical tree crops such as cocoa, oil palm, and rubber, and to the root crops yams and cassava.

Physical infrastructure. The development of rail and road networks by colonial settlers played an important role in establishing a prosperous export agriculture in many parts of Africa. It broadened input and output markets, helped disseminate critical technological know-how, ensured access to consumer goods and services, and thus provided crucial production incentives. Although comparing road densities poses conceptual and empirical problems, some useful observations on this subject are nevertheless possible. At independence, Malawi, Nigeria, and Kenya (in that order) had a higher density of roads than did Senegal, Cameroon, or Tanzania (see table 2-7).

Although Nigeria now has the highest density of roads per unit of *total* land, density per unit of *arable* land is far higher in Kenya and Malawi (in that order) than in any of the other countries. The MADIA study's detailed comparison of road density in Nigeria and in India in the 1960s (when India's population density was similar to that in Nigeria in the late 1980s) shows that current road density in Nigeria is less than a quarter of that in India in the 1960s.[15] It also shows that the quality of road maintenance in Nigeria has been poor relative to India's as a result of the deteriorating capacity of the public works departments at the local and state levels. The study concludes that the capacity for road maintenance is essential for the expansion of a rural feeder road network, that the development of such capacity has been neglected by governments and donors alike, and that privatization without the provision of such necessary public goods may not lead to market development. Unlike Nigeria, Kenya has the capacity to plan and implement the construction and maintenance of feeder roads. This explains in part Kenya's better record of smallholder development—particularly in areas of high potential such as the Central Province, where the road network is well established through such programs as the tea roads.

Kenya had the largest European settlement in Africa and consequently a relatively good transport infrastructure—including a railway connecting the White Highlands to the port of Mombasa. Even though Malawi has a reasonably good road network, this has not offset the

Table 2-7. *Roads in MADIA Countries*

Condition	Kenya	Malawi	Tanzania	Cameroon	Nigeria	Senegal
	East Africa			*West Africa*		
At independence						
Paved roads (kilometers)	2,013	413	1,300	1,231	11,053	1,658
Gravel/earth roads (kilometers)	39,934	9,697	14,292	13,122	60,818	6,851
Total classified roads (kilometers)	41,947	10,128	15,592	14,353	71,871	8,509
Population density						
Thousand	9,404	3,854	11,586	5,332	43,278	3,839
Meters per person	4.5	2.6	1.3	2.7	1.3	2.2
Total land (thousands of square kilometers)	569.25	94.08	886.04	469.44	910.77	192
Arable land (percentage)	26.0	37.0	56.0	75.0	75.0	53.0
Density of road to total land (kilometers/100 square kilometers)	7.4	10.8	1.8	3.1	7.9	4.4
Density of road to arable land (kilometers/100 square kilometers)	28.3	29.1	3.1	4.1	10.5	8.4
At present						
Paved roads (kilometers)	7,944	2,176	3,194	2,922	24,900	3,688
Gravel/earth roads (kilometers)	56,640	9,253	78,701	46,599	103,274	10,280
Total classified roads (kilometers)	64,584	11,429	81,895	49,521	128,174	13,968
Population density						
Thousand	18,791	7,044	21,497	10,555	93,402	6,036
Meters per person	3.4	1.6	3.8	4.7	1.2	2.3
Total land (thousands of square kilometers)	569.25	94.08	886.04	469.44	910.77	192.00

(Table continues on the following page.)

Table 2-7. (continued)

	East Africa			*West Africa*		
Condition	*Kenya*	*Malawi*	*Tanzania*	*Cameroon*	*Nigeria*	*Senegal*
Arable land (percentage)	26.0	37.0	56.0	75.0	75.0	53.0
Density of roads to total land (kilometers/100 square kilometers)	11.3	12.1	9.2	10.5	14.1	7.3
Density of roads to arable land (kilometers/100 square kilometers)	43.6	32.8	16.5	14.1	18.7	13.7

Source: International Road Federation, "World Road Statistics" (Washington, D.C., 1969, 1985); Government of Malawi, "Inventory of Designated Roads in Malawi" (Lilongwe, 1984, 1985); Juan Gaviria, Vishva Bindlish, and Uma Lele, *The Rural Question and Nigeria's Agricultural Development*, MADIA Discussion Paper 10 (Washington, D.C.: World Bank, 1989); Uma Lele and Steve Stone, *Population Pressure, the Environment, and Agricultural Intensification: Variations on the Boserup Hypothesis*, MADIA Discussion Paper 4 (Washington, D.C.: World Bank, 1989); World Bank Economic and Social Database (BESD); Louis Mvele, "Cooperation Nord-Sud Echecs et Succès: Les Cas des Infrastructures de Transport au Cameroun" (Geneve Institut Universitaire des Hautes Etudes Internationales, 1984).

high international transportation costs associated with being a land-locked country. These costs have more than doubled since the closure of Malawi's traditional shipping outlets in Mozambique in the early 1980s. Malawi's experience also shows that, despite its high population density and its superior record in developing feeder roads, a highly skewed distribution of income can curb the development of the means of transport and markets. The Groundnut Basin in Senegal benefited from the French investment in an effective road and rail network designed to facilitate the exchange of smallholder groundnut production and Indo-Chinese rice. In contrast, Cameroon and Tanzania—the two land-surplus countries—had a relatively poor physical infrastructure but, unlike Malawi, had good ports. In Tanzania, however, inadequate investment in rural feeder roads has been a serious constraint to growth in production.

Social infrastructure. Attention must also be given to the social services if the incentives for agricultural production are to improve. Better health services and rural water supply have a beneficial effect on productivity and reduce the number of production days lost due to sickness. Life expectancy increases, infant mortality declines, and population grows at a slower rate. Furthermore, investment in primary and secondary education increases both the supply and the quality of human capital. It improves the quality of the planning and implementation of rural development programs and increases the receptivity of farm populations to improved but complex and risky technologies.

Although the MADIA study was primarily concerned with agricultural policies and performance, the analysis of public expenditures provided important insight into the development of social services. As some of the studies in this book show, the donors' project-centered approach to these services in the 1970s overlooked critical questions relating to fiscal and administrative feasibility. Moreover, donors failed to recognize that investing in education is a way of improving the capacity for planning and implemention.

Social indicators were very poor at independence in all six countries (see table 2-8). Kenya had the most favorable ratios of life expectancy, infant mortality, and population per physician. It devoted a quarter to a third of its public expenditures to social services during 1970–86 and experienced a sustained—albeit skewed—improvement in its social indicators. The social gains accruing to the politically important agricultural constituencies (such as those in the Central Province) were disproportionately large. Broad access to primary education in Kenya has kept children in schools, maintaining a relatively high reservation price for labor.

Table 2-8. Basic Social Indicators for MADIA Countries, Selected Years

		East Africa			West Africa		
Item	*Year*	*Kenya*	*Malawi*	*Tanzania*	*Cameroon*	*Nigeria*	*Senegal*
Population (in millions)	1965	9.5	3.9	11.7	6.1[a]	48.7	3.4
	1986	21	7	23	11	103	7
Population growth rate (percentage)	1965–80	3.6	2.9	3.3	2.7	2.5	2.5
	1980–86	4.1	3.2	3.5	3.2	3.3	2.9
GNP per capita (in U.S. dollars)	1965	103	63	76	168	49	241
	1987	340	160	220[b]	960	370[c]	510
Life expectancy (in years)	1965	45	39	43	46	42	41
	1986	57	45	53	56	51	47
Infant mortality rate (per thousand)	1965	112	199	138	143	177	171
	1986	83	164	98	85	105	124
Population per physician	1965	12,820	46,900	21,700	26,680	44,230	21,100
	1981	10,140	53,000	19,810	13,990	12,000	14,200

Indicator	Year						
Percentage of age group enrolled in primary school	1965	54	44	32	94	32	40
	1985	94	62	72	107	92	55
Percentage of age group enrolled in secondary school	1965	4	2	2	5	5	7
	1985	20	4	3	23	29	13
Percentage of population with access to safe water	1973	15	33	13	26	15	37
	1980	26	41	34	53	36	42
Average annual growth rate of urbanization	1965–80	9.0	7.8	8.7	8.1	4.8	4.1
	1980–85	6.3	—	8.3	7.0	5.2	4.0

— = Not available.

a. Figure for 1968.

b. Use of overvalued official exchange rate in the case of Tanzania overstates its achievements in per capita income growth relative to other countries.

c. As a result of the recent devaluation, per capita GNP in Nigeria was approximately four times lower than amount shown above.

Source: World Bank, *World Development Report* (Washington, D.C., 1985, 1986, 1987, 1988). World Bank, *Social Indicators of Development*, (Washington, D.C., 1986). Per capita GNP for 1985 calculated from IMF, *International Financial Statistics Yearbook,* (Washington, D.C., 1987). République du Cameroun, "Enquête Nationale sur la Nutrition" (Washington, D.C., U.S. AID, 1978).

Malawi, consistent with its having the lowest per capita income of the six MADIA countries in 1965, had the lowest life expectancy, the highest child mortality, and the highest population per physician. Its social services, unlike Kenya's, accounted for a small and declining share of public expenditures—as smallholder constituencies were relatively unimportant in the 1970s. Not surprisingly, social indicators have improved less in Malawi over time in comparison with the other countries. Inadequate access of children to primary education has led to extensive use of child labor on agriculture estates, contributing to the depression of the real wage in rural Malawi. Yet the percentage of population with access to safe water was favorable at independence and still is.

Although Tanzania had poorer indicators than Kenya at independence, it made great strides in the 1970s—particularly in lowering child mortality and improving access to safe water. However, its single-minded pursuit of equity in the absence of growth made these gains difficult to sustain. Moreover, despite the emphasis on equity, Tanzania (like Malawi) placed less emphasis than Kenya on secondary education.

In West Africa, only a few data exist on Nigeria's indicators of life expectancy, infant mortality, and access to physicians and safe water, but they suggest that the indicators improved substantially after the oil boom of the 1970s. At independence, Senegal had the highest proportion of population with access to safe water. But in Senegal, as in Malawi, social indicators have shown less improvement than in the other MADIA countries.

Cameroon had by far the highest primary school enrollment in 1965, but it has since fallen behind Kenya, Nigeria, and Tanzania in this respect. Similarly, Senegal—the center of the former French empire in West Africa—had the highest level of secondary school attendees in 1965 and inherited a favorable endowment of skilled and educated personnel; yet Cameroon, Nigeria, and Kenya have made better progress in improving access to secondary school education. Malawi and Tanzania continue to have extremely low rates of secondary school enrollment.[16]

The level and pace of urbanization differ between East and West Africa but explain the rapid growth of wheat and rice imports mentioned earlier. In West Africa, about one-third of the population already lives in cities and towns of at least 5,000 persons, compared with only a tenth in East Africa. But the *rate* of growth of urbanization in the three East African countries has ranged from 8 to 11 percent annually, in comparison with West Africa's range of 3–8 percent.

Institutional development. Smallholder development depends on stable, predictable, and consistent institutional responses to agricultural research, extension, credit, and input and output marketing. Responses of this kind cannot take place unless there are institutions to represent the political and technological interests of the small farmers, and they have qualified personnel and adequate financial resources to function effectively.[17] In this section the institutional environment in the MADIA countries is considered from the point of view of their institutional stability, political representation of smallholder interests, technocracy, and the fragmentation of the institutional responsibility for policy planning.

Whereas Cameroon, Kenya, and Malawi have had a relatively stable institutional environment, Nigeria, Senegal, and Tanzania have experienced a high degree of institutional instability. In the 1980s, however, Kenya's institutions, too, became more unstable. Like Tanzania, Kenya split the ministries of agriculture and livestock in 1980 and then reunited them. It shifted the responsibility for grain marketing from the Kenya Farmers Association (KFA—a cooperative of large European and African producers) to the Kenya Grain Growers Association—a move that improved political representation but reduced efficiency. By the end of the 1980s, agricultural responsibilities were divided among as many as seven ministries.

In Tanzania, numerous changes in marketing and processing arrangements created a disruptive and unpredictable policy environment for agriculture. First, private traders were discouraged in the early 1970s. Cooperative unions were then rapidly promoted, only to be abolished in 1976. Crop parastatals came next (they numbered 400 by the end of the 1970s), but many were abolished in 1983 and replaced with cooperatives. The early 1980s also saw the creation of marketing boards, and it was not until 1985 that a degree of liberalization was introduced in agricultural marketing.

Senegal has also experienced considerable institutional instability and unpredictability. Since the early 1960s, a plethora of parastatals, agricultural cooperatives, and rural development agencies have helped the government consolidate its control over the agricultural sector. By the end of the 1970s, the growth of public employment, overextension of managerial and financial resources, and political interference began to hinder seriously the functioning of many of these agencies. When the Office Nationale de Coopération et d'Assistance au Développement (ONCAD), which managed groundnut and was the largest parastatal, was abolished in 1980, credit, fertilizer, and seed distribution services in the Groundnut Basin collapsed. The financing requirements of the numerous rural development agencies had become unsustainable by then, and in view of their unsatisfactory performance, the government began privatizing their functions in 1984. The increased politicization of cooperatives, coupled with the widespread abuse of authority, also led the government to embark on a radical transformation of the cooperatives in 1983.

The unpredictable political, administrative, and institutional environment in Nigeria was associated with unsettling political events, especially the protracted civil war in the late 1960s, followed by six changes of government (including five coups) and a redefinition of state boundaries (the number of states had increased from three to twenty in two decades).[18] A shift in the source of government revenues from export agriculture to oil following the civil war, together with the numerous coups, caused the political and administrative power to become increasingly centralized. Centralization safeguarded Nigeria's national integrity but eroded its governmental capacity.

Agricultural policy has been most responsive to grass roots institutions in Kenya, where the political process has allowed better articulation of smallholder interests. Kenya's struggle for independence was based on the assertion of land rights denied to the Africans during the colonial era and buttressed with significant administrative and financial support for smallholder development beginning just before the end of the colonial era. These events contributed to the development of a highly decentralized system that recognizes and responds to producer interests. Cooperatives represent 50 percent of Kenya's small-farm households, and the country has also produced such successful and internationally renowned smallholder organizations as the Kenya Tea Development Authority.

Governments in the other countries, in contrast, have been highly skeptical of the efficiency of small farmers and somewhat unenthusiastic about having them participate in the developmental process. Grass roots organizations often have been viewed as alternative bases of political power—a perception that has caused much institutional instability *despite* the existence of stable political regimes. For example, although Tanzania's socialist policies extolled participation, they actually promoted centralization—as reflected in numerous top-down directives. These included "Ujamma" (the forced "villagization" of some 60 percent of the population, discussed later in this chapter) and the abolition of cooperatives and were issued to counter the perceived threat to the party's political dominance. Paradoxically, despite the fall in the share of estate production in Tanzania, the political representation of smallholder interests did not improve.

In Malawi land and capital have been controlled by a few politically powerful households, including that of the president. Together with the pricing structure (as we show below), this has virtually stunted smallholder development, despite substantial investment in the sector. Economic incentives have been restricted, and cooperatives have not been permitted. However, the peaking of estate-led growth in the late 1970s, along with the onset of structural adjustment and the growing power of the technocracy, has focused attention on the need for incentives for smallholder development. The distribution of the estate leases has begun to broaden since the early 1980s with a sharp decline in the size of the estates. The question remains whether policy reforms will be able to address the problems of a rapidly immizerizing peasantry.

In much of West Africa, smallholder participation has been impeded by weak organization and ethnic cleavages. In Nigeria, where the production of individual crops can be closely identified with specific regional groups, producer organizations have been weak. On the other hand, the success with cotton production in northern Cameroon and much of French West Africa illustrates how even a top-down strategy can confer substantial benefits on smallholders if price and nonprice factors are favorable. When one of them goes out of balance, however, problems can become insurmountable. An example is the collapse of world cotton prices in 1986 and the macroeconomic difficulties following that period. These together created insurmountable problems for the cotton industry and brought some of the warts on the Francophone system of cotton development into sharper focus.

Technocrats have played a more active role in Cameroon, Kenya, and Malawi than in Nigeria, Senegal, and Tanzania. In Tanzania, ideological concerns caused the civil service to be subordinated to the party. In Cameroon and Nigeria, the differences in the technocracy's management of the oil boom in part explains the sharp differences in the economic performance of these countries. Although Nigeria made large public expenditures on agriculture, the Dutch disease effect relegated agricultural policy to a secondary role in the 1970s. A weakening of the Nigerian technocracy under successive military regimes at the state, district, and local levels also seriously limited the nation's capacity to generate responsive programs and policies for smallholder development. In Cameroon the technocracy was more effective in combining the benefits of the oil boom with the need to maintain a strong agricultural base. However, the growth of parastatals and excessive centralization constrained growth.

In several MADIA countries, fragmented responsibility for policy planning has been a serious problem. In all the countries, the president's office has often interfered in agricultural policymaking and implementation. In Kenya and Malawi, the ministries of agriculture have had relatively strong, clear roles in policymaking, even though their capacity to implement programs has been rather weak.[19] In Tanzania, after the decentralization of the government in the 1970s, the party and the prime minister's office exercised far greater influence on agricultural policy than the Ministry of Agriculture and other technical ministries. This transfer of responsibility for planning and implementation away from the parent technical ministries had an especially harmful effect on agriculture. In Cameroon, Nigeria, and Senegal, however, the responsibility for policymaking has been widely dispersed among numerous parastatal agencies and autonomous project units rather than being concentrated in government departments and ministries of agriculture.

External shocks: Losses and benefits. As a percentage of current GDP, external shocks (including the effects of terms of trade, foreign demand, interest rate on debt, and net factor income) had beneficial effects in the three West African countries because of their mineral resources, whereas the three East African countries, which depended mainly on agricultural exports, suffered substantial losses.[20] Nigeria gained most (9 percent of GDP during 1967–84), followed by Cameroon (5.6 percent) and Senegal (0.2 percent). Kenya experienced the greatest loss (4.5 percent), followed by Tanzania (1.5 percent) and Malawi (1.0 percent). The ranking of Tanzania and Malawi changes if the period since 1970 is considered.

Kenya suffered the greatest loss from adverse terms of trade (equivalent of 6.5 percent of GDP during 1967–84), followed by Tanzania (4.8 percent) and Malawi (3.9 percent). In contrast, Nigeria and Cameroon benefited because of their oil resources (until oil prices fell in 1984), with Nigeria enjoying the largest gain from favorable terms of trade (6.6 percent of GDP during 1967–84). In Senegal's case, although the world price of phosphates played a positive role in the 1970s, other external shocks relating to agriculture led to an overall loss (1.3 percent). When the French protection for Senegal's groundnut exports was removed, for example, the terms of trade went into a steep decline during 1967–69, declined again from 1974 to 1976 and 1978 to 1980, but then remained stable until 1987 (see figure 2-5).

Having expanded public expenditures and imports when the external terms of trade were favorable and aid was flowing in, all the MADIA countries except Nigeria were forced to contract imports in order to survive the external disequilibria. The import compression of the 1980s was most severe in Malawi, Senegal, Tanzania, and Kenya, in that order. It continued up to 1985 in Cameroon—whereas in Nigeria import levels actually increased (albeit at a declining rate since 1978) until the decline in oil prices.

In the 1980s, higher interest payments on foreign loans also contributed significantly to the adverse external position of all the countries except Tanzania. The other five countries increased the proportion of debt owed to private sources, which was subject to variable interest rates. Pursuing a conservative macroeconomic policy, Cameroon

Figure 2-5. Barter Terms-of-Trade Indexes for MADIA *Countries, 1965–87*
(base year = 1965)

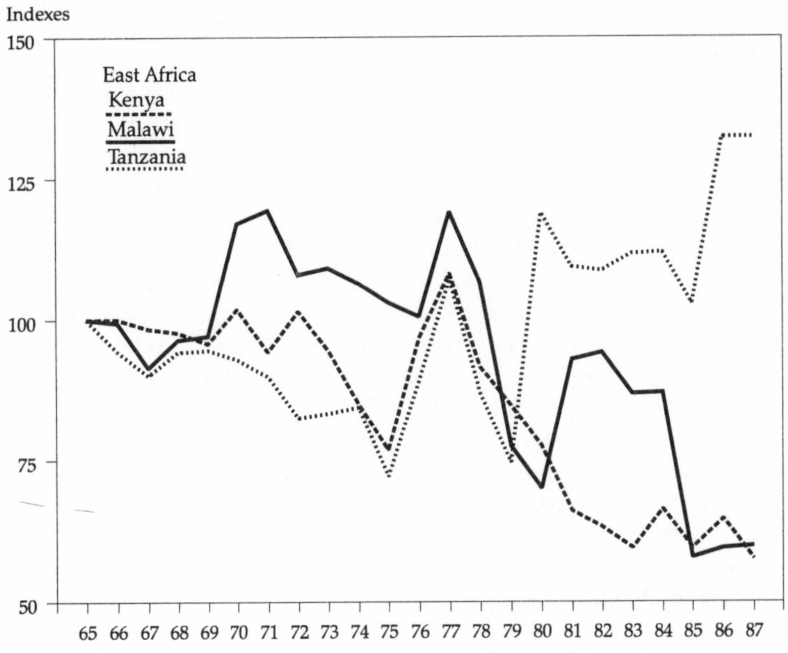

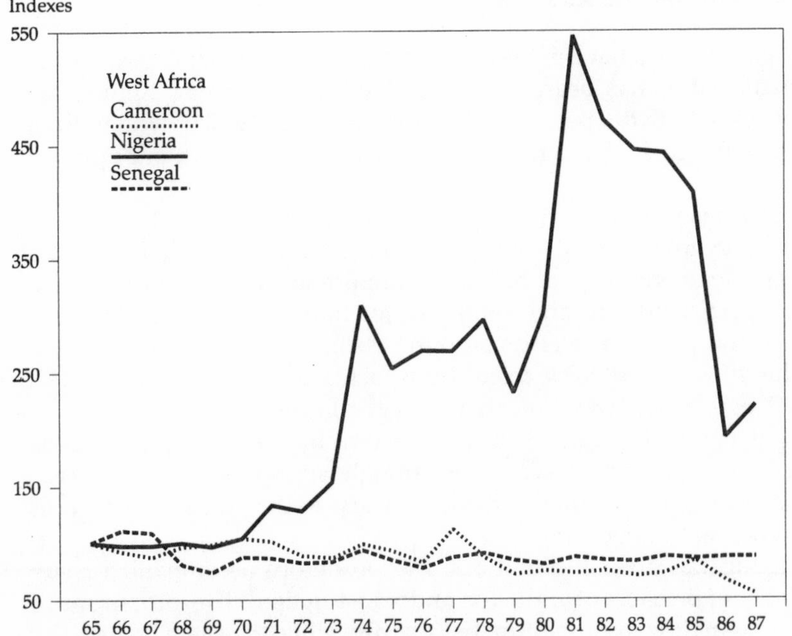

Source: Pierre Seka, Mathurin Gbetibouo and Uma Lele, "External Shocks and Macroeconomic Adjustments," MADIA Working Paper (Africa—Technical Department, Agriculture Division, World Bank, Washington, D.C., 1989).

undertook the largest repayments (equivalent to 0.6 percent of GDP during 1967–84), followed by Senegal (0.4 percent), Malawi (0.4 percent), Kenya (0.3 percent), and Nigeria (0.2 percent). Because Tanzania was able to rely more on concessional assistance from official sources, its debt profile did not change significantly.

Other shocks have also played a significant role, but they are more difficult to measure systematically. Kenya and Tanzania, for example, dissolved the East African Community and closed their common borders in 1977 in a dispute that was not resolved until 1983. Although illegal trade in consumption goods continued between the two countries, Tanzania's agricultural trade (which had relied on sales through Kenya-based traders and export markets) and agricultural research (which had relied heavily on the East African Community) suffered. Tanzania also paid a heavy price for its war with Uganda in 1979. Malawi suffered the most from external political and logistical constraints; notably, there was a sharp rise in transport costs caused by the closure of the border and a massive influx of refugees from Mozambique.

In addition, all the countries suffered from periodic droughts, but the decline in the average rainfall in Senegal (together with the withdrawal of French export price support for groundnuts) had a particularly adverse effect on its agriculture.

Macroeconomic Policies

All six countries have made an attempt to diversify out of agriculture, but the effort has been more moderate in Cameroon, Kenya, and Malawi—the better performers. In Kenya, agricultural growth brought more labor-intensive activities that broadened employment opportunities.

Tanzania represents the most extreme case of attempted diversification. The government's policy response to export pessimism was to forge ahead with capital-intensive, import-substituting industrialization, particularly in large public sector industries such as fertilizer, pulp, and paper, as well as agroprocessing. As a result, the share of industry in total public expenditures increased from 2 percent in 1972 to 11 percent in 1980. The share of agriculture, in contrast, fell from 11 percent in the early 1970s to 7 percent by the end of the decade. Tanzania's industrialization was strongly supported by donor assistance, which contributed considerably less to the industrial programs of other MADIA countries.[21]

In Nigeria, diversification out of export crops accompanied a substantial expansion of industry and construction. The proportion of GNP originating in agriculture fell sharply, while the share of manufacturing increased (although the mining sector was the most important source of growth). Senegal's drive for industrialization focused on the development of agroprocessing, fertilizers, and fisheries.

Quite paradoxically, countries that pursued an active policy of diversification out of agriculture—and therefore discriminated against agriculture—were the least successful in actually achieving it. The proportion of GDP and exports originally in agriculture was greater in Tanzania at the end of the period than at the beginning. This was in contrast to Kenya and Malawi.

Monetary policies. Of the six MADIA countries, Tanzania and Nigeria had the highest growth rates of money supply. This, combined with their high rates of public consumption, accelerated inflation and hence currency appreciation in the two countries during 1970–84 (see figure 2-6). Moreover, real appreciation hindered the production of tradables, particularly agricultural exports. Nigeria and Tanzania also showed considerable variability in the rates of inflation from year to year, which increased risk and discouraged investment. The two countries have had the poorest interest rate policy, in part because of their high rates of inflation. The negative real interest rates not only hindered the accumulation of domestic savings but also decapitalized the existing capital stock.[22]

Senegal and Cameroon have been members of the CFA zone and active monetary or exchange rate policies. They have had slower money growth and the lowest rates of inflation. Their real interest rates have not been as negative as those in Nigeria and Tanzania. Their currencies remained overvalued relative to those of Kenya and Malawi (albeit not as much as those of Nigeria and Tanzania). Because the other countries had adjusted their exchange rates by the end of the 1980s, Cameroon and Senegal suffered from considerable relative overvaluation—which reduced their competitiveness with neighboring countries.

Public expenditure policies. Compared with Kenya and Malawi, Tanzania had a higher overall share of government expenditures in GDP by the end of the 1970s, although it had started with a lower share at the beginning of the decade.[23] Kenya and Malawi had smaller expenditure programs but more balanced intersectoral expenditures. During 1970–86, Malawi had the highest share of agriculture in total government expenditures, ranging from 10 percent to 16 percent. In Kenya, the share of agriculture ranged from 8 percent to 12 percent. The share of the *recurrent* budget accruing to agriculture declined less in Malawi and Kenya than in Tanzania.

Figure 2-6. Purchasing-Power-Parity Exchange Rate Indexes for MADIA Countries, 1970–87
(base year = 1970)

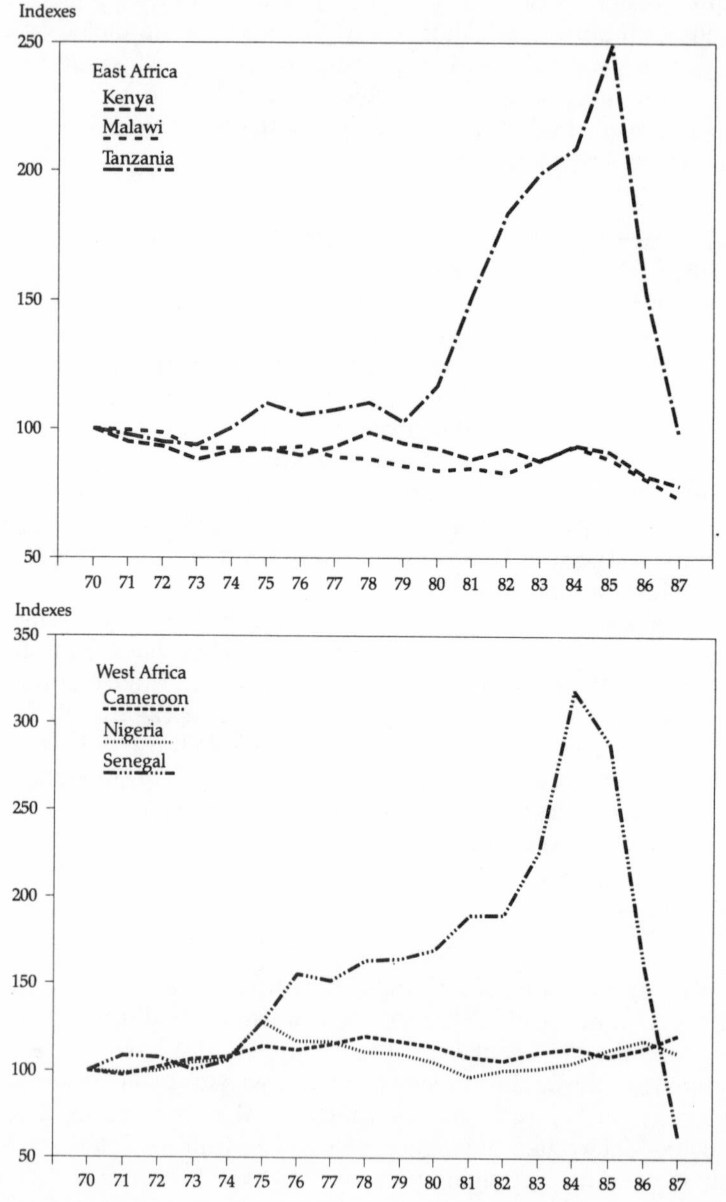

Note: Real exchange rates computed on the assumption of purchasing power parity. The rates are such that appreciation is reflected by an upward trend and depreciation by a downward trend.
Source: See figure 2-5.

In Kenya, the dynamic growth propelled by tea and coffee had important spillover effects that spurred growth in some regions. The Central Province—the agricultural heartland—dominated regional public expenditure patterns in both absolute and per capita terms until the mid-1980s. Public spending in the Central Province grew at an annual rate of 6.2 percent in real terms during 1970–83. Nevertheless, employment and wages in the less densely populated Northeast Province grew faster than in the more well-to-do regions of the Central Province and the Rift Valley. Tanzania, in contrast, pursued an income redistribution policy with more equitable regional allocations. This regional pattern of public expenditures redistributed patterns of production away from the least to the most favored in public expenditure, but with relatively little overall growth in production. In Malawi's case, there are not enough data to determine the regional bias in public expenditures.

In Nigeria, the oil boom inflated expenditures on urban services and construction. Budgeted capital expenditures in both cases were seven times higher (in real terms) during 1981–85 than during 1962–68. Agriculture was not neglected, however, and planned agricultural expenditures increased sixfold (in real terms) during this period. Large irrigation and fertilizer subsidies channeled nearly 4 billion naira into food crops until 1986. However, the poor quality of government expenditures was reflected in the lack of a well-defined strategy for smallholder development. Despite favorable price incentives for food crops, such expenditures could not offset the disincentives of the adverse policy that pulled labor out of agriculture and prevented agriculture from generating a supply response that could match the growing urban demand.[24] In Nigeria, as in the other MADIA countries, the shortage of *recurrent* expenditures has been a fundamental constraint on the development of smallholder agriculture.

In Cameroon, the overall pattern of spending in the 1970s did not help counter the large income disparities between regions. In the Fourth Plan (1976–81), for example, expenditures per capita were ten times higher in the southern Littoral and Center-South provinces than in the least favored Northwest, West, and North provinces. In the 1980s, however, planned expenditures showed a distinct redistributive bias in per capita terms, and per capita expenditures in the northern provinces increased.

In the case of Senegal, poor data make it difficult to evaluate the contribution of public expenditure policy to regional growth. In addition to Cap Vert (Greater Dakar), the Fleuve region was a prominent beneficiary in per capita terms. This is in line with the government's strategy of diversification out of groundnuts into irrigated rice to meet the growing demand for the latter.

Implicit and explicit taxation of agriculture. Only Kenya refrained from taxing tea and coffee, its principal export crops, either explicitly or implicitly through overvaluation of the exchange rate. Tea and coffee prices have been determined by the international market. Kenya has also avoided mobilizing resources by placing any heavy, direct export tax on smallholder production; it has offered smallholders the same price incentives as estate producers, since both sell their produce in the same competitive markets.

In Malawi, the right to grow burley and flue-cured tobacco, the country's primary exports, has been restricted to estates through a policy of licensing production. In contrast to Kenya, where smallholders increased their share in the production of virtually all high-value crops, Malawi has not granted smallholders licenses to grow the most lucrative crops. They have been required to sell their output at fixed prices to ADMARC, the agricultural marketing parastatal. The estates, in contrast, have been allowed to sell their output at open auctions. Smallholders have received only a third of the price that ADMARC obtained from auctioning their output. Even if the higher marketing costs for smallholders are taken into account, the difference indicates that small farmers have been taxed at rates of 50 percent or more (see tables 2-9, 2-10, 2-11, and 2-12).

Table 2-9. Ratios of Producer Prices to International Prices for East Africa, 1970–86
(nominal exchange rates)

	Kenya		Malawi			Tanzania		
	Smallholder		Smallholder	Estate		Smallholder		
Year	Coffee	Tea	Dark-fired tobacco	Burley tobacco	Flue-cured tobacco	Tobacco	Cotton	Coffee
1970	0.91	0.60	0.22	0.43	0.57	0.43	0.72	—
1971	0.90	0.67	0.25	0.39	0.68	0.50	0.61	—
1972	0.98	0.63	0.23	0.40	0.63	0.46	0.57	0.57
1973	0.96	0.60	0.22	0.54	0.86	0.44	0.35	0.43
1974	0.97	0.55	0.23	0.62	0.84	0.42	0.32	0.43
1975	1.01	0.63	0.22	0.47	0.66	0.47	0.51	0.36
1976	0.85	0.57	0.21	0.48	0.70	0.40	0.41	0.30
1977	0.92	0.70	0.26	0.60	0.76	0.42	0.45	0.35
1978	0.94	0.64	0.26	0.50	0.74	0.47	0.55	0.39
1979	0.93	0.66	0.24	0.45	0.65	0.37	0.51	0.29
1980	0.98	0.76	0.23	0.46	0.40	0.35	0.52	0.41
1981	0.84	0.62	0.19	0.73	0.56	0.33	0.61	0.53
1982	0.83	0.56	0.24	0.51	0.50	0.30	0.73	0.52
1983	0.90	0.98	0.23	0.27	0.39	0.38	0.67	0.47
1984	0.80	0.66	0.25	0.30	0.38	0.27	0.65	0.47
1985	0.88	0.76	0.21	0.26	0.34	0.36	1.07	0.53
1986	0.79	0.69	0.22	0.43	0.45	0.32	1.11	0.33

Source: World Bank Economic and Social Database (BESD).

Table 2-10. Ratios of Producer Prices to International Prices for East Africa, 1970–86
(purchasing power parity exchange rates)

	Kenya		*Malawi*			*Tanzania*		
	Smallholder		*Smallholder*	*Estate*		*Smallholder*		
Year	*Coffee*	*Tea*	*Dark-fired tobacco*	*Burley tobacco*	*Flue-cured tobacco*	*Tobacco*	*Cotton*	*Coffee*
1970	0.85	0.56	0.22	0.42	0.56	0.41	0.68	—
1971	0.88	0.66	0.24	0.39	0.66	0.49	0.59	—
1972	0.98	0.63	0.23	0.40	0.63	0.46	0.57	0.57
1973	1.02	0.64	0.24	0.59	0.95	0.45	0.35	0.44
1974	1.01	0.57	0.25	0.68	0.92	0.40	0.31	0.41
1975	1.02	0.64	0.25	0.52	0.73	0.41	0.45	0.32
1976	0.89	0.59	0.23	0.53	0.76	0.37	0.39	0.29
1977	0.94	0.71	0.30	0.70	0.88	0.40	0.43	0.33
1978	0.90	0.61	0.30	0.58	0.86	0.44	0.52	0.37
1979	0.92	0.65	0.29	0.53	0.77	0.37	0.51	0.29
1980	0.98	0.75	0.27	0.54	0.46	0.31	0.47	0.37
1981	0.86	0.64	0.21	0.81	0.62	0.23	0.42	0.36
1982	0.82	0.56	0.28	0.59	0.59	0.16	0.39	0.28
1983	0.94	1.02	0.26	0.31	0.44	0.20	0.35	0.24
1984	0.77	0.64	0.26	0.31	0.40	0.13	0.32	0.23
1985	0.87	0.74	0.22	0.27	0.36	0.15	0.46	0.23
1986	0.96	0.85	0.25	0.50	0.52	0.25	0.88	0.26

— = Not available.

Note: Seed cotton producer prices converted to lint cotton equivalent using 34 percent conversion rate. Green leaf producer prices converted to made tea equivalent using 22 percent conversion rate. World Prices are: Coffee, other mild arabica; Tea, average auction (London); Tobacco, United States all markets; Cotton, Egypt (Liverpool).

Source: World Bank Economic and Social Database (BESD).

In Tanzania and Nigeria, acutely overvalued exchange rates imposed a high implicit tax on export agriculture. In Tanzania, during the coffee boom of the mid-1970s, this implicit taxation combined with high explicit taxes on coffee, the country's main export. In Nigeria, producer price subsidies to export crop cultivators in the 1970s could not adequately offset currency overvaluation. Kenya and Malawi, in contrast, regularly adjusted their exchange rates and thus avoided taxing their agricultural sectors implicitly. Cameroon and Senegal—both members of the West African Monetary Union—also followed a relatively flexible macroeconomic policy. Cameroon and Senegal have, however, been unable to adjust their exchange rates since the mid 1980s, when their Anglophone neighbors commenced an adjustment process. This has caused severe disincentive effects on their agriculture vis-a-vis their competitors.

Under a system of French protection dating back to 1929, groundnut producers in Senegal received up to 50 percent of the French import

Table 2-11. Ratios of Producer Prices to International Prices for West Africa, 1970–86
(nominal exchange rates)

	Cameroon				*Nigeria*		*Senegal*	
Year	*Arabica coffee*	*Robusta coffee*	*Cocoa*	*Cotton*	*Cocoa*	*Palm kernel*	*Ground-nuts*	*Cotton*
1970	0.55	0.49	0.45	0.50	0.61	0.51	0.27	0.16
1971	0.60	0.48	0.60	0.44	0.77	0.59	0.27	0.14
1972	0.62	0.50	0.56	0.45	0.84	0.80	0.36	0.15
1973	0.65	0.53	0.40	0.37	0.66	0.76	0.26	0.10
1974	0.54	0.43	0.32	0.37	0.67	0.51	0.17	0.09
1975	0.76	0.50	0.49	0.50	0.86	1.18	0.45	0.14
1976	0.41	0.29	0.31	0.40	0.51	1.04	0.41	0.10
1977	0.26	0.21	0.24	0.50	0.42	0.71	0.31	0.12
1978	0.44	0.38	0.34	0.53	0.48	0.65	0.29	0.13
1979	0.43	0.40	0.41	0.57	0.61	0.60	0.35	0.14
1980	0.47	0.47	0.55	0.54	0.91	1.06	0.44	0.13
1981	0.48	0.54	0.55	0.53	1.02	1.03	0.30	0.12
1982	0.44	0.43	0.58	0.59	1.11	1.29	0.56	0.13
1983	0.37	0.37	0.46	0.48	0.91	0.87	0.53	0.11
1984	0.30	0.32	0.39	0.55	0.82	1.00	0.46	0.10
1985	—	0.38	0.42	0.77	0.75	1.57	0.51	0.13
1986	—	—	—	1.25	—	1.61	—	0.27

— = Not available
Source: World Bank Economic and Social Database (BESD).

price (which was itself about 25 percent above the world price) of groundnuts (see chapter 7). These price guarantees were removed with the signing of the Yaoundé Convention in 1967. Throughout the 1970s, the ratio of producer to international prices remained significantly below 0.5.

A comparison of export crop prices and food crop prices (see tables 2-13 and 2-14) shows that only in Kenya have the prices of export crops ensured favorable returns to land and labor relative to maize, the principal competing food crop. The higher returns to Kenya's tea and coffee producers also reflect the higher quality of tea and arabica coffee grown by smallholders in comparison with that produced by estates. This in turn reflects the strong research and extension programs that smallholders have had access to for some time.

In view of the recent emphasis on getting prices right, it is important to examine the secular movement of food and export crop prices and their relationship to each other, to input prices, and to international prices during the period covered by MADIA. Although considerable information has been available on the extent of implicit or explicit taxation of agriculture, relatively little is known about the behavior of food crop prices because food crop markets tend to be informal and

Table 2-12. Ratios of Producer Prices to International Prices for West Africa, 1970–86
(purchasing power parity exchange rates)

	Cameroon				Nigeria		Senegal	
Year	Arabica coffee	Robusta coffee	Cocoa	Cotton	Cocoa	Palm kernel	Groundnuts	Cotton
1970	0.56	0.49	0.46	0.51	0.65	0.54	0.27	0.16
1971	0.63	0.50	0.63	0.46	0.77	0.59	0.27	0.14
1972	0.63	0.50	0.56	0.45	0.84	0.80	0.36	0.15
1973	0.63	0.51	0.38	0.35	0.71	0.83	0.25	0.09
1974	0.52	0.41	0.30	0.35	0.68	0.52	0.16	0.08
1975	0.69	0.46	0.44	0.46	0.74	1.01	0.35	0.11
1976	0.37	0.27	0.28	0.36	0.37	0.74	0.35	0.09
1977	0.23	0.18	0.21	0.44	0.30	0.52	0.26	0.10
1978	0.38	0.33	0.29	0.46	0.33	0.45	0.27	0.12
1979	0.37	0.34	0.35	0.49	0.40	0.39	0.32	0.12
1980	0.41	0.40	0.47	0.47	0.56	0.65	0.44	0.13
1981	0.45	0.50	0.51	0.49	0.57	0.58	0.32	0.13
1982	0.43	0.42	0.56	0.57	0.62	0.72	0.57	0.13
1983	0.35	0.35	0.43	0.45	0.43	0.41	0.53	0.11
1984	0.28	0.29	0.36	0.50	0.28	0.34	0.53	0.12
1985	—	0.36	0.39	0.72	0.29	0.60	0.53	0.14
1986	—	—	—	1.13	—	1.35	—	0.26

— = Not available.

Note: Seed cotton producer prices converted to lint cotton equivalent using 34 percent conversion rate. World Prices are: Coffee, other mild arabica for arabica and Angolan (Ambriz 2AA) for robusta; Cocoa, ICCO average daily price (New York and London); Cotton, Egypt (Liverpool); Palm kernel, Nigerian (Europe); Groundnuts, Nigerian (London).

Source: World Bank Economic and Social Database (BESD).

fragmented. Some experts believe that food markets are competitive and well integrated, and that the primary disincentive to food crop production is government intervention, which keeps food prices low relative to international prices. The MADIA study involved a careful search for as many price series in the countries for informal markets as possible. Defining an appropriate parity price for food crops in most of the MADIA countries is difficult for a number of conceptual and empirical reasons. Although Kenya and Cameroon were marginal importers of food during 1970–85, Malawi was a perpetual exporter and Senegal a perpetual importer. Tanzania and Nigeria (where overvalued exchange rates and poor macroeconomic policies played a part) were once exporters but became leading importers. An average of the c.i.f. and f.o.b. prices seems appropriate when countries are marginal exporters or importers and when international and internal transport costs are high. The large internal costs for transportation in Africa greatly increase the band defined by cost, insurance, and freight (c.i.f.)

Table 2-13. *Trends in Ratios of Producer Prices of Export Crops to Food Crops in East Africa, 1967–85*

Year	Kenya		Malawi				Tanzania			
	Coffee/ maize	*Tea/ maize*	*Tobacco/ maize*	*Coffee/ maize*	*Groundnuts/ maize*	*Cotton/ maize*	*Cotton/ maize*	*Tobacco/ maize*	*Cashewnuts/ maize*	*Coffee/ maize*
1967	—	—	6.09	9.79	3.30	2.73	—	—	—	—
1968	—	—	4.30	10.07	3.07	3.23	—	—	—	—
1969	—	—	6.83	14.69	3.31	3.38	—	—	—	—
1970	27.2	—	7.84	11.66	3.31	3.28	—	—	—	—
1971	19.1	19.5	7.71	8.03	3.03	3.37	4.23	22.31	3.46	—
1972	20.0	15.5	7.32	9.90	3.61	2.87	4.58	24.17	3.75	18.75
1973	23.7	15.2	5.97	9.49	3.51	3.43	4.35	21.88	3.46	15.96
1974	21.7	15.5	4.86	10.73	3.59	4.34	3.42	18.91	2.73	13.33
1975	15.3	11.6	6.05	11.19	3.70	3.77	2.73	14.29	1.87	7.00
1976	32.9	13.8	5.40	8.75	3.11	2.25	2.50	9.66	1.29	10.00
1977	44.7	24.2	6.24	8.70	3.39	3.52	2.50	10.90	1.33	18.75
1978	31.7	17.8	7.80	11.28	3.70	3.94	2.71	10.67	1.31	12.81
1979	36.8	17.6	7.88	12.54	5.81	4.19	2.82	10.51	1.92	10.67
1980	27.6	16.7	6.31	0.40	4.60	3.25	3.00	8.95	1.73	11.42
1981	22.6	17.7	6.53	7.58	4.65	3.24	3.20	9.64	2.75	12.36
1982	25.8	18.0	4.03	4.50	2.87	2.45	2.47	7.41	3.09	9.93
1983	22.7	14.2	7.56	9.35	4.64	3.39	2.69	9.96	2.65	8.67
1984	22.0	29.6	6.61	8.33	4.89	3.31	2.73	7.61	2.95	10.40
1985	21.2	18.0	8.11	—	5.57	3.56	2.10	6.30	2.42	6.75

— = Not available.
Source: World Bank Economic and Social Database (BESD).

Table 2-14. Trends in Ratios of Producer Prices of Export Crops to Food Crops in West Africa

	Cameroon				Nigeria						Senegal			
	Coffee/maize													
Year	Arabica	Robusta	Cocoa/ maize	Cotton/ maize	Cocoa/ maize	Palm oil/ maize	Rubber/ maize	Cocoa/ rice	Palm oil/ rice	Rubber/ rice	Groundnuts/ maize	Cotton/ maize	Groundnuts/ millet	Cotton/ millet
1970	10.20	7.40	4.95	1.76	—	—	—	—	—	—	1.03	1.67	1.09	1.76
1971	9.40	7.10	4.80	1.71	—	—	—	—	—	—	1.28	1.67	1.36	1.76
1972	9.70	6.90	4.80	1.78	—	—	—	—	—	—	1.28	1.72	0.92	1.24
1973	10.00	6.50	4.78	1.60	—	—	—	—	—	—	1.56	1.79	0.98	1.03
1974	7.90	5.60	4.58	1.46	—	—	—	—	—	—	1.66	1.68	1.38	1.40
1975	6.70	4.10	3.53	1.00	—	—	—	—	—	—	1.19	1.34	1.19	1.34
1976	9.50	6.10	4.40	1.09	3.37	1.50	—	2.19	0.99	—	1.19	1.34	1.19	1.34
1977	7.20	5.60	3.33	0.80	3.98	1.37	1.40	3.07	1.06	1.09	1.12	1.32	1.04	1.22
1978	7.20	5.60	4.40	0.72	4.18	1.44	1.47	2.57	0.89	0.92	1.12	1.32	1.04	1.22
1979	5.80	5.20	4.42	0.61	4.12	1.54	1.44	2.49	0.93	0.87	1.12	1.49	1.14	1.37
1980	5.70	5.30	4.83	0.61	4.19	1.59	1.56	2.09	0.80	0.79	1.35	1.62	1.00	1.20
1981	5.70	5.10	4.15	0.60	2.63	1.00	1.22	1.37	0.53	0.63	1.49	1.44	1.40	1.36
1982	6.40	5.00	4.04	0.64	3.05	1.16	1.64	1.54	0.59	0.83	1.49	1.66	1.40	1.56
1983	—	—	—	—	2.62	0.93	1.30	1.83	0.64	0.92	1.49	1.66	1.27	1.42
1984	—	—	—	—	1.97	0.79	0.99	1.14	0.46	0.57	1.60	1.56	1.45	1.42
1985	—	—	—	—	—	—	—	—	—	—	1.50	1.67	1.64	1.67
1986	—	—	—	—	—	—	—	—	—	—	1.29	1.43	1.29	1.43

— = Not available.
Source: World Bank Economic and Social Database (BESD).

and free on board (f.o.b.) prices within which internal prices can fluctuate without being out of line with international prices and without trade taking place.

Viewed from this broad perspective, the producer price structure in the MADIA countries other than Kenya (and in the case of estate agriculture, Malawi) shifted over time in favor of food crops (see tables 2-13 and 2-14). This happened regardless of whether internal food markets were controlled, as in East Africa, or were relatively free, as in West Africa. Although the international prices of most primary cereals declined during this period, East African producer prices increased in local currency with the depreciation of the exchange rate while generally remaining at par with long-term average international prices. Even after correcting for the overvalued exchange rate, however, food prices in West Africa during the 1970s in general tended to be substantially higher than those in East Africa and far above international levels—the price of maize, for example, has been twice as high as the prevailing price in East Africa.

Kenya's export orientation kept the ratio of export crop prices to maize prices substantially higher than comparable ratios in the other countries. This is not surprising in view of the heavy taxation of coffee in Cameroon and Tanzania, of smallholder tobacco in Malawi, and of cocoa in Cameroon and Nigeria. Indeed, Kenya's coffee/maize producer price ratios were more than twice as high as those in Tanzania—and nearly four times as favorable as those in Cameroon.

Since the mid-1980s, some change has occurred in this general trend owing to the introduction of structural adjustment programs. The large correction of the exchange rate and of producer price distortions in Nigeria and Tanzania has led to a greater relative shift between producer prices for export and food crops than in Kenya and Malawi. In the former two countries it has caused more resources to shift from food crop production to export crop production.

Food prices in all the MADIA countries had begun to rise once again, despite the increasing food imports, because of secular food shortages, although improved rainfall in some countries, for example, in the Sahel, had led to temporary peaks in production (see chapter 10). The growing population pressure on land coupled with relatively little growth in factor productivity indicates that a growing number of rural households are becoming dependent on the market. The secular rise in the price of food crops has profound implications for food consumption by the poor (many of whom are women)—who rely on the market to sell labor and purchase food, particularly when faced with declining real wages. Yet much of the recent literature on adjustment has focused narrowly on the desirability of increasing producer prices as an incentive for production. There has also been a tendency to consider weather-induced improvements in production as due to adjustment. This tendency has ignored the fact that fundamental factors that should result in secular changes in production—that is, increased use of modern inputs and consequent increase in factor productivity—have not occurred. Quite to the contrary, at the time of the publication of this book, input distribution systems in some countries had collapsed due to the abolition of the public enterprises that handle fertilzer distribution on credit, for example, in Senegal.

Whereas smallholder export agriculture was taxed implicitly or explicitly in five of the six countries, food crops were often subsidized directly or indirectly through such measures as price stabilization, fertilizer subsidies, and the importation of food at overvalued exchange rates. Price stabilization was often undertaken at substantial cost to the treasury. For instance, in East Africa in the early 1980s, the losses or overdue payments of grain-marketing parastatals alone amounted to some 5 billion shillings in Kenya and 2.8 billion shillings in Tanzania. The costs incurred by these maize operations were substantially higher than the revenues extracted from export agriculture in either of the two countries. The government of Malawi taxed smallholder tobacco, but it subsidized smallholder maize and fertilizer. In Nigeria, fertilizer subsidies reached 1 billion naira in 1987. Although fertilizer prices were substantially lower in Nigeria than in the other countries, fertilizer did not always reach the small farmers and an extensive black market existed. Massive public sector investments also went into irrigation for food crops through River Basin Development Authorities in Nigeria and through various parastatals, such as the Société d'Aménagement et d'Exploitation des Terres du Delta in Senegal and the Société d'Expansion et de Modernisation de la Riziculture de Yagoua in Cameroon. Yet very little land was actually brought under irrigation owing to the poor policies toward this subsector. Nonetheless, when resource transfers to and out of agriculture for both food and export crops are taken into account, there was often little net taxation of agriculture, contrary to popular belief.

The above discussion is not intended to condone the agricultural policies of governments, rather it stresses the fact that in four of the six countries the poor performance of smallholder agriculture is the result of a combination of price and nonprice factors and cannot be explained by unfavorable price incentives alone. Price (and subsidy) adjustment induced by the structural adjustment programs may improve the fiscal position of governments (for example, through reduced subsidies and price stabilization for maize) and may cause a shift among competing food and export crops. But it may not necessarily increase overall agricultural production on a sustained basis unless fundamental questions related to science and technology, input distri-

Table 2-15. Comparative Crop Yields in MADIA *Countries, 1970–85*
(kilograms per hectare)

Country	*Tea*		*Coffee*		*Tobacco*				
	Smallholder	*Estate*	*Smallholder*	*Estate*	*Smallholder*	*Estate*	*Sugar*	*Cotton*	*Maize*
East Africa									
Malawi									
1971–75	231	1,399	—	—	375	1,076	10,696	406	—
1976–80	416	1,734	—	—	398	1,189	10,528	614	—
1981–85	648	1,929	—	—	342	1,238	11,290	537	1,171
Kenya									
1971–75	1,345	1,735	608	1,139	—	—	—	269	1,895
1976–80	1,199	2,289	737	1,271	—	—	—	278	1,881
1981–85	1,137	2,524	604	1,075	—	—	—	184	1,821
Tanzania									
1971–75	—	1,149	—	—	—	—	—	528	645
1976–80	—	1,356	—	—	—	—	—	592	—
1981–85	430	1,291	—	—	—	—	—	380	—

West Africa	*Cocoa*	*Coffee*	*Rice*	*Millet/ sorghum*	*Groundnuts*	*Cotton*	*Maize*
Senegal							
1971–75	—	—	1,081	549	718	1,081	823
1976–80	—	—	1,328	565	706	816	811
1981–85	—	—	1,617	654	750	1,009	990
Cameroon							
1971–75	348	325	886	773	787	541	1,151
1976–80	252	270	1,751	848	520	1,146	822
1981–85	267	295	3,699	785	266	1,308	980
Nigeria							
1971–75	3,426	—	1,679	574	516	307	764
1976–80	2,374	—	1,906	613	702	203	857
1981–85	2,037	—	2,033	709	946	120	996

— = Not available.
Source: World Bank Economic and Social Database (BESD).

bution, infrastructure, and markets discussed in this book are addressed.

Sectoral Policies

The sectoral policies in the countries under consideration provide further information on the kind of environment that aid flowed into over the past few decades.

Relative roles of price and nonprice factors. Returns to factors of production are a function of prices as well as productivity. Productivity, in turn, is a function of the quality of agricultural services available to small farmers. Coffee, tea, and maize yields in Kenya have been two to four times as high as in Cameroon, Tanzania, or Malawi (see table 2-15). Even after taking into account additional labor and other inputs, the relative return per hectare in producing coffee rather than maize in Kenya has been at least twice as great as the relative producer price differences (reviewed earlier) have suggested.

Smallholders in Kenya—in contrast to their counterparts in Cameroon, Malawi, and Tanzania—have had relatively easy access to research, extension, credit, and inputs, as well as to marketing, handling, and processing services. Traditionally, tea and coffee research has been of a high quality. The smallholder coffee cooperatives and the Kenya Tea Development Authority (a semiautonomous public sector enterprise) are among the most effective institutions for channeling export crop services to smallholders. Their clientele includes an unusually high proportion of politically conscious and vigilant small farmers. It is difficult to quantify the relative importance of these nonprice factors as determinants of the efficiency and profitability of particular crop-growing activities. However, they have clearly influenced the willingness of smallholders to apply their labor in ways that increase yields per hectare and production.

Other examples—such as cotton in Cameroon and cocoa in Nigeria—indicate that price levels are not necessarily the only important determinant of crop expansion and that technological and institutional development can help compensate for adverse price movements. Cotton producer prices, for example, were substantially lower in Cameroon than in Kenya or Nigeria throughout the 1970s—both in nominal terms and when converted at purchasing power parity exchange rates (see figures 2-7 and 2-8). Yet at the end of the decade, cotton yields in Cameroon were four to eight times as high as those in the Anglophone countries (see table 2-15). Consequently, returns to labor use in cotton production in Cameroon were significantly higher.[25]

Figure 2-7. Cotton Producer Prices at Nominal Exchange Rates

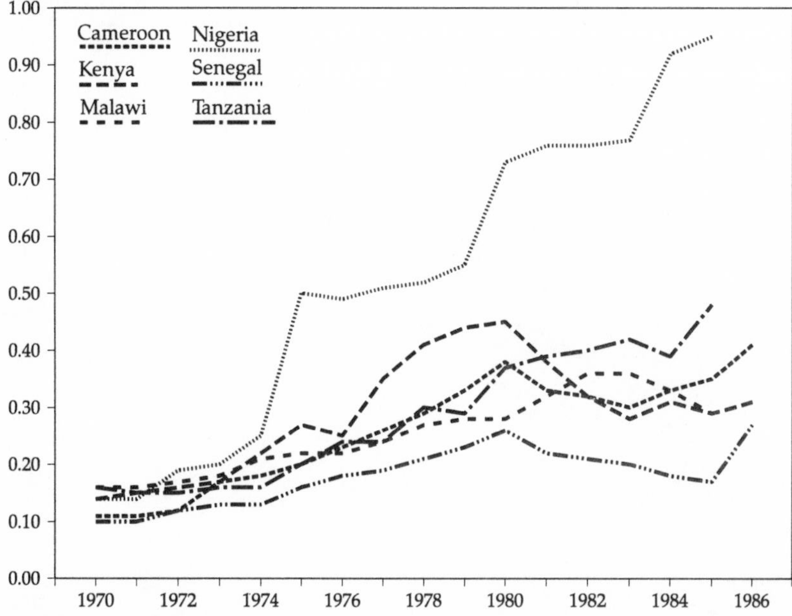

Source: Uma Lele, Nicholas Van de Walle, and Mathurin Gbetibouo, *Cotton in Africa: An Analysis of Differences in Performance*, MADIA Discussion Paper 7 (Washington, D.C.: World Bank, 1989).

Not surprisingly, the technological and organizational factors accounting for the success of cotton in Cameroon (and Senegal) have been similar to those responsible for the growth of tea and coffee production in Kenya. The Société de Développement du Coton du Cameroun (SODECOTON) is a paternalistic, public sector agency that is quite different from the participatory coffee cooperatives in Kenya. But it has had access to an excellent network of research on cotton undertaken by the Compagnie Française de Développement des Fibres Textiles (CFDT) in West Africa. Since the returns to CFDT (which has equity interests in SODECOTON) depend on the quantity of cotton exported, it has had a strong incentive to provide high-quality technical assistance and to improve the provision of services to growers in order to increase cotton production.[26] As in the case of tea and coffee in Kenya, the government's political support for the development of the northern reaches of Cameroon has been no less important. In contrast, cotton production in Anglophone Africa by and large declined in the 1970s and 1980s (except in Zimbabwe). Structural adjustment in Nigeria had begun to revive cotton production at the

Figure 2-8. Cotton Producer Prices at Purchasing-Power-Parity Exchange Rates

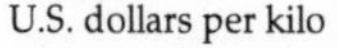

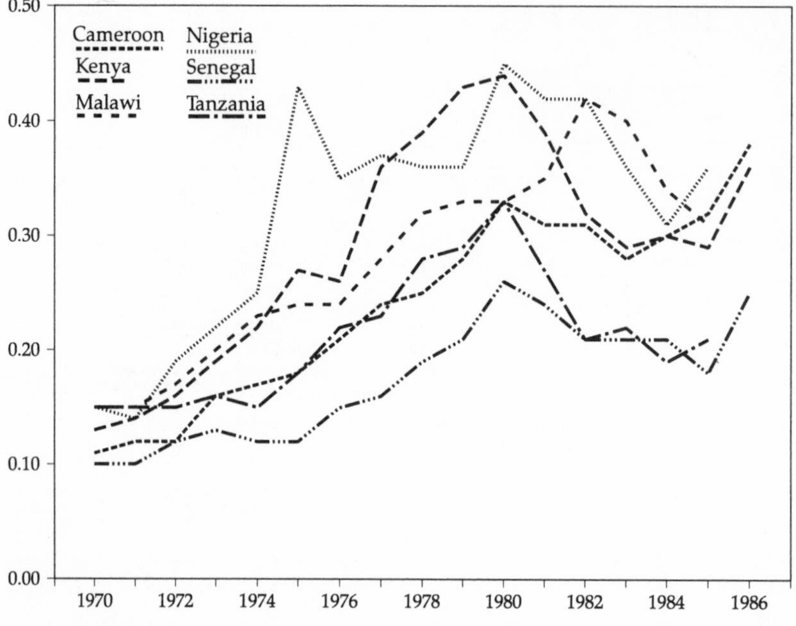

Source: See figure 2-7.

end of the 1980s, but nonprice constraints affecting the quality of agricultural research, input supply, marketing, processing, and transport facilities for cotton remained.

The two cocoa projects funded by the World Bank in Nigeria offer another example of the extreme importance of nonprice factors. The projects were implemented during the oil boom, when the crop was heavily taxed and nominal wages rose threefold. The two projects nevertheless exceeded their cocoa planting targets—a rare occurrence in donor-funded agricultural projects in Africa in the 1970s. This successful performance was partly the result of Nigeria's efficient management of the cocoa subsector. A related reason was that, even with heavy implicit taxation of Nigerian cocoa, the returns to planting *improved* cocoa strains were competitive with the already high wages in the urban sector—owing to Nigeria's strong comparative advantage in cocoa. A third cocoa project was appraised by the World Bank in 1979 but was not approved; important reasons behind this decision were the decline in the implementation capacity of the cocoa-producing states (Ogun, Ondo, and Oyo) after the breakup of the regions, the conflict between the federal and state governments regarding their respective financial contributions, and the World Bank's belief that Nigeria had lost its comparative advantage in cocoa production.

These cases raise questions about the extent to which prices matter more than various nonprice factors. As discussed earlier, they also raise questions about the role that stable and unstable prices play in increasing food production and stabilizing food consumption (especially by the poor). Whereas price stabilization has been accompanied by substantial budgetary costs in the case of food crops, it has typically been associated with taxation of export crops. Different considerations enter into the formulation of price policies for export crops.

The experience with coffee and tea in Kenya, cotton in Cameroon, and cocoa in Nigeria suggests that good production and export performance can be achieved under circumstances of both high and low taxation and stable and unstable prices. The argument favoring the payment of unstable world parity prices to perennial crop producers (as in the case of tea and coffee in Kenya) is based on the phenomenon of upswings in tree plantings occurring in periods of price booms. Countries that do not pass on international prices to producers lose out on the consequent supply response; similarly, in periods of low prices, producers tend not to uproot permanent crops, which represent long-term capital investment. They simply reduce variable expenditures—unless, of course, the low prices are sustained through adverse policies over a long period, as in Tanzania. Kenya's experience with tea and coffee supports all these arguments. It also shows that considerable revenue can be generated even at low (but mildly progressive) rates of export crop taxation. The parity prices induce increased production. Moreover, leaving incomes in the hands of individual producers rather than of the government tends to encourage households to increase their saving and investment. This stimulates even greater growth by creating a dynamic environment for the rest of the economy. Governments, however, have tended to misuse the revenues that they have earned.

It is also necessary to consider factors that support price stabilization and export taxes. If the world demand for a given crop is relatively inelastic when producer's are highly responsive and shares of individual countries in the world market are high, an excess supply can build up and world prices may fall. Taxation can restrict production in such situations. Moreover, a fall in world prices because of excess production can benefit developed country consumers if demand is primarily concentrated in developed countries. Indeed, as discussed earlier, in 1973 it was these concerns that led the World Bank through a policy to halt financing for further expansion of tea (except when countries had no other production alternatives) and to confine assistance to rehabilitating and intensifying cultivation of *existing* acreage and to processing output already on stream. Similar de facto guidelines were applied to financing of coffee. This policy adversely affected expansion of tea and coffee in Africa to a greater degree than in Asia or Latin America as these two continents were not so dependent on external assistance. Paradoxically, Kenya's smallholder tea and coffee production increased despite these guidelines. Donor investments in processing of the crop already on stream encouraged the expansion of acreage by providing a market stimulus that would not otherwise have existed. Moreover, the distinction between area expansion and rehabilitation made in donor policy toward export crop farming turned out to be irrelevant at the farm level.[27] For producers it was more profitable, at the margin, to increase acreage than to intensify existing production. Labor shortages and the lack of farm services tended to constrain intensification.

A strong comparative advantage in the production of an export commodity may entail substantial producer rents, some of which could be taxed away without adverse effect on the return to resource use relative to the next-best option. The MADIA study showed that, despite considerable taxation, groundnuts in Senegal, tobacco in Malawi, and cocoa in Cameroon offered higher returns than competing food crops. Had the taxation of the agricultural sector been compensated for by government expenditures that directly or indirectly supported the much-needed investments in physical and social infrastructure, and in increasing farmer access to technology, inputs, and information, policies of taxing the agricultural sector would not have been counterproductive. Thus neither taxation nor stabilization can be judged adequately without also taking into account a broader fiscal picture including public expenditures on agriculture that offset the revenue raised. Tanzania not only taxed agriculture but also neglected public expenditures on physical infrastructure. Nigeria spent large sums but accomplished little because of policy and institutional failures.

Some degree of stabilization may be more necessary for annual than for perennial export crops. First, at international prices, most annual export crops tend to be of lower value than tree crops, so that the return to factor use in their production tends to be relatively less attractive than it is for competing food crops. This makes switches from annual export crops to annual food crops more probable. Second, the prices and yields of annual food crops that compete with annual export crops in production vary more than those of tree crops. Consequently there are substantial switches between annual food and export crops from year to year. Fluctuations in domestic production may adversely affect capacity utilization in downstream processing activities—as, for example, in the case of groundnuts in Senegal and cotton in Kenya (where price stabilization may help stabilize supply by encouraging increased use of purchased inputs). Governments have been reluctant to import the raw materials to maintain full capacity utilization in the downstream processing industry. Moreover, rising capacity utilization of processing facilities may reduce processing margins and stimulate higher producer prices and production.[28]

These various arguments suggest that there is no unique or universal solution to the output pricing issue and that donors should not let markets determine everything. Above all they should recognize the importance of addressing country- and crop-specific production situations. Governments, in turn, face various socioeconomic and political dilemmas of their own with regard to crop pricing. The idea of stabilization plus an export tax appeals to them on the grounds that it reduces the regional income disparities and the income instability that accompany the application of international parity pricing. Their ultimate decisions depend a great deal on political considerations. Kenya seemed better able to handle the political problems arising from sharp regional income differences between the tea- and coffee-producing areas and the rest of the country—although recent experience with the reform of the price policy on export crops in Nigeria suggests that this, too, can change over time.

As for food crop pricing, donors have recently argued that market intervention—including, for example, restrictions on the interdistrict movement of grain—have adverse effects on production, as they induce illegal sales and thus raise marketing costs. Marketing outlets created by monopoly government intervention increase uncertainty. Furthermore, as discussed earlier, the fiscal costs of ensuring a uniform price across regions and seasons have been high. The MADIA study has concluded, however, that the overall production, welfare, and political effects of some degree of price stability may be quite positive.[29] Official prices tend to be bypassed by producers in years of poor harvests because of informal market sales and provide a cushion in years of good crops when market prices collapse. Furthermore, marketed maize is a large part of the consumption of low-income households, many of which are in rural areas. Purchased maize also takes a high share of the budgets of these households. Thus, food price and supply stabilization policies do help protect the consumption of the poor. This is particularly true in drought years, when the increase in market prices has substantial adverse effects on the incomes of the poor. Increased reliance on food imports to stabilize domestic prices can reduce the cost of holding domestic buffer stocks. Moreover, governments can stabilize prices and supplies by becoming buyers and sellers of last resort and by allowing greater interyear and interseasonal variability in official prices than the uniform official prices currently allow. Some degree of price stabilization is essential not only to safeguard welfare and ensure a market for producers undertaking risky investments in new productive inputs, but also to ensure political stability. Moreover, given the large budget share of food in total consumer expenditure, there is a strong relationship between the cost of food and the cost of wages in developing countries, which affects competitiveness of manufacturing. The issue then is how to minimize the efficiency cost of some amount of price stabilization. Relatively little analytical work has been done on the ways in which some of the governments' broader developmental objectives may be achieved.[30] Much experience exists on these issues in Asian countries such as Indonesia, from which Africa needs to learn.

Public sector marketing. The marketing arrangements that many African countries inherited from the colonial era represented the economic interests of European farmers and traders. But these arrangements also benefited smallholder producers by expanding food and export crop production for the market. Market intervention was seen by colonial governments and later by governments of independent countries as a means of mobilizing export tax revenue, ensuring food security, and maintaining control over politically strategic commodities—enabling the government to perform development functions, such as providing agricultural research, extension, credit, roads, and a source of political patronage.[31] To preserve and expand the benefits of state-dominated marketing structures, independent African governments retained and expanded the functions of the marketing boards and parastatals bequeathed by the colonial governments. The existing marketing arrangements were therefore not as irrational from a broad sociopolitical viewpoint as concluded during the adjustment period.

Until 1973–74, donors supported the taxation of export crops for the purpose of mobilizing revenues for modernizing the economy. They considered export market prospects for primary commodities to be limited, and therefore saw the need to limit production. Where European interests dominated production in the colonial period, the producers had received protection via price policy. Where they dominated trade, the trading interests had received protection. Where European farmers engaged in risky annual crops and asked for stable prices, marketing boards had become influential. In contrast, where small farmers dominated African production, export taxes had been the norm.

The growth of public sector marketing in the 1970s would not have been possible without the active and generous financial support of donors. Countries such as Tanzania and Senegal, which received the most foreign assistance per capita, were also those with the strongest parastatals. In Tanzania, nearly 400 parastatals were handling production, processing, transport, and the marketing of goods and services by the end of the 1970s, and the prices of nearly 1,000 commodities were controlled. During 1974–85, Sub-Saharan Africa received more World Bank support for parastatals than either Asia or Latin America. The support covered some forty-eight food crop projects, forty-five export crop projects, and seventeen livestock projects in Africa that had some marketing components.[32]

Donors tended to accept the parastatal structure for the same reasons that governments did: Because of their monopoly position, parastatals were easier to work with and control, and they could undertake tasks that the indigenous private sector was allegedly too weak to perform. African governments were unwilling to let nonindigenous communities (for example, the Indians in East Africa and the Lebanese in Senegal) achieve a prominent trading position in politically sensitive or economically powerful activities to fill the gap created by private sector weakness.

Competitive markets not only take time to develop but absorb relatively little direct financing. In a period of rapidly rising external aid the promotion of parastatals thus became the focus of donor policy. Moreover, substantial knowledge of the political, sociocultural, technological, infrastructural, and financial circumstances at the microeconomic level is required to create conditions in which the private sector can operate competitively. In a period of rapidly rising external aid—when the promotion of parastatals was the focus of policy—the steps needed to develop the legal and institutional framework (for example, free entry, information, and mobility) essential for the development of competitive markets were rarely taken. These are areas that require few financial resources but much thoughtful investment in human and institutional capacity. Kenya offers examples of successful semiautonomous agencies—for example, the Kenya Tea Development Authority (KDTA) and the coffee and dairy cooperatives that have been important to the growth of smallholder production. Among the factors accounting for KTDA's success has been the direct link between producer and world market prices and the absence of price stabilization and significant taxation. KTDA's ability to maintain organizational autonomy owes much to its financial success, to the support of the politically powerful constituency of tea growers, and to technical assistance from the Commonwealth Development Corporation and the World Bank.

The success of KTDA contrasts sharply with the problems of Kenya's National Cereals and Produce Board (NCPB). Some of the problems of the NCPB are generic to food crop marketing parastatals attempting to stabilize prices when there is no clear separation between the routine marketing activities and other, inherently loss-making, functions. The lack of effective management and control of expenditure was compounded by the doubling of its financial deficit from K Sh 312 million in 1980–81 to nearly K Sh 650 million in 1985–86. Parastatals in Malawi and Tanzania have faced similar problems—with serious macroeconomic consequences. This suggests that issues related to the intra- and interyear price stabilization in the case of cereals for the domestic market are different from those relating to export crops, where the principle of residual producer pricing tends to apply.

In Tanzania, the National Milling Corporation (the maize-marketing parastatal) alone was responsible for two-thirds of total losses, representing 31 percent of its sales. The parastatals' overdrafts had exceeded T Sh 5 billion and accounted for 80 percent of the loans of the National Bank of Commerce, the country's only commercial bank. Note that although the administrative costs connected with the growth of employment were excessive, they were a very small part of total losses. The costs of financing and sales (which reflect purchases plus transport and processing costs) accounted for 97 percent of total losses. In 1980–81, only the coffee and sugar parastatals showed a profit; the remaining ones showed combined losses of T Sh 692 million ($84 million), which was equal to 21 percent of the value of their processed commodities.

In Senegal, the high marketing costs incurred by ONCAD, the marketing parastatal, were due to mismanagement and corruption, and to the rapid expansion of staff. ONCAD's staff tripled from 400–500 full-time staff in 1966 to 1,800 in 1968, and it continued to rise—to 2,097 by 1974, and to 2,964 by 1979—while salaries came to account for more than half of the agency's operating expenses. This increase was more the result of the political pressure to expand employment than of the increases in marketing functions or groundnut transactions. ONCAD encountered financial difficulties as well because, among other things, it was required by the government to forgive the debts of drought-affected groundnut producers but was not reimbursed.

Not all the inefficiencies attributed to parastatals lie within their own control. Externally imposed pricing policies, inadequate financing to cover the legitimate costs of subsidizing grain-price stabilization operations, and pressure from governments to distribute political patronage (which leads to overstaffing) all play a part. In Tanzania and Cameroon, for example, parastatals were required to provide a number of social services for their employees (sometimes even for their households)—including educational and medical facilities, work and private transportation, prepared food services, provision stores, mechanical workshops, and sports teams. Similarly, financing for cotton roads in Cameroon came largely from SODECOTON.

In the 1980s policy reforms emphasized privatization and the need to improve parastatal performance through a combination of measures such as financial restructuring, divestiture, and greater emphasis on commercial criteria. Malawi and Tanzania liberalized grain marketing; and Nigeria and Senegal abolished their marketing boards for perennial export crops. Nigeria also turned over cotton marketing activities to the private sector. Governments have been reluctant, however, to relinquish political and economic power in these areas. Furthermore, although the private sector can provide increased competition and can clearly perform some tasks more efficiently than parastatals, the public sector must ensure that certain pricing and marketing functions are performed for political, welfare, and developmental reasons.

Thus the problem in Africa is how to develop the capacity of governments to establish clear priorities about the areas in which they should operate and to ensure that they do so efficiently. Overall, the experience with public sector intervention in agricultural marketing in the MADIA countries clearly indicates that institutional pluralism is needed to foster competition. Structural adjustment has made an important beginning in the right direction. However, with attrition of technical expertise (see chapters 5 and 8) in donor agencies, donors can provide little useful technical advice to African governments in the important area of price policy except to place a relatively straightforward emphasis on privatization.

Diversification policies within food crop agriculture. Apart from the shift in production from export crops to food crops, each of the six MADIA countries has also experienced some diversification within food crop agriculture. Most African governments have neglected the production of the traditional food crops—sorghum, millet, cassava, and yams—produced and consumed by a large majority of their citizens. Instead, they have favored the high-cost production of rice and wheat to meet the rapidly growing demand in the urban sector; indeed, rice has been the fastest growing crop in the MADIA countries. In Nigeria during the oil boom, domestic rice was encouraged through investments in large-scale irrigation, whereas the consumer prices of food imports were kept low through large imports and overvaluation of the exchange rate. A significant devaluation has made Nigeria's domestic rice production more competitive compared with rice imports especially when rice is produced on a low-cost, small-scale surface or tubewell irrigation. In Senegal national income generated from groundnut production is seven times that from rice in a normal year. Yet considerably less policy attention has been given to improving groundnut production than to promoting irrigated rice in the Fleuve (in response to rapidly increasing rice imports). Rice production has been subsidized through investments in irrigation and several other services to producers that make demands on the government budget. Exchange rate adjustment in the countries of the CFA zone will make some of the subsidies on domestic rice production unnecessary and, as in the case of Nigeria, improve competitiveness especially of rainfed rice. Nevertheless, the results of the MADIA study suggest that Senegal has a distinct comparative advantage in groundnut production under *improved* technology that it has not fully exploited.[33]

Horticultural crops provide another means of diversification. These crops generally have not been controlled by governments, and they can generate substantial income and employment for small farmers. The growth of many such crops offers impressive examples of diversification—for instance, in the highlands of Cameroon. Kenya's exports of horticultural crops grew at an annual rate of 12 percent (albeit from a small base) during 1970–85. Such crops are meeting the growing urban and export demand that has developed in response to investments in infrastructure—particularly roads. This kind of diversification is usually overlooked in evaluations of price policies and responses, and its impact on welfare gains may be understated. Thus far neither governments nor donors have paid enough attention to its implications for public policy (with regard to the development of supportive transportation, storage, information, and financial networks for private producers and trade).

Land policy. The ability of producers to mobilize additional land and labor, along with whatever capital is used in production (for example, for implements, animal traction, or fertilizer) has been crucial in raising production levels. The growing population pressure on land makes equitable access to land more urgent than ever before.

In Kenya, land policy has enabled Africans to settle on land formerly owned and operated by European settlers in the Rift Valley and the White Highlands. A land market has evolved, and large increases in land titling have occurred in areas of high potential, where rights to grow high-value tree crops such as tea and coffee (along with dairying) have been promoted. Between 1970 and 1983, the amount of land registered increased from 1.8 million hectares to 6.5 million hectares. This area constituted 97 percent of all high- and medium-potential land—or, including semiarid and transitional areas, about 44 percent of cultivable land. The share of smallholders in total registered land was 43 percent overall, but it was well above 80 percent in Western, Nyanza, Central, and Eastern provinces, where 62 percent of the population lives. Although smallholders have had recourse to legal ownership in Kenya, the process of land titling has been fraught with unequal access to capital and land because of ethnic biases, conflicting tenure customs, and registration fees.[34] This has led the population to migrate onto marginal land faster than the rate at which the population has been growing and thus has helped exhaust the soil. There may still be much underutilized land in the highlands of Kenya; access to these areas remains limited, and labor shortages in these areas constrain intensification of smallholder production of tea and coffee.[35]

In Malawi, customary rights to cultivate and transfer smallholder land are conferred by traditional tribal chiefs, while the expansion of estate farming has been explicitly determined by government policies. A licensing policy allowing leaseholds to be established on "unused" customary and public land pushed up the demand to establish estates; Between 1968 and 1984, the proportion of total arable land under estates rose from 14 percent to nearly 20 percent (of which, according to one estimate, only 6 to 8 percent was actually cultivated). Thus, less than 2 percent of the total cultivable land in Malawi produced virtually all of its agricultural exports. The area recorded as customary land had decreased since the mid-1960s, in part because of the increasing alienation of land for estates. The transfer of land from smallholders to estates has contributed to economic growth through estate production, and, although it led to a decline in average farm size in both sectors, it has worsened land distribution over time. Although the mean area of tobacco estates declined from 34 hectares in 1976 to 11 hectares in 1985, the estate sector's share in the area under tobacco increased from 24 percent in 1970 to 47 percent in 1985. However, because population has been growing by more than 3 percent per year, marginal land increasingly is being brought under cultivation. The average size of smallholdings fell from 1.6 hectares in 1968–69 to about 1.2 hectares in 1980–81, while the average size of tobacco estates fell from 40 hectares in 1967–68 to 12 hectares in 1984–85. Smallholders are being crowded out from land access just at a time that population pressure and subsistence requirements are increasing—yet estate land remains underutilized. Land policy will be the single most important factor determining the pace and pattern of future agricultural and overall economic growth in Malawi in that it will either provide or hold back the stimulus that broadly based agricultural growth can give to the rest of the economy.

In Tanzania, smallholder control over land has suffered as a result of state policy. Tanzania formally abolished traditional tribal village authority, replacing it with public ownership of land, whereby an individual has no right of ownership or sale. The ideology of the ruling party discouraged "capitalist farming" by large and small farmers alike in the 1970s. The Ujamma policy of forced "villagization" led to the resettlement of more than 9 million people—about 60 percent of the population—into 6,000 villages by mid-1975. Given the fragile soil (the reason for traditionally sparser settlements), the Ujamma policy toward land increased environmental stress and led to even greater problems of deforestation and soil exhaustion.

Yet there were also some positive aspects to land policy in Tanzania. Investments in the Tanzam road and rail links opened up areas of high agricultural potential for spontaneous settlement in the Southern Highlands. Since Western donors declined to finance the railway, Tanzania had to seek funding from China. These areas grow coffee, tea, maize, and tobacco, and are now an important source of agricultural production. Unfortunately, these gains have been offset by the government's discriminatory investment and pricing policies, which were biased toward low-income, resource-poor regions and hurt the traditional production areas in the north (Arusha/Kilimanjaro), the west (the Lake Victoria basin), and the center (Tabora). Adoption of structural adjustment programs since 1986 has been intended to resuscitate growth and the initial boost in price incentives for export and food crops had that effect. Tanzania's traditional production areas were, however, beginning to show the stress from deficits in both the road network and the transportation fleet—a direct result of neglect of investments in the past.

In Cameroon and Nigeria, large and medium farmers have been encouraged to acquire additional land by increasing their access to subsidized tractor services. Institutional and juridical aspects of land policy—such as legally specified rights to the use and ownership of land or rights to grow crops—have not been prominent issues in West Africa. Nevertheless, land policy issues have not received attention in Nigeria and Cameroon, perhaps because the overall pressure on land has not been as great as in Kenya or Malawi. In the East African countries they have been of critical importance in determining agricultural performance.[36]

Labor policy. Labor mobilization in East Africa has been greatly affected by labor policy, although labor legislation, minimum wage laws, and unionism tend to be less important in rural than in urban areas. In Tanzania, however, their impact has been considerable. Together with the political campaign to discourage the use of hired labor, these factors contributed to the decline of both smallholder and large-estate agriculture in Tanzania until 1986. Adoption of reforms by the government and greater tolerance of market prices by Tanzania's political party (the CCM) should have improved the environment for labor hire by entrepreneurs, although the issue of labor markets and employment remains greatly underresearched.

The Malawian government has not encouraged the unionization of labor, and wage employment in estate production grew at nearly 10 percent per annum in the 1970s. Employment growth in estates slackened in the 1980s and real wage rates were falling, because the discriminatory land and price policy reduced returns in farming customary areas and encouraged labor to move from the smallholder to the estate sector. Limited access to primary and secondary level of schooling by young children in Malawi has also caused a high incidence of child labor on Malawi's estates, thereby contributing to a decline in the minimum wage. Moreover, the return of the Malawian migrants from South Africa in the late 1970s and the influx of Mozambique refugees in the 1980s increased the labor force. Since 1988, declining real wages of estate labor have caused concern to donors.

By creating abundant growth linkages in the economy, Kenya's overall development strategy, in contrast, created a wide range of employment opportunities in the agricultural sector in both smallholder and estate farming, as well as in nonfarm activities. Widespread access to primary schools kept children in education. Although minimum wage guidelines were observed in agricultural employment, Kenya followed more moderate policies than the other two East African countries. Despite one of the most rapid rates of population growth, real wages in Kenya had fallen less than had been predicted in the early 1970s and to a far lesser extent than in Malawi and Tanzania, where they had declined by nearly half by 1988.

Fertilizer policy. As countries begin to run out of extensive margin lands and thus have less scope for shifting cultivation and extended fallow, they will have to increase their use of chemical fertilizers and organic materials and learn how to manage their soil better if productivity is to continue to grow. The fact that there is no positive relationship between agricultural performance and the growth of fertilizer use in the MADIA countries is not surprising in view of the important role played by macroeconomic and other sectoral policies (as discussed in this chapter). The policies include explicit and implicit taxation of agriculture, the right to grow export crops, and the ability of small and large farmers to mobilize land and labor. Kenya, which led the MADIA countries in the growth of food and export crop production, was fourth in the average annual growth of fertilizer use (6.7 percent during 1974–86; see figures 2-9 and 2-10). Nigeria showed the most rapid growth (18.0 percent during 1972–87), but it was one of the poorest agricultural performers. Tanzania and Senegal, both of which performed poorly in agriculture, also had the least satisfactory average annual growth in fertilizer use (2.2 percent and 0.8 percent, respectively). Malawi and Cameroon were in the middle—in both

Figure 2-9. Trends in Fertilizer Consumption in East Africa, 1972–87

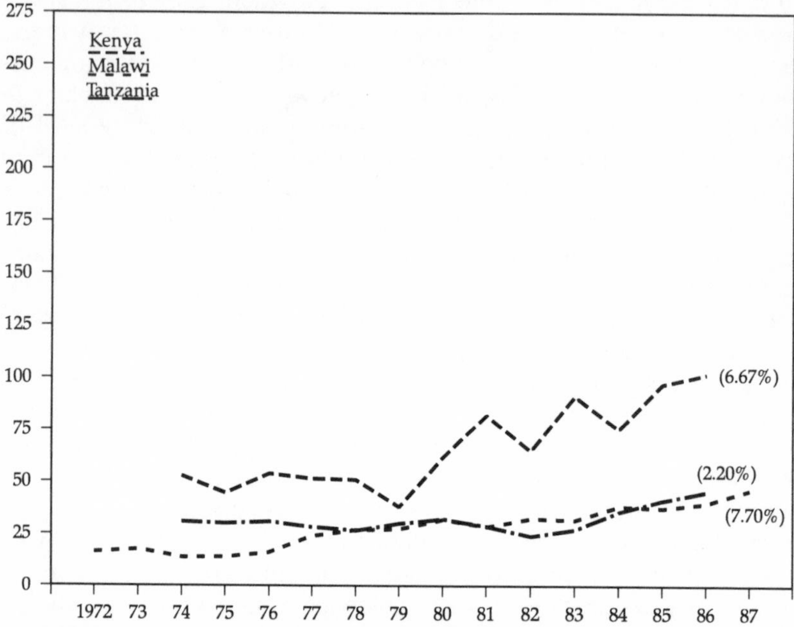

Note: Figures in brackets represent growth rates.
Source: Uma Lele, Robert Christiansen, and Kundhavi Kadiresan, *Issues in Fertilizer Policy in Africa: Lessons from Development Programs and Adjustment Lending*, MADIA Discussion Paper 5 (Washington, D.C.: World Bank, 1989).

performance and the growth of fertilizer use (11.7 percent and 7.7 percent, respectively).[37]

A number of supply and demand constraints hindered the growth and diffusion of fertilizer use. Supply constraints have included foreign exchange shortages and, where subsidies existed (e.g. in Nigeria), budgetary constraints. Other supply constraints have included restricted transport facilities and shortages of working capital for importers, wholesalers, transporters, and retailers. Distortions in the allocation of fertilizer have occurred due to fixed distribution margins and political factors. These have resulted in governments or projects directing fertilizers to particular areas of the country regardless of fertilizer responsiveness. Demand was constrained by the unpredictability of fertilizer prices, supplies, and nutrient content; low physical response to fertilizer; the lack of packaging in suitably small quantities; the shortage of working capital for small farmers; and the inability of small farmers to take risks in rainfed agriculture. Supply constraints dominated in Kenya, Tanzania, Nigeria, and Cameroon, while

Figure 2-10. Trends in Fertilizer Consumption in West Africa, 1970–87

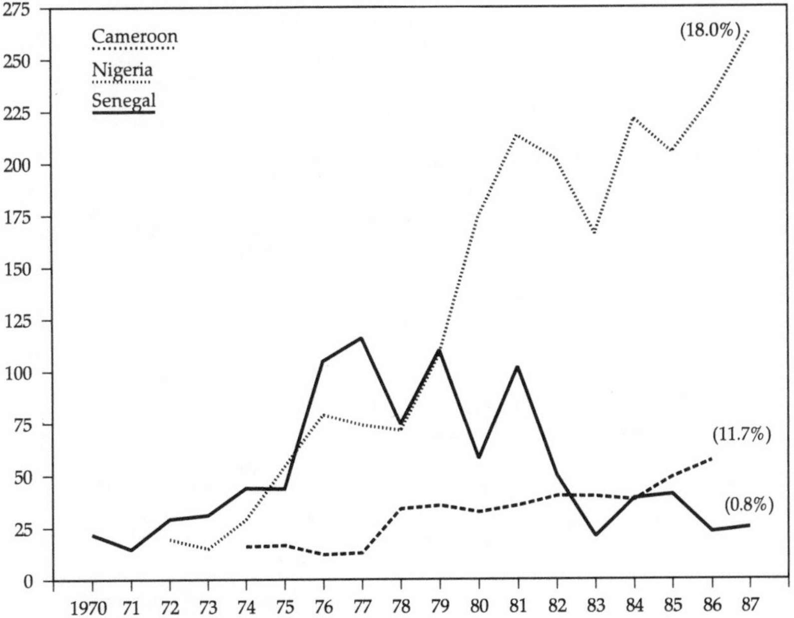

Note: Figures in brackets represent growth rates.
Source: See figure 2-9.

demand constraints were relatively more important in Malawi. Both supply and demand constraints hindered growth in fertilizer use in Senegal.

Kenya was the least reliant on explicit subsidies of fertilizers (eliminated in 1977), whereas Tanzania and Nigeria resorted to them most heavily. The rate of explicit fertilizer subsidy in Tanzania and Nigeria was similar (75 percent in the 1970s in Tanzania, after which it declined to 25 percent; 85 percent throughout in Nigeria). Explicit subsidies in Senegal (55 percent), Cameroon (54 percent), and Malawi (23 percent) have been relatively moderate.[38] Overvaluation of the exchange rate in Nigeria and Tanzania also meant implicit subsidization of fertilizers and other imported inputs.

The price of nutrients (converted to United States dollars at official and purchasing power parity exchange rates) were generally higher in the East African countries (see table 2-16). Nigeria had the lowest nutrient price because of the high subsidy. In 1985/86 the price of ammonium sulphate, for example, was $1,020 per metric ton in Malawi, $548 in Tanzania, and $398 in Cameroon. Higher internal

Table 2-16. Prices for Principal Fertilizers in MADIA Countries, 1971/72–87/88
(U.S. dollars/ton of nutrient adjusted using purchasing power parity exchange rates)

	Cameroon		Senegal	Nigeria	Malawi			Kenya		Tanzania	
Year	NPK (20:10:10)	A/S	NPK (6:20:10)	NPK (15:15:15)	NPK (20:20:0)	CAN	A/S	DAP	CAN	A/S	TSP
1971/72	—	—	122	—	—	—	—	176	247	—	—
1972/73	—	—	132	—	215	317	327	245	364	—	—
1973/74	258	—	190	—	233	343	361	367	489	—	—
1974/75	228	377	175	—	587	852	833	348	464	—	—
1975/76	477	727	203	—	543	762	669	648	955	—	—
1976/77	432	548	249	91	510	714	628	588	1,018	—	—
1977/78	326	518	243	90	547	766	673	457	824	641	409
1978/79	307	474	281	86	585	820	720	498	952	680	435
1979/80	321	498	299	87	617	867	761	531	954	684	438
1980/81	328	546	327	90	608	1,156	885	833	1,195	612	392
1981/82	275	458	276	146	525	997	1,057	819	1,227	677	347
1982/83	256	487	216	132	697	1,106	1,106	660	1,085	519	266
1983/84	245	468	370	115	697	1,036	1,099	690	776	419	215
1984/85	208	396	514	186	648	884	953	603	912	291	149
1985/86	209	398	385	180	627	894	1,020	—	—	548	344
1986/87	262	498	488	277	645	856	1,054	539	831	765	472
1987/88	—	—	—	247	822	1,066	1,335	—	—	625	386

— = Not available.

Note: Data are for official fertilizer prices adjusted using purchasing power parity exchange rates. The fertilizer type(s) listed for each country reflect what is predominantly used. Certain costs incurred within the country, such as handling cost and rebagging cost, are not affected by currency overvaluation and were not available separately for all years. Ideally these costs should not be adjusted for currency overvaluation; however, a lack of data and the fact that these costs comprise a small part of total fertilizer cost (less than 15 percent) mean the adjustment can be ignored. Fertilizer prices for Kenya are f.o.r. Nakuru. The prices in Tanzania after 1984 (when subsidy was abolished) refers to TFC's exstore prices at regional levels. Though retail prices are uniform throughout the country in both Kenya and Tanzania, the end-user prices vary according to location and depending on services rendered by retailers. NPK = nitrogen, potash, phrosphorus; A/S = ammonium sulphate; CAN = calcium ammonium nitrate; DAP = di-ammonium phosphate; TSP = triple superphosphate.

Source: Uma Lele, Robert E. Christiansen, and Kundhavi Kadiresan, *Fertilizer Policy in Africa: Lessons from Development Programs and Adjustment Lending, 1970–87*, MADIA Discussion Paper No. 5 (Washington, D.C.: World Bank, 1989).

transport costs in Malawi explain part of the variation. At purchasing power parity rates, the official prices of maize in Malawi and Tanzania tended to be about half of those in West Africa.[39] Among the six countries, Malawi thus had the most unfavorable ratio of nutrient prices to maize prices, while Nigeria had the lowest (see tables 2-17 and 2-18).

Table 2-17. Nutrient Price/Crop Price Ratios for Selected Crops in East Africa, 1980–88

Country	*Maize*	*Rice*	*Tobacco*	*Arabica coffee*	*Cotton*	*Tea*
Malawi						
1980/81	8.8	—	1.0	—	—	—
1981/82	7.8	—	1.4	—	—	—
1982/83	9.1	—	1.7	—	—	—
1983/84	9.0	—	1.1	—	—	—
1984/85	9.9	—	1.1	—	—	—
1985/86	12.2	—	1.0	—	—	—
1986/87	12.5	—	1.0	—	—	—
1987/88	10.3	—	2.3	—	—	—
Kenya						
1980/81	6.2	—	—	0.4	2.6	3.6
1981/82	7.2	—	—	0.5	3.4	4.1
1982/83	4.5	—	—	0.4	3.2	3.0
1983/84	5.0	—	—	0.3	3.1	1.4
1984/85	5.2	—	—	0.4	2.9	2.5
1985/86	—	—	—	—	—	—
1986/87	3.4	—	—	0.2	3.2	2.5
1987/88	4.5	—	—	—	—	—
Tanzania						
1980/81	5.6	3.2	0.6	—	1.9	3.1
1981/82	5.4	3.5	0.8	—	2.5	3.8
1982/83	5.1	3.0	0.7	—	2.4	4.1
1983/84	4.1	2.2	0.5	—	1.9	3.1
1984/85	2.2	1.5	0.4	—	1.5	2.2
1985/86	4.2	2.8	0.6	—	2.6	3.9
1986/87	5.0	3.3	0.6	—	2.4	—
1987/88	5.0	2.9	—	—	—	—

— = Not available.

Note: These ratios are computed using official fertilizer prices that reflect subsidies, the effect of grant aid fertilizer on cost, and the official exchange rate. The ratio does not reflect internal transport costs. The nutrient-crop price ratios for maize and rice in Tanzania have been computed for producer prices in the premium areas. For the other areas, the ratios are bound to be still higher.

Source: Uma Lele, Robert E. Christiansen, and Kundhavi Kadiresan, *Fertilizer Policy in Africa: Lessons from Development Programs and Adjustment Lending, 1970–87,* MADIA Discussion Paper 5 (Washington, D.C.: World Bank, 1989).

Table 2-18. Nutrient Price/Crop Price Ratios for Selected Crops in West Africa, 1980–87

					Coffee			
Country	Maize	Groundnuts	Rice	Millet	Arabica	Robusta	Cotton	Cocoa
Cameroon								
1980	2.2	—	—	—	0.3	0.4	1.7	0.5
1981	2.1	—	—	—	0.4	0.4	1.5	0.4
1982	2.4	—	—	—	0.5	0.5	1.6	0.5
1983	—	—	—	—	0.5	0.5	1.7	0.5
1984	—	—	—	—	0.4	0.4	1.5	0.5
1985	—	—	—	—	0.4	0.4	1.4	0.5
1986	—	—	—	—	0.4	0.4	1.4	0.5
1987	—	—	—	—	0.4	—	1.2	0.5
Senegal								
1980	1.9	1.5	1.7	1.7	—	—	1.3	—
1981	1.5	1.2	1.3	1.4	—	—	1.2	—
1982	1.5	1.2	1.3	1.4	—	—	1.0	—
1983	2.9	2.8	2.7	2.8	—	—	1.8	—
1984	3.2	3.2	3.2	3.5	—	—	2.5	—
	(4.2)	(4.2)	(4.2)	(4.5)	—	—	(3.2)	—
1985	2.4	1.9	2.5	2.8	—	—	2.1	—
	(4.2)	(3.2)	(4.4)	(4.9)	—	—	(3.7)	—
1986	2.6	2.0	2.1	2.6	—	—	1.8	—
	(3.6)	(2.8)	(2.9)	(3.6)	—	—	(2.5)	—
1987	2.9	2.3	2.3	2.9	—	—	2.1	—
	(3.6)	(2.8)	(2.4)	(3.6)	—	—	(2.5)	—
Nigeria								
1980	0.3	0.2	0.2	0.3	—	—	0.2	0.1
1981	0.5	0.4	0.3	0.4	—	—	0.3	0.1
1982	0.6	0.4	0.3	0.4	—	—	0.3	0.1
1983	0.6	0.4	0.3	0.5	—	—	0.3	0.1
1984	0.6	0.7	0.4	0.5	—	—	0.6	0.3
1985	0.7	0.6	0.4	0.5	—	—	0.5	0.3
1986	1.4	0.8	0.5	1.5	—	—	0.7	0.4
1987	1.4	—	0.3	1.3	—	—	0.5	0.1

— = Not available.

Note: These ratios are computed using official fertilizer prices that reflect subsidies and the effect of grant aid fertilizer on cost. The ratio does not reflect internal transport costs. Figures in parentheses are ratios for the unsubsidized price of fertilizer in Senegal.

Source: Uma Lele, Robert E. Christiansen, and Khundavi Kadiresan, *Fertilizer Policy in Africa: Lessons from Development Programs and Adjustment Lending,* 1970–87, MADIA Discussion Paper 5 (Washington, D.C.: World Bank, 1989).

Profitability also depends on the physical response to nutrients. The considerable variation in agroclimatic conditions between and within the MADIA countries and the poor and inconsistent data on response coefficients make it difficult to firmly establish the profitability of fertilizer use among crops and locations. Often the data mask the immense differences in response caused by climatic factors. The fundamental need for location-specific and well-articulated recommendations for the application of fertilizer—particularly micronutrients—has not received the priority it deserves from either governments or donors. Such discussion should include systematic production function analysis. In general, responses to fertilizer use on maize in the high-potential areas of East Africa were favorable and similar to those in certain areas of the highlands of Cameroon and the rain forest zone of Nigeria (see tables 2-19 and 2-20). In large parts of semiarid areas, however, the fertilizer responses of maize, sorghum, and millet have been low and highly uncertain. Similarly, varieties of arabica coffee in Kenya are reported to be roughly twice as responsive to fertilizer as the varieties in Cameroon. It is difficult to determine the extent to which Kenya's favorable soil and climatic conditions as distinct from an excellent research system may have accounted for these high responses.

Recent reform measures since the mid-1980s have been concerned with removing fertilizer subsidies and privatizing distribution networks to reduce budgetary deficits and the role of the public sector. As of the writing of this book, policy reform efforts have not, however, addressed the broader and longer-term issues of the role of fertilizer in agricultural intensification. These issues include the complexity and diversity of Africa's soils, low and fluctuating levels of nutrient use and agricultural productivity, increasing population pressure on scarce arable land, soil degradation, and increasing reliance on food imports. The issues are further complicated by stagnant exports and a poor knowledge of production response to nutrient use in specific locations, especially in situations of repeated applications.

In Senegal, the collapse of fertilizer use in the groundnut basin from a peak of 116,000 tons to only about 25,000 tons by 1987 was largely the result of the abolition of the public sector supply system and the failure of private traders to take up the supply of fertilizer. The demand for fertilizer fluctuates from year to year because of the risks associated with low and declining rainfall. Private traders are reluctant to stock fertilizers and expand distribution networks when farmer demand for fertilizer is so variable from year to year. In Nigeria, a strong supply push by the government (through a generous allocation of foreign exchange, through an active role in distribution, and through a large subsidy) led to rapid growth in fertilizer use. However, government subsidies led to wasteful use of fertilizers by increasing demand, rationing available supplies to the politically powerful larger farmers of the northern states (where responses to fertilizer application on millet and sorghum were not the most attractive). Increased demand

Table 2-19. *Response Coefficients for Selected Crops in East Africa*
(kilograms of output per kilogram of nutrient)

Country	*Maize*		*Sorghum*	*Tea*	*Coffee*	*Rice*	*Wheat*
	Local	*Hybrid*		*Green*	*Arabica*		
Malawi							
ASA	16.6	29	—	—	—	—	—
FAO	—	20–37	—	—	—	—	—
WB	14	30	—	—	—	—	—
Kenya					10.4		
East of Rift Valley	—	—	—	30–35	—	—	—
West of Rift Valley	—	—	—	15–20	—	—	—
(GOK)HPD	—	15–26	18–21	—	—	—	—
MPD	—	10–21	5–19	—	—	—	—
LPD	—	9–14	4	—	—	—	—
(FAO)(WNP)	—	15–17	—	—	—	—	—
(RVP)	—	12–22	—	—	—	—	—
(C&EP)	—	16–25	—	—	—	—	—
Tanzania							
Existing practices	—	13.5	10	—	—	13.2	11.9
Improved management	—	11.5[a]	12.8	—	—	11.5[a]	4.8[a]
(World Bank)	6	16	—	—	—	—	—

— = Not available.

Note: ASA-Annual Survey of Agriculture; FAO-Food and Agriculture Organization; WB-World Bank; GOK-Government of Kenya; HPD-High Potential Districts; MPD-Medium Potential Districts; LPD-Low Potential Districts; WNP-Western and Nyanza provinces; RVP-Rift Valley province; C&EP-Central and Eastern provinces.

a. The yields under improved practices are higher. However, data suggest that crop responses to fertilizers under improved practices are lower than under existing practices. Thus, the extent to which agricultural extension is a substitute for fertilizer use rather than a complement to it needs serious further analysis based on strong empirical research.

Source: Uma Lele, Robert E. Christiansen, and Khundavi Kadireasan, *Fertilizer Policy in Africa: Lessons from Development Programs and Adjustment Lending, 1970–87,* MADIA Discussion Paper 5 (Washington, D.C.: World Bank, 1989).

Table 2-20. Response Coefficients for Selected Crops in West Africa, 1976–85
(kilograms of output per kilogram of nutrient)

	Nigeria						Cameroon			Senegal		
		FAO			World Bank							
Crop	*Region*	*LP*	*IP*	*Falusi*	*1976–80*	*1984–85*	*Region*	*IFDC*	*FAO*	*Region*	*IFDC*	*FAO*
Maize									7.3			
	Derived Savannah	4–11					Coastal Lowlands	32.1				
	S. Guinea Savannah		5–12	6–7			Guinea Forest (Ntui)	3.8				
	Forest	7–18		6–14			Maize after cotton	30.8				
	Sudan Savannah			6	8	5.6	Maize after groundnut	20.9				
	N. Guinea Savannah			6–10	8							
Sorghum									3.9			3.8
	Sudan Savannah		3–8	2.5–7	8.5	2.5–3	Northern Plain (HYV)	7–30		North Siné-Soloum	4.3	
	N. Guinea Savannah	4–8	2–7	5–7	8					South Siné-Saloum	5.8	
	S. Guinea Savannah	5–9	5–12	3–7								
Groundnut												6.6
	Sudan Savannah	7–13				1.5–3				North Basin	4–6	
	N. Guinea Savannah	9–17	8–15	11–13						Central Basin	5–8	
	S. Guinea Savannah	10–21	9–10							North Siné-Saloum	7–9.5	
										South Siné-Saloum	8–11	
Millet												7.03
	Sudan Savannah		3–11	2.5–6		2.5				North Basin	14–20	
	N. Guinea Savannah		7–13	3–9						Central Basin	15–17	
	S. Guinea Savannah		13–21							North Siné-Saloum	17–20	
										South Siné-Saloum	17	
Rice					7–12	6						
	Derived Savannah (upland)	4–11					Northern Plain (HYV)	12–39		Casamance		5.60
	Forest (upland)	3–13										
	S. Guinea Savannah (swamp)	4–7	3–8	5–6								

(Table continues on the following page.)

Table 2-20. (continued)

		Nigeria					Cameroon			Senegal		
		FAO			World Bank							
Crop	*Region*	*LP*	*IP*	*Falusi*	*1976–80*	*1984–85*	*Region*	*IFDC*	*FAO*	*Region*	*IFDC*	*FAO*
Wheat												
	Sudan Savannah (irrigated)		3–11									
Coffee												
Arabica								5–6				
Robusta								2–3				
Yam		30		14								
Cassava		46		20–32								
Cowpeas			9–16	2–13	15–18	1–3						

Note: LP-Local practice; IP-Improved practice.

Source: Uma Lele, Robert E. Christiansen, and Khundavi Kadiresan, *Fertilizer Policy in Africa: Lessons from Development Programs and Adjustment Lending, 1970–87,* MADIA Discussion Paper 5 (Washington, D.C.: World Bank, 1989).

and a rationed supply created a black market, and in effect, the farmers paid higher fertilizer prices than intended.

In general, fertilizer subsidies should be regarded as undesirable for a variety of reasons, including their inequitable benefits and the difficulty of controlling their budgetary costs. They are often wasteful and ineffective because they address only the price dimension of fertilizer use and not the supply constraints. Nonetheless, in some cases, there are compelling arguments in favor of a fertilizer subsidy. The rationale for subsidies reflects both the need for household food security as well as market imperfections (i.e., failure of credit and insurance markets). For example, where benefit-cost ratios exceed unity but are less than 2 and are variable, subsidies may be necessary. Similarly, the increasing scarcity of arable land and growing household dependence on the market for food may on welfare grounds limit the scope for increasing output prices as a means of ensuring the profitability of fertilizer use to food deficit households. If there is little access to credit, the use of fertilizer can be made more attractive by reducing its price. In Malawi, for example, poverty in the smallholder sector has brought demand constraints as binding as supply constraints. Because subsidized fertilizer has been leaking to the estate sector, the generalized subsidy to the smallholder sector was considered to be difficult to continue. Efforts to allocate fertilizer subsidies specifically to the poorest households and fertilizer-for-work programs were under consideration, but it may be difficult to prevent fertilizer leakage to the more commercially oriented small farmers. The fact that little is known about how targeted subsidy programs work makes it important to recognize this knowledge gap and to monitor and modify policies carefully in the light of experience.

Although the private sector can improve the efficiency of input distribution, it alone cannot meet the needs of all producers. Nor can it be expected to promote or create demand for inputs where a substantial investment of time and resources is needed to foster a profitable level of demand. In addition, given the complex agronomic dimensions of soil fertility that need to be addressed in most African countries, it is unreasonable to expect the private sector alone to attempt to solve the soil management and credit supply problems for farmers. It is in these circumstances that a role exists for public distribution and subsidies in the short and medium run as a device to encourage fertilizer use until the other constraints on increasing demand are addressed.

It is still too soon to evaluate the experience with the privatization of fertilizer distribution. In Kenya, privatization and liberalization have given large agricultural units such as estates and some cooperatives in the well-organized smallholder export crop sectors (e.g., tea, coffee, and dairying) better access to fertilizers. Kenya has the highest per-hectare use of fertilizers and the most sophisticated distribution network with a relatively more dynamic private sector. But small agricultural producers, especially those in remote areas, have not benefited. This is because the private sector has tended to concentrate its attention either on the large producers or on relatively high potential areas where demand is already well established through well-organized marketing parastatals or the cooperatives.

The extremely inadequate knowledge about physical responses to fertilizers is one of the most serious impediments to effective long-term policy. Relatively little donor assistance has been directed toward understanding the determinants of fertilizer use at the farm level in Africa. This differs from the earlier experience in Asia where the spread of the green revolution was based on systematic studies of the determinents of diffusion of modern technology by small farmers. Thus policymakers and donors in Africa are poorly equipped to design and implement policies in support of intensification except on the basis of hunches, clichés, and pressure from specific lobbies such as the environmentalists or the privatizers. Given the amount of time required to generate reliable data and the confusion caused by the results of short-term trials financed by donors, governments and donors need to make a long-term commitment to the fertilizer sector—and should begin by producing better information on location-specific fertilizer responses. This means African analysts and institutions will have to develop the capacity to undertake such work on a long-term basis as a routine component of agricultural policy. This has yet to occur.

Credit policy. All six countries have subsidized agricultural interest rates, but these subsidies have been lower in Kenya and Malawi than in Tanzania, Nigeria, or Senegal. Seasonal and medium-term credit has been most advanced in Kenya, followed by Malawi, Senegal, and Tanzania.

The extent of free-standing credit projects or credit components in agricultural projects has varied from country to country. Although Kenya has had the highest number of donor-funded credit projects (followed by Tanzania, Malawi, and Senegal), Nigeria has had no credit components in donor-funded projects. This is perhaps because of the existence of a large fertilizer subsidy in the context of the World Bank Agricultural Development Projects in the 1970s. It may also arise from failure in a policy dialogue with the Nigerian government to make headway on issues related to the establishment of one or more credit institutions.

In Cameroon, credit was tied to the promotion of specific export crops, such as coffee and cotton, and this has benefited fewer farmers than in Kenya or Malawi. By and large, much of the available subsidized credit has accrued to the larger farmers. Only in Kenya and (to a lesser extent) Malawi have smallholders benefited on a large enough scale from the provision of institutional credit. Even in Kenya, however, the indiscriminate growth of inadequately supervised credit has resulted in low repayment rates and the consequent erosion of the financial capital of credit institutions—a problem also experienced in Tanzania, Senegal, and Cameroon.

Group credit in Malawi and supervised credit for cotton in Cameroon offer a few select examples of an excellent record on repayment. In Malawi targeted credit did reach nearly 20 percent of the smallholders in the communal areas. Malawi also has had one of the highest repayment rates for small farmer credit due to group pressure. This, however, also discouraged the poorest small households, typically those with less than one hectare of cultivated land, from using this mechanism. Such households tend to be concerned about their inability to pay. They are the ones who most need credit but cannot bear the risk.[40] Inequitable access to subsidized institutional credit and the erosion of financial capital because of nonrepayment gave rise in the 1970s to the view that directed institutional credit is unnecessary for agricultural development.[41] Some have also argued that the supply of informal credit in rural areas tends to be larger than is generally acknowledged, and that efforts to mobilize additional rural savings will obviate the need for specialized credit institutions. In Kenya, for instance, the erosion of the financial capital of individual institutions has nonetheless coexisted with the relatively high saving and investment rates of rural households.

In line with other studies of rural households, MADIA research indicates that, where potential economic opportunities exist, easy access to cash (for example, through remittances) has facilitated the adoption of new technologies,[42] while cash shortages have constrained the adoption of new technologies among small farmers.[43] This suggests that institutional credit can, if appropriately administered, release an important constraint on intensification. Its wholesale rejection seems unjustified. Studies have repeatedly pointed to the need for a greater supply of institutional credit—especially where hired labor and modern inputs are needed to raise productivity. Thus, though the institutional mobilization of rural savings is essential, it may be counterproductive to abolish or undermine rural credit beforehand. This is because costs of purchased inputs increase when currencies are devalued, subsidies are removed, and internal transport costs are increased as a result of the general inflation caused by devaluations but there is relatively little further scope to raise prices. The promotion of cash purchases even as input prices increase is likely to reduce input use, especially among low-income producers (as, for example, in Senegal and Malawi).

Agricultural research and technology. Factor productivity must clearly be increased in order to achieve food security and to diversify into higher value production for domestic use or for export. One of the main reasons for the poor agricultural performance in Africa is that both governments and donors have paid insufficient attention to research and technology to further this goal.

The growth of maize production in a wide range of ecological conditions in the MADIA countries provides one of the few examples of technical change in the food crop sector. At times even the traditional varieties of maize have offered higher yields than sorghum, millet, and other grains. Furthermore, more is known in general terms about the responsiveness to fertilizer of hybrid and composite maizes. Hybrids are more sensitive to growing conditions and their yields are therefore more variable, but they are higher on average than traditional varieties. Kenya's hybrid maize program has been quite successful in advancing the distribution and adoption of improved seed varieties. Adaptive on-farm research, which had made considerable strides in the high-potential areas in the 1960s and early 1970s, was not nurtured and expanded. These successes are reflected in the fact that up to 60 percent of the country's smallholder maize acreage was under hybrid or composite varieties when the MADIA study was being completed in 1988, compared with less than 10 percent in any of the other countries. Much of this gain was achieved in the 1960s, and little subsequent intensification has taken place. A central question facing Malawi's hybrid maize research program has been whether research should focus on flint maizes, which rural households have tended to prefer for their more suitable storage, handpounding, and cooking characteristics. The low adoption of hybrid varieties in Malawi even after twenty years of rural development efforts primarily reflects the inadequate resource base of small farmers and their inability to bear the risk of variable output. Other obstacles included an apparently strong consumer preference for flint maize with its better storage characteristics and farmers' inadequate access to credit and extension. Lately, easier access by small farmers to hybrid seed due to privatization of seed distribution is said to have improved maize adoption rates in Malawi. Systematic adoption studies, however, need to capture the precise relative importance of these various characteristics and their implications for fine tuning government policy. In West Africa, improved maize has done well in northern Nigeria and the better watered areas of Cameroon. Little on-farm technical change has occurred, however, in the production of other food crops although headway was being made by the IITA in tackling the problems of cassava and by ICRASAT on short-stem early maturing sorghum. The greatest weakness seemed once again to be farmer-level research on adoption, involving social scientists, that could help put in place policies and institutions to accelerate rates of adoption.

In contrast, export crop research, which has been of high quality historically, has deteriorated in some countries in the post-independence era, notably in Tanzania and Nigeria. Despite Nigeria's substantial increase in research expenditures during its oil boom, the lack of political commitment and stability seriously undermined the quality and predictability of expenditures. Thus, scarce and unpredictable operating resources for scientists, frequent changes in regional organization, and a decline in the quality of Nigeria's once-impressive scientific community were some of the problems. Some additional adverse factors in Tanzania included the breakup of the East African Community, headquartered in Kenya, on which Tanzania had depended for research, especially in tea and coffee; the sudden withdrawal of the British Cotton Research Corporation in 1975; and the primacy of ideological over technocratic considerations in the content and conduct of agricultural policy, including in the support for agricultural research. In contrast, the principal export crops in Kenya and Malawi have been backed up by excellent agricultural research systems financed through levies on these crops. This ensured a stable, predictable level of funding although Kenya's tea and coffee research had begun to show signs of strain due to political interference by the government.

In the Francophone countries, commodity research carried out by the French has continued with relatively fewer interruptions; however, there has been less training of nationals than was formerly provided by the British for export crops in the Anglophone countries (and more recently by the Americans for food crops). Although research efforts have yielded some important innovations—such as drought-resistant varieties of groundnuts, sole cropping, and the increased use of animal traction in Senegal—they have not addressed the serious problem of soil degradation, or the special need to integrate cropping, livestock, and tree farming by smallholders in order to protect the environment.

In contrast to the colonial era, the period after 1970 has seen export crop research neglected by governments and donors alike. A humanitarian concern about food security and about the environmental effects of developing export crops have dominated constituency opinion and action in the Western community. The Consultative Group on International Agricultural Research, for instance, has provided no support for export crop research.

Large resource donors have overloaded the capacity of recipients to manage such research effectively. This has occurred because they have worked in isolation of each other and developed a large number of often fragmented research programs (as observed in Tanzania, Malawi, and Kenya). They have also failed to integrate the work done by national researchers with that of donor-funded expatriates (as in Senegal). A common defect of these efforts has been excessive emphasis on the provision of bricks and mortar and expatriate technical assistance. This has tended to be at the expense of establishing long-term human and institutional capacity—or even of using an already-developed pool of human capital—to address the substance of technological issues. Identification of research priorities, and the preparation and implementation of scientific, workable plans have been major lacunae.

African political elites have not fully recognized the fundamental importance of science and technology in modernizing smallholder agriculture. Furthermore, small farmers' interests are so poorly articulated (except in Kenya) that they have not influenced research priorities. Donor efforts, including those of the Consultative Group on International Agricultural Research, have been largely supply- rather than demand-driven, and they have not adequately reflected the constraints on small farmers.[44] Through a new major initiative, the Special Program for African Agricultural Research (SPAAR) is attempting to address these problems. The success of this well-intentioned initiative will depend on the extent to which SPAAR brings substance to bear on the vast sums donors are commiting to national agricultural research. It will need emphasis on consistent, long-term implementable priorities, and the setting of high standards for the conduct and management of research.

As this chapter has shown, a complex web of macroeconomic, sectoral, and microlevel constraints (including the quality of physical resources) has impeded the expansion of smallholder production in the MADIA countries. An important question to keep in mind in the remainder of the book is to what extent donors have been able to grasp this complexity in their strategies for smallholder development.

Notes

Much of the information in this chapter is derived from the various MADIA discussion papers (see the appendix to the introduction) that contain more detailed treatment of the issues, and references to the related literature. It is also important to sound a cautionary note concerning the availability and consistency of data among the six countries. Among the Anglophone countries, Kenya and Malawi are better managed and therefore possess better data bases than Nigeria or Tanzania. The Francophone countries have done little to amass information systematically. African governments and donors, in general, have paid insufficient attention to developing effective mechanisms for collecting and analyzing even the most basic socioeconomic, agronomic, production, and trade data. Participants in the MADIA study expended considerable effort to reconcile alternate, often conflicting, data sets. Their work has clearly demonstrated that both governments and donors need to devote more resources to this area of research if they expect to see a marked improvement in the quality of planning and economic management.

1. The aid data on which this analysis is based are aggregated and do not permit breakdowns by sector (for example, the share going to agriculture and rural development). Although some of the donor studies do provide data on sectoral shares, these data are not always clearly defined and are not strictly comparable among donors (nor do they consistently match up with the aggregated data). In the following discussion, both sources have been used to the extent possible to delineate the broad trends in aid flows to the MADIA countries. The data for this section are from a MADIA working paper by Maria Cancian reviewing OECD databases on aid allocation to the MADIA countries. The data used in the paper, as well as updated data for 1985, 1986, and 1987, were derived from *Geographical Distribution of Financial Flows to Developing Countries* (Paris: Organisation for Economic Cooperation and Development, 1989). In that publication (p. 281), ODA is defined as "flows to developing countries . . . provided by official agencies for developmental purposes with a grant element of at least 25 percent."

2. See Robert S. McNamara's preface in World Bank, *The Assault on World Poverty: Problems of Rural Development, Education, and Health* (Baltimore, Md.: Johns Hopkins University Press, 1975).

3. See, for example, John C. deWilde, *Experiences with Agricultural Development in Tropical Africa*, vols. 1 and 2 (Baltimore, Md.: Johns Hopkins University Press, 1967); and Uma Lele, *The Design of Rural Development: Lessons from Africa* (Baltimore, Md.: Johns Hopkins University Press, 1975).

4. A brief beverage boom, however, did push up coffee and tea prices in the mid-1970s.

5. See World Bank, *Accelerated Development in Sub-Saharan Africa: An Agenda for Action* (Washington, D.C., 1982). The principal author was Elliot Berg.

6. See postscript to Uma Lele, *The Design of Rural Development: Lessons from Africa* (Baltimore, Md.: Johns Hopkins University Press, 1975); Uma Lele, "Tanzania: Phoenix or Icarus?" in Arnold Harberger, ed., *World Economic Growth* (San Francisco: Institute for Contemporary Studies, 1984).

7. See G. A. Cornia, R. Jolly, and F. Stewart, eds., *Adjustment with a Human Face* (Oxford: Clarendon Press, 1987).

8. All dollar amounts are U.S. dollars.

9. TRN includes ODA as well as other official nonconcessional, bilateral, multilateral, and trade-related transactions, along with export credits and other changes in bilateral long-term assets of the private nonmonetary and monetary sectors, private direct investment, portfolio investments, and loans by private banks.

10. A billion is 1,000 million.

11. See Uma Lele and Ijaz Nabi, "Aid, Capital Flows, and Development: A Synthesis," in Uma Lele and Ijaz Nabi, eds., *Transitions in Development: The Role of Aid and Commercial Flows* (San Francisco: Institute for Contemporary Studies, 1990).

12. See Uma Lele, and L. Richard Meyers, "Kenya's Agricultural Development and the World Bank's Role in It" (Africa—Technical Department, Agriculture Division, World Bank, Washington, D.C., manuscript in preparation).

13. See Uma Lele, "Structural Adjustment, Agricultural Development, and the Poor: Some Lessons from the Malawian Experience," *World Development* 18 (September 1990).

14. See Peter J. Matlon, "The West African Semiarid Tropics," in John W. Mellor, Christopher L. Delgado, and Malcolm J. Blackie, eds., *Accelerating Food Production in Sub-Saharan Africa* (Baltimore, Md.: Johns Hopkins University Press, 1987).

15. See Juan Gaviria, Vishva Bindlish, and Uma Lele, *The Rural Road Question and Nigeria's Agricultural Development*, MADIA Discussion Paper 10 (Washington, D.C.: World Bank, 1990).

16. See Richard H. Sabot and J. B. Knight, "Overview of Educational Expansion, Productivity, and Inequality: A Comparative Analysis of the East African Natural Experiment," World Bank Discussion Paper EDT48 (Agriculture Department, World Bank, Washington, D.C., 1986); Richard Sabot, "Urban Employees in Kenya and Tanzania: Educational Attainment and Its Relation to Jobs, Pay, Mobility, and Rural Links" (Agriculture Department, World Bank, Washington, D.C., 1983); and Richard H. Sabot, "Education Expansion and Labor Market Adjustment in Kenya and Tanzania: A Background Paper," Discussion Paper 81-18 (Agriculture Department, World Bank, Washington, D.C., 1981).

17. See Uma Lele and Ellen Hanak, eds., "The Politics of Agricultural Policy in Africa" (Agriculture Department, World Bank, Washington, D.C., manuscript in preparation).

18. See Uma Lele, A. T. Oyejide, Vishva Bindlish, and Balu Bumb, "Nigeria's Economic Development, Agriculture's Role, and World Bank Assistance: Lessons for the Future" MADIA Working Paper (Africa—Technical Department, Agriculture Division, World Bank, Washington, D.C.).

19. In Malawi, the increasing institutionalization of the power of the state as President Hastings Banda has aged, together with the growing importance of the technocracy (arising in part from pressure from the World Bank) in the 1980s, have strengthened the planning and implementation capabilities of the Ministry of Agriculture.

20. See Uma Lele, *Agricultural Growth, Domestic Policies, the External Environment, and Assistance to Africa: Lessons of a Quarter Century*, MADIA Discussion Paper 1 (Washington, D.C.: World Bank, 1989).

21. See also Uma Lele, "Tanzania: Phoenix or Icarus?" in Arnold Harberger, ed., *World Economic Growth* (San Francisco: Institute for Contemporary Studies, 1984); and Paul Collier, "Aid and Economic Performance in Tanzania," in Uma Lele and Ijaz Nabi, eds., *Transitions in Development: The Role of Aid and Commercial Flows* (San Francisco: Institute for Contemporary Studies, 1990).

22. See Uma Lele, Pierre-Roche Seka, and Mathurin Gbetibouo, "Agricultural Performance in a Macroeconomic Context: The Relative Roles of Luck and Policy," paper presented at the Western Economic Association Meeting, Lake Tahoe, Nevada, June 19, 1989.

23. See Uma Lele and L. Richard Meyers, *Growth and Structural Change in East Africa: Domestic Policies, Agricultural Performance, and World Bank Assistance, 1963–86*, MADIA Discussion Paper 3 (Washington, D.C.: World Bank, 1989).

24. See Lele and others, "Nigeria's Economic Development."

25. The primary difference was that, under a vertically integrated cotton production system organized by CFDT in much of Francophone Africa, Camer-

oonian cotton producers have received much more effective services. They have also been paid on time, whereas their Kenyan counterparts have experienced substantial difficulties in obtaining planting material and purchased inputs, as well as delays in payment, which in turn reflect the poor capitalization of the Kenyan cotton parastatals. See Uma Lele, Nicolas van de Walle, and Mathurin Gbetibouo, *Cotton in Africa: An Analysis of Differences in Performance*, MADIA Discussion Paper 7 (Washington, D.C.: World Bank, 1989).

26. See Lele and others, *Cotton in Africa*.

27. See Lele and Meyers, "Kenya's Agricultural Development"; and Uma Lele and Manmohan Agarwal, *Smallholder and Large-Scale Agriculture in Africa: Are There Trade-offs in Growth and Equity?* MADIA Discussion Paper 6 (Washington, D.C.: World Bank, 1989).

28. See Sidi Jammeh and Chandra Ranade, "Agricultural Pricing and Marketing in Senegal," MADIA Working Paper (Africa—Technical Department, Agriculture Division, World Bank, Washington, D.C., January 1986).

29. See Uma Lele and Robert Christiansen, *Markets, Marketing Boards, and Cooperatives in the MADIA Countries: Issues in Adjustment Policy in Africa*, MADIA Discussion Paper 11 (Washington, D.C.: World Bank, 1989).

30. An exception is Thomas C. Pinckney, "Production Instability and Food Security in Kenya: Measuring Tradeoff Between Government Objectives," Ph.D. diss. (Stanford University, Palo Alto, Calif., 1986).

31. See Uma Lele and Robert Christiansen, *Markets, Marketing Boards, and Cooperatives in the MADIA Countries: Issues in Adjustment Policy in Africa*, MADIA Discussion Paper 11 (Washington D.C., World Bank, 1989).

32. See World Bank, *Agricultural Marketing: The World Bank's Experience* (Washington, D.C., 1988).

33. See Jammeh and others, "Building Agricultural Research Capacity in Senegal."

34. See Uma Lele and Steven Stone, *Population Pressure, the Environment, and Agricultural Intensification: Variations on the Boserup Hypothesis*, MADIA Discussion Paper 4 (Washington, D.C.: World Bank, 1989).

35. See Uma Lele and Manmohan Agarwal, *Smallholder and Large-Scale Agriculture: Are There Trade-Offs in Growth and Equity?* MADIA Discussion Paper 6 (Washington, D.C.: World Bank, 1989).

36. See Uma Lele, "Sources of Growth in East African Agriculture," *World Bank Economic Review* 3(January 1989):119–44.

37. See Uma Lele, Robert Christiansen, and Kundhavi Kadiresan, *Fertilizer Policy in Africa: Lessons from Development Programs and Adjustment Lending, 1970–87*, MADIA Discussion Paper 5 (Washington, D.C.: World Bank, 1989).

38. These rates of subsidies represent averages. For Senegal, they represent the mean for 1970–82; for Cameroon, the mean for 1977–82; for Malawi, the mean for 1983–87. See Lele and others, *Fertilizer Policy in Africa*.

39. Maize is the only crop for which data are available for all the countries. Comparisons between export crops are more limited because only a few countries produce crops in common, cotton and coffee being the most important.

40. See Uma Lele, "Structural Adjustment," *World Development* 18.

41. See Dale Adams, Douglas H. Graham, and J. D. Von Pischke, *Undermining Rural Development with Cheap Credit* (Boulder, Colo.: Westview Press, 1984).

42. See William L. Collier, *Agricultural Technology and Institutional Change in Java* (New York: Agricultural Development Council, 1975).

43. In Kenya, for instance, the practice of plucking two buds and a leaf by small farmers—which ensures its high quality premiums in the world mar-

ket—is said to reduce the quantity of tea plucked per hectare. MADIA field investigations (supported by a recent survey of small tea farmers) indicate, however, that the shortage of cash for hiring additional labor is a far greater constraint on increasing smallholder yields in Kenya than other factors, such as inadequate fertilizer supply or extension. See Stanly Mwangy Karuga, "An Evaluation of Tea Productivity of Smallholders in Kenya" (Master's thesis, University of Glasgow, 1987). And yet credit policies in Kenya have discriminated against small farmers, because many have argued that credit is unimportant for small farmers. Furthermore, even if credit is provided, it is offered in kind (fertilizers and pesticides) rather than in cash (for hiring labor) on the grounds that input use will be more nearly monitored. It is only in the cocoa project in Nigeria that early World Bank projects recognized the need for cash to intensify labor use. See Lele and Meyers, "Kenya's Agricultural Development."

44. See Uma Lele, William Kinsey, and Antonia Obeya, *Building Agricultural Research Capacity in Africa: Policy Lessons from* MADIA Countries, MADIA Discussion Paper 14 (Washington, D.C.: World Bank, 1989).

3 The World Bank's Experience in the MADIA Countries: Agricultural Development and Foreign Assistance

Uma Lele and Rahul Jain

AFTER NEARLY TWO DECADES of massive support for smallholder agriculture and broad policy reforms in the MADIA countries, the World Bank is finding that these efforts have had only limited effect.[1] Apart from a few notable exceptions, these countries have not made much progress in developing the policy planning, analytical, technological, and human capacity essential for the growth of smallholder agriculture. The reasons for the lack of progress vary from country to country—depending on the initial conditions and policy responses of individual countries and on the donors' including the Bank's own responses to those circumstances. This chapter lays the groundwork for assessing the Bank's overall contribution by presenting a country-by-country analysis of its policy advice, institutional and technological choices, project investments, and macroeconomic lending.

Although the internal policies, as well as the limited human, institutional, and technological capacity, of recipient countries are in part responsible for the disappointing results, the operational style of the Bank has also played a part. This analysis is mainly concerned with the effect of the Bank's policy advice and financial assistance. Some attention is devoted to the combined effect of the Bank's operational style and the local constraints and its implications for future policies and operations of the Bank.

Bank assistance to the MADIA countries between 1965 and 1988 flowed primarily to crop production, and no more than 8 percent of its agricultural assistance went to the livestock and forestry sectors. During the early stages of this assistance, the Bank had supported a number of large ranching projects in East and southern Africa, but when they failed it moved away from livestock. In a few small projects livestock had proved quite successful (for example, one concerned with integrating livestock and forestry in northern Nigeria and another with developing the dairy industry in Kenya). Livestock productivity and production will no doubt attract more attention in the future as, with growing population pressure on the land, agriculture becomes more intensified. Improved production technologies call for integration of cropping with livestock rearing as demand for milk and meat increases in conjunction with one of the most rapid urbanizations in the developing world. As with other commodities, Africa has become a major importer of meat and milk from OECD countries, who subsidize their own production. But Africa's financial capacity to import livestock products has declined with the emphasis on the environment. Forestry, likewise, has begun to attract more attention. The Bank undertook only a few forestry projects, mainly focused on large-scale government plantations until environmental concerns mounted. But with the growing concern about deforestation as a result of the increased demand for fuelwood, more forestry projects are being considered, and their focus has changed to social forestry.

The Bank's successes and failures in achieving its stated objectives cannot be fully assessed without taking into account its institutional character, notably the centralized structure of operations at its headquarters in Washington, where, for the sake of administrative efficiency, a majority of Bank staff reside. Bilateral donors operate quite differently. The U.S. Agency for International Development (USAID), for example, operates with a large staff in the field and keeps its mission directors in the countries responsible for developing country assistance strategies. This does not make USAID operations immune to problems created by pressures from USAID in Washington. Nor does it avert the problem of sporadicity caused by shifts in aid strategies, as Johnston et al. point out in chapter 5. Nevertheless, it does allow USAID's assistance strategies to be relatively more flexible, as well as more responsive, to a country's needs—especially in the implementation of projects and programs. In contrast, the Bank oversees the development of most of its assistance strategies and project and adjustment appraisal and supervision mainly from its headquarters in Washington and to some extent from its regional offices in Nairobi and Abidjan. Because of the physical distance between Washington and project sites, not to mention the cultural and technological gap, Bank staff tend to be more optimistic about the expected pace of implementation of Bank-financed operations than the political will or the implementing capacity of the recipient countries may warrant. The number of field staff have been increasing in recent years, but from a very low base. Lending operations in Africa start with a concentration of power in Washington combined with the extremely limited planning and implementing capacity of the African countries. Thus, less is known about microlevel factors that adversely affect Bank operations and constrain the ability of countries to repay Bank funds than in the more advanced developing countries with greater ability to plan and implement their own programs. The result is a false economy in costs (as explained below).

The basic direction of Bank policy, such as the emphasis on alleviating poverty in the 1970s or on achieving macroeconomic reforms and privatization in the 1980s, is set in Washington. Although policies are formulated in response to objective and changing circumstances, they nevertheless represent a more or less "top-down" way of decision-making, which in turn influences the priorities assigned in the allocation of financial and administrative resources and incentives provided for the staff. Although the design of the individual lending operations approved by the Bank's board of directors reflects considerable decentralization of power from Washington to the mission leaders (or "task managers," in more recent parlance), policy is still formulated from the top down. Note, too, that until policy-based lending acquired the emphasis in the 1980s, the Bank was basically a project-oriented institution. Therefore the central role of macroeconomic policies tended to be overlooked in the 1970s, despite the deterioration in external circumstances. On the other hand, the major shift in favor of structural adjustment in the 1980s has undermined the Bank's substantial project lending capacity. Similarly, the emphasis on privatization became a catchword in the 1980s at the expense of the concern about the important role the government must play in economic development.

These examples of an absence of a balance between macro and micro, or the private and the public sector, are not intended to suggest that individual staff lack the scope to adapt to the specific circumstances of a country or project, as determined by the needs of their clients. Rather, they suggest that the dominant response reflects a bureaucratic culture influenced by the policy directions set at the top, at times at considerable cost to a consistent long-term approach to efficient, broadly based growth. This means that responses to the latest policy directions, many of which originate from justified concerns (such as on the environment), often are formalistic and concerned with appearance rather than substance. The remainder of the chapter will show how this same phenomenon occurred, as legitimate concerns about poverty alleviation were addressed in the 1970s.

The responses of the recipients may not be any more effective, however. Many countries in Africa lack not only the necessary capacity for policy planning and implementation but also the political will to reach a large number of small farmers on a sustained, viable basis.

Another important point to note is that the Bank underwent two extensive internal reorganizations in 1972 and 1986 and several smaller reorganizations in other years. An important consideration in bringing about these organizational changes was to increase the country orientation of the lending operations, to foster a holistic view of the recipient's development strategy, so that intersectoral links and priorities will not be overlooked, and to guard against excessive emphasis on a given project or sector. However, this country orientation has turned out to be more effective in meeting lending targets than in helping countries in the formation of long-term development strategy. Country orientation has also overlooked a variety of issues related to developing the quality of the Bank's work. For instance, regional considerations, particularly with regard to cross-border trade or agricultural research in which the comparative advantage of neighboring countries or agroecological characteristics should be the basis for determining strategies have tended to be ignored. The initiatives by the Special Program on African Agricultural Research (SPAAR) in 1989 mentioned in chapter 1 may help to correct the regional balance in agricultural research but this remains to be seen. Moreover, country orientation and attrition have brought a decline in technical excellence among staff. The problem of quality is more serious in Africa than in other parts of the world due to a lack of an internal capacity in recipient countries. Although there is no single explanation for the decline of technical expertise alongside the growth of the generalists, part of the reason is the internal concern that technicians should be able to handle a greater variety of tasks in view of the frequent changes in policy orientation that tend to take place in the institution from one period to the next. These changes are dictated not only by the changing circumstances in the recipient countries but also by the political need to respond to aid constituencies, which increasingly influence the thrust of Bank operations (such as the growing emphasis on the environment). Generalists are believed to be more flexible than technical experts and thus better able to respond to the changing expectations of performance. Due to Bank regulations it is difficult to recruit technical experts at senior grades from outside. With the emphasis on "homegrown products" it is difficult for Bank staff to remain at the cutting edge of their fields.

Still another factor to consider in an assessment of quality of work is the changing nature of economic and sectoral analysis in the Bank and its relationship to project, sectoral, and macroeconomic lending. In the 1970s, the Bank concentrated on large economic studies, the results of which appeared in comprehensive reports (known as basic economic reports) every seven to ten years. The work was updated in annual economic reports. Agricultural and other sectoral reports were issued every five years or so to identify a list of priority projects. Project identification was undertaken in consultation with countries. These reports evolved into assessments of proposed country-specific, five-year lending programs presented in a country policy paper. Projects were then prepared by teams of consultants; in the case of agriculture, the teams included consultants from the cooperative program of the Food and Agriculture Organization of the United Nations (FAO) or expatriate experts supported by technical assistance loans or credits given to the appropriate sectoral or central ministries. Since the 1980s, with the onset of internal macroeconomic problems and rapid changes in the international economic scene, the economic reports have appeared more frequently and have devoted more attention to informal assessments of particular issues, such as the need to reform public enterprises or to review public expenditures. This emphasis on particular issues increased the depth of analysis of individual issues but it took attention away from the longer term and broader issues of overall economic development and the long-term economic development strategy needed to achieve it. Policy work also became more closely tied to particular lending operations in the 1980s, which changed in character from project to subsectoral, sectoral, or macroeconomic adjustment lending. Finally, and not the least important, with greater pressure on the Bank's operational budget, the reliance of the Bank on trust funds provided by donors has increased. It is a backdoor way for individual donors to ensure recruitment of their national consultants and, in turn, of improving their chances of obtaining contracts on equipment and construction. The Bank's competitive bidding procedures remain strictly adhered to. However, technical assistance contracts have always been more difficult to evaluate objectively. The pervasive dependence on trust funds has reduced the Bank's flexibility to draw on the best international expertise, which has been its strong suit in the past. It must be emphasized that the reliance on trust funds is the result of a desire on the part of the World Bank's major subscribers to maintain control over its administrative budget with little appreciation of the unintended consequences. The links between the macroeconomic, sectoral, and microeconomic aspects of Bank work need to be strengthened further—in particular, more should be done to develop the capacity of governments for policy planning, in the context of which lending occurs. As a result of these concerns, the Bank has already embarked on a major new African capacity-building initiative (ACBI), which is directed at the recipients of aid. The relationship between ACBI and the Bank's educational sector work was not established by the time this book was completed. At the same time, the growing emphasis on "doing more with less" and on country orientation over and above technical excellence is discouraging the efforts to improve internal capacity of the Bank's own staff.

World Bank Assistance to East Africa

Between 1965 and 1988 the total World Bank assistance to Kenya, Malawi, and Tanzania amounted to more than $4.4 billion (see table

3-1). Nearly a third of this amount went into the development of basic infrastructure (energy, transport, and communications). Agricultural and rural development was the second most important category of operations; its share in this period was slightly more than 22 percent (excluding nonproject assistance to these sectors), and thus was not far off the informal guideline set by the World Bank's president, Robert S. McNamara, in the 1970s—namely, that up to a quarter of all donor assistance should be allocated to agriculture. Interestingly, in the short span of ten years nonproject assistance took on a prominent role, totaling nearly $890 million (compared with $1.02 billion in project assistance to agriculture and rural development).

During this period, the Bank approved eighty operations in support of agriculture and rural development in the three countries. These included seventy projects and ten nonproject loans or credits. The Bank's total commitment to these agricultural operations was well in excess of $1.6 billion—of which nonproject lending accounted for nearly 37 percent.

Bank assistance to agriculture and rural development in both Tanzania and Malawi in 1975–79 doubled over the previous four-year period, in response to McNamara's 1973 speech. In Kenya's case, the increase was sixfold—from $40.5 million to $257 million. This increase must be viewed in the light of the limited planning and implementing capacity pointed out earlier. The number of agricultural projects approved for Kenya and Tanzania also doubled. In both countries, the share of infrastructure, which had appropriated the bulk of Bank funds until the mid-1970s, dropped sharply. In the case of Tanzania, assistance flowed primarily to industry. The share allocated to the development of human resources—to education, population control, health, and nutrition—remained low. This was also true of Kenya. Good overall policies and a better balance in the intersectoral allocation of a country's own resources could, of course, explain or compensate for some of the imbalance in Bank assistance. In Kenya, for example, the Bank's portfolio of agricultural projects as a whole performed rather poorly, and many of the projects had to be closed down at the end of the 1970s; yet, as discussed in chapter 1, Kenya's agriculture as a whole performed well. In Tanzania, however, not only did many of the Bank-financed agricultural projects perform poorly, but so did agriculture in general. Given the distorted policy and institutional framework, relatively poor planning and implementing capacity, and the intersectoral imbalance in the Bank's lending and the donor's assistance between industry, agriculture, and the development of human resources, this is not surprising.

In the 1980s, economic conditions deteriorated, and the physical infrastructure followed suit. Consequently, Bank support for infra-

Table 3-1. East Africa: World Bank Assistance by Sector, 1965–88
(millions of U.S. dollars)

	Fiscal 1965–69			*Fiscal 1970–74*			*Fiscal 1975–79*			*Fiscal 1980–88*			*Country totals (1985–88)*			
Target of assistance	*Kenya*	*Malawi*	*Tanzania*	*Kenya*	*Malawi*	*Tanzania*	*Kenya*	*Malawi*	*Tanzania*	*Kenya*	*Malawi*	*Tanzania*	*Kenya*	*Malawi*	*Tanzania*	*Combined*
Agriculture and rural development	13.50	11.47	7.54	40.50	24.52	76.91	257.00	50.40	140.70	206.60	92.20	95.80	517.60	178.59	320.95	1,017.14
Percent of total	26.87	34.65	19.74	19.16	61.13	52.30	34.82	38.18	26.86	17.15	17.05	13.72	25.12	22.30	22.80	23.05
Basic infrastructure	28.31	14.20	25.35	139.94	13.59	50.55	210.00	45.50	75.70	428.80	108.00	268.80	806.45	181.29	420.40	1,408.14
Percent of total	56.34	42.90	66.38	65.92	33.88	34.37	28.46	34.47	14.45	35.59	18.69	38.49	39.13	22.64	29.87	31.91
Industry	—	—	—	5.00	2.00	6.00	57.00	3.00	198.00	36.00	—	43.00	98.00	5.00	247.00	350.00
Percent of total	—	—	—	2.37	4.99	4.08	7.72	2.27	37.79	2.99	—	6.16	4.75	0.62	17.55	7.93
Other infrastructure	—	—	—	8.30	—	—	151.00	7.00	35.50	35.00	20.00	26.50	194.30	27.00	62.00	283.30
Percent of total	—	—	—	3.93	—	—	20.46	5.30	6.78	2.90	3.95	3.79	9.43	3.37	4.41	6.42
Human resource development	8.44	7.43	5.30	18.23	—	13.60	33.00	26.10	23.00	112.70	122.80	25.00	172.37	156.33	66.90	395.60
Percent of total	16.80	22.45	13.88	8.62	—	9.25	4.47	19.77	4.39	8.34	24.26	3.58	8.36	19.52	4.75	8.96
Nonproject assistance	—	—	—	—	—	—	30.00	—	45.00	357.90	250.00	206.20	387.90	250.00	251.20	889.10
Percent of total	—	—	—	—	—	—	4.07	—	8.59	20.41	35.56	29.53	18.82	31.22	17.85	20.15
Technical assistance	—	—	—	—	—	—	—	—	6.00	28.00	2.50	33.00	28.00	2.50	39.00	69.50
Percent of total	—	—	—	—	—	—	—	—	1.15	2.32	0.49	4.73	1.36	0.31	2.77	1.57
Total	50.25	33.10	38.19	211.37	40.11	147.06	738.00	132.00	523.90	1,205.00	595.50	698.30	2,204.62	800.71	1,407.45	4,412.78

— = Not available.
Source: Adapted from Christine Jones, "A Review of World Bank Assistance to Six African Countries," MADIA Working Paper (Africa—Technical Department, Agriculture Division, World Bank, Washington, D.C., 1985); World Bank internal documents.

structure increased together with nonproject lending. Because of the growing disappointment with the performance of agricultural projects in Kenya and Tanzania, the number of new projects approved in the two countries decreased in the 1980s. In Tanzania in particular, where the poor performance of the Bank's agricultural portfolio was in large part a result of the proindustrial policies pursued by the government, overall commitments increased as a result of the growing importance of nonproject assistance. In Malawi, the number of projects approved in agriculture continued to rise in the 1980s. While there was considerable rhetorical support for developing policy planning capacity, the amounts approved for technical assistance increased as the demand for macroeconomic packages and for the implementation of conditionality mushroomed under nonproject assistance. Financial commitments to the development of human resources in Malawi improved substantially as awareness of the country's abject poverty became an integral part of the Bank's economic analysis in the late 1980s.

Kenya

The links between macroeconomic and agricultural policy are clearer in the Bank's work on Kenya than in its analyses of the other MADIA countries. This may be explained by a combination of factors, including the strength of Kenya's macroeconomic and sectoral policies, the stability of its institutions, and the absence of acute structural problems—not to mention the fact that the many external professionals drawn to the country because of its geographic location, good climate, superior data base, and relatively capitalistic economy broadened the scope for rigorous analysis and open policy debate. In other countries, political, institutional, technological, and data problems were more limiting to rigorous analysis and open policy debate. Unfortunately, in more recent years, the openness of public debate, disclosure on important policy issues, and institutional stability have suffered some setback in Kenya. Receptivity to Bank advice was also considerable in the early years of independence. Kenya used to ask the Bank to time missions for when the country was preparing its five-year plans, but this receptivity has waned with growing skepticism about the Bank's advice.

Bank policy recommendations. The Bank's project assistance to Kenya has not always coincided with the recommendations of its economic and sectoral analyses. For example, the Bank's 1972 report on the agricultural sector recommended that more attention be given to areas of high potential (that is, with assured rainfall and proven technologies) to obtain a reasonable return on investments. Instead, the Bank expanded its project assistance in areas of medium and low potential—and found that many of the projects had to be closed down by the end of the 1970s because they were too difficult to implement in these areas. Somewhat the same problems arose in Tanzania and in Kenya, countries whose limited planning and implementing capacity had been amply described in Bank reports. Nonetheless, projects approved individually and jointly with other donors tended to overextend and tax the capacity of both countries in this respect. Moreover, the pessimistic assessment of market prospects for tea and coffee in the economic reports did deter the Bank from financing tea and coffee production projects (see chapter 1), although Kenya's tea and coffee processing projects had by far the best rates of return and played an important role in improving the distribution of benefits to a large number of small farmers. The reasons for the growth in production—mainly area expansion—were not those anticipated in project design and revealed a rather poor understanding of the microlevel constraints, especially the shortage of labor, that affected the allocation of farm resources and inhibited intensification.[2]

In several other respects, the Bank's responses in Kenya have mirrored those in other MADIA countries, and they have persisted in periods of both project and adjustment lending. For instance, the Bank's economic and sectoral reports and project experience repeatedly stressed the government's weak analytical capacity (a serious drawback for policy formulation) and the lack of microlevel data. Its operational assistance, however, did not address these constraints. Instead, project preparation was based heavily on expatriate assistance rather than on the Kenyan expertise available locally—although this state of affairs has now begun to change. Public sector salaries have not been competitive enough to attract well-trained Kenyan personnel, and the government of Kenya has been reluctant to use the considerable number of trained Kenyan personnel who are available outside the government. Indeed, the relationship between Kenyan universities and the government has worsened over time, and the government has attracted fewer academics as a result. In recent years, however, the government has attempted to recruit Kenyan "consultants" at market prices to counteract the constraint imposed by public sector wages. Even so, this short-term solution does not address the government's basic problems with planning and implementing rural development policies, priorities, and programs.

Bank reports have repeatedly pointed out that technical packages for agricultural development in specific areas are weak, especially in areas of medium and marginal potential. The Bank's efforts at technological development in Kenya—as elsewhere in the MADIA countries—were, however, piecemeal. Adaptive trials in individual projects frequently undercut the national agricultural research system, instead of developing the system's capacity to address complex technological problems. Indeed, despite its impressive seed industry, Kenya made little technological progress since its spectacular success with hybrid maize in the early 1970s. The adoption of maize and other food crops peaked later in the decade, mainly because of the lack of effective links between research, extension, input distribution, and output marketing. The Bank financed a national agricultural extension project in 1983 and an agricultural research project in 1987. Both were expected to improve the research/extension link, unify the extension system, and improve its management. A study of the impact of agricultural extension now under way proposes to explore the extent to which these interventions reflected strategic responses to resource endowments from the viewpoint of achieving positive per capita income growth.

Bank assistance. Much of the Bank's assistance in the 1970s went to (1) parastatal-operated projects involving the agroprocessing of export crops such as tea, coffee, pyrethrum, and sugar, and (2) integrated rural development projects focusing on smallholders (see table 3-2). Kenya also received more institutional credit for agriculture than did any other MADIA country.

The first two tea projects, funded in collaboration with the Commonwealth Development Corporation (CDC) in the 1960s, helped establish smallholder production. In addition, the provision of tea processing factories through a loan of $10.4 million in 1974 alleviated a large constraint in an otherwise well-organized tea sector. The Kenya Tea Development Authority (KTDA) owes much of its institutional strength to the assistance of CDC. The Bank, for its part, made an important contribution by providing discipline to the analysis and resolution of KTDA's financial problems, caused by the unforeseen exchange rate losses that followed devaluations in the late 1970s. The Bank's decision not to finance the further development of smallholder tea because market prospects appeared limited is unfortunate; its considerable potential contribution to Kenya's smallholder tea has been lost.

Similarly, the coffee project implemented in 1980 removed a constraint on the processing of smallholder coffee by providing for the construction of cooperative factories and the rehabilitation of existing ones. Kenya's coffee cooperatives have proved highly successful in servicing smallholders. In the late 1980s the Bank assisted the coffee industry by addressing the critical problem of delays in coffee payments to producers. The remaining agroprocessing projects, which were funded in response to the government's concern about the equi-

Table 3-2. Kenya: World Bank Assistance to Agriculture, 1965–88
(millions of U.S. dollars)

Target of assistance	*Number of projects*	*Funding totals*	*Percent of total funding*	*Projects included*
Crop-oriented projects				
Tea	3	15.8	3.6	Tea Development Authority, Second Tea Development Project, Tea Factory
Coffee	1	27.0	3.6	Smallholder Coffee
Sugar	2	97.0	12.8	South Nyanza Sugar, Sugar Rehabilitation
Cotton	1	22.0	2.9	Cotton Processing
Credit	4	70.2	9.3	Agricultural Credit, Second Agricultural Credit, Third Agricultural Credit, Fourth Agricultural Credit
Integrated rural development	2	66.0	8.7	Integrated Agricultural Development, Second Integrated Agricultural Devel opment
Extension	1	15.0	2.0	National Extension
Group farms	1	15.0	2.0	Group Farm Rehabilitation
Semiarid areas	2	19.5	2.6	Narok Agricultural Development Baringo Pilot
Irrigation	1	40.0	5.3	Bura Irrigation
Research	1	19.6	2.6	National Agricultural Research
Other projects				
Livestock	3	40.4	5.3	Livestock, Second Livestock, Animal Health Services
Fisheries	1	10.0	1.3	Fisheries
Forestry	3	60.1	7.9	Forest Plantations, Second Forestry, Third Forestry
Technical assistance	2	17.5	2.3	Agricultural Technical Assistance, Agricultural Sector Management
Nonproject assistance	3	220.9	29.2	Program Loan, Second Structural Adjustment Program, Agricultural Sector Adjustment
Total	31	756.0	101.5	

Source: See table 3-1.

table distribution of regional income, were less successful. In the South Nyanza sugar project, for instance, the preparation and appraisal conducted in 1977 pointed out the drawback of situating the project in a drought-prone area, but world sugar price forecasts were relatively optimistic and promised an acceptable ex ante economic rate of return to the project for the import substitution of sugar. When unexpected devaluations caused substantial overruns in the cost of factory construction, the Bank recommended that the government raise sugarcane producer prices for the industry as a whole. No sooner did the government comply with this request than world prices collapsed. The lesson that emerged from the South Nyanza project, which ended up with a negative rate of return, was that it is essential to assess the probable risks on the international markets, not just the current ones.

The Cotton Processing and Marketing Project (1983) also encountered a host of problems that were not adequately anticipated during project appraisal. These included the poor state of research on cotton, the managerial and financial weaknesses of the cotton board and cooperatives, unfavorable prospects on the world market, unpredictable weather patterns, and pest and disease problems. Together, these factors reduced incentives to cotton producers in relation to competing nonfarm alternatives.[3]

The Integrated Agricultural Development Project (IADP), approved in 1976, was to cover four provinces but proved to be too complex to administer and also generated a negative rate of return. Thirteen institutions and five ministries were involved in the project. The Bank agreed to finance the first IADP in the Nyanza and Western provinces in part to help the government meet its political objectives, but the institutions for servicing inputs, credit, and output—such as cooperatives—turned out to be weak. Not only did the project tax the government's financial, planning, and implementing capacity, but proven technical packages were never made available to farmers. Despite the poor performance in the first phase of the project, the Bank approved a $46 million follow-on effort in 1979, but this did little to improve matters, and eventually the project had to be closed down permanently.

Numerous problems have cropped up in several other Bank projects in support of smallholder agriculture in Kenya. The Bura irrigation project, approved in 1977, was a monumental disaster. This large, capital-intensive project was expected to irrigate 6,000 hectares at $13,700 per hectare but in the end cost $32,000 per hectare. Like the South Nyanza sugar scheme, it created relatively few employment opportunities. The Bank's technical advisory staff expressed concern at every phase of project development and implementation about the effect on soils and cropping patterns and the problems of irrigation design, cost recovery, and remoteness of the location. The operational staff argued, however, that the Bura project served the government's purpose well, which was to invest in irrigation to relieve land pressure and create employment opportunities in a marginal area. Added to the escalating costs were the problems spawned by the design of the irrigation system and the decision to settle the target population in an inhospitable area. By 1979, the Bank had begun to seriously doubt that the project was financially viable and even suggested terminating it. The Kenyan government, however, was unwilling to incur the political cost. This experience is in marked contrast to the Bank's sound technical advice in small irrigation projects in Nigeria—although, paradoxically, agriculture has performed more poorly in Nigeria than in Kenya.[4] The contrasting examples of Nigeria and Kenya demonstrate the influence of expert technical staff on the quality of the Bank's own intervention.

Other activities that proved to be of marginal economic value included the Group Farms Project. Before this project was approved, the Bank's operational policy staff had expressed serious reservations about the practicality of having a large number of small farmers undertaking communal cultivation on erstwhile European farms. But the staff in the operations wing of the Bank's East Africa Region considered it workable. The farmers showed almost no interest in group farming, and virtually the entire credit had to be canceled. The group farming project revealed the weak voice of the advisory technical staff in an institution where lending pressures often led line technical staff to go along with projects of marginal value. The reorganization of the Bank in 1987 unfortunately removed even this weak instrument of quality control.

Since 1967 the Bank has supported four self-standing credit projects totaling nearly $70 million in collaboration with the Agricultural Finance Corporation (AFC). The first AFC credit project measurably increased the production of smallholder dairying and appeared to counter the concerns of Bank staff who had appraised the project and been skeptical about its prospects—but who went along at the insistence of the Kenyans. However, a succession of credit projects quickly followed, in response to implementation problems, and greatly overextended AFC's administrative and managerial capability. In general, the AFC projects were of little benefit to the poor because farmers with holdings of less than 15 hectares were ineligible for seasonal credit. By the end of the 1970s, the Bank had succeeded in negotiating an agreement reducing this limit to 5 hectares, but this still excluded the vast majority of smallholders. By 1986, the Bank was being forced to consider alternative credit mechanisms.

Bank-financed projects had a substantial effect on Kenya's pattern of public expenditures in the 1970s. Bura irrigation, South Nyanza sugar, IADP, and AFC credit (all of which had low rates of return) accounted for at least half of the development expenditure budget of the Ministry of Agriculture during 1977–82. Total gross budgetary expenditures of the ministry increased by 46 percent in these five years—that is, at an annual rate of nearly 10 percent. This restricted the scope for essential complementary investments in agricultural research or human capital development. Contrary to the popular impression that these projects were alleviating poverty in the rural sector, they did not succeed in tackling the long-standing constraints on agricultural productivity.

By 1979—in the wake of the government's expanding activities financed by the coffee boom and the substantial increase in donor-assisted projects—implementation difficulties had spread over a wide range of agricultural projects. The ensuing macroeconomic dialogue increasingly stressed agricultural issues. By 1982 the Bank also had a policy mandate to consider lending in support of structural adjustment.

The macroeconomic difficulties that emerged in the late 1970s turned out to be a blessing in disguise. They brought to an end a number of projects whose economic value was marginal at best. Nevertheless, many in the Bank attributed this failure not to the Bank's weak project portfolio, but to Kenya's poor policies.

The Bank's attempts to promote sectoral reforms in Kenya in the 1980s also met with limited success—but for quite different reasons. The first structural adjustment loan (SAL) was hastily put together in 1980 and did not include an agricultural component. A second loan/credit of $130.9 million attempted to reduce key constraints on agriculture, and provided for the liberalization of grain pricing and marketing policies, the regularization of land subdivision, and the reform of the budgetary and management aspects of agricultural marketing. The Kenyan government was not committed to most of these reforms. Notable progress occurred only in planning and budgeting in the Ministry of Agriculture, and this led to similar reforms in other government ministries.

The timing of certain policy changes also turned out to be inopportune—for example, the liberalization of the grain market in 1983 coincided with a severe drought. There was also a deeper problem of longer standing. The government had been slow to remove restrictions on the interdistrict movement of maize, even though numerous government-appointed commissions had recommended that it do so. By 1989 the interdistrict movement of grain allowed was 1 ton (on unofficial account). Whereas private millers had been allowed to trade in maize for the processing and sale of maize flour, this partial liberalization deprived the maize board of the most lucrative part of maize marketing operations and, in the short run, increased the board's financial problems.

Donors are now more aware of the need to establish a sound price and supply stabilization policy and to improve the competitiveness of the private sector as *preconditions* for further liberalization. However, they have not yet established a step-by-step plan of overall liberalization extending over several years to improve upon the relatively short-term and piecemeal methods and other problems characteristic of the adjustment loans (for example, they do not factor in drought relief measures and food aid). Different donors have focused on different aspects of liberalization. The European Communities (EC) are addressing the problems of the maize board and the United States is focusing on improving the operations of the private trade. There is relatively little interaction between the two from the viewpoint of reforming an overall maize price policy that will simultaneously address the issues of (a) food security, (b) price stability, and (c) productivity growth. Such a division of labor among donors, even pertaining to a single issue such as price policy, is a serious problem in achieving a holistic yet practical policy reform that takes into account genuine concerns facing governments.

Land titling has also been far too politically sensitive to make any headway on this issue. Even in the case of the successful budget rationalization, the problem of budget rationing persists among and within competing ministries, and there are no clear criteria for identifying expenditure priorities.

Recognizing the difficulty of eliciting a government commitment to honor the conditions attached to adjustment loans, the Bank began to provide some balance of payments support to agriculture in the mid-1980s. In an attempt to address the problems that project assistance had encountered earlier, the Bank approved two sectoral credits in 1986. The $60-million First Agricultural Sector Adjustment Operation (ASAO I) included seventy-eight conditions and reflected the same complexity that had characterized the Bank's project operations. Among other things, it sought to improve price incentives, reform parastatals, restructure public investment, and increase the flow of agricultural credit to smallholders. By stressing that everything was important, it conveyed, in effect, that nothing was priority. The Agricultural Sector Management Project credit of $11.5 million in turn financed technical assistance to strengthen the major agricultural institutions in the public sector. Although both programs have addressed issues of critical concern, they have been overoptimistic about the extent and pace of policy change that the government would be able to undertake. The multiplicity of initiatives and institutions in their purview have made it difficult to demonstrate successful results in the short term, as envisaged. The project completion report for ASAO I acknowledged the complexity of the operation and the problem in ascertaining which conditions had been met. Many of the institutional and economic management reforms are staff- and time-intensive, and it will take some time to develop the political and administrative commitment necessary for their implementation. Short-term balance of payments support does not provide the time needed to accomplish long-term sustainable reforms, unless of course reforms are undertaken before the funds are disbursed. However, not all funds are disbursed before reforms take place, and the temptation to disburse funds often overtakes the need to ensure implementation.

The Kenyan government, which was initially reluctant to accept balance of payments support on the grounds that it violated national sovereignty, has learned that quick disbursements are an easier means of obtaining the needed foreign exchange than projects that take longer to disburse. Given the country's good economic performance and the need for foreign exchange, the temptation for the Bank to provide such macroeconomic support is strong. Slower-disbursing subsectoral or project assistance of the right kind is, however, a much more appropriate means of helping complex policy and institutional systems to evolve.

Another problem with past adjustment loans was that the initial operations were clearly too broad and inadequately prepared to have any effect. A narrower focus is being considered for the future, but ways must still be found to intensify agricultural production, accelerate overall growth, alleviate poverty by creating employment, improve land access, and promote exports (especially when Bank policies do not support the financing of some of Kenya's most important crops, such as tea and coffee). These are all more fundamental issues.

Tanzania

The project problems in Tanzania were by and large related to the Basic Industry Strategy adopted in 1976, the poor macroeconomic and sectoral policies devised for the development of agriculture, and the subsequent effect of agriculture's poor performance on the Tanzanian economy. How the Bank handled the policy dialogue on macroeconomic and sectoral issues in the 1970s and the 1980s and the interrelationship between these groups of issues are of particular interest.

Bank policy recommendations. The Bank's 1974 report on the agriculture sector in Tanzania observed that the government's objectives of regional and interclass equity were being achieved at the cost of growth. The report also noted that the government's coercive villagization program—which had been launched in 1973–74 in an attempt to simplify the provision of services by congregating households into small areas (see chapter 1)—was likely to have an adverse effect on producer incentives in the broadest sense. In particular, soil fertility was expected to decline because of the growing concentration of people on fragile lands, deforestation, and the reduction of fallow. The report stressed that Tanzania needed to capture easy productivity gains by focusing on the areas of high agricultural potential with proven technical packages and recommended a sequential (as opposed to integrated) production-oriented strategy for this purpose. It represented a radical departure from the equity-centered development strategy being pursued by the government and facilitated by donors. To achieve significant productivity gains, according to the report, Tanzania needed to launch a national maize project in selected areas of high potential, to be followed by a national agricultural development program that would cover larger numbers of crops and areas. The government found this unacceptable and instead favored a quick countrywide expansion of all services for welfare, political, and ideological reasons. The report also indicated that it was important to develop and maintain feeder roads and to promote—through investment in infrastructure—voluntary resettlement in less populated areas of high potential as a means of relieving the population pressure on land in the more crowded areas. The comments about transportation and feeder roads turned out to be prophetic: One of the greatest constraints to the rapid growth of agricultural production in Tanzania has been the steady deterioration in its physical infrastructure.

Out of concern for Tanzania's national sovereignty, however, the Bank adopted a cautious attitude in suggesting changes along the lines recommended by the report. Following the severe drought of 1973–74, the National Maize Project approved in 1975 did not give priority to the six high-potential regions Bank staff had identified on technical grounds but instead spread services throughout the country. The Ministry of Agriculture found it difficult to implement the national project because of the government's policy of administrative decentralization, which increased the power of regional administrations in relation to that of the central ministries and weakened the role of technical ministries in relation to that of the prime minister's office. As had been expected by the appraisal team, the National Maize Project encountered numerous problems and had a limited effect on production.

Given the importance of agriculture in countries such as Tanzania, economic reports must inevitably explore the role of agriculture in the economic modernization of the country. The treatment of agriculture in the 1977 basic economic report, however, was at best marginal. Little space was devoted to the implications of poor agricultural performance for Tanzania's macroeconomic performance, or vice versa. The report expressed guarded support for the means by which equity objectives were being pursued by the government. For example, the policies of villagization and panterritorial pricing—criticized in the 1974 agricultural sector report—were considered to be appropriate instruments for redressing rural poverty. In contrast to the critical stance in Kenya, where the Bank had recommended liberalizing the grain trade as early as 1973, the 1976 economic report on Tanzania did not press for curtailing the growth of parastatals. The proliferation of public estates and the nationalization of private ones in the 1970s were not questioned, either. The government's basic industries policy competed strongly with agriculture for budgetary resources and policy attention, but the report only mildly questioned the pursuit of a capital-intensive, import-substituting industrialization policy.

Bank assistance. The Bank's project portfolio reflected its deference to Tanzania's chosen strategy. It actively supported the development of public sector industries such as textiles, shoes, and pulp and paper. During 1975–79, 39 percent of the Bank's total assistance to Tanzania went to industry, which was higher than the share going to any other sector. In fact, during 1965–88 industry received a greater share (18 percent) of the Bank's total assistance in Tanzania than in any other MADIA country. As in Kenya, the Bank's agricultural projects in Tanzania in the 1970s focused mainly on integrated projects and crop parastatals (see table 3-3), which was again contrary to the recommendations of the 1974 sectoral report. In this context it is instructive to note that Tanzania had the largest number of Bank-financed agricultural projects with negative rates of return, that is, eleven out of fifteen audited until 1989 (see table 3-9).

The Kigoma, Tabora, and Mwanza-Shinyanga Integrated Rural Development Projects (IRDPs) turned out to be too complex for the government to administer, and they yielded negative economic rates of return. In addition to focusing on food crops, the IRDPs often included social welfare components (for example, water supply, schools, and health clinics). They gave no attention to the development of the most important export crop in each area—for example, cotton in Mwanza-Shinyanga or tobacco in Tabora—which had been the source of smallholder prosperity in the two regions in the 1960s. Food crops remained the central concern, despite the limited technology and poor markets for these crops. In accordance with the country's decentralized administrative structure, resources were channeled to

Table 3-3. Tanzania: World Bank Assistance to Agriculture, 1965–88
(millions of U.S. dollars)

Target of assistance	*Number of projects*	*Funding totals*	*Percent of total funding*	*Projects included*
Crop-oriented projects				
Tea	2	24.8	4.5	Smallholder Tea, Smallholder Tea Consolidation
Sugar	1	18.0	3.3	Kilombero Sugar
Cotton	1	17.5	3.2	Geita Cotton
Credit	2	16.0	2.9	Agricultural Credit, Rural Development Bank
Integrated rural development	3	29.2	5.3	Kigoma Rural Development, Tabora Rural Development, Mwanza/Shinyanga Rural Development
Tobacco	3	31.1	5.6	Tobacco, Tobacco Processing, Tobacco Handling
Cashewnuts	2	48.5	8.8	Cashewnuts, Second Cashewnuts
Maize	2	61.0	11.0	National Maize, Grain Storage/Milling
Pyrethrum	1	10.0	1.8	Pyrethrum
Coconut	1	6.8	1.2	Coconut Pilot
Other projects				
Livestock	3	30.0	5.4	Beef Ranching, Second Livestock Development, Dairy Development
Fisheries	1	9.0	1.6	Fisheries
Forestry	2	19.0	3.4	Sao Hill Forestry, Second Forestry
Nonproject assistance	4	232.2	42.0	Export Rehabilitation Program Loan, Multisector Rehabilitation, Agricultural Export Rehabilitation
Total	28	553.2	100.0	

Source: See table 3-1.

the regional administrations, bypassing the technical ministries at the center, such as agriculture. However, the regional governments did not have the capacity to plan and implement projects of such complexity that had been prepared mainly by technical expatriates. Donor-funded projects had begun to proliferate, and this created a demand for counterpart resources that exceeded any realistic assessment of government revenues. By the end of the decade, virtually every region had been covered by IRDPs funded by various donors, including the EC, the United Kingdom, and the United States. Among the main problems the projects encountered was a chronic shortage of recurrent financing, spare parts, and fuel resulting from poor macroeconomic management. In 1982 the Bank reluctantly decided not to proceed with a similar project in President Julius Nyerere's Mara Region.

Until 1986, the Bank had provided loans and credits amounting to $261 million (that is, more than 80 percent of its agricultural assistance) to various parastatals involved in the agroprocessing of tea, cotton, cashews, sugar, tobacco, pyrethrum, and cereals.[5] Smallholder tea was one of the successful cases of export production in Tanzania, with a robust annual growth of 13.7 percent during 1970–85 (albeit from a small base). In other sectors, project appraisals did not fully anticipate the collapse of smallholder export crop production that would ensue from the government's policies. In 1974–75 Tanzania was the world's second largest producer of cashews, turning out 120,000 tonnes of raw nuts. By 1981–82 production had declined to a postindependence low of only 40,000 tonnes. A lack of adequate throughput caused financial problems for the cashew factories financed in the two cashew-processing projects approved in 1974 and 1978. Both projects experienced negative rates of return. Similarly, the tobacco-processing and handling projects—aimed at improving services to the tobacco subsector—generated negative rates of return.

Although the Bank provided substantial financial support for the processing of export crops in Tanzania, it took a pessimistic view of the country's export prospects (as it had in Kenya)—because of the inelastic demand and volatile commodity prices. Noting that world prices for sisal had been unfavorable since 1969, the Bank recommended a program of diversification out of sisal estates. Whether because of this advice or some other incentive, the Tanzania Sisal Authority diverted 25 percent of its investments into Bank-funded dairy farming activities—with disastrous results. By the end of the decade, the nationalized sisal estates had degenerated considerably, whereas a single private multinational company not assisted by any donor had become the principal source of sisal exports from the country.

Also, as in Kenya, the Bank refrained from financing investments in coffee, Tanzania's most important export crop.[6] Unlike Kenya, which provided ample services for its coffee producers, Tanzania had neglected the coffee industry and its export potential by adopting various discriminatory policies, such as implicit and explicit taxation, and neglect of input supplies to the traditional production areas of Arusha, Kilimanjaro, and Bukoba. The government's drive for regional equity did, however, lead to the establishment of new production in the Southern Highlands.

By the end of the 1970s, Tanzania found itself facing a domestic economic crisis of unprecedented magnitude. The breakup of the East African Community, the war with Uganda, the second oil-price shock, a fall in commodity prices following the coffee boom, and the overexpansion of public expenditures (together with the import liberalization recommended by the Bank in 1977) all contributed to a severe balance of payments crisis. The government approached the Bank for balance of payments support.

Other donors, notably, the International Labour Organisation and the Scandinavian donors, failed to share the Bank's assessment of Tanzania's economic situation. Paul Collier, who participated in the preparation of the Bank economic report, has argued that this attitude by other donors undermined the Bank's ability to carry out an effective dialogue in Tanzania without jeopardizing its presence there. Aid-coordination meetings in Tanzania came to a halt in 1977 because the government did not want donors to gang up and press for policy reforms. The Nordic donors, traditionally sympathetic to Tanzania's socialist policies, supported the government's position.

While approving an export rehabilitation credit of $50 million in 1981 to mitigate the balance of payments crisis, the Bank recommended that the government develop a program of structural adjustment and financed an advisory group to assist in the task. It also prepared a comprehensive agricultural report, completed in 1983 with a substantial contribution from Tanzanian officials, as an input into the work of the advisory group. A recent report prepared by the World Bank's Operation Evaluation Department considers the 1983 report to have been a watershed in the Bank's relations with Tanzania.[7]

While identifying the internal policies that had contributed to the poor performance of Tanzanian agriculture, the 1983 report noted that many of Tanzania's problems were the result of trying to handle massive amounts of foreign aid with weak policies and institutions. It reiterated several themes of the 1974 agricultural sector report—that is, the need to exploit areas of high potential with assured rainfall, including the Southern Highlands, where substantial production gains could be realized to reduce the reliance on food imports. The report also stressed that Tanzania would have to adjust its exchange rate before it could expect to adjust consumer and producer prices, most of which were in the domain of agriculture. It demonstrated the greater productivity of the private sector—despite the discriminatory treatment meted out to it during the previous decade. The report documented in considerable detail the problems created for economic management by the large parastatal losses, in which the overvalued exchange rate had played a part, and by the growing black market fueled by the government's efforts to control almost every item produced in the country. Ironically, the black market had taken on such significant proportions that the government had lost control of virtually the entire economy. The report argued that Tanzanian policies needed to focus less on equity and government control and more on achieving growth through private initiative and institutional pluralism; it also stressed the need to rectify the budgetary imbalance between industry and agriculture. Food production, the report stressed, could be increased through rainfed agriculture and small-scale irrigation, instead of the large-scale irrigation preferred by the government.

As in the past, the Bank exercised some caution in the presentation of these recommendations. For instance, the 1984 economic report focused on external shocks and underplayed the fundamental restructuring needed to revitalize agriculture. The most important constraint to reform in the early 1980s continued to be the overvalued exchange rate. Bringing budgetary deficits under control posed another problem. The government did begin allocating more foreign exchange to agriculture (in comparison with industry) and raised a number of producer prices. Controls on the grain market were partly relaxed. However, the Bank did not approve any agricultural projects in Tanzania after 1982 because it considered these reforms inadequate in the absence of an exchange rate adjustment, but it continued to lend to other sectors—with the ironic result that it inadvertently reinforced the bias of Tanzania's investment pattern against agriculture.

After half-hearted attempts at devaluation in 1984–85, the government devalued the shilling from T Sh 16 to T Sh 40 per United States dollar in June 1986 and agreed to eliminate overvaluation by 1988. The donor community perceived this action as a new commitment to policy reform, and aid commitments to Tanzania rose. In November 1986, after a hiatus of five years, the Bank approved a multisectoral rehabilitation credit of nearly $100 million for Tanzania. In January 1988 this was supplemented with another multisectoral adjustment credit of $30 million, followed by a $30 million agricultural export rehabilitation credit in the same year, and two industrial rehabilitation and trade adjustment credits totaling $147.5 million in 1989.

Policy reforms—including the move to raise the producer prices of both food and export crops and reduce the role of the government in agricultural marketing and input supply—together with favorable weather, have helped accelerate agricultural growth to about 4–5 percent annually since 1986, after the stagnation of the early 1980s (see chapter 1). Since 1987 food crop production outpaced population growth, with the result that Tanzania had a surplus of maize. Maize production rose from 1.65 million tons in 1982–83 to an estimated record of 3.13 million tons in 1988–89. The production of paddy, wheat, pulses, and vegetables reached record levels as well. There also was a marked recovery in the production of several export crops—for example, cotton production more than doubled since 1982–83 to reach the equivalent of 400,000 bales or more in each of the years since 1987. The decline in cashewnut and sisal production was also reversed. In contrast, both the volume and quality of registered exports of coffee, tea, and tobacco continued to fall.

The steady decay of institutions and physical infrastructure after more than a decade of neglect poses a serious threat to sustained growth. A strongly entrenched and ideologically driven party, together with President Nyerere, who relinquished his presidency in 1985 but remained head of the party, continued to dominate the policymaking process—although Tanzania's bureaucracy and its intellectual elite appear to understand the sources of Tanzania's economic problems. United donor support of internal reforms and a closer monitoring of the implementation of these reforms will continue to be essential. It is too early to judge how fast and how well Tanzania will follow through with these reforms and to what extent it will adhere to them in the long run. There is also a danger that some kinds of reforms may lead to many of the problems that a socialist Tanzania had avoided. For instance, one consequence of the reform measures adopted in 1986 appears to be that influential bureaucrats and party officials now have a free license to acquire large landholdings, on the one hand, and to maintain controls on smallholder farming, on the other. Thus inequities are likely to increase in Tanzania in the absence of a broadly based agricultural development strategy.

Malawi

The principal constraint to agricultural growth in Malawi is the sharp division between estates and smallholders and the resulting competition for the use of resources. Although the Bank was well aware of these problems, it did not directly address them in its policy recommendations until well into the 1980s, as this might have forced it to suggest that the government alter its basic strategy of estate-led growth.

Bank policy recommendations. The 1973 agricultural sector review acknowledged the government's discriminatory policies toward smallholders, which, it also pointed out, provided the financial capital for the development of the estates. Smallholder development was said to be constrained by the lack of credit, trained personnel, and marketing outlets, rather than the licensing restrictions on growing high-value export crops, the high explicit taxation of smallholder tobacco, or the lack of access to land. The report assumed that integrated agricultural development projects would alleviate these constraints. It nevertheless recommended greater smallholder participation in export production through the promotion of flue-cured tobacco schemes for the benefit of smallholders.

Whereas Bank assistance in Kenya and Tanzania during the 1970s had flowed mainly to crop parastatals, assistance in Malawi went mainly to integrated agricultural production projects (see table 3-4). The Lilongwe Agricultural Development Project, approved in 1968, was the forerunner of a series of IRDPs across Africa. Over the period 1965–88, twelve such projects were implemented in Malawi. These projects absorbed nearly $118 million and accounted for almost two-thirds of the Bank's total project assistance to agriculture and rural development in Malawi. By 1978, the Bank had begun shifting away from the relatively capital-intensive IRDP strategy. Thus the first National Rural Development Program (NRDP) introduced in that year concentrated more on the provision of agricultural inputs and farm services than on soil conservation, infrastructure, and intensive staffing. Two subsequent phases of the NRDP were approved in 1981 and 1983.

These large undertakings were designed to raise the production of smallholder crops such as maize, groundnuts, tobacco, cotton, rice, beans, and potatoes, as well as that of livestock. Their main weakness was that they failed to give enough attention to the sequencing and phasing of investments. The Bank invested large sums in infrastructure and in the expansion of agricultural staff without first ascertaining whether profitable technical packages were available for crop production. Only 6 percent of the maize acreage in Malawi was under improved maize in 1988, compared with 60 percent in Kenya. The slow rate at which improved technology was introduced is particularly noteworthy in light of the fact that early project experience in Malawi had already raised questions about the acceptability of dent maize varieties among Malawi's predominantly subsistence farmers, and a review of NRDP carried out in 1982 had confirmed the limited effect of

Table 3-4. Malawi: World Bank Assistance to Agriculture, 1965–88
(millions of U.S. dollars)

Target of assistance	*Number of projects*	*Funding totals*	*Percent of total funding*	*Projects included*
Crop-oriented projects				
Cotton	3	25.50	7.11	Shire Valley, Shire II and III (integrated projects)
Rice	2	15.81	4.41	Karonga, Karonga II (integrated projects)
Fertilizer	1	5.00	1.39	Fertilizer
Credit	2	13.70	3.82	Industrial and Agricultural Credit, Smallholder Agricultural Credit
Integrated rural development	7	76.78	21.41	Lilongwe Agricultural Development Project, Lilongwe II and III, NRDP I-IV
Extension	1	11.60	3.23	Agricultural Extension
Research	1	23.80	6.64	National Agricultural Research
Other projects				
Forestry	1	6.40	1.78	Wood Industries Restructuring
Nonproject assistance	3	180.00	50.20	Structural Adjustment Loan, Second Structural Adjustment Credit, Third Structural Adjustment Credit
Total	21	358.59	100.00	

Source: See table 3-1.

these varieties on production. It was not until after the third structural adjustment loan in 1988 that the Bank finally began to focus on improving flint maize varieties—although NRDP had by then been restructured and replaced by national agricultural research and extension projects.

Another significant problem was that the IRDPs required a planning and implementing capacity and recurrent resources well beyond what Malawi could realistically take over in the foreseeable future. Donor expenditures on infrastructure further induced large budgetary commitments on the part of the government. Once Bank funding was phased out, however, it was difficult to sustain recurrent costs—especially since productivity had failed to increase. Smallholders in Malawi have not faced the same degree of institutional instability or macroeconomic policy distortion as the small farmers in Tanzania. Also, Malawi has relied more heavily and for longer periods of time on expatriate personnel. The more favorable administrative environment in this case is reflected in Malawi's better economic rates of return. All Bank projects audited until 1989 in Malawi were estimated to have generated positive economic rates of return (see table 3-9 on page 00). It is important to bear in mind, however, that these rates were calculated immediately upon project completion, did not take into account any long-term effects, and were frequently based on inadequate data—because of the subsistence nature of smallholder crops in Malawi. The extent and length of the expatriate presence has allowed a number of well-trained Malawian nationals to obtain agricultural management experience. Nevertheless, as in Kenya, the planning and implementing capacity of the Ministry of Agriculture remains woefully thin—despite more than twenty years of donor assistance for rural development.

By the end of the 1970s there was abundant evidence of the adverse effects of producer pricing policies on smallholder production and of the limited effect of donor interventions through integrated agricultural projects. The Bank had not yet engaged in urging fundamental policy reforms, however, since its knowledge of estate farming was still superficial. Only a clause was introduced in the 1978 National Rural Development Project to alleviate in part the pricing problems in the agreement; this clause set forth both pricing and marketing criteria to which the government was expected to adhere (but which it subsequently ignored). Following the decline in tobacco prices and the external difficulties faced by Malawi, the Bank also prepared a detailed report on estate agriculture in 1979.

Bank assistance. To assist Malawi in addressing its macroeconomic problems, the Bank, together with other donors, financed three structural adjustment loans, which have come to some $224 million since 1981. The conditions attached to these loans were designed to improve the balance of payments, cut the budget deficit, and give market mechanisms greater influence in determining prices, wages, resource allocation, and the structure of production. They called for higher producer prices for smallholders, the elimination of consumer price subsidies, the elimination of the fertilizer subsidy (which proved to be difficult), exchange and interest rate adjustments, higher fees for public utilities and services, cuts in public expenditures, and a shift in agriculture away from the NRDP toward agricultural research and extension. Programs for restructuring and improving the management of parastatals included liberalization of the grain market and divestiture of public holding companies owned and operated by Malawi's elite.

As a result of the adjustment measures adopted by the government, most macroeconomic indicators had improved by 1987 (see chapter 2, page 42). The aggregate supply response of the smallholders was weak, however, as the measures did not reflect the structural constraints in Malawi's agriculture. The experience with implementing the SALs demonstrated that many of the existing agricultural interventions, including a fertilizer subsidy for smallholders, are essential, but that they needed to be made more efficient and focused.

The agricultural sector report prepared in 1981 identified the government's wage policy as the best instrument for promoting the rapid expansion of export crop production through estates. The discriminatory policies toward pricing, marketing, land access, and crop rights reduced the returns to labor in smallholder agriculture. As a result, the estates enjoyed an elastic supply of low-wage labor, which, according to the report, ensured that Malawian tobacco would be competitive in the world market. Even so, the Bank did not press the issue of the government's wage policy, although by the end of the 1970s the problem had become more acute as real wages had fallen from their already low level. Only a pricing methodology was agreed upon with the government in the first SAL.

In March 1983, several months before the second SAL was approved, the government raised the prices of export crops. Although the pricing issue appeared to have been settled, the Bank made little progress in addressing other constraints on smallholder production in its policy dialogue. For example, little had been achieved with respect to its 1974 recommendation that Malawi should promote smallholder production of flue-cured tobacco or burley tobacco on customary (as opposed to estate) land. The lifting of legal restrictions to allow smallholders to grow burley was made contingent on an analysis of world market prospects. Given Malawi's 26 percent share of the world market, the government feared a possible fall in the world price of burley tobacco if its production rose further. The Bank acquiesced in the government's decision to regulate production levels and, by implication, to leave burley tobacco production to the estate sector. The issue remained contentious, and, by the end of the 1980s, no significant headway had been made in increasing the opportunities for small farmers to grow export crops, although the average size of Malawian estates had declined. Indeed, many of the newer estates are the size of medium-scale farms rather than large farms (that is, between ten to fifteen hectares). Nevertheless, underutilization of estate land simultaneously with extreme scarcity of land in communal areas continued.

In support of the strategy of estate-led growth, Malawian policymakers have argued that scale economies and considerations of high quality to maintain competitiveness favor largeholder production of export crops. Elsewhere, it has been shown that the per hectare yields of tea, coffee, and sugar in Kenya tend to be twice as high as those on small farms, even when both estates and smallholders receive similar prices, because of the greater ability of estates to mobilize virtually all factors of production.[8] These yield differences are four times as great in Malawi. The recurrent financial and administrative costs of servicing smallholders also tend to be higher, as demonstrated by the government's National Rural Development Program. Nevertheless, domestic resource costs (which measure the efficiency of production) tend to be lower for smallholder agriculture than for estates, as small farmers use more domestic (rather than imported) inputs.[9] Furthermore, broadly based smallholder development has greater multiplier effects on the rest of the economy and therefore promotes growth to a greater degree. Donors have failed, however, to convince the Malawian government of the efficiency gains of small-farm production. Land is still being alienated for the establishment of new estates, even as land pressure in the smallholdings has intensified. The Land Policy Study carried out by the Bank in 1985 disclosed that more than 80 percent of the land on established flue-cured tobacco estates remained unutilized. Even the most conservative World Bank estimate puts it at 50 percent. The Bank has been unable to address either the restriction of rights to grow estate crops or the problem of land distribution in Malawi. Although a land tax was suggested to encourage the intensification of land, it would be difficult to collect. Even granting that the redistribution of estate land would not greatly increase the per capita availability of land in a situation of intense land pressure, land access and economic opportunities to grow high-value crops remain the most fundamental obstacles to broadly based development in Malawi.

Although (until recently) the Bank failed to make headway on structural issues, its projects in Malawi focused almost exclusively on smallholder development. The fact that a project in support of estate production was financed in 1989 suggests that the Bank has begun to accept the dualistic strategy and to aid its advancement. Some might argue that improving the utilization and efficiency of estate lands will increase employment for the marginal smallholders, especially as the size of estates has declined—but this alone is unlikely to foster broadly based agricultural or overall economic growth.

World Bank Assistance to West Africa

During 1965–88 the total World Bank assistance to Cameroon, Nigeria, and Senegal amounted to nearly $6 billion (see table 3-5). Some 39 percent of this went to agriculture and rural development, 27 percent to basic infrastructure, and another 13 percent to nonproject loans and credits. Over this period, the Bank approved seventy-one projects for agricultural and rural development in the three countries.

As in East Africa, the Bank's commitments in the three West African countries increased sharply during 1975–79 (in comparison with the period 1970–74)—rising sixteenfold in Nigeria, sevenfold in Cameroon, and twofold in Senegal. In Nigeria, most of this increase went to agriculture (which rose to 70 percent of the Bank's total commitments to Nigeria). In fact, Nigeria received nearly as much project assistance for agriculture as all of the other MADIA countries combined. In contrast, the shares of self-standing projects in basic infrastructure and human resource development dropped to zero (from 51 percent and 19 percent, respectively, in the previous period). However, as the following paragraphs explain, the Bank's agricultural development projects (ADPs) in Nigeria did have provisions for training and rural feeder roads. In Cameroon and Senegal, basic infrastructure continued to receive a substantial (but smaller) share of Bank assistance during 1975–79.

During the 1980–88 period of structural adjustment, agriculture dominated Bank assistance to both Cameroon and Nigeria—although its share in Nigeria had decreased from the levels of 1975–79. At the same time, the share of basic infrastructure fell in Cameroon, but it rose appreciably in Nigeria. Cameroon is the only MADIA country that did not receive any nonproject loans until 1989. In contrast, nonproject assistance accounted for more than 38 percent of the Bank's total assistance to Senegal and for 15 percent of its total assistance to Nigeria.

Nigeria

A striking difference between the Bank's economic reports on Kenya and Nigeria is that the central role of agriculture in overall develop-

Table 3-5. West Africa: World Bank Assistance by Sector, 1965–88
(millions of U.S. dollars)

	Fiscal 1965–69			*Fiscal 1970–74*			*Fiscal 1975–79*			*Fiscal 1980–88*			*Country totals (1965–88)*			
Target of assistance	*Cameroon*	*Nigeria*	*Senegal*	*Cameroon*	*Nigeria*	*Senegal*	*Cameroon*	*Nigeria*	*Senegal*	*Cameroon*	*Nigeria*	*Senegal*	*Cameroon*	*Nigeria*	*Senegal*	*Combined*
Agriculture and rural development	28.16	0.00	10.43	17.00	27.20	20.79	124.00	355.00	47.50	326.90	1,239.50	89.50	496.06	1,621.70	168.22	2,286.0
Percent of total	83.54	—	41.64	13.36	7.13	32.69	39.17	70.02	30.31	48.94	43.00	14.07	43.30	42.40	19.09	38.8
Basic infrastructure	0.55	65.16	14.62	90.68	192.90	29.19	166.90	0.00	45.6	245.00	603.90	121.80	503.13	861.96	211.21	1,576.3
Percent of total	1.63	70.41	58.36	71.26	50.58	45.90	52.72	0.00	29.10	36.68	20.94	19.15	43.92	22.31	23.96	26.8
Industry	—	6.00	—	—	10.00	3.60	3.00	60.00	17.80	15.00	161.00	36.00	18.00	237.00	57.40	312.4
Percent of total	—	6.48	—	—	2.62	5.66	0.95	11.83	11.36	2.25	5.58	5.66	1.57	6.13	6.51	5.3
Other infrastructure	5.00	—	—	—	0.00	8.00	—	92.00	2.50	41.00	351.30	76.00	46.00	443.30	86.50	575.8
Percent of total	14.83	—	—	—	0.00	12.58	—	18.15	1.60	6.14	12.18	11.95	4.02	11.47	9.81	9.8
Human resource development	—	21.39	—	19.57	71.30	2.01	18.20	0.00	37.00	30.10	57.30	32.50	67.87	149.99	71.51	289.4
Percent of total	—	23.11	—	15.38	18.69	3.16	5.75	0.00	23.61	4.51	2.00	5.11	5.92	3.88	8.11	4.9
Nonproject assistance	—	—	—	—	80.00	—	—	0.00	—	—	452.00	242.00	0.00	532.00	242.00	774.0
Percent of total	—	—	—	—	20.98	—	—	0.00	—	—	15.68	38.05	0.00	13.77	27.46	13.1
Technical assistance	—	—	—	—	—	—	4.50	—	6.30	10.00	18.00	38.20	14.50	18.00	44.50	77.0
Percent of total	—	—	—	—	—	—	1.42	—	4.02	1.50	0.62	6.01	1.27	0.47	505.00	1.3
Total	33.71	92.55	25.05	127.25	381.40	63.59	316.60	507.00	156.70	668.00	2,883.00	636.00	1,145.56	3,863.95	881.34	5,890.9

— = Not available.
Source: See table 3-1.

ment was far better articulated in its reports on Kenya. The Bank's analysis of Nigeria tended to focus on other macroeconomic developments, perhaps because its economy was dominated by oil. With the increase in food prices in the mid-1970s, the Bank's economic and sectoral reports began to emphasize food self-sufficiency. The reports were somewhat slow to detect the full effects of the oil boom on Nigeria's export agriculture and to stress the need for macroeconomic policy reforms. In the 1960s, in contrast, reports on Nigeria had indicated that efficiency gains in both food and export crop production would enable Nigeria to maintain its international competitiveness in agricultural commodity exports in the face of inelastic demand.

Bank recommendations. Although smallholders accounted for 90–95 percent of Nigeria's total agricultural output, the Nigerian government tended to favor large holdings and to support large capital-intensive investments in irrigation through the establishment of the River Basin Development Authorities. The World Bank, in contrast, consistently upheld the interests of small farmers—not only in its economic and sectoral reports but also in its agricultural projects (ADPs), promoting the integrated development of an area primarily through the expansion of feeder roads, extension, and fertilizer use. This difference in emphasis often led to differences of opinion between the government and the Bank on such issues as the subsidization of tractors hired to prepare land for large farmers (for which internal political pressure has been considerable) or the relative importance of small surface and tubewell irrigation projects (in which the Bank made a major contribution in Nigeria) compared with the large investments favored by Nigerians.

Bank projects in Nigeria helped improve the pattern of public expenditures in agriculture through their emphasis on smallholders. Yet greater attention to the problem of Nigeria's limited planning, implementation, and technological capacity would have ensured better returns to these investments. The Bank, like the government, concentrated more on the rapid expansion of projects than on some of the most intractable problems that need to be resolved to improve Nigeria's absorptive capacity to utilize resources effectively. An example of this is the overlooked development of planning and implementing capacity at the state, district, and local levels. This capacity proved to be a major constraint on effective project planning and implementation as it focused instead on institutional developments at the federal level, thus reinforcing the government tendency to centralize power. Such institution building helped to create the necessary planning and implementing capacity at the federal level. However, insufficient attention to simultaneous development of similar capacity at the state level and below inadvertently helped to reinforce centralization of power by the government. The Bank helped establish thirteen important institutions at the federal level—two of which are the Federal Agricultural Coordinating Unit (FACU) and the Agricultural Project Monitoring, Evaluation, and Planning Unit (APMEPU)—for the planning and implementation of rural development projects. Many of these institutions were created outside the normal government structure to attract qualified Nigerians who would otherwise not be interested in the public sector because it offered low (and, over time, declining) salaries and benefits. In Nigeria, in contrast to the other MADIA countries, the Bank encouraged academics of considerable reputation to accept long-term, five-year contracts that enabled them to make important contributions to the agricultural policy planning and implementation process. Nevertheless, it remained difficult to attract the best personnel to work in the government. The successive coups and changes in governments together with the centralization of political power following the civil war, the oil boom, and the breakup of the states have all contributed over the years to a serious erosion of governmental capacity. Ethnic tensions have reduced labor mobility among educated Nigerians. Bank projects in northern Nigeria, for example, have been unable to attract the educated Ibos and Yorubas from the south to work in the predominantly Hausa region. The northerners, for their part, have been reluctant to recruit "nonindigenes" and have often preferred to recruit expatriates rather than their fellow nationals from the south.

The Bank's reports have repeatedly pointed to deficiencies in Nigerian data and the problems this has created for policy analysis and decisionmaking. To cite an example, even the size of Nigeria's population was not known—since no census had been conducted since 1963. The establishment of APMEPU, which was to develop data bases for the ADPs, was an important step toward alleviating the data problem. APMEPU, however, is essentially a project-oriented entity and has tended to collect more data than it has been able to analyze efficiently. At the time of the completion of this manuscript, the Nigerian government had borrowed $35 million from the Bank at commercial interest rates in support of data collection. However, the exercise proved too ambitious and was not geared to providing immediate feedback to the ADP managers, whose interest in using the data-based findings has been minimal in any case. The Bank has reexamined APMEPU's role and considered strengthening the Federal Office of Statistics (the national agency responsible for data collection) instead. Yet little progress has occurred on this front.

Although projects have been difficult to plan and implement under a federal government whose role increased over time, there have been almost as many problems when political and administrative power has been decentralized—particularly from the viewpoint of achieving equity objectives, as in northern Nigeria, where the feudalistic power structure has tended to favor the politically powerful large farmers. This is in spite of the fact that the Bank planned and implemented projects from the top down (with project preparation dependent on expatriates and on FACU and APMEPU). In northern Nigeria, project implementation experience demonstrates that the more locally planned projects were still unlikely to favor small farmers. Of course, this situation would apply to a lesser extent in the south.

Bank assistance. Consistent with the Bank's economic analysis, the emphasis in early Bank lending was clearly on public goods. During 1970–74, only 7 percent of the Bank's total commitments to Nigeria went to agriculture, in support of two cocoa projects (see table 3-5). Basic infrastructure (power and transport) and education together accounted for a 70 percent share. Of the seventeen projects approved by the Bank during 1975–79, eight were for food crop development (including seven ADPs and one rice project). Of the remainder, four were for oil palm, and one each for forestry, livestock, and agricultural training.

Since 1975 new ADPs were approved in rapid succession. Nearly 60 percent of the Bank's total commitments to Nigerian agriculture (until 1988) went to ADPs (see table 3-6). The first three *enclave* ADPs (Funtua, Gusau, and Gombe) funded in the 1970s were mainly the result of the Bank's own initiative following Robert McNamara's Nairobi speech. Patterned after the Lilongwe Land Development Program in Malawi, these were resource-intensive projects employing a relatively large number of expatriates. Their visible effect—combined with the state governments' anticipation of substantial funding from the federal government as well as the Bank—helped spread them among states. The enclave ADPs were followed by statewide ADPs, which used far fewer resources. The statewide ADPs in turn were followed by multistate ADPs (the first of which was financed in 1987) that were even less resource-intensive. By the end of 1989, all twenty-one states were expected to be included in four multistate ADPs organized along ecological zones. Despite their modest use of resources, the multistate ADPs (designed to ease project processing in the World Bank and at the federal level) are relatively complex to implement. They increase the role of the federal government and make it difficult to coordinate the simultaneous implementation of complex project procedures among the numerous states.

Although the Bank did not provide support for self-standing infrastructure projects in 1975–79 or for education (since the government

Table 3-6. Nigeria: World Bank Assistance, 1965–88
(millions of U.S. dollars)

Target of assistance	*Number of projects*	*Funding totals*	*Percent of total funding*	*Projects included*
Crop-oriented projects				
Cocoa	2	27.2	1.7	Western State Cocoa, Second Cocoa
Rice	1	17.5	1.1	Rice
Oil palm	4	95.5	5.9	Midwestern State, East-Central State, Western State, Nucleus Estate
Fertilizer	1	250.0	15.4	Fertilizer Import
Agricultural development projects	15	971.5	59.9	Funtua, Gusau, Gombe, Ayangba, Lafia, Bida, Ilorin, Oyo North, Ekiti-Akoko, Bauchi, Kano, Sokoto, Kaduna, Multi State I, Borno
Management training	1	9.0	0.6	Agricultural and Rural Management Training Institute
Other projects				
Livestock	2	102.0	6.3	Livestock, Second Livestock
Forestry	2	102.0	6.3	Forestry, Second Forestry
Technical assistance	1	47.0	2.9	Agricultural Technical Assistance
Total	29	1,621.7	100.0	

Source: See table 3-1.

in any case continued to include them in its list of items for public expenditure), the share of industry rose from 3 percent in the previous period to 12 percent. Project assistance declined in the early 1980s, as the Nigerian government slowly proceeded with the currency devaluation and other macropolicy reforms that were long overdue. Another contributory factor was the technological pessimism underlying the midterm evaluations of the statewide Bauchi, Kano, and Sokoto ADPs in 1985. During 1984–88, only three new projects were approved for agriculture and rural development.

The early northern-based ADPs played an important role in promoting fertilizer use on sorghum, millet, and maize. Substantial expenditures on rural feeder roads were made via ADPs, amounting to 140 million naira during 1976–87 in the construction and maintenance of more than 9,000 kilometers of feeder roads. The maintenance of feeder roads has been a serious problem because of the weak planning and implementation capacity at the local level. Many of the new roads fell into disrepair even before the ADPs ended. About 187 million naira were committed to agricultural extension during 1976–87, but only 26 million naira went to adaptive research. Until recently, the focus remained more or less on sole cropping, even though studies of farming systems in the 1960s and 1970s had shown mixed cropping to be the rational response of small farmers in the face of risks arising from low and variable rainfall and from labor shortages. The early enclave ADPs were predicated on the assumption that the available sole crop technologies were appropriate for small farmers and simply needed to be extended. In some ADPs, even extension advice and fertilizer supplies were made conditional on the adoption of sole cropping. Whereas this practice was abandoned in subsequent projects, the de facto emphasis on sole cropping in extension continued until recently.

The ADPs succeeded in accelerating the spread of hybrid maize in northern Nigeria and progress was made in cowpeas and irrigated rice in the Middle Belt. However, for millet and sorghum (which dominate in terms of area planted), the technological possibilities for these two crops to meet all the requirements of producing farmers have been less promising. As an example, short stock hybrid sorghum has not been acceptable to farmers who used the longer stock to thatch roofs.

The Bank helped promote the use of appropriate technology in several ways, beginning with the spread of small-scale surface and tubewell irrigation technology. The Nigerian government supported large-scale irrigation, and the Bank's major role in the provision of small-scale irrigation resulted from the high quality technical assistance it brought to bear on an otherwise poorly performing agricultural sector. In contrast, in Kenya, the Bank's technical input was weak relative to a stronger overall sectoral performance. Labor, however, was a binding constraint on the adoption of new technology by small farmers in a predominantly hand-hoe agriculture, and the spread of improved tools or animal traction received relatively little attention. More generally, more attention in Bank projects was given to the large (but declining) contingent of external personnel working on technical assistance in Nigeria than on the important task of helping the public sector develop its capacity to plan and implement programs, conduct soil and water surveys, and monitor the uses of natural resources.

The ADPs' experience demonstrates the weaknesses in the planning and implementation capacity, especially at the state and local levels—of which the poor maintenance of feeder roads is but one manifestation. To avoid these problems, the ADPs were implemented in rapid succession through an apparatus of parallel institutions. Nonetheless, long lags (ranging from 27 to 67 months) still occurred between project preparation and loan and project effectiveness. Implementation was slow, loan disbursements were low, and there were too many loan conditions (they rose from an average of twenty-three for the early enclave projects to fifty-two for the third multistate ADP). These conditions reflected the Bank staff concerns about the inadequate planning and implementing environment. At the time this manuscript was completed, about 50 percent of World Bank commitments to Nigerian agriculture remained undisbursed.

Of the twelve agriculture and rural development projects audited until 1988, five had economic rates of return of 10 percent or more (see table 3-9). These include the two cocoa projects and the enclave Funtua, Gusau, and Gombe ADPs. As in the case of tea and coffee in Kenya, the first cocoa project was the only one in Nigeria in which the ex post rate of return exceeded the ex ante rate. Three other projects (the Lafia, Ayangba, and Bida ADPs) had rates of return in the range of 0–10 percent, and the remaining six projects, including four for oil palm and one each for rice and livestock, had negative rates of return.

In the case of the ADPs, it was only in Gombe that the ex post rate of return came close to approximating the expected return. For the other projects, the estimated ex post rate of return was generally less than half of that expected at appraisal. The low rates of return for ADPs are consistent with evidence that food production has performed poorly in Nigeria. Although the ADPs have played an important role in increasing the production of rice, maize, cowpeas, and vegetables, these crops are relatively unimportant in aggregate terms.

Agricultural policy reform in Nigeria has been particularly concerned with removing the massive fertilizer subsidy and privatizing fertilizer procurement and distribution. The two issues are intertwined in Nigeria because the rapid growth in fertilizer use (as pointed out in chapter 2, page 88) coincided with a uniform and high subsidy on fertilizer. The subsidy was about 85 percent over most of the period under review, and together with the overvalued exchange rate meant that fertilizer was being distributed nearly free of charge. These developments took place while the fertilizer import and distribution system was being centralized. Since 1975, the Bank has voiced increasing opposition to the financial cost and the inequity in the benefits of the subsidy, not to mention the wastage and the black market in fertilizers created by the subsidy. In 1987, for example, the fertilizer subsidies accounted for three-fourths of the federal government's total agricultural budget.

One objective of the $250 million Fertilizer Import Loan of 1983 was to help eliminate fertilizer subsidies and to commercialize the fertilizer procurement and distribution systems. Although the Nigerian government reduced the subsidy from 85 percent in 1982 to 28 percent in 1986, the overvalued naira ensured a continuing implicit subsidy. Despite the 800 percent devaluation in 1986, the government maintained the fertilizer price at predevaluation levels, thus maintaining an 80 percent subsidy. With the further depreciation of the naira since 1987–88, the unchanged fertilizer price implied a subsidy of nearly 90 percent.

With the decline in oil revenues the government was considering privatizing wholesale and retail business, with the idea of giving cooperatives a larger role at the retail level while maintaining its monopoly on fertilizer imports. Although the ADPs have done a great deal to ensure the supply of fertilizer in the states through their commercial units, they have given little attention to commercial, cooperative, or governmental institutions at the local level. Thus, institutional weaknesses will continue to pose problems unless an effort is made to gradually transfer responsibility for the distribution of fertilizer and other inputs to cooperatives. The Bank also became conscious of the importance of chemical fertilizers in increasing production and in maintaining soil fertility, for which some subsidy may well be essential.

Senegal

As pointed out in chapter 1, Senegal has the most limited agricultural resources of the MADIA countries. Two-thirds of the country's agricultural land lies in the Sahelian zone, where rainfall levels are generally low and for a while declined, although, at the completion of this manuscript, that decline had been reversed, at least temporarily. Soil fertility is also on the decline as a result of the increasing population pressure on the land and intrusion of salt water into the area of higher potential around the Casamance River (between Ziguinchor and Kolda). To add to these problems, the administered prices for the country's leading crops have fallen in real terms for the period covered by the study, per capita food production decreased at an average annual rate of 0.72 percent between 1961 and 1987, and the production of groundnuts—the commodity that put Senegal onto the world economic map—declined by 1.2 percent. During this same period per capita imports of cereals (of which rice alone represented 35.5 percent of the total food import value in 1980–86) increased by 2.2 percent annually and food aid by 7.7 percent.

Bank recommendations. From the French colonial era until relatively recent times, Senegal's overall economy revolved around groundnuts and rice (which eventually created a problem for agricultural policy). To sustain the production of groundnuts for export to the French preferential market, the government subsidized imports of rice from Indochina, another French colony, to provide a needed, cheap wage good. In the 1970s, however, the country lost its comparative advantage in groundnuts and found itself facing a high projected price of rice, the main food of the urban Senegalese (who make up 40 percent of the total population). This situation reinforced the government's desire to shift both its own support and that of donors out of groundnuts and into irrigated rice. Senegal thus lost its share of groundnuts and related products in world trade.

Since then Senegal's rice production has fluctuated between 60,000 and 150,000 tons. Only its geographic distribution underwent significant changes; between 1975 and 1980, the relative importance of the irrigated rice-growing Fleuve (St. Louis) region dropped from 66 percent to 49 percent of total production, whereas that of the rainfed rice-growing Casamance (Ziguinchor/Kolda) rose from 23 percent to 44 percent of total production. Senegal imported about 350,000 tons of rice in 1988. In the 1960s, annual groundnut exports alone could ensure as much as a seven-year supply of rice imports to Senegal. By the mid-1980s, however, they could cover only one year's supply; even though the relative producer prices of groundnuts and rice moved in favor of groundnuts, net groundnut producer prices had increased more rapidly than those for rice, and the international price ratio moved in favor of groundnuts. Despite the decreased share of groundnuts in Senegal's export basket in favor of phosphates and fisheries, the country's overall import capacity had not increased. The food import bill continued to represent a substantial share of the country's total export revenues—accounting for about 25 percent in the early 1980s, compared with 35 percent or more in the late 1960s. During this same period the share was only 5.4 percent and 6.4 percent in Cameroon and Kenya, respectively.

The cost of producing rice under the large irrigation operations of the Fleuve region is high, although an opportunity exists for developing low-cost irrigation in Casamance. One of Senegal's goals is to achieve rice self-sufficiency, but this is not too realistic, since approximately 70 percent of all rice consumed still has to be imported (and costs of domestic production are several times those in Asia, although donors have subsidized initial investment costs). Clearly, better uses of the country's scarce resources should be sought.

One factor that affected the market share of groundnuts and that has made rice self-sufficiency less feasible was the overvaluation of Senegal's currency, the CFA franc, which implicitly taxed exports and made imports cheaper than they otherwise would be. However, the country has had no unilateral ruling over its exchange rate.

There is a long-term solution to increasing the competitiveness of groundnut exports and rice production. It resides in further agricultural intensification, the improving of indigenous research capacity, and investment in soil conservation and low-cost irrigation. Donors have considered the costs of past large-scale irrigation structures as sunk.

Since the early 1960s, a plethora of public sector agencies and state cooperatives helped consolidate the government's control over the agricultural sector. Their functions covered virtually every aspect of agriculture—marketing, input distribution, credit, and extension. Most of these operated under the guidelines of the Programme Agricole, the official action plan of the Senegalese government since 1960 for the modernization of agriculture.

The program assumed that modernization could occur if farmers were encouraged to make more intensive use of the existing technical packages, fungicides, implements, and animal traction—facilitated by institutional credit. Among the national institutions supporting the program, the Office Nationale de Coopération et d'Assistance au Développement (ONCAD)—the agency managing agricultural activities in the groundnut industry—was the largest. Because of its towering presence, donors were unable to design projects that could be implemented outside its institutional framework. By the late 1970s, ONCAD had seriously overextended its administrative capabilities and technical competence and had accumulated huge financial losses. The government unilaterally liquidated the agency in 1980—acquiring a debt of CFAF 100 billion in the process.

The government had also established a nationwide network of agricultural cooperatives that came to play a central role in the groundnut system, especially in input distribution and marketing. However, these cooperatives came to be dominated by local strongmen, with the result that political control shifted toward community leaders rather than the people.[10] As in Tanzania, the increasing politicization of the cooperatives, coupled with widespread abuse of authority by the local leaders, forced the government to embark on a radical transformation of rural cooperatives that increased the role of the state and removed any possibility of grass roots representation via the cooperative movement—a situation that still persists. Before the Bank began its assistance to Senegal (in the late 1960s), only two rural development agencies existed—one operating in the Groundnut Basin, the other in the Fleuve. A number of other such agencies emerged over time in connection with the regional integrated rural development projects promoted by donors. Their rapid expansion and diversification overtaxed the technical skills and managerial capacity of the agencies—as well as the counterpart funds needed to meet their operating and maintenance costs. By the end of the decade, these costs had become unsustainable, and the Bank had begun to withdraw its support to the rural development agencies. Concern about their large operating deficits and limited effectiveness led the Bank to press for immediate and decisive institutional change. The government launched a phased reduction of the activities and personnel of the rural development agencies as part of a reform program to cut down overall public and private consumption, reduce the role of the public sector, cut the current account deficit (from more than 10 percent of GDP in 1984 to 2.8 percent in 1991–92), and eliminate the budget deficit over the same period.

The poor performance of agriculture is related in part to the fact that, nothwithstanding the large volumes of aid, the precise constraints on growth have not yet been fully understood, although some effort has certainly been made in this direction. For instance, World Bank reports have consistently attempted to identify the various technological constraints on the production of groundnuts, sorghum, and millet—which include the lack of information about fertilizer responses, the lack of yield-increasing technologies for low rainfall areas (such as the northern Groundnut Basin in contrast to the southern Siné-Saloum region), and emphasis on land-augmenting rather than labor-augmenting technological improvement. However, this has not been adequate to improve project effectiveness in the face of the risk posed by declining rainfall, declining soil fertility, and weak institutions when few resources have been used to analyze precise microconstraints.

Bank assistance. During 1965–88 the Bank lent Senegal more than $880 million, 81 percent of which comprised International Development Association (IDA) credits. A third of this total went for infrastructure—mainly transportation facilities—but relatively little, if any, was earmarked for rural roads. Agriculture and rural development accounted for a share of slightly more than 19 percent—the bulk of which was directed at crop production. Livestock and forestry, in contrast, received little assistance. The bank lent $382.1 million to agriculture during 1965–88 for eighteen projects and three structural adjustment loans (see table 3-7).

The Bank's total project assistance to agriculture and rural development during 1970–74 was double the level of 1965–69, and it doubled again in 1975–79. The growth in project commitments slackened in the 1980s, as nonproject loans and credits increased sharply. During 1980–88 nonproject assistance, comprising three structural adjustment loans, amounted to nearly $242 million—compared with only $90 million in project assistance to agriculture.

As in Tanzania, Bank assistance favored agriculture and infrastructure, whereas the government shifted its investment portfolio in favor of the industrial sector. Until the end of the Third Plan in 1972–73, 44 percent of public investment went into the rural sector. After the Fourth Plan (1973–74 to 1976–77), the share of the rural sector fell by half. Meanwhile, the share of industry increased from 4 percent during the Third Plan to 28 percent in the Fourth Plan.

The Bank projects covered all four major regions—that is, the Groundnut Basin (comprising Thies, Diorbel, Kaolack/Fatick, and Louga), Casamance (Ziguinchor/Kolda), eastern Senegal (Tambacounda), and the Fleuve (St. Louis). The discussion below focuses on important crops in each region. The Groundnut Basin received the highest Bank assistance. Casamance, which has considerable production potential and the second highest share of total population after the Groundnut Basin, received the lowest. It is often said that the politically marginal status of Casamance in Senegal explains why few donors tend to invest in that region. France has been the highest contributor to total project costs, whereas the Bank has been a relatively small financial contributor.

Farmers' lack of credit and of access to extension and inputs were assumed to be the principal constraints. This proved to be the case in three of the five projects in the Groundnut Basin. The risks posed by declining rainfall had a profound influence on the credit institutions. Severe droughts during the first credit project led the government to force ONCAD to forgive farmer debts. Not surprisingly, the first credit project had a negative rate of return. Once again highlighting the importance of weather, the second credit project realized an economic rate of return well in excess of 15 percent, mainly because of favorable weather. The improved rainfall was accompanied by a rapid increase—exceeding all targets—in the use of fertilizer and equip-

Table 3-7. Senegal: World Bank Assistance to Agriculture, 1965–88
(millions of U.S. dollars)

Target of assistance	*Number of projects*	*Funding totals*	*Percent of total funding*	*Projects included*
Crop-oriented projects				
Cotton	1	16.1	4.2	Eastern Senegal Rural Development (integrated project)
Rice	2	10.0	2.6	Casamance, Second Sedhiou
Credit	3	32.6	8.5	Agricultural Credit, Second Agricultural Credit, Siné-Saloum Agricultural Development (integrated project)
Integrated rural development	2	3.4	0.9	Terres Neuves Resettlement, Second Terres Neuves
Research	1	19.5	5.1	Agricultural Research
Semiarid areas	1	3.0	0.8	Drought Relief
Irrigation	5	70.1	18.3	Senegal Rural Polders, Debi-Lampsar Irrigation, Small Rural Operations, Irrigation IV
Other projects				
Livestock	1	4.2	1.1	Eastern Senegal Livestock
Forestry	1	9.3	2.4	Forestry
Technical assistance	1	4.9	1.3	Irrigation Technical Assistance
Nonproject assistance	3	209.0	54.7	Structural Adjustment Loan (SAL), Second SAL, Third SAL
Total	21	382.1	100.0	

Source: See table 3-1.

ment. This performance obviously could not be sustained, given Senegal's climatic conditions. After 1976, the input delivery system collapsed. ONCAD was abolished in 1980. Groundnut marketing was transferred to the groundnut mills and cereal marketing to private traders, but input distribution was to be handled by the Société Nationale d'Approvisionnement du Monde Rural, a newly created state organization that was to wind down state involvement in this field and be liquidated after three years. However, with the abolition of official credit in the wake of ONCAD's demise, fertilizer consumption fell drastically.

The Siné-Saloum IRDP (Kaolack/Fatick) was begun in 1975, but the input distribution system in the Groundnut Basin collapsed soon after, and the project generated a negative economic rate of return. Few farmers adopted the intensification package proposed under the project, which called for the destumping of cleared land, plowing every three or four years, application of rock phosphate, a heavier application of compound fertilizer, training of oxen, and promotion of ox-drawn equipment to replace light equipment that would be drawn by horses or donkeys. At the end of the project period, the area destumped was only 22 percent of the appraisal estimate. Only 23 percent of the oxen had plowed, and, except in the case of maize, plowing had done little to increase yields.

Although these projects do not appear to have made a significant contribution to agricultural production in the Basin, the situation might have been worse without them. Although production stagnated during 1970–84, the decline in groundnut production experienced in the 1960s was arrested (notwithstanding the repeated droughts), thanks to the short-duration, drought-resistant varieties of groundnuts developed and disseminated during this period. The annual growth rate of millet production improved, albeit from a very low base. The performance of the less important crops such as maize and cotton was quite impressive. However, it did not have much impact on aggregate production, as maize and cotton together occupy only 4 percent of the cropped area in Senegal. The Siné-Saloum region increased its share of maize production from 3 percent in 1960–70 to 20 percent during 1970–84; and the Basin as a whole, which did not produce any cotton in the 1960s, came to account for an 11 percent share in total cotton production over the period 1970–85.

Casamance (Ziguinchor/Kolda) had been the main area of rainfed rice production in Senegal, contributing 66 percent of total production during 1975–80 until it lost this position to the Fleuve. Two of the three Bank-funded projects in Casamance (implemented in 1971 and 1976) concentrated on rice development, but the area devoted to rice in the region declined during 1970–84 under the adverse effects of drought and water salinity as well as mistaken assumptions about the existence of yield-increasing technology for upland rice.

Of the four Bank-funded projects in eastern Senegal (Tambacounda), the Eastern Senegal Rural Development project focused on the development of cotton. This crop accounts for less than 1.5 percent of the gross cultivated area, with eastern Senegal and Upper Casamance contributing 90 percent of Senegal's cotton production. The cereals component of the project was limited to the rotation with cotton. Thanks to the many positive features of the Compagnie Française de Développement des Fibres Textiles' (CFDT) strategy for developing cotton (discussed in chapter 1), cotton production grew at an annual rate of nearly 7 percent during 1970–85. However, most of the increase occurred before 1977—and thus before the project was implemented. During 1977–89, cotton production fluctuated around an average of 38,000 metric tons, well below the Seventh Plan (1985–90) target of 60,000 tons.

The World Bank also has had difficulty in arriving at a clear-cut position on the role of irrigation. On the one hand, Bank reports have pointed out that irrigation reduces dependence on low and unreliable rainfall; on the other hand, they have also consistently criticized large irrigation projects for the high investment required. Given the low cost and greater flexibility of small, privately managed irrigation structures, these clearly need further attention and support. Nevertheless, to utilize the water already dammed by the two large irrigation schemes being undertaken jointly by Senegal, Mali, and Mauritania with the help of France and Germany, the Bank-funded irrigation projects covering about 30 percent of the total irrigated area in the smallholder sector in the Fleuve region in the 1970s. The two projects in the Fleuve were to bring new land under irrigation and to develop rice and vegetable production. The Senegal River Polders (1972) and the Debi-Lampsar (1978) projects brought about 6,340 hectares under irrigation, which constituted about 30 percent of the total irrigated area in the Fleuve's smallholdings. A third project costing nearly $34 million was approved in 1988.

The first two projects suffered a combination of technical and economic problems, including (a) salinity (which prevented double cropping); (b) high production costs for rice at the farm level, in spite of high yields, because of the high cost of pumping water; (c) the declining international price of rice; (d) the great distance from the port city of Dakar, where it is cheaper to import rice from Thailand or Pakistan after taking into account the internal costs of production and transport; and (e) in general, the institutional weaknesses of the Société d'Aménagement et d'Exploitation des Terres du Delta (SAED), the rural agency responsible for developing agriculture in the Fleuve delta. The high costs of having expatriate technical staff and of providing subsidized inputs generated huge annual losses, and SAED became dependent on government subsidies. Moreover, because the investment in human and institutional capital had been low, the government continued to rely on expatriates for the maintenance and rehabilitation of the irrigation projects, which raised questions about the economic viability of these investments. Although the economic rate of return for the Senegal River Polders Project was marginally positive (about 3 percent), it was negative for the Debi-Lampsar Project.

Nonproject assistance. At the time that the Bank provided its first structural adjustment loan to Senegal in 1980, the country was in the midst of a serious macroeconomic crisis, with a current account deficit averaging 22 percent of GDP. The principal SAL objectives were to eliminate the current account and budget deficit, increase the share of directly productive investments from 43 percent to 55 percent of the total investment program, return some parapublic activities to the private sector, introduce *contrat plans* between the government and individual state enterprises to set their medium-term objectives and give them some autonomy in their daily operations, impose ceilings on external commercial borrowing, and limit the expansion of domestic credit. In retrospect, the program was overambitious and did not anticipate the political and administrative bottlenecks in implementation. Coinciding with the severe drought of 1980–82, the SAL did not succeed in achieving the short-term macroeconomic targets relating to external debt, monetary expansion, and public finance. The government did take steps to reform the parastatal sector. By June 1983, sixteen companies (including ONCAD) were in liquidation, and another four (in textiles, farm implements, petroleum distribution, fish processing) were transferred to private ownership. Yet progress on reorganizing the central and regional rural development agencies was disappointing (except in the case of Société de Développement des Fibres Textiles—SODEFITEX).

The policy packages associated with SAL II (1985) and SAL III (1987) were a continuation of those of SAL I—aiming at short-term stabilization, while laying the basic conditions for longer-term growth. As in the case of SAL I (and in Kenya's SAL), these policy packages included a large number of measures for implementation to enable the government to strengthen public finances and public investment programming, restructure incentives in the agricultural sector to raise cereals and groundnut output, decontrol the groundnut sector, reform industrial policy, rehabilitate the financial sector, and reform the parastatals. It is difficult to assess how many of these steps have been accomplished.

Although the country's overall macroeconomic performance improved distinctly in the 1984–88 period (see chapter 1), it was in large measure the result of having started from one of the worst crop years, the better weather, and improved terms of trade. The SALs contributed to macroeconomic stabilization by imposing fiscal discipline and furthering liberalization.

At the same time, although aggregate agricultural production has increased in real terms since 1985, there is little evidence that the adjustment improved agricultural productivity and, thus, the capacity of the sector to sustain agricultural and overall economic growth over the long run.[11] During 1986–89 the production of groundnuts for oil processing and the production of millet and sorghum more or less met the targets of 800,000 and 650,000 metric tons per year, respectively, set under the Seventh Plan (1985–90). These targets were somewhat higher than the average annual production during 1976–85, the previous nine-year period. In contrast, the production of maize, rice, cotton, and cowpeas—the "diversification" crops under the adjustment program and the New Agricultural Policy implemented in 1984—remained at or below previous nine-year averages and well below plan targets. Although producer prices increased for all crops (except for sorghum and millet) in the latter half of the 1980s, input costs rose sharply and input demand declined, since little progress had been made in developing a viable alternative to the government-operated input distribution system that was dismantled under the SAL process. Contrary to donor expectations, the private sector has been reluctant to invest in agricultural input distribution. Shortage of working capital has been a pervasive problem. Overall, the increase in aggregate agricultural output by and large seems a transient phenomenon—reflecting more the temporary effects of producer price increases and favorable rains than any improvement in productivity. The SALs have not addressed the more formidable problems of soil fertility, drought, crop technology, credit, and input supply that prevent Senegal from achieving a more sustained production response. The future productivity growth of Senegalese agriculture thus appears to rest on a weak foundation.

The variable and declining rainfall—and the simultaneous withdrawal of credit, seed distribution services, and distribution of fertilizer in the Groundnut Basin following the dissolution of ONCAD in 1980 as part of a larger attempt by donors to eliminate fertilizer subsidies, reduce public sector deficit, and raise employment levels—caused fertilizer consumption to drop 88 percent from 1979–80 to 1985–86 and rice and cotton to shift outside the Groundnut Basin. Improved climate in the later half of the 1980s, however, improved agricultural production. The Bank also began to devote greater attention to the issues of sustainability of agriculture, soil and moisture conservation, and so forth.

Cameroon

Cameroonian agriculture performed well in relation to other countries until the mid-1980s, yet the Bank's agricultural project portfolio performed poorly. The Bank's sectoral and economic analysis in Cameroon has been by far the weakest among the MADIA countries when the entire 1965–88 period is considered. Bank staff have attributed this to the presence of oil and to the lack of interlocutors in the Cameroonian government. However, the quality of Bank input, which also makes a considerable difference to the quality of country analysis and dialogue, also played a part. This has improved substantially since 1986.

Bank recommendations. In view of the priority given to estate agriculture by the Cameroonian government until the late 1970s, the Bank was clearly an important catalyst in focusing attention on the smallholdings. At its insistence, several estate projects were designed to include outgrower components. But the Bank's analysis of the relative priorities to be accorded to various components of an agricultural development strategy oriented to smallholders has been weak. There was nothing to equal the ADP strategy in Nigeria or the NRDP in Malawi. In any case, the government was not in favor of complex multisectoral integrated rural development projects such as the Zapi project, which the bank financed. It performed poorly and failed to create confidence in government that this strategy would work.

Another problem for agriculture has been the policy vacuum created by the weakness of the Ministry of Agriculture and the multiplicity of parastatals involved in agriculture. Furthermore, the Bank has had a relatively small share in overall aid flows to Cameroon, and much of it has been on harder terms than to the other MADIA countries except Cameroon. Nigeria required less aid—since its economic performance was better and it had access to other sources of aid—and therefore government officials have not been readily available for policy discussion. Moreover, the Cameroonian government has had a reputation for asserting its own priorities.

The 1974 agricultural sector survey was a rather general document, and in many ways its assessment of Cameroon could have applied to several other African countries. It concluded that Cameroon's agricultural potential was good and that the medium-term prospects for its main cash crops (cocoa, cotton, palm oil, and rubber) were attractive. As elsewhere, agricultural research was considered inadequate and the institutional framework for planning and implementation (including the newly created Ministry of Agriculture) weak. The survey observed that management skills were lacking and extension services poorly equipped to communicate improved techniques to small farmers. The lack of coordination, duplication of work, and general wastage of scarce resources in the various ministries and development agencies responsible for agriculture were viewed as the main organizational and management problems.

Although the 1974 report recognized the scope for the further expansion of commercial plantation agriculture (in rubber, coconuts, and oil palm), which dominated Cameroonian agriculture, it stressed the need to focus on smallholders to reduce disparities in regional income. As pointed out in chapter 1, heavy export levies on cocoa and coffee producers (producer prices of these crops remained less than 60 percent of the international f.o.b. prices) were a problem, and given the sharp increase in fertilizer and other input prices, upward adjustments in producer prices were recommended. Land tenure was considered a barrier to the consolidation of holdings and was expected to become a serious constraint on the adoption of modern production techniques. A countrywide system of land registration was recommended, to allow land to be easily transferred and used as collateral for credit. This recommendation was not based on any analysis of the traditional land rights and their effect on producer incentives. Recent studies carried out in southern Africa by the Land Tenure Center at Wisconsin suggest that traditional land rights have a less adverse effect on incentives than generally believed. This would perhaps be the case until land pressure becomes intense and leads to the development of a land market.

Notwithstanding the analysis, few of the recommendations of the report or the Bank's subsequent lending strategy addressed the above concerns. A five-year investment program was proposed consisting of thirteen projects that cost an estimated total of $107 million, but only 16 percent of it was to be allocated to the estate sector—for a rubber plantation. The projects were intended to boost the production of coffee, cocoa, maize, and rice. Although some perfunctory recommendations were made relating to the organization of the research system, no research project was identified to improve national capacity to develop technical packages. As elsewhere, there was also no emphasis on increasing the institutional or personnel capacity of the Ministry of Agriculture.

The Bank's actual assistance deviated significantly from the program proposed in the 1974 report. Over the period 1975–84—in line with the government's own public investment program, which strongly favored the estates—58 percent of the total cost of the Bank-financed crop production projects was concentrated on rubber and palm oil plantations. In the government's own Second Plan (1966–67 to 1970–71), 72 percent of the total allocations to crop production had accrued to estates. The Third Plan (1971–72 to 1975–76) called for a greater share of funds for smallholders, and allocations to estates declined to 52 percent. Most of the investments in smallholder production, however, were devoted to two projects—the Société d'Expansion et de Modernization de la Riziculture de Yagoua (SEMRY) rice and the cocoa program in Central and South provinces. During the Fourth Plan (1976–77 to 1980–81), estates again appropriated the bulk of public expenditures on crop production, accounting for a 62 percent share.

The nonagricultural growth following the oil boom of 1979 pushed up urban wages, increased rural-to-urban migration, and ushered in a period of rising prices, especially for food, in the early 1980s. With projected oil revenues expected to decline in the intermediate future, the Bank once again began stressing smallholder agriculture and traditional crops (including maize and groundnuts) in the forest and highland zones. Most of its policy recommendations, however, continued to be couched in general terms and were not based on any specific, data-based analysis and thus were not helpful for implementation. For instance, the 1983 Agricultural Sector Report observed that the government's proposed efforts to expand the production of traditional export crops (rubber, cotton, cocoa, coffee, and to a lesser extent, palm oil) were unwarranted and that instead it needed to consolidate and reduce the underlying cost structure for export crop production. The report argued that wheat, rice, and soybean production were unable to compete with imports and therefore that the production of cereals (other than wheat), groundnuts, and rainfed rice (in the forest and highland zones) should receive priority in research and credit, input supply, and feeder roads.

The progressive reduction and aging of the agricultural labor force and the absence of planting recommendations appropriate to traditional agriculture, including animal traction and adaptive research, were seen as critical constraints on productivity. The Bank found Cameroon's mechanization policy, like that of Nigeria, to be misguided but recognized that more information was needed on the economics of estate as against smallholder production. It recommended the removal of input subsidies and a shift from public to private distribution of inputs.

The Bank continued to oppose any increase in the coverage of administered prices (then limited to cocoa, coffee, palm oil, rubber, rice, sugar, and cotton) on the grounds that past intervention had not worked, that markets are generally competitive, and that parastatals have problems with high marketing costs and uncertain payments and services.

In the 1980s the training and visit (T&V) system became an important part of the Bank's strategy, together with improvements in other agricultural services. However, numerous problems remained in consolidating and strengthening the national extension system because of the proliferation of numerous development agencies that the Bank's own project portfolio had created and expanded in the 1970s (alongside those created by other donors).

All of the Bank's smallholder projects were implemented through wholly or partly government-owned development companies. Notwithstanding the Bank's aims and criticisms of the complexity and duplication of these autonomous agencies, it consistently used them to ease project implementation and to achieve quick results, to bypass the difficulties involved in untangling functional responsibilities within the government, and to avoid the issue of developing the long-term institutional capacity of the Ministry of Agriculture to formulate and implement effective smallholder strategies.[12] Development companies became financially bloated and served only a quarter of the country's small farmers, and by the late 1980s many were abolished as part of the economic reform process.

Bank assistance. Until 1989, when Cameroon received its first structural adjustment loan, Bank assistance was heavily weighted in favor of agriculture and rural development and basic infrastructure; each of these categories accounted for more than 43 percent of total assistance during 1965–88. As in the other MADIA countries, the shares devoted to other kinds of projects, such as human resource development, were marginal. During the period 1965–88, the Bank funded twenty-four agricultural and rural development projects in Cameroon at a total cost of nearly $500 million (see table 3-8). The share of concessional (IDA) loans in this total was less than 25 percent. Of the twenty-four projects, twenty (after excluding the National Agricultural Research Project) focused exclusively on crop production. Of these, nine involved estate production (three of which had smallholder components) and eleven focused on smallholder production. All the estate projects were concerned with rubber and oil palm and accounted for more than 35 percent of total Bank assistance to agriculture and rural development in Cameroon. Among the smallholder-oriented projects, six concentrated on integrated rural development, accounting for a 23 percent share. The remaining five focused on specific crops—either cocoa or rice. A large cocoa rehabilitation loan of $103 million approved in 1988 increased the share of this smallholder crop from less than 2 percent to more than 22 percent in total Bank assistance to agriculture.

Table 3-8. Cameroon: World Bank Assistance to Agriculture, 1965–88
(millions of U.S. dollars)

Target of assistance	*Number of projects*	*Funding totals*	*Percent of total funding*	*Projects included*
Crop-oriented projects				
Cocoa	2	109.5	22.1	Cocoa, Cocoa Rehabilitation
Rice	3	34.7	7.0	SEMRY Rice, Plaine des M'bo, Second SEMRY
Oil palm	3	34.6	7.0	East Cameroon Oil Palm, CAMDEV (Supplementary), Second SOCAPALM
Rubber	3	55.8	11.2	Niete Rubber, Second HEVECAM, Third HEVECAM
Rubber and oil palm	3	86.1	17.3	CAMDEV, Second CAMDEV, Oil Palm and Rubber Consolidation
Integrated rural development	6	113.0	22.8	Rural Development Fund, Western Highlands Rural Development, Zapi Integrated Rural Development, Northern Province Rural Development, Second Western Province Rural Development, FSAR
Research	1	17.8	3.6	National Agricultural Research
Other projects				
Livestock	2	27.6	5.6	Livestock, Second Livestock
Forestry	1	17.0	3.4	Forestry
Total	24	496.1	100.0	

Source: See table 3-1.

Table 3-9. *Economic Rates of Return (ERRs) for Completed World Bank Projects*

Country	*0 percent > ERR*	*10 percent > ERR> 0 percent*	*20 percent > ERR > 10 percent*	*ERR > 20 percent*
Kenya				
	IADP	Livestock Development I	Smallholder Credit I	Tea Development I
	Group Farms	Livestock II	Forestry II	Tea Development II
	South Nyanza	Sugar Rehabilitation		Smallholder Credit II
				Tea Factory
Malawi				
		Lilongwe II	Shire II	Shire I
		Karonga I	Karonga II	Lilongwe III
		Shire III		
		NRDP I		
Tanzania				
	Kigoma Rural Development	Kilombero Sugar	Flue-cured Tobacco	Sao Hill Forestry
	National Maize		Smallholder Tea Development	
	Tabora Rural Development			
	Geita Cotton			
	Cashewnut Development			
	Tobacco Processing			
	Tobacco Handling			
	Mwanza-Shinyanga Rural Development			
	Pyrethrum			
	Fisheries Development			
	Livestock Development II			

Nigeria				
	Ondo Oil Palm Bandel Oil Palm Rice Livestock	Lafia ADP Ayangba ADP Bida ADP	Gusau ADP Gombe ADP Funtua ADP Cocoa II	Western Cocoa
Senegal				
	Siné Saloum Debi-Lampsar Irrigation Eastern Senegal Livestock Development	River Polders Sedhiou II	Agriculture Credit II Terres Neuves II	Terres Neuves I Casamance Rice
Cameroon				
	Cocoa Plaine des M'bo Rural Development Zapi Rural Development Livestock Development	CAMDEV II	CAMDEV I SOCAPALM I Niete Rubber Estate SOCAPALM II HEVECAM II Rural Development Fund Western Highlands Rural Development	SEMRY Rice I *SEMRY* Rice II

Note: The list includes only the projects that had been audited by the World Bank's Operations Evaluation Department, and therefore are the relatively earlier projects.
Source: Various project completion reports and project performance audit reports, World Bank.

In contrast, the Bank's investments in three irrigated rice projects have straddled the distinction between smallholder and plantation agriculture and have relied on capital-intensive methods of cultivation. No Bank project has concentrated exclusively on coffee or cotton—the two most important smallholder export crops after cocoa—although some of the IRDPs did include activities related to these crops.

Estate projects. The Bank became involved in plantation agriculture in Cameroon in 1967, when it assisted the Cameroon Development Corporation (CAMDEV) with financial rehabilitation and funded a seven-year program for the estate production of tree crops in the southern region of what was then West Cameroon (present-day South West Province). This was followed two years later by a loan to the Société Camerounaise de Palmeraies (SOCAPALM) for the establishment of two estates for oil palm production in what was then East Cameroon (now Littoral and Central Provinces), where, traditionally, oil palm had been a smallholder crop. Although both projects achieved modest success in raising production, they suffered from cost overruns and required further Bank financing in 1973 and 1977. The financial problems of the parastatals rested in part with the government, which had exerted tremendous pressure on them to provide physical infrastructure and social services in the sparsely populated, marginal areas of the South West Province. Clearly, estates offered fewer economies of scale than originally anticipated and were proving to be high-cost bureaucracies. Thus, in the mid-1970s, the Bank began emphasizing decentralized smallholder development in the context of a nucleus estate strategy. Estates could be used to disseminate technology and cultivation methods to neighboring areas and to serve as marketing and service centers to the outgrowers. The Bank also began emphasizing rubber development, along with oil palm.

The rubber estate projects—implemented by the Société Hévéa Cameroun (HEVECAM) in the Kribi region of the East Province—were approved in the latter half of the 1970s. They, as well as the subsequent phases of earlier oil palm projects, achieved substantial proportions of their physical planting and output targets and generated economic rates of return between 10 and 20 percent (table 3-9). The response of the smallholder components, however, was poor. Besides, all suffered from large cost overruns, and by 1982 both the rubber and oil palm producers were under severe financial strain. The Bank participated in a donor-financed joint consolidation project of the two industries to balance the deficits of the respective parastatals and redress their administrative and technical shortcomings.

Overall, the Bank's plantation projects were impeded by several obstacles. Lacking adequate microlevel information, project managers systematically overestimated production performance. The projects faced difficulties with respect to the quality of soils, suitability of terrain, attainable yields, the prevalence of plant and pest diseases, forecast international prices, and financial stability of parastatal agencies. Ethnic tensions and weak communication links restricted the interregional mobility of labor. Together with the fact that estates were located in sparsely populated areas, these problems led to a chronic shortage and high turnover of labor. Third, most of the parastatal agencies involved in plantations were poorly managed as the Bank had not devoted adequate attention to setting up long-term training and incentive systems for local managerial personnel, who used parastatal resources to support a large patronage distribution system in local communities.

Integrated rural development projects. In Cameroon, as in the other MADIA countries, the Bank's central concern in the 1970s was to promote integrated rural development projects. The Zapi Integrated Rural Development Project was located in the relatively isolated and impoverished Eastern Province, and the Western Highlands Rural Development Project in the densely populated, low-income, humid highlands of the Western Province. Both projects were approved in 1978 and used export crop parastatals to promote the development of food crops; thus they bypassed ministerial structures, especially the Ministry of Agriculture, in their operations. Similarly, the main purpose of the two Rural Development Fund projects located in the densely populated Mandara mountain area of northern Cameroon was to build institutions. They paid little attention to developing local trained manpower within the numerous regional development agencies and seriously stretched the plausibility of using parastatals for regional policy formulation.

The Zapi IRDP was undertaken against the reservations of the government. It was a complex project with many diverse social and economic activities (involving the services of five technical ministries) and required an implementation capacity well beyond the scope of Cameroon, either nationally or regionally. In the first year of operation it became evident that the project could only hope to improve the existing (French) schemes rather than cover new ground. Thus most of the project components were either abandoned altogether or seriously curtailed in the face of cost overruns, and the end result was a negative rate of return. The lack of adequate knowledge of farmers' needs and farming systems as well as organizational and management drawbacks reduced the expected benefits of the project. Limited progress was made in applied research, seed production, the construction and rehabilitation of coffee processing factories, and in the level of staff training in monitoring and evaluation. The Western Highlands Rural Development Project was designed to improve coffee production. Apart from providing rural storage, credit, and water supply, it was to strengthen the Union Centrale des Coopératives Agricoles de l'Ouest (UCCAO), the implementing agency and the apex cocoa growers' organization in Cameroon. In particular, its pest control, extension, and seed production services, as well as its field trials and demonstrations, were to be better supported. Because of implementation problems, however, the disbursement of funds was slow. The project completion report noted that most production targets had been met and a relatively high economic rate of return (between 10 and 20 percent) achieved but conceded that the project design had underestimated the obstacles to effective institution building, as well as the possibility of conflict between UCCAO and the Ministry of Agriculture over their respective roles.

Crop-specific smallholder projects. Among the first generation of smallholder-oriented projects in Cameroon were the Bank-funded projects for rice in 1972 and for cocoa in 1974. The rapid rise in urban demand for rice prompted the government and donors to invest in sophisticated irrigated rice cultivation, to ensure food self-sufficiency, and to promote employment and higher incomes in relatively underdeveloped regions such as the north. The rice scheme was implemented by the Société d'Expansion et de Modernization de la Riziculture de Yagoua (SEMRY) in 1974 in the perimeters on the Logone River, which forms the border between Cameroon and Chad. It sought to intensify rice cultivation through the introduction of pump irrigation and the rehabilitation of existing irrigation structures. The French expatriate management proved quite effective, the farmers were responsive, and double cropping proceeded much faster than foreseen. Moreover, in contrast to the situation obtaining in some of the IRDPs, strong government support existed for the project at both the national and local levels. The project recorded impressive increases in production, as yields quadrupled from 1 to 4 tons per hectare by 1980. A second project, situated 70 kilometers downstream from SEMRY I and based on a different irrigation concept (a pond gravity irrigation scheme), was implemented in 1978. Although it suffered from technical problems and a 35 percent cost overrun, like SEMRY I it performed remarkably well from an agronomic point of view.

Perhaps because of its technical excellence, the SEMRY rice scheme had a high-cost structure that rendered the output uncompetitive with imported rice at the prevailing exchange rate, although high rice prices in the 1970s appeared to suggest a favorable internal rate of return to the first SEMRY project. This problem of economic viability demonstrates Cameroon's need to adjust the exchange rate and reduce transport costs from north to south, as well as open up regional trade so that Cameroonian rice could be sold in neighboring Nigeria, instead of the distant coastal cities of Cameroon.

The Plaine des M'bo Rural Development Project was both a technical and an economic failure. The government's keenness to improve the distribution of rural income and to achieve better regional development in a remote area overshadowed the technical problems underlying the scheme. The choice of inappropriate mechanized techniques at its insistence, the problem of soil fragility, inadequate understanding of agronomic factors, among other problems, had an adverse effect on project performance. In this case, in contrast to the Zapi IRDP project, it was the Bank staff who were opposed, but they acquiesced to government demands.

Although the Bank had been advocating the development of smallholder cocoa since the early 1970s, it did not employ a consistent strategy to tackle the numerous agronomic and institutional problems confronting the small cocoa farmers until 1988. The cocoa project of 1975 aimed at improving their livelihood by rehabilitating 25,000 hectares of existing cocoa acreage and planting another 15,000 hectares with high-yielding, hybrid varieties in the Center and South Provinces. It did not, however, pay enough attention to promoting the new technical packages, or to reducing the widespread black pod disease and the critical labor shortages faced by the farmers. Coupled with erratic government policies toward industry pricing, farm inputs, and credit, these bottlenecks left the project with a negative rate of return.

The period of structural adjustment in Cameroon has seen an emphasis on four major developments: the abolition of an array of parastatals that donors helped to develop and mushroom in the 1970s, privatization of a variety of input and output marketing facilities, improvement in government services through an increased role for the T&V extension, and the involvement of the LIPVOs in agricultural services such as credit and marketing. The refusal of the French government to consider reforming the exchange rate has, however, reduced the competitiveness of export crops vis-a-vis food crops and posed a problem in resuscitating exports.

Conclusions and Policy Implications

Since the early 1970s, the Bank has consistently supported the development of smallholder agriculture in each of the MADIA countries. It has argued that smallholder agriculture can contribute to overall economic development in Kenya; it has focused government attention on the smallholders in Nigeria and Cameroon and has mobilized resources for investment in their activities; and, in general, it has continued to articulate the policies necessary for agricultural development in each MADIA country. While the Bank was slow in recognizing the fundamental importance of a macroeconomic policy environment and the role its own assistance has played in this regard, it made radical changes in its own approach to African development in the 1980s. Agricultural performance in both Nigeria and Senegal was poor but in all likelihood would have been worse in the absence of support from the Bank. Yet, with the exception of smallholder tea and coffee in Kenya or tea in Tanzania, there does not appear to have been much connection between where agricultural growth occurred in the MADIA countries and the activities that the Bank's investments supported. In general, the Bank's project portfolio performed poorly, and much of its sectoral analysis did not identify a consistent, agriculture-led strategy for long-term growth. Despite the Bank's impressive research and analytical capabilities, its economic and sectoral work did not establish strong conceptual links between recipients' macroeconomic and agricultural development strategies. Moreover, the Bank's actual lending program and policy positions often diverged considerably from its sectoral analyses. Although the occasional sectoral reports were good in some countries, analysis was by and large weak in the cases of Malawi, Cameroon, and Senegal. Thus it is not clear whether adherence to the Bank's sectoral analysis would have improved the project portfolio.

The Bank has not had a long-term strategy for broadly based growth, nor has it fully appreciated the need for the balanced accumulation of human, institutional, and technological capacity, and thus for an appropriate sequencing and phasing of investments. As a result the Bank has not—until the recent completion of the long-term perspective study and the capacity-building initiatives—paid much attention to strengthening local human and institutional capacity at the macroeconomic or sectoral level. In countries such as Nigeria and Cameroon, its operations reinforced institutions outside the normal administrative structure instead of strengthening the appropriate policymaking bodies. Moreover, Bank operations suffered from inadequate knowledge and analysis of the microlevel, location-specific constraints on long-term growth.

Adjustment lending has brought with it increased coordination among donors, although their local presence and relative strength differ, of course. The United States, for example, has performed particularly well in training. Nevertheless, donors have not yet fully exploited their comparative advantage in undertaking specific activities in support of a well-defined, long-term strategy. Instead, they have all tended to jump on the same bandwagon of integrated rural development or structural adjustment. All of these factors have reduced the benefits of their many worthwhile developmental efforts.

The reason for the massive increase in Bank assistance to the MADIA countries in the 1970s can be traced primarily to top management's initiatives in response to the 1973–74 drought and the abject poverty throughout Sub-Saharan Africa. Country-specific constraints, the Bank's rich operational experience, and the substantial expertise of its staff had less influence on the character of Bank assistance. Under the pressure to lend, the Bank opened the door to indiscriminate growth in assistance and to weak project portfolios that clearly did not reflect some of the positive features of the Bank's macroeconomic and sectoral analyses.

The Bank's concern with policy reforms in the early 1980s reflected a desire to confront the problem of country policies that discouraged broadly based growth. Nonetheless, the Bank has had limited success in convincing countries to undertake changes that they have strongly opposed—Kenya, for example, has been reluctant to liberalize grain, Tanzania to adjust the exchange rate, Malawi to limit the licensing of land for estates, and Senegal and Nigeria to remove their fertilizer subsidies. Although these are sensitive and difficult political issues, all these countries urgently need high-quality analytical support—and, most of all, they need to improve their capacity to perform the analysis themselves. The Bank has been and continues to be lax about pursuing this goal in its operations, although the recent capacity-building initiative is aimed at undertaking precisely this objective. This is an area in which bilateral donors need to work jointly with the Bank. As the foregoing discussion has demonstrated, institutional and technological problems remain by far the greatest impediment to agricultural growth. To make matters worse, the private sector and financial markets have turned out to be far weaker than had been expected.

In general, joint Bank-recipient efforts to modernize African agriculture and fine-tune policies and programs for agricultural growth will need to

- Adopt a long-term perspective (fifteen to twenty years) in articulating the requisite components and the appropriate sequencing of country-specific agricultural development strategies.
- Invest a substantial amount in human capital to create a much larger reservoir of trained local manpower for critical analytical, planning, and implementation functions.
- Establish and strengthen institutions that can provide a range of agricultural services such as agricultural research, extension, credit, and inputs essential for nurturing smallholder development.

- Expand the capacity for data collection and analysis to create a foundation of knowledge about the microlevel factors that influence producer decisions and thereby pave the way for informed and effective policymaking.
- Strengthen the local capacity to deal with science and technology.

Together with policy reform, recent efforts have focused on an agricultural services initiative, development of national agricultural research in a regional context under SPAAR, greater use of private and voluntary organizations, development of rural financial markets, and efforts to improve sustainability of agriculture. How and when these efforts will lead to self-sustaining growth remains to be seen; these various initiatives do not yet address the types of long-term development strategy issues that have been identified in this chapter as priorities, and that vary from country to country (for example, the role of low- and high-potential areas, irrigated and rainfed agriculture, large and small farmers, and so on).

Notes

1. The framework of analysis has already been explained in the Introduction and is not repeated here. The sections on Kenya, Tanzania, and Malawi are based on Uma Lele and L. Richard Meyers, *Growth and Structural Change in East Africa: Domestic Policies, Agricultural Performance, and World Bank Assistance, 1963–1986*, Parts I and II, MADIA Discussion Paper 3 (Washington, D.C.: World Bank, 1989); the section on Nigeria is based on Uma Lele, Ademola Oyejide, Balu Bumb, and Vishva Bindlish, "Nigeria's Economic Development, Agriculture's Role, and World Bank Assistance: Lessons for the Future" (Africa—Technical Department, Agriculture Department, World Bank, Washington, D.C.); the section on Senegal is based on a draft MADIA report by Sidi Jammeh, Mathurin Gbetibouo, Riall Nolan, and Uma Lele; the section on Cameroon is based on a draft MADIA report by Nicolas van de Walle. Each of these studies in turn has relied heavily on the World Bank's economic and sectoral work as reflected in Basic Economic Reports, Annual Economic Memoranda, Agricultural Sector Reports, and various project-related documents such as Staff Appraisal Reports, Supervision Reports, Project Completion Reports, and the Project Performance and Audit Reports. Field investigations, personal interviews, and interaction with the Bank's operational staff also have been invaluable sources of information.

2. See Uma Lele and Manmohan Agarwal, *Smallholder and Large-Scale Agriculture: Are There Trade-offs in Growth and Equity?* MADIA Discussion Paper 6 (Washington, D.C.: World Bank, 1989).

3. See Uma Lele, Nicolas van de Walle, and Mathurin Gbetibouo, *Cotton in Africa: An Analysis of Differences in Performance*, MADIA Discussion Paper 7 (Washington, D.C.: World Bank, 1989).

4. See Uma Lele and Ashok Subramanian, "Sectoral Strategy for Irrigation Development in Sub-Saharan Africa: Some Lessons from Experience," in Shawki Barghouti, ed., *Development of Small-Scale and Private Irrigation in Sub-Saharan Africa* (Washington, D.C.: World Bank, 1990).

5. See Lele and Meyers, *Growth and Structural Change in East Africa.*

6. The EC did initiate a coffee improvement program that resulted in a modest increase in output. See chapter 6 of this volume.

7. See World Bank, Operations Evaluation Department, *World Bank/Tanzania Relations: 1961–87,* Report 8329 (Washington, D.C., 1990).

8. Lele and Agarwal, *Smallholder and Large-Scale Agriculture.*

9. Because of the competing demands of food crop production, the lack of simple labor-saving technologies, and the lack of cash for payment to labor.

10. Taken from John Waterbury's chapter on agricultural policymaking and stagnation in Senegal in Uma Lele and Ellen Hanak, eds., "The Politics of Agricultural Policy in Africa" MADIA Working Paper (Africa—Technical Department, Agriculture Division, World Bank, Washington, D.C.).

11. See Valerie Kelly and Christopher Delgado, "Agricultural Performance under Structural Adjustment," in Christopher Delgado and Sidi Jammeh, eds., *The Political Economy of Senegal under Structural Adjustment* (New York: Praeger, 1991).

12. The 1984 Bank report on Cameroon development and planning issues concluded that "the state societies have failed to fully play their expected role and have been plagued with managerial problems. Their complex relationship with government, which finances and controls them, and with other institutions has resulted in cumbersome procedures which reduce operational efficiency."

4 *Danish Development Assistance to Tanzania and Kenya, 1962–85: Its Importance to Agricultural Development*

Ellen Hanak and Michael Loft

DANISH SUPPORT for agriculture in Africa between 1962 and 1985 went mainly to Tanzania and Kenya.[1] Over these two decades, agriculture received a quarter or more of the total aid Denmark provided for these two countries. Although the Danish International Development Agency (DANIDA) targeted only a few main agricultural activities in each country, its overall support for agriculture was quite diverse: It encompassed roughly sixty individual projects and programs covering a broad spectrum of crop and livestock activities, as well as various multisectoral and infrastructural activities closely related to agriculture.

The Danish Aid Program

Neither the Danish government nor the Danish public considers Denmark an important source of agricultural assistance. Danish aid in both Tanzania and Kenya is usually identified with social services, health, education, and water supply, largely because of the different ways in which DANIDA has approached these two kinds of activities. In the 1970s and 1980s DANIDA's strategy was to provide guidelines on the kinds of assistance it considered most appropriate (such as preventive rather than curative health care) and then to identify the particular projects or programs that fit into the country's overall sectoral plans. No such sectoral perspective was adopted for agriculture. The content of DANIDA's diverse agricultural portfolio appears to have been determined through niche identification—that is, by selecting specific groups or activities to support, rather than by carefully analyzing which activities would contribute most to agricultural development. These informal guidelines on agricultural aid (which focused on the poorer, more marginal smallholders, including women) only partly account for the composition of that aid. Much of it was also shaped by what the Danish economy had to offer in technology or inputs.

In seeking to assess the contribution of Danish aid to agricultural development, this study takes a broad view of what constitutes success. The question is not only whether a given project has succeeded in achieving its stated objectives (typically having to do with augmenting productive capacity or improving living standards in the target area) but also whether it has helped to relieve some critical bottleneck or constraint—be it institutional, technological, or financial. Thus an investment generally regarded as successful may be judged differently in this study. For example, a processing plant or an educational institution may be completed on time and at the planned cost, yet its output may be largely irrelevant for the country's development. Conversely, other investments falling short of their designers' expectations nevertheless might have been just the right effort at the right time. For readers unfamiliar with Danish aid, this first section provides an overview of the origins and buildup of the Danish aid program, the domestic constituencies that have shaped it, and the administrative guidelines by which DANIDA operates.

Forms of Aid

Denmark's total development assistance is evenly divided between multilateral and bilateral aid. Half the bilateral budget goes to untied grant aid (project aid and technical assistance, in DANIDA parlance) and half to tied soft loans (financial aid or state loans). Grants and loans are restricted to developing countries. Since the early 1980s, financial aid has also regularly included tied grants for Tanzania and Bangladesh, the two main recipients of DANIDA aid, both of which qualify as least developed countries by United Nations standards. A portion of untied bilateral aid is reserved for joint Nordic projects, which are governed by the five Nordic countries together (Denmark, Sweden, Norway, Finland, and Iceland) but are each administered on a day-to-day basis by one of the member countries. Within the multilateral allocation, Denmark has a group of projects known as multi-bi, which are administered by a specialized United Nations agency but draw upon earmarked Danish funds. In 1984 untied grants constituted 35 percent of all Danish aid, or somewhat more than their formula share of 25 percent; Nordic projects accounted for 5 percent of this, or 1.7 percent of total aid. Tied bilateral aid was nearly 22 percent of the total, multilateral aid 43 percent; and 8 percent of multilateral aid, or 4 percent of total aid, went to multi-bi projects.

Untied grants typically go to relatively small projects (those requiring several hundred thousand to several million United States dollars) with a large technical assistance component and an agricultural or social focus. Nordic projects share this basic orientation, although they tend to be somewhat larger. The tied loans are usually substantially larger (about $10 million) and are geared toward the installation of Danish capital goods. Such projects are typically industrial or agroindustrial, although they also may be civil engineering projects such as urban water systems. The tied-loan projects make use of teams of Danish technical experts, who are hired on contract through the private Danish firm that wins the project contract rather than provided as DANIDA technical assistance. Tied grants have consisted mainly of large shipments of commodities produced in Denmark, such as fertilizer. Multi-bi projects resemble the untied portfolio in size and scope.

The Aid Constituency

To a large extent, Danish efforts to assist developing countries are an outgrowth of the political support behind Danish aid. Political factors have determined not only the level of aid but also the forms in which that aid is allocated, its objectives, and the resource limitations that influence decisions on specific projects. Three kinds of interests have been paramount: foreign policy interests, philanthropic interests, and commercial interests—in that order of importance and arrival on the scene.

Foreign policy interests provided the initial impulse for the Danish aid program. Multilateral aid to the predecessor of the United Nations Development Programme (UNDP) began in 1949 as a symbolic political gesture, since Denmark was still a net recipient of aid through the Marshall Plan and the World Bank. In the early 1960s Denmark launched its program of bilateral aid as a way of establishing direct diplomatic links with some newly independent countries. In addition, bilateral aid had the potential of engaging popular support through national identification with Danish efforts. Such support was needed to sustain a planned increase in multilateral aid.

Although philanthropic interests had been active earlier through nongovernmental aid activities carried out by various religious and humanitarian organizations, they had little role in changing the Danish political consciousness until the early 1960s, when the foreign policy impetus coincided with the political consolidation of the welfare state. Among government leaders, a bilateral venture into official development assistance was viewed as a natural extension into the global arena of the state's policy of domestic equity.

To secure popular support for this policy, the government mobilized the existing humanitarian organizations in a massive national campaign to raise private funds for the benefit of the poor countries, to be matched by state funds. Rarely has a cause received stronger and broader support in Denmark. In early 1962 all the political parties, radio and television, most newspapers, labor unions, industrial organizations, the cooperative movement, churches, and a string of prominent people inundated the public with pro-aid arguments.

This campaign reached a political climax in March 1962, when the parliament unanimously adopted the Bill on Technical Cooperation with the Developing Countries, signaling the beginning of Denmark's commitment to bilateral aid. The broad parliamentary consensus that marked the passage of this legislation has more or less endured. Even compared with other elements of Danish foreign policy such as security and trade, aid policy stands out as having had an unusually broad political base.

In contrast to the pattern observed in former colonial powers, commercial interests in Denmark were relatively passive players in the early aid program. The initial enthusiasm among agricultural groups for a state initiative to establish model dairy and breeding farms soon waned (in part because the farms failed to generate demand for the export of grade cattle). Since then Danish agriculture has focused on the disposal of surplus produce through multilateral programs—a solution that has kept down the pressure for a bilateral food aid program.

The involvement of Danish industry remained insignificant until after 1966, when conditions on the tied state loans set up in the 1962 legislation were substantially softened. This was triggered by strong criticism of the Danish aid level during the annual aid review conducted by the Development Assistance Committee (DAC) in 1965, after the United States had expressed concern about allied buden sharing. At the time, state loans were the only conceivable channel for increasing disbursements, since the aid agency was already heavily constrained by the lack of manpower needed to administer regular project aid. Thus foreign policy interests again took the lead, although in the ensuing years commercial interests gradually gathered strength and in 1977 publicly demanded a larger hand in the aid disbursements. Times had changed, and with the general recession in the developed world, Danish industry took the position that since help was needed on the home front, a greater share of aid should be tied.

By incorporating a broad range of interests into its aid constituency, Denmark has been able to rise from one of DAC's worst performers in the mid-1960s to one of the best. Danish aid as a share of GDP reached the goal of 0.7 percent by 1978. In March 1985 parliament passed a resolution asking the government to steadily increase official development assistance (ODA) from the current 0.77 percent to 1 percent by 1992. These increases have taken place despite a long period of general retrenchment in public expenditures. The philanthropic interests have weathered the government's occasional threats to make small cuts in the aid budget.

At least as remarkable as the level of Danish aid is the stability of its constituency. This has been achieved primarily by giving each of the three leading interests a large stake in one form of aid: Multilateral aid continues to secure a high profile for Danish foreign policy objectives in international forums; untied grant aid maintains its philanthropic momentum thanks to generous appropriations for educating the public about the work DANIDA is doing in recipient countries; and tied aid is linked to the commercial interests through project identification and procurement.

Untied project aid looms large in the public limelight, whereas tied state loans tend to have a low, behind-the-scenes profile. This is reflected in the public literature disseminated by DANIDA, such as its annual reports; the untied project portfolio is given high visibility, whereas the uses of state loans are mentioned in passing, and this only since the late 1970s.

Guiding Principles

As a result of the broadly based philanthropic support for aid in Denmark, aid allocations concentrated on alleviating poverty well before basic needs became the center of international attention in the mid-1970s. For untied project aid, poverty alleviation has often been a sieve through which potential projects are run; more and more in the 1970s DANIDA sifted out the relatively well-off areas of a country when deciding which projects to fund. For state loans intended to export Danish technology, a direct application of this principle to project selection would have put insurmountable obstacles in the way of disbursement, so the principle was applied instead to the selection of countries. The original intention that state loans would be directed to middle-income countries, and untied project aid to the poorest ones, was dismissed. In time, state loans went only to low-income countries (corresponding to those eligible for IDA credits).

The second guiding principle—noninterference—stems from the fact that Denmark knows what it is like to be a small country and therefore is sensitive to external compromises of sovereignty. The idea behind this principle is that the recipient's priorities and strategies should shape the content of Danish aid. In practice, this has been less important for untied project aid, which DANIDA personnel have always helped design and monitor, than for state loans, in which what is known in DANIDA as the "folded-arm" policy generally persists to this day. Assuming that it was up to recipients to decide what they wanted to use the loans for (within the bounds of what the Danish economy could offer), the aid agency was initially responsible merely for formalizing the agreement between the recipient government and the Danish suppliers, who did their own outreach work. Because of a growing concern about the effectiveness of these loans, DANIDA has become more directly involved in appraisal work, particularly since the late 1970s. But a distinction is still made between untied projects and tied aid in the degree of monitoring that DANIDA provides and, indeed, in the degree of ownership it feels. State loan administrators will maintain, for instance, that DANIDA is not legally responsible for implementing these ventures, which are only rarely subject to an interim or ex post evaluation.

The third guiding principle—arising as it does from the national self-image—is more amorphous. It centers on the question, what elements of Denmark's own development history can be transferred to those to whom it is giving aid? The Danish self-image stems from two formative experiences: the agricultural-based grass roots movement in the latter part of the nineteenth century and the development of the industrial-based welfare state in the postwar period. What the Danes see as the driving force in their own history is human capital—which is not surprising in a country with scant natural resources.

The paradigms that have emerged from this history have both a sectoral focus (on education, agricultural—especially animal—production, and the development of social infrastructure) and a cultural focus (on participatory processes). Channeling assistance through cooperatives, one of Denmark's own democratizing institutions, is favored, as is reliance on other local groups, such as village organizations.

Administration

In keeping with the initial foreign policy impetus of the bilateral aid program, Danish aid continues to be administered under the auspices of the Ministry of Foreign Affairs. As with other bilateral agencies, this arrangement allows for diplomatic concerns to override the agency's professional judgment. Another ramification of DANIDA's position in the Foreign Ministry is that it is strongly inclined to avoid conflict. This is in keeping with what political scientists refer to as the "pilot fish" behavior of small powers such as Denmark. Such a posture runs counter to the use of policy conditionality in aid.[2]

Within DANIDA, the staff is composed of more regular foreign service officials than is the case in some other bilateral agencies, such as the U.S. Agency for International Development (USAID). Virtually all managers come from the ranks of the foreign service; technical input on project design and implementation is provided by a corps of advisers from professional fields, and administrative responsibilities are handled by a corps of project officers (special *medarbejdere*). A few technical advisers have moved gradually into managerial positions.

Two aspects of the staffing of DANIDA have important implications for the aid portfolio. The first is that it has been chronically understaffed, with staff increases lagging behind increases in the aid budget. Since unspent funds lapse at the end of each fiscal year, it has been necessary to find efficient methods of disbursing funds. The state loan office has been characterized as the most efficient in this respect, although in recent years an emphasis on effectiveness has led to sizable increases in this office, which got by with a handful of staff until the late 1970s.

The second and less often noted aspect of DANIDA's staff relates to the professions represented. A high proportion of managers and technical advisers have a background that emphasizes casework, the former in law and the latter in engineering. As a result of this orientation, attention has focused more on projects rather than on program, sectoral, or macroeconomic matters. Social scientists, whose training provides a more systemic orientation, are relatively underrepresented among the professional ranks and few have been assigned to sectoral or comprehensive lines of analysis. DANIDA has had very little in-house capacity to view project activities from a sectoral or countrywide perspective.

DANIDA's base of knowledge has of necessity been an eclectic one, with ideas for projects and programs coming from a wide range of international sources, including the experience of other donors. The systematic use of feedback from its own project experience began only recently with the establishment of an evaluation unit, which in addition to applying evaluation standards has been formalizing appraisal guidelines. The gradual decentralization to the resident missions in the four main recipient countries—Tanzania, Kenya, India, and Bangladesh—that began in the late 1970s has helped DANIDA become more flexible in responding to local requirements and to apply in its work the practical experiences of other donors.

Programming Constraints

The main pressure on administrators of Danish aid is to disburse an ever-increasing amount of aid. This pressure is countered, and complicated, by various constraints. First is the external accountability requirement. Public reports from the state's auditor general, in particular, have brought to light implementation problems, including those associated with state loans, that had earlier been outside the scope of inquiry. In the case of untied projects, this has led to pressures to increase the monitoring function of technical assistance and to build up implementing units, parallel to the regular government institutions, that can keep better accounts for the Danish taxpayer. In the case of state loans, the one accountability element that has always been present is a "brick and mortar" (*mur og nagelfast*) rule, under which funds were not to go to items that had a resale potential, such as bulk commodities or freighters.

A second constraint is the written and unwritten rules of tying by source. The written rules are the basis for the division between the tied state loans and untied project grants. Tying has been justified traditionally with the argument that in its absence the former colonial powers would have had an unfair advantage in getting business from the recipient countries. More recently, Denmark has taken the position that it would untie all of its aid if other donors would do so.

When the philanthropic interests objected to the additional costs of the tied aid, the problem was elegantly resolved by the enactment of the principle that tied aid can only be used for those items in which Denmark is more or less competitive internationally (although international competitive bidding is not in fact used to ascertain this). Unwittingly, this principle, combined with the brick and mortar rule, had the effect of eliminating a large pool of those items in which the Danish economy did have an export capacity (Denmark itself being a net capital importer and a commodity and service exporter).

A third constriction of the potential basket of tied DANIDA activities stems from the personnel constraints in the administration of state loans. Because DANIDA wants to involve experienced firms that can design and implement large projects (in the interests of keeping DANIDA disbursement-efficient), the spoils of tying have in practice been limited to an elite group of no more than fifty large export-oriented Danish firms dealing mostly in state-of-the-art technology, which have the surplus to invest in exploratory field visits.

The rule that applies to grant aid, which is in principle untied, is an unwritten one. Practice does not, however, fully accord with principle. With some standard exceptions (such as vehicles, which Denmark does not produce), any hardware that is needed preferably should be purchased in Denmark.[3] From a strategic point of view, what is more important than the possible variance with an internationally competitive price is the element of self-selection that accompanies project design; in fact, it is difficult to get a project with a substantial hardware component approved if the items needed are not produced (at a reasonable cost) in Denmark.

The other unwritten rule of grant aid relates to the use of technical assistance, the recruitment of which is generally limited to Denmark, or at most Scandinavia—with the obvious effect that projects (which typically have a technical assistance component) must be designed to conform to the Danish labor market. Among other things, this puts constraints on the kind of agricultural projects that DANIDA can approve, given the short supply of agricultural economists and crop specialists. The same principle applies to fellowships.

Disbursement flows are also constrained by the selection process for recipients. As already noted, poverty criteria have been applied rather rigidly to determine which countries are eligible for state loans.

For the administratively intensive untied grant aid, DANIDA has found it advantageous since the early 1970s to concentrate on a few main recipients, which together receive more than half of all Danish bilateral aid. The considerations that led it to include the two East African countries in this group and the broad characteristics of the Danish aid portfolios in these countries are the subject of the next section.

Aid to Tanzania and Kenya

It is probably more correct to say that Tanzania and Kenya chose Denmark than vice versa.

Country Selection

Tanzania and Kenya were part of a larger pool of potential bilateral aid recipients that Denmark approached at the beginning of the 1960s. Ghana had been at the top of this list, and Nigeria was another option. Neither worked out, as far as can be gleaned, because they did not take Denmark seriously as a donor, hardly responding to the official query. Tanzania, in contrast, responded with an elaborate project proposal (the Kibaha Educational Center) when approached about the possibility of a joint Scandinavian project, beginning a relationship with Denmark that would become increasingly amicable over the years.

The reasons for Kenya's selection were less clear-cut. A brush with a Francophone country (through a Red Cross hospital in Zaire) had convinced Danish aid administrators that a main recipient had to be Anglophone. Scandinavian Airways had opened up a flight connection to Nairobi. Jomo Kenyatta had attended a Danish international folk high school, and Tom Mboya had toured Scandinavia on behalf of the Kenyan cooperative movement. Kenya joined Tanzania and Uganda in the partly Danish-inspired East African Community.[4] Perhaps the most important reason, however, suggested by several of the key actors at the time, was rather more romantic. A Danish author, Karen Blixen (better known outside of Denmark as Isak Dinesen), had been one of many Danish settlers in Kenya and had managed through some of her works to establish a sentimental bond (admittedly unilateral) between her wide readership and Kenya. Fittingly, the first Danish project in Kenya was the restoration of her former farm building and its conversion into Karen College, a school for home economics teachers.

A reference to the total disbursements to the two countries (figure 4-1) reveals the evolving profile of their aid relationship with Denmark. Until the early 1970s, both received much the same level of emphasis in the DANIDA portfolio. From 1973 on, Tanzania emerged as the favored country, receiving in some years more than twice as much aid as Kenya. In the early 1980s, the large jump in Denmark's aid to Tanzania was in contrast to the already declining trend of most other major donors.[5] Denmark, too, decreased its real aid disbursements to

Figure 4-1. DANIDA *Disbursements to Tanzania and Kenya, 1962–84*

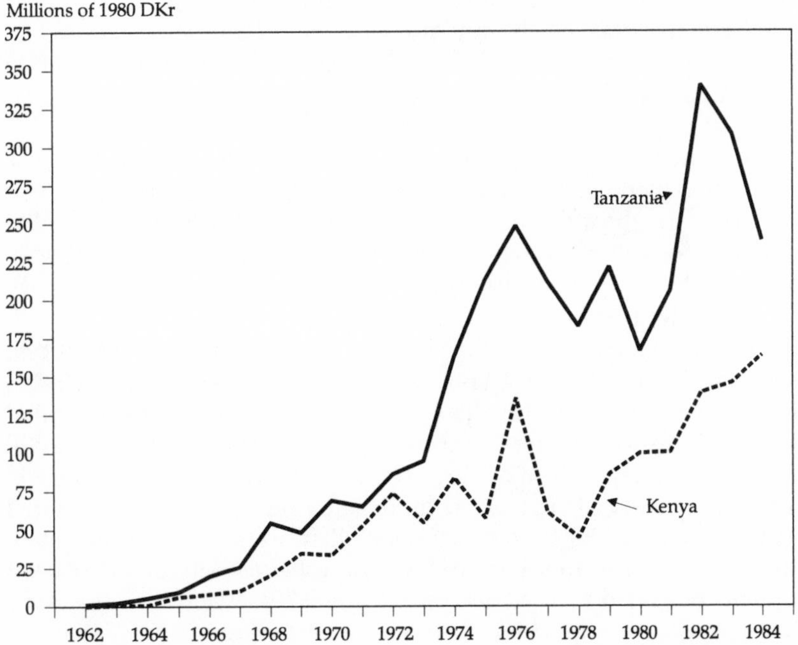

Note: Amounts for 1978 represent disbursements over nine months (April–December). *Source*: Ellen Hanak and Michael Loft, "Danish Development Assistance to Tanzania and Kenya, 1962–1985: Its Importance to Agricultural Development," MADIA Working Paper, (Africa—Technical Department, Agriculture Division, World Bank, Washington, D.C., 1987).

Tanzania in the mid-1980s. Aid to Kenya has shown a slower but steady increase in real disbursements since the relationship began.

The difference in the pattern of assistance to these two countries has had a great deal to do with the political basis of support for Danish aid in general. Tanzania's rhetoric on the primacy of welfare considerations meshed very well with the Danish philanthropic interest in aid; Julius Nyerere himself came to be perceived as a kind of social democrat, not an unfortunate perception in the era of social democratic hegemony in Denmark. Kenya, meanwhile, encountered what could almost be called public disapproval in the 1970s, with various groups in the philanthropic lobby actually suggesting that aid to Kenya be discontinued. The image problem stemmed from perceptions of Kenya as an affluent society, in which the government and the upper classes were unconcerned with basic needs and poverty.

The effect of these impulses and perceptions on the administration of aid to the two countries might be summarized as greater or lesser laissez-faire regarding the precise use of Danish funds. The basic orientation of the Tanzanian government was regarded with approval, so it was entrusted with more aid decisions. In Kenya, DANIDA took a more active role as the initiator of projects and the guardian of the focus on poverty. This difference was evident from the attention DANIDA paid to the selection of geographical areas and target groups in Kenya in comparison with Tanzania.

The laissez-faire quality of DANIDA's programming in Tanzania was heightened by the fact that the country also became a leading recipient of state loans during the 1970s. Danish industry benefited from the general goodwill toward the country, getting approvals for largely unscrutinized investments in industry (cement) and agroindustry (sugar). In Kenya, however, DANIDA was for a time reluctant to push for large state loan agreements because of some early experiences that went against the grain of Danish ethics. This difference is reflected in figure 4-2, which indicates the share of the various aid forms in total disbursements to the two countries. Since the early 1980s, Denmark has become more critical of Tanzania's policy environment and more questioning about its use of aid funds, although Tanzania still counts Denmark among its friendly donors.[6] It has also become explicitly concerned with addressing production problems—an area that DANIDA had relegated to the back seat in the 1970s, when its image was that of a leading supporter of social infrastructure.

The Recipient View

Not surprisingly, Denmark has been a more important donor for Tanzania than for Kenya—not only because of the amount of aid

Figure 4-2. Total DANIDA Aid by Form, 1962–84

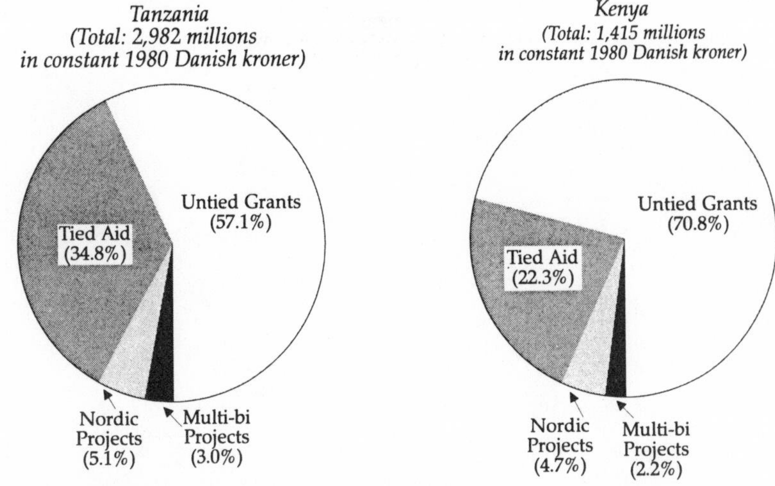

Source: See figure 4-1.

disbursed (it has provided 6.9 percent of total ODA to Tanzania and ranked fifth among donors for the period 1970–84) but also because of the strong signals it sent out indicating its fundamental sympathy with Tanzanian ideals and strategies. As keen managers of their country's relations with different donors, Tanzanian officials recognized the Danish enthusiasm for social infrastructure programs, and they let the Danes know that they looked to them for a sizable contribution in this area.

Denmark has been less significant in Kenya (ranking tenth among donors for 1970–84, with 4.9 percent of total ODA). As a result, Kenyan officials have a somewhat more vague concept of what Danish aid might offer. The Kenyan government has always been amenable to proposed poverty-oriented projects, however, since regional distribution has been an important part of the official Kenyan platform since the early 1970s.

During the recent economic crisis, the two governments reacted quite differently to Danish aid. Because of overall fiscal concerns, Kenyan officials have been somewhat reluctant to accept aid-financed loans, even on terms as soft as the Danish state loans (which have an 86 percent grant element). This may help to explain the slow pace with which DANIDA has been able to negotiate new loans now that it has a renewed interest in building up a Kenyan loan portfolio. However, the same expenditure rationalization program has led the Kenyans to welcome the addition of grant aid to items on the recurrent

Figure 4-3. DANIDA *Aid to Tanzania and Kenya by Sector, 1962–84*

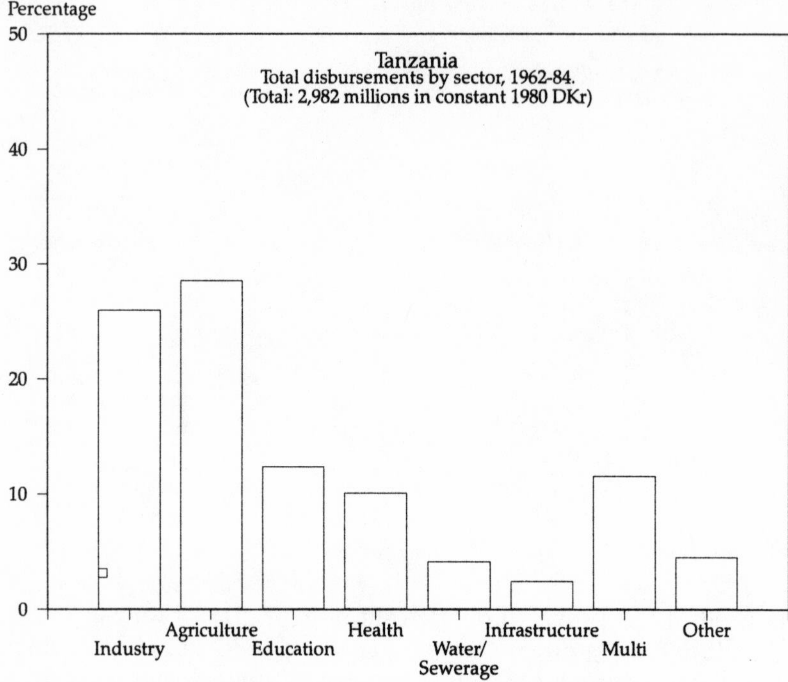

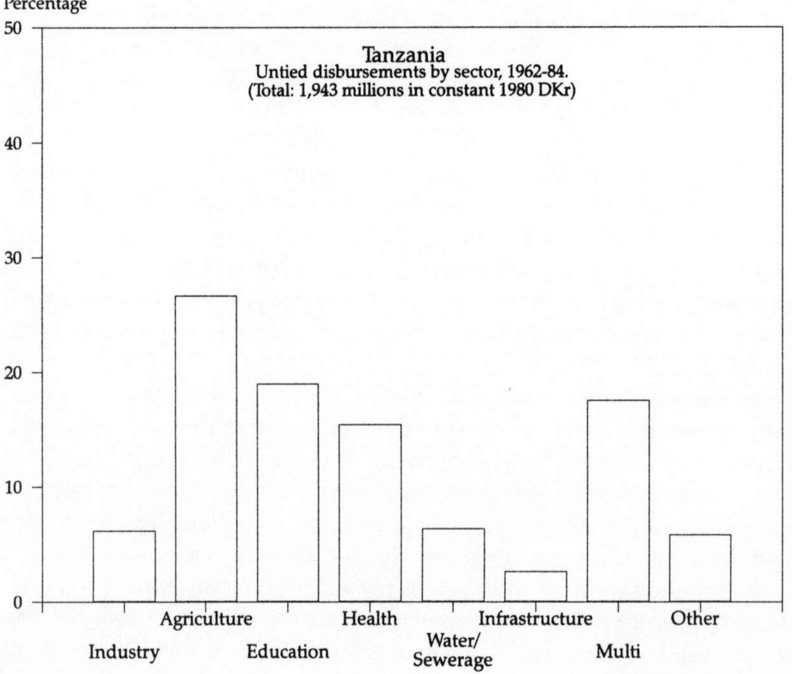

Source: See figure 4-1.

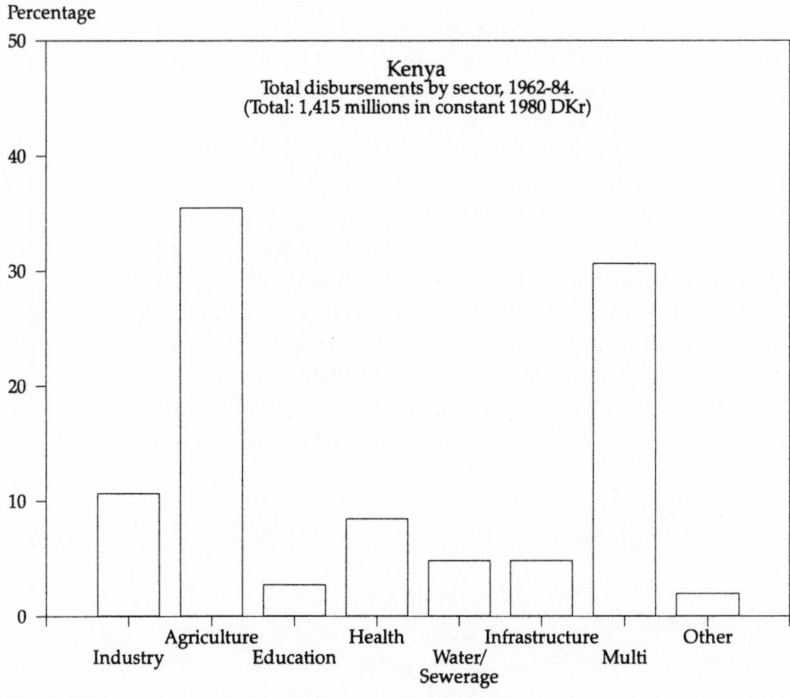
Percentage
50
40
30
20
10
0
Kenya
Total disbursements by sector, 1962-84.
(Total: 1,415 millions in constant 1980 DKr)
Industry
Agriculture
Education
Health
Water/
Sewerage
Infrastructure
Multi
Other

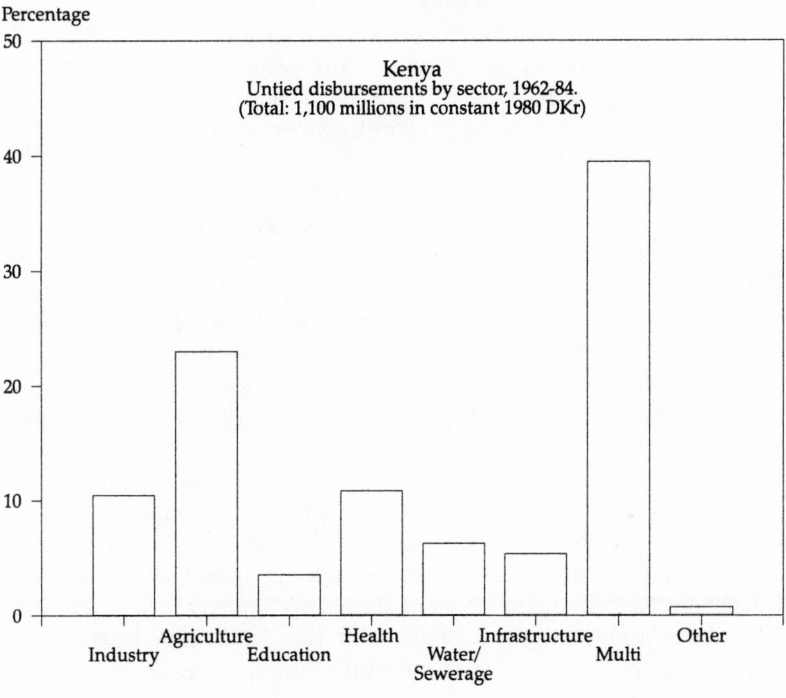
Percentage
50
40
30
20
10
0
Kenya
Untied disbursements by sector, 1962-84.
(Total: 1,100 millions in constant 1980 DKr)
Industry
Agriculture
Education
Health
Water/
Sewerage
Infrastructure
Multi
Other

budget (such as maintenance). The Kenyans have praised the Danes for their flexible approach to this matter.

In Tanzania, all Danish aid is now on a full grant basis. Denmark (together with the other Nordic countries) has distinguished itself in not joining the bilateral donors who pressed the Tanzanians for an agreement with the International Monetary Fund (IMF). Although Denmark has certainly been less harsh in its criticism of the government's policies than most other major donors, the fact that it has expressed any criticism came as a surprise to the Tanzanians, who saw this as the beginning of a more hardline attitude. They were disappointed not only about the cutback in aid that occurred when Tanzania refused to rechannel some Danish project aid to support imports in conflict with its own stated policy of structural adjustment, but also about Denmark's refusal to provide massive support for the sugar and cement industries without certain policy conditions.

Sectoral Patterns

The composition of the aid portfolios to the two countries is shown in figure 4-3. Agriculture accounted for a quarter or more of each country's share in Danish assistance programs. At the same time, the sectoral breakdowns correspond quite closely to Denmark's philanthropic agenda in their emphasis on the rural poor, through smallholder projects, and support for a wide range of social services. Indeed, DANIDA's combined support to Tanzania's social services (health, education, and water) currently amounts to 41 percent of its untied aid to that country.

The total disbursements are more likely to be of interest to the recipient countries and to others in the donor community who do not have Denmark's reason to distinguish among kinds of aid. These pies are significantly larger: by 30 percent for Kenya, and by 50 percent for Tanzania. It should be noted that the apparent larger concentration in the Kenyan portfolio on agriculture rather than on multisectoral activities is somewhat deceptive—since many if not most of the multisectoral disbursements are directly related to agriculture (the largest two items in this category being technical assistance and a project known as the Rural Development Fund). The Tanzanian portfolio, however, changes completely when loans, too, are included: Industry is on a par with social services, closely rivaling agriculture for first place. The difference hinges on the end uses of state loans in the two countries. In Kenya, the loans went almost exclusively to agroprocessing. Although this was also a facet of the Tanzanian loans, they focused primarily on industrial investments—specifically in cement.

Aid to the Agricultural Sector

The aggregate figures give the impression that agriculture fares about the same in Tanzania as in Kenya. Below the surface, however, are some pronounced differences.

Comparing the Two Country Portfolios

Foremost among these differences is the pattern of intrasectoral allocations. Figure 4-4 shows agricultural aid grouped by primary product and function. These categories are by no means the only ones the data fit into (extension, for example, often appears among functional breakdowns of agricultural aid), but given DANIDA's aid patterns, they provide some workable aggregates. Note that the scales are different and reflect the smaller overall size of the Kenyan program.

The first point to note concerns livestock, which accounts for more than half of total DANIDA aid to Kenya, but only a tenth of that to Tanzania. Tanzania has received some processing investment (in dairy activities), but more support has been to education—specifically, for a veterinary faculty at the agricultural university. By far the most funds in Kenya have gone to agroprocessing (in the dairy and meat industries), particularly to smallholder production and research.

Crop activities clearly dominate the Tanzanian portfolio, accounting for more than half of total resources. The functional orientation of both these and the nonspecific activities in the two countries is somewhat similar, with substantial aid going to crop processing (sugar or grain), financial transfers (to the smallholders' development banks), administration (principally to the renowned Nordic cooperative projects), production (especially input supply), and education (support is given to each country's principal agricultural faculty). Tanzania also received a fair amount of support for crop-related research through a Nordic project administered by Finland.

The two country programs differ in yet another respect. The far larger disbursements to Tanzanian crop and nonspecific activities mask the fact that the Kenyan program has required much greater administrative resources from DANIDA. Most of the Tanzanian program came in the form of "bulk aid"—large shipments of chemical inputs and large checks to the rural development bank. Even projects such as the above-named Nordic research project and the National Food Strategy Project (which falls under the policy category) were more in the character of bulk aid from the standpoint of DANIDA's administrative input, since they consisted of little else than signing over checks and an occasional site visit or briefing. The Kenyan program has required much more regular, individual attention that has

Figure 4-4. DANIDA *Agricultural Aid to Tanzania and Kenya by Product and Function, 1962–84*

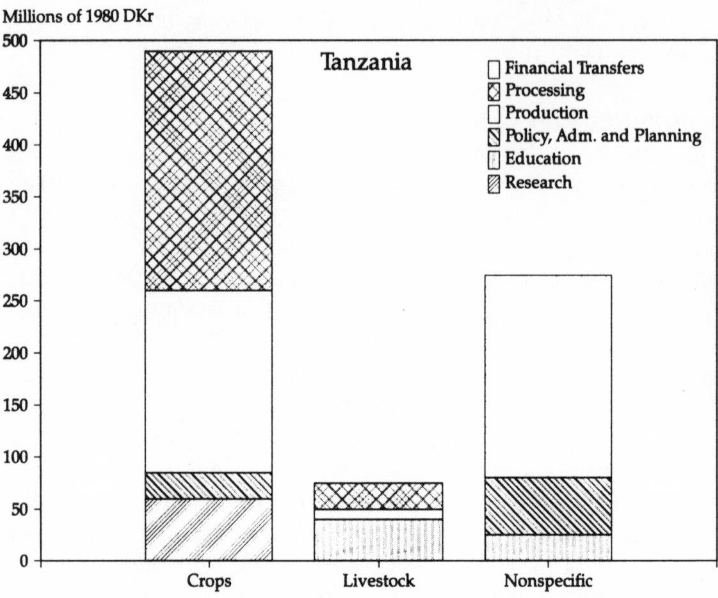

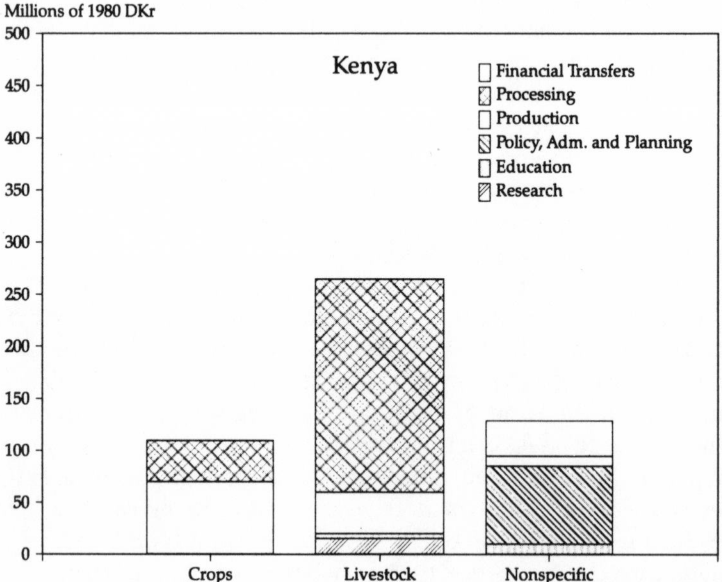

Source: See figure 4-1.

given DANIDA a better knowledge base from which to develop this portfolio.

It would appear that some of this difference in administrative intensity had more to do with Danish sensibilities regarding the two countries than any inherent differences in their need for close scrutiny. When Kenya came to be suspected in Danish pro-aid circles of questionable motives on the issue of income distribution in the early 1970s, DANIDA's response was to concentrate increasingly on the poorer segments of the population; this brought the details of aid activities in Kenya under closer scrutiny. In contrast, Tanzania's overall policy framework (or at least its expressed goals) was considered fully appropriate from the standpoint of Danish concerns about target groups. This, in turn, probably led to greater confidence that Tanzanian allocation procedures would be appropriate as well.

Important as Danish attitudes were, certain characteristics of agriculture in the two recipient countries may have also played a role in the selection of activities—and certainly in the relative effectiveness of these activities. For the purposes of the analysis that follows, it is useful to note two kinds of characteristics: (1) the kind of resource base and (2) the nature of the sectoral and macroeconomic environment. The first is of fundamental importance in identifying the means and objectives of aid intervention (for example, it is impossible to help a target group raise its income-earning potential without knowledge of its resource constraints). The second is essential not only in shaping the incentive structure for individual farmers but also in determining the extent to which project assistance is a viable form of intervention under prevailing economic and institutional circumstances.[7]

The resource base. Although Tanzania and Kenya are neighbors and grow many of the same crops (coffee, tea, cotton, pyrethrum, maize, wheat, rice, and sugar, among others), their resource bases differ, primarily with respect to the availability of arable land. It is difficult to make precise comparisons, but it can be said that Kenya's land resource base is only a small portion (4.2 percent) of its total area, yet high-quality land (zones I and II) seems more abundant in that country than in Tanzania.[8] High-value coffee, tea, dairying, and pyrethrum do best on this land. In Kenya, such areas (and crops) have enjoyed sharp increases in productivity and output since independence (1963). They lie essentially in Central Province and in the higher-elevated and better-watered parts of Eastern, Rift, Nyanza, and Western provinces.[9] Tanzania has some pockets of high-quality land in the northeast near the Kenyan border (Moshi, Arusha), in parts of Kagera in the northwest, and in the Southern Highlands (in parts of Mbeya region and

Mbinga district). All the activities noted above except dairying also grew in these areas, but the pace began to trail off by the early 1970s.

Tanzania has more vast tracts of what is typically called medium-quality land (zones III and IV), suitable for rainfed cultivation of various annual food crops, cotton, tobacco, and certain perennials such as cashews and sisal. This kind of land was in many respects the engine of growth in Tanzania in the 1950s and 1960s, when cotton, tobacco, and cashews turned in an impressive performance following the expansion of the areas under cultivation. In Kenya, nearly 60 percent of what has been classified as arable land, or about one-fourth of the total land area, is clearly marginal in character—it is semiarid or arid and thus the prospects for rainfed agriculture are rather poor. Cash-cropping in the few areas of medium potential in Kenya (devoted mostly to cotton and cashews) never took off in the same way as in Tanzania. By the 1970s, however, the situation in Tanzania also took a turn for the worse, in some cases with drastic declines in output.

It is more difficult to compare the dynamics of food crop production, given the high proportion allocated to subsistence or marketed through unofficial channels. Kenya's areas of medium potential (especially in Rift Valley) and those with high potential (the well-watered areas of Western Province) experienced a sharp increase in productivity with the introduction of hybrid maize in the mid-1960s. In the late 1970s Tanzania's Southern Highland regions (Mbeya, Rukwa, Ruvuma, and Iringa) began undergoing a similar change, which may turn out to be more extensive than that in Kenya.

The livestock industry in the two countries is also quite different, inasmuch as Kenya has had the resource base in the areas of high potential to develop an advanced, monetized dairy industry based on grade cattle, stall feeding, and regular purchases by the dairy cooperative network. In the Tanzanian highlands, there are traces of a dairy economy, although the output is essentially for the local market. Most of Tanzania's areas of medium potential are unsuitable for cattle because of tsetse infestation. In both countries, most cattle are kept in indigenous herds tended by pastoralist and agropastoralist groups in the semiarid stretches of Kenya's Rift Valley, Eastern, and Coast provinces and Tanzania's Central Plateau. So far little has been done in either country to draw these groups into the market economy.

Future prospects will undoubtedly depend in part on population factors. In Tanzania, the highlands are already quite densely populated and intensively farmed, but the medium-quality areas seem to offer considerable potential for expansion at the extensive margin. This may well be the only viable option at the moment for expanding production, since most of the improved technologies available at present have increased yields but little, typically at the expense of increasing risks. The stumbling block to expansion at the extensive margin is in part an administrative one, in that the present location of many villages prevents the farming population from moving out onto unutilized land.

Extreme population pressure in the highlands of Kenya has been pushing cultivators onto marginal soils, for which there are few known technologies. Because of this severe land crunch, coupled with a population growth rate of about 4 percent a year, Kenyan officials have been conscious of the need to create employment as much as to encourage further growth.[10]

The concentration of Kenyan land resources in a relatively small part of the country, consisting for the most part of contiguous areas, has not been without its advantages from an administrative and infrastructural standpoint. With most of its surplus-producing land spread out over a vast area, Tanzania's agricultural economy has suffered to a far greater extent from high transport costs and from breakdowns in the marketing and transport systems. The costs in moving maize from the main surplus areas in the Southern Highlands of Tanzania to the population centers have been nearly prohibitive, whereas in Kenya maize can be moved with relative ease and at reasonable cost from the surplus areas in the west to Nairobi. In addition to having these natural advantages, Kenya was much better endowed with both a physical and an administrative infrastructure, inherited from the settler-based commercial farming economy of the colonial period and the colonial government's strategy for coping with the state of emergency under the Mau Mau during the 1950s, when it added substantially to the transportation network in smallholder areas, particularly in Central Province.

Sectoral and macroeconomic characteristics. Two factors that determine the context in which donors try to operate are (1) the overall structure of incentives facing smallholder farmers (notably, real producer price levels as they pertain at the farm gate) and (2) the predictability of institutions providing services to the agricultural sector. For a small donor like DANIDA, which has defined its role primarily in terms of project assistance, these factors have had an enormous effect on the chances for success. Yet precisely because such small donors have not perceived themselves to be in the business of offering sectoral policy advice, the policy environment has not been consistently assessed or understood.

Neither Kenya nor Tanzania has had an unequivocally positive structure of farm-related incentives across the full spectrum of commodities produced. Yet for many commodities (including coffee, tea, and dairy products) the Kenyan government's policies relating to incentives have been geared toward allowing capital accumulation to take place at the farm level. By contrast, through a combination of explicit pricing policies and increasing implicit taxation through the rise in marketing margins and appreciation of the real exchange rate since the early 1970s, Tanzanian farmers witnessed a steady decline in the real purchasing power of most commodities—with the exception of a group of inferior drought staples and legumes and of preferred staples such as maize, which began to have an attractive unofficial market price by the end of the decade.[11] Large nominal price adjustments during the 1980s could barely keep pace with Tanzania's official rate of inflation, however, and the extreme scarcities of consumer goods in the countryside made that index questionable in any event. Increasingly, only the remoter areas that enjoyed subsidized transport costs continued to find that the official system offered incentive prices for commodities such as maize. By the 1980s, moreover, the problem had taken on clear macroeconomic dimensions; because of the overvalued exchange rate, the government could not pay higher prices to farmers without running higher deficits to finance the marketing authorities.

Incentives in Tanzania declined in large part because of its unpredictable marketing system rather than the price-setting process as such. A series of changes—first the scope of cooperatives was reduced, next they were replaced with parastatal marketing authorities, then cooperatives were partly reintroduced in the early 1980s—had the result in most places of worsening, rather than improving, the dependability of marketing channels. During the 1970s Tanzanian farmers were less and less able to count on timely transactions (waiting time further reduced the real value of the commodities to producers). The Kenyan marketing system on the whole has appeared more stable from an institutional standpoint, but soaring marketing margins and increasingly delayed payments characterized large parts of it—most notably cotton, but also pyrethrum and cashews.

With respect to the other institutions providing services to producers, the Kenyan system appears to have been the far more predictable one. Not only did Tanzania's farmers themselves experience a large institutional reorganization under the villagization introduced in the mid-1970s, but so did the officials whose job it was to interact with them. Since 1972 the chain of command for Tanzanian extension officers has shifted from the Ministry of Agriculture to the regional development director, in some cases to crop authorities, and then back to the ministry. At one point additional officers (village managers) were appointed to serve thousands of villages. Retail trading was affected first by the short-lived nationalization of the import business in the late 1960s, and subsequently by two campaigns to establish village shops (and close private ones) in 1976 and 1980.

On balance, it seems clear that the Kenyan agricultural environment has been more disposed to the conduct of project assistance than has the Tanzanian environment. This is not to say that inappropriate kinds of project assistance would work in Kenya; but in Tanzania even sound projects have had a much harder time staying afloat in the midst of the institutional turbulence and the deteriorating incentive structure—factors that were outside the influence of project managers. The heightening macroeconomic crisis that Tanzania has experienced since the end of the 1970s has no doubt compounded the difficulties of project assistance. The business of living has put such extraordinary demands on government and parastatal officials that the capacity of their institutions has come under severe stress. Similar problems emerging in Kenya with the onset of recession in the 1980s appear to pale by comparison.

DANIDA's assistance to the two countries has been channeled mainly into livestock activities and cooperatives, but some has also gone into production, financial transfers, and crop processing. In addition, there has been some indirect support for agriculture through transportation infrastructure and industrial imports.[12]

Livestock Activities

Livestock production holds a special significance in the Danes' economic development history and therefore has loomed large in the country's appraisal of its aid potential. The main characteristics of present-day Danish agriculture were shaped in the second half of the nineteenth century. Livestock began to dominate agriculture when crashing international grain prices spurred Danish farmers to convert from grain to animal production. The change had widespread and long-lasting economic, social, and political ramifications. For decades, livestock farmers have been supported by an impressive research and extension system (as well as favorable prices), with the result that dairy and pork products continue to be leading commodity exports.

Despite early disappointments in its effort to provide aid for dairy and breeding farms, the Danish livestock industry has managed to maintain a significant presence in DANIDA's agricultural activities—it accounts for much of the program's technical assistance and administrative input. Cattle have been the principal target of aid, with a few small exceptions in poultry and pig rearing. This emphasis is reflected in the East African portfolios.

The Kenya program has received far greater financial support and has covered a wider range of functions than the Tanzania program.

In contrast to some other donors who have run large programs to develop the dryland, pastoral cattle economy, DANIDA has focused primarily on two aspects of the highland, grade cattle, dairy economy.

First, and financially most significant, have been the periodic investments in dairy processing through state loans to the Kenyan Cooperative Creameries (KCC), the national dairy-processing company. These loans plus several export credits for the same purpose have made DANIDA the principal donor to KCC. KCC has also been the beneficiary of a number of fellowships for training in dairy management in Denmark.

Second are activities in research, education, and production, which have been oriented mainly toward improving the performance of the small dairy farmers. So far, the main concern has been to control ticks. Cattle dip rehabilitation projects have been launched in several districts for this purpose, along with acaricide resistance research (acaricide being the active ingredient used in the cattle dips). More recently, this has been supplemented by some extension work in fodder crops.

The education component (technical assistance to the Naivasha Dairy School), although small, has been significant for DANIDA's program because it provided the link between these two branches of support to the dairy industry. DANIDA-affiliated agronomists working at the school were encouraged to take more interest in the use of state loans to improve dairy processing. As a result, DANIDA commissioned the Dairy Master Plan in 1979, which brought more agricultural considerations into the appraisal of future investments with KCC. This is the only case in the two portfolios in which project and state loan policy appear to have been integrated beforehand.

In addition DANIDA has provided support for meat processing, which encompasses dryland cattle. Modern butcheries were introduced under a state loan in the mid-1970s (to Halal Slaughterhouse, Ltd., outside of Nairobi) and under project aid in the early 1980s (to eight publicly managed, district slaughterhouses). The project's principal objectives were to improve public hygiene rather than to stimulate the market in meat.

The livestock program in Tanzania started out on a similar footing, with investments in dairy processing in the Mara region through a state loan (primarily in the early 1970s) and in small dairy production projects in Zanzibar and Coast region. For reasons to be discussed, this type of activity did not gain the same momentum in Tanzania as in Kenya, with the result that the program shifted direction toward education, its present concern. The large education component is devoted entirely to the veterinary faculty at the Sokoine Agricultural University in Morogoro. DANIDA, which is responsible both for providing equipment and for establishing a veterinary teaching staff, has been the sole donor to this faculty.

Assessment of Kenyan program. On the whole, DANIDA's Kenyan livestock experience appears to have been more successful and to have shown more promise than the Tanzanian one. The support to the dairy industry appears to have had significant positive effects; meat processing, in contrast, has had disappointing results. In Tanzania, DANIDA correctly recognized the limited scope for success in the dairy industry comparable to that in Kenya. Yet it did not take into account the implications of that finding (namely, that the two countries had quite different resource bases) in its subsequent decision to help Tanzania develop a livestock health care program.

The farmer-oriented part of the Kenyan dairy program has been positive. Tick-control measures were introduced in Uasin Gishu and Kericho, districts with a high percentage of grade cattle and in which the majority of cattle diseases are tick-borne. The measures took almost instant effect, as observed by local veterinarians. Their main target was East Coast fever. An important side effect of these projects has been that the personnel providing technical assistance have helped reestablish well-functioning dipping systems. The research support also has been important. The research stations provide laboratory services for testing acaricide concentration, which is one of the crucial elements in monitoring the performance of dip attendants.

Future Danish involvement in this area will depend on the sustainability of the chosen strategy of tick control, namely, universal dipping. This in turn will depend on whether the dipping levy is collected regularly and a high standard of dipping services continues to be available. Once established, a system that breaks down can have a far more adverse effect on the mortality rates of cattle than no system at all, since cattle lose their congenital resistance to the tick-borne diseases within a generation.

Recent developments in the prevention of East Coast fever at the Kenyan-based International Laboratory for Research on Animal Diseases suggest that there may be a far less expensive and more effective means of treating cattle for this devastating disease than the current tick-control measures. The method, known as "infect and treat," consists of infecting the cattle with a live serum and then treating them before the infection becomes debilitating. The cattle acquire permanent immunity and therefore need to be treated only once. The method is not only less risky than dipping, it is far less costly (especially in foreign exchange), since standard dipping prevention requires cattle to be treated twice a week. If the early enthusiasm for this new method is warranted, DANIDA will clearly want to shift its veterinary activities into it and maintain only some strategic dipping to control the secondary tick-borne diseases.

Leaving the possibilities of alternatives to dipping aside, the ultimate verdict on this project will depend on its ability to become self-sustaining, which has been a problem thus far. Dipping fees are collected centrally by the Ministry of Agriculture and Livestock Development, which is supposed to gradually take over from DANIDA the responsibility for and financing of the salaries of the locally employed project staff. As of 1987, the ministry seemed unable to collect more than 50–60 percent of the fees and showed no interest in taking on the new obligations for current expenditures. If this situation does not change before Danish support ends, the systemic transplantation will in effect have been rejected, and the program will have had a temporary, and possibly negative, effect.

On the dairy processing side, Danish support to KCC has helped increase greatly this dairy organization's collecting and processing capability. Although KCC has had its fair share of problems, some imposed and some self-made, it has been able to secure predictable outlets and immediate payment and thereby has created a stable environment for dairy production that must be the envy of most African countries. From a production plateau of 800–900 million liters a year in the 1960s, the output of the Kenyan dairy industry rose steadily to about 1,300 million liters by the mid-1980s. Since DANIDA has been the industry's largest supporter in this period (it provided more than DKr 180 million for the loan-financed equipment alone), it would be reasonable to credit it with a correspondingly large share of the success.

It is unclear whether there is a basis for more of the same kind of investment, in line with recent DANIDA offers of additional state loans to this end. Market conditions are such that the industry may soon have difficulty disposing of its output: Domestic demand has begun stagnating and two traditional export markets have been closed off—in Uganda because of civil collapse and in the Gulf States because of competition from the European Community (EC).

The picture is less rosy for DANIDA's support for the meat economy. Halal Slaughterhouse was inaugurated in 1978 but operated for only a week or two before being closed down by administrative fiat. What happened, insofar as the story can be pieced together, was that the plant had been appropriated for private purposes. Once this was discovered, the plant's operation was blocked by other interested parties. The facilities were left standing empty for six years. The drought of 1984 prompted the Kenyan government to ask DANIDA to help reestablish it to cope with the high drought-related offtake of cattle; thus in August 1984 the plant started operating again—this time as a branch of the Kenya Meat Commission (KMC), a parastatal corporation. KMC's capacity utilization at its other slaughtering facilities at Athi River and Mombasa does not bode well for the reestablishment. In 1976, the last year in which the KMC had a monopoly over beef sales to urban areas, its capacity utilization was 80 percent. Since 1977 utilization has plummeted and has hovered at 20–30 percent in every year except 1984, which was an exceptional year. Similarly, low capacity utilization, a prime indicator of misinvestment, mars the prospects of the eight district slaughterhouses.

The fact that Danish support for dairy and meat processing has had different outcomes requires some explanation. Essentially, the reason lies in the nature of dairy and meat products and thus their different transportation and storage requirements. The movement of milk in bulk from the main production areas to the urban consumer depends on the availability of rather technically sophisticated and capital-intensive transportation and storage systems. Leaving aside local delivery (which can absorb only a portion of the current levels of milk production), there is little choice in the current technology for milk processing, whereas slaughtering technology varies widely. As a result, milk processing and packaging has to surpass certain minimum daily volumes to be economically viable. Meat processing is much more divisible and flexible.[13] These technological conditions have organizational consequences—making a legal monopoly of milk processing more justifiable and sufficiently enforceable in practice.

The opposite holds true for meat processing. As publicly managed ventures (which must follow public policy on prices, health standards, and so on), the DANIDA-supported slaughterhouses do not have the flexibility to attract a good share of the market in competition with private butchers, who can pay more for quality animals than KMC and who do not reject sick animals, as both the KMC and the district slaughterhouses are supposed to do.

Low capacity utilization of the slaughterhouses implies that the investments have had little effect on the development of the meat market in Kenya. Furthermore, analysis suggests that the public health objectives of the district slaughterhouses have not been realized. The experience of public slaughter authorities in establishing hygienic meat standards through the rejection of animals unfit for human consumption is rather uniform. In such low-income environments as those prevailing in most of Africa (including even Kenya's relatively well-off districts), efforts to control the quality of meat fail in one of two ways: by compromising meat inspectors or by circumventing the facilities themselves. Even repeated attempts to destroy unhygienic meat by burying or coloring it have been in vain.

It does seem possible to improve hygiene through the use of slaughterhouses, but only if the actual slaughtering is left to private butchers without imposing any quality restrictions on the meat itself. Hygienic standards for the meat itself can only be successfully imposed when such standards correspond to consumer priorities. It seems there is no shortcut from public campaigns and education. A differentiated system with an option for certifying the quality of the meat might be an intermediate solution, but success can only be partial until the fundamental problem of absolute poverty has been alleviated. In that sense, the project may have been premature and the investment funds might have realized higher social returns elsewhere.

Assessment of Tanzania. DANIDA did not follow up on either its early dairy production activities in Tanzania or its investment in dairy processing. The results had not been particularly favorable and in the case of the Mara dairy even drew some criticism because distribution had been so poor. Processing capacity had been installed in an environment in which milk production was low to begin with and farm households did not have a firm technological basis for increasing it—with the result that the dairy encouraged a transfer of milk consumption from rural children to urban adults.

The fact that a strategy that yielded positive results in Kenya turned out differently in Tanzania is a reflection of the different cattle economies in the two countries. The highland cattle economy of Kenya was a highly monetized farming system based on grade cattle and similar in many respects to European dairy farming. In contrast, Tanzania, like the rest of Kenya, has a pastoral or agropastoral cattle economy—with few links to the money economy. The stock are indigenous and range-fed and are viewed primarily as a risk-absorbing vehicle rather than as an investment.

Although Tanzania does have small pockets of highland areas in which the climate is hospitable to grade cattle (such as the area around the Mara dairy plant), both infrastructural and institutional obstacles put it at a disadvantage in comparison with Kenya. First, Kenya has large, contiguous areas suitable for dairy farming, which means it can realize scale economies in the provision of extension, veterinary, and marketing services, as well as in processing. Second, the Kenyan dairy economy has a long heritage that dates back to the days of European-settler farming. By independence, KCC was already an extremely well-functioning institution. The transition to servicing an industry that has become increasingly centered around smallholders has of course required skillful maintenance and institutional adjustments, but managing a transition is easier than starting from scratch.

Given the character of the Tanzanian cattle economy, the physical and curricular plans for the Morogoro Veterinary Faculty are surprisingly reminiscent of European veterinary schools. The Morogoro program has been designed to include virtually the full range of veterinary activities, including facilities for and training in surgery and anaesthesia of small animals. If DANIDA's justification for funding the veterinary faculty was the perception of an enormous untapped potential for animal production in Tanzania, the diagnosis itself would be difficult to challenge. It is harder to justify DANIDA's choice of means. Project documentation leaves this question largely unanswered, and interviews have yielded ambiguous results. The project appears to be the result of decisions influenced more by the resources Denmark could offer than by an analytical review of the demands of the Tanzanian situation. Since Denmark, for good reasons, is proud of its own level of veterinary services and education, DANIDA appears to have assumed (without much probing of the Tanzanian reality) that this system could provide an important remedy for the low productivity of Tanzanian livestock.

It is beyond the scope of this report to provide the kind of in-depth analysis that ought to have preceded the choice of a strategy for raising livestock productivity in Tanzania. However, several problems can be pointed out that seem far more vital to livestock productivity than the one DANIDA has chosen to tackle through its support for the Veterinary Faculty.

The perception that Tanzanian livestock production is far short of its potential stems mainly from discrepancies between estimates of the potential livestock carrying capacity and estimates of current livestock populations. One such assessment set the potential at 20 million livestock units, with an actual population equivalent of about 11 million units.[14] What these assessments have failed to take into account are (1) the poor distribution of water sources, (2) the lack of coordinated land use, and, especially, (3) the tsetse fly infestation. None of these factors can be addressed directly by the kinds of services veterinarians can provide.

There is no question that animal health, especially calf mortality, is a significant constraint on the productivity of the sector as well. But in light of the largely pastoral nature of Tanzania's livestock industry, intensive curative strategies for improving animal health will only cause a drain on the country's scarce resources. To be cost-effective, an animal health program in Tanzania will have to focus on *preventive* health care. DANIDA has already reached this conclusion where human health is concerned, so it may just be a question of time before the four-legged health strategy catches up with the two-legged one.

A number of professionals concerned with livestock productivity in semiarid and arid, pastorally based systems have reached the same conclusion. For instance, the Veterinary Economics Research Unit of Reading University in the U.K. has for years been concerned with assessing the economics of veterinary investments and treatment strategies for different livestock systems. Their models show that preventive vaccines against pandemic diseases can pay off, whereas just about every other kind of health care (including worm control) is at best marginally successful.

Research conducted at the International Livestock Centre for Africa (ILCA) in Addis Ababa stresses the nutritional aspects of animal health as second in importance only to the prevention of pandemics.[15] In view of such assessments, an animal health strategy based on curative treatment by veterinarians probably ranks considerably lower than other strategic priorities for the livestock industry in Tanzania.

This is not to suggest that the country does not need well-trained veterinary manpower. A small cadre with training in basic veterinary science is a fundamental prerequisite for the articulation and enactment of a preventive strategy. In the light of Tanzania's willingness to go along with the curative strategy implicit in the DANIDA project, it would appear that the cadre in question either does not exist or has not been in a position to find alternatives.[16] For the preventive strategy, it is quite unlikely that a full-scale veterinary faculty would have been the appropriate means to build up the necessary staff. Rather than an army of veterinarians, the manpower profile should include only a small corps of veterinarians, with an army of nonacademic trainees to trace and inoculate herds and work in a few serum-producing laboratories. The cost-effectiveness of building this corps locally also seems questionable, especially when compared with sending candidates to an appropriate institution outside the country for advanced training.

If the Veterinary Faculty's existence is now a foregone conclusion, DANIDA will need to address head-on the problem of how to secure a well-trained veterinary teaching faculty.[17] Two alternatives seem possible. Either a complete commitment of full institutional support must come from the Danish base of expertise (the Royal Veterinary and Agricultural University), or DANIDA will need to consider alternative sources of expertise from outside Denmark.

Both alternatives raise problems. In the first case, a core of Danish veterinary professionals would have to commit five to ten years to building a veterinary institution concerned with significantly different health care problems from those in Denmark (or in the Kenyan highlands, for that matter). This would require a professional reorientation toward African agropastoralism that many might not be willing to make unless DANIDA itself was so committed to the Tanzanian (and similar) livestock situation that it was willing to promise personnel a possible career in the field. In the second case, there would be strong objections to DANIDA using its bilateral budget to engage an appropriate counterpart veterinary institution from another industrial country (assuming one exists). DANIDA would probably need to reach agreement with another donor institution to assume financing. It would be politically easier for it to finance another developing country institution (assuming, again, that one exists) capable of interacting with Morogoro.

The time has arrived for DANIDA to assess the facilities at the Faculty on the basis of realistic, resource-conscious alternatives, in light of the type of manpower profile that a preventive strategy implies.[18] Some of the teaching facilities could possibly be used to train lower-level manpower as part of the strategy.

The Cooperative Projects

Just as livestock has provided the economic base for much of the development of Danish agriculture over the past century, cooperatives have provided the institutional channel by which the farming population has begun to reap the economic, political, and social benefits of growth. Agricultural and consumer cooperatives have had a special place in the development history of the other Nordic countries as well. It is entirely fitting that the earliest Nordic agriculturally oriented projects in both Tanzania and Kenya were designed to develop cooperatives. Through a mutual show of interest between East African leaders and the Nordic donors, two cooperative projects got under way in 1967 in Kenya and in 1968 in Tanzania. The projects have been the hallmarks of Nordic presence in the two countries ever since.

By the end of the 1960s, Denmark had assumed the administrative role for both of the projects. In practice, this has given DANIDA an edge in decisionmaking, although Nordic approval is required on important policy matters. The Nordic characteristic is perhaps most evident in the political importance of the projects' continuity, which seems to have taken on a symbolic significance. Indeed, the Tanzanian cooperative project has distinguished itself by such a strong staying power that it has managed to persist throughout the six-year period when there were no cooperatives in the country. In both African countries, the only category of support outside of technical assistance has been financing for the construction of cooperative colleges.

Projects with a history this long are difficult to assess in summary fashion. Not only have they gone through a series of permutations in successive phases, but at various times they have consisted of multiple subcomponents that have been projects in their own right. Their joint Nordic nature (with the attendant need to keep all the donors informed) has generated a vast quantity of evaluation materials. So as not to miss the forest for the trees, the discussion concentrates on some of the broader themes and issues that emerge from the two decades of experience in the two countries. In the process, some of the issues that have had prominence in project evaluation materials are sidestepped, particularly when these relate more to the specifics of project design than to broader strategic considerations.

Project overviews. By the mid-1960s, both the Tanzanian and Kenyan governments were coming to terms with the cooperatives that had grown like weeds in the years following independence (secured in 1961 and 1963, respectively). This rapid proliferation had somewhat different origins in the two countries. In Tanzania, a powerful and successful grass roots cooperative movement had begun in coffee areas before the World War II and had spread throughout cotton areas and into some tobacco areas during the 1950s. The newly independent government latched on to the idea of cooperatives as an explicit policy instrument for removing the non-African (Asian and Arab) traders in the rest of the countryside, and it promoted the idea of establishing cooperative societies across the board. Local elites quickly responded to the call.

In Kenya, the colonial government had discouraged smallholder cash cropping up until the postwar period and thus had prevented the development of an early grass roots movement. Then, in the 1950s, when the government began an aggressive coffee campaign in the smallholder highland areas (especially Central Province), it in effect imposed cooperatives on those areas. The rationale was that cooperative pulperies were the only appropriate means for primary processing of the harvest. After independence, the Kenyan government certainly seems to have looked favorably on the cooperative (and unfavorably on the presence of non-African traders in the countryside), but it did not explicitly impose the concept, as did its southern neighbor, except in the special case of group purchases of large farms. Elsewhere, aspiring local elites seem to have seen the cooperatives as an attractive means of gaining visibility in the new era of African-dominated politics. As a result they sprang up everywhere.

The substantive difference in the treatment of cooperatives in the two countries at this time seems to lie in the extent to which monopsony purchasing rights were granted to the societies. In Tanzania, once a cooperative society gained formal registration, it was vested with such rights over the surplus produce in the area.[19] In Kenya, coffee and dairy societies got monopsonies, but it appears that other societies had to demonstrate that they could attract more than half of the market (60 percent) before gaining similar status.

The net results of the proliferation were quite similar, however. Both countries had hundreds of societies and dozens of unions in financial shambles, with no reasonable system of accounts and with staff and committees being blamed for (sometimes large) misappropriations of members' funds. Commissions were established to hear and assess grievances and make recommendations to the governments. In both cases, the recommendations centered on the need for regulatory action.

Enter the Nordic cooperative projects. The projects started out with two objectives, which have more or less endured to the present: to help the government in its regulatory tasks and to encourage the cooperatives to improve themselves. The strategy consisted of sending dozens of Nordic cooperative experts to the two countries to work both with the government departments overseeing them and with the cooperative management in advisory (and sometimes executive) roles, to develop various unified financial systems and training materials. In Tanzania, the emphasis from the outset was on training members in the rudimentary skills they needed to keep the cooperative honest; this was also the trend in Kenya, although it moved at a slower pace. The magnitude of these early projects was quite striking. About fifty Nordic advisers a year were posted in Kenya and another thirty or so in Tanzania, so that by the early 1970s they overshadowed the assorted technical assistance made available by other donors in this area.

In retrospect, several premises about intervention in the cooperative system have been fundamental to the success and failure of the projects. First, the African and Nordic governments shared the view that cooperatives were an inherently appropriate institutional form for the development of smallholder agriculture. This view held irrespective of the economic base of the cooperative (or, perhaps more accurately, there did not appear to be explicit consideration of the possibility that some agricultural areas did not have the level or kind of surplus production that would be able to sustain a financially viable cooperative society or union).

Second, there was a shared view that in the end it would pay to prop up weak cooperatives (where, again, the source of weakness might be the teething pains of a society that did have a substantial economic base or might be the lack of such a base to begin with). Third, it was widely believed that government regulation was needed. Both countries adopted a set of quite extensive regulatory mechanisms to be applied across the board, including government countersigning of cooperative checks in Kenya and government approval of cooperative staff appointments in Tanzania. From the Nordic perspective, such regulation would be necessary until the movements in the two countries were mature enough to police themselves. This attitude reflected the donors' underlying desire to promote democratization through independent cooperatives. It is doubtful that either African government fully embraced this view, although over the years the Kenyan system has certainly had more scope for independence than the Tanzanian one.[20]

The projects tackled similar tasks in the two countries. Because of the national character of the projects and the belief that all cooperatives deserved support, field advisers were dispersed throughout Tanzania and Kenya, to reflect the broad geographical coverage of the cooperatives themselves. In Tanzania, an adviser was posted at each of the nearly twenty regional cooperative unions rather than in the traditional strongholds of the grass roots cooperative movement. In Kenya, advisers were posted in each of the provinces, where they began building the district unions that the government favored. Advisers at headquarters worked on developing uniform financial tools, starting with systems for basic accounting and for recording member transactions, and ultimately (in Kenya) a number of more sophisticated financial tools for banking, merchandising, financial planning, and so on.

By the early 1970s, economic and political developments in the two African countries, coupled with the more finely tuned political objectives for Nordic aid, began to push the two projects in somewhat different directions. The performance of the cooperatives clearly influenced all the governments concerned. In Kenya, the first phase of the project had corresponded to a period of healthy expansion in coffee, dairy production, and pyrethrum in Central Province and parts of Eastern and Nigeria provinces. Cooperatives had been heavily involved in the expansion, and it appeared that the management practices of these cooperatives had benefited substantially from the Nordic project's various inputs. In contrast, the cooperatives in most other parts of the country (which were based on different commodities) continued to perform poorly.

In Tanzania, performance was also poor in the majority of areas that had no tradition of cooperatives. But the Kenyan successes were not paralleled in Tanzania. By the late 1960s agricultural performance in areas of Tanzania where cooperatives were traditional was less spectacular than it had been in the 1950s and 1960s. Moreover, one of the targets of government regulatory action against financial abuses was the large and powerful network of cotton cooperatives—the Victoria Federation of Cooperative Unions.

The governments of the two countries differed on the issue of whether cooperatives were the appropriate tool for further development efforts. Kenya chose to promote cooperatives more vigorously than before, especially in areas where agricultural growth had been lagging. Tanzanian decisionmakers were disappointed by the experiences of the weak societies and unions and began dismantling the system. This culminated in the abolition of agricultural cooperatives in 1976.

Although this divergence paved the way for quite different cooperative policies in the two countries, both governments maintained a national policy on institutional form that did not recognize the different capabilities of cooperatives in different geographical areas, and both took care to maintain a channel that would give them access to the farming population. In Kenya, the cooperative system was to be the point of departure for a wide range of development initiatives being planned (in particular, credit schemes). In Tanzania, the villagization program of the early 1970s had established village governments across the entire countryside by 1975, so that the abolition of cooperatives in the following years did not leave an institutional vacuum.

Changes in the Nordic position after the late 1960s brought more attention to poorer groups, and by the early 1970s these sentiments were an explicit basis of aid to Kenya. Thus Kenya's own decision to focus on the less successful agricultural areas and to use cooperatives as a development tool meshed well with the direction that the project probably would have had to take in any case. In contrast, the general wave of support for Tanzania meant that strong Nordic feelings on cooperative principles could be overlooked (or overridden); so the project continued, despite the Tanzanian government's clear transgression of the by-laws of the International Cooperative Alliance in its 1976 action.

From this juncture, it is more appropriate of think of a shift in focus rather than a new project in the Kenyan case. System-building activities continued, and field advisers still promoted better management. The fieldwork had two specific objectives. Although management had become concerned about the weaker areas (and had moved out of Central Province), support for the union banking sections continued to be concentrated in the coffee and dairy areas—precisely because these were the only areas that had been financially sound enough to meet the fairly stringent qualifications for entering the program.

The Tanzanian project, in contrast, had to start afresh. The first objective agreed on was to provide technical assistance to help the members of the new village structure take advantage of their organizational unit. According to this plan, the Nordic project would work with several other donors to train all-purpose, village-level technical advisers. But in 1978, before things got very far with this blueprint, the government assigned people from all walks of life (ranging from drivers to regional agricultural officers) to become village managers. This new program took effect immediately and put an end to the original plan, which was to train the village advisers before assigning them. Under the circumstances, the Nordic project made the fairly pragmatic decision to concentrate on training village bookkeepers, much along the lines of the earlier lower-level training of cooperative staff and officials. The project developed teaching materials as well as a bookkeeping system for the villages, and it ran its own courses and those that were part of other donors' regional integrated projects.

By 1980, widespread dissatisfaction with the services being provided by the crop authorities that had replaced the marketing cooperatives prompted the Tanzanian government to consider reestablishing the cooperative. This idea received substantial support from the Nordic project, which was in the strategic position of being the only cooperative project at the time and therefore could provide on-the-ground support for the effort. Once the institutional and legal framework was worked out, the project shifted back into gear, posting technical staff to the unions and to the government's regulatory arm at headquarters. A new element was a special foreign-exchange credit account with the Cooperative and Rural Development Bank, set up in recognition of the inadequacy of government mechanisms to allocate foreign exchange to agricultural institutions.

Assessment. In Kenya, the more stable institutional environment in which the Nordic project has operated over the years makes it easier to assess the strengths and weaknesses of the project from a long-term perspective. Whether for this reason or because of the greater scrutiny associated with Nordic aid activities in Kenya, evaluations of the Kenyan project appear to apply a harsher than usual, and more thorough, set of performance criteria. The following remarks draw heavily on these reports, as well as on other recent work on Kenyan cooperatives.

There can be little doubt that the project can claim a large share of the glory for the progress registered in the management capabilities of the Kenyan coffee, dairy, and pyrethrum societies and unions. As noted earlier, these cooperatives got off to a somewhat haphazard start, and in the late 1950s few of them seemed likely to survive their infancy. Although not without problems, these cooperatives have become on the whole an impressive and sophisticated set of institutions in which participation is strong and active.

These cooperatives are also the beneficiaries of another contribution of the Nordic project: the cooperative banking system. An early initiative of the project in Kenya was the establishment of a system within the cooperatives for issuing production credit and holding members' savings through union banking sections. The restrictions on credit were sufficiently stringent to ensure high rates of repayment. The cooperative itself had to be on sound financial footing, and each borrower had to be guaranteed by two other cooperative members. Most of the finance was in turn provided by members' savings in personal bank accounts, which caught on like wildfire as soon as they were introduced, in no small part because the accounts could be established with a minimum deposit one-tenth the size required by the ordinary commercial banks. This union-level system was integrated with the services of the national Cooperative Bank, which provided overall financial guidance and some of its own capital for the credit program, known as the Cooperative Production Credit Scheme (CPCS).

The Kenyan Nordic project has seen the cooperative banking system through a number of growing pains with sophisticated and forward-looking changes. One of the more complex problems has been to find a way to guarantee members' savings in the event of financial difficulties at the union level. The solution that has finally been reached, and that the Nordic project is helping to implement, is to convert the union banking sections into societies in their own right. This solution not only safeguards the savings deposits but it separates the financial operations of cooperatives from their physical tasks in crop and input handling. In light of the numerous difficulties that have been endured in the financial management of many cooperatives (relating to timely crop payments, among other things), putting bankers in charge of the finances should provide the structural basis needed to tighten the system considerably.

The foresight of the planners also made it possible for the project to mitigate the effects of an even greater financial problem. In the mid-1970s the Kenyan government and a number of donors were eager to expand the cooperative credit program to serve greater numbers of farmers. Since a large part of the justification centered on making credit available to cooperative members who had previously had access to CPCS funds, the programs typically required less scrutiny of the borrowers and offered softer terms. It is difficult to know what the Nordic donors thought of the new special credit schemes as a vehicle for reaching the poor. DANIDA's bilateral support for one such system (to be discussed below) suggests that the precise mechanisms, rather than the principle itself, came under Nordic scrutiny. In any case, the project planners were quick to point out that the existing cooperative banking system had to be shielded from the risks of the new schemes, in view of the different criteria that were to be applied. In practice, this was achieved by establishing separate accounts for the special schemes within the Cooperative Bank. By this system, the Cooperative Bank did not assume risk on credit issued under other criteria.

As a result, the existing cooperative banking system was sheltered; the cooperatives that received credit from these various schemes have been less fortunate. Credit was in many cases issued on a free-for-all basis, often without much consideration for the productive uses to which it might be put. Repayment rates under many of the special schemes have been considerably below those of the CPCS and in some cases have been so poor that there is little chance of recovering the bad debts. This has left the finances of the responsible cooperative societies and unions in a terrible state. Instead of boosting the weaker agricultural areas, the credit program has further weakened their cooperative institutions.

Apparently there is no way of separating the effect of the management advice and that of the training provided for these cooperatives by the Nordic project, which may have had some marginally positive results in this interim. But the conclusion must still be drawn that, after twenty years of working with cooperatives outside the coffee and dairy belt, there is little to show for the effort.

Although much of the foregoing analysis is consistent with that found in recent evaluations of the Nordic project, this last conclusion differs in one important respect. These reports have recognized the tremendous progress made in the coffee and dairy cooperatives, in contrast with the rest of the system, but they have also assumed that the project has concentrated on those successful areas. Going back over the entire history of the project, one can identify only two respects in which the project can be seen to have favored the successful areas. First, following the development of a simple overall bookkeeping system, the so-called member transactions systems for coffee and dairy products were the earliest systems to be established. In light of the substantially higher level of transactions already occurring in these commodities, this was clearly the strategy that could have the quickest payoff as well—but those who seek a bias may find one here. Second, as already mentioned, the activities of the project's banking component tended to concentrate on these areas precisely because their banking systems were just emerging. In other respects, including the general support to management, the project was by the early 1970s clearly concerned with shifting its focus toward the weaker areas and away form the broader coverage with which it had begun.

This distinction is important because it raises more fundamental issues than those raised so far by the Nordic donors about the viability of cooperatives as an institutional form in areas with weak agricultural bases. The Nordic stand on this issue has remained much the same since the first project evaluation was completed in 1969. It has consistently been that cooperatives *are* an appropriate development channel for areas with low agricultural surplus. The only variation on this basic belief has been the suggestion that in the truly marginal areas it might be appropriate to establish multipurpose precooperatives rather than more traditional marketing cooperatives. None of the many valuations consider the issues that can arise for cooperative management when commodities are high in bulk and low in value (as are maize and other food crops), when they are grown over a more dispersed area (for example, under the more extensive farming practiced outside of the highlands), or when they have complicated and expensive processing requirements (as do cotton and sugar). Nor do any of the valuations draw upon the experience of the cooperatives that deal in such commodities elsewhere in the developing world.

This is not to suggest that there is no scope for successful cooperative development outside the few highland commodities where this institution has already secured its position. The relatively successful experience with cotton cooperatives in the 1950s and 1960s in Tanzania, as well as the success in Kenya within the dairy industry, which has more complicated processing requirements, suggests that there is much room for improvement in the Kenyan cotton industry, for instance, with the cooperative form. This is indeed the commodity on which the new phase of the Nordic project will concentrate. This is a landmark representing the project's first involvement in sectoral policy issues of pricing and marketing, which will be crucial to the success of the cotton cooperatives.

But unless the Nordic donors reassess the blanket assumption that cooperatives are a good thing everywhere, there is the danger that cooperatives will again be promoted in areas where they do not stand a chance of doing well until there are breakthroughs on the technological front or considerable advances in the sophistication of the local population's business acumen. The assumption that propping up a weak cooperative will end well needs to be challenged in the light of two decades of experience. What benefits accrue to members in poor areas when cooperatives operate with higher overheads than private traders do? Can staff and members learn how to run sound cooperatives by working in financially weak cooperatives being propped up by external means year after year? Is it any wonder that field survey after field survey reports that members are not inspired to use their cooperatives as a participatory development channel (which, after all, has been a primary goal of the Nordic project)?

Inasmuch as many of the geographic areas that received support under the Nordic project in Tanzania share the characteristics of the weaker agricultural areas of Kenya, these same issues are of concern there as well. The project's overall results in Tanzania are more difficult to assess, however, because of the tumultuous institutional environment in which it operated. Agricultural performance was waning, and the various reports from the time suggest that cooperative performance was declining even in some of the better-off areas, such as those growing cotton. A variety of policy factors, including price policy, may have adversely affected cooperative accounts and efficiency. In view of the generally proregulatory character of the Nordic project, it is interesting to note that one of the common criticisms of the cooperatives centers on the process of regulation itself. It has been argued that the introduction of the Unified Cooperative Service (under which cooperative staff could no longer be hired or fired without government approval) took away membership control, thereby reducing cooperative management's accountability to the members. At the least, it is clear that the project was ineffective in its support of the dozen or so regional unions that had been government constructs—unions that not only lacked administrative capabilities but also the very economic basis to sustain successful cooperative activities.

Perhaps surprisingly, the project appears to have done relatively well during the interim period in which the cooperative system was shut down, in large part because it had focused on village bookkeeper training. There was (and remains) a dire lack of basic accounting skills in rural Tanzania, and villages, once established, were charged with a number of tasks requiring such skills. This was particularly true once the cooperatives were abolished. The parastatal structure that replaced the regional unions and primary societies relied on the villages' ability to serve as self-managing buying points. As a result, the project probably helped prevent an even worse decline in peasants' exchange relations under the parastatal marketing system than would have taken place in its absence. In addition, of course, people acquiring the training were in a position to provide other useful functions in their villages, and in the wider economy.[21] In all likelihood, there would be substantial benefits from continuing this type of training, since the demand for these highly fungible skills in the rural economy certainly was not exhausted in the short time the project was engaged in it. From the perspective of the broader socioeconomic goals of the Nordic donors, such activities may provide one of the most direct channels for empowering the rural population in a country where the institutional policies and structures have tended to constrict rather than widen their opportunities.

The project that has emerged to serve the new cooperatives is too young to assess by any other criteria than its objectives. From the beginning, the Nordic project has supported the idea of reintroducing independent, voluntary cooperatives. No doubt it had some influence on the final wording of the new cooperative legislation, which now conforms to international principles on voluntary membership. In today's Tanzania, the significance of this particular point is doubtful, since cooperatives have been granted monopsony rights to purchase the produce of members and nonmembers alike. However, some battles are being waged between the reemergent movement (which until now has consisted mainly of unions and societies in former cooperative strongholds) and the party structure over the question of whether the movement should be independent of the party's political monopoly at the village as well as the national level.

Although this struggle will need to be waged among the domestic participants, it is significant that the new Nordic project reflects a greater independence from the will of the central Tanzanian authorities than did its predecessor. The distinct break with the earlier pattern of blindly following Tanzanian government priorities is seen in the regional selectivity of the project. On the grounds that one should first see whether the cooperative structure can work in the regions where cooperatives have traditionally performed better, project support has been confined to the seven regions in which the old movement is trying to regain a footing. These are also the areas in which it is hoped that production will respond quickly to the new institutional arrangements for marketing and for distributing input.

In view of the chronic problems the Nordic projects have experienced in both Kenya and Tanzania in supporting weaker agricultural areas, this selectivity provides an interesting contrast to the typical project pattern of pressing on in the face of adversity. The decision to focus this project on the relatively stronger agricultural areas initially was the result of a great deal of footwork by a few individuals who had a substantial background in Tanzanian agriculture. It was not the result of an institutional learning process based on the past experience of DANIDA or the Nordic group. Indeed, stronger winds could easily have convinced these donors to provide support for the entire national system, as Tanzania had officially requested. Unless DANIDA and its Nordic partners conduct more in-depth analysis of the conditions likely to ensure the success of agricultural marketing cooperatives, it is altogether possible that the next round of Tanzanian requests to extend the project will receive a positive response. The blanket suggestion that cooperatives are inherently suitable institutions has surfaced, for instance, in DANIDA's discussions with the Tanzanians concerning another recently approved project, which is to provide inputs for the four Southern Highland regions. Several of these regions did not begin to register any considerable grain surpluses until their (government-imposed) cooperatives were abolished and replaced by the National Milling Corporation in the mid-1970s. This suggests that they will not be in any position to successfully manage the movements of these grains and the input trade at the low marketing margins that are absolutely essential when one is dealing with such low-value crops.

The prospects for the project, as it is currently constituted, will depend to a great extent on the institutional outcome of the movement's independence. At best, the project may have the scope to meet the democratization objective, as well as the economic objective of helping to revive crop-marketing structures. It would be natural, perhaps, for the project to revive membership training (which had been a casualty of the 1976 abolition) and to support an independent research budget for the Cooperative College that would enable it to do empirical studies on cooperative-related issues. What seems obvious at this juncture is that if the party wins the current battle, the socioeconomic objectives and main legitimization of the project will be abandoned.

Cooperative management is showing signs of wanting to get into a range of production activities that are uncertain from the economic standpoint—for example, it has expressed an interest in taking over large farms. In this respect, the fact that the Nordic project does not have a monopoly in supporting the cooperatives is significant. Given the likelihood that other donors will want to put money into relatively better cooperatives (with the risk of overcommitting them, as was part of the problem in the last round) it will be extremely important for donors to coordinate their support for the movement.

Production

DANIDA has directed its production-oriented assistance through two channels: projects in support of smallholders, mainly in Kenya, and (far more costly) bulk deliveries of chemical inputs, mainly in Tanzania. Quite different issues are raised by the two kinds of aid.

Projects in marginal areas. In keeping with DANIDA's policy of helping the poorer groups in Kenya, its production-oriented projects have concentrated on the less developed agricultural areas. These areas are by and large composed of marginal lands, as defined by the rainfall they receive, but they also encompass some geographically remote areas with medium potential, as in western Kenya. Little agricultural progress has been achieved here, despite numerous donor-assisted projects since the mid-1970s.

DANIDA has pursued two strategies to raise productivity: it has encouraged farmers to adopt existing technological packages (especially chemical inputs) and, more recently, it has encouraged aid recipients to learn how to manage their soil and water to improve their natural resource base. The first of these strategies has been followed in the Farm Inputs Supply Scheme (FISS), in operation in Kenya since the mid-1970s. FISS is one of the special credit schemes (mentioned above in the discussion about cooperatives) designed to raise output by subsidizing cooperative distribution mechanisms for various farm inputs and other rural amenities. The project has been heavily staffed with technical personnel, has been well managed in general, and has had a high (but falling) level of recovery compared with most of the other special credit schemes.

Thanks to its emphasis on management, FISS will not have the adverse effect on the financial position of weak cooperatives that credit schemes such as the World Bank's IADP have had throughout the western cotton-growing areas. But the project's conceptual framework raises some doubt about whether its benefits will go much beyond the project period itself. Underlying the project design is the basic supply-side philosophy, not uncommon in development circles, that if farmers have access to inputs, they will develop a taste for using them. Unlike the more typical case in which subsidies promote new technology, FISS hinges on the assumption that a technology Kenyan farmers have been aware of since the 1960s will fail in the retail markets; the inputs have not been stocked in local stores because demand has been too low to achieve scale economies in marketing.

DANIDA's evaluations of FISS do not look explicitly at the validity of this assumption, but there are some indications that it should be questioned. In the dryer areas, the project appears to have been far more popular for its provision of building materials than for inputs, which suggests that farmers have declined to use high-risk chemical inputs where rainfall is unreliable. At the other extreme, in the areas with relatively high agricultural potential, the project proved to be largely redundant, inasmuch as shops already existed to meet input demands. For the areas in between, the program may have helped increase the use of inputs in the short term. Although the stores established by FISS were running with a small surplus on their operating costs, the inputs continued to need heavy subsidization by the project, despite their high turnover.

DANIDA's area-based irrigation, water, and soil management projects in several of Kenya's marginal districts have followed another strategy in implementing the traditional input credit project. The oldest of these, in Garissa, is based on the standard technology for pumping water from a river, but a project in Mutumo introduced a prototype design that has been followed in the more recent Taita-Taveta project.[22] This technology is based on the concept of entrapping precipitation before it runs off the soil, so it can be stored in subsurface or other natural reservoirs. These projects represent an important departure from the more common "blueprint" approach to area-based development in that they treat it as a learning process, which in this case consisted of identifying catchment areas and establishing self-help groups.

So far, participants have responded more enthusiastically to the water management activities than the afforestation activities. It is too early to assess the effect on production, or the cost-effectiveness of this project, but in principle, the strategy is exciting because it has the potential to reach poor smallholders in marginal areas. By augmenting the local resource base directly under the producers' control while reducing risk, the project has improved upon the input credit schemes that add to the uncontrollable risk factors, such as the weather and pests, the risk of unpredictable timing of input supply and of severe crop failures in the event of inadequate rainfall.

Bulk input supply. Tied support for imports of chemical inputs has accounted for a large share of the annual disbursements to Tanzania since 1979. DANIDA has been one of many donors shipping fertilizers and the sole provider of coffee pesticides. This practice raises several questions—about the fungibility of government funds, the role of sectoral policy constraints, and the constraints imposed by tying by source.

On the first point, it seems clear that the Danish grants have added to the total amount of inputs available in Tanzania, given the extreme scarcity of foreign exchange. Yet the inputs may not have been enough to meet the quantities that would have been purchased in the absence of aid. For instance, the Tanzanian treasury has used the alibi of donor support to withhold from coffee growers access to foreign exchange that was rightfully theirs under the export retention scheme guaranteeing exporters a share of their earnings in hard currency to meet import needs. The result is an almost complete dependence of the coffee industry on donor funds. This renews questions about the Tanzanian government's willingness to give agriculture higher priority in its development efforts.

Second, the policy framework for import distribution has been severely marred by a restrictive, publicly run retail system (with fewer than twenty outlets on the entire mainland) and a distorted pricing system arising from a costly domestic fertilizer industry.[23] Although DANIDA, like most other input donors, has expressed concern about these problems, it has not made its deliveries contingent upon policy changes. Although it would be unreasonable to expect small donors singlehandedly to spearhead policy dialogue, their overall significance collectively puts them in a position to discuss more seriously with the Tanzanian government the measures required to free up distribution and to spare farmers from having to pay the costs of inefficient domestic production. There are compelling reasons for coordinating the donors' own supply programs on timing, kind of fertilizer, and destination. DANIDA and other input donors will need to be convinced that these issues are worth addressing.

On the third point, the consideration being given to shifting to denser (and more cheaply transported) kinds of fertilizer raises questions for longer-term Danish support, since these varieties are not produced in Denmark.

Financial Transfers to Development Banks

The development banks in both Tanzania and Kenya are primarily concerned with the rural economy. For many years Tanzania's bank was known as the Tanzania Rural Development Bank, although recently it was renamed the Cooperative and Rural Development Bank (CRDB). The Kenyan counterpart is the Cooperative Bank of Kenya (CBK). These development banks have had similar objectives: namely, to provide financial services for the part of the rural economy that would not be particularly attractive to the regular commercial banking system. In practice, the scope of Tanzania's CRDB has been wider than that of Kenya's CBK because the Kenyan cooperatives have been responsible for much of the credit in the field, whereas CRDB has had full responsibility down to the village level.

Both banks have enjoyed a reputation for professionalism, which accounts for their being saddled with substantial administrative burdens as the implementing agencies for a myriad of donor-financed credit projects. Of the two, the Tanzanian bank appears to have been somewhat less sheltered from the deleterious effects of the many unsuccessful credit programs, in that political directives have frequently overridden its collection attempts.[24]

Denmark has funded both banks. CRDB has been one of DANIDA's largest recipient institutions, receiving large capital grants annually since the early 1970s. Support for the capital budget of the CBK began in 1976, on a far smaller scale. Beyond this, the two institutions reflect the distinction between the bulk character of the Tanzanian portfolio and the more administratively intensive Kenyan one.

The origins of CRDB support appear to stem from a stamp of good health by the World Bank (which subsequently used it as an agent for a number of its input credit activities) and a joint Nordic review early in the 1970s. For almost a decade, DANIDA stayed virtually out of CRDB's sphere of influence, providing no technical assistance and being content to receive quarterly reports on the bank's activities. During the 1970s CRDB provided an administratively efficient channel for undisbursed funds from the entire DANIDA project budget at the end of each fiscal year. DANIDA's remoteness from the CRDB's day-today problems is reflected in the fact that it did not even safeguard the bank's access to the foreign currency that was being transferred to Tanzania on its behalf. This practice was modified somewhat in 1970, and since then about one-third of the total allocation has been reserved for CRDB in informally tied foreign currency.

Support to the Cooperative Bank of Kenya followed other DANIDA involvement in cooperatives, which gave DANIDA a clear sense both of the CBK's needs and of its own abilities to meet these. Some capital support has been earmarked for specific activities in coffee and dairy production, with the remainder entering the bank's own capital budget. These funds have been accompanied by a handful of Danish financial advisers throughout the project period. Although the capital support appears to have been useful, the project's strong point is its technical assistance. As the Kenyan cooperative banking system becomes more sophisticated (through, among other things, the development of the union banking system discussed above), the tools of the financial officers need to grow correspondingly. Over the years the Danish advisers have filled a need felt by the Kenyan staff for on-the-job training in the use of more refined investment analysis and general banking practices. More recently, the advisory staff has been in a position in CBK's rationalization exercise to create a unified credit scheme out of the chaotic institutional apparatus left behind by the special credit schemes of the 1970s.

In the Tanzanian case, DANIDA's support has not been distinguished from the general activities of CRDB, so it is appropriate to assess aid effectiveness within this overall context. Although CRDB has been a relatively sound institution, it is appropriate to question the basic orientation of this financial transfer. Credit does not stand out as a principal constraint to agricultural potential with respect to the range of incentive problems that have been facing Tanzanian producers since the 1970s. This holds for seasonal inputs (for which, as noted, there have been fewer than twenty retail institutions on the entire mainland), and it holds for a range of investment items such as oxplows, mills, bicycles, and corrugated iron sheeting. Note that in Kenya the basic institutions in the agricultural sector appear to be more or less in working order, and the retail markets can meet the demands of those with cash. Under such conditions, it makes sense to refine at the margin the capacity to assess the creditworthiness of potential investments, so that loan officers can serve more fully as economic advisers to agricultural producers.

Crop Processing: Support to the Sugar Industry

A substantial part of the crop-related donor activities in both Kenya and Tanzania are centered on processing, which is assisted mainly through loans for sugar extraction and grain storage equipment. The experiences in the two countries raise similar questions concerning the appropriate use of technology supplied through state loans. Tanzanian sugar investment is the example discussed here.[25]

Overview. DANIDA, along with the World Bank and the Netherlands, has been one of the three leading donors to the Tanzanian sugar industry. This is one of the rare occasions when Danish commercial investments preceded the aid program (in contrast, the practice was quite common for the colonial powers). The Tanganyika Planting Company (TPC) was established in the interwar period by one of Denmark's leading shipping magnates and soon attained a prominent position in the country's sugar industry, which it has maintained to the present.

TPC was initially supplied with non-Danish milling equipment, but in the early 1960s it began to employ a prototype of a new technology for cane processing developed by the leading Danish beet sugar processor, De Danske Sukkerfabrikker (DDS). The technology was based on diffusion, the method normally used for processing beet sugar. This collaboration was important in subsequent DANIDA involvement. In the late 1960s, DDS supplied a cane diffuser to the Ramisi estate in Kenya's Coast Province and in the mid-1970s to the publicly owned Kilombero estates in Tanzania in collaboration with the World Bank, which financed the production. These investments were all made as state loans. With the continuing investments in the TPC, Denmark was a major participant in the general expansion taking place in the Tanzanian sugar industry in the 1970s.

By the late 1970s, TPC's parent firm in Denmark wanted to divest itself of the sugar estate after being starved for some time of the foreign exchange allocations needed to maintain its capital stock. DANIDA smoothed the transition by financing a management contract for the initial period of public control and by providing some new equipment (mainly spares).

Although this sequence of events may give the impression of a logical progression of DANIDA's sugar policy, in fact DANIDA had no ex ante sense of sectoral involvement. Rather, it first became sectorally concerned with its role in sugar after making these investments. In 1981 Denmark joined the Netherlands in the World Bank initiative, which was designed to take a unified stand on the rehabilitation of the sugar industry. By this time the industry had fallen into a general decline because of factors such as the lack of foreign exchange for maintenance activities and the poor management of production and processing. The donors jointly requested changes in the government's sugar polices, including a block on further expansion until performance on the existing estates improved. On the implicit (if not explicit) understanding that the donors would support rehabilitation of the estates in which they had already invested DANIDA fully expected to come up with substantial additional financing. But over the next two years the World Bank changed its position because further analysis of the agricultural sector concluded that sugar was not an investment priority for scarce rehabilitation funds—in view of other, more structural problems in agriculture (such as the entire management system under agricultural parastatals) and estimates that other crop enterprises had a higher net foreign exchange earnings/savings content than sugar. The Danes followed the Bank's lead and closed the books on sugar in Tanzania.

Assessment. In assessing DANIDA's involvement in sugar, it is important to go beyond the general information on the decline of the Tanzanian sugar industry since the mid-1970s to Danish investments. DANIDA has little information on these investments, because they came at a time when state loans were subject to little or no monitoring. The information gap did not improve with the joint donor initiative, since DANIDA left the analytical work to the World Bank, which focused on overall performance rather than issues specifically related to individual donor investments. Interviews with a number of sugar experts suggest there are grounds for concern about the specific nature of DANIDA involvement. At issue is the choice of technology for sugar processing.

Today there are basically three ways to process cane sugar: (1) open-pan sulphitation (OPS), (2) the vacuum pan (VP), and (3) diffusion. The OPS and VP technologies differ in the way the boil extracts cane juice to induce crystallization (a difference reflected in their name) and in scale—the VP requires a large cane throughput if it is to be efficient (minimum 3,500 tons per day) and the OPS is to run on a much smaller throughput (60–150 tons per day).[26] The diffusion technique differs from the others in the way it extracts the sucrose from the cane. Whereas they crush the cane mechanically (with mills) to obtain the sucrose, diffusion extracts it through a leaching process. This principle was developed for sugar beets, where it is the dominant method of processing. The Danish DDS introduced the prototype cane diffuser at the TPC estate. Although some small versions are available (and as yet untried in Africa), the scale of the standard diffusion technology depends on the VP.

From a given quantity of cane, the diffusion technique can in principle extract 5–6 percent more sugar than VP, which in turn leads OPS by at least 10 percent. But for a given output of sugar, the small OPS may require less than one-quarter the investment of the large VP and may provide more than six times the employment. By contrast, what distinguishes diffusion from VP is not so much capital as management intensity. Although diffusion is mechanically simpler, its tolerance margin for unsteady production is much lower and a production stop much costlier (because of restart time and losses due to fermentation).

The unpredictable production environment prevailing in most of Africa suggests that the diffusion technique might have difficulty there. A choice between OPS and VP technologies would be somewhat less transparent, since it would depend on many variables, including the scale of production, national price policies, and given infrastructure. The geographically concentrated, high-volume production of sugar definitely favors VP technology. Yet other conditions, such as the abundance of labor with respect to capital, the feasibility of extensive as against intensive cane cultivation, and the scarcity of foreign exchange point in the opposite direction. Thus it is important to consider the various options in sugar processing technology in making investment decisions, whereas in the dairy industry there is basically only one technology available for industrial processing. For Danish tied aid, however, the choice of sugar technology is a nonissue, since Denmark can only deliver the diffusion technique.

Not surprisingly, the technology has performed dismally. Management was unable to concentrate on maximizing extraction rates since its full attention was devoted to ensuring that extraction took place at all. As a result, diffusion technology has been put out of commission. According to DDS, the technology was never employed in the one Kenyan estate receiving a Danish diffuser—at least initially because cane production was too low to keep the equipment in operation. At TPC in Tanzania (which had a large expatriate professional staff during the period under consideration), the diffuser was found to be too sophisticated and was eventually abandoned. The Kilombero estates, which have had far worse management problems, have not been able to cope with diffusion, either.

It is significant that not a trace of this lesson seems to have been imprinted in DANIDA's institutional memory. DANIDA closed the book on sugar in Tanzania for macroeconomic reasons. But because it never conducted a technological evaluation of the sugar investments, there are no grounds for avoiding the technology in the future should Tanzania or another country request it at a more propitious time. Although this lesson has been registered by the company that had developed and provided the technology, it would be too much to expect a commercial firm to decline a contract of similar magnitude, were it offered in the future.

Other Activities Supporting Agriculture

DANIDA has financed numerous activities to promote agriculture indirectly, including transportation infrastructure and industrial imports.

Support to transportation infrastructure. DANIDA has been among the donors to recognize the links between transportation investments and agricultural production in its portfolio and future plans. It has commissioned a comprehensive study of the bottlenecks in Tanzania's transportation infrastructure that should be of use to donors in general. So far, it has supported transportation in both countries through labor-intensive, rural, road-building projects. In Kenya, DANIDA has been an important donor in the ILO-inspired Rural Access Roads Program (RARP) since 1977. This program has helped the country organize a system for constructing dirt and gravel roads with labor-intensive methods. In addition to facilitating rural trade, the 7,500 kilometers of all-weather roads established under the program (through some 60,000 man-years) have boosted purchasing power in the twenty-six districts in which they have been constructed by virtue of the employment generated.

The long-term significance for agriculture will, however, depend on how and to what extent the government resolves the financial and organizational problems surrounding the maintenance of access roads. For a period of three years from 1985 to 1988, DANIDA was among the donors that supported the transition to a maintenance program. The fact that the roads are situated in relatively more productive districts increases the probability that political pressure will resolve the problems.

In Tanzania, the labor-intensive feeder roads program is in Ruvuma region, in the Southern Highlands. Unlike the RARP, which is administered by Kenya's Ministry of Works, this project is administered directly by the ILO, which was the source of inspiration for the similar idea of providing temporary wage employment in rural areas. Whereas the RARP appears to be making a substantial contribution to agriculture, the Ruvuma project appears to have less chance of being effective, primarily because the labor resources are poorer in this project area. Although agricultural land is abundant in Ruvuma, labor in the peak farming seasons may be in short supply. Thus a labor-intensive feeder roads program might have a negative effect on agricultural output unless an effort is made to identify the labor peaks of the farming system and to employ unskilled labor only in the slack periods. These questions were not even considered until several years after the inception of the project, and the results of surveys conducted then downplayed the finding that there had already been some adverse effects on agriculture.

Moreover, project documents provide no substantive evidence that the roads themselves would have a net positive effect on agriculture; indeed, the low traffic flow suggests otherwise. An analysis of whether other constraints (such as the lack of fuel, trucks, spare parts, or storage) have not been more binding than the roads themselves, or whether alternative logistical systems (such as bicycles, local storage, or all-weather trunk roads) might not have been more appropriate, does not appear to have been done. Rather, the strategy chosen seems to reflect the ILO's preoccupation with logging the wage hours it has created, irrespective of the local conditions. In contrast, population density or land shortage (typically an inverse indicator of year-round surplus labor) was an explicit criterion for the allocation of RARP activities in Kenya.

Industrial import support. In addition to chemical inputs, DANIDA has provided Tanzania with increasing industrial support—to the soap industry since 1979 (technical fat) and to the local engineering and smithing industry since 1985 (steel plates and rods). The aim has been to support the production of end products rural producers need.

Aid to the soap industry was considered support to incentive goods. DANIDA took care to provide the quality of fat that could only be used to make the low-grade washing soap not in demand among higher-income urban dwellers. Monitoring as of early 1985 found the soap (albeit at high prices) in shops in distant villages, many of which had not seen this basic commodity for years.

The steel imports were intended to alleviate bottlenecks in production and contribute to the repair of infrastructural items (such as vehicles) and production inputs (such as hoes and plows). Informal reports in late 1986 suggested that this objective was thwarted in part by the type of steel sent. The steel rods were absorbed by the local construction business, a booming inflation hedge for urban dwellers. The experience suggests that more care will need to be put into the selection of the kinds of commodities to be provided (as was done in the case of soap).

On the whole, import support is a creative and potentially positive response to a wide range of problems affecting aid to Tanzania: rampant shortages of most items because of the scarcity of foreign exchange; the near impossibility of running successful agricultural projects in the context of both the economic crisis itself and the policy environment in which projects must operate; the formal and informal restrictions on Danish aid that make financial transfers more difficult to provide than Danish-based commodities; and the Tanzanians' long-standing inability to set priorities among the agricultural imports and various industrial investments it needs. Yet commodity aid to Tanzanian industries sidesteps some fundamental questions about the overall soundness of the government's trade and industrial policies. A recent World Bank study that surveyed more than 100 Tanzanian industrial enterprises found numerous firms producing a negative value added, in many cases irrespective of the level of capacity utilization.[27] Part of the blame for this situation rests with the long overvalued currency, which has underpriced industrial imports. These distortions have been compounded by the administrative allocation procedure for foreign exchange, which has been unable to take into account the relative efficiency of the various firms' use of resources. Poor performers were found in the private and public sector alike, with considerable variation among firms in the same industry.

The only way to sort out fully which firms are financially viable and which are not would be to get the exchange rate to its market value. Otherwise, donors providing industrial import support need to conduct detailed economic and financial analyses to ensure that they are not bolstering firms whose economic prospects will diminish once macroeconomic health is restored. If a donor's ultimate objective is to reach the rural areas, it may at times be more appropriate to sidestep the Tanzanian industrial capacity altogether and to provide the end products directly.

Policy Conclusions

DANIDA's future support of East African agriculture should be guided by the lessons of past experience. In particular, it appears that policy changes are needed to forge a stronger link between the agriculture in the recipient countries and the resources from which the donor can provide assistance.

Assessing the East African Portfolios

DANIDA has provided four kinds of resource transfers, each with somewhat different implications for aid effectiveness: (1) Danish capital goods (hardware), through state-loan-funded projects; (2) Danish commodities, provided as balance of payments support; (3) Danish know-how (software); and (4) international know-how, provided through Danish financing. The first category broadly encompasses the tied state-loan program (and some project aid), the second the more recent shift to import support (whether formally tied or untied), the third the majority of project aid, and the fourth the contracting out to United Nations agencies through multi-bi projects. The following discussion concentrates on the first of these four kinds.[28]

Transfer of Danish capital goods. The opportunities for Danish investments in Tanzania and Kenya using tied state loans have been rather unsatisfactory. The main obstacles to such aid are the limited capacity of the recipient country to determine which industrial and agroindustrial investments are needed and the erratic production environment, which makes it difficult to run and maintain sophisticated Danish equipment.[29]

It is widely recognized in DANIDA that the first problem was to blame for the misplaced investments in the expansion of the Tanzanian cement industry. Tanzanian officials were either unable or unwilling to base their financing requests on realistic projections of demand and cost, with the result that many millions of Danish kroner have gone into cement factories that cannot keep running without large subsidies from foreign donors. Slaughterhouse investments in Kenya appear to fall into the same category, since the economy cannot readily absorb them.

The second type of problem has surfaced in Tanzania in the case of sugar equipment, which requires much more stable conditions than Tanzania can provide. Only in the case of dairy processing in Kenya does there appear to have been a clearly positive role for Danish state-of-the-art capital goods.

This mediocre experience in the two African countries in which DANIDA has had the greatest opportunity to understand the economic context of its investment decisions raises questions about the chances for success of state loans in the rest of Sub-Saharan Africa. DANIDA cannot assume that these countries are able to determine what kinds of capital investments their economies can manage; and yet DANIDA does not have the resources to make these judgments for or in conjunction with them. Although the state-loan office has substantially upgraded its project appraisal capacity since the late 1970s, the discrete investment's rate of return is still the main concern. The means for assessing the viability of investments in the sectoral and macroeconomic context—that is, from a *strategic* point of view—do not rest with DANIDA.

Transfer of Danish commodities. On the whole, the experience with commodity aid has been far more positive than that with the export of capital goods, although Denmark's special mix of products does not readily lend itself to the developing economy. When care is taken to identify the appropriate products required and a suitable channel is found for them, they can be an extremely helpful form of crisis aid. In Tanzania, in fact, this may be a better form of support for agriculture than a blank check to the Ministry of Finance, since the government has not yet sorted out its priorities for allocating scarce foreign exchange. To find the appropriate channels, DANIDA obviously needs to have a strategic sense both of the economy's needs and of the internal channels by which the commodities in question are allocated. The instances of import support to the Tanzanian soap industry show extreme sensitivity to both of these issues. The experience with steel imports has apparently been less positive because these channels were less carefully assessed. In the case of support for chemical agricultural inputs, which has become a regular part of the Tanzanian portfolio and has also occurred briefly in Kenya, policy questions concerning internal distribution need to be addressed to improve the effectiveness of the aid. Since many donors are involved in input supplies, DANIDA will have to show continued willingness to join the leading suppliers in discussing policy reform with government officials.

The potential of commodity aid could be increased if the market was opened to a wider basket of Danish commodities. Two fairly rigid procedures of aid administration would need to be relaxed for this to occur. First, present inhibitions on the application of tying prevent Denmark from providing commodities that are not viable commercial exports. Second, DANIDA's practice is to send only production inputs; yet in a country such as Tanzania, where many industrial enterprises are not financially viable, the intended rural recipients may benefit more from having finished goods than from having their domestic production subsidized with Danish intermediate inputs. Were these two procedures relaxed, DANIDA would be able to draw from a number of home goods such as consumer durables (bicycles, batteries, and so on).

Of course, in an ideal world DANIDA would be able to provide whatever commodities it identified as essential to agricultural recovery and would purchase them by international tender. But assuming that tied Danish commodity aid adds to the total amount of imported resources, more expensive Danish commodity support (appropriately identified) would still be better than none and might well have a greater economic impact in the recipient country than those Danish products that are internationally competitive. This principle has already been well established for subsidized Danish agricultural commodities channeled through the food aid programs of the EC and the World Food Program.

Enthusiasm for the potential of commodity aid does not, however, extend to countries that are not main recipients of Danish aid. In these cases, the state-loan office's policy not to move into commodity aid is probably a sound one. Without a DANIDA mission in the country, the transfer would be impossible to monitor (in line with perceived accountability requirements). The issue is seen less as one of monitoring than one of DANIDA's ability to appropriately identify the economy's needs. With proper identification, monitoring is necessary only to verify, not to steer, the domestic allocation of the goods in question.

Transfer of Danish know-how. A common belief in Denmark is that technical assistance is one of the strengths the country has to offer, and this is certainly reflected in the composition of many projects reviewed in this study. Happily, there seems to be no cultural barrier to close cooperation between Danish technical assistance personnel and personnel in East Africa. The effectiveness of technical assistance therefore has depended on how good the match is between the abilities of the Danish personnel and the needs of the recipient economy. That this match is not always satisfactory is detected in a review of the three kinds of projects concerned primarily with the transfer of knowledge: livestock, financial management, and engineering projects.

Danish livestock expertise is more likely to have a positive effect in Kenya than in Tanzania. In Kenya, there has been a fruitful interaction in the area of cattle disease control, and there are signs that work in fodder development can also have a good payoff. In Tanzania, the investments in veterinary medicine education seem fraught with problems. The outcome of these aid projects has been a function of the role of cattle in the two economies, as already noted. Cattle rearing in Kenya is not much different from livestock rearing in Europe, whereas the Tanzanian case is still closer to a tropical subsistence economy, in which livestock are treated as a savings and insurance device. Unless some expertise is acquired in managing livestock under these latter conditions, the future contribution of Denmark in this area will remain limited.

A number of Danish projects concerned with financial management have had important advisory components. Danish experts in this field have been able to provide organizational advice adapted to a range of institutional forms. But the success of the intervention has depended on a correct assessment of the need for or relevance of this type of input in the context of a particular project. In all likelihood, most of the advisers to the regional cooperatives up to 1976, when cooperatives were abolished, made little difference because they were placed in nonviable institutions. In Kenya, those aspects of the cooperative project that focused on marginal areas had similar problems, with the result that expensive advice was sown on barren ground. In contrast, the support given to economically viable cooperative activities in the two countries seems to have constituted an important Danish-Nordic contribution. This contribution has been most effective in Kenya, where institutional stability has allowed the project to provide sustained support for management practices in cooperative societies and unions with high potential, and for the development of a cooperative banking system. In Tanzania, policy instability eroded the earlier years' effective support to the cooperatives in highly productive areas. Village bookkeeper training, which began subsequently, seems to have been less susceptible to the institutional turbulence and hence more successful. Although assessments of the Kenyan Farm Inputs

Supply Scheme do not provide enough information to arrive at firm conclusions, it would appear that this project, run with a core team of financial advisers, had the same problems as the cooperative project in Kenya because it used an inappropriate mechanism for assisting marginal producers. Advisers to the Cooperative Bank, in contrast, have proved highly valuable in helping to develop that institution on sound financial principles.

Although Danish capital goods exports have a fairly restrictive technology, the engineering sector has shown itself to be flexible, if not neutral, on the question of technology transfer. The usefulness of the Danish contribution in this regard has depended on DANIDA's ability to define the appropriate parameters for engineers to do their work. Two examples of successful infrastructural activities have been the Rural Access Roads Program in Kenya and the Rural Water Supply (Southern Highland) Project in Tanzania. In the roads program, the project design specified the use of a labor-intensive technology for road construction; an appropriate method was then developed and executed by the project engineers. In the water project, specifications took into account the likelihood that recurrent foreign exchange would be scarce and therefore concluded that the schemes should be based on gravity-drawn rather than pump-drawn sources. In contrast, in the less successful donor-financed schemes in Tanzania in the early 1970s engineers leaned toward schemes using diesel pump technology (which typically costs less to install than the gravity-drawn technology).

Comparison of the East African experiences. Successes and failures can be identified in each category of aid to the two East African countries. Grouping the successes by country, one finds a striking imbalance in favor of Kenya's portfolio, the smaller of the two.

In Tanzania, the bookkeeper training element of the cooperative project stands out in an otherwise barren project landscape. Commodity aid for chemical inputs and soap seems to have been appropriate crisis aid and undoubtedly it has had some short-term benefits in stemming economic deterioration. The effect of the new Cooperative Project will depend on the outcome of policy debates within the Tanzanian government.

The successes in Kenya are more numerous. The multifaceted support to the production, research, processing, and marketing aspects of the dairy industry might top the list, but certainly the coffee and the pyrethrum cooperatives have benefited just as much from the Nordic project's strengthening of their general management systems. Another cornerstone in the country's cooperative edifice has been laid by DANIDA's support for the Cooperative Bank's staff development and for the strengthening of its operational procedures. Projects in more specific areas also may have a longer-term effect. The Rural Access Roads Program and the Rural Development Fund have in different ways contributed to the country's rural infrastructure. Although it is premature to give a final verdict on the more integrated methods being applied in Mutomo, Taita, and Taveta, the preliminary results and the flexible learning strategy employed in harnessing locally controlled resources leave ample room for optimism.

The different success rates in the two countries may be attributed to historical factors. In Kenya's dairy industry, it appears that past success has been responsible for the present success. The climatic conditions, genetic resources, organizational and spatial forms of production, marketing, price incentives, credit availability, and, not least, the "see, but not touch" policy of the colonial era[30] have produced one of the few instances of successful livestock development in tropical Africa.[31] In other words, the Danish investment in milk processing came to fruition because of all the features that were already in place.

DANIDA's assessment of the resource base was an important element in its dairy investments, as in its other successful aid projects. The question is, why was more of this assessment done in Kenya than in Tanzania? The answer seems to lie in the interaction between the donor—Denmark—and the political systems of the two recipient states. As noted earlier, DANIDA had a different perception of the policy framework in the two countries and therefore adopted a different strategy in identifying the projects for each. The Tanzanian government's basic orientation was seen to fit with DANIDA's own concern with poverty. This led it to adopt a more laissez-faire attitude toward the precise use of Danish funds and to pay little attention to assessing resources. In Kenya, DANIDA saw itself as the initiator and guardian of a program to alleviate and in exploring the feasibility of pursuing this objective it had to assess resources.

Denmark's compensatory reaction was compounded by operational necessities stemming from the different structures of the two economies. The broader the scope of a recipient country's policies and the more centralized the method of implementing them, the less opportunity there is for a donor to participate in identifying specific targets for aid. Although both Kenya and Tanzania have had their share of blanket policies that are insensitive to the specific conditions of different areas (as, for instance, in cooperative policy), Tanzania clearly surpasses Kenya in the extent of centralized decisionmaking and detailed intervention in the workings of the agricultural economy down to the farm level. Even if DANIDA had wanted to, it could not have replicated successfully in Tanzania the case-by-case scrutiny carried out in Kenyan projects. The systemic weaknesses in the Tanzanian policy and institutional environment can only be addressed through policy conditionality, a task for which DANIDA is not well equipped.

Basically, the nature of Danish aid to East African agriculture up to the present can best be described as supply-side assistance. To a large extent, its contours have been shaped by Denmark's own domestic and international concerns—whether cultural, economic, or political. Seen from the perspective of maintaining a comprehensive aid constituency and of increasing real aid levels, the Danish aid policies may be regarded as something of a masterpiece. The record with regard to aid effectiveness is somewhat spottier, however. When aid has been effective, it has met at least three conditions on the demand side: It has corresponded to the needs of the intended beneficiaries, has added an incremental but critical resource to a local constellation of otherwise underutilized factors of production, and has fitted in with the national policies of the recipient country.

More often than not, at least one of these conditions was absent. Agricultural aid can only be made more effective by ensuring that the resource base of the donor matches the needs of the recipient. This means, first, that more attention should be devoted to identifying the demand situation; second, it is vital to recognize that the donor's resource base is not a fixed parameter, but can itself be developed to respond to the identified needs; and, third, some kinds of aid may have to be restructured to ensure better delivery.

Toward More Effective Aid to Agriculture

Some of the obstacles to effective agricultural aid are familiar to all donor and recipient governments; they arise because understanding of the developmental process has been embryonic or incomplete. In addition there are some institutional constraints to greater aid effectiveness that are particular to the Danish methods of allocating aid. These constraints arise from contradictions inherent in the various objectives or motivations that have shaped the overall aid policy. The three constituency-generated objectives of Danish aid are related to foreign policy, philanthropic, and commercial interests. Since these interests at times clash—not only with each other, but also with the primary objective of development itself—it is necessary to define a fourth interest that allows the development objective to be distinguished from the constituency-generated ones. In this discussion, the term "professionalism" is used to refer to an exclusive concern with the demand side of the equation, completely detached from any cultural, political, or commercial determinants on the supply side.[32] In determining the demand side, professional analysis cannot disregard recipient government requests, but must assess whether they coincide or conflict with the self-perceived interests of the target population in the given agricultural system.

The most significant conflicts among these four kinds of interests originate in one of three ways: among different interests outside the aid agency; among different interests inside the agency, as represented by different personnel groups or organizational cultures; and within the internalized value system of individual staff members.

The first conflict arises from the long-standing differences between commercial and philanthropic interests over the allocational procedures for the tied aid portfolio. As noted earlier, the originally intended recipients of state loans were the middle-income countries. Under popular pressure to make all aid poverty-oriented, this soon gave way to a policy that allowed only low-income countries to have access to these funds. In effect, this compromise maintained the volume of aid benefiting Danish industry while curtailing its outlets. The compromise has greatly handicapped the search for an appropriate use for Danish state loans. It also necessitates more work on DANIDA's part, since many of these recipients do not have the analytical capacity to handle certain functions and the agency must (or ought to) take them on.

This chapter has already pointed to one possible procedural modification to heighten aid effectiveness in the Kenya and Tanzania and at the same time keep disbursements up: namely, to extend the use of tied commodity aid. At the same time, there is some question as to the advisability of DANIDA's continued promotion of regular capital-export loans elsewhere in Africa—since neither DANIDA nor the recipients have the capacity to adequately analyze the macroeconomic and sectoral context of the investments.

The institutional mechanism by which the Danish capital exporter and the recipient government identify and agree on a DANIDA-financed state-loan contract tends to favor installations that are too sophisticated for African conditions, have greater capacity than necessary, and are overpriced. Of the three involved parties, DANIDA has the least vested interest in such an outcome. But DANIDA seems also to have the least manpower invested before the signing of the contract. The representatives of the recipient government tend to choose the most modern option. And a private contractor, needless to say, tends to want to secure the largest possible contract.

Ironically, the direct export of sophisticated capital goods through the aid budget to countries as poor as most of the African recipients affords the contractor only a one-time financial shot in the arm. The purchasing power of at least a middle-income country is required to promote the industry's long-term interest in helping to develop steady, self-capitalizing markets for Danish equipment. The recent opening of the Chinese market to Danish state loans should help considerably in alleviating disbursement problems. But since the pressure to disburse is bound to persist, it would be worth considering lifting the per capita income limit of eligibility (and perhaps charge modest interest rates). By extending the list of eligible countries to those able to use Danish technology more effectively, both the recipients and the Danes would be further ahead.

The second conflict emanates from the growing professionalism of the aid administration, on the one hand, and the foreign policy environment that permeates its modes of operation, on the other. The foreign policy platform has made DANIDA become concerned with avoiding conflict. Yet in order to increase the effectiveness of some aid activities, DANIDA will need to ensure that recipient-country policies are conducive to development. With some hesitation, the agency got its feet wet on conditionality in the Tanzanian case (over cement): the experience was painful for relations between the two countries.

In achieving the foreign policy objective of creating goodwill through bilateral aid, a generous aid portfolio risks putting the donor in a hostage position: Denmark can only maintain full goodwill if it does not raise any questions. But project identification and design, and the effective use of import support, are bound to suffer if it follows a course of least resistance.

The constraints imposed by the foreign policy environment on the development of professionalism may well have been the most serious long-term impediment to the effective use of Danish untied aid. Since the Foreign Ministry subsumed DANIDA upon the retirement of the agency's first director in the late 1960s, this tension has gradually risen, culminating in an administrative review, completed in early 1986.

The review produced recommendations concerning personnel policies and operational procedures, chief among which were a longer minimum time commitment for diplomats wanting to serve in the agency; greater accessibility to management positions for technical advisers; greater emphasis on the functions of the resident missions; and a new emphasis on country studies, strategies, and planning, which would provide specific enough guidance to allow for an effective decentralization of decisions to the missions and would provide foreign service officers with more operational instructions than hitherto. These recommendations, if followed, would resolve the conflict between the professional and the foreign policy interests by professionalizing the agency's personnel and modes of operation.

The third conflict stems from the tension between professional and philanthropic values or perceptions within the people shaping the content of Danish aid. Earlier in the chapter, this was described as a conflict between the Marshall Plan aid paradigm and the Albert Schweitzer syndrome. On one side is the desire to achieve a growth-oriented, catalytic effect comparable to the results of America's post-war aid to Europe, the goals of which were centered on GNP growth, the litmus test being that the aid should become superfluous after a short time. The second philosophy considers the alleviation of human suffering and uplifting of human dignity to be ends in themselves.

To varying degrees, all Western aid agencies have devoted attention to meshing these two strands of thought—the widely endorsed Basic Needs Strategy of the mid-1970s being the most explicit push to integrate the two. The point here is not that there *need* be a congruence, but that the present course has not been too effective in meeting either objective.

In the DANIDA portfolio, the incongruence expresses itself in two ways, depending on whether the activities are oriented primarily toward production or toward social services. Where aid has been oriented toward production, which includes agricultural production, the Albert Schweitzer syndrome has had a muting effect on productivity in several cases. Although the social services portfolio was not examined in detail in this study, it does seem that elements of the Marshall aid paradigm have adversely affected the design of welfare-enhancing activities.

Some agricultural projects that have had an explicit poverty orientation—and thereby have focused on marginal producers—have not proved to be either replicable or sustainable. Those that supported marginal cooperative societies and the Farm Inputs Supply Scheme in DANIDA's Kenya portfolio are cases in point. The Christian Michelsen Institute arrives at the same conclusion in its evaluation of Kenya's Rural Development Fund, observing that "the widespread belief that the promotion of production-oriented projects is a convenient shortcut for uplifting the rural poor seems to be based on unrealistic assumptions."[33]

Moreover, it is likely that DANIDA could have done more with the same money in the way of addressing the welfare concerns of these population groups had it not attempted to focus directly on production increases. A single female head of the household in a semiarid area of Kenya is much less likely to be helped by the purchase of a subsidized plow from a FISS store than by health and education programs that increase the likelihood of her children's survival and their chances for gainful off-farm employment. Moreover, production-oriented projects designed to uplift the rural poor frequently increase their dependence on external resources and conditions beyond their control. This demonstrates the importance of selecting appropriate technologies and methods of reaching poor farmers. One of the main reasons for being optimistic about DANIDA's strategy in Mutomo, Taita, and Taveta is precisely that it focuses on developing resources that are under the control of the producers themselves.

As noted earlier, social services are heavily emphasized in DANIDA's East African portfolio, particularly in Tanzania. The problem with these investments is the time frame; the donor is still under the influence of the Marshall aid syndrome: for DANIDA, the ideal social project seems to be one that local authorities can take over after the initial aid-financed capital investment.

During the recent crisis in Tanzania, DANIDA has been extremely flexible in assuming the recurrent costs of programs in both health and education (the former through drug supply and the latter through a large school maintenance program). Nevertheless, it has yet to make the explicit long-term commitment that involvement in the social service sector implies. To be effective, DANIDA (or another such donor) might need to be in the health sector for up to two decades, during which time institutions could be built up and resources made available. Short of this, a stop-gap intervention to provide essential drugs for a few years can only temporarily postpone the time when the clinics are empty. Thus it appears that if the aid program were to adopt broad welfare objectives (an option this chapter does not contest), a long-term commitment might be essential.

Although the stability of Danish aid depends on maintaining the existing three-legged bias in domestic interests, that aid will not help countries attain the broad objective of development unless more effort is put into disentangling these interests. What this boils down to is *maintaining balance in the overall portfolio*—but not necessarily in the design of individual projects or programs.

Notes

This chapter is an abridged version of a more detailed report by Ellen Hanak and Michael Loft, "Danish Development Assistance to Tanzania and Kenya, 1962–1985: Its Importance to Agricultural Development," MADIA Working Paper (Africa—Technical Department, Agriculture Division, World Bank, Washington, D.C., 1987). The work has been sponsored by DANIDA as part of a multidonor endeavor to examine the role of aid in agricultural and rural development in Africa under the auspices of the World Bank research project, Managing Agricultural Development in Africa (MADIA). Detailed references to internal evaluation materials are provided in the full report. The authors gratefully acknowledge the contributions of the many persons who were interviewed and who commented on earlier drafts. Maria Cancian and Sara Sidenius Johansen provided research assistance, and Jeanne Rosen editorial suggestions. Responsibility for the interpretations rests solely with the authors.

1. This chapter followed the OECD convention in defining aid as official development assistance (ODA) that has a grant element of at least 25 percent. This encompasses all flows from DANIDA, which are full grants or soft loans with a grant element of 76–86 percent. It excludes export credits and other official flows such as equity contributed by the Danish Industrialization Fund for Developing Countries.

2. This by no means implies that Danish diplomats shy away from conflict. Given instructions or well-defined guidelines, they will (in the words of one of them) "fight like scorpions." Aid policy generally is not, however, an issue on which the Danish Ministry of Foreign Affairs would want to risk a confrontation with recipient governments.

3. DANIDA, in its 1982 and 1984 annual reports to DAC, estimated that approximately 60 percent of its total bilateral grant assistance was used to purchase Danish goods and services.

4. Kjeld Phillip, a prominent figure in Danish aid circles, was head of the commission that recommended the establishment of the East African Community.

5. The mustering of additional, quick-disbursing flows of commodities out of the tied aid budget accounted for most of this increase in aid.

6. Tanzanians have coined this phrase to refer to the group of important bilateral donors whose aid has been on the softest terms and most in line with the Tanzanians' own sociopolitical philosophy.

7. For a fuller treatment of these issues, see Uma Lele and L. Richard Meyers, *Growth and Structural Change in East Africa: Domestic Policies, Agricultural Assistance, and World Bank Assistance, 1962–86*, Discussion Paper 3 (Washington, D.C., World Bank, 1989).

8. The measurement tools have varied between the countries. On the whole, there has been considerably more attention to measurement in Kenya, which reflects the fact that land resources are a greater constraint there.

9. In Western and Rift Valley provinces, the higher-quality areas are distinguished by their rainfall patterns, although the soils are poorer and less suitable to some of these export crops than they are to improved varieties of maize.

10. Many would argue that this could include subdivision of the larger farms in the areas of higher potential that are fairly extensively farmed.

11. See Yaw Ansu, "Macroeconomic Shocks, Policies and Performance: A Comparative Study of Kenya, Malawi and Tanzania—1967 to 1984," MADIA Working Paper (Africa—Technical Department, Agriculture Division, World Bank, Washington, D.C., 1986), pp. 109–17. Ansu documents the progressive overvaluation of the T Sh from 1972 to 1984, during which time the K Sh broadly kept within the bounds of its earlier real value (calculations based on purchasing power parity real exchange rates). Devaluations of the T Sh since spring 1986 have partly redressed the imbalance, but the currency remains considerably overvalued in the opinion of most analysts.

12. For information about activities omitted here, such as research, see Hanak and Loft, "Danish Development Assistance to Tanzania and Kenya."

13. Currently the minimum for pasteurized milk is 20–30 tons a day, which equals 2,000 liters an hour and 250 tons a day for ultra-heat-treated (UHT) milk.

14. Jack Frankel, "The Role of Livestock," background paper to the "Tanzania Agricultural Sector Report" (Africa—Technical Department, Agriculture Division, World Bank, Washington, D.C., May 1982).

15. In some Ethiopian and Kenyan pastoral areas, ILCA has been conducting on-site trial research on the types of crops that could supplement the nutri-

tional intake of calves, for instance. In the semiarid zones that are home to most of Tanzania's cattle, perennials would seem to be the most promising.

16. The fact that the Tanzanians did not object to using aid resources in this manner also may relate to the political implications of this project as a preventive strategy. Precisely because of their marginality, veterinary programs tend to imply relatively nonthreatening kinds of measures. In contrast, preventive and nutritional measures typically would demand sweeping changes in land use or stocking policies, as well as considerable restructuring of the administrative machinery dealing with animal health care.

17. The upgrading of the Morogoro campus to an independent university several years ago, as well as the fact that the majority of investments in facilities have already been made, suggests that this is the only politically feasible assumption.

18. DANIDA reports that in the second half of the 1980s there was an unofficial shift in the curriculum in favor of preventive health courses. Although this change is surely welcome, it does not appear to address the fundamental, structural alteration of the objectives of the program (such as the composition of manpower output or the research orientation of the Tanzanian teaching staff), which is necessary to attain substantial social benefits, and not just a marginally improved performance on this investment.

19. The colonial tradition lay with the granting of monopsony rights, although it is probably true to say that this was done with a somewhat greater assurance of a society's viability than was the case following independence.

20. In Kenya there is, for instance, a reluctance to relax the regulations for the parts of the cooperative system that have become quite sophisticated. In Tanzania the cooperatives reintroduced in the early 1980s have built-in government and party control measures at the union management level, which suggests that an independent movement is at best a long way off.

21. See M. Loft, E. Hanak, and A. Ndyeshobola, "The Evaluation of the Kigoma Rural Development Project" (University of Dar es Salaam Economic Research Bureau, 1982). The authors noted, for example, that a large number of bookkeepers had found work in a wide range of both public and private regional activities.

22. On the technology, see Erik Nissen-Pedersen, *Rain Catchment and Water Supply in Rural Africa: A Manual* (London: Hodder and Stoughton, 1982).

23. Before 1984, the pricing system was also distorted by a transport subsidy heavily subsidizing consumption in distant regions.

24. As in Kenya, the repayment for seasonal credit is collected as a deduction from crop payments to borrowers. In the Tanzanian case, the crop parastatals responsible for handing over these funds to CRDB were frequently remiss. In addition, it was not uncommon for them to continue to make in-kind input credit available to farmers with outstanding debts to CRDB. World Bank, "Tanzania Agricultural Sector Report" (Africa—Technical Department, Agricultural Department, Washington, D.C., August 1983), chap. 5.

25. For information on grain storage, see Hanak and Loft, "Danish Development Assistance to Tanzania and Kenya, 1962–85."

26. For a recent evaluation of the open-pan sulphitation (OPS) technology see Raphael Kaplinsky, *Sugar Processing: The Development of a Third World Technology* (London, Intermediate Technology Publications, 1984).

27. World Bank internal documents.

28. For a full discussion of the fourth category, see Hanak and Loft, "Danish Development Assistance to Tanzania and Kenya, 1962–85." In short, the

analysis shows that Denmark cannot necessarily solve its own expertise shortages by farming out the activities to the specialized agencies. To avoid inappropriate projects (like the ILO road project in Tanzania), DANIDA will need to assess carefully the capabilities of each agency to do the work it does not feel it can do itself.

29. A third problem, inappropriate factor intensity of investments, may be exhibited by capital-intensive grain storage facilities in Kenya, a labor surplus economy. See Hanak and Loft, "Danish Development Assistance to Tanzania and Kenya, 1962–85."

30. Philip Raikes, *Livestock Development and Policies in East Africa* (Uppsala: Scandinavian Institute for African Studies, 1982).

31. Kenya's unusual success is contrasted with other experiences on the continent in Hans E. Jahnke, *Livestock Production Systems and Livestock Development in Tropical Africa* (Kiel: Kieler Wissenschaftsverlag Vauk, 1982).

32. This is clearly an "ideal" in the Weberian sense, hopefully as analytically useful as it is empirically empty!

33. Christian Michelsen's Institutt, "Kenya's Rural Development Fund: A Study of its Socioeconomic Impact" (Bergen, Norway, August 1985), p. 70.

5 *Swedish Aid to Kenya and Tanzania: Its Effect on Rural Development, 1970–84*

Marian Radetzki

THIS CHAPTER is about Sweden's aid to Kenya and Tanzania in the field of rural development during the period 1970–84.[1] Six projects—comprising support for rural water and rural health in both countries, for land care in Kenya, and for forestry in Tanzania—are the focus of the investigation. These projects account for an overwhelming share of Swedish aid for rural development in the two countries during this period: 36 percent of total Swedish disbursements went to Kenya and 20 percent to Tanzania.

Sweden's Overall Aid to Kenya and Tanzania

Swedish aid had a relatively late start. Before 1962 the amount was insignificant, but the volume rose during the 1960s, and in 1969 the global total reached $100 million (which amounted to 0.43 percent of the country's GNP).[2] That year Sweden's official development assistance exceeded the average share of the Development Assistance Committee (DAC) for the first time. Swedish foreign assistance expanded rapidly in the subsequent years, and since the mid-1970s it has ranged from 0.75 to 1.02 percent of GNP—which is two to three times more than the average for the DAC group. Aid from Sweden rose from 1.7 percent of the total DAC flows in 1970 to a peak of 5.0 percent in 1977, but then gradually fell to 2.5 percent in 1984. In comparison with aid from other major donors, the flows from Sweden have been a large though declining multilateral share with high concessionality and a low level of formal tying.

Kenya and Tanzania were among the early recipients of Swedish aid. Between 1962 and mid-1984, Kenya received a total of SKr 1.1 billion and Tanzania SKr 3.8 billion (for annual disbursements after

1970, see table 5-1). The two countries together have absorbed about 10 percent of the overall aid flow from Sweden—and 15–20 percent of the bilateral flow. Swedish aid has played a significant role in the national economies of the two countries. Throughout the period under scrutiny, Swedish disbursements corresponded on average to roughly 0.5 percent of GNP in Kenya and 1.5 percent in Tanzania (table 5-2). In the early-to-mid-1970s Sweden contributed about 15 percent of total aid receipts in Kenya and some 25 percent in Tanzania. More recently, it has played a less prominent role, since the Swedish flows to the two countries have declined. The aid to Kenya (in 1980 SKr) rose from 51 million in 1971–72 to a peak of 136 million in 1973–74 and then fell to 67 million in 1983–84; the flow to Tanzania rose from 137 million in 1971–72 to 373 million in 1976–77, and then stagnated below the peak, hovering around 304 million in 1983–84.

Terms

Since 1975–76 Swedish aid to Kenya and Tanzania has been entirely in grant form. Before that, a proportion of the aid was provided as loans on soft terms, but these loans were written off in 1977–78. Until that year, total service payments amounted to SKr 3.0 million in the case of Kenya and SKr 9.8 million in Tanzania.

Formal tying, first introduced by Sweden in its overall aid program in 1971–72, rose from a mere SKr 21 million in the global aid expenditure in 1971–72 to about SKr 600 million in 1976–77, and to more than Skr 1,100 million in 1983–84. The last two figures corresponded to some 20 percent of the total Swedish aid budget.[3]

Tying to purchases in Sweden was imposed on Tanzania in 1977–78 and on Kenya one year later, but initially the recipients were free to choose any goods and services exported by the donor country (table 5-3). In the early 1980s, pressure for double tying increased; that is, Sweden wanted to determine the composition of goods to be supplied. As in the global Swedish aid program, the formally tied aid component has reached about 20 percent of total disbursements to Kenya and Tanzania in recent years.

In addition there are a variety of aid practices that amount to informal tying, particularly in the use of personnel. The expatriates engaged in Swedish aid endeavors have been almost exclusively recruited in Sweden. The cost of such personnel amounts to some 15–20 percent of total aid disbursements, substantially raising the proportion of tied aid.

The sectoral distribution of Sweden's assistance to Kenya and Tanzania is presented in tables 5-4 and 5-5. An overview of the most important sectoral shares is provided in figures 5-1 and 5-2.

Table 5-1. Sweden's Aid Disbursements to Kenya and Tanzania, 1970–86
(millions of Swedish kroner and percent)

Country	*1970–71*	*1971–72*	*1972–73*	*1973–74*	*1974–75*	*1975–76*	*1976–77*	*1977–78*	*1978–79*
Kenya									
SKr millions	18.5	24.3	36.0	74.6	81.5	86.1	85.6	79.3	76.8
Percent	2.6	3.3	4.0	5.7	3.7	3.5	2.9	2.3	7.4
Tanzania									
SKr millions	51.1	65.9	96.6	132.7	202.6	232.6	278.4	255.6	255.6
Percent	7.2	9.0	10.6	10.2	9.2	9.4	9.6	7.4	9.1
		1979–80	*1980–81*	*1981–82*	*1982–83*	*1983–84*	*1984–85*	*1985–86*	*1986–87*
Kenya									
SKr millions		101.3	90.2	87.2	99.4	105.6	169.8	136.9	127.8
Percent		2.5	2.1	1.7	1.8	1.8	2.7	1.9	1.8
Tanzania									
SKr millions		346.5	310.6	444.5	458.2	464.7	494.3	524.8	517.7
Percent		8.5	7.2	8.9	8.2	7.7	7.8	7.1	7.1

Source: SIDA, *Bistand i siffror och diagram* (Aid in numbers and figures), 1982 and 1983; SIDA Annual Reports, 1970/71–1976/77.

Table 5-2. Kenya and Tanzania: Share of Swedish Aid in GNP and in Foreign Aid Receipts, 1970–86
(percentage)

Country	*1970*	*1971*	*1972*	*1973*	*1974*	*1975*	*1976*	*1977*	*1978*
Kenya									
Swedish aid/GNP	0.2	0.3	0.4	0.8	0.7	0.7	0.6	0.4	0.3
Swedish aid/total aid	5.4	7.0	10.4	17.7	15.4	16.8	12.3	10.8	6.9
Tanzania									
Swedish aid/GNP	0.7	0.8	1.2	1.7	2.0	1.8	2.5	1.8	1.7
Swedish aid/total aid	17.6	21.1	34.5	30.3	27.9	20.2	18.6	13.4	12.4
		1979	*1980*	*1981*	*1982*	*1983*	*1984*	*1985*	*1986*
Kenya									
Swedish aid/GNP		0.4	0.3	0.3	0.3	0.2	0.2	0.3	0.2
Swedish aid/total aid		6.8	5.2	3.8	3.3	3.8	3.5	4.5	3.2
Tanzania									
Swedish aid/GNP		1.8	1.5	1.5	1.4	1.3	1.2	1.2	2.6
Swedish aid/total aid		12.1	10.9	11.6	10.4	11.7	9.9	10.1	15.6

Source: OECD, Development Assistance Committee Review, annual supplemented by SIDA, United Nations, and World Bank statistics.

Table 5-3. Composition and Relative Importance of Tied Aid, 1977–87
(percentage)

Country	*1977–78*	*1978–79*	*1979–80*	*1980–81*	*1981–82*	*1982–83*	*1983–84*	*1984–85*	*1985–86*	*1986–87*
Kenya										
Tied aid/total import support		100.0	71.9	70.2	76.5	55.3	77.5	100.0	100.0	100.0
Tied aid/total aid		7.2	9.9	10.2	22.8	10.0	18.9	7.3	13.6	9.4
Tanzania										
Tied aid/total import support	51.2	50.1	37.6	58.3	34.4	67.2	78.7	83.9	70.6	72.5
Tied aid/total aid	5.8	11.5	9.5	12.9	12.8	21.8	26.7	28.0	31.1	25.5

Source: See table 5-1.

Table 5-4. Swedish Aid to Kenya: Sectoral Distribution, 1970–87
(millions of Swedish kroner)

Sector	*Until and including 1970–71*	*71–72*	*72–73*	*73–74*	*74–75*	*75–76*	*76–77*	*77–78*	*78–79*	*79–80*	*80–81*	*81–82*	*82–83*	*83–84*	*84–85*	*85–86*	*86–87*	*Total until 1 July 1987*
Agriculture	21.2	3.2	9.8	12.4	13.2	15.4	7.8	12.0	16.8	11.9	12.8	8.3	10.5	17.4	32.2	23.8	34.0	262.8
Artificial insemination	12.9	2.3	2.4	2.6	3.4	1.0	0.1	0.1	—	—	—	—	—	24.8	—	—	—	24.8
Agricultural finance	—	—	—	—	—	8.0	—	1.5	6.5	2.0	—	—	4.0	25.7	8.5	7.0	15.6	56.9
Land care	—	—	—	—	—	—	—	3.4	3.1	3.5	—	8.3	6.5	46.0	17.3	13.9	13.1	90.3
Sector support	—	—	—	—	—	—	—	—	—	—	5.3	—	—	76.2	6.4	2.9	5.2	14.6
Other	8.3	0.9	7.4	9.8	9.8	6.4	7.7	7.0	7.2	6.4	—	—	—	—	—	—	—	76.2
Rural development, excluding agriculture	12.8	5.9	4.4	33.1	15.2	28.2	36.5	30.3	41.1	45.5	30.3	38.9	49.3	40.2	72.3	69.7	62.3	616.0
Rural water	1.1	3.7	1.5	27.6	9.2	20.5	17.8	17.8	37.4	25.9	14.7	10.9	18.2	223.5	17.7	21.4	26.8	289.4
Rural cooperatives	11.7	2.2	2.9	2.8	2.4	2.8	4.4	1.4	1.8	3.6	5.3	7.0	5.3	57.6	2.5	3.8	0.0	63.8
Rural infrastructure	—	—	—	2.7	3.6	0.6	0.4	0.7	0.7					8.7				8.7
Rural health[a]	—	—	—	—	—	4.3	13.9	10.4	1.2	16.0	10.3	21.0	25.8	121.9	52.1	44.5	35.5	254.1
Industry	—	—	—	0.6	5.7	1.5	1.6	1.1	0.9	7.8	0.9	1.1	2.9	1.0	0.2	—	—	25.3
Transport	—	—	2.8	4.8	8.8	5.0	6.0	2.6	0.3	—	—	—	—	—	—	—	—	30.3
Energy	—	4.8	9.7	9.3	3.1	4.6	—	—	—	—	—	—	—	4.9	25.1	—	—	61.5
Health and family planning	1.4	0.9	1.9	2.3	1.1	4.7	6.5	9.1	—	—	—	—	—	—	—	—	—	27.8
Education	32.7	6.8	5.2	8.7	18.0	21.2	20.8	15.4	7.2	13.9	22.1	7.3	13.9	7.2	5.7	—	—	206.1
Planning and administration	2.3	2.5	2.0	3.0	3.7	3.4	3.4	5.4	1.2	0.4	—	—	—	—	—	—	—	27.3
Commerce and finance	—	0.2	0.2	0.3	11.0	0.6	1.5	2.0	2.4	2.9	—	—	—	—	—	—	—	21.1
Import support	—	—	—	—	—	—	—	—	5.5	13.9	13.1	26.0	17.9	25.8	12.4	18.6	12.0	145.2
Tied to purchases, in Sweden	—	—	—	—	—	—	—	—	5.5	10.0	9.2	19.9	9.9	74.5	12.4	18.6	12.0	117.5

(Table continues on the following page.)

Table 5-4. *(continued)*

Sector	Until and including 1970–71	71–72	72–73	73–74	74–75	75–76	76–77	77–78	78–79	79–80	80–81	81–82	82–83	83–84	84–85	85–86	86–87	Total until 1 July 1987
Miscellaneous										2.1	3.7	—	—	1.4	4.2	8.0	6.2	25.5
Subtotal	70.4	24.3	36.0	74.5	79.8	84.6	84.1	77.9	75.4	98.4	82.9	81.6	94.5	97.8	152.2	120.1	114.5	1,449.0
Aid through non-governmental organizations	—	—	—	0.1	1.7	1.5	1.5	1.4	1.4	2.5	4.3	5.6	4.9	7.8	14.1	16.7	13.3	76.8
Emergency aid	—	—	—	—	—	—	—	—	—	—	—	—	—	—	3.6	—	—	3.6
Food aid	—	—	—	—	—	—	—	—	—	0.4	3.0	—	—	—	—	—	—	3.4
Total	70.4	24.3	36.0	74.6	81.5	86.1	85.6	79.3	76.8	101.3	90.2	87.2	99.4	105.6	169.8	136.9	127.8	1,532.8

— = Not available.
a. From 1979–80, includes family planning.
Source: See table 5-1.

Table 5-5. Swedish Aid to Tanzania: Sectoral Distribution
(millions of Swedish kroner)

Sector	*Until and including 1970–71*	*71–72*	*72–73*	*73–74*	*74–75*	*75–76*	*76–77*	*77–78*	*78–79*	*79–80*	*80–81*	*81–82*	*82–83*	*83–84*	*84–85*	*85–86*	*86–87*	*Total until 1 July 1987*
Agriculture	7.2	6.6	17.8	23.6	20.8	20.9	15.8	18.1	14.0	12.7	7.3	9.6	8.1	7.5	6.1	3.5	2.3	201.9
Agricultural education	4.6	1.9	4.4	5.2	5.5	6.5	0.8	2.0	3.1	2.6	1.1	5.4	5.2	5.2	4.3	0.0	0.0	57.8
Agricultural finance	—	2.0	9.5	9.0	8.5	8.0	8.0	8.0	6.0	6.0	3.0	—	—	—	0.0	0.0	0.0	68.0
Grain storage	0.6	2.0	3.5	6.3	4.5	0.7	2.4	—	—	—	—	—	—	—	0.0	0.0	0.0	20.0
Other	2.0	0.7	0.4	3.1	2.3	5.7	4.6	8.1	4.9	4.1	3.2	4.2	2.9	2.3	1.8	3.5	2.3	56.1
Rural development, excluding agriculture	52.6	29.9	40.8	46.5	46.8	93.7	64.9	74.5	71.8	70.9	49.2	57.4	64.0	59.5	89.2	68.4	79.6	1,059.7
Rural water	48.2	24.3	26.0	32.2	22.2	62.5	38.9	49.0	45.0	32.2	12.2	30.5	26.6	34.6	39.2	33.3	30.8	587.5
Rural cooperatives	3.9	2.2	1.5	1.9	1.1	2.3	2.6	0.6	0.6	11.4	3.4	5.2	9.4	2.9	17.0	11.5	15.0	92.5
Rural infrastructure	—	—	0.2	2.0	0.1	0.1	—	—	—	—	—	—	—	—	—	—	—	2.4
Rural health	—	—	4.0	3.3	8.4	7.9	11.8	8.6	11.3	7.1	11.3	3.0	1.9	2.0	3.5	2.4	0.3	86.8
Forestry	0.5	3.4	9.3	8.9	13.3	20.9	11.5	16.3	14.9	20.2	22.3	18.7	26.1	20.0	29.4	21.3	33.5	290.5
Industry	5.3	1.4	1.7	6.6	—	0.3	14.0	15.9	35.7	52.6	93.2	100.7	102.6	118.9	97.5	78.3	89.4	814.1
Transport	39.0	—	—	—	8.0	—	—	—	—	—	—	—	—	—	0.0	0.0	0.0	47.0
Energy	8.6	12.5	13.6	8.6	19.2	7.6	8.0	16.7	27.6	29.2	14.8	4.0	1.7	6.4	16.0	25.2	28.4	248.1
Health	1.2	0.3	—	—	—	0.2	—	—	—	—	—	2.6	3.7	1.0	1.2	0.6	0.4	11.1
Education	36.0	12.6	14.0	18.1	21.6	36.2	25.9	35.2	45.2	39.1	52.7	63.3	71.7	55.9	52.8	40.8	51.1	672.3
Planning and administration	7.4	1.8	1.8	1.9	2.9	4.9	13.9	6.2	8.4	7.9	10.9	8.7	15.1	16.9	22.7	24.9	17.8	174.1
Commerce and finance	1.0	0.8	1.9	12.8	11.9	8.4	66.2	56.1	38.3	16.5	5.0	6.5	15.2	14.2	5.7	14.6	24.3	299.3
Import support	—	—	4.0	3.9	62.5	53.7	65.2	28.9	75.0	87.2	68.6	165.5	153.3	157.5	165.3	231.3	181.8	1,503.7
Tied to purchases in Sweden	—	—	—	—	—	—	—	14.8	37.6	32.8	40.0	56.9	103.0	123.9	138.6	163.4	131.9	842.8

(Table continues on the following page.)

Table 5-5. (continued)

Sector	*Until and including 1970–71*	*71–72*	*72–73*	*73–74*	*74–75*	*75–76*	*76–77*	*77–78*	*78–79*	*79–80*	*80–81*	*81–82*	*82–83*	*83–84*	*84–85*	*85–86*	*86–87*	*Total until 1 July 1987*
Miscellaneous	4.0	—	—	10.2	6.2	2.3	0.4	0.2	—	0.4	—	1.9	5.7	7.9	13.7	9.5	5.6	67.9
Subtotal	163.3	65.9	95.6	132.2	199.9	228.2	274.3	251.8	316.0	316.5	301.7	420.2	441.1	445.7	470.2	497.0	480.6	5,099.3
Aid through non-governmental organizations	2.6	—	0.6	0.2	2.7	4.4	4.1	3.7	4.4	4.6	8.8	14.3	15.8	19.0	19.6	24.8	35.2	164.8
Emergency aid	—	—	0.2	0.3	—	—	—	0.1	5.0	25.4	—	10.0	—	—	4.5	2.9	1.9	50.3
Food aid	0.1	—	0.2	—	—	—	—	—	1.4	—	0.1	—	1.3	—	—	—	—	3.1
Total	165.0	65.9	96.6	132.7	202.6	232.6	278.4	255.6	326.8	346.5	310.6	444.5	458.2	464.7	494.3	524.8	517.7	5,317.5

— = Not available.
Source: See table 5-1.

Figure 5-1. Sectoral Distribution of SIDA *Aid to Kenya, until July 1, 1987*

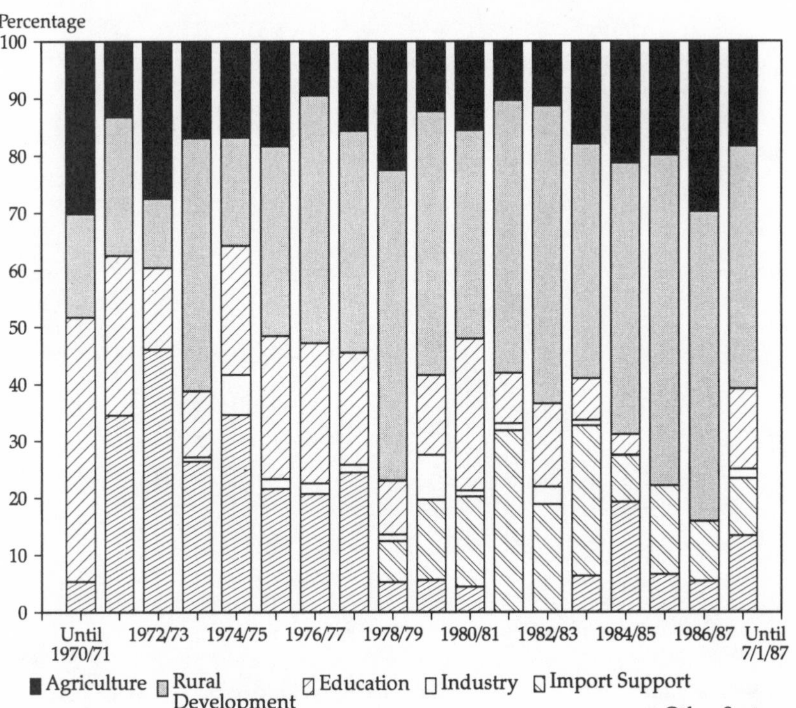

Note: Rural development includes, in order of importance, assistance for rural water, health, cooperatives, and infrastructure.
Source: Table 5-1.

Agriculture, rural development, and education dominated the flows to Kenya until 1971. In the 1970s, the sectoral allocation was greatly diversified, but from about 1980 on agriculture, rural development, and imports accounted for the lion's share. Note, too, the gradual decline in the allocations to agriculture, the large increase in the rural development share (largely as a result of the expansion of water and health programs), the continuous decline in aid to education, and the rapid growth of a predominantly tied import support program since the late 1970s.

In Tanzania, in contrast, agriculture and rural development have declined in importance, whereas industry has registered the largest growth since the late 1970s. Industry and imports account for more than 50 percent of the country's total aid allocations.

Figure 5-2. Sectoral Distribution of SIDA Aid to Tanzania, until July 1, 1987

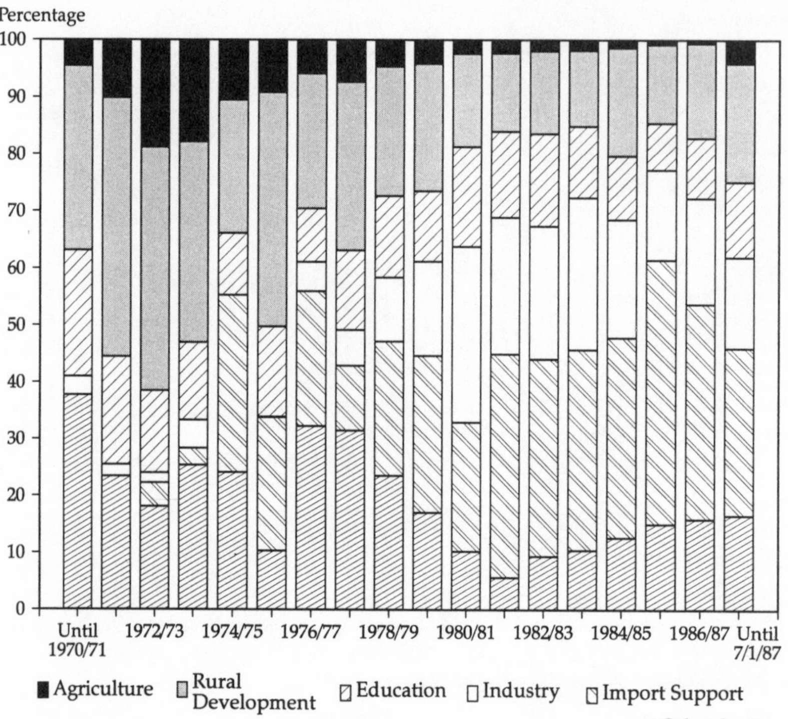

Note: Rural development includes, in order of importance, assistance for rural water, forestry, cooperatives, health, and infrastructure.
Source: Table 5-1.

Project Aid as against Other Assistance

In the early years of Swedish aid, project assistance dominated the flows. Over time, there has been a shift to less specific activities in both countries, but the share of project aid has remained lower in Tanzania throughout the period.

The fact that project aid is less flexible with respect to allocation—and that a larger proportion of aid to Kenya was made available in this form—in part explains the lower efficiency in disbursing aid commitments to Kenya. Only 76 percent of the total aid committed to Kenya between 1980–81 and 1983–84 was actually disbursed in that period. For Tanzania, the figure was 99 percent.

Swedish Aid Allocations

The fundamental rationale for Swedish aid has been a feeling of solidarity with the poor people in low-income countries. The justification for Sweden's involvement was strengthened by the popular perception that Swedish aid could in some measure counterbalance the capitalist and neocolonialist forces that threatened equitable development in poor countries. There was also a strong belief that the lessons of Sweden's own development experience could be usefully applied in the other countries. Furthermore, the development of the poor nations was regarded as a prerequisite for global peace. These motives explain Sweden's preparedness to spend—compared with other donors—a high proportion of its GNP on foreign assistance.

Goals

Since the early 1970s, Swedish aid programs have had four clearly defined goals: to promote the growth of resources, increase economic and social equity, help countries acquire economic and political independence, and promote democracy in society.[4] The relative weights attached to the goals have varied over time—although the last goal has not had much influence on aid policies in the main recipient countries over the period examined in this study.[5] Resource growth was emphasized in the late 1960s and then was replaced in the 1970s by equity.[6] This coincided with a shift in the internal economic policies of Sweden. However, the economic stagnation or decline that affected both Sweden and its aid recipients in the 1980s has made resource growth a primary goal once again.

These official goals provide a general idea of the intended direction and thrust of Sweden's aid, but they do not specify the precise objectives needed to guide operations in practice. In response, the Swedish International Development Authority (SIDA) has issued over the years a series of papers identifying the intended structure and purposes of, for instance, its support for rural water or rural health worldwide.[7]

Other goals have also helped shape aid policy at times. For example, aid has sometimes been used to promote investment, on the assumption that Sweden could withdraw once the investment phase, defined in a broad sense, was completed and national resources could ensure continued operations. The underlying motive in this case is the desire to promote the recipient's independence and the donor's reluctance to enter into perpetual engagements.

Another objective that gained prominence in the written policy statements of the 1970s but that faded into the background in more recent years was that recipients should have complete freedom in determining the allocation of aid. In practice, this objective was never fully implemented.

A further objective, primarily concerned with the donor's interests, has given preference to the use of Swedish resources in aid programs.

The growth of tied aid after the mid-1970s is explained by the economic stagnation and the current account deficits experienced by Sweden at that time. The result was a weakening of the altruistic aid constituency and a strengthening of the groups that wanted to use aid to promote Sweden's commercial interests. In addition Sweden was disappointed to find that other donors were unwilling to untie their aid flows.[8]

There has been little public discussion in Sweden of the existing tradeoffs among aid goals. The obvious possibility that goals might conflict—and that no one goal will be achieved if several are pursued at the same time—often was not recognized, even in central policy statements.[9] The image of harmony among the different goals and the costs of the overall program (with respect to the loss of efficiency if all of them were pursued) may have been the price for attaining a broad consensus for the large and generous assistance program.

Two strategies have been employed to attain the professed goals and objectives. The first has been to choose countries whose domestic circumstances ensured that the goals would be attained. On these grounds, Cuba and Vietnam were added to the list of recipients because of their egalitarian policies, and Botswana, Lesotho, and Mozambique were included because of the threat to their independence caused by the policies of the United States and South Africa. Choosing countries with the "right" development policies became particularly important during the 1970s, when the recipients were given increased freedom in the use of aid. Reluctant to break off existing aid relations, Sweden was induced to redistribute aid among established recipients in favor of those whose development policies were in line with Swedish goals.[10]

The second strategy was to select and design activities so as to promote Swedish goals, particularly in recipient countries whose development policies were thought to be out of line with the Swedish goals. In several cases, the promise of support was used to encourage policy reorientation.

These strategies were not always easy to follow. In some cases, the choice of a country or the emphasis in the aid package was motivated by the belief that the recipient's policies (for instance, Cuban and Tanzanian policies concerning the evening out of income distribution) ensured that Swedish aid would be highly productive in reaching its goals. In other cases, the fact that a goal had not been met was used either as an argument in favor of or against aid—without explicit consideration of the effect of the aid flow on attaining the goals (Botswana's lack of economic and political independence would be a case in favor, and Kenya's uneven income distribution a case against). This ambiguity might well be due to the fact that the goals were used later to justify country choices that in effect had been made on other grounds. Aid activities were selected on the basis of a variety of factors, some of which were clearly related to the Swedish goals, but others less so. The most important of these factors are listed below:

- The recipient government's requests. As noted earlier, this was a prominent factor during the 1970s, although in a limited number of situations; the shift in emphasis from rural development and agriculture to industry in Tanzania in the late 1970s reflects this factor at work.
- The donor's assessment of what will help achieve its goals. Support for rural water and rural health illustrate Swedish initiatives motivated by the donor's perception that public services to poor groups constitute a crucial component of development.
- Donor belief that a certain activity is being neglected. Until the early 1970s, support for family planning in Kenya was pursued primarily on this ground. Support programs for women's activities in both countries have come into being mainly because of the donor's perceptions in this regard.
- Special competence possessed by the donor country. A number of the Swedish ventures—including support for cooperatives, vocational training, forestry, and hydropower—have been spawned by this motive. The donor preferred them because they eased the strain aid was putting on its balance of payments. The recipient favored such choices both because the donor's competence was believed to ensure efficient execution and because compliance with donor wishes smoothed aid relations.
- Supplies available in the donor country. The most obvious example of this rationale is the import support tied to purchases in Sweden that has been extended to Kenya and Tanzania since the late 1970s. Swedish supplies and competence sometimes led to an inappropriate choice of technology. Examples include grain storage in Tanzania and the diesel-powered rural water installations in the two countries, both of which proved unserviceable because of inadequate technical facilities in the recipient countries.
- The executing capacity of the donor agency. Constraints arising from SIDA's administrative capacity have led both to the preference for large projects that make it possible for each administrator to handle sizable amounts of money and to the shift from project to program support in both countries.
- Donor collaboration. The desire to collaborate with other donors has sometimes influenced the content of Swedish aid. For instance, Nordic collaboration managed by Finland has involved Sweden in an agricultural venture in Tanzania. In 1984, as the crisis in that

> country deepened, the Nordic aid agencies coordinated their assistance more closely. Collaboration with the World Bank has prompted Swedish support of the Mufindi pulp and paper complex in Tanzania and of dryland ranching in Kenya.

In many cases, the content of aid was determined by some other factor—such as what the recipient believed the donor was prepared to offer.

Evaluation of Aid Performance

Most of the formal evaluations of Sweden's aid have had a microeconomic character. A series of reports from annual joint missions by SIDA and a recipient ministry have evaluated individual projects. These and other similar assessments point to achievements and indicate means to overcome observed problems. By describing the projects' outputs, they provide a partial measure of the contribution to resource growth. Few of the evaluations, however, compare the total costs expended with the recorded achievements through a formal and detailed cost-benefit analysis. Although cost-benefit analysis has its limitations (which are taken up later in this chapter), it nevertheless provides a framework for a thorough assessment of the benefits and costs. Without such a framework, important considerations tend to be overlooked on both sides of the balance sheet.

Past studies have by and large failed to take into account the role of the macroeconomic circumstances in Kenya and Tanzania in determining the climate for Swedish aid—either with respect to the effects of the macroeconomy on project and program effectiveness or to the priorities for aid implied by these circumstances. The discussion of goal fulfillment is usually vague. As already mentioned, microeconomic evaluations do assess the contributions to resource growth. The impact on equity, admittedly more difficult to measure, is said to stem from the fact that the activities aim at the poorer population, but there is rarely an in-depth analysis in support of the claims. The remaining two goals are typically referred to only in passing.

For a donor whose contributions weigh as heavily in Kenya and Tanzania as Sweden's do, it would have been valuable to see analytical attempts showing that the ventures undertaken and the mode of executing them would contribute to development, however defined, better than alternative sets and modes of execution. It would have been equally important to know how the Swedish assistance affected overall national resource allocation—and how it affected growth, equity, or other development objectives. There is little evidence of such work having been conducted or commissioned by SIDA, which, like other donors, has been slow to recognize that broader evaluations can be a guide to more effective aid portfolios. Several factors have probably contributed to these shortcomings.

First, there is a notion that the recipient governments, not SIDA, are primarily responsible for the evaluation of aid.[11] This may have appeared to be a constructive idea in principle. In practice, the two recipients made little effort to evaluate Swedish aid. Second, during the 1970s evaluation issues were of little interest to SIDA's chief executives and the politicians involved with aid policy. Sweden's aid grew rapidly during that time, and efforts were focused on expanding spending, rather than on past activities. Since resources were not a problem, policymakers and executors could afford a relaxed attitude toward evaluation. Third, a proper evaluation is difficult to undertake and requires large inputs of qualified personnel. And fourth, the accounting systems employed by SIDA have not been conducive to formal cost-benefit evaluation of the Swedish endeavors.

As a result of these various problems, there has been little feedback from evaluations to the aid activities at both the aggregate and individual project levels. Administrative shortcomings within SIDA, including a short institutional memory, have also also been to blame for this lack of feedback.[12]

In the 1980s, aid grew at a slow pace and there was increasing pressure to improve its effectiveness. Swedish policy statements during that period stressed the donor's role in allocating and evaluating aid. Consequently the evaluation function has recently been reassessed, and the quality of the evaluation exercises improved.[13] Despite the limited feedback from evaluation, some lessons have obviously been learned from experience, as discussed later in the chapter.[14]

The Different Treatment of Kenya and Tanzania

Equity has been the most important goal behind Swedish aid to Kenya and Tanzania, but the size and content of this aid has differed in the two countries because of the donor's perception rather than formal analysis of these economies. According to official policy documents, the difference can be attributed to the importance Tanzania's government attaches to social and economic equality.

African socialism, as defined by President Julius Nyerere, had great appeal to the Swedish aid constituency. Protection of Tanzania against neocolonialist foreign powers assumed special importance after the country's showdown with a group of large aid donors in the late 1960s and provided an opportunity for Sweden to assume a leading donor role. Equity was a less evident concern in Kenya, and the corresponding political opportunities for Sweden did not emerge; hence, Swedish enthusiasm for providing aid was more muted there. Swedish aid authorities did not commission their own studies on the income and wealth distribution in Kenya and Tanzania but relied instead on the general perceptions in the donor community at that time.[15] Nor did they attempt a thorough macroeconomic analysis to establish the incidence of equity from the internal policies and aid programs in the two countries.

This difference in Swedish perceptions and attitudes is the main reason that Sweden was more generous toward Tanzania, that it had more of a laissez-faire attitude in its relations with Tanzania, and that the greater share of aid resources was allocated to the modern industries in Tanzania. The last two points reflect the donor's trust that Tanzanian policies would ensure that the overall allocation of national resources would be consonant with the Swedish goal of equity.

It took more than a decade of practical experience for Sweden to perceive fully—and to voice—the problems that Tanzania's internal policies were causing for national development in general and for the Swedish aid effort in particular. From 1983 onward, however, SIDA reports expressed the view that serious negligence on the Tanzanian side, along with inappropriate pricing, trade, and exchange rate policies, had hampered its aid efforts. Swedish attitudes toward Kenya have remained more stable.

Six Experiences with Project Assistance

Six SIDA projects are reviewed in the following paragraphs to illustrate the impact of Swedish aid on development in Kenya and Tanzania.

Rural Water in Kenya

Kenya's decision in the late 1960s to launch a large program of rural water supply was mainly the result of Swedish persuasion and the promise of generous aid.[16] The programs started in 1970. By mid-1984 SIDA's expenditure in this area had reached SKr 224 million—which accounted for 20 percent of all Swedish aid disbursements to Kenya and for 38 percent of the flows to agriculture and rural development. Until about 1977 Sweden was the only donor to rural water and provided about 40 percent of its total funds.[17] By 1980–81 the Swedish contribution had declined to about 13 percent of overall expenditures, corresponding to some 30 percent of total aid funds.[18]

Until 1979–80, some three-quarters of the Swedish contributions were expended on construction, particularly on piped supplies in areas of high agricultural potential and above-average income levels.[19]

Other activities included technical assistance to the Ministry of Water, the training of personnel, and the preparation of surveys and master plans.

Over the 1970s, a number of controversial issues emerged from this collaboration:

During most of the period, SIDA was dissatisfied with the inefficiency of the Ministry of Water, through which the Swedish programs were executed.[20] A particular complaint was the slow progress in construction. In 1974 the ministry and SIDA agreed that Sweden would finance seventy-five water installations, to be completed by 1979. By 1983, only twenty-two of the units had been installed.

Another perennial complaint was that the ministry never allocated enough funds for operations and maintenance. A study published in 1977 concluded that on account of such deficiencies almost one-half of the target population residing within the reach of the Swedish-financed projects did not use the water facilities at all, and that less than 30 percent of this population had access to reliable facilities.[21]

Later it was discovered that many installations had been delivered with serious faults. Apparently the controls put in place by SIDA had not functioned satisfactorily. For example, one water scheme was delivered without water tanks, although tanks were necessary for its operation. Another scheme produced water unfit for human consumption.

The issue of water tariffs has continuously marred relations between SIDA and the ministry and has never been properly sorted out. The views of both parties have undergone changes over time. The gist of the early Swedish position was that water should preferably be free to the poor and that any fees imposed should be so low as to be affordable by this group. When the faults of the system were recognized, SIDA began to emphasize a tariff structure that would ensure adequate funds for operations and maintenance. The Kenyan position oscillated between proposals for flat and differentiated tariffs. A Kenyan goal was that user charges in areas of high agricultural potential should cover all operation and maintenance costs, but given the low level of fees and Kenya's inability to collect them, only a small fraction of the costs was recovered.[22]

The diesel-operated piped systems that were established supplied water through both individual connections and communal water points; the latter, usually more marginally located, were intended to serve the poor. The flat water rates led to excessive consumption through individual connections, leaving little water for the poor. Less money was spent on maintaining the communal points, so they decayed faster. Many were disconnected because the water fees were not paid. The discovery that the poor were increasingly excluded from access to water caused great concern within SIDA.

These problems led SIDA to redirect its activities around 1980.[23] The construction of new facilities was sharply reduced. Almost half the funds were reallocated toward meeting recurrent costs in a broad sense—for activities such as the training of personnel and the construction of repair workshops. This helped prevent the further deterioration of the rural water system. By mid-1986, however, there were still no reports of any substantial improvement in the system. Nor was there any indication that the ministry had accommodated SIDA by redirecting the program in favor of the poor.

Beginning in 1984, there was a further reorientation of SIDA's support. The nationwide program was by and large discontinued and replaced by geographically focused activities in the Eastern and Coast provinces, which included the rehabilitation of existing installations and sociotechnical experiments with communal water at the local level in dry areas. These experiments have emphasized participation by the local population, although it has not been clear precisely how assurance can be obtained that this is in fact taking place. It is too early to know what effect these experiments have had on development.

The national efforts supported by Sweden have not been too successful. The results of SIDA's institutional support to the ministry continue to disappoint, and the scope of this support is being reduced.[24] Recent studies have revealed that more than one-half of the schemes established under the program continue to operate poorly.[25] One-half of the water produced is lost or unaccounted for. Only a small fraction of the resident population covered by rural schemes are able to obtain water at communal points. All this is far below the original plan to cover a majority of the rural population. The system that has been established is rapidly deteriorating. The technology employed is beyond the capability of Kenya's personnel and financial means, and the water that is supplied benefits mainly the richer population.

The shift in SIDA's efforts between 1980 and 1984 was a result of these negative experiences. Although the new strategy may well be the most promising avenue to follow, it does not reflect a systematic evaluation of alternative options (and hence a deliberate choice based on prospects for long-run success).

Rural Water in Tanzania

Swedish support for rural water development in Tanzania began in 1965. By mid-1984 SKr 484 million had been spent, representing 13 percent of overall Swedish disbursements and 48 percent of the spending for agriculture and rural development. Until the late 1970s, Swedish support played a dominant role in the Tanzania's national program, but this has changed in more recent years as other donors have expanded their involvement.[26]

Initially, Swedish support was comprehensive. More important, Swedish thinking played a critical role in the evolution of Tanzanian policies. The crucial document in this respect is the Rimér report of 1970.[27] Its optimistic conclusions, along with the prospects for extensive Swedish support, led the Tanzanian government to adopt a program that was expected to provide the entire rural population with free piped water by 1991.[28] The political eagerness to get this program started was boosted by the attractiveness of rural water as a carrot in the national villagization scheme that the government was launching at the time.

Beginning in 1972, a number of other donors joined in the support of rural water activities. At the instigation of the government, these donors were directed to specific regions. Although the Swedes continued their nationwide activities, they restricted their new endeavors to three regions on Lake Victoria. By the early 1980s most of Sweden's nationwide programs had been phased out.[29]

The effect of Sweden's aid is difficult to isolate from other assistance. But because Sweden played a dominant role in this endeavor, national statistics do provide a feel for the achievement. The Tanzanian plan to supply free water to the rural population within a twenty-year period was clearly unrealistic. In 1984 the facilities installed covered 38 percent of the rural population. However, only one-half of these facilities were functioning and another 20 percent were operating erratically.[30] Thus, after thirteen years of implementation, less than 12 percent of the rural population had access to reliable drinking water. This achievement constitutes only a fraction of the original plan. Despite sizable and costly planning exercises, the activities finally adopted were technically inappropriate or misconceived, and inadequate attention was devoted to operations and maintenance.[31]

Diesel-run, piped water facilities have dominated the system. These have proved inappropriate on both economic and technical grounds. Because foreign exchange has long been scarce, the diesel fuel has not always been available. Managerial and technical resources for servicing the facilities also have been inadequate. Swedish efforts to build up such competence by providing training have proved inadequate. In the 1980s the aid effort shifted toward shallow wells operated by hand pumps. The problem with shallow wells is that their water supply drops during normal dry seasons. Out of more than 3,000 shallow wells established in Tanzania with assistance from the Netherlands and Finland, barely more than one-half were found to be reasonably reliable.[32]

The system could not function properly without funds for operations and maintenance. Public financing of the recurrent costs would have been a formidable task, even if appropriate low-cost solutions had been chosen. The cost of the existing system was clearly beyond the government's means, although it might have been less of a burden if local communities had become involved in the program. In fact, local participation has been conspicuously absent.[33] Through most of the period, SIDA's view was that water should be a "free good" to the users. Only in the 1980s did it reverse its position, after realizing that the program could not survive without the financial support of consumers.[34]

Another disappointing outcome is that the anticipated health benefits from clean water have not materialized. Traditional water sources continue to be used since the facilities installed function erratically. Moreover, the main beneficiaries of the rural water schemes, contrary to both government and SIDA intentions, have been the relatively better-off rural farmers, traders, and civil servants.[35]

Sweden began implementing its regional water projects only in 1984, and no achievements can yet be reported. One component has been designed to rehabilitate existing installations. Another component, still at the trial stage, provides selected villages with shallow wells driven by hand pumps along with support for community development and health-related projects. As in Kenya, there is a great emphasis on local participation. An important goal is to keep recurrent costs at a level that local authorities can afford.

The rural water development program in Tanzania suffers from severe functional problems. Given the low capacity utilization, the cost per unit of water actually supplied is exceedingly high, and the system is likely to get worse. Since Sweden is the central donor in this activity, it has to assume a substantial part of the blame, in that SIDA's actions encouraged the government to launch an unrealistic program. SIDA insisted that water supply should be free. When it became clear that the government was unable to operate the system, SIDA withdrew its support at the national level and restricted its activities to narrow geographical areas. It is too early to judge the impact of this decision.

Rural Health in Kenya

Sweden became involved in rural health in Kenya in 1975, although it had already contributed to health-related activities, including family planning, that were not specifically directed toward the rural areas. Total expenditures on rural health up to 1984 amounted to SKr 122 million. This accounted for 11 percent of total Swedish aid flows to Kenya and 21 percent of the flows to agriculture and rural development.

SIDA has made significant contributions to rural health expenditures in Kenya. For instance, in the period 1979–80 to 1981–82, the SIDA programs financed 25 percent of the total.[36] In recent years, Sweden's relative importance has declined as a result of the growing involvement of other donors. As in the case of rural water, Sweden's involvement in health was preceded by a persuasion campaign, coupled with promises of generous aid.

Construction, rehabilitation, and the equipping of health institutions account for about one-half of the total resources expended. The building program (two district hospitals, twenty-three health centers, and three dispensaries) experienced substantial difficulties and delays. Of these twenty-eight rural health facilities, only nine had been completed by 1984.[37] Realizing that the rural health system was greatly in need of recurrent funds, SIDA decided to change the emphasis in its program and in 1981 started distributing basic drugs to the rural health facilities.[38]

Family planning and mother-child health care have been central components of Swedish assistance since 1969. For many years SIDA has been the main supplier of contraceptives to the Kenyan family planing centers.[39] More recent Swedish endeavors in rural health include the building and running of schools for medical personnel.[40] Since 1982 it has been supporting an experimental program aimed at simplifying and reducing the cost of constructing rural health centers. A large portion of this financial support is expended through nongovernmental organizations.

The shift during the 1980s from construction and hardware toward the provision of necessary inputs, management, and other software has been motivated by the emerging evidence that Kenya is unable to service and run the installed capacities. Sweden's aid to rural health is fully integrated into the overall national programs, and its share of the total is far less than it was in the two water programs discussed above. This creates special problems for evaluation, but some comments can nevertheless be made about Sweden's contribution.

Table 5-6 presents health-related indicators for Kenya and Tanzania, along with the averages for Sub-Saharan Africa. On most counts, Kenya appears to have benefited, but this does not necessarily imply that the overall national or Swedish resource allocation to health has been efficient. A recent evaluation by SIDA concludes that "the rural health center and dispensary program and family planning support have been extremely inefficient. . . . Insufficient implementation planning, indicated by such [matters] as the absence of objectives and

Table 5-6. Health-Related Indicators for Kenya and Tanzania

Indicator	*Kenya*	*Tanzania*	*Sub-Saharan Africa*
Female life expectancy at birth, 1983 (years)	59	52	49
Percentage change from 1965	+16	+18	+9
Infant mortality under 1 year, 1983 (per thousand)	81	97	119
Percentage change from 1965	−35	−30	−24
Population per nursing person, 1980	550	3,010	3,148
Percentage change from 1965	−69	+43	−32
Crude death rates 1983 (per thousand)	12	16	18
Percentage change from 1965	−29	−27	−18
Crude birth rates 1983 (per thousand)	55	50	47
Percentage change from 1965	−2	+8	+2

Source: World Bank, *World Development Report 1985* (New York: Oxford University Press, 1985).

targets as well as an efficient monitoring system" are identified as the main causes of inefficiency.[41]

At a more general level, one may question the appropriateness of having a system that originates in the dispensary, operates through the rural health centers and the district and provincial hospitals, and culminates in the Kenyatta National Hospital in Nairobi. In practice, such a system is infeasible because Kenya does not have the resources to maintain and operate it. Moreover, standards for the facilities were set too high. Even if this was the decision of the recipient, the aid agency—given its initiatives and important role in the endeavor—cannot escape its responsibility for the inappropriate technological choices.

An indication that the present rural health system is beyond Kenyan means is that although only 30 percent of the rural population have easy access to the facilities, the system has already exhausted its finances.[42] Despite sizable Danish and Swedish operations and maintenance support, two-thirds of the centers are reported to be lacking essential equipment. In hindsight, both the Kenyan government and the donors agree that a much simpler health system, emphasizing preventive medicine, would have been more affordable and cost-effective.

So far, the results of the family planning efforts have not been encouraging. In 1985 only 13 percent of Kenyan females of reproductive ages used modern family planning methods. Birth rates have continued to increase.[43] Only in recent years has the government come out clearly in support of family planning. This change in attitude has improved the prospects for family planning and could well be the main achievement of SIDA's insistence on this activity.

Rural Health in Tanzania

Sweden's contribution to Tanzanian rural health has been limited. Between 1973, when the program started, and mid-1984, SKr 81 million—or barely more than 2 percent of total Swedish disbursements—had been expended. During the 1970s, the program corresponded to 3 percent of the total budget spending in the Ministry of Health.

In the early to mid-1970s, the Tanzanian government decided to construct some 300 rural health centers before 1980, and SIDA agreed to contribute by establishing 135 of these units and equipping them with the necessary facilities.[44] This activity, which absorbed close to 60 percent of Swedish disbursements, was plagued by extended delays and cost overruns of several hundred percent, and the health centers actually established seldom had adequate resources for operations and maintenance.[45] In the early 1980s a majority of the units were reported to lack essential supplies such as clean water, electricity, or refrigerators. That they functioned at all was due to a massive effort by Denmark and the United Nations International Chidren's Emergency Fund (UNICEF) to provide the system with essential drugs. SIDA, in contrast, assumed limited responsibility for maintaining and operating the centers that it had established.

In addition Sweden has contributed small amounts for technical assistance to the ministry, for the provision of medical doctors for Tanzanian health institutions, for building hostels for medical students, and for the preparation of evaluation studies and health campaigns.[46]

About 30 percent of Swedish rural health aid has been expended on establishing and running the Tanzania Food and Nutrition Center (TFNC). This research center is held in high regard both in Tanzania and internationally, and its advice is followed by several government institutions.[47] A unique feature of this institution is that it is run almost exclusively by Tanzanian employees, who are able to fill its sophisticated manpower needs.

Swedish support to the TFNC is expected to continue, but a decision was made in 1983 to move out of national rural health activities once the current construction program is completed. The following assessment of rural health activities has only small bearing on the Swedish endeavors, in view of SIDA's limited aid in this area, which in any case was closely integrated with Tanzanian programs.

As in the case of Kenya, most of the health-related development indicators registered improvements much above the Sub-Saharan Africa average (see table 5-4). As expected, the general status of health in Tanzania is inferior to that in Kenya, given the lower per capita GDP there. And whereas the availability of nursing personnel recorded a gain in Kenya, in Tanzania it declined sharply in the fifteen years before 1980.

The emphasis in the health programs in rural areas has been impressive. Over the 1970s the rural share of the total health budget doubled and in 1980–81 surpassed 40 percent.[48] At that time, 70 percent of the rural population had to travel no more than 5 kilometers to the nearest health institution.[49] However, the severe malfunctioning of the system suggests that the national economy could not afford to sustain it. The impact of what Sweden has done has obviously been affected by these performance problems.

According to SIDA, Sweden provided only a modicum of support for operating the health centers because other donors seemed prepared to provide such support. SIDA's more recent decision to withdraw completely from rural health at the national level has been motivated by the need to reduce the number of areas in which Sweden is involved. It leaves behind a deteriorating physical structure, on one hand, and valuable contributions to the training of medical personnel, on the other.

In contrast, the support to the TFNC must be regarded as a considerable success—both for its contribution to institution building and to the center's programs. Much of this success appears to be related to the initial choice of the personnel that have managed the center.

Soil Conservation in Kenya

Soil conservation is by far the smallest of the six Swedish assistance projects under scrutiny, amounting to SKr 46 million, or 4 percent of the total Swedish aid flows to Kenya. Nevertheless, Swedish initiatives have been instrumental in launching soil conservation in Kenya. The program forms part of the agricultural extension services in the Ministry of Agriculture. Sweden is the sole donor at the national level, and its contribution covers about one-half of total costs.

Swedish assistance started up in 1974–75, when an expert was engaged to advise the ministry; an expanded program was gradually conceived under this expert's guidance. Since 1977–78, Swedish assistance has comprised three to four experts on a continuing basis and financial support to the Soil Conservation Unit in the ministry. This support has been channeled into designing suitable soil conservation measures, developing training and education material, training extension staff, providing materials and equipment for program implementation, establishing nurseries, and actual fieldwork.[50]

The implementation consists of extension workers going out from the ministry to visit farmers and persuade them to build terraces, plant grass and trees, establish cutoff drains, and undertake other measures to conserve the soil on their land. Simple tools are provided for farmers free of charge. Although soil conservation had been practiced in colonial times, it fell into disrepute at independence because of its association with colonial compulsion.

The program has addressed a crucial developmental issue: If no action had been taken, the country would have risked losing a large part of its agricultural potential. By December 1984, soil conservation measures had been introduced on 365,000 farms—or about one-half of all farms requiring such measures.[51] On this count, at least, the program can be judged highly successful.

An overall assessment must also consider whether the program would be able to survive without Swedish aid. The financial support from Sweden has been small and its import component limited. The technical assistance has consisted of relatively simple technology. Hence, the Kenyan government should not have great difficulty taking over, should the Swedes decide to leave. Sweden's current intentions are to stay.

Another question that should be considered relates to the recurrent features of the program. Soil decay cannot be fully prevented unless extension workers make repeated visits to each farm to persuade the farmers to maintain the conserving installations. Two recent studies of selected districts provide some tentative insight into this issue.[52] Although the initial acceptance rates by farmers were quite high, the participation rates in follow-up work were less impressive. Up to 80 percent of the landholders enrolled in the program, but only about 60 percent completed the terracing work. A few years after, only one-third of the farmers continued to maintain their terraces properly. Although a positive net yield to participants was clearly confirmed, the measures were adopted mainly by farmers who were better off, in part because the poorer landholders had problems in providing the required cash or labor inputs.

Four factors appear to distinguish this relatively successful activity from the other SIDA-supported efforts in Kenya. First, the project had a slow start. In contrast to the headlong rush into rural water and rural health, this project evolved gradually, after careful consideration of possible alternative options. Second, the strategy was relatively simple and the work labor-intensive. Hardly any heavy machinery was employed, and the tools used were familiar to the farmers. Third, farmers participated in implementation voluntarily. This can only happen if the participants perceive the private benefits that they can reap. Fourth, soil conservation has had strong political support at the highest levels of government.

Forest Development in Tanzania

Sweden has provided support for industrial forest planting and care, sawmilling and related activities, technical assistance, and village afforestation throughout Tanzania. In addition to supporting forest activities, it has contributed financial support to the pulp and paper industry at Mufindi.

Sweden's aid to forestry began in 1969. By mid-1984, SKr 206 million had been expended—which corresponds to 5 percent of overall Swedish aid and 20 percent of Sweden's total support to agriculture and rural development. SIDA has contributed as much as two-thirds of the total Tanzanian budget for forestry development over several extended periods[53] and on occasion has contributed as much as 90 percent.[54]

One of Tanzania's crucial problems is rapid deforestation. The annual sustainable wood production from the 44 million hectares of forested land has been assessed at about 20 million cubic meters. However, total wood consumption is about 40 million cubic meters per year. More than 95 percent of this amount is used for fuel.

Although overall wood consumption vastly exceeds the output of Tanzania's forests, there is a huge excess capacity in logs and pulpwood from two sources. First, there are 10 million hectares of forest reserves, with an annual output capacity of 5 million cubic meters of logs and an equal amount of pulpwood. In addition, roughly 80,000 hectares of industrial forest plantations provide an annual yield of 400,000 cubic meters each of logs and pulpwood.[55] However, forest reserves and plantations are not intended to be a source of fuelwood, although in practice a substantial take for this purpose cannot be avoided.

The demand for logs is determined by the requirements of sawmills. In 1985 the demand for logs was about 500,000 cubic meters, of which 150,000 cubic meters was supplied by plantations. The demand for pulpwood will reach 300,000 cubic meters when the Mufindi project becomes fully operational.[56] Thus Tanzania's industrial demand for logs and pulpwood is only a small fraction of the annual capacity of forest supply, particularly on forest plantations. Throughout the period under study, a small share of Swedish aid to forestry has been expended on training programs and institutional support in the Forest

Division of the Ministry of Lands and in the Tanzania Wood Industries Corporation (TWICO), a parastatal holding company for forest processing industries. The remaining Swedish forestry allocations experienced two fundamental shifts during the 1970s.[57]

Until about 1976, most of the Swedish resources were employed in forest plantations. SIDA's activities financed the establishment of some 20,000 hectares, that is, 25 percent of the present stock. When it was realized in the mid-1970s that the industrial forest capacity vastly exceeded the forest industry's needs, the program to expand plantations was replaced by assistance to TWICO to establish mobile sawmills and thus expand the industrial demand for logs. Support for the maintenance of plantations was continued.

From about 1980 on, village afforestation became an additional component in Sweden's aid. The aim was to increase the supply of fuelwood in rural areas. Apart from technical assistance to the Forest Division, SIDA has financed the establishment of nurseries, the production and import of plastic tubes for seedlings, and campaigns to persuade the rural population to plant trees. In the 1980s, SIDA regarded village afforestation as the most important component in its support to forestry.[58]

An assessment of the first component of Swedish aid to forestry in Tanzania, the expansion of its forest plantations, reveals that this effort was misconceived because a proper analysis of demand had not been undertaken. Consequently it was not until after a number of years of work that authorities recognized plantation trees do not live much beyond thirty years and have to be harvested at that age. The need to cut, in turn, revealed that the industrial demand for wood in the country was limited.

The second component has been concerned with rectifying the growing imbalance between the supply of and the demand for logs. SIDA financed the establishment of eleven small mobile sawmills, adding appreciably to the national sawmill capacity and to the demand for logs. Because of the prevailing prices for sawn wood products, sawmilling has the potential to provide good profits. The mobility, small capacity, simple technology, and labor-intensive activities of the sawmills makes them appropriate for the conditions on Tanzania's plantations.

The third component, the technical assistance extended to the Forest Division and TWICO, has not been too successful, although the contribution of the expatriates in the ministry is not entirely clear. For some years TWICO continued to run at a loss despite its near-monopoly position, the excess demand for its products, and the many reorganization plans proposed by the foreign advisers. Since 1983, however, it has become increasingly profitable, but the turnaround was not related to the technical assistance received. Instead it was the result of the toughness of the new management appointed in 1981 by Tanzania's president, with a mandate to slash unprofitable units and redundant labor and to reward or penalize managerial performance.

Village afforestation has become an extremely important and clearly poverty-oriented task in national development. Although it is too early to evaluate the impact of this activity, Tanzanian authorities and their Swedish supporters rushed headlong into it about 1980, after village afforestation became politically fashionable. Instead they should have spent more time on the design of these endeavors and could have avoided some of the problems that are now emerging concerning, for example, the suitability of the species being propagated. If the trees do not thrive, there may be a backlash. Some aspects of the program's operations also need to be improved. For instance, seedlings are supplied from large nurseries rather than from local village units. Timely deliveries, crucial to successful planting, cannot be guaranteed because of unreliable transport. Political campaigns supported by Sweden have been used to persuade (or mildly coerce) the farmers to take part in communal afforestation. A large number of the seedlings have been planted on collective plots, where the survival rates are about 0–40 percent, in contrast to 50–80 percent on individual plots.[59] Under the pressure of these campaigns, many farmers enrolled unwillingly in the collective programs, but subsequently did not participate enough to make the programs a success.[60]

The Impact of Sweden's Aid on Development

Against the background of the aid objectives and their application, the impact of Swedish aid can be assessed from the actual and potential additional income generated by the aid activity—particularly among the poor. Actual additional income can in principle be derived by evaluating the current service flow (for example, the water provided or the forest grown) from the aid endeavors. Potential additional income can be estimated by examining the role of aid in capital formation, including learning, and in the establishment of institutions and the encouragement of policies that permit the efficient utilization of that capital. The sustainability of the capital and institutions must also be taken into account. The last step in this exercise is to identify the beneficiaries of the additional income and to assign a higher value to that part that accrues to the poor. These are not easy tasks, and the following analysis employs, in the main, qualitative methods.

Allocation of Aid to Specific Purposes

An earlier section of this chapter explained how Swedish aid has been allocated; the question explored here is the appropriateness of the allocations. The project surveys revealed one clear instance of inappropriate allocation: the effort to expand forest plantations at a time when the forest industries did not have the capacity to absorb the output of the plantations. This question is not as easily answered in the case of the other projects.

In principle, the optimal allocation of aid resources is arrived at by assessing the effect of alternative activities within a well-defined macroeconomic framework. The fact that Swedish aid planning did not proceed in this way suggests that allocation was suboptimal. In practice, however, even a firm grasp of the macroeconomic circumstances is no guarantee of optimal allocation.

Two striking allocational features stand out in the Swedish aid flows to Kenya and Tanzania. The first is the emphasis on subsidized public services. Such services can help improve agricultural productivity and the well-being of the poor. Expectations of this nature motivated SIDA to provide assistance for rural water and rural health projects. In retrospect, these expectations were not met. Implementation problems along with inappropriate project designs—not to mention the economic crises that the two recipients suffered in the 1980s—reduced the benefits these projects were expected to generate. It is possible that more penetrating macroeconomic analyses beforehand would have revealed that the proposed project technologies were too advanced and the recurrent costs too high for the prevailing circumstances.

The second allocational feature is the preponderance of "standard" as distinct form "innovative" activities. Innovative aid is defined here as ventures aiming to establish and use new technical, administrative, institutional, or other relevant knowledge in a manner especially adapted to the recipient environment. Such aid can often function as a catalyst in mobilizing dormant or underutilized resources into highly productive efforts. With a few exceptions, notably the aid provided for the TFNC, Sweden has put most of its money into straightforward construction, and technical assistance in the main has involved the transfer of standard professional skills and administrative know-how by experts working on short-run contracts.

Problems in Implementation

The delays and cost overruns in the implementation of the construction programs financed by Sweden's aid, as well as the poor quality of the facilities delivered, have been a disappointment. Many other aid programs in Africa have experienced similar difficulties. In Sweden's case, limited experience with the recipient environment led planners to push ahead with overambitious programs and to expect them to be implemented at an unrealistically high pace.

Some of the problems can also be traced to the fact that the responsibility for implementation has not been clearly defined. In the early days, Sweden's role was to provide turnkey projects—that is, complete facilities in operating order. Later, the responsibility for execution was shifted to the recipients on the grounds that they would benefit from learning by doing. Yet the Swedes were unwilling to relinquish responsibility for execution, and implementation came under dual control. Although formal responsibility for implementation is usually vested in the recipient ministry, Swedish experts attached to that ministry, as well as SIDA itself, commonly hold important executing functions.

SIDA considers the turnkey practice inappropriate, yet it is also opposed to the idea of transferring all responsibility to the recipient for fear that such a move would affect performance standards.

In cases where a sophisticated technology is being transferred, the economic gain from turnkey delivery—in the speed and efficiency of execution—could more than outweigh the benefit of having the recipient learn by doing. In technically less complex endeavors, however, the arguments against giving the recipient complete responsibility for implementation are not convincing. If direct donor involvement in execution did not make a great difference, a clearly inferior performance would be apparent in those parts of the economy of Kenya and Tanzania that did not receive aid, such as postal services and road transport. In fact, no such difference is noticeable. Furthermore, over the period between 1970 and 1982, aid has financed, on average, only 21 percent of the investment expenditures in Kenya and 46 percent in Tanzania.[61] If the donor claims were true, then the majority of investments in both countries should have yielded a poor return. In fact, the incremental capital output ratio, (ICOR, which is the gross investment ratio over the GNP growth rate) works out to be an average of 4.5 in Kenya and 5.4 in Tanzania over the twelve-year period. These figures are in no way exceptional. The ICOR for the entire developing world is 5.0, whereas for industrial countries it is as high as 8.0—indicating a lower return to investment in heavily capitalized economies.

On this evidence, it is hard to maintain that recipient institutions are generally inefficient in implementing or operating projects. Like executing donor agencies, these institutions of developing countries have to grapple with inadequate infrastructural facilities and economic policies that often provide perverse signals.

Achievements and Costs of Aid

Swedish aid has indeed contributed to the formation of physical capital. The installations for supplying water in rural areas, the facilities for storing agricultural products, and the structures that prevent soil erosion or that house rural health centers and educational institutions are but a few examples. Similarly, the training programs for medical staff, water engineers, forest technicians, and other professionals have helped build up human capital, although this contribution is less apparent on the surface.

Sweden's contribution to the establishment of institutions and policies that facilitate the utilization of this capital is less clear. The TFNC and the Soil Conservation Unit in the Kenyan Ministry of Agriculture are admirable examples of useful institution building in which Swedish aid has played a crucial part. In contrast, the heavy Swedish manpower inputs in the ministries of water and health in both countries has had little effect. In the 1980s, host countries began to voice concern about some of these technical assistance programs, with the result that several of the programs are being scaled down.

In a longer-term perspective, there is probably a close connection between the conceptual soundness of an aid project and the impact of the technical assistance provided in its support. Another prerequisite of success is that the recipient government must be committed to the task at hand. Both factors help explain the different performances of Swedish technical assistance in the land care, soil conservation program in Kenya, on the one hand, and in the rural health and rural water projects in both countries, on the other.

Throughout the period surveyed, Sweden did not intervene in recipient country policies. A rare example of an attempt to interfere can be seen in Sweden's quarrel with the Kenyan government over rural water tariffs. In a broad sense, Swedish policy can be said to have influenced the decisions in both Kenya and Tanzania to launch large rural water programs.

SIDA has not made any overt efforts to bring about policy change in areas such as the exchange rate or agricultural pricing and marketing, where serious policy-induced distortions have been common. Only in the early to mid-1980s, in consequence of the economic crisis that afflicted both East African nations, did the Swedish aid agency start to question crucial policies of this kind, especially in Tanzania.

Sweden has been reluctant to impose policy conditions for both practical and ideological reasons. Practically speaking, it believed that if different conditions were imposed by many donors the recipient governments would be unable to satisfy them all. And as a matter of principle, broad policy conditionality was regarded as an undesirable infringement on the recipient's sovereignty. SIDA, along with other Nordic aid agencies, was hesitant to join the "hardliner" donors for fear that it might become hostage to policy recommendations that were contrary to its equity principles. When policy reform in Tanzania emerged as a crucial precondition for the continued functioning of

SIDA's assistance, the Swedes chose to present their views not as strict conditions, but in the form of a seminar.[62] As the Tanzanian crisis deepened toward the mid-1980s, Swedish aid policymakers adjusted their policies to accommodate the views of the hardliners.

The flow of goods and services from the capital created by Swedish aid has not been impressive. In the programs surveyed, the physical capital stock is declining and the capacity utilization is low. SIDA's reaction to such problems has been slow. There must be a link between the output of goods and services and income generation. If the former is unimpressive in relation to production capacity, the same will be true of the latter. The Swedish aid endeavors under study were designed to benefit low-income groups. Much of the additional income generated by Swedish aid should therefore have accrued to the poor and thereby should have improved equity. In some cases, the outcome was far from the intended objective, which was clearly the case in the Kenyan rural water supply program, the benefits of which were reaped mainly by the well-off.

A full-fledged evaluation must relate the achievements of aid to the resource costs. In the case of Swedish aid, the costs are almost as difficult to quantify as the benefits. In most ventures, donor and recipient funds have been mixed, and it is seldom possible to disentangle the value of the resources that the recipient has expended on each aid activity from other values. Ideally, achievements and costs should be compared in some kind of cost-benefit analysis. For the projects under scrutiny, such efforts would have to start from scratch and would require a substantial amount of work to collect the necessary data.

The sums that are quantifiable are those disbursed by Sweden—summarized in tables 5-5 and 5-6. To these should be added substantial but unknown sums paid by the recipients, and the interest on the money expended until the start-up of production. This resource spending led to the aid achievements described in the preceding section. Additional—but even harder to quantify—benefits may have accrued in the form of learning by donor and recipient in the process of aid implementation.

Whether the aid resources have been productively spent is impossible to answer with any degree of certainty. The fact that construction was slow and the capacity utilization low in the four large programs surveyed suggests that the cost-benefit ratio was substantially below the level (whether assessed or not) that led planners to go ahead with the projects. But then, as already noted, the underlying assessments may have been unrealistically optimistic.

Adverse Effects on Society at Large

Aid may produce several adverse effects on society at large.

Overgrown government. Virtually all Swedish aid has been channeled through the central governments of Kenya and Tanzania. This practice is not exclusive to Sweden; other donors tend to follow the same procedure. SIDA's insistence that recipients should launch particular activities, coupled with the promise of aid, led these countries to overexpand their administrations. Knowing that aid would be available and hoping that it would continue after the aid facilities had been delivered, recipients paid somewhat less attention than desirable to the implications of the investment expenditures and recurrent costs. For example, if Kenya and Tanzania had had to develop their rural water supply without external assistance, the programs would certainly have been more modest and the consumer asked to share a greater part of the financial burden—simply because the governments could not have afforded anything else. As a result, the central government would have remained smaller and less likely to overextend itself administratively and financially.

To claim, as donors do, that the excessive cost of installations is due to recipient insistence is to miss the point. If the donor agency is footing the bill, it is obviously going to be asked to provide the best—especially when it is uncertain that any "savings" from choosing lower standards will be available for other purposes.

Operations and maintenance costs. Recipient governments are often unable or unwilling to provide adequate funds for the recurrent costs of aid projects or to ensure against capital decay. This problem arises because it is widely believed that aid is intended for investment purposes only. Consequently the budgets of Kenya and Tanzania—which rely heavily on aid—stress investment. The aid-financed capital stock and the recurrent costs needed to keep it operational have grown much faster than the government's recurrent revenues. The investment bias of aid has therefore diverted attention from recurrent cost funds.

The recipient government may be unwilling to finance recurrent costs in part because it may never have wanted the aid venture at all, or may feel that, although the venture itself is useful, it has poor prospects in the given country—because of, say, the technology chosen. Or the recipient may calculate that the donor will provide the recurrent funds after all, rather than see the aid project disintegrate.

Swedish aid projects provide some examples of this kind of attitude in recipients. The recurrent costs of the rural water and rural health programs were probably beyond the means of Kenya and Tanzania. In Kenya, the lack of funding for the recurrent costs of family planning reflected the government's lack of interest in this activity. In Tanzania, some of the rural water installations are nonviable because their operating costs are higher than the investment plus operating costs of alternative installations. Kenya's reluctance to provide funds for operating the rural health centers was clearly related to the Swedish (and Danish) indications of possible support.

The operations and maintenance issue raises two important questions for the donor: What should be done about past aid investments that are deteriorating? Should the principle of "aid for investments only" be revised?

If the sole objective of aid is to maximize recipient development, then the principle should go. Recurrent costs should be funded wherever this would mean production and income flows would be greater than the expenditure on new capital formation. Such a policy may be difficult to adopt on political grounds: If other donors continued to apply the "aid for investments only" principle, Sweden's aid would contribute best to development by being spent entirely on operating the aid projects of other donors. Although Sweden has been more liberal and flexible than most donors on the issue of recurrent cost, such an extreme policy clearly would be unacceptable to the domestic aid constituency.

Even in less extreme cases where only Swedish-financed projects were concerned, one must consider the possible negative consequences to development from long-run donor commitments to pay for operations. Such commitments could reduce the recipient's sense of responsibility for these projects and lead to the perpetuation of activities having a low priority on the recipient's agenda.

In a broad sense, there has been a fundamental adjustment in Swedish assistance flows over time in response to the inability of its recipients to operate and maintain the investments provided by aid. Early on, the Swedish programs did indeed consist mainly of investments in areas such as power, roads, buildings, water, and industrial equipment. Later, the emphasis shifted toward the software needed to run these installations (for example, training programs, health plans, operating systems, and instruction). The recent acceptance of greater responsibility for management and operations costs is but a last step in this adjustment process.

The appropriations-in-aid technique. Swedish aid funds used to be channeled through the Ministry of Finance to the specialized ministry and then on to the organization in charge of project implementation. Since about 1980, this procedure has been changing because of complaints that projects have difficulty obtaining the funds transferred from Sweden. Delays in forwarding the funds or allocating the foreign exchange to the project administration have disrupted project work. The foreign exchange crisis plaguing the two countries and the ensuing pressures to reallocate resources to resolving the crisis explain why the flow of funds through the recipient administrations was disrupted.

To ensure that its projects will run smoothly, SIDA has introduced the practice of appropriations-in-aid. This means that Sweden sends funds as well as imported equipment directly to the project organization and that both the Ministry of Finance and whatever other ministry is involved are bypassed.

The practice became quite common among donors to Kenya and Tanzania during the 1980s. No doubt it has helped speed up aid implementation, but it also raises some fundamental issues that have not been discussed much by the donor community. Although it has been introduced to expedite donor contributions, the practice is turning around the whole philosophy of aid giving. International aid traditionally has been seen as a government-to-government relationship. Where a large part of the recipient governments' budgets are aid-financed, the spread of appropriations in aid could seriously compromise the authority of the central government. Although aid formally remains the government's responsibility, in reality the appropriations-in-aid along with the increasing regionalization of the donors' interests turn foreign assistance into an activity more akin to private foreign investments—or missionary activities—in which the government has limited say over the content or mode of operation.

Another consequence of appropriations-in-aid is that it gives precedence to microeconomic considerations in the allocation of resources. During the extended economic crisis in Kenya and Tanzania, scarce foreign exchange resources had to be used to keep the economy functioning, for example, by importing the diesel fuel or spares needed to operate the road transport system—rather than in maintaining a timely implementation of Swedish health or rural water investments. Appropriations in aid would give priority to the latter. The following SIDA view is probably close to what the donor community in general believes: "Appropriations-in-aid has become a must now that the Kenyan government, impelled by the IMF, has had to make heavy cuts in its development budget."[63] The implication is quite clear: The implementation of aid projects has precedence over national development.

Will the consequences of this attitude be good or bad for national development? Although the answer is not entirely clear, the efficiency of resource allocation at the national level is bound to decline. The economic sovereignty of the recipient government is bound to be circumscribed. And institutional development in the recipient administration will no doubt stagnate. On the positive side, the reach of an overgrown government may be reduced. What is clear is that this change in aid practice will have ramifications far beyond the issue of expediting donor contributions.

Gains in donor experience. The aid experience in Kenya and Tanzania has taught SIDA some valuable lessons. The fact that these lessons can help it improve future aid effectiveness provides some compensation for the failures and inadequacies of many past programs.

At the broadest level, Sweden's experience with the economic crises that befell Kenya and Tanzania in the 1980s has demonstrated that a large donor cannot be passive about the national economic policy environment. An aid-financed activity cannot function well in an environment of severe policy-induced scarcities and distortions. Import-dependent projects will fail if there is no foreign exchange to satisfy their needs. Projects designed to improve agricultural productivity and output will not succeed if agricultural pricing discourages farmers from producing more. When national economic policies are clearly counterproductive to aid, the donor's choice will be either to try to persuade the recipient to change such policies or to discontinue the aid.

Donors cannot expect to influence broad policy matters without a comprehensive grasp of the macroeconomic circumstances of the recipient nation. Such a grasp is also needed to ensure that aid will be allocated efficiently.

Although gains in this area certainly have been made over the past two decades of aid activity, Sweden has yet to reach the requisite level of understanding of the recipients' social and economic environment. Past experience points to the dangers of rushing into this environment with a new activity on a large scale; it is better to proceed step by step, taking the experiences gained in the process into account as the activity is developed. Experience with water and health assistance in Kenya and Tanzania also points to the inadvisability of using generous aid offers to induce the recipient government to undertake projects that it can ill afford and the consequences of which have not been fully considered. Users must help finance, execute, and maintain social service activities such as rural water or rural health if these activities are to succeed. It is essential that the technology for operating such service programs be simple and cheap enough for local communities to afford. The best method of gaining such participation still remains to be defined.

The problem of financing recurrent costs points to the importance of identifying the recurrent costs before new aid ventures are launched.

The interests of the donor and recipient must coincide to a large degree if the donor's objectives are to be reasonably satisfied in aid activities that are completely integrated in broader national programs. Thus Swedish aid to family planning in Kenya was ineffective because the recipient authorities did not share the Sweden's interest in this endeavor; and Swedish support for rural water in Kenya did not reach the poor because the recipient authorities did not share Sweden's concern about equity.

Another lesson from Sweden's aid projects in Kenya and Tanzania is that even when broad public service programs are oriented toward alleviating poverty, this is no guarantee that equity will improve. Direct measures to reach the poor are usually required to prevent benefits from finding their way mainly to the better-off groups.

The actual demand for the output from aid ventures must be carefully assessed in advance to avoid failures such as Sweden's expansion of Tanzania's forest plantations.

Expectations about the speed of aid implementation and about the ratio of outputs to resource inputs have been excessively optimistic in most past projects. More realistic assessments of what is achievable will reduce future disappointments. This is true whether underachievement is the result of incompetence within the aid agency, the difficult social and economic environment in recipient countries, or other factors.

SIDA's occasional experience with channeling aid through nongovernmental organizations is, on the whole, encouraging. These organizations have proved less bureaucratic and more flexible than the government as instruments for putting aid to useful work.

Policy Conclusions for Future Aid

The economic crisis affecting Kenya and Tanzania since the early 1980s constitutes a serious deterrent to development. Since the objective of aid is to promote development, it is appropriate to seek opportunities to employ aid to resolve such crises.

Aid for crisis resolution. The use of aid resources to fight economic crises is important for the effectiveness of normal aid programs, because the latter are difficult to implement while the crisis is going on. Another point to note is that the causes of such crises are usually external as well as internal. Unfavorable climatic conditions and depressed demand for the commodities exported by Kenya and Tanzania, along with distorted economic policies, for example, produced a number of bottlenecks that paralyzed their economies. One of their more serious problems was the lack of foreign exchange.

Foreign aid could play a constructive role both in relaxing the resource bottlenecks and leveraging change in some of the internal policies that contributed to the crisis. This implies that most of the aid not immediately related to resolving the crisis should be deferred and that the released resources should be spent on an expanded program of import support without ties to specific purposes, but should be contingent upon policy reform. The primary purpose of the policy change promoted by the donor would be to remove existing bottlenecks, for example, to reduce the scarcity of foreign exchange by increasing its price, or to augment the domestic availability of food by permitting agricultural prices to rise.

Swedish aid has in fact been redirected along such lines in the recent past. More aid is being provided for import support. SIDA is exerting more pressure for policy change—but the shifts have been only partial and appear inadequate. Governments have been responding cautiously perhaps because they are uncertain about how to tackle the new situation. Undoubtedly many are also reluctant to slow down or arrest aid ventures already under way.

Aid can help resolve economic crises by relaxing resource constraints and acting as a catalyst for policy reform. Its effectiveness in this regard will be greatly increased if the leading donors can coordinate their policies. The first basic task for a coordinated donor group would be to sit down with the recipient and hammer out a feasible path out of the crisis and to determine the most constructive role that foreign assistance could play in the process. As a leading donor in Tanzania and a prominent one in Kenya, SIDA could well take a lead in coordinating donors and redirecting aid in the suggested directions.

Longer-run issues for Swedish aid. The acute economic crisis from which Kenya and Tanzania are struggling to extricate themselves will eventually be resolved. In the meantime, it is important to consider the policy measures that could improve the effectiveness of Sweden's aid in the longer run. A number of such measures that emerged from the analyses in earlier sections of this chapter are restated in the following paragraphs.

Sweden should endeavor to improve its understanding of the macroeconomic circumstances in the recipient countries. One means of doing so might be to support the establishment of independent economic policy think tanks of high academic standing in each recipient country and to encourage collaboration between these and Swedish institutions. Apart from strengthening Swedish knowledge about Kenya and Tanzania, these independent institutions could fulfill useful roles in formulating alternative policies for the government to consider.

Careful macroeconomic analysis is indispensable if Sweden hopes to determine whether its aid allocations are appropriate. Such analysis would reveal the extent of the investment bias that aid has introduced in government budgets. It would also throw valuable light on the recurrent costs of aid projects and would indicate where it would be appropriate to expend aid on recurrent costs. This could help SIDA formulate long-run policies for recurrent cost financing. To avoid heavy commitments and yet to encourage the recipient to provide sufficient resources for operations, SIDA might consider the strategy—sometimes adopted by the United Kingdom—of assuming only the incremental recurrent costs on condition that the recipient provide the base load.

The developmental implications of all proposed aid activities should be carefully assessed against the macroeconomic circumstances of the recipient countries to weed out ventures that do not fit. This would reduce the need for SIDA to be involved in detailed decisions about aid allocations. Macroeconomic analysis ought to reveal neglected comparative advantages that aid could help to mobilize for the purpose of generating additional income. The guidelines provided by such analysis might reorient the content of Sweden's aid in favor of agriculture or of activities with an export potential.

This is not to say that a better understanding of the macroeconomic and of the social and economic environment of recipient countries—although exceedingly important as a framework for the delineation of an appropriate aid program—is by itself a panacea. A variety of other conditions must also be satisfied to achieve a high level of aid effectiveness.

The short institutional memory of SIDA needs to be extended. Historical analyses of past aid provided by SIDA, assessing what went right and wrong over time, could serve this purpose. Making such analyses required reading for relevant personnel groups could increase the feedback from past experiences of this agency.

SIDA should also devote more attention to evaluating its activities at the microeconomic level. The agency's accounting systems should be adjusted with a view to facilitating cost-benefit analyses of projects and programs.

The circumstances under which Sweden should apply policy conditionality to its aid should be clearly identified. Widespread coordination among donors is necessary to avoid inconsistencies that the recipient cannot reconcile. Clearer rules on when and where policy conditionality will be applied would help the recipient government anticipate the consequences of its own alternative actions and minimize the risk of opportunism on the donor side in the use of this instrument.

A greater emphasis on innovative activities to develop new scientific, technical, or institutional knowledge—appropriately adapted to the recipient country—could improve the effectiveness of Swedish aid in helping to increase output and generate income. The research centers financed by the Rockefeller and Ford foundations, which gave birth to the green revolution, come to mind as examples. The Tanzanian village afforestation program to which SIDA is a prominent contributor could provide an opportunity for innovative aid from Sweden. The program could be strengthened if a forest research institute was set up to identify the species most suited for planting around villages and to clarify the sociopolitical circumstances that must prevail to ensure plant survival. Sweden may have a comparative advantage in this area, given its long tradition of forest research. To launch innovative activities Sweden would have to call for more careful research into the recipient environments than has been common under its aid programs. The standard two-year technical assistance contract is an unsuitable means of pursuing innovative aid. To be effective, the core personnel provided by SIDA probably would have to commit their lifetime careers to such tasks.

The causes of the disappointing performance of the rural water and rural health programs launched by SIDA are easy to summarize. They employed technologies that were not manageable at the local level, incurred operating and maintenance costs that the central governments could not afford, and failed to provide for local participation.

What kinds of rural water and rural health facilities would be more appropriate—in the sense that they could serve a substantial part of the population in Kenya and Tanzania and be operated and maintained without continuous foreign support? This question has not yet been sufficiently investigated. Innovative aid efforts could make a valuable contribution by supporting the development of technologies in these areas that are simple enough and cheap enough to operate. Some aid-supported research should also be devoted to investigating the practicalities of ensuring local participation without using coercion.

These may be tricky tasks. To satisfy the above conditions, the facilities might have to be so simple and rudimentary that an advanced country like Sweden might not be prepared to support their establishment. Public opinion in the donor country might disapprove of, say, a national health system that could not help sick people because the available resources were all used for disease prevention. Or the donor might disapprove of a system of rural water that has acceptably low recurrent costs (gravital system), for example, because its total costs are much higher than those of another system (drilled wells run by diesel pumps)—even though this other system runs up unacceptably high recurrent costs. On strictly economic grounds, it might be cheaper for the donor to install the diesel-run system and pay for its operation, rather than to finance the high design and installation costs of the gravital system and have the consumers cover recurrent costs. Such issues require careful research in which Swedish aid could play a useful role. Indeed, the slow progress of SIDA's more recent rural water endeavors at the regional level may be attributable to attempts to tackle these complex problems.

As already mentioned, Sweden's traditional, altruistically motivated aid constituency has been losing some ground to the proponents of aid that is commercially useful to Sweden. As a result, increasing attention will have to be devoted to identifying the tradeoffs between a larger aid program containing commercial features that may have less effect on development, on one hand, and a smaller program directly concerned with development, on the other. If Sweden was to concentrate its aid on a few activities in which it has had distinct comparative advantage, coupled with innovative efforts to adapt Swedish excellence to the conditions of the recipient countries, it might come up with a program that is commercially beneficial to Sweden but simultaneously contributes to income generation and equity.

The executive responsibility in SIDA's projects should be clarified. Standard aid with only a few high-tech inputs could probably be managed by recipient institutions, as long as performance standards were clearly spelled out and their fulfillment was a condition of continued support. Implementation is more complex in innovative aid and therefore warrants more extensive Swedish involvement. High-tech ventures might best be delivered as turnkey projects.

The encouraging experience of providing aid through nongovernmental organizations suggests that such collaboration should be expanded. At the same time, careful consideration has to be given to the role of the government in the aid process, so as to safeguard against compromising the central authorities, as has occurred through the practice of appropriations in aid.

Another important step for SIDA would be to further coordinate its aid with that of donors in other Nordic countries and elsewhere. Such coordination is vital if donors expect to pursue purposeful policy conditionality. When donors coordinate their efforts, there are fewer administrative hurdles to contend with in the recipient government, duplication is avoided, valuable experiences are shared and the information from them spreads faster, and efficiency in the allocation of the overall aid to recipient countries can be vastly improved.

Notes

This study was prepared between late 1985 and early 1986, using documentation available at that time. Since then a number of important policy changes have taken place that were just on the horizon in the mid-1980s. In the light of the experiences of the latter half of the 1980s, Swedish aid programs to East Africa have shifted their emphasis from project lending to an expansion of import support, cofinancing with other development institutions, and more frequent employment of conditionality where aid is granted—provided that the recipient country undertakes essential policy reform. In recent years more attention has also been given to evaluating aid efforts. The chapter would have required extensive revision to take all these changes into account and so only the statistical tables have been updated. Therefore some of the conclusions and criticisms expressed in the study do not apply to the Swedish aid performance of the late 1980s. The valuable research assistance of Apollo Njonjo and Lars Rylander in the preparation of this chapter is gratefully acknowledged.

1. Throughout the chapter, aid, or assistance, is defined in accordance with the reports of the Development Assistance Committee (DAC) of the Organisation for Economic Co-operation and Development. Between 1970 and 1981 the annual average exchange rate of Swedish kroner (SKr) with respect to the United States dollar varied between 4.15 and 5.17. It rose thereafter to a peak of 8.99 in 1984. Constant SKr values have been obtained by using the Swedish consumer price index as deflator. Split years refer to the Swedish budget year, starting July 1. In addition to the works quoted, the analysis is supported by numerous interviews in Sweden, Kenya, and Tanzania.

2. Marian Radetzki, *Aid and Development* (New York: Praeger, 1973).

3. SOU, *Sveriges samarbete med u-landerna* (Swedish collaboration with developing countries) (Stockholm, 1977), 13; SIDA, *Bistand i siffror och diagram* (November 1984).

4. Ibid.

5. O. Stokke, *Sveriges Utvecklingsbistand och bistandspolitik* (Sweden's development aid and aid policy) (Nordiska Afrikainstitutet, 1978) concludes that this goal has been insignificant—except at the rhetorical level. However, SIDA's long-standing support for refugees of political struggles and conflicts can be seen as a manifestation of the democratization goal. In recent years, attention increasingly has turned to integrating the democratization objective into the regular development aid portfolio—for instance, through literacy programs and support to decentralized local government structures.

6. Ibid.

7. SIDA, "SIDA's Strategi for Lansbygdsutveckling," (SIDA's strategy for rural development) (1981); SIDA, "Policy for SIDA's Halsobistand" (Policy for SIDA's health sector support) (1982); J. Stymne, "Importstod—Principer och Problem" (Import support: principles and problems) (SIDA, 1984); and SIDA, "Vattenstrategi, Landsbygdens Vattenforsorjning" (Water strategy rural water supply) (1984).

8. Ruth Jacoby, "Idealism versus Economics: Swedish Aid and Commercial Interest," in P. Fruhling, ed., *Swedish Development Aid in Perspective* (Stockholm: Almquist & Wiksell, 1986).

9. Regeringen's proposition, Swedish Government Budget Proposal (1977–78), 135:11.

10. SIDA's anslagsframstallning 1977–78 (1976).

11. Swedish National Audit Bureau, SIDA *in Tanzania* (1974), 23: 128; and Swedish Ministry of External Affairs, *Effektivare Bistandsadministration* (More efficient aid administration) (DS UD, 1984), 1:201.

12. Ibid., 207.

13. Examples of more comprehensive evaluations include recent studies of health in Kenya and Tanzania and of forestry in Tanzania.

14. The conclusions drawn here about the limited feedback of evaluation are called into question by Kim Forss, "Planning and Evaluation in Aid Organization," Ph.D. dissertation, Stockholm School of Economics, 1986. Forss argues that the more informal, learning-by-doing evaluations used in SIDA have been valuable inputs into SIDA's operations and that they have usefully augmented SIDA's institutional memory and knowledge.

15. SIDA's views on Kenya were most likely inspired by the influential ILO report, *Employment, Incomes, and Equality* (Geneva, 1972). The findings with regard to income distribution have been heavily criticized since by various studies; see, for example, P. Collier and Deepak Lal, "Why Poor People Get Rich: Kenya 1960–79," *World Development* 10 (1984). Donor perceptions of Tanzania's favorable record on income distribution were widespread, as reflected, for instance, in various World Bank reports from the 1970s.

16. Ulf Rundin, *Tio Ars Bistand till Kenya* (Ten years of aid to Kenya) (SIDA, 1978).

17. SIDA, Samarbetsprogram med Kenya (Collaboration program with Kenya) 1979/80–1980/81 (1978).

18. SIDA, Samarbetsprogram med Kenya 1981/81–1982/83 (1981).

19. SIDA, Samarbetsprogram med Kenya 1977/78–1978/79 (1977); SIDA Samarbetsprogram med Kenya 1983/84–1984/85 (1983).

20. SIDA, Samarbetsprogram med Kenya 1975/76 (1975); SIDA, Samarbetsprogram med Kenya 1983/84–1984/85 (1983).

21. "Evaluation of the Rural Water Supply Program," a report for SIDA referred to as the VIAK Report (1977).

22. SIDA, *Summary of Recent Recommendations on the Rural Water Sector* (Nairobi, May 1985).

23. SIDA, Samarbetsprogram med Kenya 1987/80–1980/81 (1978).

24. SIDA, Samarbetsprogram med Kenya 1985/86–1986/87 (1985).

25. SIDA, *Summary of Recent Recommendations on the Rural Water Sector.*

26. SIDA, Samarbetsprogram med Tanzania (Collaboration program with Tanzania) 1983/84–1984/85 (1983); World Health Organization/World Bank Cooperative Program, *Rural Water Supply Sector Study* (1977), Annex 7:80–81.

27. O. Rimer, "Tanzania Rural Water Supply Development," Report prepared for the Tanzanian Ministry of Agriculture (April 1970).

28. O. Therkildsen, "Planning and Implementation of Basic Needs Activities: The Case of Donor-Funded Rural Water Supplies in Tanzania," (Copenhagen, June 1985, draft).

29. SIDA, Samarbetsprogram med Tanzania 1985/86–1986/87 (1985).

30. Tanzania National Committee on Drinking Water Supply, Minutes of Meeting, 25 April 1985 in Dar es Salaam.

31. Interview with Roger Anderson, UNICEF, Dar es Salaam, September 1985.

32. Therkildsen, *Planning and Implementation of Basic Needs Activities.*

33. Ibid.

34. SIDA, Samarbetsprogram med Tanzania 1981/82–1983/84 (1981).

35. Bureau of Resource Assessment and Center for Development Research, *Water Master Plans for Iringa, Ruvuma and Mbeya Regions* (1983) 12:6.19–6.20.
36. SIDA, Samarbetsprogram med Kenya 1981/82–1982/83 (1981).
37. SIDA, Samarbetsprogram med Kenya 1985/86–1986/87 (1985).
38. SIDA, Samarbetsprogram med Kenya 1983/84–1984/85 (1983).
39. SIDA, Samarbetsprogram med Kenya 1985/85–1986/87 (1985).
40. Ibid.
41. SIDA, *Evaluation of Swedish Assistance to Health Sector Development in Kenya 1969–1985*, 1986/3, part 1.
42. Government of Kenya, Ministry of Health, *Development Plan 1984–88* (Nairobi, August 1983).
43. SIDA, Samarbetsprogram med Kenya 1976/77 (1976).
44. SIDA, Samarbetsprogram med Tanzania 1974/75 (1975)
45. SIDA, Joint Swedish-Tanzanian Health Sector Review (February 1984); SIDA, Samarbetsprogram med Tanzania 1981/82–1982-83 (1981).
46. Report from a joint Swedish-Tanzanian Health Sector Review (February 1984).
47. SIDA, Samarbetsprogram med Tanzania 1985/86–1986/87 (1985).
48. Government of Tanzania, Ministry of Health, "Country Report on Tanzania" (Dar es Salaam, 1982).
49. SIDA, Samarbetsprogram med Tanzania 1985/86–1986/87 (1985).
50. SIDA, Samarbetsprogram med Kenya 1981/82–1982/83 (1981).
51. Government of Kenya, Ministry of Agriculture, Soil Conservation Project Semiannual Report (Nairobi, July-December 1984).
52. L. Hedfors, "Evaluation and Economic Appraisal of Soil Conservation in a Pilot Area" (Ministry of Agriculture, Nairobi, 1981); and "Evaluation and Economical Appraisal of Soil Conservation in Kalia Sub-Location, Kitui District" (Ministry of Agriculture, Nairobi, draft, 1985).
53. SIDA, Samarbetsprogram med Tanzania 1981/82–1983/84 (1981).
54. Joint Tanzanian-Swedish Review Mission in the Forest Sector (Dar es Salaam, 1980).
55. Ibid.
56. Ibid.
57. The sources to the following three paragraphs include SIDA, Samarbetsprogram med Tanzania, several issues; interviews with E. M. Mnzawa, director, and Arnold Ahlbeck, expert, Forestry Division, Dar es Salaam; and with Roland Oqvist, SIDA's office in Dar es Salaam. The interviews were carried out in September 1985.
58. SIDA, Samarbetsprogram med Tanzania 1981/82–1983/84 (1981)
59. SIDA, Samarbetsprogram med Tanzania 1985/86–1986/87 (1985).
60. M. McCall Skutsch, *Why People Don't Plant Trees: The Socioeconomic Impacts of Existing Woodfuel Programs: Village Case Studies, Tanzania*, Discussion Paper D-73P (Resources for the Future, March 1983).
61. The sources for the figures in this paragraph include Organisation for Economic Co-operation and Development, *Development Assistance Committee Annual Review* (various issues); United Nations, *Yearbook of National Accounts Statistics* (various issues); *World Bank Atlas* (various issues); World Bank, *World Development Report 1984* and *World Bank Annual Report 1983* (Washington, D.C.).
62. G. Edgren, "The Changing Aid Relationship: Terms, Conditions and Working Methods," in P. Fruhling, ed., *Swedish Development Aid in Perspective* (Stockholm: Almquist & Wiksell, 1986).
63. SIDA, Samarbetsprogram med Kenya 1985/86–1986/87 (1985).

6 *United States Activities to Promote Agricultural and Rural Development in Sub-Saharan Africa*

Bruce F. Johnston, Allan Hoben,
and William K. Jaeger

THE EMPHASIS in this chapter is on the activities of the United States Agency for International Development (USAID) in support of agricultural and rural development in the six countries included in the MADIA study. The topics of particular interest are the regional and international programs devoted to agriculture and USAID's support of road construction and other infrastructural projects and health and population programs for rural areas.

United States Assistance for Sub-Saharan Africa in a Global Context

During the 1963–84 period covered in this review, USAID allocations for agricultural development projects and programs in the six study countries amounted to slightly more than $900 million in constant 1983 dollars (see table 6-1). Allocations for rural development were not quite $520 million. These two areas of development accounted for more than half of the $2.4 billion USAID spent in the six countries. Total United States assistance for the six was nearly $3.6 billion for the same period—including, in addition to USAID's funding of projects and programs, P.L. 480 food aid, Economic Support Funds (ESF), and the Peace Corps.

For the six countries, and for Sub-Saharan Africa in general, these amounts are modest, compared with the general importance of the United States in the foreign assistance initiatives since World War II. As explained later in the chapter, the role of USAID and its predecessor agencies in Sub-Saharan Africa has been (a) limited, (b) relatively late, and (c) subject to large variations over time and in country focus. That contrasts sharply with the dominant role that the United States

Table 6-1. Total U.S. Assistance to the MADIA Countries, 1963–84
(millions of constant 1983 U.S. dollars)

Assistance	*Cameroon*	*Kenya*	*Malawi*	*Nigeria*	*Senegal*	*Tanzania*
Total U.S. assistance	278.6	835.8[a]	190.8	1,209.4	429.5	645.2
All projects and programs	213.8	519.5	146.7	944.0	174.3	341.5
Agriculture	85.2	269.3	25.5	284.2	114.7	126.3
Rural development	90.7	135.9	84.1	36.1	13.4	157.6
Other	37.9	114.3	37.1	623.7	46.2	57.5
PL 480 food aid	19.7	181.2	12.2	182.5	192.7	247.7
Other economic assistance	44.1	135.1	31.9	82.9	61.8[b]	56.1
Total U.S. assistance, per capita (average)	$1.36	$2.10	$1.33	$0.61	$3.25	$1.46
Total assistance as percent of GDP	0.17	0.77	0.65	0.09	0.76	0.64
Assistance to agriculture and rural development as percent of GDP	0.11	0.37	0.37	0.02	0.21	0.28
Share of total U.S. assistance to Africa, 1963–84 (percent)	1.43	4.31	0.98	6.23	2.21	3.33
Share of USAID assistance to Africa, 1963–84 (percent)	1.97	4.78	1.35	8.7	1.61	3.14
Share of United States in receipts of total ODA	6.1	15.4	8.5	22.0	10.4	7.3

a. Excludes military aid ($245 million for Kenya).
b. Includes Peace Corps.
Source: See figure 6-1.

assumed in foreign aid programs in other developing regions, especially Asia, during the 1950s and 1960s. Looking back over the entire span of development assistance, it seems clear that the unprecedented size and success of the Marshall Plan was a critical factor leading to the innovation in international relations represented by the substantial and sustained foreign assistance provided by the Organisation for Economic Cooperation and Development (OECD) countries since the OECD and its Development Advisory Committee (DAC) were created twenty-five years ago.[1] Yet between 1975 and 1985, official development assistance (ODA) provided by the United States declined from 0.58 percent of United States GNP in 1965 to less than 0.25 percent between 1979 and 1985. Equally striking, however, is the extent to which the decline in the United States contribution to foreign assistance has been more than offset by increases in the ODA provided by other DAC countries. Thus it is estimated that annual ODA from all donors for all developing countries (expressed in United States dollars) rose from about $20 billion to $29 billion (in constant 1983 prices) between 1966 and 1985, in spite of the fact that the United States contribution itself declined from 82 percent of the total ODA from the DAC countries in 1965 to 30 percent in 1985.[2]

USAID's Role in Sub-Saharan Africa

United States aid to Africa has been primarily economic aid, with less than 10 percent going to military assistance. Traditionally, Africa has not been the focus of United States economic assistance; before 1978 Africa received only about 5 percent of United States aid, but since that time, Africa's share has risen above 10 percent. The economic aid has been provided primarily for development programs, food aid, and for budgetary support under the Economic Support Fund (ESF); during most of the 1970s, this type of funding was referred to as "security supporting assistance."

The role of the United States in assisting Sub-Saharan Africa has been modest in comparison with assistance from the World Bank and other multilateral and bilateral donors. Among the six MADIA countries, it was only in Nigeria that United States aid for the period 1970–84 exceeded 20 percent of total ODA, followed by Kenya at 15 percent. For the other four countries, the United States share ranged from 6 percent of ODA in Cameroon to just over 10 percent in Senegal (where food aid accounted for 45 percent of total United States assistance).

The figures on the United States' share in total ODA, however, understate the importance of the United States' role in support of agricultural and rural development. A relatively large share of USAID's bilateral assistance was allocated for agricultural and rural development activities. Furthermore, that assistance was directed in considerable measure toward building institutions of higher education in agriculture, such as the three faculties of agriculture in Nigeria. Although United States assistance for those and other institutions was sporadic, its contribution to building educational institutions in Kenya, Malawi, and Tanzania as well as in Nigeria seems to have had a clearly positive and lasting impact. It is too early to tell if the same will be true of more recent technical assistance for the establishment of Dschang University in Cameroon.

It is also emphasized, however, that the potential payoff to investments in postsecondary institutions for agriculture and veterinary medicine has yet to be realized because of limited progress in establishing effective national agricultural research systems. In considerable measure the creation of educational institutions is an intermediate product, and the return on that investment cannot be realized fully until the locally trained agricultural scientists and other specialists begin to make important contributions to generating profitable and feasible innovations for a large and growing percentage of a country's small farmers—and also to policy research and analysis.

In contrast, USAID bilateral support for agricultural research has remained a small component of its assistance until recently. For a donor grappling with problems of periodic surpluses at home, the development of agricultural colleges in Africa was less controversial than was directly productive research. In any case, the impact on production would be long in coming, and thus less likely to threaten United States interest groups. Although USAID and other donors have missed some important opportunities to support the difficult but essential process of developing research capacity, it is important to recognize that this process is inherently a long-term phenomenon. The substantial assistance that the United States has provided for the Institute for Tropical Agriculture in Nigeria (IITA), International Center for Maize and Wheat Improvement (CIMMYT), International Crop Research Institute for Semi-Arid Tropics (ICRISAT), and other international agricultural research centers has had, and will continue to have, an important impact on agricultural progress in Sub-Saharan Africa.[3]

In the early 1960s the level of United States assistance to Africa was more than $1 billion per year (in constant 1983 dollars); it then declined until the mid-1970s, when the level began to rise again. Only in 1983–85 did United States assistance reach levels similar to those of the early 1960s (figure 6-1). USAID funding has consistently accounted for between one-half and two-thirds of total United States economic assistance to Africa.

Figure 6-1. U.S. Economic Assistance to Africa, in Real Terms, 1963–84

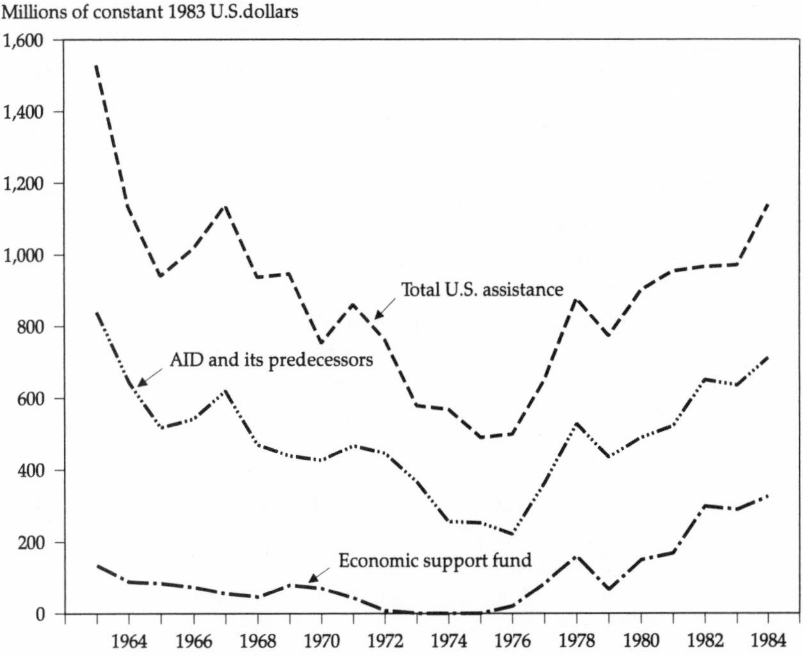

Source: B. F. Johnston, Allan Hoben, D. W. Dijkerman, and W. K. Jaeger, *An Assessment of AID Activities to Promote Agricultural and Rural Development in Sub-Saharan Africa*, USAID Evaluation Study 54 (Washington, D.C.: USAID, April 1988).

The composition of United States economic assistance to Africa has changed greatly since the 1960s, when development programs dominated. Since the mid-1970s both food aid and ESF have grown in both relative and absolute terms. Since 1980 the two together have comprised more than half of all United States economic assistance to Africa: Of the total $1.1 billion in aid to Africa in 1984, $333 million was food aid and $346 million was ESF. ESF programs are intended to serve United States political, security, and economic objectives and they provide a rapid and flexible disbursement instrument. ESF was used in Africa for a brief period in the early 1960s, but reemerged in the mid-1970s as an important part of the aid program. ESF programs can take the form of commodity import programs, cash/budget support, or project aid.[4]

A Comparative Assessment of USAID in Six African Countries

This review of USAID's programs in six African countries also provides a fairly good picture of the nature of USAID's support for agricultural and rural development in Africa in general. The kinds of USAID support in these countries are representative of USAID assistance in Africa as well. For example, the share of USAID funding going to education and agriculture in the six countries is similar to the overall shares for Africa as a whole; and food aid represents one-fourth to one-third of United States assistance for the six countries and for Africa overall.

The selection of countries for the MADIA study was influenced by the fact that they have experienced relatively more stable political and policy environments than countries such as Zaire, Ethiopia, or Uganda. Only Zaire and Sudan have received more assistance from the United States than Nigeria; and Kenya, Tanzania, and Senegal also rank among the top eleven African countries that received assistance from the United States between 1946 and 1985.

The analysis is focused on four principal questions about the effectiveness of USAID's activities in promoting agricultural and rural development:

- Were the activities that USAID chose to promote appropriate–that is, were they critical elements of a well-conceived strategy for agricultural and rural development and were they capable of having a catalytic effect on efforts being made within the recipient country itself?
- Was the country situation favorable with respect to the policy environment, the timing and sequencing of the activities, and the commitment of the country's political leadership to the objectives of the programs undertaken?
- To what extent are United States experience, technical expertise, and institutional models appropriate to the host country's needs and context?
- Does USAID have, or can it obtain, the institutional capacity to effectively plan and implement the activities necessary for the success of this kind of program under host country conditions?

The first question turns out to be especially difficult and important because of the lack of consensus concerning the kind of development strategies that should be promoted by USAID. For example, a recent survey of United States aid to Africa carried out by the Congressional Research Service argues that there is a continuing "tension in the debate over United States assistance for African development between 'top-down' and 'bottom-up' strategies of economic growth."[5] A central thesis of this chapter—and of the study on which it is based—is that this polarization of the debate is based on the unfortunate and misleading perception of a dichotomy between growth and equity. Over the past thirty-five years, a good deal of progress has been gained in our understanding of the complex processes of agricultural and rural development. Asian experience especially has emphasized that the tradeoffs between growth and equity objectives can be minimized if serious attention is given to devising and implementing development strategies that are well balanced and effective in furthering multiple objectives.

The present study seeks to draw upon the most important lessons of the past thirty-five years in order to outline an analytical framework for assessing USAID's effectiveness in supporting agricultural and rural development. In spite of the continuing controversy, there is an emerging consensus among development specialists that policies and programs should be effective in attaining multiple objectives. In particular, there is a need for agricultural strategies that are effective in simultaneously accelerating the growth of agricultural output and in generating opportunities for productive employment for a large and growing labor force. The remainder of this chapter takes up these questions, relying heavily—but not exclusively—on USAID's experiences in the six MADIA study countries.

Overview of USAID's Assistance to the Six Countries

The six MADIA study countries differ considerably in the size, pattern, and content of United States assistance. Nigeria has received the highest total assistance. Between 1963 and 1984, United States assistance to Nigeria came to $1.2 billion when valued in constant 1983 dollars (see table 6-1). Kenya, with $836 million, has had the second largest program, followed by Tanzania ($645 million) and Senegal ($429 million). The smallest programs have been those in Cameroon and Malawi, receiving $278 million and $191 million, respectively.[6] Looking at country shares, Nigeria has received more than 6 percent of total United States assistance to Africa, and nearly 9 percent of the USAID total, whereas Malawi has received less than 1 percent of total United States assistance to Africa, but a slightly larger share (1.35 percent) of USAID's funding.[7] The ranking of the six is quite different in terms of per capita aid averaged over the twenty-two-year period. With a population of only six million, Senegal's average annual assistance was by far the highest, $3.25 per capita. Kenya ranked second, with an average of $2.10 per capita. Nigeria, with a population of ninety million (which is 50 percent larger than that of the other five combined) is lowest, with an average of $0.61 per capita per year.

When compared with national GDP, United States aid to both Senegal and Kenya has averaged approximately 0.75 percent of GDP, followed closely by Tanzania and Malawi at about 0.65 percent. Cameroon and Nigeria, the two petroleum exporters, received much smaller amounts relative to their GDP.

Patterns of United States Assistance to the Six Countries

The levels of assistance to the six countries over the past twenty-five years have fluctuated (figures 6-2 and 6-3)—in part because of changes in United States funding levels for Africa as a whole. Although USAID's experience in each of the six countries differs, a number of events (and responses to them) affected several of the countries. The recommendations of the 1966 Korry Report that USAID concentrate on a small number of priority countries resulted in the phasing out of bilateral programs in Senegal, Cameroon, and Malawi. But in both Senegal and Cameroon, the USAID program was later enlarged and redirected as a result of the Sahel drought in the early 1970s—although the effect on USAID's Senegal program was more pronounced. Malawi, Cameroon, and Senegal all had low and somewhat erratic funding levels until the mid-1970s (figure 6-3). The large spikes in figure 6-3 between 1969 and 1975 were for regionally funded infrastructural

Figure 6-2. U.S. AID *Project and Program Assistance to Nigeria, Kenya, and Tanzania, 1963–84*

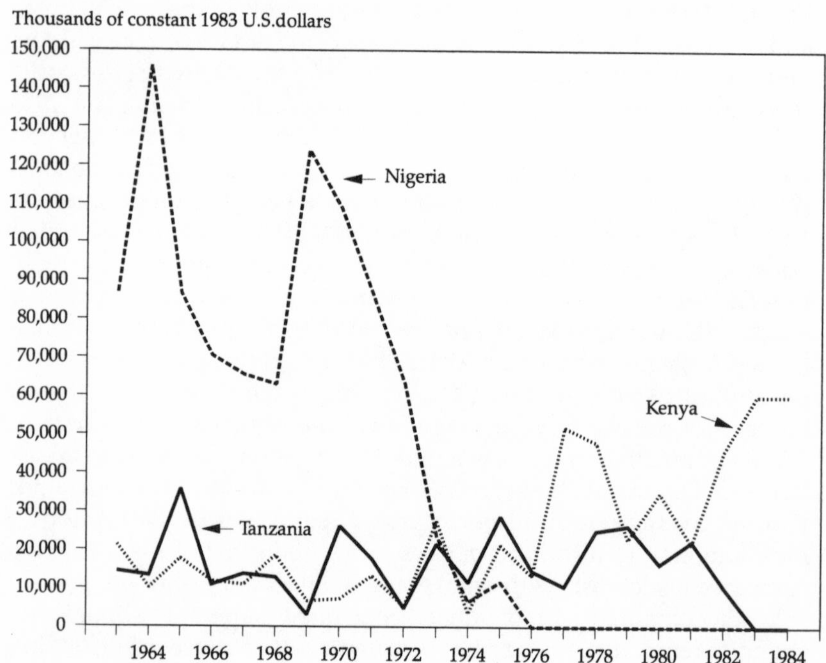

Source: See figure 6-1.

Figure 6-3. USAID *Project and Program Assistance to Senegal, Cameroon, and Malawi in Real Terms, 1963–84*

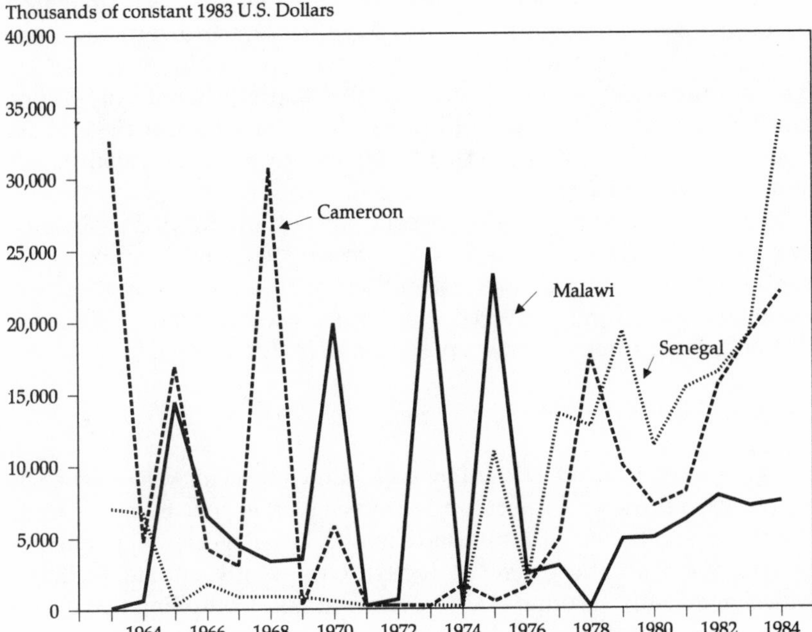

Source: See figure 6-1.

development—for railroads in the case of Cameroon and for highway construction in Malawi.[8]

Because of its size and the priority that it received during the years of the Kennedy administration, aid for Nigeria dominated United States assistance to the six countries until the early 1970s (figure 6-2). United States project and program aid for Nigeria peaked at $145 million in 1964. Beginning in 1972, the United States rapidly phased out its bilateral aid to Nigeria because of large increases in petroleum revenues. By 1977 the USAID mission was closed, and since that time Nigeria has benefited only from a small program grant and from regional and centrally funded USAID programs such as support for IITA in Ibadan and some health and population activities. Both Kenya and Tanzania have received relatively steady levels of USAID assistance over most of the period under consideration, although USAID's program in Tanzania recently has been phased out. Kenya is the only country among the six to receive a generally growing United States economic assistance program—as a result of its increased political importance to the United States. In addition to the country USAID missions, regional accounts and centrally funded programs contribute importantly to USAID's total assistance program for Africa. More than 10 percent of United States assistance to Africa has been obligated through regional accounts. Since 1963, seven different regional accounts have been used for specific regions within Africa or for special purposes. Several of these accounts administered only minor amounts and have been discontinued. Between 1963 and 1984, $1.35 billion was disbursed through USAID's Africa regional accounts (in constant 1983 dollars).

In addition to these regional accounts, centrally funded assistance plays an important role in USAID's Africa programs. For example, centrally allocated funds to support the Consultative Group on International Agricultural Research (CGIAR) are used in core funding for IITA and other international centers active in Africa.[9]

Sectoral Distribution of USAID Funds

USAID funding is broken down by sector and subsector below for each of the six countries.[10] Project funds are assigned to specific subsectors, depending on the activities undertaken.[11] The categories were chosen to coincide with the intended focus of the study and to facilitate consistency with the other MADIA donor studies. Compiling these data proved to be a complex and time-consuming task because of missing or conflicting data, especially for the earlier period. Assigning annual project funds to specific categories was an immense undertaking and would have been impractical for all of Sub-Saharan Africa.

The shares of USAID funds allocated to agriculture in these countries have fluctuated enormously from year to year, although there was a trend toward increased emphasis on agriculture during the 1970s (figure 6-4). The average share of USAID obligations for agriculture plus rural development was 60 percent for the six countries (table 6-2). Within those two categories, the largest subcategories have been agricultural education and training, and rural infrastructure—each with about 13 percent of the USAID total. These are followed by input supply (6.7 percent)—which includes both seed multiplication farms and fertilizer import programs—and livestock (5.3 percent). Agricultural extension, research, management and planning, and health and population have all received from 2 percent to 4 percent of the total USAID funds.

In several cases, individual countries diverge considerably from this average profile. Agricultural education is not as predominant in Senegal as in the other countries. And rural infrastructure has only been of minor importance for Nigeria and Senegal, but has been the largest subcategory for Malawi, Cameroon, and Tanzania. Funding

Figure 6-4. USAID *Agricultural Assistance to the* MADIA *Countries in Real Terms, 1963–84*

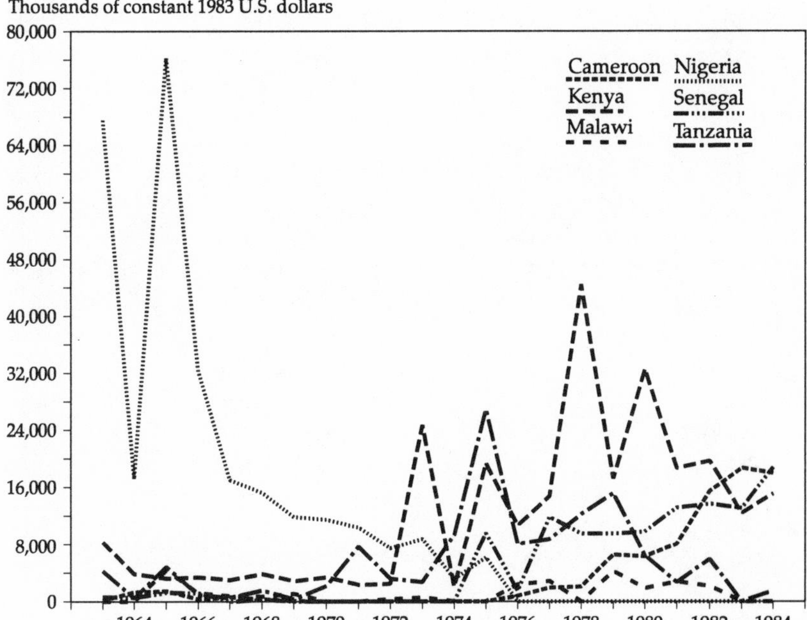

Source: See figure 6-1.

levels have been highest for input supply in Kenya, and for agricultural extension in Senegal, where most of the agricultural projects had large extension components (table 6-2). The patterns of emphasis over time for several of these subcategories are shown in figures 6-5 to 6-10. The high share of total obligations for agricultural education is explained by the Nigeria program in the 1960s and early 1970s, and by Kenya and Cameroon in the late 1970s (figure 6-5). USAID's focus in the area of extension was reduced at the end of the 1960s but then expanded in Senegal and Cameroon after the Sahel drought.

USAID bilateral support for agricultural research is recent; earlier funding in agricultural research was made through regional and centrally funded accounts. Figure 6-7 indicates that, by 1979, four of the five existing missions (the Nigeria mission had closed) expanded their support in this area. The levels, however, have been relatively low. The support for agricultural research in Nigeria in the 1960s shown in figure 6-7 amounts to less than 2 percent of the total USAID program during that period. As discussed below, research has been an important part of regional and centrally funded programs for Africa.

Table 6-2. Sectoral Composition of U.S. Assistance to the MADIA Countries, 1963–84
(millions of constant 1983 U.S. dollars)

Sector and subsector	*Total*	*Percentage*	*Cameroon*	*Kenya*	*Nigeria*	*Malawi*	*Senegal*	*Tanzania*
AID projects and programs	2,407.7	100.0	213.8	550.1	943.0	152.2	174.3	374.2
Agriculture	905.2	37.6	85.2	269.3	284.2	25.5	114.7	126.3
Crop production	0.0	0.0	0.0	0.0	0.0	0.0	0.0	0.0
Storage and processing	21.9	0.9	0.0	8.1	4.0	0.0	9.9	0.0
Input supply	161.6	6.7	13.5	89.6	0.0	0.0	15.3	43.2
Credit	11.9	0.5	1.6	5.5	3.2	0.0	1.5	0.0
Research	55.9	2.3	6.2	5.8	14.3	10.1	4.7	14.9
Extension	77.4	3.2	5.5	2.6	36.0	0.0	26.4	6.9
Education and training	311.9	13.0	36.0	80.5	136.0	15.5	11.8	32.2
Planning and management	80.6	3.3	6.0	27.5	26.8	0.0	15.1	5.2
Irrigation	40.0	1.7	7.2	0.0	23.2	0.0	9.5	0.0
Marketing	3.2	0.1	0.0	0.0	0.0	0.0	0.0	3.2
Livestock	127.3	5.3	8.3	43.7	38.5	0.0	16.0	20.9
Forestry	9.6	0.4	0.0	5.3	0.0	0.0	4.3	0.0
Fisheries	3.9	0.2	0.8	0.6	2.1	0.0	0.3	0.0
Rural development	517.8	21.5	90.7	135.9	36.1	84.1	13.4	157.6
Infrastructure	308.7	12.8	78.4	48.4	28.3	69.1	6.6	77.8
Health and population	84.8	3.5	4.5	27.7	7.7	0.0	6.7	38.2
Education	6.5	0.3	6.5	0.0	0.0	0.0	0.0	0.0
Water supply	7.0	0.3	0.8	0.0	0.0	6.2	0.0	0.0
Community development	41.7	1.7	0.4	29.0	0.0	3.3	0.0	8.9
Other	985.6	41.0	37.9	144.9	623.7	42.6	46.2	90.3
Food aid	836.0		19.7	181.2	182.5	12.2	192.7	247.7
Other economic assistance	411.8		44.2	135.1	82.9	32.0	61.5	56.1
Total[a]	3,586.5		277.7	835.7	1,208.4	190.9	428.6	645.3

a. Excludes military assistance.
Source: See figure 6-1.

Figure 6-5. USAID *Assistance to Agricultural Education in the* MADIA *Countries in Real Terms, 1963–84*

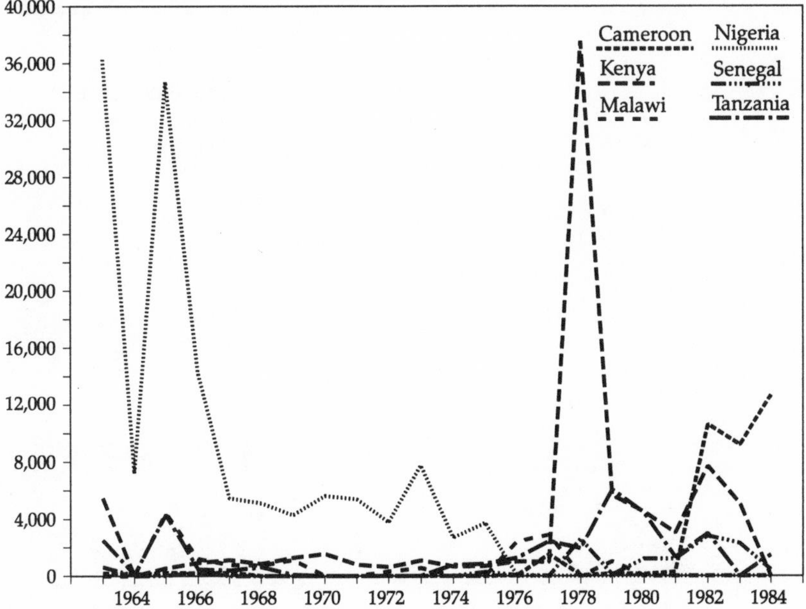

Source: See figure 6-1.

Significant programs for developing livestock were undertaken in Nigeria and Kenya in the 1960s (figure 6-8). The Kenya livestock program was continued and expanded in the 1970s, and new programs were introduced in Senegal and Tanzania. Input supply (which includes both input support and commodity import programs) did not receive much attention from USAID until the early 1970s, when Kenya and Tanzania received large amounts in this subcategory. In Tanzania this was mainly for seed multiplication activities, whereas in Kenya the funds were for fertilizer import programs (figure 6-9).

Investments in rural infrastructure (figure 6-10) represent an important part of USAID's assistance programs in four of the six countries (Senegal and Nigeria being the exceptions). Development loans and grants for highways, rural roads, and a railroad in Cameroon were important components of many of USAID's country programs in the 1960s and early 1970s. Since then very little has been done in this area—largely because the Africa Bureau has been avoiding this kind of aid following the shift in emphasis to poverty-oriented programs.

In the 1980s, nonproject assistance tied to policy reform issues became an important part of the USAID program in Kenya, Malawi,

Figure 6-6. USAID *Assistance to Agricultural Extension in the* MADIA *Countries in Real Terms, 1963–84*

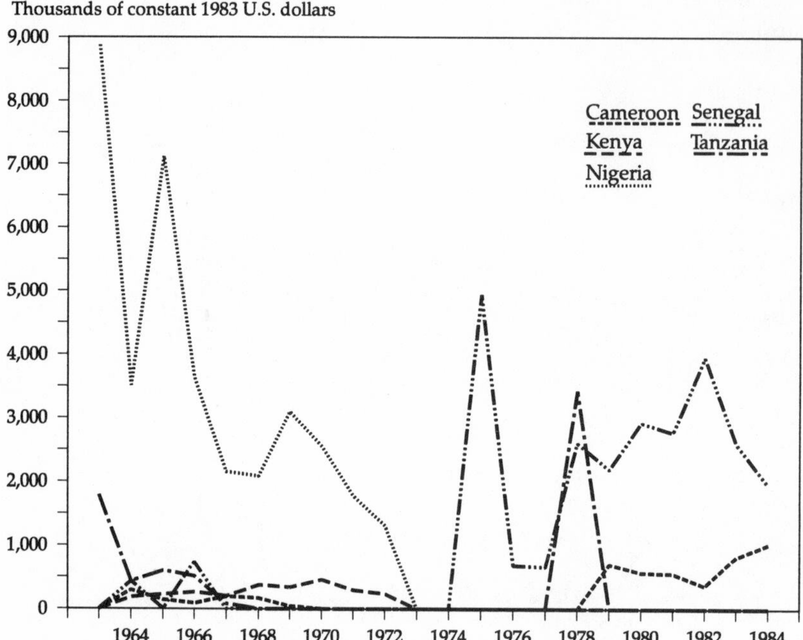

Note: U.S. AID has not given any assistance to Malawi in this category.
Source: See figure 6-1.

and Senegal. Such assistance most often took the form of commodity import programs.

Impact of USAID's Project and Nonproject Assistance

This section is based on the conviction that efforts to increase the effectiveness of USAID's future activities will require a better understanding of the kinds of activities that merit priority, as well as improved implementation of the activities that USAID decides to support. In brief, it needs to reach an understanding of what should be done and of what can be done, given the severe financial and personnel constraints faced by local governments and the limited extent to which USAID assistance can overcome those constraints.

To provide a framework within which USAID's activities can be placed and judged, it is necessary to make a few points about the process of development. One of the most significant advances in economic understanding of the development process during the past

Figure 6-7. USAID *Assistance to Agricultural Research in the* MADIA *Countries in Real Terms, 1963–84*

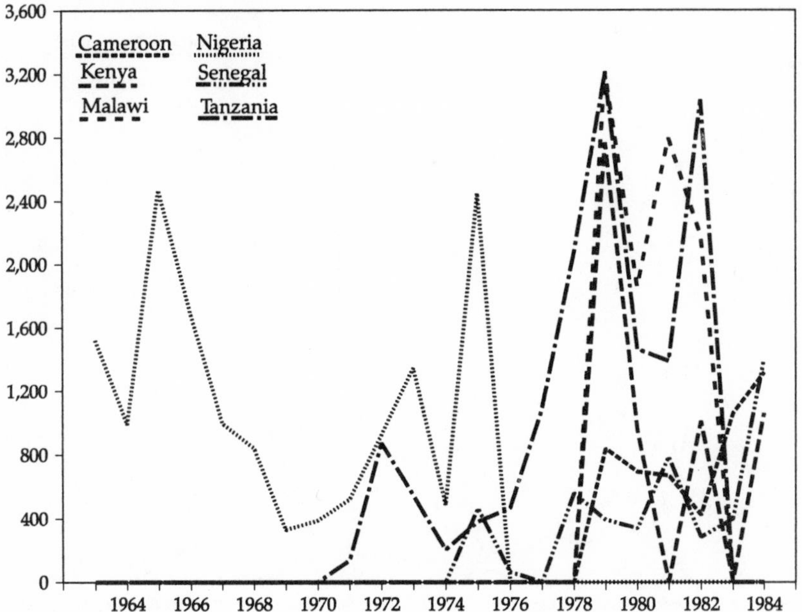

Source: See figure 6-1.

thirty-five years has been the recognition that increases in conventional inputs of labor, land, and capital frequently account for less than half of the increases in national output.[12] In virtually all countries that have achieved impressive progress in agricultural development, technological change leading to increases in total factor productivity—that is, in output per unit of total inputs—have been a principal source of the growth of agricultural production.[13]

These observations yield a set of general propositions that can be used to assess United States aid activities. Clearly, USAID's effectiveness in furthering agricultural and rural development depends not only on how well its activities have achieved their specific goals, but also on whether the activities it chose to support constitute critical elements of a well-conceived strategy for agricultural development.

As a point of departure for identifying those crucial elements of the development process, development has been conceptualized in this chapter as a "generalized process of capital accumulation" in which capital is defined broadly to include not only physical capital (plant and equipment, natural resources), but also human capital (in the

Figure 6-8. USAID *Assistance to Livestock in the* MADIA *Countries in Real Terms, 1963–84*

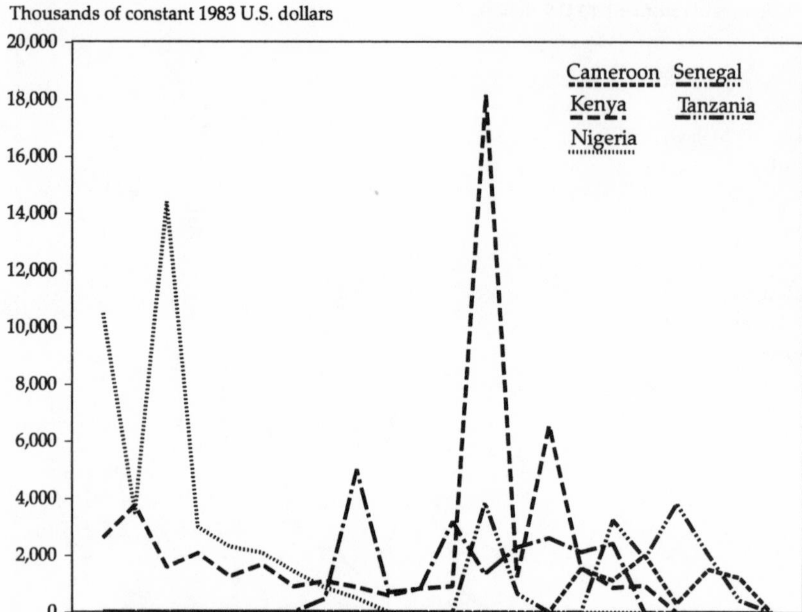

Note: U.S. AID has not given assistance to Malawi in this sector.
Source: See figure 6-1.

form of skills and professional competence) and social capital (in the form of economically useful knowledge, organizations, and organizational competence). This view of development emphasizes the role of efficient social and economic mechanisms for maintaining and increasing large per capita stocks of capital, including policies and institutions that permit and encourage efficient use of that capital. Thus H. G. Johnson characterizes the process of economic growth as

> a generalized process of capital accumulation, that is, of investment in the acquisition of larger stocks of the various forms of capital; and the condition of being "developed" consists of having accumulated, and having established efficient social and economic mechanisms for maintaining and increasing large stocks of capital per head in the various forms.[14]

In order to achieve this kind of growth, a reasonable balance must be achieved among activities that foster growth in these various kinds of capital, and at the same time the various mechanisms that permit efficient use of those forms of capital must be strengthened. USAID's

Figure 6-9. USAID *Assistance to Input Supply in the* MADIA *Countries in Real Terms, 1963–84*

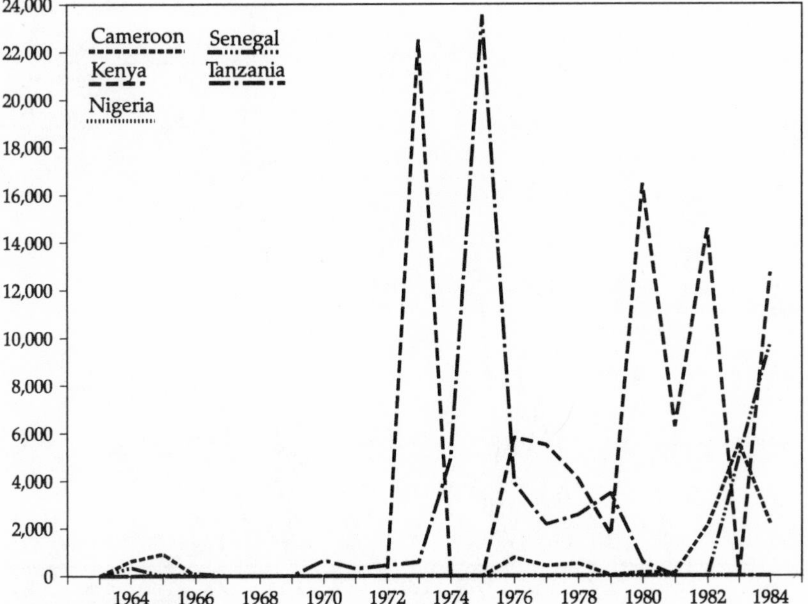

Note: USAID has not given assistance to Malawi in this sector.
Source: See figure 6-1.

emphasis on "policy dialogue" and the current concern of donors and African governments alike with structural reform are of great importance as preconditions for achieving development based on a balanced and generalized process of capital accumulation.

This view of development does not ignore the importance of welfare and equity as criteria for judging development. Rather, it incorporates the lessons learned from the "basic needs" strategy popularized in the mid-1970s. Thus it emphasizes that public investments in education, health, and nutrition can contribute in important ways to increased human welfare and to economic growth.[15] It is, however, the growth in the economic base that makes it possible to finance those investments. Moreover, it is the kind of development strategy—including the pattern of agricultural development—that largely determines the extent to which a country's rural and urban populations will participate in the increases in productivity and income that will enable them to more adequately satisfy their basic needs for food and other essential goods and services. This view of the development process is now widely held among development specialists.[16]

Figure 6-10. USAID *Assistance to Rural Infrastructure in the* MADIA *Countries in Real Terms, 1963–84*

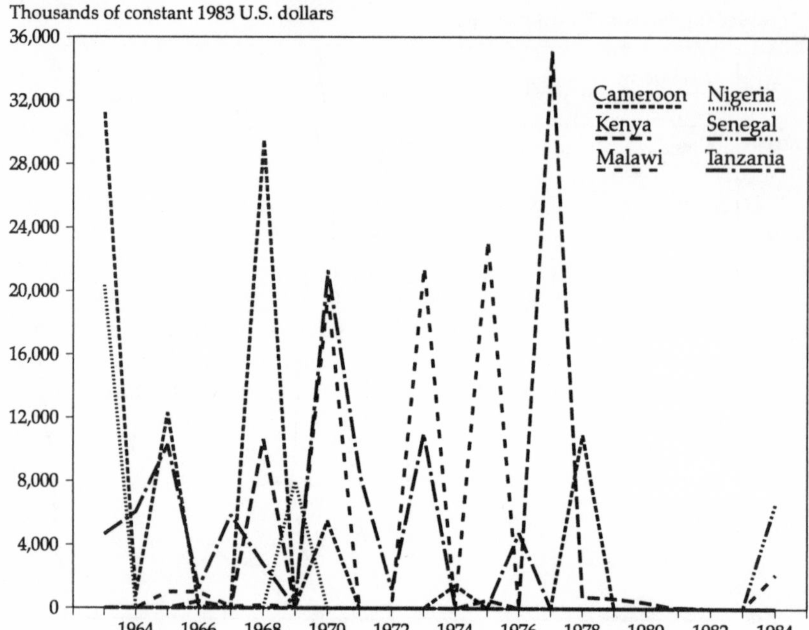

Source: See figure 6-1.

This cumulative advance in understanding provides a basis for drawing some important conclusions about the critical elements that need to be considered in the pursuit of a coherent development strategy.[17] With respect to the role and limits of government action, a wealth of experience in many countries has demonstrated the efficiency of decentralized decisionmaking by independent farm units. If markets and prices are used to allocate most kinds of goods and services, the outcome is by and large more efficient than that achieved by hierarchical social processes. The problems that such processes can cause are especially serious in Sub-Saharan Africa, where the scarcity of the critical resources of administrative capacity, analytical skills, and government revenues makes the imbalances already present that much worse. This underscores the need to make the most efficient use of those scarce resources, to seek institutional arrangements that minimize government involvement, and to enlarge the stocks of vital human resources. But, clearly, certain strategic public goods and services can play a catalytic role. Public support for agricultural research, education, and basic health services, including family planning, is crucial. Because they are public goods, private investment in such activities would be far below the level that is socially desirable. Public support for strategic investments in infrastructure is also essential, and the decisive role of government in macroeconomic management is inescapable.

Much has been learned about the importance of complementarities and efficient timing and sequencing for many investments in physical, human, and social capital to accelerate the expansion of agricultural output. People are also more aware of the importance of the price of capital, foreign exchange, and farm products and inputs that reflect their scarcity value. Their prices influence not only the decisions of farmers and firms but also the allocative decisions of agricultural administrators and scientists and the rate and bias of technological change.[18] Given the multiple growth paths developing countries face, the direction of both technical change and institutional change will be influenced by distortions in the economy, such as those that favor a subsector of large and capital-intensive farms.

On the basis of the cumulative progress that has been made in advancing understanding—which is beginning to include a better understanding of the basic characteristics of African farming systems—it seems possible to define some general priorities that would now be widely accepted among development specialists. The eight propositions listed below should not be taken as a list of what USAID should do. USAID's activities as one of many donors will have to be further restricted by a recognition of the limits on its resources and of its comparative advantage.

- Support the efforts by host governments to define carefully their development priorities and to coordinate the activities of USAID and other donors so that they fit national priorities and do not exceed a country's financial and administrative capacity for effective implementation.

- Invest in the formation of human capital by supporting rural schooling and literacy programs and building the institutions of higher learning needed to strengthen agricultural research systems, support policy research and analysis, and improve the management of agricultural and rural development.

- Assist in the development of effective national agricultural research systems oriented toward the needs of smallholders. Farming systems research and other techniques for improving the two-way flow of information between farmers and research workers represent important supplements to formal research, but they clearly are not substitutes for on-station and commodity-oriented research.

- Strengthen the capacity for policy analysis and policy research and assist in establishing information systems that provide the most essential data needed to improve the quality of governmental decisionmaking.
- Improve the quality of policy dialogue to foster policies favorable to effective and sustained agricultural and rural development; constructive dialogue can only emerge if USAID and host country participants engage in better policy research and analysis. Such dialogue is obviously important for macroeconomic policies and also appears to be a source of vital encouragement for initiatives in rural nonfarm activities as well as in agriculture.
- Promote a more accurate understanding of the respective strengths and weaknesses of public and private activities, so that their roles are defined with a view toward maximizing the relative advantage of each.
- Make and facilitate investments designed to extend and improve a country's rural infrastructure of roads, communications, electric power, and water supplies for farm and household use and for rural manufacturing and service firms.
- Provide encouragement and support for affordable rural health and family planning programs with an emphasis on the interrelated objectives of improving child health and survival prospects and reducing fertility.

Clearly, USAID's priorities should take into account the activities of other donors as well as the programs of the host government. These priorities should be established within and among categories. The main concern in all instances should be to maintain a sensible balance between objectives and resources so that projects and programs are sustainable. In some instances, that should probably include highly selective commitments by USAID to provide assistance over a number of years for meeting recurrent costs in local currency and similarly selective allocations of foreign exchange. In the long run, however, external resources cannot substitute for local resources—which once again underscores the importance of a generalized and balanced process of accumulating physical, human, and social capital.

Successes and Setbacks

The evidence from the six country studies indicates USAID's activities in support of agricultural and rural development have met with mixed success. In a number of cases, successful implementation, combined with intermediate indicators of impact, suggest that these activities have contributed to agricultural and rural development, as broadly defined. In other instances, USAID's efforts have been less successful, for a variety of reasons.

In agricultural education and training and in the development of infrastructure, all six countries have scored some significant successes. Some progress has also been made in agricultural research, although until recently USAID had not contributed much to this area; as a result, and because of the long gestation period that is characteristic of research, it would be premature to draw any conclusions about the contribution of these activities. USAID's involvement in nonproject assistance to promote policy reform—such as commodity import programs—is also relatively recent and therefore difficult to evaluate fully. In contrast, many of USAID's activities in other areas (such as extension-based production projects, integrated rural development, seed multiplication, and livestock) did not turn out as well. The degree of success and the reasons for it vary from country to country and project to project, as explained below.

Agricultural education and training. Between 1951 and 1966 USAID and its predecessor agencies initiated sixty-seven institution-building contracts with thirty-five United States land-grant institutions in a total of thirty-nine countries.[19] The clearest examples of USAID's success in this area are from Nigeria, where institution building was undertaken at three Nigerian universities shortly after independence. A faculty of agriculture was established in each of the new universities with support from a United States land-grant university: at the University of Nigeria in eastern Nigeria, under a contract with Michigan State University (MSU); the Ahmadu Bello University (ABU) in northern Nigeria with support from Kansas State University (KSU); and the University of Ife in western Nigeria under a contract with the University of Wisconsin. KSU also entered into a contract with USAID for the establishment of a faculty of veterinary medicine at ABU.[20]

The most successful of these ventures was at ABU, which USAID began supporting in 1962. A total of $21.2 million was obligated for six separate projects connected with ABU's Faculty of Agriculture, Faculty of Veterinary Medicine, the Institute for Agricultural Research (IAR) adjacent to the university, the Extension and Research Liaison Service, and agricultural schools at Kabba, Samaru, Mando Road, and Vom.[21]

USAID's seventeen-year involvement with ABU demonstrates the importance of sustained support over a long period of time. Even then some argued that the relationship was terminated prematurely and too abruptly. USAID's mode of operation in this early period made it possible for qualified and dedicated specialists to play a central role in planning and implementing activities and for the agency to provide more continuing and flexible support than has generally been the case since then. These early institution-building efforts were successful, too, because they occurred at a time when Nigeria's government and people were convinced of the value of education. Thus the timing of these particular investments was appropriate not only in that they were part of a well-conceived strategy for agricultural development, but also that they were backed by a host government that was genuinely committed to these efforts.

How those endeavors affected agricultural development is difficult to judge. There is no doubt that agricultural and rural development cannot proceed without an indigenous capacity to train agricultural scientists and administrators. It seems equally clear that the USAID-funded assistance by the United States land-grant universities enabled Nigerian institutions to develop the capacity needed to provide that training. The USAID-KSU project is given much credit by Nigerians and other informed observers for coordinating teaching, research, and extension at ABU. The Nigerians, who now fill virtually all faculty and research positions in both ABU and IAR, have been able to mold the institution to fit Nigeria's needs and resources.

A number of Nigerians trained in the institution-building programs at those universities have helped establish other Nigerian universities in recent years. Especially noteworthy is the work of ABU's Faculty of Agriculture and of Veterinary Medicine in this regard in other states of northern Nigeria.

In contrast, the established universities received less than adequate support from the government during the oil boom. In that heady climate, the emphasis was on creating new colleges and universities and an excess of agricultural research institutes, it seems. With the sharp decline in foreign exchange receipts and government revenue in recent years, these institutions are now being crippled by severe funding constraints.[22]

Efforts to establish an agricultural university at Dschang in Cameroon are still in the early stages, but the agricultural colleges supported in Kenya, Tanzania, and Malawi have all met with some success, even though the assistance they have received has been quite sporadic. Policy shifts are largely to blame for this situation. When Tanzania passed its New Directions legislation, for example, the USAID mission there rejected a government request for support for advanced training in agriculture, noting that Washington preferred projects that "benefit the poor directly in the shortest amount of time possible."[23]

In Kenya, USAID's support for agricultural education has concentrated on the Egerton College of Agriculture. Established initially to provide agricultural training for European farmers, the college had earned a reputation as a high-quality educational institution, attracting students from other African countries, as well as from donor programs. USAID, assisted by ten other donors, engaged in a long-term program of expanding and strengthening the institution in the 1960s. The college's leadership, originally expatriate but Africanized by 1966, played a crucial role in this expansion and in coordinating donor assistance.

Similarly, Tanzania received USAID support for the development of the Morogoro College, launched in 1961 with additional assistance from the Rockefeller Foundation. In 1962 USAID entered into a contract with West Virginia University to assist in establishing a college that would be capable of meeting the country's need for diploma-level agriculturists. Over time, Denmark and other donors helped offset the effects of USAID's fluctuating support.

Participant training for Morogoro, however, proceeded slowly, primarily because Tanzania had fewer secondary educational facilities before independence than Kenya. In addition, Tanzanian policy explicitly emphasized primary education and limiting the number of secondary schools. The relative shortage of qualified candidates for overseas training has limited the pool of undergraduate applicants, so that more training needs to be financed at that level before any postgraduate programs can be launched, thus "lengthening the time needed to build a cadre of people who can serve as trainers to the next generation of Tanzanians."[24] The government recently reorganized Morogoro College and renamed it Sokoine Agricultural University, thereby indicating that it recognizes the need to educate agricultural scientists and other specialists and administrators.

USAID has also supported agricultural education through long-term training. Since the early 1960s it has funded university training through programs such as the African Graduate Fellowship Program (AFGRAD), the African Scholarship Program for American Universities (ASPAU), and the InterAfrican Fellowship Program (INTERAF). Between 1956 and 1984 an estimated 1,681 Tanzanians completed degree and nondegree training, and 1,839 participants from Kenya received training in the United States. In Cameroon, 575 participants were trained in the United States between 1961 and 1982. Roughly 60 percent of all participants received their training in fields related to agriculture—agronomy, animal sciences, biology, entomology, general agriculture, livestock production, plant breeding, range management, veterinary medicine, and agricultural economics.[25]

Follow-up studies on trainees from AFGRAD and other programs indicate a high degree of success, with 87 percent of the alumni from these programs living and working in Africa. Educational and research institutions have employed about half of these graduates. A high percentage of those trained for positions at Egerton and other

USAID-supported institutions have in fact taken up those positions, and about a fourth have worked in governmental and parastatal organizations. Most important, the survey concludes that "over half of the older alumni now have major responsibility for policy formulation and decisionmaking in their respective places of employment."[26]

Through the International Agricultural Research Centers (IARCs) of the CGIAR system, USAID contributes to a wide range of agriculture-related educational programs. IITA alone provided training for 2,860 participants from forty-two African countries between 1970 and 1984.

Investments in human capital tend to complement other critical elements of strategies for agricultural and rural development. They are more durable than investments in many other projects more vulnerable to changes in government policies or in circumstances affecting project implementation, such as changes in international prices. This is an area in which USAID appears to have a comparative advantage. It is able to rely on a large number of United States institutions of higher learning that rank with the best in the world and that are especially strong in the agricultural sciences.

There are, of course, questions about the relevance of training in the United States for future work in African countries. Indeed, that is one of the reasons why helping to establish and strengthen African institutions of higher education is so important. Their existence should make it possible to limit future participant training in the United States to advanced or specialized training not yet available in Sub-Saharan Africa. At the same time, it seems important for dissertation research to be carried out in Africa so that the problems addressed and the laboratories and other resources available will be relevant to scientists' future research there.

Although agricultural development can make much better progress when the country has an indigenous capacity to train agricultural scientists, the training capacity alone is not enough. As noted earlier, the teaching role of universities is essentially an intermediate product. To fulfill their potential, these institutions must also have the capacity to contribute, directly and indirectly, to the development and testing of the technical innovations that spark agricultural development.

Rural infrastructure. USAID's support for rural infrastructural development in Africa has been primarily in transportation. During the 1960s USAID participated in a multidonor project for major extensions of the TransCameroon railway, as well as Farm to Market Roads and Highway Development projects in that country. In Tanzania USAID also funded large parts of the TANZAM highway connecting Zambia with the port of Dar es Salaam. In Malawi, USAID's support for road construction accounted for 47 percent of all USAID projects and program assistance between 1963 and 1984.

It can reasonably be asserted that USAID's investments in improving transportation networks have had a significant long-term impact in improving market access, reducing costs, and facilitating the integration of rural economies. These activities from the 1960s appear to have been implemented with relatively few difficulties, whereas more recent infrastructural projects, such as the construction related to the agricultural university in Cameroon, have been more problematic, especially because of the increasingly complex requirements in the contract bidding and awarding procedures within USAID. Provided that maintenance has been supplied—and in many of these cases it has—these investments appear to have had a lasting impact, in part because they are unaffected by changes in governments, policies, or international prices, and also because they are relatively straightforward to implement, in that they do not require extensive and prolonged supervision and management. Furthermore, they are investments in Africa's physical capital and a prerequisite to the growth of market-oriented agricultural economies.

There is no reason to believe, however, that the United States has a comparative advantage any longer in providing assistance for rural infrastructural projects. However, investments in road construction are likely to be reasonably effective uses of USAID funding on occasions when it becomes politically attractive to act quickly to provide increased assistance for a country, as appears to have been the case with Tanzania at the time that the United States provided substantial assistance for the TANZAM road project.

Agricultural research. USAID has supported agricultural research in Africa only to a small extent. Its share of assistance has amounted to 2.3 percent in the six MADIA countries—and many of its activities have been short-term, fragmented efforts that could not be expected to make a significant contribution to the necessarily long-term task of building a national capability for research.

In the 1960s USAID provided technical assistance to help establish a comprehensive breeding improvement program at Kitale, Kenya. However, the support for maize research was not continuous and there were a number of shifts in priorities, with the result that aid effectiveness was lower than in other parts of Africa. Particularly unfortunate was USAID's failure to complete the job that was started at Kitale in building the capacity for a strong and sustained national maize-breeding program. A shift in emphasis from the high-altitude to the medium-altitude regions appears to have been justified by the success achieved; the spread of new hybrids of maize adapted to the medium-altitude areas of the Central Province matched the earlier rapid spread of hybrids suited to the high altitudes of western Kenya. However, the emphasis on breeding for protein content and quality appear to have diverted scarce resources away from more important objectives. A shift in the emphasis of USAID-supported maize research to semiarid areas of eastern Kenya also appears to have been questionable.[27]

Similar problems have limited the effect of USAID's efforts on agricultural research. By the late 1960s, the need to strengthen Tanzania's agricultural research system had been identified as a priority for USAID assistance. The research project, finally initiated in 1973, suffered from several implementational problems, including unsatisfactory communication between researchers and farmers, the lack of qualified trainees for the project, and various systemic problems that were making it more and more difficult to undertake development work in Tanzania.[28] In 1982, an $8.3 million Farming Systems Research Project was initiated, and the government agreed to reorganize research activities under a Tanzanian Agricultural Research Organization. In view of the economic situation in the country at the time and the problems of recurrent financing faced by the government, USAID had to eventually channel local currency generated by its food aid program to the maintenance and operation of the research station.

Two factors in particular appear to account for USAID's relative neglect of agricultural research: the persistent tendency toward technological optimism that has given rise to an extension bias in Africa and other regions and the emphasis in the New Directions legislation on directly satisfying the basic needs of the poor, which diverted attention from longer-term institution-building efforts. The contribution of research was regarded as too slow, and there was a stubborn tendency to assume that technical solutions were available and could be readily transferred.

The reasons for the lack of success in research programs are also numerous. The difficult and diverse physical environment for agriculture is one obvious factor. A number of the assumptions behind American and Asian models of food crop research were misleading. The relative abundance of land in Sub-Saharan Africa led to the widespread view that a direct shift from hand-hoes to tractors would greatly increase agricultural productivity and output; this ignored the constraints imposed by cash income on purchasing power and by other factors that usually make it uneconomical to shift directly to tractor-based technologies.[29] Impressed by the results of the green revolution in Asia, many development planners began to focus on improved seed-fertilizer combinations and other yield-increasing innovations, overlooking the fact that such innovations are not attractive to farmers when land still has little scarcity value. More generally, the complex farming systems evolved by African farmers were poorly understood. As a result, many of the innovations recommended by research scientists and extension staff were neither feasible nor profitable, given the labor and cash income constraints that farmers faced.

The fact that Malawi is the only country in the MADIA sample in which agricultural research has been a prominent component of total agricultural assistance for the period 1963–84 reflects the fact that USAID channeled relatively little assistance to this area until the late 1970s. In Malawi, a contract for a $9 million agricultural research project with the University of Florida in 1979 exceeded the sums allocated for extension as well as for education and training. This was a basic research project with a farming systems component and it was intended to strengthen the capability of the Ministry of Agriculture's Department of Agricultural Research to develop technical innovations for Malawi's smallholders.

The process of designing a follow-on agricultural research project was a good example of a joint effort by the government and two donors (USAID and the World Bank) to build a more effective research and extension system. In 1986 USAID approved $14 million for a Malawi Agricultural Research and Extension Project to round out a program that also comprised two World Bank–IDA projects totaling $35.7 million, and a $33.1 million contribution by the Malawian government. The purpose of the USAID project is to improve Malawi's institutional capacity to increase the productivity of traditional crops and to identify the most viable crops for diversifying smallholder production. The Ministry of Agriculture was directly involved in project design and insisted that the new projects incorporate lessons learned from the previous project.[30]

The USAID-funded National Cereals Research and Extension Project in Cameroon is of considerable interest as a possible model for other parts of Sub-Saharan Africa. It was designed mainly to implement research programs for maize, sorghum, millet, and rice and to create a testing liaison unit to facilitate communication and feedback among researchers, extensionists, and farmers. A midterm evaluation in 1983 was favorable.

In recognition of the long time it takes to develop an effective national agricultural research system, USAID approved the ten-year Phase II project in 1984. This $39 million project provides for three additional Technical Liaison Units. In addition, the Cameroon government is currently negotiating a $46 million project with the World Bank for agricultural research that will cover areas not included in the cereals research project, such as research on export crops.[31]

In spite of the formidable difficulties, the current situation is rather encouraging and indicates that USAID has learned much from experience. In recent years, USAID/Washington has shown increased interest in supporting agricultural research in Sub-Saharan Africa. This interest is reflected in the projects in Malawi and Cameroon, where careful attention to design and to the lessons of earlier experiences has provided a strong foundation for the implementation of current projects, which have longer-term, realistic goals and show considerable promise as a result.

It is still too early to evaluate these projects, although it can be said that USAID's Africa Bureau has produced a new strategy paper for agricultural research that is in many ways exemplary.[32] It incorporates lessons from earlier failures, is well attuned to the needs and capacities of various nations, and provides a coherent plan for implementation.

Extension-based production activities. Over the past twenty-five years, USAID has allocated a substantial portion of its funds in Africa for activities intended to affect agricultural production directly. These projects have often been based on technology transfers and have generally relied on extension workers to transmit information to farmers about specific farming methods or the use of inputs expected to increase productivity and thus give farmers higher incomes. During the mid- to late 1970s, more attention was placed on such activities since the New Directions legislation had called for greater assistance for the rural poor. It was hoped that these kinds of activities would offer a solution to the food shortages of semiarid Africa, which had become dire during the Sahel drought.

This category includes crop-specific production projects, components of integrated rural development projects, livestock projects (discussed separately below), irrigation projects, and rural training activities. Nearly all these efforts in the six countries studied failed to achieve their objectives and their outcomes reflect a consistent pattern of exaggerated assumptions about the benefits and appropriateness of the technological solution. Except in a few cases—notably cotton research in a number of countries and the development of hybrid maize in Kenya, Zimbabwe, and Zambia—extension programs have had relatively little to offer that was relevant and attractive to smallholders in most parts of Africa, given the constraints they face. Moreover, agricultural extension programs have had an inadequate research base.

Among the notable extension projects were two in Senegal, which set out to increase millet yields 50 percent by promoting fertilizer use, early planting, and other agronomic techniques. Another was Cameroon's Small Farm Family Training Centers project, which was designed in the belief that a year of training in the use of agronomic techniques and animal traction would permit farmers to return to their villages and increase their income by 50 percent. In Nigeria, the Maize and Rice Production Project epitomized technological optimism—its staff set out to devise improved packages and to persuade farmers to adopt them, with almost no specific information about what was available or what might be appropriate. Still another project, this one in Tanzania, was to use the Ministry of Agriculture Training institutes and establish rural training centers for farmers on the assumption that if a sample of farmers was offered short courses, the farmers would not only apply the knowledge directly and increase their production and incomes, but would also have an important demonstration effect for their neighbors, thus helping to reduce the need for large extension staffs.

Several conclusions can be drawn from the outcomes of these activities. First, it is virtually impossible to determine the appropriateness of technologies for the African context; the direct transfer of technologies to Africa is unlikely to succeed in part because agricultural research in much of the world is focused on increasing yields (because land is the scarce factor of production), whereas in Africa labor, not land, is still the scarce factor of production. As a result, farmers will be unwilling to adopt technologies that require additional labor in order to raise production per unit of land area.

Second, these kinds of activities, which are prone to exaggerated assumptions and technological optimism, persist because of one of USAID's weaknesses—that is, it is unable to enforce realism and objectivity in the analyses of the project papers and evaluations that determine whether such activities are approved or continued.

Livestock. Livestock accounted for 5.3 percent of USAID's project and program assistance for agriculture, but it is now recognized to be the agency's least successful investment. Other donors have had much the same experience. Recently, USAID management suspended its contributions to pastoral livestock.

Most of the projects USAID had funded in this area were concerned with range management. The projects were carried out in all the MADIA countries except Malawi, but none appear to have made any progress toward their range management, production, or human welfare objectives. Although their training components have contributed to the formation of human capital, they have contributed little to institution building. It seems curious that lessons learned in earlier projects in Nigeria and Ethiopia were not incorporated into the programs in Kenya and Senegal, since the earlier experience was known to USAID design officers.

Apparently one of the main reasons they did not follow up on this information was that the African governments, USAID, and pastoralists all had different objectives. Governments tend to view pastoral nomads as a nuisance and would generally prefer that they settle and take up cultivation. Their weak commitment to livestock projects has been manifested in a lack of support for recurrent costs, diversion of equipment, and strained relations between host country officials and USAID contractors.

USAID's livestock planners have viewed pastoralists as backward and inefficient. With the exception of projects in Niger and Senegal, USAID-funded livestock projects have all been based on the direct application of a range management model derived from successful American experiences in regulating the use of the open range by competitive, commercially oriented livestock producers. This range management model was given theoretical backing by the untested belief that African pastoralists caused serious degradation through overgrazing because their herding practices exemplified the tragedy of the commons.

This uncritical acceptance of the American range management model in the design of pastoral projects led planners to devote almost no attention to collecting site-specific data on current livestock and range management practices, climate cycles, and stocking levels, and their effect on range condition. It was simply assumed that livestock were deteriorating everywhere and that it would be possible to increase offtake by improving herder practices, altering herd composition, and establishing and enforcing an appropriate carrying capacity for the range.

Input supply. Input supply ranks next to agricultural education and training in USAID expenditures on agriculture, accounting for 6.9 percent of project and program outlays in the six countries. The largest expenditures in this category have been for commodity import programs for fertilizer, which are better discussed in conjunction with nonproject aid, policy reform, and policy dialogue. Other than commodity import programs for fertilizer, the principal expenditures have been for seed multiplication projects in Tanzania and Cameroon.

There is an attractive logic to the proposition that a seed multiplication project is an essential ingredient of a crop improvement program. In the case of hybrid maize, it is true that seed multiplication and distribution are necessary conditions for success because of the rapid decline in yield if hybrid seed is not replaced each year. (The rapid diffusion of hybrids among Kenya's smallholders was dependent on the competent performance of a private company that had previously specialized in producing grass seed for European farmers in the highlands.)

The North Cameroon Seed Multiplication Project illustrates many of the problems that make it exceedingly difficult to design and implement a seed multiplication project that will have a favorable cost-benefit ratio. Phase I of the project began in 1975, with a $1.5 million grant to develop a system for producing improved seed for peanuts, maize, sorghum, and millet and distributing the seed to farmers. The project goals could not be achieved, however, because its resources became overextended. A much larger Phase II project, begun in 1982, also suffered from slow implementation, lack of coordination among government agencies, and poor management. Although it did succeed in distributing substantial quantities of seed to farmers, the seed was sold at subsidized prices that were 50 to 100 percent below local market prices. Apart from the problem of economic viability, a more fundamental constraint has been the unrealistic assumption (underlying both phases) that research would be able to develop improved varieties of the four crops promptly.

The seed multiplication project in Tanzania also appears to have been out of sequence because of the limited availability of improved crop varieties. USAID assistance began in 1970 and continued until 1982. Although the government strongly supported the project in principle, its financial support declined as economic difficulties mounted. A review in 1982 declared that the project "was in complete disarray."[33] With the benefit of hindsight, it now appears that the project was probably premature, given the indications that it would not be sustainable once USAID assistance was withdrawn.

Seed multiplication and distribution is a highly specialized activity, and therefore any conclusions drawn here must be considered tentative. However, it does seem that most seed specialists consider seed multiplication programs to be an essential component of agricultural development strategies, without regard for the economic returns of that activity, compared with other activities that might merit a higher priority. Thus it appears that the USAID outlays for seed multiplication in Tanzania and Cameroon were out of proportion to other more fundamental elements of their agricultural development strategies. In particular, those outlays appear to have been large relative to the modest level of investment in agricultural research. This is also another example of the technological optimism mentioned earlier. A high social rate of return cannot be obtained unless the varieties to be multiplied have a substantially higher yield than local varieties, and thus far there has been no convincing evidence that such varieties are available in these countries—although cotton and maize may be exceptions, and a new sorghum variety in northern Cameroon seems promising. In addition, both the Cameroon and Tanzania projects were designed to use inappropriately capital-intensive technologies and both suffered from serious management problems.

Planning, Management, and Statistics

This rather mixed category received 3.0 percent of total USAID project and program outlays, making it fifth in outlays for agriculture and only a little less important than extension. All of the six countries except Malawi had significant projects in this category, but there were large differences in the nature and timing of the projects.

Tanzania, for example, received considerable support for agricultural analysis and planning activities in the second half of the 1960s and again in the early 1980s.[34] During the earlier period, the Agricultural Production Surveys Project led to the commissioning of studies on agricultural marketing, seed multiplication and distribution, livestock and range management, land consolidation, smallholder tea development, and agricultural education and credit. During the early 1980s, USAID's Tanzania Mission again initiated some valuable analysis and planning activities. A special policy unit known as the Office for Policy Analysis was established. But the idea that the government's policies were partly to blame for the country's agricultural problems was controversial, and because of the sensitive nature of these issues, the mission's approach was to undertake analyses, commission studies by consultants, and support the efforts of Tanzanian scholars and organizations.

Another means of strengthening agricultural management and planning capacity was tried out in the Kenya Rural Planning Project, implemented by the Harvard Institute for International Development (HIID). In this case the technical assistance team, acting as advisers, and the introduction of microcomputers appear to have helped the Ministry of Agriculture carry out its budget management responsibilities more efficiently.

In Cameroon, one task of the Agricultural Management and Planning Project, initiated in 1978, was to help the Agriculture and Planning ministries conduct an agricultural census for the entire country. The census was carried out in 1984 and received excellent support from national, regional, and local governments. The project was extended to June 1987. Some useful studies have been carried out, and with the establishment of the Département des Etudes et Projets in the Ministry, good progress has been made in institutionalizing a capacity for economic analysis and for the collection, processing, and analysis of statistical data.[35]

The Agricultural Research and Planning Project initiated in Senegal in 1981 has followed a different path. Its objectives are to develop Senegalese macroeconomic research capacity in the area of food and agricultural policy and to build up a production systems research capacity at the microeconomic level. Financed by the World Bank and France in addition to USAID, the project has a strong participant training component that has included graduate training at United States universities and field research on policy-related matters carried out in Senegal with young but able United States collaborators. The resulting studies have made a valuable contribution to the policy dialogue over agricultural issues in Senegal.[36]

Although USAID has had mixed success in this area, probably the most glaring deficiency in the African countries is the lack of reasonably accurate statistics on crop areas, yields, and production. Local governments and donors alike are bedeviled by the lack of factual information about the agricultural economies of Sub-Saharan Africa. The value of these kinds of projects is undeniable, but difficult to measure. Strengthening the ability of African governments to plan and monitor their own agricultural development is essential, and it can be a costly error to base agricultural planning on inaccurate data or poor analysis.

Integrated Rural Development and Area Development Projects

USAID-funded projects of this nature have been relatively unimportant in the MADIA countries, except in Senegal and Tanzania. They have, however, played a large role in the assistance programs of the World Bank and several other donors. The $24 million Casamance Regional Development Project in Senegal and $15 million Arusha Regional Planning and Village Development Project in Tanzania were the two main projects of this nature reviewed in the separate country studies. The Tanzania project had some special design features that gave rise to considerable friction between the USAID mission and the contractor. Moreover, the general economic decline in Tanzania makes it especially difficult to assess the project's potential contribution to regional development.

In the case of the Casamance project in Senegal, the learning process within the mission, together with evaluations and audits, indicates that the project was based on overly optimistic assumptions, that it ignored existing services, and that it failed to take into account the structural weaknesses and inappropriate functions of the parastatal organizations it sought to strengthen. There is much to be said for an integrated perspective on agricultural and rural development, but the Casamance project seems to provide additional evidence that the effort to administratively integrate a variety of rural development activities in a single project exceeds the administrative capacity of the host country. It also seems clear that USAID does not have the institutional capacity to implement projects of that nature.

Nonproject Assistance, Policy Reform, and Policy Dialogue

In many countries of Sub-Saharan Africa, the success of projects seeking to increase productivity by investments in physical, human, or social capital appears to depend in large part on structural reforms to improve the policy environment. The conceptual framework outlined above includes the important notions of "induced innovation" and "induced institutional change." Arbitrary and discretionary intervention—especially the kind that encourages governments to underprice capital and foreign exchange and to ration the scarce resources of a favored subsector of atypically large and capital-intensive farm units—tend to induce a dualistic pattern of agricultural development. Furthermore, price distortions and poor macroeconomic management, parastatal controls of marketing systems, and overstaffed government agencies encourage the inefficient use of some of Africa's scarcest resources and inhibit private initiative.

Policy dialogue and structural reform programs became the focal point of USAID's programs in a number of African countries in the 1980s—including four of the six examined here—as attention shifted away from the basic human needs mandate of the 1970s. Economic assistance to Kenya grew considerably because the United States had a strong political interest in having its naval vessels use the port of Mombasa. This assistance included a $117 million structural adjustment program in 1983, with a $30 million economic support fund grant for the first year of a three-year program. The conditionality of this program was aimed at overcoming structural weaknesses in the Kenyan economy through economic stabilization, reduction of trade barriers, institutional reforms related to budgeting and parastatals, population policy, and liberalization of fertilizer distribution and grain marketing. The initial $30 million grant appears to have contributed significantly to the success of Kenya's macroeconomic stabilization efforts in that year: Kenya's annual inflation rate and budget deficit were cut by about one-half, the effective exchange rate was lowered, the real rate of interest increased, and the current account deficit and foreign borrowing were reduced.[37] In the area of agricultural policy, however, little was achieved in promoting liberalization of fertilizer distribution and the marketing of maize and other staple foods.[38]

Liberalization of fertilizer pricing and distribution has been a common theme of USAID policy reform initiatives but it has been undertaken to varying degrees in Malawi, Senegal, and Cameroon. Malawi and Cameroon were encouraged to shift to high analysis fertilizer and to reduce fertilizer subsidies. Such a change poses a difficult challenge for extension staff, however, because farmers have to be trained in the more demanding techniques of applying high analysis fertilizers.

In Senegal, a severe financial and economic crisis left the government little choice but to accept the aid and conditions of the International Monetary Fund, the World Bank, France, and USAID. Since the early 1980s these efforts have made little progress in liberalizing agricultural marketing and pricing, restructuring credit, and reducing government debt.

Two conclusions can be drawn about USAID's involvement in nonproject assistance for policy reform:

First, USAID needs to handle policy dialogue in a new way. There has been too much emphasis on using leverage—which is really lecturing to government officials—to ensure that the right decisions are made. Instead policy dialogue should be geared toward improving a country's capacity for policy research and policy analysis so that its own policymakers will be able to make the critical decisions. But this objective will not be achieved without educational institutions to train people for such tasks or mechanisms to institutionalize that capacity. Stronger links need to be forged with government ministries so that policymakers will be motivated to demand and get relevant information and good analysis. It appears that USAID's Agricultural Research and Planning Project in Senegal is making a notable contribution to this kind of institution building.[39]

Second, it also needs to be emphasized that policy reform represents a transitional strategy. Once price distortions and other large policy problems are resolved, the gains to be realized from further reforms will be limited, as will the willingness of African countries to adhere to donors' conditionality when there is less need for additional balance of payments support.

It will be a pity if the present enthusiasm for policy dialogue and policy reform diverts attention from the continuing need for development in the sense of "a generalized process of capital accumulation."

Review of Policies and Constraints on Aid

Among the major donors, USAID is unique in the extent to which it has assigned its staff to overseas missions and given them broad programming responsibilities. This arrangement is said to give the agency a comparative advantage in collaborating with host countries, in developing strategies well suited to local needs, and in implementing projects. In view of the growing pressure to reduce the size of missions for fiscal and security reasons, some attention should be given to the strengths and weaknesses of the system.

The strengths are difficult to document, however, because many of the agency's achievements are the result of informal contacts, friendship, and patient persuasion that are not featured in official reports or documents. Yet there is clear evidence from the MADIA country studies that this informal process, reinforced by seminars, conferences, and visits to the United States or to selected developing nations, has significantly altered the attitudes of host country officials toward higher agricultural education, research, health, and population issues. USAID's mission system also allows its field staff to have a considerable degree of flexibility in marshalling or redeploying resources in response to changing circumstances, unforeseen difficulties, or unexpected opportunities. Indeed, it is not in the mission's interest to reveal the degree of its flexibility to a distant and often hostile Congress, or to a worried Washington bureaucracy.

This review also leads to the conclusion that USAID's African missions have had some difficulty in translating its general policies and available resources into a development assistance program that addresses the host country's needs and capacities. The agency is constantly subjected to pressures that reduce its effectiveness, the greatest of which is the pressure to obligate appropriated funds in a timely manner. It is also under pressure to select and package its activities in accordance with the current policy climate in Washington; to comply with ever-increasing, complex, and time-consuming documentation, contracting, and procurement requirements; to fend off or accommodate numerous claims for support from domestic special interest groups; to accommodate the State Department's political and strategic concerns; and to support the political and developmental agenda of host country leaders. In each of the countries examined, there are clear examples in which these pressures (from Washington) led missions to compromise long-term development goals. A case in point is the bias in the New Directions policy introduced during the 1970s, which led the agency to eliminate support for agricultural higher education in Tanzania and delayed it several years in Cameroon. For similar reasons, support for agricultural research was delayed in Cameroon and Kenya. The combined pressure to obligate funds and to focus projects on rural and low-income people had an adverse effect on project design and performance in livestock projects in Kenya, Cameroon, and Senegal, and in other production-oriented projects in Senegal (and other Sahelian states). The largest USAID project in Senegal, which was based on a number of questionable assumptions and performed poorly, was undertaken not only to assist rural people directly, but because of pressure from the State Department to help the host government cope with a separatist movement in the Casamance region.

Mission management is also constrained by the size and skills of its work force. Given the complex, time-consuming, and time-driven nature of USAID's programming procedures, it is simply not practical to engage in extensive analysis or in exploring alternative projects in more than a cursory fashion. The mission is under more pressure to put together a plausible program and to obligate available funds than to consider the opportunity costs of potential options.

In Africa, the ability of USAID missions to develop and maintain effective program strategies also has been constrained by the need to plan without facts and by a loss of mission memory, exacerbated by mission instability. During the 1970s, USAID's heavy emphasis on projects and on contracting out all but bureaucratic tasks severely limited the staff time and skills that could be devoted to analytical tasks. This change over the past twenty years or so appears to have made it difficult for USAID to recruit highly qualified, technically skilled individuals as it is widely recognized that USAID staff must devote nearly all their time to administrative tasks.

In addition, the agency's employees in Africa are part of an expatriate community with limited local contacts outside the bureaucratic and technocratic urban middle-class groups and therefore are often unaware of the perspectives of the farm population. Mission personnel also vary in their ability to obtain information from the available sources.

These competing, and at times conflicting, pressures have affected mission strategies in many ways. Although USAID goals have remained consistent throughout the period under review and have continued to emphasize agriculture, food crops, and smallholders, the strategies devised to achieve these goals have been ineffective and project-level support for specific institutions and activities has been intermittent.

Whether USAID programs and projects are continued or terminated often seems to depend more on the pressures from Washington than on project performance or changes in host country conditions. Accordingly, the institutional capacities and political priorities of the host countries receive inadequate attention. This seems to be a central difficulty in USAID's country strategies. Pressures from Washington also have the effect of discouraging missions from coordinating their activities with other donors. Because of the multiplicity of donors operating in African countries, it is vital for them to work together—but difficult to coordinate their efforts. In principle, USAID's country missions have a comparative advantage in collaborating with host countries and in helping local governments develop policies and programs well suited to local needs. The constraints summarized above and some of the factors affecting USAID's programming system examined in the next section have the effect of impairing the ability of USAID missions to work collaboratively and constructively with host governments.

Pressures from Washington or the embassy at times vitiate the mutual learning that occurs through discussions with government officials at the operational level. When this happens, high-level host government leaders may be urged to agree to programs that are not clearly understood or desired by planners and technicians in the implementing ministries. This problem is exacerbated by policy changes, fluctuations in funding levels, and windows of opportunity created by the unexpected availability of funds in particular functional accounts late in the obligation period.

These problems are stressed here because the USAID country missions have the potential to play a an important and constructive role. The fact that the problems are surmountable seems to be demonstrated by the way in which health and population officers in the country missions have been able to work patiently and persistently with host governments and other donors, notably in helping to reduce the opposition to family planning and in encouraging donors and recipients to collaborate on the development of health and population strategies. By focusing on relatively simple measures such as immunization and oral rehydration to improve child survival prospects, the health activities appear to be manageable and complementary to efforts to bring fertility levels into a more manageable balance with drastically reduced mortality levels. In Malawi, and especially in Kenya, there also appears to have been significant progress in working with the local government and with the World Bank and other donors in developing plans for strengthening agricultural research and mechanisms for attracting more agricultural scientists in university faculties of agriculture to research.

Effectiveness of USAID's Programming System

USAID's experience in Sub-Saharan Africa indicates that, to be effective, assistance for agricultural and rural development must be based on technical and analytical skills; familiarity with what has worked in the host country; a comparative perspective; and a patient, persistent, flexible, and error-embracing attitude, which is particularly important because it takes a good deal of experimenting, groping, and mutual learning to adapt Western technology and organizational forms to Africa's unfamiliar, distinctive, and diverse conditions.

Over the past quarter-century, USAID has contributed greatly to the available pool of appropriate skills by broadening the disciplinary and technical breadth of its work force and by providing long-term support for relevant sectoral and topical investigation and training at universities and other research centers in the United States and Africa. USAID has also developed an evaluation system that has produced comprehensive assessments of USAID's experience and impact and has provided managers with useful information during project implementation. In addition, the agency has made substantive progress in developing assistance strategies that are better suited to African social, economic, and agronomic contexts. At the same time, changes within USAID have made it more difficult for the agency to adopt a flexible, error-embracing attitude and to fully capitalize on these favorable developments in implementing its programs.

Ironically, USAID's organizational structure, procedures, personnel system, and incentives were, in some respects, better suited to its task in the early years than at present. The agency was more decentralized then and more authority was delegated to the missions. Contracting and procurement procedures were less restrictive. Programming technical assistance was less time-consuming and more flexible, as it required little documentation and was reviewed in Washington by a small, technically oriented staff.

Most personnel were employed under a special authority that enabled USAID to hire professionals with special skills on a temporary basis. The lines between USAID and contract employees were not clear, and many USAID employees worked closely with their counterparts in the host country. The fact that they had less time to map out and implement their projects encouraged them to innovate, take risks, and to identify with their profession to a degree not characteristic of professional career services.

USAID's organization has become far more complex, and the country missions are oriented more toward Washington than the host country and its problems. New structures have been created to show compliance with new objectives, regulations, directives, and oversight from the Congress as well as from USAID/Washington. USAID's programming, project design, contracting, and procurement requirements have become vastly more detailed, standardized, and time-consuming. More time has to be spent preparing forward-looking advocacy documents to obtain funding. Less time can be devoted to project implementation and evaluation. Resource allocation decisions are still shaped by the entrepreneurial efforts of USAID's employees, but more and more of them are concerned with USAID's burdensome bureaucratic requirements rather than host country needs.

USAID's defensive posture also creates incentives to select or ignore information in project evaluation and to be wary of bringing independent country or technical experts into decisionmaking processes unless they are known to understand USAID's needs. The agency's personnel system has become more bureaucratic, although it remains less hierarchical than that of many other large organizations. Promotions are linked by and large to general bureaucratic skills and performance rather than to technical skill or ability to work effectively with host country counterparts. The only clear career ladder is in management. Together, USAID's internal work incentives and career pattern tend to frustrate its most able and committed employees and make it difficult for them to maintain their professional skills.

Attention has been drawn to these institutional problems to explain many of USAID's well-recognized problems with designing and implementing projects, achieving program continuity, and maintaining a balanced focus on the host country's problems and prospects rather than its own.

Conclusions and Recommendations

The USAID assistance programs examined in this study have been handicapped by the distinctive conditions in Africa, by the agency's lack of a domestic constituency, and by certain organizational and procedural constraints.

All of the MADIA countries have diverse agroclimatic environments and extensive areas in which physical conditions are harsh. Their agroeconomic systems vary greatly from one location to another, are complex, grounded in unfamiliar social institutions, and often oriented toward avoiding risk more than toward optimizing returns. Moreover, because of the overwhelming importance of rainfed agriculture and the high cost of the investments required to expand the irrigated areas, agricultural research programs find it particularly difficult to produce innovations adapted to Africa's diverse and changing environments. In many areas rainfall is inadequate and unreliable, whereas in other areas it is so heavy that the soil is rapidly leached of its nutrients. Fallow periods usually become shorter and trees and shrubs are destroyed in the transition from abundance to scarcity of agricultural land, a process that leads to the degradation of soils and adds immeasurably to the challenge confronting agricultural research systems.

At independence, transport systems were poorly developed; education and social services rudimentary; trained manpower scarce; region-specific research, data collection, analysis, and planning capacity virtually nonexistent; and manufacturing limited. With two or three exceptions, the region's economies depended almost exclusively on the export of primary agricultural products. Few Africans had experience in central government institutions. Attitudes toward professionalism and accountability were weakly institutionalized. Leaders had to contend with arbitrary boundaries and numerous ethnic constituencies and had no precedent for legitimate political activity within the newly created nation-states.

Encouraged by the promise of rapid development, the optimism of foreign development experts, and the unbounded expectations of their constituents, all of the region's countries succumbed in greater or lesser degree to the attractions of centralized economic planning and control; accepted development assistance uncritically; rapidly expanded governmental organizations, parastatals, project authorities, and government payrolls; and established a troublesome pattern of ethnic patronage to maintain political balance.[40]

Another constraint on the effectiveness of USAID programs in all African nations is the fact that Africa has had lower priority than any other region in United States foreign policy, as is evident from the low absolute levels of assistance, the lack of continuity in country focus, program size, and shifts in emphasis between bilateral and regional assistance.

The absence of a clear political constituency for long-term foreign assistance has left USAID vulnerable to faddish policy shifts, to pressures from an increasing variety of special interest groups advocating their objectives or seeking contracts, to management by individual congressmen, and to constant—and not necessarily well-informed—criticism. Although these problems have affected USAID programs in other regions as well, it appears that they have been less constraining elsewhere because in Asia and Latin America programs began earlier, and because host governments there had longer traditions of education and greater administrative capacity and thus were better able to draw upon USAID assistance selectively and hence to incorporate it into their plans. Furthermore, coordinating United States aid with assistance from other donors was less difficult because the United States usually played a dominant role, either alone or in partnership with the World Bank.

USAID's effectiveness in Africa also has been limited by the lack of consensus on the kinds of strategies needed for agricultural development, the persistent overoptimism concerning the appropriateness of the technologies and institutions being transferred, and various factors that have led planners to disregard the lessons of experience. These problems have been made all the worse by the agency's complex organization and procedures and by the weaknesses in its institutional incentives.

Effectiveness of USAID's Procedures

As the evidence from USAID's activities in these six African countries clearly shows, aid to agriculture will have a less than desirable outcome unless it proceeds from a well-conceived agricultural development strategy designed to produce a balanced increase in the per capita availability of material and human capital. It is no coincidence that the activities that were successful and that appear to have contributed to agricultural development in these countries are also the ones that fit the analytical framework here and constitute the critical elements of a well-conceived development strategy. These include agricultural education and training, rural infrastructure, and the creation of economically useful knowledge through agricultural management and planning activities, particularly the collection of agricultural statistics. Not only are these all examples of vital components of the development process, but they also represent investments in areas in which Africa clearly lags behind the developing countries of Asia or Latin America.Therefore these are also areas in which the returns to those investments are likely to be high. Although many of USAID's activities in Africa have not been successful, it should be pointed out that USAID has provided the largest shares of its agricultural assistance (13 percent each) to agricultural education and to infrastructural development—the two subsectors that are both essential elements of agricultural development and activities in which USAID has shown significant success.

As has been clearly demonstrated in other parts of the world, agricultural research represents an important element of agricultural development. However, because of the long gestation period before results can be expected and because USAID and other donors have neglected agricultural research in Africa until recently, no clear evidence of the effect of these investments is yet apparent.

The success of USAID's efforts in Africa is limited by its own institutional procedures and the external constraints brought to bear by Congress and specific interest groups. USAID is an agency without a strong supportive constituency and therefore has tried to secure support by responding to the desires of a large number of small interest groups and to congressional views.

These pressures are transmitted from Washington to the country missions. Whether USAID programs and projects are continued or terminated seems to depend more on the pressures from Washington (such as the "basic needs" orientation of the 1970s) than on project performance or changes in host country conditions. This, rather than USAID's inability to sustain an effort over time, seems a central difficulty in USAID's country strategies. The Washington orientation of the country missions frequently leads them to give inadequate attention to host country institutional capacities and political priorities.

Recommendations

Africa's diversity makes it is impossible to state which specific activities should be promoted in the countries of this continent without intimate knowledge of each country's policy environment, the strengths of its existing institutions, and the nature of its current problems and opportunities. At the same time, there is little doubt that missions need to pay more attention to host country needs, work more closely with their host country counterparts, and seek better coordination with other donors. Although some steps in this direction are possible now, USAID would find it easier to move ahead with such changes if it simplified its programming procedures and linked further funding to a review of what has been accomplished with obligated funds, rather than to unrealistic promises of what will be done if funds are obtained.

The eight activities singled out for attention earlier in the chapter should be thought of as activities that facilitate effectiveness rather than create a direct impact. Their purpose is to help developing countries form human, social, and physical capital—and to do so by helping these countries strengthen the capacity of their own institutions to address their distinctive needs. Planning, coordination, and resource allocation must therefore be firmly planted within host country institutions, rather than in USAID. This is a task that calls for patient, long-term, flexible support; experimentation; risk taking; and an error-embracing process of learning.

USAID's current programming system, implementation procedures, and incentives are not well suited to carrying out these activities. But even without organizational or procedural changes, USAID's performance in Africa could be improved by avoiding projects that assume it will be possible to transfer directly existing American technologies and forms of organization to rural African populations; projects that depend on extensive logistic support, the timely procurement of commodities, or American-made equipment that cannot be serviced by existing facilities; projects that entail complex management, create new administrative units, or assume it will be easy to alter existing institutional patterns, including those established during the colonial period; projects that require American contractors to live in remote rural areas and work more or less directly with local people;[41] and projects that depend on the outputs of other planned projects, rely on inputs to be provided by ministries not responsible for the project's implementation, or require substantially better interministerial coordination than already exists.

Although these general guidelines also apply to support for rural infrastructure, they can be relaxed here, if necessary, because USAID's past efforts in this area have been comparatively successful and because of its catalytic, facilitating role. Moreover, rural infrastructure can usefully absorb unanticipated windfall funding. For these reasons, it is advisable for USAID to have shelf projects in this category of assistance.

Although USAID's institution building and participant training have achieved a good deal, their impact could be increased. More support should also be given to developing institutions *after* the initial infusions of technical assistance, training, and construction have been completed. This can be done by providing additional and continuing support for the following activities:

- Research by Africans on many aspects of agricultural and rural development, including population, health, natural resource tenure, energy, and environment.
- The maintenance of American equipment for which spare parts and service are not locally available.
- Workshops, publication, travel, networking, and midcareer and in-service training to enable Africans to maintain their professional competence and morale.
- Policy-relevant, applied research and the interchange of information between political leaders, administrators, and African technical experts to inform government decisions and institutionalize the process of technically informed dissent. The principal objective of such support should be to enable faculties of agriculture to make a greater contribution to national research programs. Nonproject assistance should continue to be used to expand successful host country initiatives and to reduce the costs and risks associated with changing government policies, procedures, organization, and responsibilities.

These recommendations entail a shift in the mission's work, procedures, and staffing pattern. Less effort would have to be devoted to designing and managing new and complex projects and to the inevitable problems associated with contracting and procurement. More effort would have to be spent analyzing country needs and working with host country counterparts to arrive at the best ways to help existing institutions meet these needs. By shifting mission attention to existing institutions, the agency would encourage better coordination with other donors. The increased effort needed to make institutions more effective—a need already recognized by USAID management—would also mean that donor assistance would be less likely to foster the proliferation of projects and the expansion of government.

Although some of these modifications are possible even now, they would be facilitated, as already mentioned, by greatly simplifying USAID programming procedures, and, with Congress's approval, by linking further funding to a review of what has been accomplished with obligated funds rather than to unrealistic promises of what will be done if funds are obtained. Such changes would increase incentives for carrying out better monitoring and evaluation. Adopting a less defensive, more flexible, error-embracing approach would also encourage USAID to welcome more participation by non–USAID African and United States experts and expert bodies such as the National Academy of Sciences.

To implement this strategy and thereby ensure effective, informed, and patient policy dialogue, as well as effective nonproject assistance, the agency must expand the analytical skills and country knowledge of its missions, but reduce its total personnel. This action would motivate mission staff to update their skills and broaden their understanding of the host country and region. USAID could help them do this by providing opportunities for short- and long-term training and for advancement along coherent career ladders.

Notes

This analysis draws heavily on country studies for Cameroon, Nigeria, and Senegal carried out by William Jaeger, and studies of USAID activities in Malawi, Kenya, and Tanzania, prepared by Dirk Dijkerman, as well as a more detailed comparative report drawing on all six studies. See William K. Jaeger, "U.S. Aid to Cameroon: Its Impact on Agriculture and Rural Development," "U.S. Aid to Nigeria: Its Impact on Agriculture and Rural Development," and "U.S. Aid to Senegal: Its Impact on Agriculture and Rural Development," MADIA Working Papers (Africa—Technical Department, Agriculture Division, World Bank, Washington, D.C., 1987); Dirk Dijkerman, "Agricultural Development in Southern Africa: An Assessment of AID Assistance to Malawi," "Agricultural Development in East Africa: An Assessment of AID Assistance to Kenya," and "Agricultural Development in East Africa: An Assessment of AID Assistance to Tanzania," MADIA Working Papers (Africa—Technical Department, Agriculture Division, World Bank, Washington, D.C., 1987); and Bruce F. Johnston, Allan Hoben, Dirk W. Dijkerman, and William K. Jaeger, *An Assessment of AID Activities to Promote Agricultural and Rural Development in Sub-Saharan Africa*, USAID Evaluation Special Study 54, (Washington, D.C.: United States Agency for International Development, April 1988).

1. Rutherford M. Poats, *Twenty-Five Years of Development Cooperation: A Review* (Paris: OECD, 1985).

2. World Bank, *World Development Report 1986* (New York: Oxford University Press, 1986), p. 218.

3. Sub-Saharan Africa and Africa are used interchangeably throughout this chapter.

4. Commodity import programs have been the most common use of ESF since 1975, although cash/budgetary support has risen since 1983. Project aid has accounted for about 20 percent of Africa's ESF programs since 1980. See Congressional Research Service, *U.S. Aid to Africa: The Record, the Rationales, and the Challenge*, prepared for the Committee on Foreign Affairs, Subcommittee on Africa by R. W. Copson, T. W. Galdi, and L. W. Nowels (Washington, D.C., January 1986).

5. Congressional Research Service, *U.S. Aid to Africa*, p. xi.

6. Military aid—relevant only for Kenya—is excluded from these figures.

7. A recent report of the Congressional Research Service (1986) provides a convenient summary of USAID assistance to Sub-Saharan Africa for the period 1946 to 1985. The following table, in millions of 1985 dollars (rather than 1983 dollars used in this chapter) shows the position of four of the six MADIA countries:

1. Zaire	1,895	7. *Kenya*	951
2. Sudan	1,687	8. Somalia	812
3. *Nigeria*	1,305	9. *Tanzania*	665
4. Ethiopia	1,298	10. Zambia	537
5. Liberia	1,181	11. *Senegal*	508
6. Ghana	1,128		

A breakdown by five-year periods from 1960 to 1985 included in the Congressional Research Service report shows the sharp changes in country emphasis over time.

8. Only those obligations that are clearly attributable to the country in question are represented in the figures and tables. Further discussion of regional accounts is found below.

9. William K. Jaeger, "U.S. Aid to Nigeria: Its Impact On Agriculture and Rural Development," MADIA Working Paper (Africa—Technical Department, Agriculture Division, World Bank, Washington, 1987).

10. For the period 1978–84, extensive use was made of the "Agriculture and Rural Development: Functional Review FY 1978–84" prepared by USAID's Africa Bureau to attribute project totals to different subsectors. In the three West African countries—Senegal, Cameroon, and Nigeria—funds for individual projects are divided among several subsectors when they contain different components. These shares are estimated from project papers and end-of-project financial data, and are invariant between years. For Kenya, Tanzania, and Malawi, each project was assigned to one subsector. Additional detail is given in the country studies by Jaeger and Dijkerman.

11. Moses Abramovitz, *Resource and Output Trends in the United States since 1870*, Occasional Paper 52 (New York: National Bureau of Economics Research, 1956); and Simon Kuznets, *Economic Growth of Nations: Total Output and Production Structure* (Cambridge, Mass.: Harvard University Press, 1971), p. 73.

12. Yujiro Hayami and V. W. Ruttan, *Agricultural Development: An International Perspective* (Baltimore, Md.: Johns Hopkins University Press, 1985), chap. 8; and Bruce F. Johnston and Peter Kilby, *Agriculture and Structural Transformation: Economic Strategies in Late-Developing Countries* (New York: Oxford University Press, 1975), chaps. 5–6.

13. This conceptual framework, derived from H. G. Johnson, is elaborated in greater detail in his "Comparative Cost and Commercial Policy Theory in a Developing World Economy," *The Pakistan Development Review* 4(1) Supplement (Spring 1969):1–33; and Johnston and others, "An Assessment of AID Activities."

14. Johnson, "Comparative Cost and Commercial Policy Theory," 9.

15. Bruce F. Johnston and William C. Clark, *Redesigning Rural Development: A Strategic Perspective* (Baltimore, Md.: Johns Hopkins University Press, 1982), chap. 4.

16. Definitions of the essential elements of development put forth by Anne O. Krueger, "Aid in the Development Process," *The World Bank Research Observer* 1(1,1986):57–78; and G. L. Johnson, "Institutional Framework for Agricultural Policy Monitoring and Analysis," prepared for the Economic

Development Institute (World Bank, Washington, D.C., 1986) differ only slightly from the definition presented here. Johnson refers to the four driving forces of rural development as "technical change, institutional improvements, human development, and growth in the biological and physical capital base" (p. 1). Krueger stresses the importance of promoting "accumulation and efficient use of resources, the development of well-functioning markets, efficient governmental provision of infrastructural services, and institutional development in both the private and public sectors" (p. 58) in order to achieve development goals.

17. See Johnston and others, "An Assessment of AID Activities," chap. 4.

18. Hayami and Ruttan, *Agricultural Development*.

19. David C. Wilcock and George R. McDowell, *Building Colleges of Agriculture in Africa: U.S. University Experiences and Implications for Future Projects* (Washington, D.C.: Board for International Agricultural Development and Agency for International Development, 1986).

20. Jaeger, "U.S. Aid to Nigeria."

21. Ibid., pp. 42–43.

22. W. K. Gamble, R. L. Blumberg, V. C. Johnson, and N. S. Raun, "A Review of the Impact of AID Assistance to Three Nigerian Universities" (Morrilton, Ark.: Winrock International, 1986), p. 6.

23. Dijkerman, "An Assessment of AID Assistance to Tanzania."

24. Ibid., p. 99.

25. Dijkerman, "An Assessment of AID Assistance to Kenya," pp. 169–265.

26. USAID, "AFGRAD African Graduate Fellowship Program," Phase III Project Paper 698-0455 (Washington, D.C., 1984), p. 22.

27. Dijkerman, "An Assessment of AID Assistance to Kenya," p. 84.

28. Dijkerman, "An Assessment of AID Assistance to Tanzania," pp. 88–91.

29. Johnston and others, "An Assessment of AID Activities," chap. 4.

30. Dijkerman, "An Assessment of AID Assistance to Malawi," pp. 72–74.

31. Jaeger, "U.S. Aid to Cameroon," pp. 76–77.

32. USAID, "Plan for Supporting Agricultural Research and Faculties of Agriculture in Sub-Saharan Africa" (Washington, D.C., 1985).

33. Dijkerman, "An Assessment of AID Assistance to Tanzania," p. 44.

34. Ibid., pp. 85–92.

35. Jaeger, "U.S. Aid to Cameroon."

36. Jaeger, "U.S. Aid to Senegal," pp. 75–80.

37. Elliot Berg, Walter Hecox, and Jim Mudge, "Evaluation of the AID 1983–84 Structural Adjustment Program in Kenya," draft report commissioned by USAID/K (Washington, D.C., 1985), p. ii.

38. Ibid.

39. Jaeger, "U.S. Aid to Senegal."

40. Political instability, which is often cited as an impediment to economic development in Africa, has not been a characteristic of the countries in this study, except in the case of Nigeria. It is worth recalling that the growth of government payrolls posed an especially serious problem because at the end of the colonial period the principle was adopted, in the name of nondiscrimination, that African civil servants should receive the same salaries as their European predecessors. The real value of those salaries has now been reduced substantially by inflation, which has not been matched by salary increases, but that legacy contributed significantly to the exceptionally large gap between incomes in the "modern sector" and the incomes earned by rural households.

And in the 1960s and 1970s donors encouraged the proliferation of parastatals and project authorities.

41. Activities implemented by the Peace Corps and private and voluntary organizations (PVOs) constitute a partial exception.

7 *European Communities Assistance for Agricultural Development in Cameroon, Senegal, and Tanzania, 1960–87*

Walter Kennes

AGRICULTURAL COOPERATION between the European Communities (EC) and Sub-Saharan Africa dates back a number of years—to 1960 in the case of Cameroon and Senegal and to 1975 in the case of Tanzania. The historical origin of EC development assistance is a provision in the Treaty of Rome, which founded the European Economic Community in 1957. This foresaw EC involvement in trade matters and infrastructure investment in the regions and territories that were at that time colonies of the founding member states. These investments were financed through a fund set up for this purpose, which became the first European Development Fund (EDF).

Starting in 1964, after these territories had gained their independence, a series of five-year agreements—or conventions—dealing mainly with trade and aid were concluded between the Community and a group of sovereign African states. With the entry of the United Kingdom to the Community in 1973, many Commonwealth countries joined the agreement. Sixty-six African, Caribbean, and Pacific (ACP) countries signed the third Lomé Convention (1986–90). Each convention has a corresponding EDF replenishment. The sixth EDF is linked to the third Lomé Convention. Both Cameroon and Senegal have participated since the first EDF, Tanzania only since the fourth (1976–80). Outside the ACP group, there are also cooperation arrangements by the EC with countries in Latin America, Asia, and North Africa.

The constituency for EC cooperation is broader and more complex than the one for bilateral aid programs because it comprises diverse interests from the twelve EC member states. As a result, EC cooperation has generally been free from the historically linked biases that sometimes characterize bilateral programs. The EC philosophy concerning development cooperation emanates from a continuous dialogue between the group of ACP states and European institutions and member states. The member states are involved in all decisionmaking procedures. The part of total development assistance of member states that is handled by the EC has been steadily rising and is currently close to 12 percent. In recent years, payments in millions of European Currency Units (MECU) have been greater than 1,600 million. The European Parliament has been consistently in favor of increasing EC development assistance.

It should be noted that agricultural cooperation in this chapter is interpreted broadly—so as to take into account rural development. Nevertheless, actions that are rural, but predominantly nonagricultural (for example, support for schools, hospitals, water supply, and road infrastructure) are not included in the review. Food aid is included, because it relates to agriculture in at least two ways: It affects the supply of food, and its counterpart funds can be used to stimulate rural development. The system for the stabilization of agricultural export earnings (STABEX) is also discussed.

Background on EC Cooperation with Cameroon, Senegal, and Tanzania

Cameroon, Senegal, and Tanzania are members of the group of sixty-six African, Caribbean, and Pacific countries that signed the third Lomé Convention. The financing is provided through the sixth EDF, which covers the period 1986–90. The EDF is managed by the Commission of the European Communities (CEC), except for some components that are handled by the European Investment Bank (EIB).

EDF resources can be subdivided into "programmed" and "nonprogrammed" aid. The package of programmed aid allocated to a country is determined at the beginning of each convention and consists mainly of grants and a smaller quantity of special loans (with a grant element of more than 80 percent). The allocation is determined largely on the basis of population and per capita GDP and also takes into account whether the recipients are landlocked or insulated and the level of past EDF assistance. At the beginning of each five-year convention, the broad allocation of programmed resources is determined through a negotiation between the ACP states and the EC. The result is an indicative (country) program that constitutes the first stage of the EDF decision cycle. Subsequently, specific programs and projects are appraised, decided, and implemented.

Nonprogrammed aid is not allocated in advance to specific countries. Countries may benefit from it, depending on circumstances. An important type of nonprogrammed aid is STABEX, which serves to compensate for downward fluctuations in earnings from exports of agricultural products to the EC. A comparable system for stabilizing mineral exports (SYSMIN) exists. Another kind of nonprogrammed aid is risk capital, which is used to acquire temporary minority holdings in companies and is managed by the EIB. Nonprogrammed aid also includes emergency assistance to help countries cope with natural disasters or exceptional circumstances of a similar nature.

Outside the EDF, but within the convention framework, there are "normal" loans provided by the EIB. These loans are offered at market conditions, but they are usually softened by interest subsidies from the EDF. Apart from the resources linked to the conventions, there is also grant aid financed on the annual budget. The most important form is food aid, followed by cofinancing provided for nongovernmental organizations (NGOs).

Composition and Evolution of Aid Commitments

A summary of EC aid to Cameroon, Senegal, and Tanzania is provided in table 7-1. When the figures are converted to constant 1983 purchasing power and further into United States dollars, the cumulative aid flows to Senegal and Cameroon equal more than $1 billion. For Tanzania, the 1983 constant value is above $500 million. Table 7-1 also shows that normal EIB loans have been particularly important to Cameroon and that Senegal has received high STABEX transfers.

Not represented in table 7-1 are the regional projects. These involved more than one country and have generally focused on transport links with landlocked countries. In the case of Senegal, funds were also provided for the dams on the Senegal River (MECU 55). Other regional funding covered training facilities, agricultural research, and, particularly, animal disease control.

Procurement for EDF projects is mainly done by international competitive tendering open to all ACP and EC member states, to ensure a wide degree of competition. The third Lomé Convention contains provisions to favor contracts in ACP states. Their share in the total value of EDF contracts has increased from almost 15 percent in the 1960s to approximately 30 percent by 1984. About 2 percent goes to third countries not belonging to the European or to the ACP group.

Sectoral Composition

Table 7-2 shows that up to the third EDF (1971–75) funding was concentrated on physical infrastructure. In Cameroon, this included roads, port facilities, and railways (the EC financed a large part of the Trans-Cameroonian Railway). In Senegal, trunk roads and bridges accounted

Table 7-1. Overall European Communities Aid Commitments
(millions of European currency units)

Country	EDF 1 1958–65	EDF 2 1966–70	EDF 3 1971–75	EDF 4 1976–80	EDF 5 1981–85	EDF 6 1986–90
Cameroon						
Programmed aid						
(allocations from EDF)	(51.3)	(53.9)	(58.8)	(55.3)	(69.0)	(96.0)
Grants	51.3	39.4	49.9	32.8	29.7	27.8
Special loans	0	14.5	8.9	20.8	17.9	0
Subtotal	51.3	53.9	58.8	53.6	47.6	27.8
Nonprogrammed aid						
Interest subsidies	0	0	0.5	4.2	20.9	0
Risk capital	0	0	0.5	5.0	0	0
Exceptional aid	0	0	0	2.3	1.6	0.2
STABEX	0	0	0	4.1	29.6	0
Subtotal	0	0	1.0	15.6	51.2	0.2
Total EDF commitments	51.3	53.9	59.8	69.2	99.7	28.0
Budget commitments[a]	0	0	0.5	2.7	1.8	1.1
European Investment Bank loans	0	11.3	6.0	32.6	95.7	0
Total	51.3	65.2	66.3	104.5	197.2	29.1
Senegal						
Programmed aid						
(allocations from EDF)	(42.9)	(67.4)	(57.1)	(59.0)	(69.0)	(97.0)
Grants	42.9	61.5	52.8	39.4	38.3	87.0
Special loans	0	5.9	4.3	19.3	20.1	10.0
Subtotal	42.9	67.4	57.1	58.7	58.4	97.0
Nonprogrammed aid						
Interest subsidies	0	0	0	1.8	5.6	0
Risk capital	0	0	0.8	7.4	4.2	25.5

Exceptional aid	0	0	9.2	4.6	2.1	0.9
STABEX	0	0	0	65.1	90.6	82.1
Subtotal	0	0	10.0	78.9	102.5	108.5
Total EDF commitments	42.9	67.4	67.1	137.6	160.9	205.5
Budget commitments[a]	0	0	14.3	14.9	28.5	2.5
European Investment Bank loans	0	2.4	1.4	12.0	21.0	0
Total	42.9	69.8	82.8	164.5	210.4	208.0
Tanzania						
Programmed aid						
(allocations from EDF)	0	0	0	(103.4)	(120.7)	(169.0)
Grants	0	0	0	70.3	109.2	103.6
Special loans	0	0	0	32.9	11.6	0
Subtotal	0	0	0	103.2	120.8	103.6
Nonprogrammed aid						
Interest subsidies	0	0	0	0.1	0	0
Risk capital	0	0	0	7.8	9.7	0
Exceptional aid	0	0	0	0.3	0.5	18.0
STABEX	0	0	0	20.7	20.9	8.9
Subtotal	0	0	0	28.9	31.1	24.9
Total EDF commitments	0	0	0	132.1	151.5	130.5
Budget commitments[a]	0	0	7.5	14.1	43.2	7.2
European Investment Bank loans	0	0	0	5.0	0	0
Total	0	0	0	151.2	194.8	137.9

Note: EDF = European Development Fund. The figures represent financing decisions up to 31 December 1987 and are expressed in current prices.
a. Food aid, NGO cofinance, and special programs.
Source: Commission of the EC.

Table 7-2. Sectoral Allocation of European Development Fund Aid
(percentage)

Country	*EDF 1 1958–65*	*EDF 2 1966–70*	*EDF 3 1971–75*	*EDF 4 1976–80*	*EDF 5 1981–85*
Cameroon					
Agriculture and rural development	11.5	28.8	29.1	43.9	51.6
Transport infrastructure	66.3	48.2	48.8	31.5	32.6
Social infrastructure	18.9	14.5	15.4	6.3	4.6
Industry (nonagricultural)	0.0	3.0	0.0	9.7	6.9
Other	3.3	5.6	6.7	8.6	4.3
Total	100.0	100.0	100.0	100.0	100.0
Total value (MECU)	51.3	53.9	59.8	65.1	69.6
Senegal					
Agriculture and rural development	21.7	78.5	55.7	36.4	52.6
Transport infrastructure	51.7	8.0	31.4	20.1	7.3
Social infrastructure	25.6	10.2	2.2	23.6	16.1
Industry (nonagricultural)	0.0	0.0	1.6	13.4	12.3
Other	0.9	3.3	8.9	6.5	11.6
Total	100.0	100.0	100.0	100.0	100.0
Total value (MECU)	42.9	67.4	67.1	72.5	68.2
Tanzania					
Agriculture and rural development	0	0	0	44.2	51.4
Transport infrastructure	0	0	0	36.8	22.1
Social infrastructure	0	0	0	5.7	17.8
Industry (nonagricultural)	0	0	0	12.2	7.6
Other	0	0	0	1.1	1.1
Total	0	0	0	100.0	100.0
Total value (MECU)	0	0	0	110.8	119.5

Note: Situation 30 September 1986, excluding STABEX transfers.
Source: Commission of the EC.

for the bulk of physical infrastructure (the EC financed 25 percent of the trunk road network). Agricultural and rural development—broadly defined to include processing, rural roads, rural health centers, irrigation facilities, and agricultural schools—has been the second most important area of funding up to the third EDF. More recently, especially for the fifth EDF (1981–85), it was the most important, covering about 50 percent of project funds in Cameroon, Senegal, and Tanzania. Social infrastructure, mainly in the form of school and hospital buildings, constituted the third most important area of funding.

There have been drastic shifts over time in the shares of the different categories within agricultural and rural development (see table 7-3). The most striking shift in Senegal and Cameroon has been from export crop production and processing toward food crop production. Livestock, fisheries, and forestry have on the whole absorbed a relatively small part of EDF aid. An exception is livestock in Senegal, which accounted for 25 percent of agricultural aid under the fourth EDF. It is noteworthy that the fifth EDF (1981–85) maintained a larger share for export crops within total agriculture for Tanzania than for either Senegal or Cameroon.

The importance of technical assistance for agricultural and rural development cooperation in Senegal and Cameroon has fluctuated between 10 and 15 percent up to the fourth EDF (1976–80). In all three countries, however, the fifth EDF (1981–85) had a high share of technical assistance (almost 20 percent). This is a result of the shift toward food crops, which require more extensive preparation and much closer follow-up.

The factors explaining the sectoral breakdown of EDF funding and its evolution over time are diverse and often reflect specific country priorities. However, in a more general way, they also reflect the changes in development thinking. In the 1960s, the lack of basic infrastructure was seen as the greatest constraint on economic growth. Another such constraint was the lack of human resources—which justified EDF investment in educational and health facilities. At the same time, export crops were seen as the only expandable source of foreign exchange and government revenue.

The 1972–74 world food crisis had a strong influence on the allocation of funding. In many African countries (for example, Senegal) food imports had been rising rapidly and were absorbing a large share of export revenue. The high level and volatility of food prices on the world market provided the justification to move aid funds toward food crops. Furthermore, fluctuations—and in some cases downward trends—in the prices of major export commodities discouraged further support for these crops. The shift is clearly applicable to EDF funding in Cameroon and Senegal.

Table 7-3. European Development Fund Aid for Agricultural and Rural Development
(percent)

Country	EDF 1 1958–65	EDF 2 1966–70	EDF 3 1971–75	EDF 4 1976–80	EDF 5 1981–85
Cameroon					
Subsistence crops	0.0	0.0	6.0	26.3	25.8
Export crops	0.0	78.9	47.4	28.6	10.5
Crop processing	0.0	14.2	33.0	11.5	11.8
Livestock	14.2	0.0	0.0	3.1	4.8
Fisheries	0.0	0.0	0.0	0.0	5.6
Forestry and conservation	12.2	0.0	0.6	2.9	2.0
Physical infrastructure	25.4	0.0	12.1	3.9	27.0
Social infrastructure	8.1	0.0	0.0	17.6	4.3
Other	40.1	6.9	0.9	6.1	8.2
Total	100.0	100.0	100.0	100.0	100.0
Total value (MECU)	5.9	15.5	17.4	28.6	35.8
Senegal					
Subsistence crops	10.2	6.9	42.0	30.9	41.8
Export crops	0.0	81.5	27.6	26.8	9.0
Crop processing	0.0	1.4	2.6	3.0	0.0
Livestock	0.0	1.4	18.3	25.8	4.6
Fisheries	8.2	0.0	0.0	0.0	5.1
Forestry and conservation	0.0	0.8	0.0	0.0	6.7
Physical infrastructure	30.6	0.0	8.0	0.9	27.7
Social infrastructure	42.4	0.0	0.7	8.9	2.5
Other	8.6	8.0	0.8	3.7	2.7
Total	100.0	100.0	100.0	100.0	100.0
Total value (MECU)	9.3	52.9	37.4	26.4	35.9
Tanzania					
Subsistence crops	0	0	0	8.2	18.4
Export crops	0	0	0	23.6	36.6
Crop processing	0	0	0	64.1	13.5
Livestock	0	0	0	0.0	15.3
Fisheries	0	0	0	0.0	0.0
Forestry and conservation	0	0	0	0.0	1.7
Physical infrastructure	0	0	0	3.8	4.1
Social infrastructure	0	0	0	0.0	6.6
Other	0	0	0	0.4	3.8
Total	0	0	0	100.0	100.0
Total value (MECU)	0	0	0	49.0	61.4

Note: As of 30 September 1986.
Source: Commission of the EC.

A list of specific projects in the area of agricultural and rural development is provided in appendix tables 7A-1 to 7A-5 at the end of this chapter. For clarity and brevity these tables do not include the large number of small actions that were also taken (for example, studies or small technical assistance projects). For the fourth and fifth EDF (see tables 7-8 to 7-10), the values are given for two stages: the amount decided (primary commitments) and the amount paid or disbursed. (Projects that are examined in detail in text are marked in all appendix tables by an asterisk.)

Direct Support for Agricultural Development

This section covers direct support for agricultural development; STABEX and food aid affect the agricultural sector more indirectly and are discussed later in the chapter. Only projects that are in one way or another representative of the EC cooperation effort are included. Especially in Cameroon and Senegal, each with a history of more than twenty-five years of agricultural cooperation with the EC—but even in the case of Tanzania—it was necessary to leave out several important actions.

Direct support can be subdivided into four main categories: export or cash crop production, irrigated crop development (mainly rice), integrated rural development, and small-scale projects. Each of the following subsections describes the background of a representative project (or program), the main project activities, and their effect.

Export Crop Production

Groundnuts in Senegal. At the beginning of the 1960s, groundnuts dominated the agricultural economy of Senegal, accounting for more than 80 percent of commodity exports and approximately 40 percent of government revenue. Groundnut processing was the main industrial activity. More than 75 percent of farmers' cash income depended on groundnuts. The bulk of groundnut exports were granted access to the French market at prices above world market levels. When France became a member of the EC, Senegal found it was going to lose its privileged groundnut products export market. It was clear that any strategy to promote economic growth in Senegal would have to pay attention to the groundnut industry. At the same time, without substantial cost reduction, Senegalese groundnut exports would not be competitive and would lose their share in world exports.

These considerations led the EC to finance a comprehensive five-year groundnut program, which was approved in 1965. Subsequently, other actions in support of groundnuts were approved. Overall, almost ECU 60 million (nominal value) were spent to support the groundnut industry. Most of the disbursement took place between 1966 and 1975. The program had two basic components: structural support of the supply side and export price support. About 55 percent was earmarked for the structural components designed to reduce production costs.

The elements of the structural component were extension, improved implements, fertilizer distribution, better seed, storage infrastructure, animal traction, and soil conservation measures. Credit for inputs and implements were channeled through the cooperative system. The price support amounted to an export subsidy scheme compensating Senegal for the gradual reduction of French import prices to the world market level. It was designed to be phased out by the fifth year, when the structural improvements were expected to have their effect on production. Actual disbursements under the program deviated from original intentions: Less was spent on structural improvements, and export subsidies were not phased out after five years. Both components were extended beyond the period foreseen.

The difficulties that had to be faced during execution of the program were partly economic (world price movements), climatic (drought), and institutional (inefficiency of parastatals). The 1970–71 season was particularly bad because of a drought. The marketed surplus declined drastically, and in several producing areas no seed was available. This led to a separate project to set up a seed service. This project was quite successful, and the marketed surplus recovered quickly.

In the wake of the 1970 drought, the EC approved emergency support for groundnuts; this was designed not only to combat the effects of drought, but also to improve the policy and institutional environment. The specific government measures to which the program was linked were spelled out in detail. These measures were negotiated through a policy dialogue and included a rescheduling of the cooperative debts and an increase of the producer price. At the time, this was an innovation. After 1975 the EDF did not continue direct support for groundnut oil production, since attention shifted toward food crops. However, indirect price support was continued through the export revenue stabilization scheme, as explained later in the chapter.

Complementary to EDF funding, the European Investment Bank provided a loan (MECU 3) to the Société Nationale de Commercialisation des Oléagineux de Sénégal (SONACOS) to modernize and extend the groundnut processing capacity in the Casamance region. An interest subsidy associated with that loan was granted using resources of the fourth EDF.

As part of the effort to diversify Senegalese agriculture, the EC also supported confectionery groundnuts. Other diversification actions included cotton and horticulture. In the early 1970s the demand for confectionery groundnuts was growing rapidly, especially in Europe, and substantial export gains were expected. Projections were to increase the area from less than 3,000 hectares in 1968 to about 70,000 in 1978. The projects were integrated, providing support from seed and extension to processing and packaging.

It is important to mention that the 1965 groundnut program as well as the subsequent emergency and exceptional support were closely coordinated with French bilateral cooperation. Mainly French organizations were involved in implementation. The technical package introduced by the program was well accepted; however, for a variety of reasons—including the inefficiency of parastatals involved with marketing—it was not possible to reach the targets. Many of the infrastructural and input distribution targets were reached, but yields did not improve, partly because of adverse weather conditions. Most important, between 1965 and 1969 the income of groundnut farmers declined by 25 percent, despite the substantial price and structural support.

A factor that strongly affected the results of the groundnut program was the increasing competition of soybean oil, which is only a by-product of soybean cake and which led to a decrease of Senegal's export prices. Although the export of groundnut cake was rising, it could not compensate for the losses on oil revenue. Groundnut cake exports were hampered by the presence of a toxic substance, aphlatoxine, linked to a fungus. The EC contributed to research on aphlatoxine, and the problem is now generally under control.

In sum, even though the targets of the groundnut program were not reached, by compensating for the effects of drought and world price decline, the EC projects probably prevented a complete collapse of groundnut production. Such a collapse would have created massive unemployment not only in the rural areas but also in related processing and transport activities. In Nigeria, groundnut production did collapse, but there, petroleum revenue made it possible to absorb labor (at least during the 1970s). For Senegal, another benefit of groundnut maintenance was nutrition. Because of the continued availability of groundnuts, even the poor households have always been assured of a reasonable supply of vegetable oil. Many other developing countries have to spend scarce foreign exchange on imports of vegetable oil.

The introduction of confectionery groundnuts was initially successful, and many farmers were attracted to the crop. The acreage target of 70,000 hectares in 1978 was met. Given that holdings range from 1 to 2 hectares, some 50,000 smallholders were reached. Production growth was less satisfactory because of several years of drought. Furthermore, it was not possible to organize efficient processing. Since

1980, there has been little further expansion of confectionery groundnuts. Nevertheless, the crop is now established and continues to generate some export revenue.

Cotton in Senegal. After experiments carried out in the early 1960s by French researchers, the EC decided to support the introduction of cotton as part of the effort to diversify Senegalese agriculture. Cotton cultivation had been successfully introduced in neighboring Mali, but Senegal had no tradition of cotton production. The projects to introduce and support cotton had to start from scratch and to provide an integrated package, from extension and input delivery to processing and export. Cotton is a labor-intensive and delicate crop, so that the quality of support must be good in order to avoid failure. The EC financed two-thirds of the cost of the government's cotton program (approximately MECU 17)—the balance being provided directly from Senegalese resources.

The program started in 1966, initially covering Siné Saloum and Casamance and later also eastern Senegal. Up to 1974, responsibility for the operations was entrusted to the Compagnie Française de Développement des Textiles (CFDT). Starting in 1974, the Senegalese parastatal Société de Développement des Fibres Textiles (SODEFITEX) took control. In addition to diversifying exports, the cotton action had two further objectives: to provide raw material for the domestic textiles industry and to contribute to regionally balanced development.

The introduction and adoption of cotton continued well up to 1976, when the area planted reached 45,000 hectares and more than 70,000 farm households were producing cotton. Fiber production reached 17,000 tonnes, 80 percent of which was exported. The rapid development was the result of a well-organized extension effort that was tightly supervised by CFDT. Development was facilitated by the favorable cotton/groundnut price ratio during the first half of the 1970s. Cotton prices were also more stable than groundnut prices. After 1976, production and area declined for various reasons: low yields as a result of the drought, the spread of cultivation to less suitable areas, difficulties in sustaining the comprehensive extension effort, difficulties in maintaining quality, and depressed world market prices. During the 1980s, some recovery took place, so that the area under cotton stabilized at almost 40,000 hectares.

Following the world food crisis of 1972–74, attention shifted from export crops toward food crops. Even the fourth EDF project was no longer solely a cotton project, but rather a project to develop the cotton areas in eastern Senegal, with a focus on rice production.

Cotton cultivation appears to have made a modest, but nevertheless sustainable, contribution to the diversification of Senegalese exports.

Between 1982 and 1986, its export value averaged $17 million against $104 million for groundnut products and $117 million for fisheries products. Because cotton is labor-intensive, it has made a significant contribution to employment, creating about 60,000 jobs. The crop rotations with cotton, cereals, and groundnuts that were propagated by the fourth EDF project have proved to be agronomically sound and economically interesting—whenever rainfall is adequate. In addition, SODEFITEX has emerged as one of the better-managed parastatals in food and agriculture.

Palm oil in Cameroon. During the 1960s Cameroon's exports were dominated by coffee and cocoa, but traditional palm oil production remained widespread in the south of the country. The yields were low, however, and the rewards for the hard work of collecting and processing the fruits were equally low. To diversify the economy and to ensure the availability of a basic food item at a reasonable price, the government decided to modernize palm oil production, mainly by creating large estates and processing facilities. Since the mid-1960s several donors—including the World Bank, France, and the EC—have supported oil palm development in Cameroon. Total EC finances for oil palm amounted to about MECU 40, using different kinds of funding: grants, special loans, risk capital, and normal EIB loans in combination with EDF interest subsidies. All projects were located in the southwest of the country. The main objectives of EC support for palm oil were to satisfy the growing urban demand for oils and fats, contribute to export earnings, increase rural revenue by introducing high-yielding oil palms and improved processing techniques, and contribute to the profitability of the enterprises engaged in palm oil production and processing.

Two-thirds of EC support went to the Dibombari agroindustrial complex managed by the Société Camerounaise de Palmeraies (SOCAPALM) and one-third was allocated to the Cameroon Development Corporation (CDC), both parastatals. In collaboration with CDC, 4,300 hectares of oil palm plantation were established between 1967 and 1977. CDC also obtained a loan for a processing factory that went into operation in 1972. With a World Bank loan the capacity was subsequently doubled. More recently, the original factory was modernized, and the building of a second factory was financed by an EIB loan in combination with an EDF interest subsidy. The work was completed by early 1986.

CDC was established before independence in the part of Cameroon that was administered by Great Britain. When that part of Cameroon joined the federation in 1962, CDC became ineligible for financial support by the Commonwealth Development Corporation. CDC also faced adjustment problems because of a decline in the profitability of banana cultivation. EC support for palm oil came at a critical moment to support CDC's diversification policy. Both plantation and processing components were implemented more or less according to schedule. Oil palm has made positive contributions to overall CDC results. In contrast, other CDC activities have been much less successful (for example, tea, which also received EC support).

EC assistance for the Dibombari complex consisted of a high-yielding oil palm plantation (target 6,000 hectares), an outgrower's scheme (target 800 hectares), a processing factory, and village feeder roads. Establishment of the plantation took place from 1974 to 1977—according to schedule. The outgrower scheme was started in 1977 and completed in 1982. With 1,200 hectares, the acreage target was exceeded by 50 percent. The number of growers who participated (400) was much higher than foreseen. The first stage of the Dibombari oil mill was put into operation in 1979 and the second stage was completed by the end of 1984. Actual cost of the oil mill was below what was budgeted, and no serious problems were encountered.

According to an evaluation carried out at the end of 1984, the palm oil operations, financed by the EC, have in many respects been successful.[1] With 11,000 hectares established, they account for more than 20 percent of the present acreage in Cameroon. The physical targets (plantation and infrastructure) that were foreseen were usually attained and sometimes surpassed.

The palm oil operations have effectively contributed toward fulfilling the country's requirements for edible oils. The increase in export revenue has been modest, especially because the government has given priority to supplying the domestic market. Employment creation in a densely populated area has been significant: 1,350 workers are employed in the Dibombari complex. The outgrowers' scheme has improved the livelihood of smallholders in the project area. It has also encouraged them to rely less on shifting cultivation and thus has helped to slow down the process of deforestation and ecological degradation. However, the scheme has not been in operation long enough to judge whether there is any lasting positive environmental impact.

There have also been several weaknesses and problems. The Dibombari plantation has experienced a high turnover of labor. Plantation work is seen as an intermediate stage between work in the village and in the town (Douala). The SOCAPALM deserves credit for coping rather well with this problem. In contrast to the success the outgrowers' scheme has had with planting, the plots have been poorly maintained. The evaluation study referred to earlier recommended strengthening the extension services. The land tenure system has also given rise to some problems. It has been difficult to establish equitable compensation to the local communities for the plantation land. Outgrowers who, for one reason or another, discontinued their participation have been difficult to replace, and land tenure has also been a problem. A more thorough socioeconomic analysis of the project area might have reduced these problems but would also have delayed implementation.

On the whole, the positive contributions outweigh the problems so far. However, the long-term viability of the oil plantations depends mainly on the relative price of palm oil versus other edible oils. In 1987 the palm oil price hit a record low level, squeezing the cash flow of CDC and SOCAPALM, discouraging the outgrowers, and making the future look uncertain.

Coffee in Tanzania. Under the first Lomé Convention, signed in 1977, it was agreed to provide MECU 12.7 for the four-year Coffee Improvement Program (CIP), for which Tanzania would also contribute the equivalent of MECU 12, to be raised by a levy on coffee growers. The program was designed to raise production from the smallholder coffee growers by upgrading the extension services. The main component of both the EDF and local contribution, accounting for two-thirds of the total, was the supply of chemicals (pesticides), as well as mechanical inputs and equipment; the remaining one-third of the EDF financing covered vehicles for the extension services, feeder road improvement, the rehabilitation of coffee pulperies, the construction of a number of stores, and technical assistance.

The CIP was expected to help Tanzania increase extension service coverage (its target was 1 extension worker per 300 hectares, or 600–800 growers), and thereby lead to a gradual improvement in yields—so that by the end of the project, yields would be 30–50 percent higher (depending on the region) than the rather low levels (240–350 kilograms of coffee per hectare) obtained at the time. A total production increase of 23,000 tonnes of coffee was projected by the 1981–82 season. The organization was centered on the Coffee Marketing Board, subsequently to become the Coffee Authority of Tanzania (CAT), which in 1977 took over all the duties of the disbanded cooperative unions, including input delivery, extension services, and crop collection.

In 1982, under the second Lomé Convention, the two-year Coffee Development Program (CDP) was approved to strengthen coffee production in areas where performance in the earlier CIP had been poor—and also to establish a more effective institutional framework for implementation. Among the major changes was the increase in technical assistance personnel from three to an average of twelve, in order to cover local management and technician shortages. Whereas the CIP had simply provided a temporary injection of resources, the CDP emphasized the strengthening of all the critical aspects of coffee operations, including research, the training of extension officers, input delivery, the repair of CAT vehicles, and the rehabilitation of the Bukop processing factory. The EDF contribution per year was more than twice that during CIP (MECU 6.75 versus MECU 3.15). To increase effectiveness, a number of special conditions—for example, on coffee pricing and project accounting—were also negotiated.

Following an evaluation of CDP, it was agreed in 1984 that EDF support would be continued for another two years (to the amount of MECU 9.5), but with certain changes that can be summarized as follows:

- Imported inputs no longer included chemicals, but were concentrated on the purchase of mechanical inputs (notably hand pulpers for improving on-farm processing and hence coffee quality) and on equipment for smallholders, and for the first time an allocation also was included for equipment and spares to be sold to estates—both nationalized and private. The total allocation for inputs accounted for about one-half of the funds.
- Technical assistance personnel were further increased—to fourteen per year—and accounted for about one-third of the costs.
- More emphasis was given to research and training, with less for transport, and with no construction component.
- The government agreed to discuss with CEC any proposed changes in the institutional arrangements affecting the coffee industry and to ensure that CAT would have access to sufficient foreign exchange to obtain inputs.

Any assessment of EC support for coffee must take into account that producer prices for coffee in Tanzania were at historically high levels in 1976–77, and that they fell in real terms by about 50 percent during the following five years. Given this price trend and the fact that Tanzania's general economic situation deteriorated rapidly from 1979 onward, with severe foreign exchange shortages and the curtailment of many basic imports (fuel, fertilizers, and pesticides), the coffee industry faced an increasingly hostile general economic environment.

It must also be noted that from 1960 to 1976 smallholder production appeared to be on a long-term upward trend, with erratic fluctuations from year to year and between regions. By 1970, however, production from the estates, most of which had been nationalized in the late 1960s and early 1970s, had started to decline. For the three years, 1983–84 to 1985–86, average annual smallholder production was about 47,600 tonnes—7 percent higher than in 1975–76 to 1977–78, but 12 percent lower than in 1980–81 to 1982–83. Even allowing for the long gestation period of an extension-oriented project and some direct sales by producers of the north and west in neighboring countries, it is clear that production has not increased much since the program began. There is a difference in regional performance, suggesting that the actions have been more successful in the south than in the north and the west. However, the production rise in the south mainly reflects increased acreage (up 85 percent from 1977 to 1985, but not promoted under the EDF programs) and the absence of alternative cash crops. Yield, the main target variable of the programs, does not appear to have improved much.

The success with which any program is carried out inevitably depends to a considerable extent on the effectiveness of the institutional framework. The Coffee Authority of Tanzania (CAT)—a parastatal under the Ministry of Agriculture—was the nominated executing agency. Established only in 1977, following the dissolution of the cooperative unions, CAT was a new organization at the beginning of the CIP, yet it was responsible for the management of the entire coffee industry, including input supply, extension services, crop collection, processing, and marketing. Its total staff in 1980 was about 1,500—most of whom were employed in extension work and in buying posts and procurement offices throughout the widely dispersed coffee-growing regions. The management and financial control of this large new operation clearly presented enormous problems, given Tanzania's limited manpower resources.

As a parastatal, CAT was by no means autonomous: Coffee pricing decisions, for example, were taken by interministerial committees. The drawing up of CAT's annual plans and budgets was closely supervised by the Ministry of Agriculture. Clearly, given the complexity and coverage of the programs, the management and control of the operations posed a considerable administrative and communication problem. Several policy and management problems were more or less permanently present, particularly in the system of access to foreign exchange for CAT, the reform of the producer payment system (to include greater quality differentiation), and the reform of the producer levy system for recovering input costs.

In 1985 confusion and difficulties were arising from the policy of reintroducing cooperatives, which called for a total restructuring of the coffee industry, but was not discussed with CEC as explicitly requested in the special conditions of the CDP financing agreement. The changes have meant the dissolution of CAT and the distribution of its former functions to three institutions: the cooperatives for input supply and distribution, the Ministry of Agriculture for extension services, and the Tanzanian Coffee Marketing Board (TCMB) for transport, processing, and marketing. Many program-trained extension workers have been dismissed or transferred outside coffee areas. Confusion continued in 1986 and 1987, particularly on the distribution of responsibilities between the cooperatives and TCMB.

An evaluation conducted in 1986 concluded that the conception of the programs on a national scale, covering all smallholders, was too ambitious, given the large area to be covered, the huge distances between these areas, their different agricultural characteristics, and the weak administrative and technical capacity of the Tanzanian coffee operations.[2] Nor was the average annual EDF contribution of MECU 4 sufficient for the task of sustaining such a nationwide operation. The palm oil and cotton operations in Cameroon and Senegal were, in comparison, much more focused. These weaknesses have been amplified by an uncertain policy and institutional environment. Since 1986, however, there have been signs of greater consistency and decisiveness, that is, devaluations and sharp rises in coffee producer prices.

In summary, there is little evidence of a clear, positive impact on yields, but considering the unfavorable overall circumstances and the increased relative attractions to many farmers of the food crops for sale on unofficial local markets, the fact that smallholder coffee output has on average been above preprogram levels can be considered a modest success, which can probably be attributed largely to the delivery of crucial inputs. In this context, it should also be noted that the production of most other export crops declined sharply during the same period.

Irrigated Crop Development

The principal crop targeted for irrigation support was rice.

Irrigated rice in Senegal. Even before independence, Senegal was importing significant quantities of rice—first from Southeast Asia (Indochina) and later from Mali (Niger scheme). Rice imports steadily increased from about 100,000 tonnes in the early 1960s to more than 300,000 tonnes in the early 1980s. Especially at times when world rice prices were high (for example, 1974–75 and 1980–81), these imports constituted a heavy burden on the balance of payments. From 1981 to 1983 rice alone accounted for 10 percent of Senegal's commodity imports. Quite naturally, rice has been a target for import substitution.

Upland rice is traditionally produced in the Casamance area. However, yields there are low, and virtually all the rice is used for subsistence. Already in the 1960s, the EC supported this kind of rice cultivation, but the results were disappointing. The marketed surplus was hardly raised. Labor availability turned out to be one of the main constraints.

The greatest potential for irrigated rice production, in association with other corps, lies in the Senegal River Valley. More than 250,000 hectares are suitable for fully controlled irrigation, making it possible to produce more than 1 million tonnes of rice—an amount that largely exceeds import requirements. Up to now, however, despite sizable investments involving several donors, only a small fraction of the potential has been realized.

Three main operations that have been financed by the EC are the Nianga plain scheme, a large operation; the village irrigation perimeters around the Senegal River near Podor; and the intensive rice production project in eastern Senegal, which is a continuation of the development of the cotton-growing areas.

The background study on the Nianga scheme was done in 1968. The proposal to embank 9,000 hectares and to create 2,000 hectares of paddy fields under controlled flooding was approved in 1972. Shortly thereafter, however, it was decided to introduce fully controlled irrigation with double-cropping on a reduced area of 750 hectares. The EDF contribution of almost MECU 6 included the embankments, the pump station, the leveling of the land, and technical assistance. The complete management of the scheme (input supply, mechanization, marketing) has been carried out by the parastatal Société d'Amenagement et d'Exploitation des Terres du Delta (Senegal) (SAED). Inputs are provided on credit, and the cost is recovered through sales by the farmers to SAED. The main objective for the Nianga scheme was to have 600 farmers producing 5,000 tonnes of paddy per year.

Following the Sahelian drought of the early 1970s, a number of small village irrigation perimeters (VIPs) of 20–50 hectares were constructed along the Senegal River. The main objective of these schemes was to strengthen food security at the village level. The EDF finance of about MECU 8 covered 2,500 hectares, of which 900 hectares was part of the a program promoting small-scale projects. For these projects, the EDF financed equipment, material, and technical assistance; and SAED carried out the development work, with an important contribution by the farmers themselves (mainly labor). For the other part (1,600 hectares), EDF finance also included the land development work and training.

The concept of a VIP is that the water is pumped from the river with a small diesel pump and distributed through earthen canals with simple concrete division structures. Rice is grown in the rainy season mainly for subsistence; in the dry season, tomatoes, onions, and other vegetables are grown as cash crops. The area per farm household is 0.25 hectares, but sometimes households can benefit from more than one scheme. As with the large scheme, services and inputs are provided on a credit basis by SAED, but in this case management is left to the farmers.

It was mentioned above that the fourth EDF cotton area project also included rice production using the VIP approach. The latter project target was to develop 750 hectares for the double-cropping of rice. The fifth EDF project (MECU 4.7) for rice production in eastern Senegal was designed to consolidate and extend the cotton area development project. The project became more "integrated" and now took in animal traction development, village repair, and implement production workshops, as well as a literacy and health program. Again the farmers contributed by providing labor. SODEFITEX was responsible for the development and management of the scheme.

In 1985 a sectoral evaluation of EC-financed irrigation projects was carried out by the Dutch Institute for Land Reclamation and Improvement (ILRI).[3] The study covered projects in Senegal, Cameroon, Niger, Ethiopia, Burundi, and Madagascar. The rest of this section draws heavily on this study. As far as rice production is concerned, the results of the Nianga scheme are satisfactory, even though the initial targets have not been reached. A net irrigated area of 630 hectares was available from 1977—that is, within three years—and production reached 3,500 tonnes of paddy. Each farm household was allocated approximately 1 hectare of fully irrigated land. The financial results for the farmers have been quite favorable. However, this has only been possible through large subsidies on the cost of inputs and irrigation services (up to 60 percent). Furthermore, the farmers have not participated in the initial investment cost, or in the administrative overhead of SAED. The viability of the scheme, therefore, appears doubtful.

The progress of the village irrigation perimeters near the Senegal River has been satisfactory with regard to area, cropping intensity, and yields obtained (4.8 tonnes per hectare of paddy and 15 to 20 tonnes per hectare of tomatoes). Many farmers have been very motivated to participate because crop growing in the irrigation scheme is financially attractive. Nevertheless, for the irrigation parastatal SAED—and even for the VIP—there is still a sizable recurrent cost deficit, estimated at ECU 235 per hectare in 1985.

Because the VIPs are relatively new, it is still difficult to judge their long-term viability. Much will depend on the performance of paddy price, on the flexibility with respect to crop rotations, on the possibilities for integrating some livestock activities in the farming system, and on reducing the losses of SAED, or on making the schemes independent of SAED by allocating more tasks to the farmers. Experience with the village schemes on the Senegal River up to now has been, on the whole, satisfactory.

In contrast, the results of the small irrigation schemes in eastern Senegal have been disappointing. Area development has been far below its target. Progress has been slow, in part because the farmers have shown little interest and in some cases have been unwilling to execute their part of the work, in sharp contrast to the farmers in the Senegal River Valley. The cropping intensities on the reclaimed areas also have been below target, but the paddy yields obtained were satisfactory. The poor results in eastern Senegal cannot be blamed on the technical nature of the schemes or on water availability, and so the reasons must be sought elsewhere—for example, in the locations of the perimeters, which are often far from the villages. More important, according to the evaluation, the farmers had clearly indicated a preference for rainfed agriculture, whereas SODEFITEX had been strongly promoting rice production. Since the climate in the region generally permits modest, but acceptable, yields of cotton, sorghum, millet, and groundnuts, farmers did not feel obliged to introduce radical changes in their way of life.

When the project became integrated, irrigation was no longer the sole objective. The results for the other project components have been mixed. The literacy program and the introduction of animal traction have developed satisfactorily. The production of farm implements, however, has been difficult due to lack of raw materials and because the strong barter trade makes it difficult for blacksmiths to establish themselves. Results for the health component have also been less positive than anticipated.

The description of irrigated rice production in Senegal illustrates that a favorable social environment (that is, motivation and participation of the farmers—as in the VIP) and a demonstrated technical potential for rice cultivation (through the yields obtained) are important and necessary, but by no means sufficient conditions for a viable operation. For long-term viability, it must be possible to pay for real production costs and for maintenance of the investment without subsidizing input prices—unless there are important noneconomic objectives that can be financed from external resources.

Irrigated rice production on the Ninaga perimeter started in 1975—that is, at a time when world rice prices had risen by more than 400 percent over three years. Senegalese imports of rice were growing rapidly at exorbitant cost. Most of the EDF village irrigation perimeters became productive during 1981–84, when drought in the Sahel drastically cut the production levels of rainfed crops, particularly millet and sorghum, ensuring instant success. However, in 1985, and even more in 1986, the weather in the Sahel was more favorable for rainfed crops and also for livestock. At the same time, world rice prices were on a steep decline.

As a result of these developments, the policy problem in relation to rice production in Senegal has become formidable. At a time when the government is trying to reduce the deficit of the parastatals by charging the full cost of inputs and maintenance to the farmers, the price of rice imports has declined. Senegal must now decide whether to continue subsidizing rice cultivation—either explicitly, as in the past, or implicitly, by raising the tariff on rice imports—or whether to encourage alternative crops or activities.

The issue is further complicated by the fact that Senegal can import inexpensive broken rice, which fits the country's consumption patterns well. In considering tariff protection at the national level against cheap rice imports, the government must weigh the interests of close to 2.5 million urban dwellers against the interests of about 0.5 million people in the Senegal River area. Ecological issues must also be taken into account: Irrigated production will on the whole put less pressure on the physical environment than extensive cropping and grazing and thus preserve future resources. Regardless of how the government will cope with the policy problem at the national level, it is clear that the village schemes have better prospects than the large schemes—because their costs are lower and because they can be more readily integrated with other farm activities.

Irrigated rice in Cameroon. Investment in irrigated rice production in northern Cameroon started about 1970, after a long period of study and experimentation. Northern Cameroon belongs to the Sahelian climatic zone, with a long dry season (November to June) and a short wet season characterized by highly variable rainfall (400–600 millimeters). The region's border with Chad is formed by the Chari River and its tributary, the Logone, which drain part of southern Chad and the Central African Republic into Lake Chad and provide opportunities for irrigation. In 1971, the Société d'Expansion et de Modernisation de la Riziculture de Yagoua (Cameroon) (SEMRY) was founded as an autonomous public corporation, supervised by the Ministry of Agriculture, to manage the planned irrigation schemes. SEMRY I, comprising about 5,000 hectares, was established between 1972 and 1977; SEMRY II with 6,000 hectares, was installed during 1978–82. The bulk of the external finance for SEMRY I and II was provided by the World Bank and France.

The success of SEMRY I, the drought in the Sahel, and the record high prices of rice on the world market around 1975 provided strong arguments in favor of SEMRY III—and in 1978 the European Communities approved a first phase, costing ECU 4.7 million. SEMRY III is located in the Logone and Chari district, which is the most northerly district of Cameroon. Phase I was executed from 1979 to 1982. An interim phase was financed on a STABEX special project grant of ECU 1.1 million and implemented in 1983. By the end of 1983, approximately 800 hectares of irrigated land were available, together with the necessary infrastructure, including a rice mill. Financing for the second phase of SEMRY III (amounting to ECU 9 million) was approved in 1984. By the end of 1987, about 70 percent of these funds were disbursed, and the total irrigated area was about 1,800 hectares. This area is not continuous, but spread in 5 perimeters along the Logone and Chari over a distance of more than 100 kilometers. This characteristic has increased the cost of project follow-up. The fact that refugees from Chad have temporarily resided in the project area (1984) has not significantly delayed the progress of the project.

The specific objectives of the SEMRY III operations were to reduce the risk of famine in the extreme north of the country, increase the income of the peasant population in the district (by selling the marketed surplus of rice); improve the regional balance in the province; and contribute to the national availability of rice. These objectives are not only economic; to a large extent, they are also social (improving food security and regional balance). This is important for subsequent evaluation of the results.

Altogether, the EC provided ECU 15 million in support of irrigated rice production in the Logone and Chari district. For Lomé III, the district has been chosen as one of the areas of concentration, and the government has requested further EC support for consolidating and extending the SEMRY III operations. However, the circumstances in 1987 were quite different from those prevailing at the time of appraisal for Phase I (1975) or Phase II (1984). With the better rainfall in 1986 and 1987, the traditional crops were more abundant and the demand for rice fell. Moreover, cheap import rice had become available as a result of changes in the international markets. These circumstances make it difficult to formulate an economically viable extension of SEMRY III.

The SEMRY scheme, as it developed during the 1970s, introduced double-cropping, complete water control, and detailed management supervision. SEMRY is responsible for the mechanized preparation of land, the central nurseries, and the provision of inputs and irrigation water. Farmers are allocated individual plots (0.5 hectares for SEMRY I and II, 0.25 hectares for SEMRY III). Each season they build small dikes around their plots and carry out all crop operations, from transplanting to harvesting. A specific share of the paddy crop is sold at a guaranteed price to SEMRY. The cost of inputs advanced by SEMRY is then recovered. After processing the paddy into rice, SEMRY sells it on the national market.

Thanks to good farmer motivation, yields for SEMRY III have been high, close to ten tonnes of paddy per hectare over two seasons. The cropping intensity for the rainy season has generally been in excess of 80 percent. For the dry season, it has fluctuated between 20 and 70 percent. The original one-quarter hectare per family has been increased to one-third—so that 5,000 farm families, or almost 20 percent of the district's population, benefit from the scheme. The project clearly has improved food security in the district.

From a technical and management point of view, the three SEMRY irrigation schemes can undoubtedly be called successful. In 1985–86, they produced more than 100,000 tonnes of paddy, which accounted for 90 percent of Cameroon's production. The rice equivalent of the paddy significantly exceeds average rice imports over the past five years (around 30,000 tonnes, 1981–85). It looks as if Cameroon could easily become self-sufficient in rice. However, beneath the surface, it is not so clear whether this would be desirable.

In the past, the Upper North Province of Cameroon could export rice to Nigeria. Recently, these export possibilities were drastically reduced because of better harvests and import restrictions in Nigeria. To transport SEMRY rice to the main Cameroon consumption centers, Douala and Yaoundé, is an expensive and difficult undertaking because of the long distances and bad transport conditions. At present, the c.i.f. Douala price of imported rice is extremely low. Furthermore, better rainfall in the Sahelian region since 1985 has increased the availability of traditional staple foods, particularly sorghum and millet. As a result, SEMRY farmers need to keep less rice for subsistence, and they obtain a low price for what they try to sell on open markets. Thus a blessing for the region leads to drawbacks for the irrigation projects.

SEMRY is now facing a shortage of rice milling capacity so that large quantities of paddy must be stored (around 100,000 tonnes beginning in 1987), and the quality of rice is going down (large share of brokens), which makes marketing even more difficult. These problems have led to increasingly high losses (about MECU 1 for the 1986–87 season for SEMRY III)—a situation that is certainly not sustainable. Especially in view of a possible extension of SEMRY III, it is worthwhile to digress briefly on actions that could be taken to alleviate these problems.

At the local level, some of the problems could be reduced by extending the milling and storage capacity; restricting rice production to the wet season, when variable production cost is lowest (however, average fixed cost will increase); diversifying the cropping pattern (perhaps growing vegetables for export); diminishing the farmgate price (farm income would not go down because revenue from nonirrigated crops and livestock would be higher); allocating more of the tasks to the farmers to reduce costs (for example, using animal traction for land preparation); and introducing cheaper technology (this appears to be difficult for the expensive element of pumping).

At the national level, most of the measures that can be considered imply some form of protection of the rice market—by tariffs, quota, or, as is already done, by so-called twinning (that is, requiring traders to buy locally at production cost a certain quantity of rice for each ton that they import). Clearly, protection measures imply a loss of welfare for rice consumers in urban areas and a danger of fostering inefficient production if world market prices recover.

There are also some noneconomic questions to consider when dealing with the rice issue in Cameroon. As already mentioned, SEMRY III had two important social objectives—to protect the population from famine and to redress income inequality in the region—but other noneconomic objectives could be added, such as preserving the environment or preventing people from migrating by providing a livelihood. To the extent that a country is willing to pursue such objectives it should also be willing to pay the cost in reduced economic benefits in other regions or for other population groups. Such choices are difficult to make.

Integrated Rural Development Projects

By the 1960s, certain districts in the Upper North Province of Cameroon had very high population densities, in excess of 100 people—sometimes even more than 200 people—per square kilometer. In a semiarid environment dominated by subsistence agriculture, such densities imply a high vulnerability to famine. In contrast, the northeastern part of the Bénoué district, because of its relative isolation, was underpopulated, with fewer than 5 people per square kilometer, and since the 1950s there had been some spontaneous migration toward the region. To improve the regional population balance, the Cameroonian government decided to encourage and support this migration.

Northeast Bénoué, Cameroon. The integrated rural development project in the northeastern part of the Bénoué district has been carried out over three phases, starting in 1973. Two-thirds of the financing, or MECU 25, was provided by the EC. External contributions also included French and NGO participation (mainly for the health component). Complementary food aid for arriving migrants has been provided by the World Food Program (WFP).

The main objective of the project has been to help the migrants settle and earn a living in a new environment. The project includes basic economic infrastructure (bridges, access roads, village water supply); social infrastructure (schools, dispensaries, village pharmacies); intensification of food production (animal traction, improved seed, inputs); extension for cash crops, particularly cotton (carried out by the Société de Développement du Coton [Cameroon], (SODECOTON); support for farm associations; and reforestation.

Throughout Phases I and II (1973–78 and 1979–82, respectively) the project area was 6,700 square kilometers. With the third phase (1983–86) the area was increased to 11,000 square kilometers. During that phase, a separate project was started to support fisheries on the 700-square-kilometer Lagdo Lake, which was formed after completion of a dam on the Bénoué River (financed by China) in 1981. All three phases, as well as the fisheries project, have had a sizable input of technical assistance. In 1983, the project staff consisted of sixteen expatriates, including ten from the participating NGOs, plus eleven Cameroonian staff. The fisheries project has another three expatriate staff.

Organized migration into the project area between 1973 and 1986 amounted to approximately 42,000 persons, to which should be added the spontaneous migration, estimated at 34,000 persons. Taking into account the effect of natural growth, the population of the extended area went up from 70,000 in 1972 to almost 170,000 by the end of 1986. In recent years spontaneous migration has reached high levels (probably 7,000 in 1986—partly as a result of drought conditions in exit areas) and has made it necessary to stop support for organized migration. According to recent estimates, the agricultural potential of the region would allow a further population increase of 150,000–200,000 persons.

The main physical targets of the project have been achieved without great delays. The social components of the project, particularly schooling and medical care, are generally considered a success, thanks mainly to the important input of NGO volunteers. Agricultural production targets were exceeded for cotton because of the good extension effort of SODECOTON. However, production targets for food crops were not reached; nevertheless, food availability has kept pace with population growth.

The fish catch on Lagdo Lake greatly exceeds expectations based on experience in other African countries. Production went up from 2,500 tonnes in 1983 to an estimated 10,000 tonnes for 1986. This production contributes significantly to the animal protein availability in the Northern Province (of which Bénoué district is a part) and to the livelihood of approximately 2,500 fishermen and their families. It is expected that maximum sustainable production will be reached in 1988. The growth of fisheries production cannot be attributed solely to the presence of the project—since it started only in 1985. However, the project can have an important impact on the economically and environmentally sustainable exploitation of this natural resource.

The Bénoué project has faced a number of difficulties. Migration and resettlement is a socially and economically delicate process, and there are many examples of complete failure. In addition, some people are reluctant to leave the densely populated areas, and those arriving in the destination area run into problems with land tenure. Nevertheless—despite the limited success so far with food production—good results with some cash crops and fisheries and, above all, the extensive social and economic infrastructure that has been put in place and maintained imply that the project is supporting a viable operation.

Iringa: Tanzania. In 1972, to strengthen the development of the regions, the government of Tanzania introduced measures to decentralize their administration. Donors were invited to provide assistance at the regional level through integrated rural development projects. The first project of this nature was implemented by the World Bank in Kigoma region starting in 1974. Others were carried out by Germany (Tanga), USAID (Arusha), the United Kingdom (Lindi/Mtwara), and Japan (Kilimanjaro). Iringa region was assigned to the EC. The Iringa region agricultural development project was carried out in two phases: The first, financed under Lomé I, covered 1977–81, and the second, financed under Lomé II, covered 1982–86.

Iringa region is part of the Southern Highlands and covers an area of almost 60,000 square kilometers and has an estimated population of 1.3 million (1987). Access to the region from Dar es Salaam is easy because of the TANZAM highway and the TAZARA railroad. Within the region, however, access to particular districts is problematic because of insufficient infrastructure and maintenance. Agriculture is dominated by approximately 200,000 smallholders growing mainly maize, sorghum, and beans. The cultivated area per farm is between 1 and 3 hectares. Export crops include tobacco, pyrethrum, and tea. Currently only 7 percent of the total land area is cultivated, although an estimated 25–30 percent is very fertile. Thus there is considerable potential for expanding production.

The financing agreement of MECU 6.6 for Phase I was signed in 1977. No Tanzanian counterpart funding was foreseen. The main components were technical assistance (25 percent) and infrastructure (45 percent for stores, workshops, pyrethrum driers, and feeder roads). Smaller provisions were made for extension, oxen equipment, fertilizer, seeds, insecticide, water supply, dairy cattle, and reforestation.

Execution of the project was seriously hampered by delays in the arrival of equipment and by frequent changes in counterpart staff. Nevertheless, by mid-1981 most of the physical targets had been reached. However, an evaluation report of Phase I concluded that the project's effect on farming in the region was limited.[4] The overemphasis on physical targets had prevented the technical assistance from establishing adequate working relations with local government agencies and farmers. The program to increase the use of oxen with 5,000 pairs of oxen trained to plow the land was well received, but due to lack of complementary equipment, its impact on production was small. Most important, the profitability of the production mix (especially sunflower and pyrethrum) that was extended declined and turned out to be so low that farmers were unable to refund inputs on obtained credit. Revolving funds could not be established. Oxen training centers, dip tanks, and dairy units also faced management problems.

Despite the difficulties encountered in Phase I, the major objective—to increase agricultural production and living standards for smallholders in a region with considerable potential—certainly was consistent with Tanzanian as well as EC priorities. A second phase was agreed upon in 1982, again for four years. The Phase II project was, on the whole, more realistic than Phase I. Its targets were less ambitious, and the level of financial commitment was more significant (MECU 21.3 as compared with MECU 6.6). The project components had two important additions: more attention for livestock development (dipping and veterinary services and dairy production) and a small irrigation project (fifteen village systems).

Another important change from Phase I to II was the extension of project activities from seven areas of concentration (approximately 15,000 square kilometers) to the whole region (60,000 square kilometers). This was in response to an explicit Tanzanian demand to maintain an overall balance among the districts, but it meant that the project's resources, especially the input and implement components, had to be spread too thinly for any visible effect. Phase II, unlike Phase I, contained a government contribution (MECU 1.1) that was to be financed from food aid counterpart funds and a contribution from the Tanzania Pyrethrum Board (MECU 0.9).

The first two years of Phase II continued the focus on physical targets, as Phase I had. Some of the more important achievements were the improvement of the regional road network by upgrading and maintaining feeder roads, including the construction of twenty-eight bridges; the construction of another twelve village warehouses (in addition to the twenty-eight of Phase I), which responded to a clearly expressed need; the rehabilitation and construction of eighty-eight dip tanks; and the establishment of four oxen training centers. During Phase II, supply of complementary implements and inputs for the farm support program was better organized than during Phase I.

Midway through Phase II (1984), following an internal review and with the approval of the government as well as the European Communities, an important realignment of activities took place. These changes occurred against the background of the government's new agricultural policy. The realignment was centered along three axes: Extension and land-use planning activities were concentrated on eleven agroecological zones (and "safe land use" was introduced in those zones); a regional survey of resources was used to prepare a detailed regional development plan; and the general farm support program was phased out.

The planning exercise was not part of the original scheme and was in effect a different sort of project. It was added because of the need for more baseline and monitoring data. However, it came too late to be useful for the project itself, and it diverted attention from regular activities. The decision to focus on specific zones again was in reaction to the difficulties of carrying out a large set of activities over a vast region; it was a return to the Phase I strategy, which was meant to increase the impact and visibility of the project.

Project activities were in effect closed down by mid-1986. An evaluation carried out at that time criticized the project for its lack of design, for insufficient monitoring provisions, and most strongly for the fact that it was set up and managed as a separate institution, with only small links to the regional development authorities and farmers.[5]

The planning exercise carried out toward the end was considered to be done in a hurried, top-down way without enough local involvement. But some of the physical results were judged successful: the warehouses, the road improvements, and the village nurseries for reforestation (some of which were installed by NGO projects).

In view of the similar problems encountered in other regions of Tanzania, the above criticisms appear to be somewhat exaggerated. Any assessment should also take into account the following local conditions: the macroeconomic deterioration throughout most of the project period; the frequent institutional changes (villagization, communal production, redefinition of the role of parastatals and cooperatives); a policy environment that discouraged marketed production through official channels and reduced the profitability of export crops; and the complexity and diversity of the project components and the limited resources in relation to the tasks, especially when the project area was extended in Phase II.

It is rather doubtful that better project design and planning could have offset the negative effects of the above factors. Nevertheless, more clearly circumscribed objectives (for example, concentrating on the dominant staple food, maize) might have produced more sustainable results despite all the difficulties of the Tanzanian institutional and economic context.

Small-Scale Projects

Micro project programs. To respond in a practical way to the needs of local communities, Lomé I introduced financing for what are known as micro projects. These are normally carried out in rural areas and must be undertaken on the initiative and with the active participation of the local community.

Micro projects have to be grouped into programs that are submitted for approval to the EC. Financing decisions on individual projects are then taken by the beneficiary country in agreement with CEC through a simple procedure. In view of the success of this form of assistance, which was experimental under Lomé I, its scope has been enlarged under Lomé II and III. Since Lomé II there has been no limit on the overall amount (within programmable resources) that a country may spend in micro projects. The one stipulation is that the combined contribution of the government and the local community must be at least equal to the amount requested from the EDF. The ceiling for this amount has been increased from ECU 75,000 (Lomé I) to ECU 150,000 (Lomé II), and ECU 250,000 (Lomé III).

Of the three countries under consideration, Senegal has made the most use of the micro projects facility. A first program for Senegal, amounting to MECU 0.3, was approved under Lomé I and was used for a variety of small activities: vegetable growing, the provision of agricultural equipment for young farmers, livestock vaccination, and village water supply. Under Lomé II, seven subsequent programs have been implemented for a total value of MECU 4.3. A great variety of actions have been financed—ranging from a delivery of irrigation equipment (ECU 14,000) to the rehabilitation of banana production in the Casamance region (ECU 820,000). A large amount (ECU 440,000 from the second program and almost ECU 600,000 from the fourth) was allocated as complementary finance for the village irrigation perimeters near Podor on the Senegal River.

In the case of Tanzania two micro project programs were implemented under Lomé II, amounting to MECU 1.5. In contrast to Senegal, Tanzania has nominated a single executing agency: the Communities Development Trust Fund (CDTF), which is supervised by the prime minister's office. Technical assistance (one expatriate) was provided to help CDTF manage the programs. Altogether more than one hundred projects have been financed under the two programs. The average EC contribution has been about ECU 15,000. The most important actions financed have been concerned with village water supply, livestock development, grain processing, and equipment for an agricultural school. In some cases, projects were cofinanced from food aid counterpart funds.

In Cameroon, micro projects were used only on a limited scale, with three relatively small programs amounting to MECU 0.7 together. They focused mainly on rural roads and village water supply, agricultural production, and food storage.

Because of the wide geographic and sectoral dispersion of micro projects it is hardly possible to describe results and judge their viability. Some evaluation studies, dealing with a sample of projects, were carried out, particularly for Lomé I in Cameroon and Senegal.[6] Micro projects vary greatly, both within and across countries, which makes it difficult to reach firm conclusions. Nevertheless, the experience in Cameroon, Senegal, and Tanzania supports a few general observations. First, micro projects can be used to complement other activities, as this reduces the cost of follow-up and management (note, for example, the success of the VIPs in Senegal). Second, it is desirable to concentrate micro projects geographically. And, third, the supervision of micro projects is greatly facilitated when a specific agency is made responsible for the management; such an agency will then require some technical assistance (as in the case of the arrangement with the CDTF in Tanzania).

Nongovernmental projects. In recent years, NGOs have had a larger role in EC development cooperation, principally in four kinds of actions: food aid (mainly project and emergency food aid), emergency aid (apart from food), refugee aid, and small-scale development projects. This section concentrates on their role in development projects.

Recently, EC aid disbursement through NGOs totaled about MECU 140 per year. Since 1976, the annual EC budget has included an allocation for the cofinancing of projects with NGOs, and the allocation has steadily increased—from MECU 2.5 in 1976 to MECU 62 in 1987. More than 500 European-based NGOs are involved in these activities. On average, the EC contribution is 40 percent of the project cost.

For the period 1976–87, some cumulative data are as follows:

	EC Financial Support (MECU)	Number of Projects	ECUs per Project
Cameroon	3.7	76	49,000
Senegal	5.3	92	58,000
Tanzania	5.8	115	50,000

The NGO-cofinanced projects have focused on providing social and economic infrastructure for local communities in rural areas. NGO projects have been similar in content to micro projects. Both rely on the direct participation of local communities. However, the developments described above also show some differences. Micro projects tend to be less import-intensive and to have less of a Western technology bias; micro projects are also more directly involved with the population. In contrast, NGO projects virtually always have an expatriate input. NGO projects tend to be better organized and technically more efficient, but also more expensive; they generally have a training component; they are often more innovative (socially as well as technically), but sometimes experimental; and because NGO projects are cofinanced, there is a multiplier effect on the use of EC aid funds (currently this multiplier is 2.5).

Both NGO projects and micro projects constitute a useful complement to normal projects, mainly because they focus on direct improvements of the living conditions of local communities and because they rely on community participation. From the point of view of managing development resources, the small size of such projects and the fact that they are widely dispersed can be a disadvantage. Consequently, small projects need to focus on a certain theme or kind of intervention that is relatively easy to supervise and manage. Some thought should also be given to linking the two kinds of small-scale projects.

Food Aid

EC food aid started toward the end of the 1960s and increased considerably during the world food crisis (1972–74), at which time the EC became the second most important food donor after the United States. Since 1975, food aid has accounted for about one-quarter of total EC aid disbursements. Its budgetary value is expressed at world market prices and is not influenced by internal EC price setting—the difference being charged to the agricultural budget. In recent years the value of EC food aid has been upward of ECU 500 million.

Neither Senegal nor Tanzania have been among the big food aid recipients. Nevertheless, the cumulative value of EC food aid is important: more than MECU 50 for Senegal and more than MECU 60 for Tanzania, counting only direct aid (that is, food aid allocated to governments, which amounts to approximately 75 percent of the total). Indirect aid is handled by international or nongovernmental organizations and is generally for projects or emergency cases. The rest of this section deals with EC food aid for Senegal and Tanzania. Both countries illustrate how food aid has gradually been adapted in a variety of ways from an instrument of surplus disposal to a resource for development that complements other resources and contributes to food security. Cameroon, apart from some shipments via NGOs and an emergency allocation to cope with drought in the Upper North in 1971, did not receive significant amounts of food aid. Indirectly, Cameroon was involved through deliveries for Chad that were bought from SEMRY in 1985.

Food Aid to Senegal

Senegal has long been a large importer of food. Since the beginning of the 1970s, imports have accounted for 40 to 50 percent of the supply of cereals, the dominant staple food. Average annual cereal imports for 1981–85 have been about 530,000 tonnes. An all-time high of 600,000 tonnes was reached in 1984. Recently, however, the growth appears to have leveled off, even though it is too early to judge whether the long-term trend has changed. The main explanations for this dependence on food imports are historical, climatic, and geographic. The division of labor within the French colonial empire was based on groundnut exports from Senegal and imports of rice from Indochina. The population was concentrated near the ports, and so cereal imports were relatively cheap and easy to deliver. Urban, and to some extent rural, consumption became dominated by imported rice and to a lesser degree by imported wheat. Other cereals, particularly maize and millet, the main traditional staples, were imported in years of crop failure.

Only after 1973–74 did food aid become a significant part of imports. Gradually, the share of food aid within total cereal imports went up from less than 15 percent to almost 25 percent in recent years. The commodity composition of food aid has differed from that of commercial imports, with relatively large shares of wheat and coarse grains in comparison with rice. For fourteen consecutive years, up to 1985, Senegal received direct EC cereal food aid. The EC contribution to total cereal food aid to Senegal declined from more than 20 percent in the 1970s to about 15 percent in recent years. One could say that EC food aid paved the way for food aid by some other donors. Maize and wheat have dominated EC aid with respect to quantity, each accounting for 37 percent of the total, whereas sorghum and rice each represent 13 percent of the total. Rice, maize, and sorghum have generally been distributed free, whereas wheat has been sold to the milling industry, with the receipts credited to a counterpart fund.

Apart from cereals, Senegal also imports sizable amounts of dairy products. Between 1981 and 1985 average imports of dried skimmed milk were 15,000 tonnes. Most of this was used to produce reconstituted milk for urban areas. Food aid accounts for only 10 percent of this quantity, implying there is a strong effective demand for milk in Senegal. Dairy product food aid has been dominated by the EC.

Indirect food aid, mostly through NGOs and in the form of dairy products, has also been important—mainly in nutritional and food-for-work projects, particularly for vulnerable groups. In some cases, NGOs have carried out long-term programs. For example, for almost ten years, SOS SAHEL has run a well-organized program of supplementary feeding for schoolchildren and lactating mothers. Apart from its nutritional benefits, the program has also increased school attendance.

But EC food aid operations in Senegal, particularly the free distribution of direct aid, have been criticized for various shortcomings. An evaluation study carried out in 1982 observed that, even though free distribution generally focused on the vulnerable populations in rural areas, its effectiveness often was limited by organizational and logistical problems:[7] the difficulty of reaching outlying regions, excessive distribution at harvest time, high transport cost (to be paid by being deducted from the amount that is freely distributed), and illegal export to neighboring countries. The study's main recommendations were that free distribution should be limited to exceptional situations, counterpart funds should be integrated with food strategies and policies, and delivery should be c.i.f. rather than f.o.b.

The most important recent development has been the establishment in 1985 of a joint (multidonor) counterpart fund (fonds commun de revente: FCR). The agreement on the FCR was reached after almost two years of negotiations. Before 1985, each food aid donor had separate rules and the funds were usually allocated in a rather ad hoc way—mostly financing the Senegalese contribution to bilateral projects, and, in the case of EC aid, often the international transport cost. The FCR was conceived to support the Cereals Plan, a component of the New Agricultural Policy launched by the Senegalese government in 1984. The main objectives of the fund are to support the farmgate prices of cereals, strengthen rural grain storage, and encourage the consumption of local cereals.

In 1985 a two-year interim program for the FCR was agreed upon, focusing on agricultural input delivery and seed production. Because its implementation was not satisfactory, the donors insisted on a medium-term program that would be more directly linked to the cereal policy and would benefit farmers rather than parastatals. It was agreed that for the 1986–87 season, most of the available funds (70 percent) would be allocated to the marketing of local cereals, including transport from surplus to deficit regions.

The overall cereal situation at the end of 1986 did not warrant additional food shipments. Therefore, the EC decided to replace the equivalent of 10,000 tonnnes of cereals by a direct foreign exchange grant to the FCR. This substitution operation provided further support for the marketing of local cereals (particularly millet and sorghum).

Even though the setting up of a joint counterpart fund can be considered an important step in using food aid as a resource for development, the experience has not been entirely positive. So far, the EC members have been the only donors to put all their counterpart funds in the common basket and, as a result, together are by far the largest contributor (60 percent). Other contributions come from Canada, Germany, France, the Netherlands, and Japan.

Although it is open to the EC to conduct triangular food aid operations—that is, to buy food in a developing country for shipment to a (neighboring) country asking for food aid—the production and logistical conditions within the Sahel are such that the potential for organizing triangular food and thus stimulating regional food trade are rather limited. Most countries have surpluses of similar corps (millet and sorghum) at the same time. Clearly, there is more scope for developing trade between Sahelian countries and coastal countries. As early as 1982 the EC decided to buy 14,000 tonnes of millet in Senegal for delivery to Chad and Niger. Buying the grain and shipping it to Douala and Lomé turned out to be relatively easy, but the further transportation to landlocked Chad and Niger was very difficult and costly. Apart from 11,000 tonnes of sorghum delivered from Thailand in 1985, there have been no triangular food aid operations with cereals going to Senegal.

Food Aid to Tanzania

The differences between the agricultural economies of Tanzania and Senegal have important implications for the role and handling of food aid in Sub-Saharan Africa. Unlike Senegal, Tanzania has not been a big food importer. Its agricultural production capacity in relation to its population is vast, and even though certain regions are facing land degradation, this bears no comparison with the advance of the desert in Senegal. In fact, up to the early 1970s, Tanzania exported significant quantities of maize and even rice. Until about the same time, only wheat was imported regularly, while limited amounts of other cereals were imported occasionally to make up for fluctuations in yield. Imports of cereals suddenly rose to more than 400,000 tonnes in 1973–74, when Tanzania experienced a bad drought and for the first time received massive food aid. Adverse weather conditions also prevailed in 1981 and 1982 and led to high food imports. Nevertheless, it has not been the weather, but the need to feed a rapidly growing urban population, combined with stagnating marketed production, that has made Tanzania into a structural food importer. Among the underlying causes of this trend have been a strong deterioration of production incentives and an inefficient marketing and transport system.

The share of food aid in total cereal imports has been much higher in the case of Tanzania than in that of Senegal. Between 1981 and 1985, average cereal imports were almost 300,000 tonnes, of which two-thirds were provided as food aid. Senegal had to import much more on commercial terms. Over the same period, the share of direct EC food aid in total cereal food aid was somewhat above 10 percent.

The most important component of total cereal food aid has been maize (43 percent) followed by rice (33 percent) and wheat (24 percent). In the case of EC cereal aid, the share of maize is higher (65 percent), reflecting an attempt to deliver goods that correspond to the normal consumption pattern, partly through triangular operations. Three triangular shipments of white maize were decided: from Zimbabwe in 1981, and from Malawi in 1984 and 1986.

Imports of dairy products largely consist of dried skimmed milk and butter oil to make reconstituted milk for consumption in urban areas. There are few data on commercial imports, but one can assume that they declined over the past decade because foreign exchange was scarce. The European Communities provide the bulk of dairy product food aid—both as direct aid and as indirect aid—for NGOs or international organizations (particularly WFP).

A distinction between the EC food aid to Tanzania and Senegal is that there have been no free distribution programs in the case of Tanzania, where all direct food aid is handled by parastatals—cereals by the National Milling Company (NMC), dairy products by the Livestock Development Authority (LIDA) as well as Tanzania Dairies Limited (TDL). Since 1975 the receipts (after the deduction of handling cost) have had to be transferred to the Central Bank. The conditions stipulated that the counterpart funds would be allocated through the development budget to agricultural projects (livestock projects in the case of the dairy aid). Information on these projects was only required afterward. In 1981, less than one-third of the accumulated value of NMC food and grain sales had been used to finance development operations. A small sum (T Sh 2 million—approximately ECU 110,000) was provided as cofinance for the Iringa project. One of the reasons for the Central Bank to hold back counterpart fund money was the huge overdraft of NMC (close to T Sh 2 billion). The situation for dairy products sold by LIDA was more or less similar.

In 1982 the Commission of the EC started negotiations with the Tanzanian government with a view to improving the management of counterpart funds. These discussions were parallel to the food strategy initiative and to the efforts elsewhere to integrate EC food aid into cooperation on agricultural development. In 1984 a memorandum of understanding was signed stipulating that food aid deliveries were to be sold to an administering agency (such as NMC) at a price corresponding to the c.i.f. price in Tanzania of commodities of similar quality bought on the world market; the proceeds of the sale were to be lodged in a special account with the National Bank of Commerce (rather than the Central Bank), and the fund used in financing agricultural development projects to be agreed upon in advance jointly by the Tanzanian government and the CEC. Although the agreement did not prescribe the time lags for depositing and disbursing the money and did not touch upon the issue of interest payments, it represented an important step forward. In 1985, a committee with representatives from three ministries (agriculture, finance, planning), the Cooperative Rural Development Bank, and the CEC was formed to supervise and recommend expenditures from the counterpart fund.

The agreed priority areas for spending were in line with the recommendations of the National Food Strategy study that had been prepared by the Ministry of Agriculture and completed in 1984: promoting food production in outlying areas, strengthening input delivery systems and agricultural research, improving agricultural data, and reducing postharvest losses and improving storage conditions.

A recent evaluation concluded that the counterpart fund is functioning reasonably well.[8] Gradually, payments into the fund have become more prompt. The disbursement of approved funds has also been speeded up, although it is still rather slow. The main weakness lies in the capacity to formulate and follow up projects. However, the fact that there is prior discussion on the allocation of funds rather than simply notification afterwards is a significant achievement.

Assessment

The EC food aid programs in Senegal and Tanzania have evolved from an ad hoc response to government requests for help toward the setting up of mechanisms to use food aid as a resource for development in coordination with other development actions. This strategy works only if the food shipments are well planned (with respect to the timing, kind, and quality of the product) in relation to the crop situation and other imports, and if the food products are sold at a normal market price. Once these conditions are fulfilled, it is up to the management of the counterpart funds to ensure that the food aid has the desirable effect on development. The allocation of counterpart funds makes it possible to target the resource transfer embodied in food aid. In Senegal, as well as in Tanzania, there has been significant progress with respect to the management of counterpart funds.

Because of the fungibility of monetized aid resources, including food aid, the management of counterpart funds should emphasize sound advance planning and monitoring of the actions and avoid a pure accounting appraisal, which usually amounts to drawing up a list of past activities. The arrangements now in place in both Senegal and Tanzania are satisfactory except for the lack of an administrative capacity to formulate and follow up projects.

It also appears that in both Senegal and Tanzania indirect food aid via NGOs is directed toward the most vulnerable groups. However, local NGOs need to be better trained in the handling of food aid (storage, transport, and processing).

STABEX

Basic Rules of the System

The STABEX system—which was designed to mitigate the adverse effects of fluctuations in export earnings—has been in operation since the first Lomé Convention (1975) but was improved under the second and third conventions. In essence, STABEX compensates for shortfalls in export earnings for tropical agricultural products on the EC market. For some countries that traditionally have had only limited trade with the EC and that would otherwise hardly ever benefit from the system, exports to all destinations are covered. At present, thirteen countries are in this situation (Ethiopia being the largest).

Transfers to compensate for shortfalls in earnings are normally determined on a commodity-by-commodity basis. In several cases, however, primary commodities and those produced by the first stage of processing are both covered, and such related commodities may be aggregated. This treatment is distinct from the International Monetary Fund's Compensatory Financing Facility, which compensates on the basis of the total export position. The justification for the STABEX practice is that, in principle, the compensation should serve to restore financial flows in the specific sector hit by the shortfall.

Earnings can be affected by international price movements as well as quantity changes. Quantity fluctuations are usually the result of domestic problems (for example, a crop failure or processing bottlenecks), although they may also arise from international factors.

Two basic conditions must be fulfilled to trigger a STABEX transfer for a specific product (or group of related products). First, the country's exports must depend significantly on the particular product; that is to say, the share of the product in the total value of export goods must exceed a dependence threshold (export to all destinations). Second, the percentage shortfall of export earnings in the year of application, when compared with the average of the four preceding years (that is, the reference level), must exceed the fluctuation threshold (the export normally to the EC).

Under the third Lomé Convention, the dependence and fluctuation thresholds are both 6 percent, except for the landlocked, insular, and poorest countries, for which they are 1.5 percent. In fact, the "normal" 6 percent applies only to thirteen of the sixty-six ACP countries. Both Cameroon and Senegal belong to this group, whereas Tanzania is part of the group of poorest countries.

Normally, the transfer payment covers the full shortfall between exports for the application year and the reference level. However, if there are significant changes in the ratios between production, marketed production, export to all destinations, and exports to the EC, the transfer may be reduced. As a rule, the kind of change that would warrant a reduction would be one precipitated by circumstances within the control of the countries concerned.

There is a large degree of freedom on the use of the funds. The convention stipulates that transfers must be devoted to maintaining financial flows in the sector hit by the shortfall or to diversification. The transfer request must include information on the specific actions to which the funds will be allocated. Within a year of the signing of the transfer agreement, the ACP state must submit a report on the actual use of the funds, including an assessment of the impact of the allocation.

If the circumstances that led to a transfer improve significantly, the beneficiary country must repay the funds. This replenishment obligation contributes to future STABEX resources and increases the sustainability of the system. The poorest countries are exempted, so the transfers for them are always grants. At present, forty-three of the sixty-six ACP states are in this category. Even for countries that must contribute to the replenishment, the conditions are such that there is still an important grant element. The question of whether a transfer must be repaid is examined in the year following the year when the payment was made and the answer is arrived at by comparing the preceding year with averages for its four previous years. Both unit values and quantities exported must have recovered, and earnings must have increased by at least 6 percent. If these three conditions are fulfilled, the repayment obligation is determined as the difference between earnings for the control year and the four-year average, without exceeding the value of the original transfer.

Actual repayment is spread over five years, preceded by a two-year grace period. No interest is charged. Repayment conditions are checked over a period of seven years, after which there is no further obligation to replenish. It is possible to use a new transfer in whole or in part for repayment. Furthermore, the third Lomé Convention made it is possible to replenish in local currency, which can be used as counterpart money for EDF-financed projects.

Currency fluctuations can create a special problem for the system. The implicit principle of STABEX is to compensate for losses in local currency. Therefore the basis of calculation is the local currency (f.o.b.) export value. But the actual payment is in ECU—so that the exchange rate is important in deriving the value of the transfer. Under Lomé III, shifts in exchange rate between the reference period and the application year are restricted to 10 percent upward or downward (tunnel method).

STABEX is designed to be a quickly disbursing support facility. Therefore the procedures are carried out within a strict time schedule. Requests for a particular year must be submitted during the first quarter of the following year and, except for cases where cross-checking is difficult, the CEC makes its decision before the end of July. Upon receiving information from the beneficiary country on the use of the funds, a transfer agreement is signed, and funds are released almost automatically. There is also a possibility of advance payment in the course of the application year or later. The smooth and rapid functioning of the system, particularly for the payment of advances, depends on a regular flow of information from the ACP country to the CEC.

STABEX in Cameroon

Up to 1987 Cameroon has received approximately MECU 34 worth of STABEX transfers (see table 7-1). Under Lomé I, two transfers were paid: one for wood, amounting to MECU 3.6; and a small one for cocoa paste, amounting to about MECU 0.5. Important STABEX transfers in favor of Cameroon were granted for the application year 1981 (MECU 9.1 for coffee and MECU 8.1 for cocoa). Unfortunately, 1981 was a crisis year: World commodity prices were at extremely low levels, and the overall value of approved STABEX claims far exceeded the resources of the system for that year (less than 50 percent of the claims were covered). Almost all transfer claims had to be reduced. As a partial compensation for the lack of funds, a special project grant of MECU 40 was approved in 1982. Out of that grant, Cameroon received MECU 1.5 for coffee and MECU 2.3 for cocoa products.

After 1982, mainly because the bad years 1980 and 1981 were included in the reference period, the total value of STABEX transfer claims decreased drastically, so that when the Lomé II STABEX accounts were closed in 1986, a surplus remained that was used to further compensate for the lack of resources in 1980 and 1981. Consequently, Cameroon was allocated another MECU 3.5 for coffee and MECU 5.2 for cocoa products–making its total for the 1981 application year MECU 14 for coffee and MECU 15.5 for cocoa. Most of the 1981 transfers were used to finance agricultural inputs and rural roads, as well as to support the cooperative movement.

Cameroon did not benefit from STABEX transfers for the application years 1982 to 1986. This was partly because of the growth of oil exports, which pushed several agricultural products below the dependency threshold, but mainly because fluctuations had not exceeded the threshold for several years. In 1987 the prices for many commodities were extremely low, and Cameroon's export earnings from coffee and cocoa fell sharply (more than MECU 100). The situation for 1987 was similar to that in 1981: The STABEX system did not have enough resources to cover all claims—even taking into account an additional MECU 120 made available from the reserves of the EDF. Consequently all claims had to be reduced. Furthermore, Cameroon had replenishment obligations of MECU 18 that were deducted. The resulting net transfer for 1987 amounted to MECU 8 for cocoa and MECU 34 for coffee. These amounts were paid in 1988.

STABEX in Senegal

Senegal's export earnings strongly depend on groundnut products destined for the EC. This fact, combined with the vulnerability of groundnut yields to drought and with the volatile nature of the world vegetable oil market placed Senegal in a position to be a leading beneficiary of STABEX. Indeed, among the sixty-six beneficiary coun-

Table 7-4. Time Patterns of STABEX Transfers to Senegal
(millions of European currency units)

Payment year	Type of payment	Application year				
		1978	1980	1981	1985	1986
1978	Advance	19.0	0	0	0	0
1979	Balance	46.1	0	0	0	0
1980	Advance	0	25.0[a]	0	0	0
1981	Balance, advance	0	13.6	18.0	0	0
1982	Balance	0	0	2.5	0	0
1983	Project grant	0	0	5.7[b]	0	0
1984	0	0	0	0	0	0
1985	Advance	0	0	0	15.0	0
1986	Reliquat,[c] balance	0	0	25.7	12.6	0
1987	Advance, balance	0	0	0	0	54.5[d]

a. 18 MECU paid in June, 7 MECU paid in October.
b. Disbursement started in 1983.
c. Amount received when the Lomé II accounts were closed.
d. Advance of 30 MECU was received at the beginning of the year.
Source: Commission of the EC.

tries up to 1988, Senegal has been the largest recipient of STABEX funds, with an accumulated total of transfers amounting to MECU 238 over the period 1978–87. Because Senegal has to contribute to the replenishment of the system, however, net payments received have been slightly lowered (by MECU 26). Moreover, even though Senegal is the largest STABEX beneficiary in absolute terms, this is not so in per capita terms: Swaziland, The Gambia, and several small island states benefited more than Senegal in per capita terms.

An overview of STABEX payments to Senegal is given in table 7-4. Although claims relate to only five application years, payments have been made over nine years, with two periods of concentration: 1978–81 and 1985–86.

The importance of (net) STABEX payments for the Senegalese economy can be assessed by expressing them in relation to some macroeconomic variables:

	1978–81 (percent)	1985–86 (percent)
Share of total export revenue	7.1	4.4
Share of total government revenue	6.9	4.7
Share of net aid disbursement	17.3	15.0

The stabilizing effect of STABEX has been greatly increased by the payment of advances within the year of the export shortfall, which amounts to a very rapid disbursement of funds. This has been made possible by the good cooperation between Senegal and the CEC on export statistics.

The data in table 7-5 reflect the timeliness of STABEX transfers. On the whole, the transfers provided support when it was most urgently needed. The timeliness of Lomé II application years (1980–81) appears to have been slightly better than that for Lomé I or Lomé III. However, the 1980–81 transfers were impeded by the system's lack of resources referred to above. Senegal received only about 45 percent of its established claim, and to add to the problem, the transfer value had already been reduced, because of a decline in the marketed surplus and a fall in the EC share in total exports. The amount received in 1986 when the Lomé II accounts were closed covered only a small part of the remainder. As table 7-5 also shows, the decline in production because of the drought has been the dominant cause for export revenue shortfalls (except in 1986).

For the application year 1987, Senegal chose to use the transfer right for groundnut products, largely to offset the amounts due to replenish earlier transfers. As in the case of Cameroon, all transfers for 1987 had

Table 7-5. Senegal: STABEX Receipts, Groundnut Export Value, and Prices

Year	Net STABEX payment[a] (billion CFAF)	Export value Groundnut production[b] (billion CFAF)	Production[c] groundnuts (thousand metric tons)	Unit value groundnut oil exports (CFAF/kilogram)	Producer price groundnuts[d] (CFAF/kilogram)
1975	0.0	40.3	980.0	159.0	40.0
1976	0.0	64.5	1,412.0	164.0	40.0
1977	0.0	75.5	1,208.0	215.0	40.0
1978	5.3	23.5	519.0	252.0	40.0
1979	13.5	40.2	1,061.0	215.0	40.0
1980	7.4	14.9	650.0	181.0	46.0
1981	9.5	9.1	521.0	287.0	50.0
1982	0.8	42.1	867.0	205.0	70.0
1983	1.9	55.3	1,145.0	230.0	70.0
1984	0.0	54.5	575.0	460.0	70.0
1985	5.1	23.7	490.0	461.0	80.0
1986	14.5[d]	24.4	601.0	211.0	90.0

a. The Lomé II balance allocated in 1986 was used to replenish part of the 1980–81 transfers and is not included in the table.
b. Exports to all destinations, usually more than 85 percent, is to the European Communities.
c. 1975 = 1974/75 season, 1976 = 1975/76 season, and so on.
d. Including advance paid beginning of 1987.
Source: Except first column, "Senegal: An Economy under Adjustment," Report 6454.SE (Africa—Technical Department, Agriculture Division, World Bank, Washington, D.C., 1986).

to be reduced because of the lack of resources in the STABEX system, leaving a net transfer of only MECU 1.

Because of the complexity of the Senegalese groundnut system and the fungibility of funds that are transferred, it is difficult to evaluate the effect of the transfers. The reports provided by Senegal itself are rather sketchy. They only show the allocation of STABEX funds in a general accounting sense, and give little indication of the economic effects on groundnut producers. An evaluation of Lomé I carried out in 1981 indicates that most STABEX transfers to Senegal were channeled to the Caisse de Péréquation et de Stabilisation des Prix (CPSP), a government body that is responsible for price stabilization of groundnuts and several other agricultural products.[9] If, after taking into account transformation and transport costs, export prices are below the officially guaranteed producer prices, CPSP covers the deficit. If export prices exceed official prices, it collects the surplus through a levy.

The drought-related declines in production indicated in table 7-5 have undoubtedly been a serious problem for groundnut producers, making it difficult for them to repay the advances obtained for seed and fertilizer. As a result, a large part of STABEX funds have had to be used to cancel farm debts. Some of these funds were also used to finance the fertilizer subsidy and cover the cost of the dissolution of the Office Nationale de Coopération et d'Assistance pour le Développement (ONCAD), another parastatal, to pay its debt to cooperatives and input suppliers. Even though ONCAD stopped functioning in 1981, the 1985 transfer was still officially allocated to cover the financial consequences. Smaller amounts have been used as counterpart contributions to various rural development projects, to buy millet for an emergency food reserve, to pay for animal feed to help cattle farmers hit by drought, and to improve rural water supply. The special project grant (MECU 5.7) was used mainly for the microprojects program and rural water supply.

In conclusion, most of the STABEX transfers allocated to Senegal have contributed to maintaining the revenue of groundnut producers—largely indirectly, by canceling debts on input supply (especially in 1978, 1980, 1981, and 1985); partly directly, by guaranteeing a higher price than the export market allowed (especially in 1985 and 1986); and through emergency relief operations. The rural community (for example, through the water supply facilities) further benefited indirectly from the investments financed with STABEX money. The support of the groundnut system also helped to maintain economic activity in the rest of the economy by linking demand and supply. For a good period of time, however, STABEX has also facilitated some parastatal inefficiency (particularly by paying for the liquidation of ONCAD).

STABEX in Tanzania

There are some important differences in the STABEX operations in Cameroon and Senegal, on the one hand, and Tanzania, on the other. To begin with, Tanzania, is one of the poorest countries, so that it qualifies for the lower thresholds and does not contribute to replenishment; Tanzanian exports do not concentrate on the EC as much (its average share is around 40 percent); and fluctuations in the exchange rate of the ECU to the Tanzania shilling can have a strong influence on the size of transfers.

Tanzania has received a large number of relatively small transfers totaling MECU 50. STABEX certainly did not have the macroeconomic impact there that it had in Senegal. Nevertheless, the more or less regularly available untied foreign exchange provided by STABEX was useful for the government's development budget—to cushion against delays in donor disbursements, to cope with cost overruns, or, sometimes, to remove supply bottlenecks.[10]

About 60 percent of STABEX transfers were provided for sisal. Yet sisal export earnings have almost continuously declined since independence, with only a brief upswing in the second half of the 1970s when prices followed the upward move of synthetic fibers. In 1986 sisal exports went below the dependency threshold of 1.5 percent, and the fall in earnings could no longer be compensated. The coffee transfers of 1980 and 1981 would have been substantially higher if STABEX resources had been sufficient and if the Tanzania shilling—pegged to the United States dollar—had not appreciated with respect to the ECU.

About 75 percent of the Lomé I transfers went outside agriculture—financing two cement factories, a large mineral survey, and power transmission lines. The remainder was allocated to the grain-marketing parastatal, NMC, for storage facilities. The agencies that received STABEX money were not aware of the origin of the funds.[11] Later transfers were more concentrated on agriculture, including the sector that triggered the transfer. A large part of the 1983, 1984, and 1985 sisal and cashew transfers were allocated to the rehabilitation plans of these sectors carried out by the relevant parastatals. The data are insufficient to judge the effectiveness of these actions.

STABEX resources also have been used to pay EIB arrears (MECU 1.9), as complementary finance for various projects (including the EDF vehicle repair project), and to finance the petroleum imports urgently needed for the transport of agricultural inputs and products.

For the application years 1986 and 1987, STABEX requests for sisal, tea, coffee, and cotton were all rejected, primarily because the tunnel method was applied to restrict exchange rate movements. The method, introduced in Lomé III, worked out very unfavorably in the case of Tanzania.

Assessment

The role of STABEX has been different in each of the three countries under consideration. For Senegal, STABEX transfers represented a significant proportion of export revenue, government revenue, and aid disbursements. They enabled the government to mitigate the effects of disastrous crop failures on the economy. The STABEX transfers to Cameroon were much smaller in relation to macroeconomic indicators. However, because most transfers took place at a time when the economy was less strong, the effects have been positive. STABEX transfers for Tanzania also were small compared with macroeconomic variables—but they were all in the form of grants and certainly helped Tanzania cope with its acute foreign exchange problems.

Some general observations nevertheless can be made about the varied experience of Cameroon, Senegal, and Tanzania:

- STABEX is a quick-disbursing and flexible source of funds. The use of funds is untied and virtually unconditional (funds are to be used within the sector hit by the shortfall or to foster diversification).
- A considerable advantage of STABEX is that it covers shortfalls regardless of their source (excluding those arising from explicit government policy decisions).
- The operational rules of the system virtually ensure that it will not distort the trade flows. This was confirmed by the Lomé I evaluation study.[13] STABEX is neither designed to save nor capable of saving a part of the economy that is facing a declining market (such as sisal in Tanzania). It can, however, help a country reorient itself toward more profitable lines of activity. In this respect, STABEX compares favorably with commodity agreements, which usually compensate only price effects and may lead to the spread of quotas that distort production patterns.
- STABEX transfers should be as neutral as possible with respect to exchange rate fluctuations. It is the loss of purchasing power that should be compensated—a restriction being the transparency and manageability of the operating rules. Tanzania has suffered from the way its exchange rate changes were handled. The tunnel method introduced in Lomé III punishes countries applying an adjustment program that includes substantial devaluation. Because both Senegal and Cameroon participate in the Communauté Financière Africaine (CFA) system, there have been no problems in their case, because CFA currency has been rather stable in relation to the ECU.

- Without diminishing the flexibility of the system, it would be desirable in certain cases to link STABEX more closely to project aid, especially when the funds are channeled to the sector with a shortfall. In Tanzania's case, this would have meant integrating STABEX resources in EDF support for coffee. In the case of Senegal, it would have implied some follow-up to the substantial EDF involvement in groundnut production in the 1960s and 1970s.
- Projections of STABEX flows should be taken into account when designing structural adjustment packages, even though such projections are technically rather difficult to arrive at. When the projected flows are large, this would imply a corresponding EC involvement in adjustment discussions.
- The smooth functioning of the STABEX system depends foremost on the availability and quality of statistics (production levels, marketed surplus, export value, and quantity). Especially in the case of Tanzania, but also in Cameroon and sometimes Senegal, it has been difficult to establish statistical data accepted by both parties with which to compute the transfers. A country project for improved data collection, management, and training would help to avoid these problems.

Recent Developments

Following the 1972–74 world food crisis, more aid funds were channeled toward food production. This clearly applied to EC cooperation with Cameroon and Senegal. Nevertheless, it became clear by 1980 that this quantitative change did not fundamentally improve the food situation, particularly in Sub-Saharan Africa. In 1981, in reaction to this state of affairs, the EC launched an initiative to support food strategies in a number of African countries.

This initiative is designed to concentrate on the basic objective of food security; define and implement coherent policies to promote food security through a process of policy dialogue; strengthen coordination among donors; and integrate instruments for the same objective (for example, food aid sold at market price and the resulting counterpart funds used for supporting rural development).

These characteristics subsequently became central features of the third Lomé Convention; in this way, the food strategy approach was generalized. In Lomé III, this is referred to as sectoral concentration—the chosen sector usually being agriculture or rural development. The policy dialogue, as a rule, centers on the sector of concentration.

This new strategy has generated large rural development programs, usually costing between MECU 20 and 100. These Lomé III programs are different from the earlier "integrated rural development projects," mainly because of the element of policy dialogue. By their very nature, such large programs are not spelled out in detail during appraisal. As a result, although the commitment of funds has been speeded up, because of the size of the programs, there has been a slowdown in the implementation and disbursement of Lomé III funds in comparison with previous conventions. To some extent, the slower disbursement also follows from the increased concentration on food security and rural development, which generally leads to more complex actions focused on a dispersed group of smallholders. Large infrastructure projects, which used to account for the greatest share of EC funding, are much easier to appraise and implement.

The possibility of financing sectoral import programs (SIPs), introduced by Lomé III, may compensate for the slow disbursement of the large rural development programs. Recently, several import programs have been worked out. Such SIPs are normally linked to the concentration sector. For Cameroon, a fertilizer import program (MECU 15) is under preparation (see the next section). For Senegal, fuel imports will be financed, and the resulting counterpart funds will be used to support groundnut production (MECU 11.5). In the case of Tanzania, plans are being made to finance imports of raw materials and spare parts to increase capacity utilization in industry and transport (MECU 24.5). The Senegal and Tanzania import programs are financed from a special budget approved at the beginning of 1988 to assist debt-distressed countries. With this budget, it is also possible to fund general import programs within the context of economic adjustment operations.

Cameroon

The indicative program for the third Lomé Convention was signed in May 1986 and stipulated a concentration of 80 percent on rural development. Later the rural development share was lowered to about 70 percent to free funds for the 160-kilometer Yaoundé-Ayos road. Noncommitted funds as well as unspent amounts of closed projects from the fourth and fifth EDF also have been earmarked for the road, bringing available resources to about MECU 60. Since the road forms part of the vital link between the north and the center of the country, it will reduce the price at which local food is available in Yaoundé, and it should have an important stimulating effect on the agricultural sector.

The rural development component consists mainly of a few large programs that build on past experience, as well as a sectoral import program. One specific program, for the Bénoué Basin (MECU 25), was approved in 1987 and continues the earlier EDF activities in that region.

In contrast to the Bénoué program, progress on the continuation of irrigated rice activities is rather slow. The main reason for the delays has been that the government needs to take appropriate measures to protect its rice market, so that production from North Cameroon can compete with imports. Beginning in 1988, and following extensive consultation with the European Communities, the government decided to set up a price stabilization agency.

At the end of 1987, the government requested support for a fertilizer import program that complements a similar USAID program. The European Communities reacted favorably because the program is linked to important policy reform measures: the phasing out of fertilizer subsidies, and the liberalization and privatization of fertilizer trade. The program (valued at MECU 15) was approved in October 1988 and the first fertilizer shipment had already arrived in December 1988.

Senegal

The Lomé III indicative program signed in July 1985 stipulated both a thematic and geographic concentration of funds on food security and the struggle against desertification in the lower Senegal River area. The full indicative program (MECU 97), committed to the development of the Podor region, was approved in the spring of 1987 and strengthens earlier EC activities in the Senegal River area. It contributes to the investment that is necessary to exploit the potential created by the two dams recently completed on the Senegal River.

About half of the Podor program is earmarked for the construction of irrigation facilities and a quarter is for infrastructure (including road rehabilitation, the construction of access roads, and water supply for Podor town). Smaller program components are reforestation (MECU 5); supplies for small enterprises (MECU 4); social infrastructure for villages (MECU 9); and management, monitoring, and evaluation (MECU 8). The main output of the program will be in the form of rice to be used for subsistence and for marketing in the rest of the country. The economic and financial results of the program depend on the future condition of the market for cereals. During and after appraisal, therefore, a policy dialogue concerning cereal pricing and marketing has involved the EC. The Podor program is consistent with the cereals plan that the government worked out in 1984 and that foresees incentives for locally produced cereals (at production and processing levels), the limitation of rice imports at 1984 levels, and a tariff on cereal imports.

The Podor program cannot be judged solely on the basis of its economic return at the currently prevailing low world prices for rice

(1988). Its contribution to a better regional balance of welfare within Senegal and to the preservation of the environment should also be taken into account. This applies equally to the rice program in Cameroon.

Tanzania

The Lomé III indicative program for Tanzania was signed in July 1985, as it was for Senegal. It was agreed to concentrate 90 percent of the resources on food security and agricultural development. The policy intentions of the government in areas directly relevant to the program were spelled out (for example, there was to be an increase in producer prices, prompt payment, and adequate retention of foreign exchange in the coffee sector).

The agricultural sector support program (ASSP) embodied the ideas of the indicative program; in fact, it became the first Lomé III–style program to be submitted to the EC member states. The allocations for the main components are as follows:

	MECU
Food security	21
Coffee production and marketing	23
Assistance to cooperative unions	8
Vehicle and tractor repairs	26
Feeder roads	10
Institutional support	6
Total	94

Apart from the foreign exchange component, there is a local currency contribution equivalent to MECU 35 to be provided to a large extent from food aid counterpart funds. The ASSP is concentrating on the areas with good potential for maize and coffee production in the Southern Highlands. The coffee component also includes follow-up of previous actions in other coffee areas. The vehicle and tractor repair component builds on a similar successful project carried out between 1982 and 1984.

Approval of the ASSP toward the end of 1986 was speeded up because of the favorable attitude prevalent among the aid agencies in the wake of the Economic Recovery Program that Tanzania had agreed to in mid-1986. Implementation of the ASSP has been slow, however, and by the end of 1987 only a very small part of the funds had been disbursed (a delivery of fertilizers for about MECU 1). This slow disbursement is in part characteristic of this method of assistance, which allows a great deal of flexibility at the implementation stage, but thereby leaves many details to be worked out at this stage. Important policy issues that affect the program—for example, the pricing of fertilizers and the distribution of responsibilities between the marketing board and cooperatives in the coffee sector—remain unresolved.

Concluding Observations

Although agricultural development issues are complex, a few general observations can be made about the EC experience that may help improve cooperation in this area of economic development.

On the whole, projects focused on export crops have been more successful than those aimed primarily at food production. Export crops have, in many cases, made important additions to farm revenue, including the revenue of smallholders. A possible explanation is that export crops could build on more institutional and other resources. It is generally easier to attract progressive farmers to a new venture than to upgrade traditional crops for a large, dispersed group of subsistence producers.

Consequently the shift within the EC project portfolio from export crops toward food crops (particularly in Cameroon and Senegal, and to a lesser extent in Tanzania, where support for coffee has been continued) may reduce its overall rate of return. Contrary to views that sometimes dominate policy thinking, a food security strategy can be compatible with export or cash crop development—providing additional farm revenue can be used to improve food consumption and nutrition. There are also cases in which the development of export crops is directly complementary to the production of subsistence crops; for example, the export crop revenue makes it possible to buy inputs and to obtain credit that can be used for food crops. For the future, it may be desirable to reemphasize export crops with a view to exploiting these complementarities.

Export crop activities have been more successful in Cameroon (palm oil, cotton) than in Senegal (groundnuts, cotton) and Tanzania (coffee, pyrethrum), where frequent institutional and policy changes have been among the main constraints. The situation has been aggravated in Senegal by adverse weather and in Tanzania by an overambitious project design.

Integrated rural development projects became more or less a standard practice during the 1970s. The idea behind integration was to tie agricultural development to its socioeconomic setting. As a result, project activities were broadened to include health, training, credit systems, and local infrastructure, in addition to crop development. Even though the basic arguments in favor of integrated rural development are valid, the strategy has often produced disappointing results (for example, Iringa in Tanzania). Although it has generally been possible to reach physical targets in, for example, the construction of feeder roads, it has been difficult to make a lasting effect on farm household revenue. Typically, integrated projects have tried to achieve their objectives over too short a period in relation to the complexity of the task. They have tended to overstretch local management capacity and have not succeeded in sufficiently involving local community members, especially women.

The results of integrated projects have also been affected by more general problems that relate mainly to the overall policy environment. Even the best integration cannot compensate for a lack of production incentives. This may not be apparent at the height of a project when the extra resource inflow (for example, in the form of inputs and technical assistance) leads to positive physical results. However, once the resource flow is phased out, farmers may be forced to return to their traditional strategies.

The success of the Northeast Bénoué Settlement Project may be attributable to the relatively modest targets, the geographical concentration, and the rather undistorted economic conditions in Cameroon by comparison with Tanzania. The lack of success in eastern Senegal demonstrates the importance of involving local communities in basic decisions (for example, on the cropping pattern).

Active support has been provided by the EC for irrigation schemes. Although such schemes have been important technical successes—relating to yields, for example—their capital and recurrent costs have often been high, leading to frustrating overall economic results. Small schemes have done much better than the larger ones, mainly because the farmers' participation reduced the overhead costs and improved sustainability.

To some extent, these problems with irrigation schemes have been the result of the artificial conditions that sometimes prevail on the world market for cereals. In the cases of Cameroon and Senegal, the appraisal of major irrigated rice projects took place in 1974–75 and 1980–81—a time when rice prices were at record high levels. Full production was attained in 1986 and 1987, when world rice prices were depressed and when good rainfall had pushed up the yields of traditional cereals. Appraisal methods cannot cope well with high price uncertainty. It is doubtful whether project funds should be earmarked in advance to absorb losses that may result from price movements.

In connection with further investments in irrigated rice production, countries have been encouraged by the EC to stabilize and protect their rice markets, and some measures have already been taken to this end. Price stabilization may help farmers overcome their risk aversion. It is possible to support price stabilization with the counterpart funds from a general import program or from food aid. Some form of protection will often be required to achieve a lasting effect on production. An important distinction should be made between protection on economic grounds and protection introduced to achieve noneconomic objectives. Protection on economic grounds should be temporary—applied to bridge the period before the newly introduced farming system can operate at minimum cost (the infant industry argument). In agriculture, this can take a long time. Protection for noneconomic objectives (for example, environmental conservation, the creation of rural employment, and balanced regional development) should be compared with other ways of reaching those objectives (for example, through increased support for traditional crops, livestock, or fisheries activities and investment in human capital in the form of better rural health care and education). The objectives should be clearly identified. A judgment should be made on who should bear the burden: the consumer paying more for food as a result of a tariff or the taxpayer when support is financed through the budget.

In the three countries under review, but more so in Senegal and Tanzania than in Cameroon, small projects—both the micro projects handled entirely by the beneficiary country and NGO-cofinanced projects—have experienced considerable success. The small-scale projects have acted as catalysts to trigger local initiatives. They have also been less affected by administrative delays. The main constraint has been that local groups do not have the full capacity to prepare, manage, and monitor these projects. Because of their success, the potential for small projects should be exploited as much as possible. There should be adequate attention for the programming and management aspects of such projects, as well as for training. Whenever feasible, local organizations such as farmers' association, credit unions, or cooperatives should be involved. Particular attention should be paid to creating employment for women, to the development of rural infrastructure, and to the processing of agricultural products. Moreover, in view of the pressing need for conservation, it is essential to integrate crop, livestock, and forestry activities. Conservation measures should stress tangible benefits for local communities.

The handling of food aid has undergone some important changes in relation to agricultural development. In many countries, including Senegal and Tanzania, arrangements have been set up to use food aid counterpart funds primarily for rural development. In this way food aid is an additional resource that complements other funding for rural development. The discussions related to the use of food aid also have been a useful entry point for a more general food policy dialogue.

The STABEX system, now in operation for about fifteen years, has proved its viability. It is a quickly disbursing instrument of EC funding, and its functioning does not distort trade and production patterns. In the case of Senegal, the STABEX transfers have had an important stabilizing effect on the groundnut sector, and therefore on the economy as a whole. In Cameroon and Tanzania, they have been used for a variety of purposes, sometimes outside agriculture. The STABEX transfers should be used more directly for the benefit of agricultural producers. When projected STABEX flows are sizable, they should be linked to economic adjustment discussions.

Traditionally, there has been no attempt by the EC to provide policy advice for developing countries. Toward the beginning of the 1980s, the constraining effects of a deficient agricultural policy environment became all too clear in many Sub-Saharan African countries. The EC did not have the opportunity, for lack of a mandate and for lack of the necessary skills, to engage in policy-based lending. Nevertheless, the food strategy initiative, launched in 1982, introduced a food policy dialogue to help the EC reach agreements with recipients on the implementation of specific policy measures that will ensure the success of agricultural projects. The EC policy dialogue has generally been concerned with price incentive issues (for example, protection) and the reform of agricultural parastatals. Senegal, Tanzania, and Cameroon have not been among the countries in which the EC's food policy dialogue has had a strong impact. In some other countries—for example, Mali and Kenya—the results have been more significant.

The EC policy dialogue has remained focused on specific areas of the economy and has not led to conditionality where implementation would be automatically linked to specific policy measures. The substantial STABEX transfers to Senegal, for example, were made without consideration of the policy measures that might improve the performance of the affected sector.

The introduction under Lomé III of sectoral import programs as well as the 1988 EC Council resolution on structural adjustment may increase the possibilities for policy-based lending. Moreover, general import support is being provided through the Special Program of Assistance for debt-distressed countries in Africa, which was also approved in 1988 with the participation of the EC. In the area of structural adjustment, EC concern has been particularly with integrating social considerations in the design of adjustment packages. In addition to food security, emphasis is on the maintenance of health and education services for vulnerable segments of the population, as well as employment schemes for employees of the public sector who were laid off. The sectoral import programs or food aid help finance tergeted social intervention either directly, through the goods supplied, or indirectly, by channeling the counterpart funds from the sale of imported goods to the government budget.

The main agricultural projects supported by the EDF in Cameroon, Senegal, and Tanzania are set out in appendix tables 7A-1 to 7A-5.

Appendix

The following five tables list specific agricultural and development projects. Those projects that are examined in detail in this chapter are marked by asterisks.

Table 7A-1. Cameroon: Main Agricultural Projects, European Development Fund 1–3
(thousand European currency units)

Title of action	*Amount*
EDF 1 (1958–64)	
Health training, Northern Cameroon	1,200
Soil conservation	717
Livestock improvement, Adamaoua	500
Rural roads (two projects)	1,102
Hydrogeological study, Northern Cameroon	920
Agricultural school	474
EDF 2 (1965–70)	
Agricultural production: groundnuts, coffee, cotton (5 annual shares plus extension for two crop years)	7,068
*Palm oil plantation (4,380 hectares at Mondoni)	6,482
*Rural development, northeast Bénoué (preparatory study)	637
EDF 3 (1971–75)	
*Palm oil plantation (6,000 hectares at Dibombari)	2,790
*Agroindustrial complex, Dibombari (special loan)	8,850
Sugarcane plantation and mill (grant)	772
*Continuation rural development, northeast Bénoué	4,050
*Irrigated rice, Logone and Chari	391

Note: Projects marked with an asterisk are discussed in the text.
Source: Commission of the EC.

Table 7A-2. Cameroon: Main Agricultural Projects, European Development Fund 4 and 5
(thousand European currency units)

Title of action	Decided: Year	Decided: Amount	Situation April 1988: Paid	Situation April 1988: Percent paid[a]
EDF 4 (1976–80)				
*Dibombari (grant)	1977	2,192	2,192	100.0
*Dibombari (risk capital)	1977	2,300	2,300	100.0
*Micro projects	1977	403	403	100.0
*Village palm oil (grant)	1977	329	329	100.0
*Village palm oil (loan)	1977	688	688	100.0
*Northeast Bénoué (second phase)	1978	4,087	4,087	100.0
Djuttitsa tea (grant)	1978	1,420	1,396	98.3
Djuttitsa tea (special loan)	1978	1,233	1,233	100.0
*Irrigated rice, Logone, Chari	1978	4,471	4,250	95.0
Northwest Province, rural development	1981	8,920	5,019	56.2
Total		26,043	21,897	84.1
EDF 5 (1981–85)				
*Interest subsidy, SOCAPALM	1982	1,038	660	63.6
Interest subsidy, CAMDEV	1982	1,911	1,340	70.1
*Rural development, Bénoué Valley	1982	13,180	12,991	98.5
*Micro projects	1982	457	394	86.2
*Irrigated rice, Logone, Chari	1983	1,080	913	84.5
*Continuation, Logone, Chari	1984	8,970	6,376	71.0
Continuation, Djuttitsa tea	1984	713	713	100.0
Interest subsidy, HEVECAM	1984	2,260	2,260	100.0
*Fisheries, Bénoué, Lagdo	1984	2,000	1,628	81.3
*Village palm oil, Dibombari	1986	1,110	157	14.1
Northwest Province (Bafut rural development)	1986	1,500	482	32.1
Interest subsidy, SODECOTON	1986	1,188	0	0.0
Total		35,407	27,914	78.8

Note: Projects marked with an asterisk are discussed in the text.

a. Amount paid (or disbursed) as a percentage of the amount decided ("primary" commitment).

Source: Commission of the EC.

Table 7A-3. Senegal: Main Agricultural Projects, European Development Fund 1–3
(thousand European currency units)

Title of action	*Amount*
EDF 1 (1958–64)	
Fisheries wharf, Dakar	611
Livestock research center	2,110
Drilling and construction of wells	2,431
Construction of 30 rural development centers	2,094
School for rural advisers	506
EDF 2 (1965–70)	
*Groundnut program (5 annual shares plus extension for two crop years)	30,980
*Groundnut program (special loan)	5,900
*Cotton development, Siné Saloum	3,448
*Cotton development, Casamance, eastern Senegal	1,072
Rice and bananas, Casamance	2,063
Rice production, Casamance	1,731
*Confectionery groundnuts, Siné Saloum	996
*Groundnut seeds (1971)	492
*Setting up of seed service	2,972
Vegetable production	1,000
Millet improvement program	1,207
Construction of two slaughterhouses (St. Louis, Thies)	466
EDF 3 (1971–75)	
*Exceptional aid for groundnut producers	7,185
*Continuation cotton	4,656
*Cotton processing plant	957
*Continuation confectionery groundnuts	2,219
Agricultural development, Casamance	712
*Rainfed rice, eastern Senegal	1,008
Drought relief operation	1,800
Livestock development	5,865
*Nianga irrigated perimeter	5,797
Village water supply	3,008
Commercial vegetables and fruits (BUD Senegal)	3,322

Note: Projects marked with an asterisk are discussed in the text.
Source: Commission of the EC.

Table 7A-4. Senegal: Main Agricultural Projects, European Development Fund (EDF) 4 and 5
(thousand European currency units)

	Decided		Situation April 1988	
Title of action	*Year*	*Amount*	*Paid*	*Percent paid*[a]
EDF 4 (1976–80)				
*Continuation cotton	1976	6,538	5,660	86.5
*Confectionery groundnuts	1976	4,040	4,040	100.0
*Micro projects	1977	340	316	92.8
Fruit production	1977	4,563	4,563	100.0
Hydrogeological study	1978	988	988	100.0
Exceptional aid	1978	3,673	3,673	100.0
Continuation livestock	1980	2,963	2,963	100.0
*Village irrigation, Podor	1982	480	453	94.2
Total		23,585	22,656	96.1
EDF 5 (1981–85)				
*Village irrigation, Podor	1982	6,620	4,307	65.1
*Micro projects (7 programs)	1981	4,310	3,257	75.5
*Cereals production, eastern Senegal	1982	4,680	3,387	72.3
Dams on Senegal River	1982	10,300	5,505	53.4
Gum tree planting	1982	2,450	2,194	89.5
Drilling of wells	1983	2,300	2,293	99.6
Continuation livestock	1982	692	692	100.0
Vegetable production, Thies	1983	2,250	1,121	49.8
Livestock relief operation	1984	797	797	100.0
Emergency drought victims	1984	2,000	2,000	100.0
Coastal fisheries, Casamance	1986	1,600	0	0
Total		37,999	25,553	67.2

Note: Projects marked with an asterisk are discussed in the text.

a. Amount paid (or disbursed) as a percentage of the amount decided (primary commitment).

Source: Commission of the EC.

Table 7A-5. Tanzania: Main Agricultural Projects, European Development Fund 4 and 5
(thousand European currency units)

	Decided		Situation April 1988	
Title of action	*Year*	*Amount*	*Paid*	*Percent paid*[a]
EDF 4 (1976–80)				
*Coffee improvement program	1977	12,572	12,572	100.0
*Agricultural development, Iringa (I)	1977	6,593	6,593	100.0
Morogoro canvas mill (grant)	1977	14,900	14,900	100.0
Morogoro canvas mill (risk capital)	1977	4,900	4,900	100.0
Kiltex-Arusha textile mill	1978	6,550	6,229	95.1
Total		45,515	45,194	99.3
EDF 5 (1981–85)				
*Agricultural development, Iringa (II)	1982	19,325	18,559	96.0
Morogoro canvas mill	1982	2,500	2,500	100.0
*Coffee development program (I)	1982	13,500	12,839	95.1
Training irrigation engineers	1982	920	815	88.6
*Micro projects (2 programs)	1983	1,500	954	63.6
*Coffee development program (II)	1984	9,500	8,308	87.4
Rinderpest control	1984	1,400	1,305	93.1
Morogoro canvas (risk capital)	1984	3,500	3,500	100.0
Morogoro canvas mill management	1984	2,200	2,200	100.0
Banana improvement	1985	3,000	211	7.0
Cooperative Rural Development Bank	1986	3,150	409	12.9
		60,495	51,600	85.3

Note: Projects marked with an asterisk are discussed in the text.

a. Amount paid (or disbursed) as a percentage of the amount decided (primary commitment).

Source: Commission of the EC.

Notes

This chapter is an abridged and updated version of a report prepared in December 1987 as part of the World Bank study on managing agricultural development in Africa. Helpful comments on earlier drafts by Ciaran Dearle, Thiery de Saint Maurice, Marc Franco, Robert Gregoire, Gerhard Hild, Friedrich Nagel, Andreas Papadopulos, Martyn Pennington, Serge Pivetta, André Van Haeverbeke, and Heiko Wolle have contributed to the text. The part on coffee in Tanzania is based on a more elaborate paper by Brian Greey. Without the encouragement and useful comments of Uma Lele, the MADIA team leader, the text would not have been completed. The views expressed herein are those of the author and not necessarily those of the CEC, the World Bank, or other organizations affiliated with the MADIA study.

Values in the text are expressed in European Currency Units (ECU), a basket of European currencies. Up to 1970, the ECU was defined as being equivalent to the United States dollar. From 1971 to 1981, the ECU was strong against the dollar, with a peak of ECU 1.0 = \$1.40 in 1980. Between 1981 and 1986 the ECU weakened down to ECU 1.0 = \$0.81, but the situation turned around in 1987, and by July 1988 the ECU was equal to \$1.15. In the text, MECU refers to millions of ECUs.

In addition to the references cited in the notes, the following sources provide evaluations of EC assistance in Sub-Saharan Africa: Africa Asia Bureau and Institute of Development Studies, "An Evaluation of the EC Food Aid Program" (Brussels, 1982); CEC, "Comprehensive Report on the Export Earnings Stabilization System Established by the Lomé Convention for the Years 1975 to 1979," SEC (81) 1104 (Brussels, 1981); CEC, *STABEX User's Guide* (Brussels, 1985); CEC, "Report on the Operating during 1985 of the STABEX System," COM (86) 622 (Brussels, 1987); CEC, "Community Food Aid Policy and Management in 1984: Report from the Commission to the Council and the European Parliament" COM (86) 622 (Brussels, 1986); V. Drachoussoff, "Développement rural dans la vallée de la Bénoué," evaluation report prepared for the United Republic of Cameroon and CEC (Brussels, 1984); A. J. Hallbach and H. Michel, "Evaluation globale de l'aide communautaire au Sénégal," IFO Institut für Wirtschaftsforschung (Brussels, 1980); Adrian Hewitt and C. Oxby, *STABEX: The United Republic of Cameroon: A Case Study* (London: Overseas Development Institute, 1981); Josse Kestemont, "Contribution de la CE a l'économie rurale du Cameroun de 1958 a 1984" (Brussels, 1986); Charles Van der Vaeren and G. Lejeune, "A Quick Evaluation of Community Food Aid to Tanzania" (CEC), Brussels, 1982; and André Vanhaeverbeke, "Evaluation des projets de développement du coton au Sénégal" (CEC, Brussels, 1973).

1. SOTESA/SHAWEL, "Evaluation of Oil Palm and Tea Projects Financed by the European in the United Republic of Cameroon" (Brussels, 1985).

2. Bureau de Développement de la Production Agricole, "Evaluation of the Implementation of the Coffee Development Programs in Tanzania" (Brussels, 1986).

3. International Institute for Land Reclamation and Improvement, "Evaluation of Irrigation Projects Sponsored by the European Community" (Wageningen, 1985).

4. N. H. Vink, "Evaluation of Iringa Region Agricultural Development Project, Phase I" (Brussels, 1981).

5. Société d'Etudes du Développement Economique et Social, "Evaluation of the Iringa Region Agricultural Development Project, Phase II" (Brussels, 1986).

6. On Cameroon, see Marc Franco and Pierre Monkam, "Evaluation comparative des microprojets et des projets cofinancés par la CE et des ONGs au Cameroun" (1980); on Senegal, see Bernard Lecompte and Albert Peeters, "Evaluation des microprojets et des cofinancés par la EC et des ONGs" (1980). In fact, these studies were specifically set up to compare micro projects with NGO projects.

7. John Lynton-Evans and A. Ruche, "Evaluation de l'aide alimentaire de la CEE au Senegal," report prepared for CEC, Africa Bureau (Cologne, 1982).

8. Edward Clay and Charlotte Benson, "Evaluation of EC Food Aid in Tanzania" (1988).

9. G. Chambas and others, "Le STABEX au Senegal," Centre d'Etudes et de Recherche sur le Développement International (University of Clermont-Ferrand, 1981).

10. Adrian Hewitt and A. Weston, *STABEX: The United Republic of Tanzania: A Case Study* (London: Overseas Development Institute, 1981).

11. Ibid.

12. Adrian Hewitt, *Synthesis Report on the Global Impact of STABEX Operations from 1975 to 1979: Based on Ten Case Studies* (London: Overseas Development Institute, 1982).

8 French Economic Cooperation with Senegal and Cameroon: Rural Development from Independence to the Present

Claude Freud

FRENCH ECONOMIC COOPERATION has a longer history than most aid relationships. The transition from France's colonial system to independence was prepared for by a framework of law that put into place a development plan financed by the colonial power. To implement this plan, the French government created a whole battery of instruments: FIDES, or Fonds d'Investissements pour le Développement Economique et Social des Territoires d'Outre Mer (Overseas Territories Economic and Social Development Investment Fund); CCFOM, or Caisse Centrale de la France d'Outre-Mer (Overseas Territories Central Fund); a number of study and project companies; and various research institutes.[1] As a result, at independence all of these cooperation instruments, with their specialist staffs, were already in place—except that their names were changed. The CCFOM became the Caisse Centrale de Coopération Economique (CCCE), or the Central Economic Cooperation Fund, the FIDES became the Fonds d'Aide et de Coopération (FAC), or the Aid and Cooperation Fund—and the colonial administrators became technical advisers. The study and project companies and research institutes continued to operate as if nothing had changed, and it was not until the 1970s that the research institutions were nationalized and national study bureaus were created. Cooperation policy developed around two main themes: (1) the training of local managers and supervisors to take over from technical assistance and (2) the installation of productivity-enhancing projects, intended to permit the countries' economies to bear the shock of the fall in export product prices after the former French colonies became associated members of the European Communities (EC) in the mid-1960s, and of diversification projects to end dependence on a single export crop.

The costly infrastructure investments were ceded to the European Development Fund (EDF).

Ministry of Cooperation aid was characterized by a high proportion of technical assistance (70 percent of lending). This technical assistance was not integrated into projects but was provided at all levels of administrative life (teachers in secondary schools, technical advisers in ministries), often in executive or line positions. Thus the intervention by France often could be regarded as substitution rather than development activities.

Initially (1960–70), the Ministry of Cooperation was able to keep pace with its partners' requests for both technical assistance and project aid. This was not the case, however, from the 1970s onward. The ever-increasing technical assistance (which included higher salaries after 1968) and the ever-growing number of project requests compelled the Ministry of Cooperation to favor one over the other. It opted for technical assistance. The CCCE then took over responsibility for projects, particularly in agriculture—an area in which it had not operated until then. The fact that the CCCE found it increasingly difficult to come up with bankable industrial projects contributed to this change.

The development model chosen was one that had succeeded in France itself after World War II: modernization through the adoption of the latest technologies. The model included a flexible planning framework and a free trade environment. The objective was welfare (free education and health); the image was that of the European consumer society.

Francophone Africa had chosen its camp—that of the Western World—and to prevent it from becoming a field of rivalry among competing external interests, France entered into defense agreements, accompanied by military aid, with each partner in the region.[2] This community of interests would be united by the cultural bond of the French language.

At the same time, the economic links between France and Africa were weakening. French private capital began withdrawing at independence, and trade with Africa embarked on a steady decline. Today it represents only 3 percent of France's external trade, compared with 30 percent in the 1950s. And although the volume of French aid in constant francs has been maintained, the French share of total aid to the countries within its area of influence has fallen sharply—from more than 75 percent before 1970 to less than 25 percent today.

As other donors appeared on the scene and became involved in various areas of the economy, French aid shifted to fill any gaps that were appearing. French aid is therefore regarded by its partners as aid that can be called upon to act as a catalyst for other external financing operations or to fill financing gaps. As a result, French aid sometimes does not finance certain activities to which French funding agencies assign priority because financing is provided by other suppliers of funds; however, it sometimes finances nonpriority activities because they provide continuity in the political links that have been forged between France and its former possessions. With its heavy emphasis on technical assistance, French aid can at best only be spread among all sectors of economic activity. Having lost its position of leadership, French aid often finds itself giving way to the international organizations—not being in a position to recommend a different development policy that would cause other donors to withdraw when France in any event lacks the means to take their place.

The Ministry of Cooperation's rural development aid to Senegal accounts for 9 percent of all aid to that country. The efficiency of this 9 percent is not representative of that of all aid—particularly since these operations often are not representative in themselves, in that they provide support for operations financed by other sources of funds. Conversely, foreign aid as a whole finances all of the country's rural development investment. Thus evaluating rural development progress in Senegal amounts to evaluating the efficiency of foreign aid.

To try to find out which donor deserves credit for the success of a rural development project is no better than guesswork, since all large projects are cofinanced. Is it attributable to the quality of the personnel paid by French aid or to the sums expended in the rural areas by the project grants or loans (for example, from the International Development Association)? That raises the basic question of the fungibility of government receipts and consequently that of expenditures.

This study is based on the evaluations of development in Senegal and Cameroon performed by the Ministry of Cooperation in Senegal and Cameroon between 1982 and 1985, as it related to agricultural activities surrounding rice, cotton, groundnuts, millet, and maize in Senegal, and rice, cocoa, cotton, and food crops in Cameroon.[3] The central question explored in this analysis is whether these newly independent countries have succeeded in their efforts to increase their productivity and diversify their agriculture. The projects examined have all been based on the same model and implemented by the same project companies. Since most of these projects inherited colonial policies or policies contemporaneous with independence, they are in essence extensions of earlier projects.

Central Features of the French Projects

The French projects have three distinguishing features relating to the methods used to increase productivity, their emphasis on extension, and the method of implementation.

Methods used to increase productivity. The projects are to raise productivity by applying the advanced knowledge and techniques gained through research. The purpose of research is to furnish development operations and projects with plant material that has the highest yield potential and is adapted to natural conditions; to define levels of input required; and to develop technical packages. The most efficient technical innovations are tested at experimental stations and constitute the basis for extension messages disseminated by the projects.

Thus, the IRCT (Institut de Recherche des Cotons et Textiles Exotiques or Cotton and Exotic Textile Research Institute) has undertaken research in cotton genetics (new seed selection), agronomy, plant health treatments, and technology with the object of furnishing selected seed and a package of techniques adapted to each environment for this important commercial crop. This research has introduced new varieties that have made it possible to raise cotton ginning yields substantially (from about 28 percent in 1946 to about 40 percent today), to improve fiber quality (length, fineness, strength, elongation, color), and to raise potential yields greatly. The current norms of the various projects range from 1.5 to 2.0 tons per hectare, compared with some 300 kilograms per hectare in the postwar period.

Similarly, IRHO (Edible Oils and Oil Crops Research Institute) has set up testing stations to experiment with the general research formulas for oil seeds in different bioclimatic environments and on different soils, and to search for regional solutions. Varieties giving agronomic yields 20 to 25 percent higher than the yields of local grains and 23 to 30 percent higher oil production were available even before 1960. By 1960, two-thirds of the seed used was selected seed.

Innovations in animal traction and the use of fertilizer were introduced in groundnut production in the period 1965–68 and met with great success, as did the use of the mechanical seeder (from then on, 43 percent of the area sown to groundnuts in Senegal was seeded mechanically). These innovations permitted substantial increases in the area under cultivation. Yet groundnut yields increased more slowly. In manual cultivation, the average net yield rose from 700 kilograms per hectare before World War II to 800 kilograms per hectare after 1950 because of the dissemination of selected seed.

Extension. A system of continuous communication with the farmers is used to disseminate technical information. Initially, the projects were organized into operational units that were both unwieldy (in some cotton projects, there was one extension agent for every fifty small farmers) and hierarchical (they had several intermediate levels). This mode of organization tended to favor a small number of the more dynamic small farmers.

In the second phase (from about 1968 on) a new system based on participation by the farmers was developed by channeling local extension services through the cooperatives. However, the same energetic farmers and notables appeared in the command posts of these institutions—and the second approach produced the same results as the first.

Method of implementation. The project is managed by a project implementation agency. The agency is usually of French origin: Société Centrale pour l'Equipement du Territoire (SCET-AGRI) in the case of rice farming development works in the Senegal River Valley and the Société d'Expansion et de Modernisation de la Riziculture de Yagoua (SEMRY) rice project in Cameroon; Société d'Aide Technique et de Coopération (SATEC) for groundnuts in Senegal; and Compagnie Française de Développement des Fibres Textiles (CFDT) for cotton projects in Senegal and Cameroon. These companies participate in the overall organization of production from extension and dissemination to processing, marketing, and, in the case of cotton, export. They are amply provided with technical assistance staff, which ranges, depending on the project, from a staff of about 100 for cotton in Cameroon, to one of about 30 for the Cameroon rice project (pre-1985 figures), and of 40 for the Senegal rice project.

Aid to Senegal

Aid flows from the Ministry of Cooperation to Senegal averaged F 73 million annually over 1960–65, rising to F 450 million annually over 1980–85 (table 8-1). In real terms, volume remained more or less 80 million in constant 1960 CFA (Communanté Financière Africaine) francs. The share of rural development aid remained about the same–about 10 percent over this period.

Over 1960–65 the average composition of Ministry of Cooperation aid was investment, 25 percent; technical assistance, 60 percent; and operating subsidies, 15 percent. Over 1980–85, the average share of investment had fallen to 12 percent, whereas that of technical assistance had risen to 66 percent, and that of operating subsidies had risen to 22 percent.

A look at total French aid to Senegal, including aid from other ministries and the CCCE, shows that net CCCE aid, which was negligible in the 1960s, had become significant in the 1980s and now accounts for roughly half as much as the aid provided by the Ministry of Cooperation. Thus, at the present time, two-thirds of total French aid to Senegal is in the form of grants and one-third in loans, whereas at the time of independence nearly all of it was in the form of grants.

Table 8-1. Senegal: Net Disbursements of French Aid, 1960–85
(thousands of current and constant French francs)

Allocation	*1961*	*1965*	*1970*	*1975*	*1980*	*1985*	*1985 (constant 1960 francs)*
Ministry of Cooperation							
Investment aid (IA)	29,600	4,000	21,700	19,300	26,700	64,400	9,900
Percentage for rural development	18	8	28	70	25	48	
IA as percent of total Ministry of Cooperation aid	34	5	25	9	7	12	
Technical Assistance (TA)	47,000	55,000	47,000	110,800	254,600	295,700	45,500
Percent for rural development	—	—	—	2	3	4	
TA as percent of total Ministry of Cooperation aid	66	76	53	54	67	57	100
Operating aid (OA) (including financial assistance)	—	13,700	19,900	73,700	96,300	161,700	24,900
Percent for rural development	—	—	35	23	27	—	
OA as percent of total Ministry of Cooperation aid	—	19	22	36	26	31	
Total Ministry of Cooperation aid	87,600	72,700	88,600	203,800	377,600	521,800	80,300
Percent for rural development	10	2	16	14	9	9	
Other ministries[a]	—	76,800	12,200	19,200	18,700	151,600	23,300
CCCE	11,400	9,400	10,800	10,400	388,500	255,300	39,300
Percent for rural development	—	1	13	49	26	66	
Total AID	99,000	158,900	111,600	233,500	784,800	928,200	149,900
Percent for rural development	10	2	14	16	18	27	

— = Not available.
a. Ministry of Education, Ministry of Finance, and so on.
Source: Claude Freud, "*25 ans de coopération en chiffres*" (Yaoundé Ministère de la Coopération, 1985).

Investment, including CCCE projects, represents 40 percent of total aid flows, with rural development aid accounting for 25 percent.

Characteristics of French Aid in 1985

In 1985 project grants supported by the Ministry of Cooperation experienced considerable erosion and dispersion. Apart from the project in support of the Société d'Aménagement et d'Exploitation des Terres du Delta (SAED), which amounted to F 11 million, only one operation reached F 5 million; the others rarely exceeded F 2 million. The grants approved in 1985 were in fact merely to permit the continuation of existing projects and thus indicated a gradual shift out of grant investment aid in favor of CCCE loan assistance, which was six times as large on average over 1980–85.

Decrease in technical assistance. The French Senegalese Ministerial Committee decided in 1985 to continue the process begun in 1980 (involving 500 teachers and 250 technical assistants) of cutting the number of French aid personnel by 1989 by half—from 1,500 to 750. Advantage will be taken of this adjustment phase to revitalize the plan for nationals to fill many technical assistance posts and to redirect the technical assistance that remains toward more advisory roles.

In 1985 the cost of technical assistance (F 300 million) remained practically unchanged from the previous three years because the staff cutbacks were offset to a significant degree by increases in salaries and related costs.

Significant increase in financial aid. Financial aid reached a peak of roughly F 700 million in 1985—owing to the combination of an adjustment loan of F 200 million by CCCE, a grant of F 40 million from the French Treasury, a budget subsidy of F 100 million granted at the end of the year, and, in particular, a Paris Club rescheduling operation of F 370 million.

This large contribution from France enabled Senegal to meet the performance criteria prescribed under the current International Monetary Fund (IMF) stand-by agreement by the December 31, 1985, deadline and to achieve a (fragile) balance in its public finances. But this commitment was undertaken to the detriment of financing for productive projects that could launch an economic recovery. The French government has proposed remedying this by involving French private or public enterprises in the investment effort through a joint investment fund.

Evaluation of Rural Development

Production results can be analyzed under four main topics: (1) the physical results observed, (2) the production conditions that explain the physical results, (3) the behavior of farmers in choosing crops in response to incentives, and (4) the development policies implemented by the Senegalese government to improve rural living conditions.

Physical results. Groundnut production continues to be at the mercy of fluctuations in the climate and is no higher than the level attained twenty or twenty-five years ago. Yields are stable or diminishing, and the area under cultivation is falling slightly, owing to the increase in food grain, which in turn is linked almost entirely to the home consumption in rural areas.

Cotton production, which reached 41,000 tons in 1981–82 under an area of 32,000 hectares, with an exceptional yield of 1,280 kilograms per hectare, fell back to 28,000 tons in 1985.

For rainfed crops in general, yields, areas under cultivation, and production volume have scarcely increased in ten years—an indication that the functioning of the production system has not improved and that productivity remains low and at the mercy of the climate. The only change worthy of note seems to be some development in food grains at the expense of groundnut farming.

Over the past twenty years, production of paddy rice in Senegal has ranged from 100,000 to 140,000 tons (from 60,000 to 105,000 tons of hulled rice), whereas imports of hulled rice, which were about 200,000 tons a year between 1970 and 1979, have moved up to 360,000 tons per year since 1980. Bottomland rice production, under a project supervised by the Textile Fibers Development Company SODEFITEX (Société de Développement des Fibres Textiles), is now only 3,000 tons of paddy rice. Production in the Senegal River Valley irrigation schemes has reached 70,000 tons of paddy, but traditional rice production in the lower Casamance has plummeted.

Although production in the Senegal River area has increased now that total water control has been achieved, it remains lower than expected. One of the goals of rice farming along the Senegal River has been to sell rice to the towns, and this goal has not been achieved: Only 10,000 tons of paddy are being sold to the Delta Development and Operation Company (SAED). The village project areas consume almost all their production themselves.

In conclusion, the production figures, although not disastrous, are disappointing. A review of the prevalent production conditions explains the physical results obtained and their trend over time.[4] The influence of the various factors of production varies according to the subsector.

Production conditions. One of the most important factors affecting agricultural production in Senegal has been climatic uncertainty. Rainfall plays a crucial role in rainfed cotton, groundnut, and grain farming. Generally speaking, yields and production are good when rainfall is high (as in 1978–79 and 1981–82) and poor when it is low (as in 1977–78, 1979–80, and 1980–81). In the case of cotton, it should be added that parasite activity has been low in recent years except for 1978–79, which explains the poor yields in that crop year.

In the case of irrigated rice, climatic fluctuations should have little effect, since the land area is under total water control. In fact, however, poor water management and inadequate maintenance of the irrigation network and pumping stations are creating a new risk. As a result, 40 percent of the improved area is not cultivated; only 80 percent of the crop on the cultivated area is harvested; and there is relatively little double-cropping (70 percent utilization of equipped areas in the Delta and the Middle Valley, and 120 percent in the village schemes—giving 80 percent for the schemes as a whole, compared with a possible 150 percent).[5]

Production has also been influenced by seed availability and quality. In the cases of cotton and rice, seed does not seem to present a problem with respect to quantity (about 1,000 tons needed annually for each crop) or quality. For groundnuts, the seed program has guaranteed distribution of a sufficient quantity of seed—that is, 120,000 tons a year—even in poor years. The quality of the groundnut seed is less clear. Only 50 percent of the seed distributed is selected seed, and it appears that in some regions, such as Siné Saloum, the varieties used do not adapt easily to the fluctuations in the climate.

The availability of technical information is yet another factor to consider in assessing Senegal's agricultural production. In groundnut cultivation, technical messages relating to extensive cultivation—selected seed, sowing date, chemical fertilizers and treatment, and animal traction—have been disseminated successfully. Farmers seem to have a good technical grasp, and failures are due mainly to problems in managing the projects. For example, some projects were abandoned recently because of budget constraints. Fertilizer deliveries fell sharply when government aid was reduced or eliminated, and deliveries of animal traction equipment ceased altogether after agricultural credit was abolished in 1979. With the elimination of government subsidies, barely 30,000 tons of fertilizer was used for groundnuts, millet, and sorghum in 1981–82, and less than 10,000 tons in 1982–83, compared with 100,000 tons a few years earlier. This drastic fall has not brought about any spectacular reduction in yields. Is this because the fertilizer formula is unsuitable and causes soil acidification? Is it because this is an area with poor rainfall and the effects of the fertilizer are not always apparent? Research is needed to answer these questions. The future trend of soil fertility remains a central concern, since the soils are often overused and not allowed to lie fallow.

Although the extensive technical messages pertaining to cultivation have met with obvious success in the groundnut area, the more complex messages about production intensification seem to have failed—particularly those explaining how to maintain soil fertility (for example, by deep phosphating, plowing in organic matter, organic fertilization, cropping patterns that permit high-density cultivation, or reforestation with *Acacia albida*). This failure is can be traced in large part to a poor grasp of the economic constraints on farmers, who have no resources available to invest.

One can therefore say that an almost total impasse has been reached in groundnut cultivation. Inputs other than seed are no longer distributed, intensification messages are rejected by the farmers, the use of animal traction is obstructed, and capital is shrinking rapidly following the suspension of the agricultural credit farmers need to purchase equipment. The situation may become catastrophic if the supply of animal traction equipment is not renewed—for it must not be forgotten that this equipment makes it possible to sow groundnut and grain seed rapidly and at the optimum date—after lightly working the soil to ensure better use of rain, which is always scarce in groundnut areas. Furthermore, in certain operations (groundnut seeding and harvesting) animal traction can to some extent offset the loss of manpower due to the emigration of large numbers of young people.[6]

The situation is less serious for the cotton or the rice grown along the Senegal River. SODEFITEX and SAED have continued to deliver fertilizer and pesticides, which are particularly cost-effective in the well watered cotton areas and in the irrigation schemes. SODEFITEX was also able to deliver animal traction equipment in 1982, and the rice farmers along the river have benefited from the cultivation work done by SAED equipment—these activities having been financed by aid projects. In cotton and rice production, therefore, the outreach activities and technical channels are not called into question, as they are in the case of groundnuts. Because the technical messages offered here do in fact produce good agronomic results, the problems are, at least in the short term, more economic than technical in nature, or are related to management (to SAED's inefficiency in water management or in the plowing and threshing service).

Choice of farming activities and producer prices. The behavior of farmers in the three areas of production is remarkably stable. Under the present socioeconomic circumstances, farmers have little choice in the crops they grow, and so the area sown to groundnuts varies little, holding at about 1 million and 1.2 million hectares seeded annually. This low elasticity of area seeded to production conditions is due to the fact that, out of a cultivable area of about 2 million hectares, 1 million is devoted to millet, 90 percent of which is consumed on the farm. Millet and groundnuts are the only crops that can do well in this region since rainfall is too low to grow cotton or maize. It is only when rainfall is poor or in the year after a bad harvest that larger areas are planted to millet—the maximum increase being 200,000 hectares; in these circumstances groundnut cultivation is reduced, for manpower and land shortages keep the total area under cultivation practically constant from year to year. The fact must be stressed, although it is not universally recognized, that groundnut cultivation does not jeopardize the food equilibrium of rural populations in the Groundnut Basin, except when there is an exceptional drought.

In the south, the percentage of area under cotton is small in comparison with that under other crops: 11 percent in eastern Senegal and 13 percent in upper Casamance, compared with about 50 percent for food grains and more than 35 percent for groundnuts in both areas.[7] Thus here, too, there is little room to maneuver and the total area under cultivation remains about the same. The choice between cotton and groundnuts remains fairly stable. The farmers generally try to maintain diversified production that minimizes risk and optimizes use of the factors of production—particularly since there is no significant difference between the monetary incentives in cotton and groundnuts, or rice.

Small farmers in the Senegal River Valley still rely heavily on rainfed crops and stockraising and employ more than half the work force. In the Upper Valley of the Senegal River, emigration and workers' remittances provide funds for the wages and inputs in the village schemes and thus provide food security for households. Generally speaking, labor constraints remain substantial—despite the use of seasonal workers and recourse to SAED for a number of cultivation tasks, particularly in the large schemes. As a result, considerable difficulty is experienced in maintaining the schemes and ensuring appropriate production conditions. For these reasons, and also for technical reasons relating to the establishment of irrigation infrastructure, the areas under cultivation are not increasing significantly and remain stable at around 20,000 hectares. The important fact is not so much whether the area has increased as the transition to total water control that has been achieved under the projects.

As for producer prices, their influence varies fairly widely across products and therefore the subsectors. As already mentioned, farmers have a limited choice of rainfed crops, so that unless the price systems change radically, the choices between crops cannot be expected to change greatly. Groundnuts will continue to be grown on 1 million hectares, as will food grains, and cotton will probably not exceed the 60,000-hectare long-term projection unless world cotton prices are much more favorable than groundnut prices and make it possible to grant an attractive cotton producer price. Barring this, the only effect of manipulating producer prices would probably be to boost groundnut sales on the parallel market, as happened in 1980–81, if official prices are too low in comparison with parallel market prices.

At the same time, it is quite clear that if a new policy were adopted allowing true commercialization of food grains at an attractive producer price, their share would increase substantially. The combination of the commercial and the food aspects would constitute a decisive advantage for the farmers—who are constantly concerned with minimizing risk. At present, there is little marketing of grains such as millet, sorghum, and maize, and the official grain purchase price can be described as meaningless, since there is no supply at that price.

Moreover, the expansion of export crops such as groundnuts or cotton has its limits. Although the historical trend has led to this preference for commercial crops—with Senegal's towns buying imported rice and wheat at low prices—it seems out of the question for farmers to abandon grain growing for subsistence needs at a time when the export price of groundnuts or cotton is stagnating or falling. Because of both food security concerns and trends in terms of trade, therefore, it seems that the production of rainfed food grains cannot decrease in the future.[8]

With regard to irrigated rice, it seems clear that the purchase price of paddy has no effect on the quantities marketed, since the areas allocated to it barely suffice to supply farm consumption needs.

Senegal's sectoral and development policies. The three crops studied are produced with scarce resources that must be put to the best possible use: these consist of the factors of production (land, water, inputs, labor), on one hand, and macroeconomic resources (foreign exchange, public savings, foreign debt), on the other. The production activities of all three crops contribute to the goals of various policies and of development strategy more generally: They help supply foodstuffs to urban centers, through the increase and regularization of domestic grain production; fuel the national economy through agricultural purchases and the value added created; promote regional development planning through the judicious siting of agricultural development projects; and, in general, help improve rural living conditions and endeavor to make the best use of scarce resources.

As for the regional impact of projects revolving around these crops, groundnuts supply most of the agricultural monetary income of Senegalese farmers virtually throughout the country, even in the cotton-growing area. Groundnuts thus play a considerable role in activating the rural economy. In a normal year groundnuts provide CFAF 45 to 50 billion in monetary income to groundnut producers—which is 20 times as much as cotton and 150 times as much as rice.[9] Hence, abandoning groundnut cultivation is at present tantamount to eliminating rural monetary trade. Cotton is a supplemental source of income, which is sometimes substantial in areas where it is the principal source of cash. Rice growing makes it possible (admittedly at a high cost) to ensure the food security of the Senegal River populations, particularly in years of poor rainfall. The Senegal River schemes thus mainly serve to make production for home consumption secure, although one of the goals was to market rice in the towns.

This goal of supplying food to the towns is in fact impossible to achieve at present, not only for the technical reasons already noted but also for economic reasons, which are tied in with Senegal's food strategy and agricultural policy choices. For some time, the country's agricultural strategy has been based on three assumptions, although they were not always spelled out as such: (1) groundnut cultivation can furnish income to the farmers, revenue to the government, and foreign exchange to the country; (2) the farmers can provide their own subsistence needs in grain; (3) urban consumers can buy imported broken rice at low prices. This situation is ideal as long as groundnut products continue to command a high price on the world markets and broken rice can be imported at a low price: Transportation and marketing costs make the purchase of imported rice by farmers or of local grain by town dwellers economically unattractive.

This development model has produced the expected results, particularly the near disappearance of the consumption of millet, sorghum, and maize in the towns. Barely 10,000 tons of millet have been marketed through official channels in recent years (and that mainly on account of substantial subsidies), whereas more than 320,000 tons of broken rice and 118,000 tons of wheat are imported annually (not counting food aid).

In recent years, a fundamental change has been taking place in the world commodity markets: The price of groundnut products has been falling, bringing it more and more into line with competitive fatty substances such as soybeans and sunflower seed. Nonetheless, from the point of view of the national economy, there continues to be no advantage to producing millet, sorghum, or maize to replace imported broken rice on Senegal's urban market. Thus, the consumer price of broken rice is CFAF 160 per kilogram (table 8-2). Although unprocessed millet can be purchased at CFAF 70 per kilogram, millet flour costs the consumer in Dakar CFAF 180 per kilogram.[10] This high price includes transportation, marketing, and milling costs. The consumer price for broken maize would also be close to CFAF 160 per kilogram.[11] Consumer prices for domestically grown millet and maize are thus, respectively, even higher than, or the same as, the price of imported rice; to replace rice, they would probably have to be 20 to 30 percent lower. Increasing the consumer price of rice is politically explosive and severely penalizes the underprivileged urban classes.

If it is virtually impossible to sell rainfed millet or maize in the towns at present, the same is true of irrigated rice from the Senegal River area, since marketed production is low and is consumed within that region. The cost price of SAED rice is about CFAF 250 per kilogram.[12] Costs remain high because (a) double-cropping has not yet come about, owing to the length of the rice cycle, and (b) almost all the water is supplied by pumping (as rainfall amounts to only 0.3 meters per year). The substitution of irrigated SAED rice for imported rice therefore cannot be justified economically.

The decision to introduce irrigated rice projects is the outcome of regional development policy and may be justified in the long term—provided that SAED's costs are stabilized, that maintenance costs are reduced, and that production is increased with two crop cycles on 100

Table 8-2. Cost of Domestically Consumed Foodgrains, 1986
(CFAF/kilograms)

Cost item	*Millet*	*Maize*	*SAED rice*	*Imported rice*
Producer price or import price	70	70	85	45
Primary collection or miscellaneous forwarding costs	30	30	—	15
Transportation to place of consumption	25	25	—	—
Processing	40	20	—	—
Finished product	165	145	—	60
Wholesale/retail markup	15	15	—	15
Retail price (at full cost), Dakar	180	160	265	75
Actual consumer price (net of tax or subsidy	160	160	160	160
CPSP margin tax (+) or subsidy (−)	−20	0	−105	+85

— = Not available.

Source: Pierre Thenevin, "Synthèse des Evaluations Riz-Coton-Arachides au Sénégal" (Paris: Ministère des Relations Extérieures, Coopération et Développement/Caisse Centrale de Coopération Economique, 1982). Updated with 1986 prices (c.i.f.)

percent of the equipped areas (once the Diama dam is completed). However, in view of the high recurrent costs and Senegal's large budget deficit, the country will have great difficulty finding a way to repay the loans taken out for the capital costs of these investments (including project areas, dikes, and dams). These costs have not even been included in the calculations presented here.

In the medium term, any initiative in the Senegal River Valley will have to be financed by external resources, since neither the government nor the farmers are in a position to pay for the current operating costs—let alone repay the obligations on the investments. Ten years ago, groundnuts and cotton brought the budget of the state CFAF 30 billion in direct and indirect revenue or revenue induced by wage earners' and farmers' consumption. Since 1981 the agricultural sector as a whole has presented a negative balance sheet for the government. Meanwhile, government expenditure has more than doubled in ten years, to more than CFAF 200 billion. The loss of agricultural revenue is extremely serious for the government; since it cannot increase the burden on farmers, whose purchasing power is stagnant or even declining, it has no choice but to go heavily into debt.[13]

Aware of the current impasse, the Senegalese authorities have instituted the New Agricultural Policy (Nouvelle Politique Agricole, NPA) to redress the rural situation. The NPA forms an integral part of the medium- and long-term adjustment program (1985–92), which was the subject of the general economic policy declaration of the Government of the Republic of Senegal in October 1984. The NPA calls for the reorganization of rural life, which hinges on setting up grass roots *village sections* and producer groups; government withdrawal from the project companies within five years (starting with the abolition of the Société Nationale d'Approvisionnement du Monde Rural and the Société des Terres Neuves in 1985 and entry by the private (or semiprivate) sector into a number of fields; a new policy for inputs, particularly for groundnut seed and fertilizers; a food grain policy that employs incentive prices to promote food self-sufficiency and raise production levels; and a long-term policy for the conservation of the natural environment, soil regeneration, reforestation, and for combating desertification.

Although these measures are expected to have a positive impact, the NPA leaves some important problems unresolved. The specific, restrictive context in which the NPA was drawn up bears restating. Increasingly higher costs—both to society at large and to the government—of agricultural activities are a part of this context; there is no short-term hope of redressing this problem because agriculture is battling soil exhaustion, deteriorating terms of trade, and drought, on the one hand, and is working with inappropriate implementing structures (cooperatives, regional development companies, and the Caisse de Péréquation et Stabilisation des Prix [CPSP]), on the other. Further complicating the situation are pressures from donors, chiefly the IMF, to reduce costs in the short term, but they do little to encourage Senegal to recover production or to strive for consistency in its long-term goals. Nor is there a consensus (either internally or among the various donors) on the recovery measures to be taken—whether in dealing with technical issues (such as the benefits of irrigation as against rainfed crops, the returns to fertilizer use on different crops, and so on) or socioeconomic issues (income distribution, price policy, or the interests of the various pressure groups, CPSP, religious sects, oil and sugar manufacturers, and staff of the regional development companies).

The NPA can only be a weak compromise in that it consists of contradictions (since it endeavors to satisfy conflicting opinions or interests), refuses to choose between certain options, and contains serious omissions. Broadly speaking, the goals of the NPA merit support, subject to the following reservations.

First, the decision to give the producers greater responsibility and to phase out the supervisory companies (*sociétés d'encadrement*) is a courageous and positive step. However, some doubts remain about the organization of the village sections and producer groups. The haste with which the 4,472 village sections were set up and the constraints placed on their membership (minimum levels are required) suggest that the causes of the failure of the cooperatives have not been eliminated. This is all the more worrying in that a new failure would make it difficult to set up producer organizations for several years to come—and consequently to restore agricultural credit, one of the top priorities of the NPA.

Second, since the phasing out of the regional development companies, little has been done to ensure that other bodies will provide the services necessary for agricultural development (technical messages, information systems, extension, research and development, plant health control, and antidesertification measures). These services, which were poorly performed by the regional development companies, appear likely to be abandoned altogether.

Third, the authorities need to clarify the links between the food grains policy and the goal of food self-sufficiency. The current structural grain deficit, about 500,000 tons per year, can at best be made up only in the long term. The self-sufficiency goal thus seems to have no operational validity in the medium term. It would probably be better to set medium-term goals that recognize the present constraints.

Fourth, the decision to increase the area developed for irrigation in the Senegal River Valley from 2,000–3,000 hectares per annum to 5,000 hectares should be examined more closely to verify its feasibility. With regard to financing, will it be possible to raise the CFAF 10 to 20 billion a year required to carry out the investments? What will be the impact on the finances of the various operators (the government, SAED, and the producers)? What will be the final cost of the outputs (paddy and vegetables)?

Fifth, the grains policy must be a global policy that addresses every aspect of agriculture: production (rice, millet, maize), imports (broken rice, wheat), and relative prices. With regard to physical resources, does the SAED possess the capacity to carry out this enormous program? Are the communities involved ready to adapt to this new pace and to this new mode of production? The outlook for maize seems promising with regard to production, processing, and consumption. This is undoubtedly a possibility to be exploited, even if its benefits can be expected only in the long term.

Financing of the NPA and the price policy it implies (with respect to input, output, and consumer prices) are closely interlinked. Yet the NPA itself scarcely touches on this topic. The fact is that a policy of market prices for inputs (including investment) and incentive prices for producers with administratively set floors would shift the burden of financing to the consumer. Is this the intended course? Price consistency has not yet been studied. Moreover, the amounts and methods of financing the measures advocated by the NPA are scarcely outlined, and urban rural tradeoffs have not been discussed.

Aid to Cameroon

Unlike Senegal, a country poor in agricultural potential and severely limited in its choice of crops by the lack of rainfall, Cameroon is a highly diversified country with good rainfall and therefore good potential for the substantial expansion of agricultural production. Cameroon's experience is unique in two ways: It did not set up a Rural Development Ministry until fairly recently (in 1973), and it finances half its rural development investments out of its own resources.

The relative newness of its institutions explains by and large why it is difficult to retrace the rural development policy of the Cameroonian authorities. The fact that they finance the better part of their projects makes them extremely reluctant to disseminate information to third parties, which merely complicates the analyst's task. For these reasons, the analysis of Cameroon in this chapter goes into less depth than that of Senegal and passes over the coffee, palm oil, rubber, and banana subsectors to focus on rice, cocoa, and cotton. This will permit a comparison with Senegal using identical products (rice and cotton) and two low-density crops (cocoa and groundnuts).

A comparison of annual averages for 1960–65 and 1980–85 indicates that aid flows from the Ministry of Cooperation to Cameroon tripled in nominal terms over the interval, but fell by 50 percent in real terms. The share of rural development aid remained stable at about 10 percent (table 8-3).

Between 1960 and 1965 the average composition of Ministry of Cooperation aid was investment, 45 percent; technical assistance, 33 percent; and operating subsidies 22 percent. Twenty years later, the share of investment had fallen to about 15 percent, that of technical assistance had risen to more than 80 percent, and that of operating subsidies had fallen to only 5 percent.

Looking at total French aid to Cameroon, including aid from other ministries and the CCCE, it is evident that CCCE aid (negative in the 1960s) is now about equal to that provided by the Ministry of Cooperation. The composition of total French aid is now half grants and half loans, whereas at the time of independence it consisted entirely of grants. Investment, including CCCE projects, represents nearly 50 percent of total aid flows, with rural development aid accounting for 20 percent.

Characteristics of French Aid in 1986

Since 1986, France has been providing three kinds of aid to Cameroon: technical assistance and training fellowships, support for diversification, and support for infrastructure.

Technical assistance and training fellowships in France. The technical assistance furnished to Cameroon has declined from 627 technical assistants in 1973 to 528 in 1986. This is still largely a substitution type of aid. However, that is the form in which the Cameroonian authorities wish to receive it. From France's own point of view, this technical assistance is an important factor in its role in the Cameroonian economy. Cameroonian students constitute the largest contingent from the Sub-Saharan African community being trained in France.

Diversification of domestic production. FAC (Aid and Cooperation Fund) and CCCE have a number of diversification projects: rice farming in northern Cameroon and the Noun Valley, the development of the cocoa area, the promotion of soybean cultivation, and the development of the cotton area.

Infrastructure. France is helping to develop infrastructure through a mix of FAC subsidies and CCCE loans to telecommunications, energy, and transportation works being undertaken by Cameroon. Examples

Table 8-3. Cameroon: Net Disbursements of French Aid, 1960–85
(thousands of current and constant French francs)

Allocation	*1961*	*1965*	*1970*	*1975*	*1980*	*1985*	*1985 (constant 1961 francs)*
Ministry of Cooperation							
Investment aid (IA)	48,100	39,800	27,700	39,100	45,900	29,900	5,000
Percent for rural development	23	8	10	4	28	43	
IA as percent of total Ministry of Cooperation aid	58	47	47	28	23	13	
Technical Assistance (TA)	24,000	34,000	34,000	73,900	125,000	183,200	30,500
Percent for rural development	—	—	4	3	4	9	
TA as percent of total Ministry of Cooperation aid	29	40	45	53	62	81	
Operating aid (OA) including financial assistance)	10,900	11,200	13,500	25,800	31,500	13,500	2,200
Percent for rural development	—	—	34	33	23	8	
OA as percent of total Ministry of Cooperation aid	13	13	18	19	15	6	
Total Ministry of Cooperation aid	83,000	85,700	75,200	138,900	202,600	226,600	39,500
Percent for rural development	16	6	13	9	12	13	
Other ministries[a]	—	—	—	6,400	4,100	122,000	20,300
CCCE	−10,000	−22,300	19,600	6,400	312,400	228,000	38,000
Percent for rural development	—	—	—	24	7	32	
Total AID	73,000	62,700	94,800	151,700	519,100	576,600	97,800
Percent for rural development	16	9	10	9	9	20	

— = Not available.
Note: Not including guarantees.
a. Ministry of Education, Ministry of Finance, and so on.
Source: Claude Freud, "*25 ans de coopération en chiffres*" (Yaoundé: Ministère de la Coopération, 1985).

are access roads in Yaoundé, the Trans-Cameroonian Railroad, satellite telecommunications, television, and hydroelectric plant and water supply facilities. This participation in the expansion of the Cameroonian economy reflects France's "bet" (before the oil crisis) on the development of Cameroon, which was to replace Côte d'Ivoire as the up and coming economy and was therefore designed to enable French enterprises to share in that success.

Evaluation of Rural Development

Agriculture occupies a central place in the Cameroonian economy. Directly or indirectly, it employs nearly three-fourths of the population, even though its share in GDP fell from 40 percent in 1960 to 20 percent in 1985. Until 1980, agriculture contributed the largest share of exports—close to 75 percent. Since the rise in oil production, its share of exports (mostly coffee and cocoa) has fallen to 27 percent, and it has been displaced by oil as the leading source of foreign exchange earnings. However, agriculture is still an important contributor when import substitution (rice, sugar, millet) is taken into account.

Until 1980, export crops furnished 40 percent of government revenue. Although the oil income has since reduced agriculture's share, it continues to be a source of revenue and one that will be appreciated all the more as oil income diminishes.

Agriculture's modern sector. Cameroon's system of agricultural production continues to be divided between the great mass of traditional small farmers and the "modern" farms, which are oriented toward food production and are under the control of the government.

Even though the modern farms contribute only 10 percent to agricultural output, they receive nearly two-thirds of agricultural financing under the country's Fourth Plan. This study focuses on these operations (primarily those that produce cotton, cocoa, and rice), since they are the ones that have benefited from external financing and are the barometer of the Cameroonian government's development intentions.[14]

Cotton. After a difficult start in the late 1920s, cotton production climbed to 47 tons in 1931 but then dropped to 6 tons in 1936. Cotton growing was not launched on a large scale until the 1950s, when it was made possible by the liberal course chosen—which was in contrast to the forced cultivation instituted in Chad and the Central African Republic. The French administration entrusted this task to the Compagnie Française de Développement des Fibres Textiles (CFDT), which from the outset modeled its operation on the strictly controlled system of production, processing, and marketing in the other countries of French Equatorial Africa and which rapidly demonstrated its efficiency.

In the initial phase, production increased mainly because the area under cultivation was expanded. Average yields were low: about 400 kilograms per hectare. After reaching 100,000 hectares by 1966, the area under cultivation stabilized because land became scarce. Cotton is still an itinerant crop that exhausts the soil and is therefore a large consumer of arable land.

In view of the situation, the CFDT decided to switch over to high-density cultivation. The results were striking: Yields reached 840 kilograms per hectare in 1969, and production rose from 41,000 tons in 1963 to 99,000 tons in 1970. This success was due to the combined effect of several favorable factors. This was a period of good rainfall. Research had disseminated more productive varieties. Animal traction had developed (more than two-thirds of the land was tilled semimechanically), breaking the deadlock of the labor shortage. Above all, producers had become enthusiastic about cotton, which brought them an ever-increasing cash income.

The boom was then interrupted by a drought. Yields fell back to 400 kilograms per hectare beginning in 1970, and in 1973 production collapsed to 28,000 tons—its 1960 level. But the drought was not the whole story. To the extent that it directly compelled farmers to expand the area under food crops (to limit the climatic risks), it operated to the detriment of cotton because manpower and land were scarce. However, the decline in the area under cotton was also due to a drop in cotton receipts compared with food crops, whose prices soared, spurred by the strong demand from neighboring Nigeria.

As a result, farmers expanded the cotton-growing area toward the south, where the climatic risks are less great, and stepped up the shift to intensive cultivation. In 1974 the Société de Développement du Coton du Cameroun (SODECOTON) took over the activities of CFDT, to which it continued to be linked through its equity holdings and through technical and commercial assistance agreements. Intensive farming progressed rapidly to reach an average of 1.3 tons per hectare. It was based on the latest research gains—in particular on substantial increases in fertilization and antiparasite treatments.

The cotton area and production both rose steadily, reaching 89,000 hectares and 115,000 tons, respectively, in 1985–86. This spectacular recovery was apparently due to the availability of efficient plant material, developed by research; optimum use of fertilizer and antiparasite treatments; a highly disciplined extension and supervision service, which supplied credit for the purchase of inputs only on condition that the farmer had carried out the recommended cultivation operations; expansion of animal traction and even the beginnings of motorization in the south, where the prevalence of trypanosomiasis makes the use of animals impossible; and high producer prices—averaging 40 percent higher than in other African countries.

The aggregate product of the cotton and textiles operations is CFAF 38 billion, including national value added of CFAF 24 billion.[15] Although the greater part of value added is created by the farmers, they receive only 25 percent of domestic revenue from the crops; cotton activities mainly benefit SODECOTON and textile industry wage-earners.

Cotton contributes only 1.5 percent of GDP, but its effect on the trade balance has been positive: Exports in 1985 rose to CFAF 21 billion (3.2 percent of Cameroonian exports) in comparison with imports of CFAF 14.4 billion. This was made possible by a substantial state subsidy (CFAF 18 billion in 1985). The reason for this intolerably heavy burden on public finances is that in 1983, a year when cotton production broke even, producer prices rose 50 percent whereas export prices were halved.

Restructuring is in progress to lower the costs of production, with expatriate supervision being reduced by 50 percent and the farmers bearing 100 percent of input cost (currently subsidized by 40 percent). But much more will have to be done before cotton producers can break even—unless international cotton prices rise and producer prices fall.

Cocoa. Cocoa production in Cameroon has been stagnant at barely more than 110,000 tons since the 1960s. There would seem to be two causes for this: the producer price and the age of the cocoa trees.

A comparison of price trends in Cameroon and Côte d'Ivoire, where production has been rising sharply since 1960, shows that Cameroonian producer prices have averaged CFAF 50 per kilogram lower. Cameroon finally caught up with Côte d'Ivoire prices in 1977 and then exceeded them in 1980, when the Cameroon government, thanks to its oil receipts, was able to do without the cocoa levies. Until 1979, the producer price was less than 20 percent of the world price. Today, it is 50 percent, a ratio that still allows the state to make a profit.

Remunerative prices encourage growers to establish new plantations. A study of the age pyramids shows that the period 1960–77 was marked both by a low replanting rate and by a fall in producer prices in constant francs. Because the cocoa tree takes seven years to mature, the impact of a low replanting rate on production is not felt until seven years later. The leveling off of production from 1970 onward therefore can be explained by the low replanting rate. In contrast, a rise in producer prices has an immediate impact, since it encourages farmers to give greater attention to maintenance and to resume the operation of old plantations.

The purchasing power of Cameroonian growers stagnated between 1960 and 1970, when world prices were such that producer prices could have been raised. It seems possible that this policy of low producer prices limited the replanting rate and led to the aging of the plantations and the stagnation of production.

One of the main problems in growing cocoa continues to be the increasing age of both the farmers and the plantations: More than half the growers are more than fifty years old, and two-thirds of the plantations are more than twenty-five years old. This phenomenon is due in part to the extensive flight from the land and in part to the fall in profits brought on by the appreciable decline in producer prices in real terms and the spread of brown rot. Brown rot continues to be the greatest obstacle to the development of cocoa production in Cameroon. Antiparasitic measures must be improved if cocoa production is to move ahead. Yet the farmers are not at present applying the standards recommended by research because they lack the manpower and the equipment. Consequently, cocoa farming has become a low-density operation—largely limited to pod-picking by retired people.

Cocoa production costs CFAF 575 per kilogram of beans exported.[16] This leaves the state with a profit even when world prices are depressed, as they are at present. Farmers' remuneration is the principal cost, accounting for more than 50 percent of total cost.

In 1982–83 the value of cocoa production was CFAF 68 billion—or 5 percent of GDP. With export sales of CFAF 67 billion, cocoa accounts for 10 percent of Cameroon's exports. The included import cost is CFAF 13 billion, leaving a positive balance of CFAF 55 billion, which is equal to 25 percent of the trade balance figure. Cocoa thus yields a good return to the state. A world bean price of CFAF 750 (the average rate in constant value over the past fifteen years) would yield a profit of CFAF 22 billion.

At present the industry is still trying to make the transition to high-density planting. As in Togo and Côte d'Ivoire, when the majority of growers opt for extensive cultivation, they do so at an equivalent rate of profit since in principle the loss rate with brown rot is 50 percent; low-density planting of 2 hectares is probably less constraining to the farmer than high-density planting of 1 hectare.

Rice. The first agricultural water resource improvements in northern Cameroon date from 1951–52. Until 1970, little had been done in this area: 6,000 hectares were under cultivation, with a paddy yield on the order of 1 ton per hectare.

In 1971 the government set up SEMRY, which took over the previous development works and was entrusted with the development of 5,300 hectares. SEMRY maintains and manages the scheme. It carries out the land preparation (by mechanized tilling) and furnishes all services to the growers (seed, fertilizer, water supply, and extension). It also has a monopoly on paddy purchasing and milling. The farmers carry out planting, weeding, and harvesting and transport the paddy to the points of sale, where the levies are collected.

Since 1975 yields have averaged 4.5 tons per hectare per cycle. Farmers quickly made the transition to two growing cycles a year. Yields improved substantially because of better water control and the general practice of transplanting. Although transplanting was not provided for in the project, it took place fortuitously and was immediately adopted by most of the rice farmers. This testifies to the ability of the farmers to incorporate even an exacting technique quickly if they see that it offers an immediate return.

Between 1975 and 1985, the area developed multiplied threefold—from 4,500 to 13,100 hectares, and paddy production rose form 23,000 to 103,000 tons. Average yields henceforth ranked among the highest in Africa. Paddy production bought by SEMRY in 1985–86 covered nearly two-thirds of the domestic rice demand, estimated at 90,000 tons (equivalent to 130,000 tons of paddy).

The value added created by SEMRY is about CFAF 10 billion.[17] This is hardly representative of rice production at the national level, but it is roughly in line with the level of the northeastern region where the scheme is located. Until 1985, however, 70 percent of rice sales took place on the external markets (chiefly Nigeria). The SEMRY project therefore strikes one as an export project and not an operation geared to domestic demand. With the closing of the Nigerian border, the rice can no longer be sold. On-farm consumption accounts for only 10 percent of the value of production. This project is thus firmly integrated into the money economy, and many rice growers are not self-sufficient in food. SEMRY employees receive a higher share of rice income (52 percent) than the growers (35 percent). In this sense, this is indeed more an agroindustrial than a rural development project.

Despite good technical results, the incremental value added created by the project over the past ten years is still below operating costs. The poor economic results bring to attention the cost of rice production, which in 1983 was CFAF 185 per kilogram, whereas the selling price to merchants was CFAF 150 and the state subsidy therefore CFAF 35 per kilogram.

SEMRY's rice-marketing difficulties stem from the fact that its market is not protected against competition from imported rice. Counting transportation costs and margins, imported rice arrives in northern

Cameroon (the region in which SEMREY rice is produced) at CFAF 150 to 155 per kilogram, that is, at a price below that of SEMRY rice sold by merchants, who charge CFAF 165. And this is not to mention the Yaoundé and Douala markets, where its price would be augmented by transportation costs.

Because SEMRY rice is not competitive, unsold stocks of rice (in July 1986) amounted to 65,000 tons of paddy and 11,000 tons of milled rice—meaning that a total of CFAF 7 billion was tied up. As a result, SEMRY sold off 5,000 tons of rice at CFAF 70 to be able to pay its employees, and it withheld payment to the farmers for the last paddy harvest, which amounted to 50,000 tons.

All this transpired because the linked sales system (*jumelage*) performed poorly. Under Cameroon's method of cross-subsidization, each dealer's import permit is tied to a compulsory SEMRY rice purchase quota. Until 1985, the fact that dealers skipped their obligations to purchase SEMRY rice did not matter because there was a demand for it in the Nigerian market. When the border trade was officially cut off, the dealers did not honor their obligations any more than they had done before, and SEMRY rice sales slumped.

The validity and success potential of the SEMRY system of managing agricultural water resources remains questionable, in that the technical standards applied (mechanization with technical assistance and by and large two crop cycles) call for control and authoritarian supervision, which up to now have left little room for initiative by the farmers.

Have the original goals been achieved? At the national level, rice self-sufficiency is well on the way to being achieved technically. At the regional level, the result is beyond dispute: Farmers' incomes amounted to CFAF 6 billion in 1985. But the capital and operating costs of the project are high. Its self-sufficient, inward-looking nature remains a goal on paper alone—in that only 10 percent of the rice consumed in the project area is grown under the scheme. Rice imports have not been reduced, and the central problem of how to sell SEMRY rice on the domestic market has not been resolved.

This project has been orphaned: The external financing sources have been withdrawn (although French technical assistance is still provided) and the government of Cameroon has not been able to take the essential steps of taxing imported rice or suspending SEMRY.

Limits on the Growth of the Modern Agricultural Sector

The growth of the modern agricultural sector is hampered by structural difficulties. The setting up of large agroindustrial complexes presupposes the availability of both land and labor. In the densely populated areas, manpower is available, but not land. The large agroindustrial complexes are in conflict with local production systems, which are all based on the possibility of long fallow periods. The mobilization of local labor, usually young people, works to the detriment of traditional agriculture. It is a problem of how to integrate these enclaves of high productivity, which up to now have demonstrated more of an ability to destroy the environment than to become nuclei of development.

Conversely, in the empty areas, the land problem does not arise, but labor does have to be brought in. This calls for heavy investments in roads, housing, and social infrastructure, which impose a large burden on the economics of these projects. Generally speaking, the cost per job created becomes prohibitive in the modern agricultural sector: CFAF 7 to 10 million, with high recurrent costs and an uncertain return.

Traditional Food Production

Traditional food crops: a neglected area. Government intervention has focused on export crops (cocoa, coffee, cotton) or import-substitution crops (rice), neglecting traditional food crops—even though these constitute agriculture's most important source of value added and jobs.

Cameroon does not fare badly when it comes to food self-sufficiency, in comparison with many other African countries: Food imports are only 5 to 6 percent of total imports. At the beginning of the 1970s, each member of the active population produced for 2.5 persons; in 1985, the figure was 3.5 persons. Since extension and supervision have remained minimal in food crops, it appears that the growth in food production results from spontaneous intensification by the farmers, spurred by a sharp rise in food crop prices.

A context of favorable urban prices. Food crop prices in the major urban centers have risen faster than inflation over the past twenty years—indicating that the equilibrium between supply and demand has become increasingly precarious. In central and south Cameroon, for which statistics are available from a long period, demand pressure has been high in the markets for the five principal consumer products (beans, macabo, cassava, bananas, and maize). Prices rise in steps and stabilize, but they do not fall in subsequent years. Rice and bread, the prices of which remain relatively low, play a substitution role in response to price rises of other products. Nevertheless, judging by price and income elasticities, consumers remain attached to their food habits, and the demand for cassava, bananas, and macabo remains rigid. The speed of urban growth and the resulting demand pressure have created a context of favorable prices that up to now has sustained the growth of food production.

The profitability of food crops also stems from the marketing system, in which fragmentation and sharp internal competition systematically limit margins. Generally speaking, the net margin is 14 percent, and the producer receives 50 to 55 percent of the consumer price, which is fairly favorable. Moreover, until about 1977, food crops benefited from the low producer prices of the principal export crops.[18]

Thus the traditional food sector so far has responded to and profited from the pressure of demand. But productivity gains are becoming more and more difficult to achieve.

Weakness of government interventions. Historically, marketing has been the focus of government action in the food sector. The objective was to regulate the prices of food products and to ensure a regular supply to the towns. Generally speaking, government agencies have not been able to control a large enough share of the market to be able to regulate prices. Being far less efficient and flexible than private dealers, they have suffered heavy operating losses, and most of them have trimmed their activities.

The Mission Interministerielle du Développement des Cultures Vivrières (MIDEVIV) provides an example. When it was established in 1976, its objective was to control 20 percent of the food crop market in Yaoundé (about 25,000 tons). Yet in its best years, MIDEVIV has not marketed more than 3,000 tons—at an average net cost to the national economy of CFAF 24,000.

Production interventions. On the production side, rainfed food crops have been neglected for a number of reasons. Research gains in food crops other than rice and maize have been limited. This is in part due to research policy, which up to the end of the 1970s focused on export crops. In Cameroon, as elsewhere, research on food crops is a good ten years behind (this is particularly true of bananas, beans, and all tubers). To add to this problem, little is known about the constraints on and the strategies of local production systems, and the liaison between research and extension is inadequate.

Subsidies on food crop inputs cannot—as in the case of export corps—be recovered downstream by taxes on the final producer price. To intensify traditional food crop production Cameroon will have to install a system of rural credit or aid that functions without the need for direct reimbursement to government—which probably explains the timidity of government action in this field.

Food Self-Sufficiency Policy

Although the investments made in sugar, rice, and palm oil production undoubtedly have limited the import burden, they are far from fully meeting domestic demand. Moreover, all of these crops suffer from acute marketing difficulties. This is in part due to the unsuitability of supply: crude palm oil, for example, does not meet the urban demand for refined oils—just as (in the case of exports) cheap granulated sugar does not meet the demand for lump sugar.

Domestic production costs are higher than world market prices, and the domestic market is poorly protected. This leads to massive and often clandestine import flows that cannot be justified by a supply deficit—not only of rice, but also of sugar and oils.

SEMRY exemplifies this situation, as it is both a model of technical development and a commercial failure. Production costs, although lower than those of similar schemes elsewhere in Africa, remain above the cost of imported rice delivered to northern Cameroon. In the absence of duties on imported rice, the project increasingly depends on government subsidies to maintain its financial equilibrium.

Broadly speaking, SEMRY's difficulties raise a fundamental problem: how to match cyclical economic policies to specific operational needs. Rice finds itself in a competitive and rapidly changing economic environment (with respect to the price of imported rice, the volume of imports, and demand by or closure of the Nigerian market). Nor does the Cameroonian government err on the side of haste in making decisions: It usually takes more than six months to alter an administered price (SEMRY prices remained stable for seven crop years at a time when production costs were rising), and the present linked-sale system cannot be efficient in the face of such large discrepancies between domestic and imported rice prices. Responses to the market therefore should take place faster, and make the best possible use of economic policy instruments such as the modulation of customs duties and changes in the selling price of rice.

Conclusions

The rural development policies of Senegal and Cameroon appear to have neglected traditional food crops in favor of export crops. These policies are a legacy of those followed by France in colonial times and derive from what has been called the colonial pact, which was based on the principle that the colonies were to produce the raw materials needed by the home country.

To achieve this goal, the French government instituted taxes payable in money and thereby compelled farmers to produce for the market.

This system worked satisfactorily because these territories were self-sufficient in food production and their labor force was not employed full time (since there were no outlets for the produce). In compelling the territories to produce materials needed for the French market, the colonial system did not upset the food equilibrium of their populations. Export crops came to be added to the traditional crops, making use of the farmers' surplus labor capacity.

The French government guaranteed economic services to the French private sector, which it called upon to invest in ports, road and rail networks, and extension services to improve production conditions. With the collapse of the price of raw materials after 1929, it was feared that these advances would be wiped out and that farmers would refuse to produce for such low prices. France thereupon set up a preferential area in which the home country granted a premium on production from the colonies—imposing import duties on similar products from other countries and passing their amount on to producers in the colonies. This policy, the effect of which was to raise prices 25 percent above world market rates on average, stimulated a substantial increase in production. The system was continued during the first years after independence, with preferential access to the French market under price-premium conditions.

Change came in the mid-1960s with the signing of the Yaoundé Convention, which associated the former colonies with the European Economic Community and provided for the abandonment of price premiums and the introduction of production subsidies designed to raise productivity and thereby compensate for the fall in prices. At the same time, a production diversification policy was instituted, both for export crops (to do away with dependency on a monoculture) and for food crops (to ensure self-sufficiency and to eliminate the need to import food products). Among export crops, only cotton recorded productivity gains, with the result that farmers' incomes fell. Among food crops, irrigated rice cultivation received all the attention, in the hope that it would replace imports. The course decided upon was the most sophisticated one possible, with prohibitively expensive development works and high operating costs in areas of low rainfall, where pumping was necessary year-round—and this strategy was pursued even though rice could be obtained cheaply on the world market and domestic efforts were therefore not competitive.

The inescapable conclusion is that the situation in Cameroon and Senegal has changed little since the colonial period—except that their economies are no longer protected, and the prices of their raw materials must bear the full brunt of the deterioration in terms of trade. Yet these countries need foreign exchange, which they can only obtain by continuing to exploit their natural resources in the form of export crops. They must therefore continue to bank on these crops, at any rate in the short and medium term. But under what conditions?

The development of export crops depends on four factors: producer prices, input subsidies, research results, and project management. For all products, a good producer price motivates farmers to increase the areas under cultivation. This is what happened to all products before 1964, without any need to subsidize inputs.

When producer prices are low and inputs are subsidized, the situation changes, depending on whether one is looking at an extensive crop such as groundnuts, or an intensive crop such as cotton. In the case of groundnuts, the increase in productivity due to subsidized inputs is insignificant and does not offset the reductions in area (as in Senegal in 1967–69). In the case of cotton, the increase in productivity offsets the reductions in area.

The contradictory responses of the two crops to intensification can be traced to the other two factors that also govern increases in production: research results and project management. Research results are not convincing evidence to the groundnut, coffee, or cocoa farmers. These farmers will always prefer the logic of extensive cultivation, which guarantees a certain income, to the risk of attempting to increase productivity through more intensive cultivation practices—a gamble that they are not certain to win and that is expensive for them. For example, in the Senegal Groundnut Basin, the sharp fall in fertilizer consumption did not lead to any spectacular drop in yields. This has not been true of cotton, however, where the farmer can see that one or more fertilizer treatments can bring productivity gains of 25 to 30 percent.

The other crucial factor is project management. On the one hand, groundnut, coffee, and cocoa grown on small farms respond individually to the market and depend on its smooth functioning (input supply, credit, marketing). It can happen that this market is held by government companies that do not perform their role properly and do the farmer a disservice (as in the case of groundnuts in Senegal), or that no market exists (as in the case of groundnuts in Mali after the government company was dismantled) and production collapses.

On the other hand, there are government plantations (rubber, palm oil) managed by technical agencies with proletarianized growers, among whom one can include cotton growers. Like the government plantations, at the functional level, cotton production is controlled from upstream of farm production to the c.i.f. stage by the CFDT apparatus, leaving farmers little room for initiative. The small farmer in this case does not really operate from a production function, but from a labor-supply function. This highly centralized, highly capitalized organization, which achieves good technical performance but at the price of high factor costs, is condemned to intensive production. In a situation of low producer prices and no input subsidies, production falls sharply as happened with groundnuts after 1967. This certainly would be the case with cotton at the present time if the producer price had been aligned on the world price and if subsidies had been abolished. The price that could be paid to the cotton growers would be so low that, in contrast to what happened in the recent period, it would have a deterrent effect and would wipe out twenty years of efforts to achieve intensive cultivation.

This points to the problem of world prices, which—more often than not—today bear no relation to production costs and correspond to dumping prices.

Notes

1. The study and project companies are the Bureau Central des Equipements d'Outre-Mer (BCEOM, overseas plant); Compagnie Française de Développement des Fibres Textiles (CFDT, textile fibers); Bureau de Développement de la Production Agricole (BDPA, agricultural production); Société d'Aide Technique et de Coopération (SATEC, technical assistance and cooperation); Société d'Etudes du Développement Economique et Social (SEDES, economic and social development); and Société Centrale pour l'Equipement du Territoire (SCET-AGRI, equipment development, agriculture). The research institutes are Office de la Recherche Scientifique d'Outre-Mer (ORSTOM, Overseas Scientific Research Institute); Institut de Recherche des Huiles et Oléagineux (IRHO, Edible Oils and Oil Crops Research Institut); Institut de Recherche d'Agronomie Tropicale (IEAT, Tropical Agriculture Research Institute); and Institut de Recherche des Cotons et Textiles Exotiques (IRCT, Cotton and Exotic Textiles Research Institute).

2. In fact, those former colonies that entered into cooperation agreements with France (that is, excluding Guinea until recently).

3. The study on Senegal was produced with the assistance of P. Thenevin, and that on Cameroon with the assistance of P. Baris and J. Zaslavsky.

4. P. Thenevin, "Synthèse des évaluations riz, coton, arachide" (Summary of rice, cotton, and groundnuts evaluations) (Ministry of Cooperation, Paris, 1983).

5. J. M. Funel and others, "Evaluation économique de l'aménagement de la rive gauche du fleuve Sénégal" (Economic evaluation of development of the left bank of the Senegal River) (Ministry of Cooperation, Paris, 1982).

6. P. Thenevin and J. M. Yung, "Evaluation de la filière arachide au Sénégal" (Evaluation of the groundnut subsector in Senegal) (Ministry of Cooperation, Paris, 1982).

7. J. Benhamou and J. Zaslavsky, "Evaluation de la filière coton au Sénégal" (Evaluation of the cotton subsector in Senegal) (Ministry of Cooperation, Paris, 1982).

8. P. Bonnefond and Annie Loquay, "Evaluation de la filière riz en Casamance" (Evaluation of the rice subsector in Casamance) (Ministry of Cooperation, Paris, 1985).

9. C. Agel, P. Thenevin, "Filière arachide, réactualization" (Groundnut subsector, update) (Ministry of Cooperation, Paris, 1983).

10. J. M. Yung, "La filière mil dans le bassin arachidier" (The millet subsector in the groundnut basin) (Ministry of Cooperation, Paris, 1984).

11. C. Agel and J. M. Yung, "La filière maîs au Sénégal" (The maize subsector in Senegal) (Ministry of Cooperation, Paris, 1985).

12. P. Bonnefond and C. Raymond, "Analyse économique de la filière riz SAED, réactualization" (Economic analysis of the SAED rice subsector, update) (Ministry of Cooperation, Paris, 1983).

13. G. Durufle and others, "Politique d'ajustement structurel au Sénégal" (Structural adjustment policy in Senegal) (Ministry of Cooperation, Paris, 1985).

14. Government of Cameroon, Ministry of Agriculture, "Bilan diagnostic du secteur agricole 1960–1980" (Diagnostic balance sheet of the agricultural sector, 1960–1980) (Yaoundé, 1980); Government of Cameroon, Ministry of Agriculture, "Bilan du secteur agricole interne du 5ème Plan" (Balance sheet of the domestic agriculture sector of the Fifth Plan) (Yaoundé, 1985).

15. CCCE, "La filière coton" (The cotton subsector) (Paris, 1984).

16. P. Baris and J. Zaslavsky, "L'impact et le coût de la SODECAO dans la filière cacao" (Impact and cost of SODECAO in the cocoa subsector) (SODECAO, Yaoundé, 1984).

17. C. Arditi and P. Baris, "Evaluation socio économique du projet SEMRY" (Socioeconomic evaluation of the SEMRY project) (Ministry of Cooperation, Paris, 1983).

18. P. Baris and J. Zaslavsky, "La demande et le marché des vivres dans les villes du centre et du sud" (Food crops demand and market in the towns of central and southern Cameroon) (SODECAO, Yaoundé, 1984).

9 *British Aid to Agriculture in Malawi, Tanzania, and Kenya*

John Howell

THIS CHAPTER is primarily concerned with the effect of aid from the United Kingdom on the agricultural development of three countries: Malawi, Tanzania, and Kenya. This aid is examined in the context of British colonial support for African agriculture and in the wider context of U.K. aid policy and its administration after these countries gained their independence. The distinctive characteristics of U.K. aid intervention in these countries can be seen in the support provided for agricultural research and for agricultural technical services and inputs supply; the investment in smallholder export crop schemes; support, particularly in the 1970s, for area-based "integrated rural development" projects; and the supply, in the 1980s, of program aid in support of economic policy reform directed at agriculture.

The Context of Agricultural Aid

The bilateral program that the United Kingdom has been operating since the 1970s to disburse agricultural aid can be divided into several categories.

Components and Trends in Expenditures since 1970

Under the general heading of financial aid, the most important categories are project aid, program aid (or import financing for countries with balance of payments difficulties), and concessionary finance made available to the Commonwealth Development Corporation (CDC), a statutory body established in 1948 to promote development by commercial investment in agriculture and other sectors. Under the general heading of technical cooperation, the most important categories have been the supply of personnel to governments or other public bodies overseas and the training of developing country nationals in the United Kingdom.

Another important category of agricultural aid (that is not allocable by country) includes grant support for tropical agricultural research and other services based in the United Kingdom. This expenditure is channeled primarily through research and development funds to the scientific units of the Overseas Development Administration (ODA), notably the Tropical Development and Research Institute (TDRI) and the Land Resources Development Centre (LRDC), which were amalgamated in 1987 to form the Overseas Development Natural Resources Institute (ODNRI).

In the period since 1975 (when contributions to European Economic Community [EEC] aid began), there has been a substantial growth in the United Kingdom's multilateral aid. By 1987 the share of multilateral aid had risen to 42 percent of the total program, from around 10 percent in the early 1970s. Partly as a consequence, the U.K. bilateral program in Sub-Saharan Africa has dropped to eighth place, after having ranked with the programs of France and the World Bank, in the early 1970s.[1] However, within the shrinking U.K. global bilateral program, the share of aid directed to Sub-Saharan Africa has risen from about 30 percent in the 1970s to 47 percent in 1987, making this region the largest recipient.

Within this provision to Sub-Saharan Africa, project aid generally maintained its importance over the period since 1970, although since 1985 there has been an increase in the share of nonproject aid due because of disaster relief and a new emphasis on program aid. Within project aid, expenditures in most subsections in agriculture and natural resources have declined in the 1980s (see table 9-1).

Similarly, the level of CDC commitments to agriculture in the Sub-Saharan region has declined since the late 1970s.[2] For example, in Kenya and Malawi (two of the most important countries for CDC agricultural investment) there was a sharp decline in investment opportunities in those smallholder crops with which CDC is most closely identified. However, this was partly compensated for by new opportunities in the estate subsector (see table 9-2).

The number of technical assistance personnel working in Sub-Saharan Africa also has declined steadily. In 1972, 740 officers were in agricultural posts, mostly supplemented government posts; by 1985, there were only 154, mainly on a fully funded advisory basis. After 1980, there was also decline in real expenditure to support tropical agricultural research in the scientific units, although the grant position stabilized after 1986, and grants to the International Agricultural Research Centers increased over the period.

The data on U.K. aid since 1970 does not, however, indicate any major changes in priority accorded to agriculture in Sub-Saharan Africa. Although there are some indicators of diminishing support

Table 9-1. Agricultural Project Aid Expenditures in Kenya, Malawi, and Tanzania (combined), by Subcategory, 1980–85
(thousands of pounds sterling)

Target of assistance	*1980*	*1981*	*1982*	*1983*	*1984*	*1985*
Agriculture						
Crop production	7,296	3,553	1,918	2,612	1,047	2,955
Storage and processing	637	575	743	5	123	1,064
Inputs and marketing	165	15	10	1,411	2,925	599
Research	305	86	70	0	0	0
Irrigation and water resources	532	664	810	558	339	208
Livestock	462	160	151	326	139	57
Forestry	1,044	462	1,394	100	98	554
Fisheries	0	0	0	0	0	81
Rural development						
Road utilities	1,219	972	475	31	0	7
Rural roads	352	337	206	684	291	417
Other rural development	573	1,418	1,689	763	391	15
Total	12,585	8,242	7,466	6,490	5,353	5,957

Source: Commonwealth Development Corporation.

Table 9-2. Commonwealth Development Corporation Agricultural Commitments in Kenya and Malawi (combined) by Subcategory,[a] 1970–85
(thousands of pounds sterling)

	Smallholder crops and nucleus estates				
Year	*Tea*	*Sugar*	*Tobacco*	*Coffee*	*Estates*
1970	75	0	600	0	0
1971	913	0	0	0	0
1972	210	0	0	0	78
1973	8,715	1,746	0	0	0
1974	0	0	0	0	0
1975	0	800	0	0	0
1976	650	4,561	3,000	0	0
1977	0	0	0	0	2,328
1978	6,840	1,530	0	10,400	0
1979	0	0	560	0	0
1980	0	500	0	0	3,900
1981	0	0	0	0	0
1982	0	1,360	0	0	1,360
1983	0	0	0	0	0
1984	0	0	0	0	6,459
1985	0	0	0	0	3,400

a. Excluding agricultural inputs, for example, National Seed Company (Malawi).
Source: Commonwealth Development Corporation; Statistics Department, ODA.

for particular forms of aid at different periods, aid to multilateral institutions (such as the World Bank, IFAD, and the European Development Fund) that have given emphasis to African agriculture has increased steadily, and there has been a substantial increase in the mid-1980s in bilateral program aid, which in large part is intended to facilitate policy reforms in support of agriculture.

Within the category of agricultural support, ODA priorities for Sub-Saharan Africa have seen some adjustments over the period, although there are a number of areas of long-standing interest. In the period immediately after independence, national and regional agricultural research services were given U.K. assistance in the form of budgetary support and staff. Project aid began to be substituted for budgetary aid in the late 1960s, and ODA moved away from sustaining research programs and institutions toward solving specific problems. Moreover, research and development funds were allocated toward projects intended to have a regional applicability, and grants increasingly have been concentrated on U.K.-based research.

There had been a particularly strong colonial legacy of export crop research and services, but direct ODA support declined after independence, as the industries concerned and the Commonwealth Development Corporation assumed relatively more importance, although often with some U.K. technical assistance. In the 1970s, emphasis shifted toward food staples, although by this time the emergence of the Consultative Group on International Agricultural Research (CGIAR) centers reinforced the British decision to remain apart from long-term research programs of plant breeding and to concentrate upon problem solving—where the strengths of the scientific units, particularly the former Tropical Development and Research Institute, have been particularly evident. TDRI itself had been formed by the merger in 1983 of the Centre for Overseas Pest Research and the Tropical Products Institute, both of which had their origins in the colonial period.

The former TDRI was particularly concerned both with postharvest technology—quality control, processing, storage, and marketing—and with pest and vector management, and its work straddled both research and technological services more widely. These services, however, were only one part of ODA's involvement in public sector agricultural supply, for which there have been several different forms of aid support. In project aid, the most important components have been the provision of planting materials and breeding stock, animal health services, crop protection services, and soil conservation services and minor irrigation.

In training aid also, British Council data indicate a strong bias toward courses at ODA-supported research centers on seed technology, pest management, crop storage, agricultural engineering, and veterinary services.[3] In this chapter, it is argued that the main successes of U.K. agricultural aid have been in technical services and inputs supply—particularly in the work of the CDC, which has made large contributions in the provision of farm inputs for selected crops and in the development of seed industries.

Since the mid-1960s CDC has specialized in extending to smallholders the production of exportable crops such as tea, coffee, sugar, and flue-cured tobacco. This has generally involved the provision of capital for the development of scheme infrastructure, processing capacity, and working capital, along with technical and managerial support to provide the supply of inputs and production services (such as field preparation, extension, and crop marketing). CDC, together with ODNRI and its predecessors, provide U.K. agricultural aid with much of its distinctiveness; and CDC, in particular, represents the main financial source of British agricultural support for several African countries. For example, CDC's loan finance for the production and processing of sugar and tea constitute a large part of agricultural project aid in Malawi and Kenya.

Despite this emphasis, critics of U.K. agricultural aid (such as some of the nongovernmental organizations and the environmental lobbies) are wrong in claiming that British aid has supported mechanized farming, modern irrigation, plantation crops, and the use of imported chemicals, vaccines, and fertilizers—to the neglect of "peasant" agriculture and the production of food staples. Although it is true that expenditure on integrated rural development has fallen away in recent years (see table 9-1), and that, within such projects, the returns to peasant incomes and production have been disappointing, it simply is not the case that the Overseas Development Administration has given priority in its aid allocations to modern, commercial agriculture of the sort associated with plantation companies and large estate owners at the expense of food staple production by peasant producers.

Nor is it the case that ODA has neglected to finance investment in the export crop sector because of an overemphasis on improving the welfare and incomes of cultivators and herders in the traditional sector and in marginal environments. Within a generally shrinking program of bilateral project aid support for agriculture, proportions of spending in the period since 1970 have been broadly maintained between traditional and modern agriculture, between areas with high potential and those with low potential areas, and between export crops and domestically consumed staples.

Changes in the Overall Aid Policy Context

The broader aid policy underlying U.K. support for agriculture in Sub-Saharan Africa has changed its emphasis since 1970. In 1975, a White

Paper entitled *The Changing Emphasis in British Aid Policies* committed the government to a poverty-oriented program that would have "the most effect in alleviating the worst poverty over the long term." This end was to be achieved by increasing bilateral aid going to the poorest countries—especially those most affected by the rise in the prices of oil and other commodities. A subsidiary objective was to assist the poorest people in the poorest countries, particularly in the "large, very poor, and mainly rural, traditional sector."

One element of the new strategy was support for a number of Integrated Rural Development Projects (IRDP), particularly in Sub-Saharan Africa. Many of the concerns for developing subsistence farming in Africa were voiced in the United Kingdom in the 1960s, before donors began to recommend the poverty focus for integrated rural development projects. These concerns were later evident in the White Paper, which represented a more comprehensive statement of the IRDP case than either the World Bank or the Food and Agriculture Organization (FAO) had formulated at that time. The White Paper explained why it was important to address the constraints on production and welfare in several subsectors simultaneously; to develop local planning and implementation capabilities; to accept the need for patience and flexibility in technological development and in institutional arrangements; to consider more finance for local cost components; and to look for new skills in understanding rural household economics.

In practice, however, it proved difficult to initiate ODA integrated rural development projects with a focus on poverty, and "more help to the poorest" in practice often meant either conventional projects that fitted poverty focus requirements or support for area-based programs already identified by governments or by other donors, particularly the World Bank. A number of IRDPs in Africa were started in these circumstances, and this similarity served—as discussed below—to oversimplify the lessons that were drawn from the disappointments of the projects begun in the mid- to late 1970s.

The primary policy change of the new government from 1980 onward was to introduce a stronger commercial and domestic industrial element into the aid program. This reflected the concern of virtually all aid donors that the aid program should be used to help secure or protect their market share in developing countries. One element of this policy, the Aid Trade Provision (ATP), was in fact introduced in 1977 before the change of government and before the deepening of the world recession.

The impact of the emphasis upon U.K. commercial considerations on aid allocations to African agriculture is difficult to capture. The share of ATP allocations in the aid program has continued to expand, but none of the eighty-two ATP-related sales between 1978 and 1985 were in agriculture in Sub-Saharan Africa. Furthermore, the share of the agricultural sector in project aid declined in Africa after 1980 with the growth in aid to the power and transport categories. Yet against this evidence has to be set the difficulty experienced by ODA in identifying suitable opportunities for agricultural project investment. It was this difficulty, rather than commercial and industrial pressures, that contributed to a shift in emphasis away from project aid support toward program aid.

This shift can be traced to the early 1980s, when evidence on Africa's deteriorating economic performance pointed to the poor returns to aid-assisted project investments. ODA, like other donors, took the view that most African governments were proving incapable of maintaining at economic levels much of the physical infrastructure and public services that had been built with external aid, and that both productive investments and domestic financing capacity were being undermined by public policies inimical to growth. The agricultural sector was considered to be particularly disadvantaged by prevailing government policies.

In ODA, these constraints on effective use of project aid funds led to a renewed interest from 1981 in "sector aid," whereby several aid instruments are used together. Sector aid is designed in part to rehabilitate production in sectors such as agriculture. After 1983 there was also an attempt to regenerate manpower aid. Although the reduction of manpower aid had been deliberate policy since the late 1970s, an ODA review in 1983 made the case for an enhanced program in training and manpower provision. The withdrawal of expatriate manpower was seen as a factor contributing to the deteriorating performance in public institutions, and the review argued that U.K. aid should be directed toward rebuilding those institutions whose "efficient functioning is critical to development." Much more important in financial terms, however, was a substantial shift into program aid linked to conditions of policy reform designed to enhance agricultural output and, in particular, agricultural export earnings.

None of these instruments of policy were new, but together they represented a move away from identifiable project initiatives. A ministerial Commons statement in 1985 confirmed this emphasis in relation to Sub-Saharan Africa, calling for fast-spending program aid to support economic policy reform, the strengthening of public institutions through increased manpower and aid training, and a package of assistance to rehabilitate vital areas of the economy.

Current U.K. policies on program aid mirror, albeit imperfectly, other forms of nonproject aid that were important in the 1960s and the early 1970s and that included formal, nonproject-related conditions agreed upon with the recipient government and relating to agricultural and domestic public expenditure policies. Examples include the Land Transfer Program in Kenya and the last years of budgetary aid in Malawi. In the 1970s, there were fewer examples of program aid, and these often were designed (as in Tanzania) largely to relaunch a suspended bilateral program and to provide balance of payments assistance. Moreover, such program aid allocations did not have either a specific agricultural focus or a framework for macroeconomic policy change.

Aid Mechanisms

The initiative for identifying and developing new agricultural projects and programs is left substantially to officers working in ODA's Development Division within the main regions (which include eastern Africa, based in Nairobi, and central and southern Africa, based in Lilongwe). In countries such as Malawi in the early 1970s, when ODA had a large number of technical cooperation officers (TCOs) serving in governments, and a spread of small projects in the agricultural sector, project proposals often were instigated by TCOs working within their ministries. However, in the late 1970s, a number of ODA agricultural projects in the region had their origins in preparation or appraisal documents prepared by other donors, particularly the World Bank. For example, the Tabora Land Use Project (in Tanzania) and the Bura Irrigation Project (in Kenya) were components of larger projects prepared in advance of a formal ODA identification mission. The large area-based projects in all three of the countries discussed in this chapter were also a response to national programs in which individual bilateral donors were invited to consider support for specific regions or districts.

An ODA evaluation of the procedures in 1983 argued that particularly in the more complex agricultural projects, the design and appraisal stages should be more carefully prepared, and a broader disciplinary approach should be adopted (meaning additional advisory inputs were needed).[4] Although other agencies (such as the World Bank) have been willing to commit more substantial resources of time and staff to project preparation, they have also run up against the difficulty of designing projects for developing the traditional systems of crop and livestock production in Africa.

Despite some reductions in the advisory cadre following a 1980 management review, the ratio of ODA natural resource advisers to the volume of agricultural spending has in fact increased over the period, as has the ratio of advisers to technical assistance posts overseas.[5] But this apparent lightening of the load of these advisers should not be taken at face value. They have a larger monitoring program than in the past, when smaller projects were often monitored by reports from ODA-appointed TCO project managers and when ODA projects often were administered by British-supplemented staff within ministries.

Agricultural Aid to Kenya

European settlement and colonial administration had a much more profound effect on agriculture in Kenya than in either Tanzania or Malawi.

The Colonial Legacy

During colonial rule Kenya came under a program of land alienation that led to rapid growth in European commercial farming in the Central Highlands. This, in turn, stimulated the establishment of agricultural research laboratories and other services. Most of these services (for example, in veterinary care and artificial insemination and in the processing of export crops) later played a large role in the growth of African commercial farming. Kenyan agriculture also benefited from a regionally established research system. The East African Agriculture and Forestry Research Organisation (EAFFRO) and the East Africa Veterinary Research Organisation (EAVRO) were established at Muguga in the early 1950s and eventually became the Kenya Agricultural Research Institute (KARI) in 1977.

Yet, because of settler pressure on the colonial government, African smallholder production was by and large neglected, in comparison with that in neighboring Uganda and Tanganyika, for example. It was not until the 1950s that initiatives were undertaken to boost African export corp production, and that, in particular, restrictions on such productions were lifted.

It was in farm planning and land consolidation that colonial initiatives in the early 1950s were to have their greatest impact. One such initiative (in Rift Valley Province) developed a model of balanced farming on holdings of about 4 hectares that eventually provided one of two main props of The Plan to Intensify African Agriculture (the Swynnerton Plan) in 1953. The other prop was the reform of customary African land tenure. Land registration was considered an essential condition for the development of African agriculture, and so the issuing of land titles became the central feature of the Swynnerton Plan. The first step of the plan was to consolidate holdings in areas of higher potential that were capable of sustaining mixed farms with some export cropping, where appropriate.

It was the increase in smallholder tea and coffee production that had the greatest long-term impact on African agriculture. Until the 1950s, tea had been a plantation crop, and the companies had set up and financed their own Tea Research Institute at Kericho. At first, the industry was somewhat skeptical about the viability of smallholder production, but by the early 1950s it had begun to participate in the financing and management of smallholder production and of new factories. During the main period of investment that followed, the CDC and the World Bank financed both field and factory development under the Kenyan Tea Development Authority.

With an estimated 15,000 growers, coffee was already a smallholder crop by the early 1950s, but it was confined to areas remote from European plantings (to avoid infestation and crop theft). In the 1980s the number of smallholders rose to an estimated 250,000. Thus development began in the colonial period, sparked by the efforts of the Departments of Agriculture and Co-operative Development to establish nurseries and construct pulperies. Coffee research was undertaken at the National Agricultural Laboratory (partly financed by an export cess), and a spraying program for berry disease was instigated. After independence, the responsibility for research passed to the Coffee Research Foundation.

These colonial policies led, from the late 1950s to the mid-1960s, to substantial increases in marketed output in the areas where land was being consolidated and export crops cultivated. With the approach of independence, however, the transfer of ownership of land in the "European Highlands" became the most important issue for agricultural policy. Beginning in 1960 the Land Transfer Program (LTP) financed the buying of mixed farms and, through the Land Settlement Department, the subdivision of plots and the settlement of African smallholders. The initial thrust of the policy was high-density settlement—priority was given to the landless and the British government ultimately provided finance to compensate the European farmer. But "low-density settlement" on larger units attracted additional CDC and World Bank support for relatively progressive farmers and, in some cases, land was acquired for commercially managed national farmers under the Agricultural Development Corporation (ADC), which was established in 1965 and which continues to manage a number of seed and pedigree stock farms.

Trends in Agricultural Aid

The LTP continued to supply funds until the mid-1970s and came to dominate the U.K. aid program. In the 1966, 1970, and 1973 aid agreements, the LTP constituted the largest item (some £ 23 million out of a total of £ 46 million of capital aid). With the phasing out of the grants for land purchase and settlement, there was some expansion of project aid commitments (see table 9-3). CDC loans contributed the major share of British agricultural aid from the early 1970s on, most of it going to tea, coffee, and sugar. However, the only significant new CDC commitment in the 1980s was equity finance to the National Oilseeds Development Company, with private capital and management being supplied by East African Industries (part of the Unilever Group).

There has been a greater CDC concentration on smallholders in Kenya than in either Tanzania or Malawi. The contribution to the Kenya Tea Development Authority (KTDA) is discussed below. CDC support for the coffee industry, as for tea development, has been devoted mainly to developing processing facilities; new pulperies have been constructed or improved for the 140 smallholder cooperative societies involved in coffee marketing. The other major CDC agricultural investment has been in sugar. In 1976, £ 5.4 million was committed to a factory extension and to road building in the area under cane in the parts of western Kenya with higher rainfall, where some 28,000 cane growers were supplying the factory at Mumias.

CDC's role as a venture capitalist in Kenyan smallholder agriculture is less important than it once was. Kenya's tea and coffee industries are now well established and close to their limits where land development is concerned; Mumias will shortly meet most of Kenya's sugar requirements. CDC's role in institution building is also now less important, although in the case of tea the CDC has had considerable influence in the design of the KTDA and its early management. In the case of the Mumias Sugar Company, a U.K. private consultancy (Bookers International Agricultural Services) has been responsible for design and management, and CDC has played simply a financial role. And in the case of coffee, CDC has had little influence on either the design of the institutions to assist smallholder production or the management of the industry.

Another feature of the shift into project aid support for agriculture in the 1970s was the emphasis on specific research initiatives. Previously, U.K. aid had provided budgetary support for both EAFFRO and EAVRO. In EAFFRO, except for work on crop virology, all of the new research projects were of short duration (three to six years). As a consequence, scientific work was frequently passed on to a small number of experienced Kenyan scientists with limited funds. The examples of maize and potato agronomy indicate the limitations of project aid in support of agricultural research.

There has, in fact, been a substantial decline in U.K. support for crop research in Kenya. Whereas in 1975 twenty-four TCOs were engaged in

Table 9-3. United Kingdom Bilateral Aid to Kenya, 1970–85
(thousands of pounds sterling)

Component	*1970*	*1971*	*1972*	*1973*	*1974*	*1975*	*1976*	*1977*
Financial aid								
Project aid								
including aid-trade provision (ATP)	6,166	4,118	3,653	2,329	1,926	1,912	1,715	4,912
Program aid	0	0	0	0	0	0	2,150	1,032
Debt cancellation	0	0	0	0	0	0	0	0
Other nonproject	42	0	1,458	1,086	2,304	810	2,161	0
CDC loans	1,620	2,810	1,028	3,512	7,606	1,949	6,408	4,273
Subtotal	7,828	6,928	6,139	6,927	11,836	4,671	12,434	10,217
Technical cooperation								
Wholly financed personnel	227	230	231	237	310	332	472	476
Partly financed personnel	2,743	2,419	4,035	3,842	3,529	3,339	7,011	4,579
Students and trainees	154	176	191	276	286	407	522	611
Other TC	147	66	42	386	474	724	562	469
Subtotal	3,271	2,891	4,499	4,741	4,599	4,802	8,567	6,135
Total	11,099	9,820	10,638	11,668	16,435	9,473	21,001	16,352

	1978	*1979*	*1980*	*1981*	*1982*	*1983*	*1984*	*1985*
Financial aid								
Project aid including ATP	5,510	7,563	6,792	10,610	8,754	11,419	16,806	12,002
Program aid	8,562	2,816	456	6,910	8,459	3,283	1,204	103
Debt cancellation	2,100	3,646	4,035	4,832	5,126	5,103	5,079	4,929
Other nonproject	1	1	0	537	557	118	148	232
CDC loans	7,277	7,843	10,164	4,492	5,499	2,086	2,725	5,606
Subtotal	23,450	21,869	21,447	27,381	28,395	22,009	25,963	22,873

(Table continues on the following page.)

Table 9-3. *(continued)*

Component	*1970*	*1971*	*1972*	*1973*	*1974*	*1975*	*1976*	*1977*
Technical cooperation								
Wholly financed personnel	750	804	939	1,130	837	1,106	1,296	1,627
Partly financed personnel	5,838	7,840	6,548	4,775	3,916	3,539	3,181	2,121
Students and trainees	710	901	1,709	1,731	2,311	2,930	3,950	4,880
Other TC	532	791	591	4,668	1,991	2,270	3,172	2,937
Subtotal	7,830	10,337	9,786	12,304	9,055	9,845	11,599	11,565
Total	29,180	28,560	31,233	39,685	37,450	31,854	37,562	34,438

Source: British Aid Statistics: Statistics of the U.K. Economic Aid to Developing Countries (London: Government Statistical Service, annual).

various aspects of research, by the mid-1980s the work was confined to pest management, and ODA's research and development funds for regional application became increasingly concentrated in the United Kingdom itself. In the case of animal health projects, however, these funds have continued to be directed to Kenya and have helped to maintain the strength of the former EAVRO. A considerable effort has also been put into research on East Coast fever, where long-term project support from ODA has alleviated a difficult staffing and budgetary situation in the veterinary research services.

ODA agricultural aid has been deployed in support of poorer agricultural regions, particularly those with low and erratic rainfall. The main direct involvement in drylands projects began with the Second National Livestock Development Project in 1975. The ODA component consisted of livestock marketing, but little progress was made in increasing commercial offtake from the pastoral areas, and the World Bank–led project was wound down in 1982. More recently, ODA has been involved in the national Arid and Semi-Arid Land Program (ASAL), under which the three districts of Embu, Meru, and Isiolo (EMI) are supported by what could be termed an ODA integrated rural development project consisting of several components, including health centers and minor roads.

There has been a substantial decline in the number of agricultural projects supported by ODA in the 1980s. This is partly a reflection of the reduced opportunities for CDC investment. More important, ODA support for agriculture shifted, after 1982 in particular, toward foreign exchange difficulties within the agricultural sector. This eventually became termed "natural resources private sector project aid." It provided £ 6.5 million, primarily for agricultural machinery and spare parts from U.K. suppliers. This was also held to be ODA's contribution to a coordinated donor effort led by the World Bank in support of policy reform in Kenyan agriculture.

Emphasis also shifted toward sectoral aid, which in practice has meant a package of aid instruments (including program aid) designed to improve the weak commercial performance of the ADC, established in 1965. More than £ 4 million was awarded to ADC on the condition that it implement an agreed divestiture program and concentrate on trading and production activities that could not be adequately undertaken by the private sector. These activities included the production and distribution of seed maize, stock breeding, and the replacement of machinery, as well as technical assistance.

Project Aid for Agricultural Research: Maize and Potato

After budgetary aid to research institutions ended in the 1960s, ODA instigated a number of specific research projects. These included the

Maize Agronomy Project, which initially ran from 1968 to 1971 but was subsequently extended in phases until 1978; and the Potato Research Project, which ran from 1970 to 1976. As elsewhere, such relatively short-term support failed to establish programs and institutions capable of sustaining themselves without external support.

It was not until the mid-1950s that a systematic breeding program was started in maize at Kitale (in 1956) for an early maturing variety. Several hybrids were developed, but there was little immediate adoption by smallholders, and ODA was asked to support a project to investigate the agronomic and physical characteristics of new hybrids and to recommend measures to improve yield performance and farmer returns from maize cultivation.

The ODA-supported work was confined to Kitale and was successful in several respects. By 1975 most farmers in the area with 8 hectares or more had land under hybrids, and on-station trials showed potential or substantial yield improvements. In both the Kitale area and elsewhere in Kenya, however, smallholder production of maize remained well below yield expectations. An evaluation for ODA in 1984 concluded that the project had concentrated too much on achieving record results, at the expense of applied agronomic work in smallholder conditions, and that insufficient support had been given to strengthening national research capability.[10] In particular, the government-funded regional maize agronomy units contributed little to research output. Since the end of the ODA project, maize agronomy research at Kitale has continued, but the shortage of funds and frequent staff changes have severely constrained activities. This has meant that a further project has become necessary (with USAID support) to strengthen the national maize research capability.

In the potato research project, the aim was to instigate a breeding program to provide both (a) new and better varieties resistant to blight and other diseases and (b) the information necessary for the control of bacterial wilt. The research station at Tigoni was designated a potato research station in 1972, and it was here that a disease-free center was developed for raising and screening seedlings for blight resistance and for multiplication purposes. A new variety, selected from hybrid seed supplied by the Scottish Plant Breeding Station, was officially approved for commercial production and released in 1973 under the name Kenya Baraka. In 1974 five further clones were bulked up and certified from virus-free stocks.

ODA ended support for potato work in 1976, when it was considered that an effective commodity research station had been established. Potato research in Kenya has, however, deteriorated since 1976. Once again, funds have been inadequate, and the station has reported breakdowns in its tractors, cold stores, and irrigation system. In addition, staff have often left for more remunerative posts with better facilities, at such institutions as the Coffee Research Foundation. As for building local research capacity, the ODA project might well have not existed.

Theileriosis (East Coast Fever) Research

U.K. aid for research into the cattle disease East Coast fever has involved the sustained use of specialized expertise in support of a national research program, which in this case has been supplemented by postgraduate training and by support for field extension of the research results.

Theileriosis is a complex of diseases transmitted by ticks. In eastern and central Africa, *T. parva*, which causes East Coast fever (ECF), is the most prevalent and is responsible for an estimated 0.5 million cattle deaths a year, as well as losses due to reduced growth and fertility. The first attempts to control ECF came during the colonial period with the mandatory dipping (or spraying) of cattle infected by acaracides in disease-prone areas together with regulations on cattle movement. However, such measures were, and remain, difficult to apply on a national scale; and, in the period before independence, an immunization method was developed whereby animals were infected and the development of the disease was blocked by treatment with tetracyclines.

This infection and treatment method was further developed after independence in the FAO-UNDP Tickborne Diseases Project at Muguga, and in the 1970s the Veterinary Department asked ODA to conduct investigations before establishing a field program. These investigations covered the effects on the productivity of immunized cattle, the possible discovery of strains of *T. parva* that did not cross-immunize, the danger of the treatment leading to carrier animals that would spread the disease, and the overall practicality and safety of the method itself. Two ODA projects were established at Muguga—one concerned with the epidemiology, the other with the therapy of the disease. There has also been substantial ODA support for training animal research scientists at Muguga, including Ph.D. candidates in virology and protozoology supervised by project staff.

As a result of this work, the infection and treatment method was adopted, and recommendations were released for the use of two drugs for therapeutic purposes. Following up this work, ODA agreed in 1985 to support a team at the Veterinary Department that is responsible for an extension program of ECF treatment among stockkeepers.

Smallholder Export Crops: KTDA

The development of smallholder tea production in Kenya through KTDA is generally regarded as one of the great successes in tropical agricultural development. In fact, it was the Department of Agriculture's work in the 1950s on a number of small, subsidized, and closely watched pilot schemes in Central Province that encouraged, first, the establishment of the Special Crops Development Authority (SCDA) in 1960 and, subsequently, the large leap into what is now an industry of 145,000 smallholders providing green leaf to thirty-nine factories operating without subsidy.

Much of the success of KTDA can be attributed to the Department of Agriculture and SCDA, and to subsequent work by U.K. technical officers attached to the KTDA. This work included, most notably, the development of the plucking regime that came to be known as "two leaves and a bud," which helped establish the premium quality of Kenya tea, and the extension to growers of vegetative propagation techniques.

CDC provided loan finance to the SCDA and the successor to KTDA, but it was the Department of Agriculture, not the CDC, that was the main architect of KTDA, a forerunner of similar smallholder crop authorities. CDC's involvement in KTDA management was also less intensive than in other smallholder projects subsequently. For example, the post of general manager was never held by a CDC officer but successively by British colonial administrative service officers until the first Kenyan general manager was appointed in 1969.

Yet, loan finance apart, CDC had an important role in the rapid expansion of KTDA in the late 1960s and early 1970s. For example, CDC was particularly insistent on the establishment of the growers' committees, which eventually assumed ownership and control over the factories; and it was a CDC accountant who developed the computerized system that handled anything up to 200 delivery slips in a season from individual growers and still managed regular monthly payments. Under Kenyan management in the 1970s, the KTDA successfully extended its function into factory management and domestic tea marketing through its subsidiary company, Kenya Tea Packers. Furthermore, while other public agricultural agencies were going through periods of damaging cost escalation, KTDA maintained relatively high levels of operating efficiency.

The success of KTDA cannot be put down entirely to effective management. The rise in incomes to smallholder tea growers over the period as a whole is also attributable to good natural growing conditions, the generally favorable prices for Kenya tea on the world market, and the support of estates,which provided a strong technical base for tea research and development at both the field and factory levels.

Yet CDC's involvement in the management of KTDA has been important to its success. CDC has helped KTDA maintain its commercial autonomy, generate revenue from its own (rather than government) cesses, and remain accountable to growers. These management characteristics have been difficult to establish elsewhere, as the Malawi evidence has shown.

Embu-Meru-Isiolo (EMI) Districts Program

The emphasis on poverty alleviation in the mid-1970s focused attention on the drier regions of countries such as Kenya, where agricultural production and incomes lagged behind more favored, wetter regions. Following the earlier Special Resource Development Program (SRDP) pattern of donor-designated areas of operation, the government began seeking support for selected dryland districts in 1977; by the time that the 1979–83 Development Plan was launched, it had in place agreements in principle to finance a series of regional rural development programs. ODA agreed to support what became the EMI Districts Program, which meant, in practice, the poorer areas of the marginal cultivation and nomadic pastoralism. ODA advisers accepted that the main thrust of agricultural aid spending should be on soil and water conservation, forestry, and stock improvement, but they wanted to ensure that projects were carefully prepared in collaboration with the district authorities.

The ODA approach to arid and semiarid lands therefore developed into a slow buildup of specific interventions largely under the supervision of TCOs. In the fist three years of the program, the main responsibility for preparing projects (and ensuring their incorporation into central ministry and district budgets) fell on a TCO appointed to the post of adviser to the Provincial Planning Office for Eastern Province, in which the three districts lie.

The initial work on soil conservation was based on a small catchment in lower Embu, with earthworks to reduce runoff into farmers' fields. With an engineer and land-use planner in the post, a program of research and development began in four catchments linking physical works to on-farm conservation and rehabilitation measures (including afforestation) in collaboration with farmers. The training of field staff in soil and water conservation planning was also part of the ODA program, and these activities were continued into a second phase (from 1986) that was termed the dryland farming project.

The forestry work involved tree planting, nursery development, and research into species and planting methods. Support for stock improvement has meant the development of a sheep and goat breeding center that has led to sales of animals (with, it is hoped, greater disease resistance and faster growth rates) to local farmers, some of whom have been trained as outbreeders. ODA has been unable to identify any significant initiatives for cattle or camel development—apart from some finance for postdrought restocking and a number of investigations in Isiolo on grazing management and water development.

Given the relatively modest level of U.K. aid in the EMI Program, there have been some significant achievements. A number of physical changes are attributable to ODA support: the goat and sheep station, soil and water conservation works, and forest nurseries. But the main achievement has been the enhanced capacity of line departments in Meru and Embu districts to undertake technical work in support of farmers. Financial aid supported by long-term technical assistance and consultancy (much of it based on the work of LRDC staff) bolstered the work of the Departments of Agriculture (in soil conservation and agronomy), Livestock Development, and Forestry.

The conditions for such institutional strengthening appear to be twofold: recognized U.K. competence (which permits acceptance of expatriate manpower) and technical intervention that is appropriate to field services capability and management. It is because such conditions are lacking that it is difficult to envisage, at present, any similar institutional strengthening in the animal health and range management services in Isiolo district. However, in the one explicit institution-building component of the program, ODA has not been particularly successful. The post of adviser to the Provincial Planning Office was designed to develop the capacity of district and provincial authorities to effectively manage a decentralized planning system, but there is little evidence that planning capacity has been enhanced or, more to the point, that decentralized planning has become an effective instrument of policy.

A narrower form of institutional development is represented by EMI, whereby ODA support for technical services has improved their capacity to address local constraints. This form of support is a feature of ODA's involvement in EMI more than in ODA-assisted integrated rural development projects in Kenya and Tanzania; in Malawi, there has not been the technical assistance support, and in Tanzania the large volume of technical assistance generally has not been incorporated into the day-to-day work of technical departments. The lessons of EMI, therefore, are not confined to IRD projects; they also suggest some U.K. strengths more generally in the provision of agricultural technical services.

Natural Resources Private Sector Aid

U.K. aid for natural resources private sector projects is, in effect, program aid by another name. In 1983 the United Kingdom met Kenyan requests for balance of payments support with a £ 2.9 million foreign exchange allocation for the purchase of essential imports for the agricultural sector. This was the beginning of what was later termed natural resources private sector project aid, which in 1985 was to provide a further £ 6.5 million for imported agricultural inputs. Both operations were regarded as projects, rather than program aid, which they more typically represented. However, these operations, although quite unlike conventional project aid, were directly targeted on specific private sector demands for agricultural imports—in contrast to the £ 15 million allocated as program aid in 1975 and 1976 for a range of U.K. capital goods and to offset repayments on land transfer loans.

This earlier aid had been subject to an ODA evaluation that found, in the absence of a foreign exchange problem, that it was not adding to Kenya's U.K. imports and may simply have been displacing commercially financed orders. The more recent batch of natural resources private sector aid allocations had their origin in different economic circumstances, and they were linked to adherence to the terms of the new IMF standby agreement and the release of funds under the World Bank's second Structural Adjustment Loan (SAL II).

When Kenya requested new emergency assistance at the end of 1984 to cope with the severe drought, the pattern had already been set. The United Kingdom responded with a package of £ 6.5 million of natural resources import financing to be directed to the private sector. The content of the goods was specified: agricultural spares, fertilizer and other agricultural chemicals, veterinary drugs, and "other mutually acceptable imports." Most of the capital equipment was intended to be for replacement use (pumps, diesel motors), on the grounds that it would have a less displacing effect on commercial orders, and a more direct effect on relieving bottlenecks).

Unlike the 1982 allocation, however, the provision of natural resources input aid was not specifically linked to the government's adherence to an IMF standby or a World Bank SAL. The aid was offered as the United Kingdom's contribution to structural adjustment, in which operation the World Bank was acknowledged to be the lead donor. But ODA's objective was to supply fast-disbursing drought relief, which it did not wish to be hedged around by multilateral conditions beyond the capacity of the Kenyan government. An example of these conditions was World Bank insistence on the liberalization of grain marketing, which ODA did not regard as an appropriate issue on which to base bilateral aid allocation decisions. In the event, Kenya coped with its drought better and more speedily than its neighbors; and after failing to resolve its disagreement with the World Bank over grain marketing, Kenya did not take a third SAL.

Disbursements under natural resources private sector aid proved slower than expected, because there was little immediate demand and the foreign exchange shortage eased up after 1985, as coffee and tea export prices enjoyed a boom. In this context of relative foreign exchange abundance, the terms of the aid appeared unattractive. Credit terms for local purchasers were more onerous than under normal commercial arrangements, and in addition they were obliged to procure through a third party, the crown agents.

In these circumstances, the targeting of program aid on a particular sector or end-user had only limited relevance. As shown in ODA support for the ADC, earmarked foreign exchange can alleviate the difficulties of particular agencies and facilitate the introduction of new measures. Yet taken overall, the main effect of natural resources private sector project aid had been simply to expand the foreign exchange resources available to the government and the private sector combined. It is difficult to argue that such aid is either directly beneficial to the private sector or even directly employed within natural resources.

Agricultural Aid to Malawi

Agricultural aid to Malawi cannot be fully understood without some details of its colonial legacy.

The Colonial Legacy

The main agricultural legacy of the British colonial period in Malawi (or Nyasaland) were the export-oriented estates whose growth had been facilitated by transport investments and supported by research services in crops such as tea, cotton, and tobacco. Smallholder export crops also received some official encouragement. For example, by the end of the 1930s, the cotton industry had become reliant primarily upon African smallholder production, and dark-fired tobacco production had been stimulated by the Native Tobacco Board established in 1926. It was not until the 1950s, however, that the colonial government promoted African smallholder production on any scale.

Broadly speaking, the colonial government followed a two-pronged strategy. First, it instituted production schemes for export crops (such as tea, tobacco, and confectionery nuts) that were based on expanded research, marketing services, and transport improvements. Second, it launched a few small, intensive area development projects based on land consolidation and some soil conservation.

Chitedze Research Station was established in 1950 to serve small farmers in the Central region, and five smaller stations were opened to cover the main ecological regions. A program of cattle selection and management also was begun. A new station for tea research (which became the responsibility of the Tea Association in 1959) was opened at Mulanje in 1949, and Malawi joined the Federal Tobacco Research Board in 1954. An Agricultural Research Council of Rhodesia and Nyasaland was founded in 1959 to reinforce agricultural research in Central Africa. This survived the breakup of the federation but was ultimately dissolved in 1967, when Malawi responded by setting up its own Agricultural Research Council.

In the 1940s, the extension services provided for Malawi were largely confined to soil conservation measures. In 1946, legislation was introduced to prescribe and enforce such practices when authorities became alarmed by the rate at which the prevailing cultivation and tenure arrangements were exhausting the land. It was held that, in areas of high density, fundamental changes were necessary in husbandry practices, the physical layout of landholdings, and land tenure before sustained increases in productivity could occur. As a result, a number of intensive land schemes were introduced that subsequently often involved the settlement of Malawi "young pioneers" from agricultural training centers. But the most important scheme of land consolidation and development was the Lilongwe Land Development Project (LLDP).

The four Integrated Rural Development Projects instigated after independence with World Bank support followed the intensive area development model and were a direct legacy of the colonial schemes. ODA continued to support the LLDP, although it was not until the late 1970s that British agricultural aid expenditure became heavily concentrated on the National Rural Development Program (NRDP), which itself had evolved from IRDP experience.

Trends in Agricultural Aid

At independence in 1964 the U.K. budgetary grant of £5 million to Malawi represented one-third of total recurrent expenditure. By 1970 the grant was down to £ 2 million (and 10 percent of expenditure), and from that time on, project aid (and particularly CDC loans) became the main instrument of support for the agricultural sector until program aid was introduced in the early 1980s (see table 9-4). These program aid allocations have an agricultural focus in that they have been linked, in part, to donor-prescribed economic policy changes (including changes in agricultural pricing and farm input subsidies). But attempts have also been made to target program aid directly on agriculture by addressing the position of foreign exchange availability

Table 9-4. United Kingdom Bilateral Aid to Malawi, 1970–85
(thousands of pounds sterling)

Components	*1970*	*1971*	*1972*	*1973*	*1974*	*1975*	*1976*	*1977*
Financial aid								
Project aid								
including aid-trade provision (ATP)	2,959	2,766	4,846	3,366	3,085	5,339	7,608	4,585
Program aid	0	0	0	0	0	0	0	0
Debt cancellation	0	0	0	0	0	0	0	0
Other nonproject	2,945	692	0	0	0	0	842	0
CDC loans	120	575	529	1,375	1,741	2,075	3,239	7,505
Subtotal	6,024	4,033	5,375	4,741	4,826	7,414	11,689	12,090
Technical cooperation								
Wholly financed personnel	63	129	173	151	115	80	137	134
Partly financed personnel	1,337	1,306	2,343	1,624	2,661	2,734	3,679	3,279
Students and trainees	176	189	159	195	244	366	433	484
Other TC	109	117	146	190	225	132	76	82
Subtotal	1,685	1,742	2,822	2,160	3,244	3,312	4,326	4,429
Total	7,709	5,774	8,197	6,901	8,071	10,727	16,015	16,519

	1978	1979	1980	1981	1982	1983	1984	1985
Financial aid								
Project aid including ATP	6,060	8,854	3,894	2,845	3,670	2,515	3,161	3,277
Program aid	0	0	0	3,612	1,645	214	224	1,054
Debt cancellation	0	1,457	1,364	1,615	1,777	1,833	1,889	1,917
Other nonproject	233	1	0	0	0	23	0	0
CDC loans	5,647	9,004	5,012	1,736	3,369	3,076	748	1,092
Subtotal	11,940	19,316	10,270	9,809	10,461	7,661	6,022	7,340
Technical cooperation								
Wholly financed personnel	186	214	390	449	428	490	552	534
Partly financed personnel	3,065	4,181	4,204	4,220	4,023	3,941	3,482	2,904
Students and trainees	655	912	1,055	922	1,382	1,923	1,936	2,406
Other TC	132	148	602	555	688	593	904	642
Subtotal	4,039	5,455	6,273	6,190	6,523	6,959	6,938	6,486
Total	15,979	23,314	16,543	15,999	16,984	14,620	12,959	13,825

Source: See table 9-3.

for agricultural importers. A more enduring form of aid has been technical cooperation, which by the mid-1980s had risen to about 50 percent of the total U.K. aid disbursement. The composition of U.K. manpower aid to the Malawi public service has changed since the 1960s and 1970s when postings of aid-funded British permanent secretaries and similar officials were common. Yet U.K. nationals still have a much larger presence in Malawi than in Kenya and Tanzania, although there have been significant reductions in recent years. The number of TCOs and supplemented posts in Agriculture and Natural Resources stood at eighty in 1975, rose to ninety-one in 1980, and fell to thirty-one in 1985.

The pattern of project aid has been much influenced by manpower aid. Apart from large CDC investments and an unsuccessful attempt to establish a pulpwood industry at Viphya based on softwood forests planted in the 1950s, the U.K. agricultural aid portfolio in the 1970s consisted of relatively small contributions. In agricultural research a number of research teams were established—in grant legumes, cotton, and pastures, for example—following the decision to end budgetary aid to the Agricultural Research Council and to substitute project aid.

Apart from research, the main thrust of the agricultural aid program in the 1970s was a series of attempts instigated by TCOs or supplemented staff either to establish new activities in a specific part of the country or to support particular specialist services within the national system. Examples of the former activities are the Mzuzu poultry scheme, the smallholder irrigated settlement in Hara, and the Integrated Livestock Project, which established marketing infrastructure, as well as artificial insemination and other technical services in selected districts. Examples of the national specialist services are the dipping and vaccination program (which received a favorable evaluation report in 1983 for its reduction of cattle mortality rates) and the Seed Technology Unit.

The only project of this varied portfolio that continues to receive British aid is the animal disease work, which is primarily concerned with rinderpest control. The decline of small projects set in around 1980. Few were evaluated in any formal sense, but the issue was not whether the projects were individually successful. Indeed, it was felt (within the U.K. government and among influential donors such as the World Bank) that small donor-assisted projects were difficult to replicate and did not fit any national strategy to build capacity to assist large numbers of smallholders. For ODA, there were also the factors of declining TCO influence and of a declining aid program—and, more broadly, the value being attached to donor coordination and cofinancing arrangements. The upshot was ODA decided to support NRDP. Its main component was the Phalombe Rural Development Project, which provided for increased expenditure on extension, credit, and rural roads.

U.K. aid for Malawi's research programs has declined substantially since the early 1970s. There were about twenty British personnel working in established agricultural research posts from independence through the early 1970s, but by 1981 there were only two supplemented posts, including the chief agricultural research officer; today there are none. Also by 1981 ODA project aid for agricultural research had been reduced to a few projects, in export crop research. Support for tobacco research, and for cotton research, was sustained over a long period, and this continuity has been an important ingredient in the establishment of local institutional capability. Support for maize research has been less successful and relatively short term.

CDC's agricultural investment in Malawi is larger and more diversified than in either Kenya or Tanzania. Its main role in agricultural development has been to act as the leading agency in promoting tea, sugar, coffee, and flue-cured tobacco among smallholders. The uptake among smallholders has been widespread, particularly in tea and tobacco, but the CDC schemes have not obtained the expected increases in farmer incomes, number of producers, or commercial viability of the authority concerned. The lessons of the CDC experience in Malawi point in particular to the difficulty of covering the costs of managing tenancy-based schemes.

The CDC has also contributed a significant amount to the large estates. Since 1980, the corporation has invested in three new estate projects: Vizara Estates Rubber, Karuzi Tea Company, and the Kawalazi Estate (which produces tea, macadamia, and coffee). In addition, since 1977 CDC has provided three loans to the government of Malawi to subscribe shares in the Dwangwa Sugar Corporation, which manages a 5,200-hectare irrigated estate in the Central region, of which 660 hectares are under lease to about 300 smallholders under the Smallholder Sugar Authority (SSA).

The SSA's Dwangwa Smallholder Sugar Project is a modest scheme for irrigated smallholder development, when set against the original objectives for the Dwangwa Delta. In 1969, ODA established a pilot rice scheme, and the subsequent British Irrigated Rice Project produced a proposal for 4,300 smallholder settlers. However, in 1973 the government decided to expand national sugar production, and the Dwangwa Sugar Corporation was established.

Investment in sugar in the Dwanga Delta (the overall investment includes the construction of a road north of Nkhotakota under ODA project aid) has proved unsatisfactory to date. Projected land development costs soared in the period 1977–81, partly because the land had to be redeveloped and flood protection works built after an unanticipated rise in the level of Lake Malawi. More important in the long run, however, were the downturn in the world sugar price in the 1980s and sluggish domestic demand. For SSA producers, the ex-mill prices were some 20–30 percent below CDC appraisal report projections from 1982 onward. The government has provided price support (and ODA an effective subsidy—as the costs of the expatriate CDC manager are met from aid funds); but there have been more than seventy resignations and evictions from the scheme, and the commercial viability of SSA is uncertain.

The record of SSA is repeated, in broad terms, in all four of the smallholder crop authority projects in which CDC has been involved as both financier and manager. The Kasungu Flue-Cured Tobacco Authority illustrates the problems for commercial management in circumstances where smallholder production is subject to large price fluctuations. Yet the first of the CDC smallholder projects, the Smallholder Tea Authority, which began in 1967, also shows positive price responsiveness, with significant yield improvements from 1983–84 (following world price increases) after several years in which poor husbandry and plucking standards had caused some despair among managers. The current poor performance of the Smallholder Coffee Authority also reflects the difficult and long-term nature of establishing a significant base for a smallholder export crop industry in a particular region.[6] As in the SSA, ODA finance has been provided to cover part of the management costs, but the necessity of government subventions on the operating costs of the authorities runs counter to CDC objectives of establishing self-financing enterprises.

Crop Research: Cotton, Tobacco, and Maize

U.K. technical assistance has played a vital role in the development of both cotton and tobacco in Malawi, particularly in resistance breeding and the development of cotton pest-management practices. Under the Colonial Development and Welfare Fund, a cotton pest research program was established in Malawi in 1956; it was to work specifically on two major pests, the red bollworm and the stainer bug. In a successful period of work, the biology of the main pests was determined and recommendations developed for the control of the cotton pest complex. Together with the release in 1961 of Albar 637, which had a high degree of resistance to bacterial blight, the growing use of recommended insecticides provided the basis for a rapid expansion of the cotton crop in Malawi and elsewhere in the Central African Federation.

After independence, cotton pest-management research was continued by the Malawi Agricultural Research Council (which received support through U.K. budgetary aid); when this form of aid was ended, support for research in cotton breeding, agronomy, and pest management became available from ODA's research and development funds. For example, support was provided by the former TDRI in the design of traps to monitor bollworm populations; and in breeding, selection work continued to improve Albar 637 and another improved variety, Makoka 72, released in 1972. This work was undertaken by the staff of the Cotton Research Corporation (CRC). The CRC was a legacy of the Empire Cotton-Growing Corporation established in the early part of the century. Its finance was provided from the U.K. aid program and from cotton-growing member countries. However, subscriptions were not always paid and the corporation ended in 1975, when contributions from member countries and ODA itself could no longer match operating costs. U.K. aid support has, however, provided help to develop a significant Malawian research capability to replace the earlier CRC work.

In 1986 the Ministry of Agriculture had a five-person research team, based at Makoka, four with postgraduate degrees from the United Kingdom. The strength of the team has been demonstrated by its shift in emphasis toward the development of varieties suited to specific areas. In 1985 a new variety was released for the Shire Valley, with a significant lint yield superiority over Makoka 72, and a further variety has been developed for estate production with a high ginning percentage.

The establishment of a strong technical base for cotton production in Malawi has resulted from the long period of U.K. support and from the continued commitment of the Malawi government to provide an infrastructure for research. In Malawi, unlike Tanzania, the end of CRC support did not lead to a rundown of cotton research since Malawi staff had gained experience working with the CRC and were provided with specialist training in the United Kingdom.

A similar record of effective aid is evident in the tobacco industry. Of the crop research projects set up in Malawi when budgetary aid was brought to an end, tobacco research has been the longest. Support was provided from ODA's research and development funds from 1971 to 1977, when the project was extended as part of the bilateral aid program. The project was then transferred from the Ministry of Agriculture to the newly established Malawi Tobacco Research Authority in 1980.

During the first three years of the project, it was found that the standard of management of the fire-cured crop was the principal factor affecting quality. The yield and quality characteristics could be influenced by manipulating fertilizer and spacing treatments so that greater returns could accrue to the small grower without increasing inputs. In the breeding program, attention was paid to the diseases brown spot and wildfire, which were serious constraints to burley (a tobacco variety) production. The problem was by and large solved by the release in 1976 of Blanket A-1, and cultural recommendations established by agronomic trials enabled the more efficient growers to double their yields.

One main thrust of the breeding program on fire-cured tobacco for smallholder production has been the development of a disease-resistant variety. A cross-breeding program was started under the project that led to the release of DRV (disease-resistant variety) 7. The variety resembles the old in growth habit and carries resistance to brown spot, wildfire, and mosaic virus. By 1985–86 the whole of the fire-cured tobacco area had been planted to the new variety.

The U.K. project was brought to an end in 1985. It had been in operation long enough to achieve its objectives, and the control exercised over the issue of seed enabled the breeding work to make a rapid impact as soon as new disease-resistant varieties were available. Today the Malawi Tobacco Research Authority is relatively well staffed with national scientists, and there are good facilities for work. As in the case of cotton research, U.K. long-term support has contributed to a strong institutional base.

In maize research, however, a different picture emerges. Maize is the staple food and principal crop of Malawi with respect to planted area and volume, and from the early 1970s U.K. technical assistance was provided to improve yields and develop new maize varieties. In particular, the five-year project aimed to develop higher-yielding varieties of white-seeded maize and to establish fertilizer requirements. During the first two seasons of the project, thirty varieties were tested at about 100 sites. The existing hybrid SR52 gave much the best yields, but SR52 (and its successors) are dent types not favored for food use. Compared with flint types, they are difficult to pound, susceptible to weevil damage, and store poorly under high moisture conditions. The project was remodeled to emphasize composites. Two of these, Tanzanian Ukiriguru Composite A (UCA) and Malawian Chitedze Composite A (CCA) were identified as giving improved yields at medium to high altitudes and at lower altitudes, respectively. Both are flint types, and a program of recurrent selection was initiated to improve their yield and agronomic characteristics. They remain the only two maize varieties recommended for domestically consumed crops, and there has been little progress in maize breeding since the mid-1970s, when the ODA project ended. In retrospect, the period of the ODA project was too short; it provided no formal training and when it was closed down in 1976 a large gap was left in national maize research work.

Seed Development

The seed industry had two phases of U.K. support: first, in the establishment (from 1976) of a Seed Technology Unit under the director of agricultural research, and second, in the creation (in 1978) of the National Seed Company of Malawi (NSCM) under the Agricultural Development and Marketing Corporation (ADMARC) and CDC ownership. The aid took the form of technical and capital assistance for the Seed Technology Services project and CDC loans and ODA-supported management consultancy for the NSCM.

U.K. aid initially concentrated on a technical service responsible for maintaining parent lines, field certification, and seed testing. Capital aid was given for the laboratory and buildings of a seed technology unit (STU); support for recurrent costs was also provided, and technical assistance took the form of a chief technical officer (CTO) to establish the STU. ODA took the view in 1975 that commitments should be limited to three years, and the government of Malawi was expected to take the STU onto its recurrent budget by 1978. In fact, by late 1977—when the CTO's contract was due to expire—equipment was still arriving, and the building work had not been completed. One item that had been delayed was a Swiss-manufactured humidifier, which had been held up for five months while permission for a Department of Trade and Industry waiver was sought.

A request to extend the contract of the CTO was granted by ODA but in the meantime a CDC mission had reported on the proposed National Seed Company, and CDC was looking to ODA to provide the services, under consultancy terms, of the same CTO as general manager. On leaving the STU in 1978, the CTO stressed the need for an experienced expatriate replacement and saw that the fledgling unit was in great need of technical direction. In the event, ODA was unable to provide a suitably qualified replacement and did not press the matter as aid finance for Malawi had become constrained. In 1983 the agricultural adviser found that the STU still lacked a trained seed analyst and suggested that an ODA-supplemented appointment should be considered. The matter was not followed up, and no request materialized.

A more substantial U.K. investment was involved in the establishment in 1978 of NSCM, which owns a 450-acre seed farm, processing plant, warehouse, head offices, and cold stores. In addition to loan finance, CDC provided, up to 1986, the core management of NSCM with four posts: general manager, company secretary, seed production manager, and seed-processing manager.

The company has greatly reduced Malawi's dependence on imported seed and now exports small amounts of maize, vegetable, and rhodes grass seed. Although it has yet to achieve the shareholders' target of a 15 percent return on invested capital, NSCM has made small operating surpluses in each year since it was established. The company is well managed, the contract grower system is working efficiently, and (below senior management level) there has been a satisfactory development of local staff capacity.

NSCM represents a successful U.K. aid intervention. Yet seed development for smallholder production in Malawi remains at a disappointingly low level. In particular, the sales of seed maize, by far the single largest commodity in which the company deals, have grown little since the company became fully operational in late 1979.[7] One factor frequently mentioned within the company concerns the demand collection and distribution capabilities of ADMARC. But the low margins in seed trading that the government imposes on ADMARC inhibits the holding of large stocks at its local sales point and CDC has been unable to influence government policy in this area. Of more long-term importance has been the failure of the Research Department and (to a lesser extent) the STU to develop a range of varieties suited to the economies and consumption patterns of Malawi's smallholders. As the CDC visiting adviser noted in 1983, NSCM does not receive enough new inputs of breeder seed, which reflects a shortage of qualified staff, poor maintenance of research equipment, and a general lack of research funding, especially for maize breeding and agronomy research. Although the current level of efficiency of the Malawi seed industry clearly owes much to U.K. aid in various forms, the industry could become even more effective with a more sustained U.K. aid effort to lay the foundation for the seed industry, particularly in its main commodity, maize.

Kasungu Flue-Cured Tobacco Authority

In its initial feasibility study of the smallholder tobacco production on Kasungu, CDC emphasized that "smallholders should be at least self-supporting in food crops" and that CDC should "provide sufficient help and supervision at the start; but aim to progressively withdraw it so that the African farmer, individually or as a group, becomes more self-reliant."

CDC has now provided six loans (a total value of £ 4.16 million) to the authority (KFCTA) since its establishment in 1970, and it has also provided management under contract. During most of the 1970s and early 1980s there were four CDC staff members in senior positions in the authority (general manager, workshop manager, production manager, and financial controller). In 1986 there were still two senior posts filled by the CDC: financial controller and production manager.

In 1986, 900 Malawian farmers were benefiting from the opportunity to grow flue-cured tobacco, a crop previously dominated by large commercial growers. By 1985–86, 1,225 hectares had been brought under production by the authority, producing 2,114 million kilograms of tobacco (or approximately 8.5 percent of national production), with a further 1,078 hectares under maize. KFCTA carries out a wide range of services on behalf of smallholders (1 hectare) and growers (4 hectares), including the procurement and delivery of fertilizer and chemicals; the provision of extension services; the maintenance of the road, electricity, and water services; and the organization of tobacco grading and its transport and presentation on the auction floors. The costs of such services are recovered—in theory—from tobacco sales handled by the authority.

The tobacco schemes have had some notable successes. Yields have continued to rise steadily (from 1.19 tons per hectare average in 1971 to 1.92 tons per hectare in 1985), and both yield and selling price have been consistently higher than the national average. Against this, however, there has been a contraction in the number of settled farmers (the number fell form a peak of 1,247 in 1980 to 754 in 1984, although it rose again to 930 in 1986), and also in the cropped tobacco area (down from 2,011 hectares in 1978 to 1,226 hectares in 1986). Furthermore, returns to tobacco growing have weakened, and farmer incomes in many cases have proved a disincentive to continued production. Up to 1977, the costs of production of flue-cured tobacco were relatively low in relation to tobacco prices. After 1977, however, crop costs started to rise, and tobacco prices went through a period of marked deterioration. From 1978 to 1981, the majority of farmers were unable to generate sufficient revenue from tobacco to pay KFCTA for the cost of services and to retain an adequate income. Although from 1982 onward the majority of remaining farmers have made a profit, this disguises the fact that substantial numbers of farmers have continued to operate unprofitably and have either left the project or reduced their input into tobacco cultivation.

These difficulties for farmers have had a serious impact on the financial viability of the authority. All of KFCTA's permanent capital has been provided through redeemable loans, mainly from the CDC. Repayment was intended mainly from farmers' accumulation of a capital stake, whereby individual farmers were required to contribute 40 percent of their profits. In practice, most farmers were unable to pay, and in 1981 the stake system was replaced by a rental system, whereby farmers pay a rent designed to cover interest on development loans. There is at present no charge contributing to repayment of principal, which KFCTA is thus unable to meet. Similarly the authority has been unable to cover the recurrent costs of its operations in every year but one since 1975, and the costs themselves have risen sharply because of vacant land, farmers' losses, and the rising expense of maintaining welfare and technical services.

In 1981 the government introduced a subvention payment to KFCTA and discontinued the carryover of farmers' debts. These measures, together with an increase in tobacco prices in recent years, have improved farmer incomes. The use of input packages has increased and the high yields necessary for the continuation of the project are now being achieved—but only at the cost of an effective government subsidy.

The case of KFCTA illustrates not only the general benefits that can accrue from such a scheme, but also the problems that may arise (especially in years of poor commodity prices) and that can, as in Malawi, limit their potential for further expansion. This experience—like that of the more successful KTDA project in Kenya—shows the need for smallholders to achieve high yields to cover the relatively high costs of smallholder schemes; it also shows the close correlation between farmer incentives, production performance, and the financial viability of the scheme itself.

It is evident from the KFCTA experience that the careful design of smallholder projects undertaken by CDC does not invariably produce—even where direct CDC management is provided over a long period—the sort of successful enterprise exemplified by the KTDA in Kenya. With farmers still dependent upon KFCTA to service their tobacco crop, and KDCTA itself still dependent on regular government subventions, the initial objectives of farmer self-reliance and scheme financial viability have not been realized and the spread of wealth from tobacco production is narrower than originally anticipated.

Phalombe Rural Development Project

The Phalombe RDP has been the largest component of ODA's support for the Malawi NRDP: The two other components have been assistance to the Blantyre Agricultural Development Division (in which Phalombe is located) and to the National Sample Survey of Agriculture. World Bank technical assistance has been important to the evolution of NRDP but the commitment of ODA was seen by the Malawi government in 1977 as critical to the arrangements of coordinated donor support for a £ 40 million program requiring £ 35 million in external finance over five years. In the 1977 U.K.-Malawi aid talks, £ 4.8 million was earmarked to NRDP, and eventually ODA became the third largest (and largest bilateral) donor.

The NRDP strategy, to which ODA subscribed, was regarded as an extension of the LLDP strategy. A long-term commitment was envisaged, with a twenty-year time scale for developing infrastructure and support services and for expanding these from the initial selected area. The term used to describe provision was "extensive" rather than "intensive," and LLDP was generally seen as too costly and overmanaged for long-term replication.

But in fact the NRDP strategy was substantially different from the earlier land development projects. In Lilongwe, for example, a constraint to increased production was the scattered and insecure nature of landholdings and the low level of land husbandry. The project emphasized resettlement, land registration and consolidation, soil conservation and, in places, irrigation measures. NRDP, in contrast, identified more manageable and short-term goals: input supply (particularly improved seed and fertilizer), credit, extension, and—in support of these—rural feeder roads, stores, and staff housing. Thus the Phalombe RDP has been essentially an agricultural services project with a "poverty focus" on the smallholder sector, which is primarily cultivating mixed stands of food crops, with only occasionally some land down to crops such as cotton or tobacco.

The decision to support NRDP was based on confident assumptions about rates of uptake of trial-based recommendations across a range of crops. Farm input costs were expected to rise substantially (thereby necessitating new credit facilities) with a doubled output value of about 20 percent of farmers. The NRDP (and thus the Phalombe project) strategy assumed the availability of improved technologies attractive to smallholders.

The costs of the Phalombe RDP arise largely from its extension services. The number of extension workers has doubled, and provision has been made for staff housing and training centers. The project has also covered the costs of supporting the increased extension effort: administration, fuel and vehicles, and rents. A large part of the extension effort has consisted of credit administration, but ODA support for loans has been limited to about £ 200,000 made available to ADMARC on the understanding that the equivalent value would be expended on U.K. procurement of agrochemicals and fertilizer. Other expenditures have gone into improving feeder roads and building storage depots.

The project was designed to be incorporated into the government system. The annual project budget, 90 percent of which is covered by ODA, has been agreed upon each year with the Development Division in Lilongwe. ODA was concerned at the outset about the recurrent costs of Phalombe and resisted government requests that it provide for more posts and mileage allowances. However, the calculated internal rate of return of 12 percent assuaged some of ODA's concerns about the financing of extension expenditures. On the question of local capital and recurrent costs, ODA agreed that under special circumstances the guidelines on U.K. procurement could be liberalized, and more than 50 percent of the Phalombe allocation has been for local costs. On local recurrent costs, it was accepted that project posts and related allowances need not be placed on the government revenue account until the end of the financing period.

The most pressing issue for an extension of support to the project (into a new phase and an expanded area) has been the high recurrent cost and management implications for the Ministry of Agriculture. The government of Malawi's initial request for an extension included almost 400 new posts, 300 staff house units, and 90 vehicles. ODA has been unwilling to countenance this request, especially in view of the staff demands of a similar agricultural development project elsewhere in the district. Yet it has been the lack of confidence in the direction and likely outcome of Phalombe RDP that has raised so sharply the questions about the size of public sector employment against the returns of the services being provided.

As a 1985 evaluation of Phalombe RDP indicates, it is impossible to judge how the project will affect agricultural output.[8] Maize production increased sharply form 1981 to 1982, but this increase appears to have been largely attributable to price changes; and it occurred in both project and nonproject areas of the district. Furthermore, a survey in the fifth year of the project showed that only 2 percent of the maize area (as against an anticipated 8 percent) was down to the recommended hybrids and composites. However, the number of registered tobacco growers had increased, and sales of insecticides to cotton farmers had climbed up. There had been also a big expansion in the uptake of credit, and fertilizer sales had increased correspondingly.

The 1985 evaluation did note, however, that in general farmers did not welcome crop recommendations. Extension agents also reported that, in mixed stands, improved varieties had not sufficiently outperformed local varieties to justify the attendant risks, including the problems of lodging and pest damage. The greatest weakness in agricultural support in the Phalombe areas has thus appeared to be in research, where trials did not begin until 1985 and were confined to screening cowpea and pigeon pea varieties. ODA has had little technical involvement in Phalombe. It is evident that the lack of economically sound technical messages has held up agricultural improvement; recommendations were expected to be tailored to different extension planning areas, for example, has meant little of this has been done in practice, and a centrally determined package has remained the dominant pattern.

Program Grants, 1980–85

The introduction of program aid to Malawi in the 1980s occurred when the first of three World Bank structural adjustment loans was under negotiation and when an IMF standby program, later to be supplemented by a three-year IMF Extended Fund Facility, already had been agreed. Program aid was thus first supplied at a time of unusually severe balance of payments difficulties for Malawi. The first program aid agreement of 1980 (for £ 6 million) was explicitly designed to help relieve a foreign exchange constraint by supporting the flow of imports to sustain existing productive capacity, particularly in the agricultural sector. The second agreement of 1984 (for £ 2.5 million) was made, less explicitly, "in support of measures undertaken by the IMF and the IBRD."

Under the first grant, agricultural inputs (particularly requests for fertilizers and machinery) were favored by ODA, and the main beneficiaries proved to be government departments and parastatals. Even so, the end disbursement date for this new stream of fast-spending program aid had to be extended from the end of September 1982 to the end of September 1984. The take-up of the second program grant of 1984 was even less rapid, despite initial applications totaling £ 4 million for a grant covering imports of £ 2.54 million.

Many of the initial applications for funds were subsequently withdrawn, including requests for agricultural equipment, and several large importing firms did not apply to the Reserve Bank for a tranche of U.K. program aid, as they feared this would disrupt their normal access to foreign exchange under existing arrangements. This indicated that the foreign exchange shortage was no longer severe in the 1984–85 period, and an internal ODA appraisal of the second program grant expressed doubt that the aid was relieving a critical foreign exchange position.

Conditions for the use of the second program grant were much tighter than the first. This time the U.K. government insisted that procurement should come from the private sector rather than the government and the parastatals, and that it should be in the form of raw materials, spares, and replacement equipment. Yet, unlike the first grant, it did not prescribe a particular agricultural input share, and, in the event, only £ 1 million of the £ 2.5 million available was related to agricultural use. This amount was largely made up of sales to three firms: Shell Chemicals (Malawi), Farming and Engineering Services, and Agricultural and Auto Spares.

The introduction of the "private sector procurement" condition into the second program grant ignored the reality of the Malawi economy, much of which is only nominally in private hands. Furthermore, if one of the objectives of U.K. program aid had been to assist Malawian smallholders with a regular supply of imported inputs, this would have necessarily involved procurement by government agencies, so that the restriction of procurement to private firms tended to reduce the flow of direct benefits to the smallholder subsector. In practice, however, a large order for Shell's Ripcord pesticide represented the total annual requirement of the Malawi market for the product, indicating that much would be supplied not to the private sector, but to the parastatals.

Experience with five years of program aid to Malawi has proved that it can be faster to disburse than conventional project aid, but it was less fast-spending than had originally been anticipated, and there was regularly pressure to elicit suitable requests for allocations in the three months before the close of each financial year to avoid underspending. Furthermore, inasmuch as foreign exchange was not in short supply after the first two years of program grant applications, program aid also had only limited effect in filling a foreign exchange gap and directing imports into areas of high priority, in the spirit of the structural adjustment programs.

It is also evident that program aid had less direct impact on agriculture than anticipated. Agricultural suppliers and producers had priority access to foreign exchange under existing Malawi government guidelines, and many of the larger firms serving the estates had no difficulty in procuring imports through the normal channels. The stricter requirement to direct allocations to the private sector under the second grant had the effect of extending access to foreign exchange to small firms in transport and manufacturing, rather than to smallholder agriculture.

Agricultural Aid to Tanzania

Tanzania inherited a potentially strong agricultural sector from the colonial period.

The Colonial Legacy

Research and services for sisal, cotton, and coffee production were well established, although research on food staples had not made the same progress. Partly because there was less pressure for protecting the farming interests of European settlers in Tanzania than in either Malawi or Kenya, there was earlier colonial government support for smallholder production that involved considerable intervention in the sector, including encouragement for cooperative processing and marketing arrangements.

The marketing of crops grown by Africans was initially undertaken by Asian traders, but as early as the 1920s, African coffee producers organized to break the Asian monopoly and established the Kilimanjaro Native Planter's Association (KNPA, later the KNCU), the first such organization in East Africa. With the encouragement of the Colonial Office, the cooperative movement as a whole underwent substantial expansion in the 1940s and 1950s, and some of the cooperatives were among the largest commercial enterprises under African control in the entire continent.

After 1945 a strongly interventionist policy developed toward African agriculture. Apart from schemes for large mechanized groundnut cultivation to serve the needs of the British edible oils market (a cause célèbre of its time), there were also resettlement schemes, such as Sukumuland, based on the expansion of its cotton production. Increased emphasis also was given—against nationalist opposition—to enforcing soil conservation and livestock control.

In agricultural services, the most important legacy of the colonial period was the building of an agricultural research system. The East African Agricultural Research Station was established at Amani in 1921; the Cotton Research Corporation assisted with the establishment of cotton research stations; and a veterinary laboratory and livestock research station were also established on the site of a former German rinderpest serum institute at Mpwapwa.

The colonial research effort benefited coffee, cotton, and sisal in particular, and selection work was initiated on sorghum. A maize breeding program started by the Tanganyika Agricultural Corporation in collaboration with the East African Agricultural and Forestry Research Organisation (EAAFRO) had notable success in the 1950s with the development of locally adapted varieties resistant to *Puccinia polysora* rust, which first appeared in East Africa in about 1941. Despite this progress in food staples, however, the main feature of colonially administered agriculture was the considerable export base that had been developed by and was primarily in the hands of African smallholders. Tanganyika was thus regarded by the colonial agricultural service as having a greater farm potential than Kenya. Furthermore, unlike Kenya and (to a lesser extent) Malawi, independent Tanzania did not inherit a farm sector in which European settlement had competed significantly with African land needs. But of particular significance was the legacy of state intervention in all areas of farming, including cultivation practices, resettlement, marketing, and price control. This laid the basis for the further extension of public regulation after independence, when radical policies to transform traditional agriculture were introduced.

Trends in Agricultural Aid

Since independence, bilateral relations between the United Kingdom and Tanzania frequently have been strained, and the U.K. aid program has also developed an erratic profile (see table 9-5), with periods in which new aid commitments are suspended.[9] The United Kingdom has not had the same long-term involvement in Tanzanian agriculture that has characterized aid to Malawi and Kenya, although there are two exceptions to this—cotton research and dairy development. As a result, ODA agricultural aid decisions have been instigated by government requests for project finance in line with development policies already determined with other donors; assistance for specific projects has dominated the aid program since the late 1970s. For example, ODA has given support both to Tanzania's decentralized integrated rural development initiatives and to its grain reserve strategy. In Mtwara and Lindi regions, ODA became the lead external aid agency, and in Tabora, ODA was responsible for a land-use component of a project in which the World Bank took the lead. ODA support for strategic grain reserves—through the building of large regional depots—also was a main item in U.K. agricultural project aid from the late 1970s, although it became evident in the 1980s that low levels of maize output, together with a shift in policy emphasis toward village-level storage, had diminished the utility of the depots for grain storage.

In the case of support for integrated rural development projects (IRDPs), ODA was influenced in its assessment by the 1975 White Paper, which stressed the need for both an "integrated and decentralized approach to agricultural development." Within the Tabora Integrated Rural Development Project (TIRDP), ODA financed (between 1978 and 1984) a land resource survey that identified the nature of Kenya or Malawi in some detail. The total financial commitment to Tanzania in the period 1970–84 was £ 27 million—well below that to both Malawi (£ 59 million) and Kenya (£ 78 million)—and of that £ 27 million, only £ 5 million went to agriculture, primarily to TANWAT and TANSEED. CDC's main agricultural interest has been a plantation company, TANWAT, established in the 1940s to produce tanning extract from wattle. In the 1960s CDC (faced by a declining world demand for wattle) also went into the production of beef, wheat, timer, and seed maize. It has been CDC policy worldwide to divest ownership of established companies such as TANWAT, but the government has been unwilling to assume responsibility for what has become a diverse enterprise.

The Tanzanian brand of socialism implied a degree of hostility toward individual farmers producing relatively high-value export crops, and the CDC smallholder authority model was not adopted. In the 1980s, however, the deteriorating performance of crops such as sisal, tea, and coffee led the government to revise its attitude toward the management of agricultural exports. In 1985, the CDC agreed to finance and rehabilitate a number of estates and a factory and was

Table 9-5. *United Kingdom Bilateral Aid to Tanzania, 1970–85*
(thousands of pounds sterling)

Component	*1970*	*1971*	*1972*	*1973*	*1974*	*1975*	*1976*	*1977*
Financial aid								
Project aid including aid-trade provision (ATP)	0	0	0	0	0	835	147	48
Program aid	0	0	0	0	0	0	1,520	3,850
Debt cancellation	0	0	0	0	0	0	0	0
Other nonproject	0	0	0	0	0	980	895	362
CDC loans	238	715	347	111	205	210	0	0
Subtotal	238	715	347	111	205	2,025	2,562	4,260
Technical cooperation								
Wholly financed personnel	9	1	2	—	—	7	84	218
Partly financed personnel	1,764	1,378	1,362	1,342	1,194	1,750	1,293	1,454
Students and trainees	19	26	14	45	110	240	460	613
Other TC	0	0	0	0	2	32	41	141
Subtotal	1,792	1,405	1,378	1,387	1,307	2,029	1,878	2,426
Total	2,030	2,120	1,725	1,498	1,512	4,054	4,440	6,685

	1978	*1979*	*1980*	*1981*	*1982*	*1983*	*1984*	*1985*
Financial aid								
Project aid including ATP	1,012	8,462	19,289	16,482	15,283	21,694	15,595	10,467
Program aid	5,573	4,793	3,548	1,366	0	0	0	0
Debt cancellation	0	517	433	415	362	362	362	362
Other nonproject	5	1,148	0	0	469	150	0	0
CDC loans	70	2,145	94	2,436	3,780	1,470	8,022	225
Subtotal	6,660	17,024	23,365	20,699	19,895	23,676	23,980	11,054

(Table continues on the following page.)

Table 9-5. *(continued)*

Component	*1970*	*1971*	*1972*	*1973*	*1974*	*1975*	*1976*	*1977*
Technical cooperation								
Wholly financed personnel	648	1,461	2,046	1,886	1,452	1,677	1,311	1,160
Partly financed personnel	1,501	2,507	459	377	420	662	664	641
Students and trainees	828	1,345	2,470	2,317	2,226	1,483	1,301	1,791
Other TC	726	1,739	3,779	4,761	3,336	2,885	2,975	3,321
Subtotal	3,703	7,051	8,754	9,341	7,434	6,707	6,251	6,913
Total	10,363	23,559	32,119	30,040	27,328	30,384	30,230	17,967

Source: See table 9-3.

also encouraged to prepare proposals for financing and managing a rehabilitated coffee industry.

Cotton Research

Cotton growing was introduced into Tanzania in 1904, but efforts to improve productivity did not begin until the mid-1930s, with selection work on the mixed stock of seed then sown. This led first to the development of Mwanza Local, the first cotton variety to be developed in Tanzania, and subsequently to the selection of MZ 561, which was released in 1939. In the same year the CRC provided staff to organize cotton research at the Ukiriguru Research Station in the western cotton-growing area (WCGA). The corporation continued to provide staff support until it was dissolved in 1975, at which time U.K. aid was extended until 1982. The research done in the period from 1939 to 1974 was responsible for the rapid development of the Tanzanian cotton industry. Production in the WCGA rose from 50,000 bales of lint in the 1950s to about 190,000 bales in the early 1960s and 390,000 bales in the mid-1970s.

The most serious constraint to production identified in 1939 was the cotton jassid, and work began on the selection of jassid-resistant cottons. An important aspect of the breeding work, as with the associated agronomic research, was a program of trials on farmers' fields throughout the region to ensure the adaptability of material. The work led to the release of a series of jassid-resistant varieties from 1948 to 1959, each showing better jassid resistance, lint yield, and ginning percentage than its predecessor. A further breeding program began to confer resistance to bacterial blight by means of a hybridization program with a resistant variety obtained from the corporation's breeding work in Uganda. A variety with greatly improved blight resistance was released in 1961.

The WCGA was then divided into two varietal zones, northern and southern. In a practice still followed, varieties with longer, finer fiber were grown in the northern zone, where the growing conditions were better. Four additional varieties from the breeding program were released to the northern zone between 1963 and 1977, and another five to the southern zone between 1963 and 1947. The progress made in breeding was consolidated by an efficiently managed cottonseed multiplication and distribution scheme based on the strict control of seed issued to the growing area of each ginning.

During the 1960s yet another disease, fusarium wilt, became a problem on light soils in the northern area. A breeding program to confer resistance to the disease was begun and led to the release in 1977 of UK 77. While the plant-breeding work was proceeding, supporting research was undertaken in agronomic practices, crop nutrition needs, and other crop protection practices. This led to recommendations on sowing dates, cross-tying of ridges for water conservation, fertilizer requirements, and crop-spraying regimes. Research was also carried out by CRC staff based at Ilonga Research Station for the eastern cotton-growing area along the coast. Reselections of the better-quality Uganda UPA cotton were developed for the area, and recommendations were made for cultural methods and pest control measures. By the end of the 1960s cotton production had risen to almost 27,000 bales a year.

In the period after independence, cotton research was largely undertaken by the CRC. The corporation supplied a multidisciplinary team of seven to eight research cotton workers to staff all of the senior research positions at Ukiriguru and Ilonga. However, little provision had been made for developing local staff at the professional levels. The first Tanzanian cotton breeder and plant pathologist were not appointed until 1973. An entomologist was appointed in 1974. Two national agronomists had worked in Ukiriguru in the 1960s but had subsequently left; another agronomist was not appointed until 1973.

When the CRC was abolished in 1975, the government was faced with the collapse of its cotton research capability, and ODA was approached for assistance. As a consequence, two ex-CRC cotton breeders were posted to Ukiriguru (for two- and four-year contracts, respectively) and four other research posts were filled at different times of a project that lasted from 1976 to 1982. Training was also provided—through the British Council—for four nationals at the M.Sc. level (a breeder, soil scientist, entomologist, and a plant pathologist).

The main technical output in this period was the release for the southern zone in 1982 of a variety that produced about 15 percent more lint than its predecessor. But at the end of the period of ODA support, the national cotton program was still not able to sustain a strong research effort. In 1984 the FAO attached a cotton breeder and a socioeconomist to the cotton research team, but the work of the station generally remained constrained by manpower deficiencies in areas such as agronomy and soil science. In addition, the cotton program suffered a severe shortage of operational funds and a lack of foreign exchange to purchase new equipment, spare parts, and chemicals.

Cotton production declined from about 400,000 bales a year in the early 1970s to about 250,000 bales in the mid-1980s. Yields likewise declined, from about 600–700 kilograms seed cotton per hectare in the early 1970s to about 300–350 kilograms per hectare in 1986. Despite the earlier advances in agronomic recommendations, a survey of six villages around Ukiriguru in 1984–85 showed that less than 10 percent of the cotton crop was effectively sprayed, and only about 5 percent of the cotton farmers were using fertilizers.

A task force on cotton rehabilitation examined this performance in 1985 and pinpointed a number of problems: the organization and financial structure of the Tanzanian Cotton Authority, the criteria by which prices for lint and cottonseed were calculated (resulting in poor economic returns to the farmers), late payments to farmers, the poor quality of cottonseed (linked to ginning), poor engineering management at ginneries, inadequate and erratic fuel supply, and deterioration of the road and rail transport system. The task force also noted that the government had not given enough priority to cotton research.

Thus four decades of U.K. aid for cotton research in Tanzania can be said to have provided the catalyst for the development of a considerable cotton industry and a sound basis for future cotton research and development. However, in 1974 eight of the nineteen research scientists at Ukiriguru were expatriates, and when the CRC closed down, Tanzania was left with little capability for cotton research. Even by 1982, when ODA support ended, local staffing was inadequate.

In retrospect, ODA project support should have been phased out over a longer period and stronger provision made for training national scientists. Yet it is unlikely that, on its own, U.K. aid would have made a substantial impact on the current poor performance of cotton if it had continued after 1982. Such support would not have been effective unless buttressed by a stronger Tanzanian commitment to research and to the rehabilitation of the cotton industry (for example, through the provision of high-quality planting seed and payments). The price structure and the performance of the Tanzanian Cotton Authority were clearly factors in declining cotton production and incomes, and the adverse impact of such factors has inhibited the effectiveness of a substantial U.K. contribution in research and development.

TANSEED

The Tanzanian Seed Company Ltd. (TANSEED) was established in 1972 as a joint venture between CDC and the parastatal National Agriculture and Food Corporation to expand the production and supply of certified seed, particularly maize and sorghum. At that time the cereals seed industry consisted primarily of a breeding station at Ilonga, with a number of regional multiplication stations under the Ministry of Agriculture distributing certified seed mainly to its regional offices and to the Tanganyika Farmers Association. In the early 1970s, however, the U.S. Agency for International Development (USAID) decided to support the establishment of foundation seed farms (replacing the poorly functioning regional stations), and it made the creation of TANSEED a condition of this support. Simultaneously, the government enacted seed legislation, under which the ministry established a seed certification agency TOSCA (Tanzanian Official Seed Certification Agency).

Thus the early 1970s saw some new cultivars such as the composite UCA being developed; the foundation seed farms (with other contract growers) were taking this breeders' seed and multiplying for TANSEED to process, certify, and market. The system was similar to the one already described in Malawi. CDC's role was also similar to its role in the National Seed Company of Malawi; although in Tanzania there was a stronger base of expertise and involvement in seed production—particularly at TANWAT, which was producing seed maize and wheat.

CDC itself was involved in TANSEED from the outset, originally holding a 50 percent share and providing a general manager, a company secretary, and a seed production manager under a managing agency contract. The general manager post was localized after four years (although CDC still provides the company secretary), and until 1986 the post of seed production manager was also held by a CDC appointee under World Bank financing.

The company established four processing plants—at Arusha, Iringa, Morogoro, and Njombe—with a total annual production capacity of 9,000 tons. Four years later, TANSEED sales were 5,224 tons (1976–77), but the annual sales figure then fell back to a low of 3,922 tons in 1982–83; although a recovery followed, the figures for 1983–84 and 1984–85 were still only a little over 5,000 tons.

Nonetheless, TANSEED appeared to be trading successfully until 1982–83, although a CDC mission found that earlier profits had been somewhat exaggerated in that and losses on seed stock that were no longer salable had not been taken into account in the calculations. TANSEED finances have continued to deteriorate under the weight of growing debts, not to mention the difficulties it has had meeting payments to contract growers and for service equipment. Seed processing and packaging in particular has suffered because machinery has been going down, although both Dutch and Canadian aid is now being provided to rectify this.

The question is whether the seed industry's problems are the result of wider factors affecting the agricultural economy (suppressing both the demand for seed and the efficiency of its supply), or have been caused by industry itself and the way it has been managed and supported—or not supported—with external assistance.

U.K. support to the industry has been channeled mainly into TANSEED itself, but the problems of TANSEED cannot be divorced from wider difficulties in the industry—particularly in quality control, retailing, and seed production. For example, the USAID–supported foundation seed farms were run inefficiently, and when the project ended a large proportion of the mechanical equipment was in need of refurbishment. The government of Tanzania felt that the scale and cost of the foundation seed farm operation (when set against its seed output) could not be sustained without external grant support and TANSEED was approached (unsuccessfully) with a view to letting the company take direct control.

Meanwhile, TANSEED was having difficulty with its own contract growers, who were not attracted to the price paid by the company, especially compared with prices the same grain could attract on the parallel market, and who were confronted by late and irregular payments. But it was not the retail side of the seed industry that was causing the most serious problems. Although a CDC review mission found that the overall quality of TANSEED seed was "not especially bad," many farmers thought that seed originating from TANSEED was of poor quality and at times might not germinate. This problem stemmed from the poor stock control and management under the regional agricultural development officers (who had become the main outlet for TANSEED with the decline in the national role of the Tanganyika Farmers Association). According to the CDC mission, seed was often poorly stored, held over without retesting, and occasionally incorrectly labeled.

Such shortcomings in management are compounded by the difficulty of operating a seed industry in Tanzania. Unlike the National Seed Company of Malawi, TANSEED has four factories to manage, and its seed producers often are far from the processing facilities. Distribution is also a problem because of Tanzania's size and deteriorating transport systems. Moreover, Tanzania's postharvest period—unlike Malawi's hot and dry postharvest season—is generally humid, making storage that much more difficult.

The poor trading performance and weak management of TANSEED has led CDC to conclude that, without a substantial injection of new capital, the company cannot become financially viable. But such an injection has been difficult to justify when other components of the seed industry are underperforming and thereby suppressing any significant increase in demand. As in the Malawi case (which is a more successful U.K.-aided industry), it is evident that CDC could have a large role to play in the establishment of a structure for a publicly controlled, yet commercially viable, seed industry. But the potential effectiveness of CDC depends largely on whether other parts of the industry can be expanded to include activities such as plant breeding and farm input supply services.

U.K.-Based Scientific Support: Armyworm Control

U.K. support for African armyworm research and development in Tanzania (and Kenya and Uganda, in fact) is an example of aid funds being used to support home-based scientific expertise—in this case ODA's TDRI. Like the desert locust, armyworm is a migrating pest, and it is difficult to control without regional cooperation. Thus in 1961 the East African Agricultural and Forestry Research Organisation was the initial focus of U.K. involvement, and ODA's former Anti-Locust Research Centre participated from 1966 to 1971 in an armyworm research project that established an embryo forecasting service in East Africa to warn farmers when they could expect infestations.

In continuing work at TDRI in the United Kingdom during the 1970s, researchers identified the components of the female sex pheromone of the armyworm moth and showed a synthetic pheromone to be an effective attractant in traps. Since then large numbers of pheromone dispensers have been provided by TDRI for an extensive trap network in East Africa, which, together with data on wind systems, makes it possible to forecast primary outbreaks in recognized areas at particular times of the year. The rate and direction of subsequent dispersion that might form secondary and tertiary epidemics can also now be predicted.

In controlling armyworm, TDRI scientists in 1977 launched a new program of ground and aerial spraying in several countries, including Tanzania. In addition to four TDRI staff members located at the Desert Locust Control Organisation headquarters in Nairobi, there is also an ODA-supported program of armyworm control in Tanzania with two TCOs attached to the Plant and Crop Protection Services Department of the Ministry of Agriculture in Tanzania.

The control program provides training for national personnel at all levels, and the capabilities of TDRI are particularly evident in this area of endeavor. The training unit of TDRI organizes courses in the biology, detection, reporting, and control of armyworm for trap operators at the regional and district level. Extension aids have also been prepared and include an African armyworm training package for the Ministry of Agriculture.

Integrated Rural Development Projects (Mtwara and Lindi Regions)

The Mtwara-Lindi U.K. aid program consisted primarily of an attempt to support regionally based planning and implementation. The main impetus to external aid to IRDPs was decentralization policy and regional equity considerations (which led to the establishment of the

Regional Development Directorates) rather than agricultural development as such.

In 1975, a U.K. aid mission led by Minister Judith Hart agreed to support broadly based rural development in the remote and poor southeast regions of Mtwara and Lindi. Following up this decision, an identification mission visited the area but could not see any immediately supportable projects beyond road maintenance, rural water supply, and (drawing upon existing commitments) research and development in oilseed. This mission suggested that two TCOs be appointed, largely to develop stronger proposals. The prime minister's office (which is responsible for IRDPs) did not regard this as a suitable ODA response and emphasized the existing guidelines for donor support for IRDPs. These different views were reconciled in the 1977 Reconnaissance Mission that led to the Regional Development Technical Cooperation Program.

The natural resources component of the program included resource surveys undertaken by ODA's LRDC and a number of small projects that were identified and implemented as a result of U.K. aid participation in the regional planning exercise. In this respect, Mtwara-Lindi—like EMI in Kenya—represents an aid strategy for difficult environments. Under this strategy technical assistance staff are assigned to work within decentralized government structures partly to strengthen planning and executive capabilities and partly to discover any specific aid opportunities that are not evident at the onset of the program. In Mtwara-Lindi, the initial TC appointments meant an implicit commitment to identify crops and livestock projects; subsequently, fisheries staff were also appointed with a similar commitment.

Projects in all sectors were approved within the framework of the regional plan or the annual capital budget for each region. The main capital expenditures were on the Veterinary Investigation Centre (£ 75,000), rural water supplies, and village stores. By 1980 twenty-five projects—most costing less than £ 50,000—had been approved. Few of these projects involved any ODA contribution to local recurrent costs, and the planning program itself financed only a small number of incremental local posts and allowances. Nonetheless, even this relatively small U.K. contribution to recurrent costs could not be matched by the government, and often the planned Tanzanian contribution failed to materialize. A number of initiatives—such as the poultry feed mill, the hatchery at Mtwara, and the tractor hire unit—failed to provide adequate staff, fuel, and water supply.

Most visiting advisers and TCOs found the range and scale of the small projects unsatisfactory on the whole and felt that any significant improvement in natural resources would be unlikely in the long term unless the overall system of government agricultural support was improved. This view was accepted by the 1981 review, which stressed the importance of dealing with the constraints in extension research, along with credit and inputs delivery.

The original project proposal envisaged "substantial increases" in marketed output of cassava and noted that rice could be "expanded greatly" and that there were "good" prospects for introducing improved sorghum varieties. The 1981 review team saw the scope for an extension program in crops (and livestock) since "recommendations" already existed. As a result of this confidence, the second major phase of Mtwara-Lindi was closely linked to decisions on a proposed extensions and training program (ETP). This came to be regarded as the core project of ODA's natural resources aid in Mtwara-Lindi, one that would require a relatively high level of support for staff, vehicles, and buildings for the Ministry of Agriculture's field operations. But by 1984 the case for the ETP had collapsed. Reviewing the evidence from LRDC and from the TCO agronomists on the existing land preparations, fertilizer use, seed selection, disease control, and agronomic practices, ODA concluded that "there are no extension packages that would markedly improve farmers' living standards" and that the individual practices proposed would be of "insufficient merit to justify an extension of the [crop] extension service."

Rather different issues were raised by the performance of the crop research program. With ODA assistance, the Naliendele Research Station was given national responsibilities for research on sesame, groundnut, and sunflower. Yet it was located in an inaccessible area with difficult working conditions. Thus it is not surprising that the majority of field trial results in the early 1980s were lost because transport difficulties prevented them from reaching sites at the appropriate time. In the case of sunflower, it was evident that the crop was performing poorly compared with trial locations at higher altitudes, and in due course a new project, supported by ODA, relocated sunflower research at Ilonga.

By 1987 the level of ODA agricultural aid in Mtwara-Lindi had been reduced to a few small programs: a pilot extension services project for goat husbandry, collaboration with several other donors on health services for cattle, a fisheries survey, and trials and demonstration work on rice in a few valley sites. Contributions to the institution-building area of regional planning and implementation capacity had ceased.

This reduction in ODA support was deliberate. The office had, in effect, moved away from the IRDP concept to what it termed "project-oriented interventions." It was not surprising, therefore, that the form and level of ODA support became a bone of contention with the Tanzanian government. The government had anticipated ODA support for the RIDEPs, which were a centerpiece of the National Five-Year Development Plan. The ETP, in particular, signaled ODA intentions, and its subsequent rejection was a source of some acrimony.

Without a substantial aid program, ODA's contribution to strengthening regional government generally became peripheral, although this aspect of U.K. aid had never been a satisfactory component of the Mtwara-Lindi program. At least one senior officer involved in strengthening local capacity was reported to have had "negative working relations" with the Tanzanian counterpart; and plan preparation became largely an expatriate exercise. Furthermore, the regional planning units remain weak professionally, with frequent transfers of local staff.

At the outset, insufficient consideration was probably given to the most appropriate form of ODA support, particularly in the natural resources sector. Unlike EMI, Mtwara-Lindi was not a series of relatively well-prepared and restricted technical interventions reflecting U.K. expertise—although it eventually came closer to this; unlike Phalombe, it did not represent an endorsement of government agricultural service and input supply initiatives in a specific area. In the circumstances, it was inevitable that the program would suffer because U.K. and Tanzanian perceptions of ODA's role were vastly different.

Program Aid

The main instrument of U.K. agricultural support in Tanzania at present is program aid, which is intended as a prelude to more direct agricultural assistance. The United Kingdom's position is that government policy changes encouraging private enterprises, switching resources from social services into production, and managing the exchange rate at a level that makes exporting attractive to agricultural producers constitute the conditions for a new period of U.K. aid project funding. In early 1987 an offer of an additional £ 25 million aid grant over a three-year period was made, £ 12 million of which was earmarked from development projects giving high priority to agriculture.

This marked a significant shift in the United Kingdom's aid policy toward Tanzania, following a period in the early 1980s when little effort had been made to instigate U.K. aid initiatives. On the U.K. side, the aid standoff had been partly influenced by poor diplomatic relations following earlier disagreements over U.K. intentions in Zimbabwe and U.K. policies for bringing about change in South Africa; but ODA also disapproved of the government's economic policies; in particular, it had grave reservations about the forced nature of villagization and was exasperated by Tanzania's refusal to abandon state controls, notably in agriculture.

Tanzania established its own domestic structural adjustment program in 1982 and in 1984 conceded large increases in producer prices for both food and export crops. Although the government refused to accept IMF-recommended economic policy changes, the United Kingdom—along with others—refused to provide program aid or to initiate new capital projects. This was altogether a much more robust use of program aid in support of policy reform than in either Kenya or Malawi. The issue eventually hinged on a matter as specific as the size of the agreed Tanzanian devaluation, and it was after an IMF agreement was signed in 1986 that the United Kingdom allocated the first £ 10 million tranche of program grant to support "essential imports."

Of this allocation, £ 3.74 million was specifically earmarked for agriculture—agricultural chemicals, veterinary drugs, and small diesel engine spares—and the remainder for road and rail transport. Since agriculture would obviously benefit if marketing efficiency and the supply of agricultural inputs by road and rail were improved, most of the program's aid allocation can be deemed to be directed toward supporting the agricultural sector.

Lessons

In all three countries under consideration in this chapter the pattern of agricultural development has been influenced both by their colonial inheritance and by U.K. aid in the period immediately after independence. In this respect Kenya is in a special category, particularly because its African farmers inherited a commercial and technical infrastructure from settler agriculture that the other countries lacked. There are, however, a number of common colonial agricultural legacies with differing degrees of longevity. All three countries inherited a system of public regulation of much of the marketed output, with a structure of price controls, movement restrictions, and some monopsony powers. The ways in which this system has been employed have varied from country to country, as this chapter has pointed out, but most of the system has remained in place and been consolidated.

The United Kingdom also bequeathed to the three countries a structure of support for smallholder export crops that placed emphasis on producer responsibility for the financing of services such as research and extension. This structure has survived well, but research efforts in crops such as tea, tobacco, and coffee are still organized by industry-financed foundations, and the decline in cotton production can be partly attributed to the failure of the industry to finance its work.

Furthermore, the most successful extension services in the region are still financed from cesses and charges levied through crop authorities.

ODA had considerably less influence on domestic agricultural policies in the 1970s and, as a matter of policy, aid allocations came to be influenced by the priorities agreed upon by the government with the World Bank and other donors. The attachment to the World Bank was deliberate in the case of project aid in the late 1970s and early 1980s and reflected confidence in the much larger World Bank professional input into agricultural planning. It also reflected ODA support for notions of cofinancing and donor coordination over nationally agreed strategies (such as NRDP in Malawi and ASAL in Kenya).

Although ODA's independent influence on agricultural policy in the three countries has been relatively unimportant, domestic agricultural policy frequently has played a major role in determining the effectiveness of U.K. aid. In particular, several of the projects instigated by ODA have been constrained by the lack of effective government support. In some cases, this is where prices regulated by government have posed a disincentive to production (for example, for cotton in Tanzania) or where public marketing organizations have been allowed to trade inefficiently (for example, in seed in Malawi or livestock in Kenya). But the more widespread constraints have been the inability or unwillingness of governments to provide appropriate budgetary and staff resources to activities to which ODA has committed aid.

There is little evidence from U.K. aid to agriculture in the three countries to suggest that either aid tying or local costs provisions have seriously diminished aid effectiveness or that commercial factors have seriously distorted aid allocations. There is some evidence that ODA's procedures for preparing and supervising agricultural projects, particularly in marginal environments, fit uncomfortably with the complexity of the task of assisting peasant farming, but the main difficulty appears to be not the procedures themselves, but the numbers of staff available to ensure that they are promptly and effectively undertaken.

Program Aid

These limitations on the effectiveness of agricultural project aid have contributed to a shift into program aid in the 1970s, and in all three countries ODA has seen program aid as a mechanism for supporting the agricultural sector. Program aid has been used to relieve balance of payments and import constraints that have been perceived to adversely affect the agricultural sector. It has also been used as part of a coordinated effort with other donors to encourage changes in agricultural policies and institutions designed to create a more favorable environment for subsequent agricultural aid investment.

These two agricultural aspects of program aid–agricultural inputs aid and policy reform—do not invariably sit together. In the case of the 1984 Malawi Program Grant, there were no specific agricultural targets, and finance went largely to manufacturing industry and services—which at the time of actual disbursement were not experiencing any serious foreign exchange problems. But the grant was part of ODA support for a World Bank–led program of adjustment measures in agricultural policy and institutions in a series of SALs. In Kenya, program aid provided as natural resources private sector project aid was directed at dealers supplying U.K. farm machinery and production requirements. This was less attached to SAL negotiations than in Malawi, and when difficulties arose for the World Bank because the government was reluctant to deregulate the domestic grain trade, U.K. aid was not discontinued. In Tanzania, an altogether more robust strategy was adopted—with both program aid and new project aid withheld pending IMF agreement, and despite a series of domestic agricultural reforms in mid-1982. Upon agreement with the IMF, program aid included a substantial agricultural inputs package.

Such agricultural inputs aid (however fast-disbursing and helpful to governments in the generation of counterpart funds) has not, in practice, always been of direct benefit to agriculture, as it has not proved possible to predict foreign exchange requirements to the sector itself. In both Kenya and Malawi, there was less demand than anticipated from importers of agricultural inputs, who in effect had privileged access to foreign exchange, and who had no incentive to use the relatively cumbersome process of procurement under program aid.

The impact of program aid from individual donors is difficult to assess in an area such as agriculture. But the growing use of bilateral U.K. program aid raises the question of whether, as a form of aid, this represents the best use of available resources, given U.K. strengths and capabilities. A related question is whether the specific ODA priorities within project aid—the main alternative form to program aid—are those that represent the best use of U.K. resources available for agricultural development.

There have been four areas of substantial U.K. project aid investment—integrated rural development, agricultural research, agricultural technical services, and smallholder crop authorities—and it is on the evidence of these four areas of aid that a case has to be sustained for a program of more directly targeted U.K. support for agriculture.

Integrated Rural Development Projects

Over the late 1970s and early 1980s a clear spending priority for ODA in African agriculture was a series of area-based IRDPs, often in marginal environments and invariably concentrating on low-technology, low-income farming. That generation of IRD projects is now frequently criticized as too ambitious and inadequately prepared to improve agricultural technology, and too expensive to comfortably handle the future recurrent costs of extension and farm service infrastructure. However, the three ODA-assisted projects examined in this chapter do not support the argument that design was overambitious and poorly prepared.

The design and content of the three projects varied greatly. In the most successful of them, namely EMI, the ODA strategy consisted of a slow buildup of specific interventions largely under the supervision of TCOs. In Mtwara-Lindi, the ODA project had some capital components, but it was primarily a regional planning exercise. And Phalombe, the largest of the three in expenditures, was primarily an agricultural services project designed to provide credit, extension, physical infrastructure, and transport. "Overambitious" and "poorly prepared" inadequately describe all the IRD projects. It is the case that Phalombe largely accepted an existing package of agricultural services—despite ODA reservations about the economic and technical assumptions on which it was based. However, in Mtwara-Lindi ODA established a detailed series of resource studies and finally found few opportunities for economic investment in agriculture. And in EMI, ODA selected a small number of interventions for support within the district agricultural services.

The lessons of ODA's poverty-focused agricultural projects suggest that ODA is correct in reducing its emphasis on multisectoral rural development. It is also evident that the particular technical difficulties of marginal and remote areas require an enormous research effort, and that ODA support has been most effective where specific technical services have been supported. In the three cases reviewed, ODA has not been successful in firmly establishing regional planning and implementation mechanisms, and it has had difficulty administering a number of locally managed infrastructure projects and welfare services in remote rural areas. However, where ODA has concentrated on specific technical interventions and worked to assist the line departments in the ministries involved in natural resources, its project work has generally been effective.

Agricultural Research

When the three countries became independent in the 1960s, their agricultural research services were still staffed mainly by British expatriates, and continued manpower and financial assistance were needed to strengthen and maintain their research capability. In response, the United Kingdom provided personnel to fill key scientific posts for the Agricultural Research Council and the Agricultural Research Services of the Ministry of Agriculture of Malawi, and for the regional centers of EAFFRO and EAVRO. Budgetary support was also provided, although this was phased out from the 1970s onward. The number of long-term research postings also declined as greater emphasis was placed on specific research projects.

The general record of government research performance in the three countries suggests that the basis provided by the colonial period and budgetary aid after independence has not been consolidated. Project aid has had only a limited effect; training has been deficient; and longer-term institutional development has not occurred. In several projects, the contribution of governments to local costs has been inadequate, and at the end of U.K. involvement the level of funding and activity in the project's field of research declined further.

Yet this chapter has recounted several examples of relatively successful U.K. research aid. These include support for cotton and tobacco research in Malawi, for veterinary work in Kenya, and for cotton in Tanzania in the early 1970s. All of these cases illustrate the importance of long-term research aid, with a series of initiatives to assist institutional capacity to address problems. In contrast, other cases of research aid, such as maize in Kenya and Malawi and the potato in Kenya, have involved significant initial technical advances, but ultimately this aid has had less effect than it should have had because of discontinuity and a limited range of support measures.

It is not surprising that the greatest impact has tended to be made by the longest supported research projects. The length of support provided by the CRC—more than fifty years in Malawi and nearly forty years in Tanzania—was the main factor in the development of the cotton industries in all three countries, and it has left a continuing mark on subsequent research. Long-term support also has been most effective where institutes have been well supported nationally—for example, the Tea Research Foundation and Tobacco Research Authority of Malawi and the Coffee Research Foundation of Kenya.

The case of cotton research also illustrates a wider trend in donor research support. There has been a large input into food corp research by the CGIAR centers but a lack of similar international support for nonfood crops. This factor, together with recognized U.K. expertise, provides sound reasons for strengthened U.K. aid for research into the leading export crops of Africa. Similarly, there appears to be scope for expanded support for forestry and fisheries research in the three countries, since this has been modest since independence (except in postharvest fishery technology) when set against the United Kingdom's substantial experience, especially, for example, in tropical forestry research in support of plantation development.

Smallholder Crop Authorities

Much of the interest in CDC's contribution to African agriculture has focused on the design and management of the Smallholder Crop Authorities (SCAs). In practice, the SCAs vary considerably. In the case of tea in Kenya and coffee in Malawi, the CDC concentrated on building processing plants and facilitating marketing as a means of encouraging smallholder production on existing farms. In the case of sugar in Malawi, a settlement scheme model of supervised production has been instigated. And, also in Malawi, the tobacco scheme involves both supervised settlement schemes and an attempt to stimulate smallholder production outside the scheme area.

The overall record of CDC investment in the smallholder production of crops such as sugar, tobacco, and coffee has shown that the level of factory throughput and the ability of smallholders to pay for services is frequently constrained by their low yields (compared with estate performance, for example) and by their readiness to switch labor and other inputs away form the export crop once returns show signs of deterioration or uncertainty.

The outgrower schemes (such as KTDA) have been more successful in increasing production than the settlement schemes, which are also normally more costly to establish and administer and thereby place heavy financial burdens on tenants within the scheme. In irrigated smallholder sugar in Malawi, for example, loan repayments have been poor, and it has proved difficult to retain tenants on the scheme. In the case of the Kasungu Flue-Cured Tobacco Authority, substantial annual subsidy payments have become a feature of an authority designed to be self-financing.

The requirement on CDC that its projects in the longer run be commercially viable and produce a financial return means that its opportunities to develop new smallholder schemes are restricted—even where capital aid is provided to cover development costs and where technical cooperation funds are used to cover some management costs. It is significant that the level of private sector investment in similar schemes is modest. BAT in Kenya and, more recently, East African Industries in collaboration with CDC on oilseeds, are among the exceptions. Nevertheless, CDC venture capital and management skills clearly have made a significant contribution to African smallholder production of a narrow range of export corps, and the agricultural staff of CDC remain an important resource in the U.K. aid program.

Agricultural Technical Services

U.K. agricultural aid in the thee countries scored its main successes in the provision of expertise and training in agricultural technical services and associated farm inputs. This includes the supply of planting materials and breeding stock, animal health services, crop protection services, and soil conservation services and minor irrigation. Some of these successes are attributable to the work of ODA's Overseas Development Natural Resources Institute (ODNRI), and the case of armyworm control in support of local research and extension services exemplifies the value of home-based scientific units. Similarly, the work on East Coast fever in Kenya shows the importance of long-term support involving capital and technical assistance aid. There is also evidence of the effectiveness of ODA assistance in the development of seed industries. The availability of specialist skills under the aid program has had a major impact in Malawi (and to a lesser extent in Tanzania) in production, multiplication, testing, processing, and storage.

In EMI in Kenya, ODA support has enabled the Departments of Agriculture, Livestock Development, and Forestry to undertake technical work of direct relevance to farmers. A condition for effective support in this case, and also in the case of Mtwara-Lindi, is that technical intervention be appropriate to the capabilities of existing field services. It is because this condition is lacking that it is difficult to envisage, at present, any similar institutional strengthening in the animal health and range management services in Isiolo district; this is also why it has proved difficult to support extension services in southern Tanzania.

Conclusion

The overall evidence of U.K. project aid indicates that domestic policies have diminished the effectiveness of directly targeted support for agriculture. Yet the current level of donor support for program aid, linked to policy reforms designed to assist agricultural output, provides the basis for a revival of more targeted mechanisms of support. Among the large number of donors currently operating in African agriculture, ODA appears to be particularly well placed to move its policies forward into investments in technical services and research. It is such investments that will constitute the most important foundation for significant increases in farm production and incomes in the continent.

Although the United Kingdom's scientific manpower with experience in African conditions has been depleted since the 1960s, ODA is still able to respond to the challenge of strengthening agricultural services and developing productive investments in the sector. If there is one area in which ODA could claim a comparative advantage among donors, it is in the range of technical services and research that it is able to provide. The record of performance in Kenya, Tanzania, and Malawi and the continuing availability of specialist manpower suggest that ODA has a particularly important role to play in providing direct assistance for African agriculture.

Notes

This chapter draws on an evaluation study entitled "U.K. Agricultural Aid to Kenya, Tanzania, and Malawi," EV 388 (Overseas Development Institute, London, 1988) written by a team from the institute consisting of John Howell, Adrian Hewitt, and Kenneth Anthony. This does not necessarily represent the views of the Overseas Development Administration.

1. Organisation for Economic Co-operation and Development, *Development Cooperation 1986 Report* (Paris, 1986).
2. "U.K. Agricultural Aid," tables 2.2 and 2.3.
3. Ibid., table 2.6.
4. Overseas Development Administration, "Project Identification: An Evaluation of ODA's Procedures and Practices," EV 291 (London, 1985).
5. "U.K. Agricultural Aid," table 3.1.
6. Overseas Development Administration, *Evaluation of CDC Projects: Malawi Smallholder Coffee Authority* (London, 1985).
7. "U.K. Agricultural Aid," table 4.9.
8. Overseas Development Administration, "Evaluation of Phalombe RDP," EV 387 (London, 1986).
9. "U.K. Agricultural Aid," table 5.1.
10. Overseas Development Administration, "An Evaluation of the Maize Agronomy Research Project, 1972–78," EV 241 (London, 1983).

10 German Aid to Agriculture in the MADIA Countries of Cameroon, Kenya, Malawi, Senegal, and Tanzania

Christian Heimpel and Manfred Schulz

ALTHOUGH GERMAN AID has a generally accepted conceptual framework, diverse perceptions and judgments of aid issues nevertheless exist even within the German aid administration. This variety of opinions gives only a hint of the complexity of the task of the present analysis: to analyze aid from Germany to agriculture in the MADIA countries from 1962 to 1986. If one considers African agriculture in relation to the continent's critical overall economic situation, its population growth rates, the food crisis, the desertification threat, not to mention its long-standing and emerging political tensions, it becomes evident that no one knows a single right way for a better future—since neither Africans nor non-Africans disregard the historical experience and since there is no universally proven global policy prescription for agricultural development.

Yet empirical evidence does indicate that success rates of agricultural projects and programs are higher in other regions of the world than in Africa. Thus it is important as a first step toward improving project design to find out why Africa is such a problematic field of action. In view of the growing demands for more donor coordination and cooperation in the aid that goes toward development, the MADIA study's comparison of the diverse experiences of donor-aided development in agriculture should prove helpful.

German Aid to Agriculture in the MADIA Countries, 1962–86

In all the MADIA countries except Senegal and Nigeria, Germany is among the top four donors in terms of official development assistance (ODA).[1] During the period 1962–86, Germany disbursed DM 5,070 million in the six countries (table 10-1). The first question is how this amount is distributed.

Volume of Aid Flows

In 1986, German bilateral and multilateral development aid amounted to DM 8,317 million. From 1950 to 1986, the total amount of German assistance to particular countries came to DM 69.2 billion. Of this sum, Africa received DM 25.3 billion, or 36.5 percent. At that time Asia's share was even larger (39.5 percent), but in recent years the distribution has shifted in favor of Africa because of the continent's severe problems. Now 42 percent of all means for development cooperation are spent in Africa.

In Africa (northern Africa included), fifty-four countries and territories are beneficiaries of German aid. The six MADIA countries have received roughly one-fifth of all aid to Africa over the past quarter-century, although they only represent one-ninth of all countries aided; hence the MADIA countries received an overproportional share of German aid to Africa.

As the aid figures to the West African countries and to Malawi are relatively similar, it must be asked why Kenya and Tanzania have been proportionately so much more important in German development aid

Table 10-1. Aid Disbursements to the MADIA Countries, 1962–86
(millions of deutsche marks)

Country	*Financial cooperation (gross)*	*Technical cooperation*	*Food aid*	*Total*
Cameroon	372.8	357.3	0.4	730.5
Kenya	604.7	582.7	26.1	1,213.4
Malawi	307.3	189.1	0.0	496.4
Nigeria	271.2	334.0	1.7	606.9
Senegal	264.1	166.0	50.2	480.3
Tanzania	664.6	831.9	46.0	1,542.5
Total	2,484.7	2,461.0	124.4	5,070.0

Source: Internal government documents.

(table 10-2). It is because these two countries, of all African countries, receive the highest attention from the German public, although for different reasons. Kenya, in the German view, is one of the rare exceptions (together with Côte d'Ivoire) of a successful example in Africa of a development scheme following a free market and entrepreneurial economy. Moreover, Kenya is widely known in Germany because it has succeeded in attracting a large number of German tourists, following the development of its tourist potential. Tanzania, on the other hand, has impressed the German government for a long time by the outstanding leadership of President Julius Nyerere, by its development rhetoric, and by the high expectations of its rural development policy. When in recent years it became clear that these expectations could not be met, German development aid to Tanzania was reduced.

The amount of German aid to Kenya and Tanzania is less impressive if one takes population figures into account. The per capita aid figures show that Senegal and Cameroon received relatively more aid, although not much more than Kenya and Tanzania (table 10-3). Because per capita aid for the MADIA countries does not vary greatly (except in the case of Nigeria), this appears to be a fairly good indicator of what the countries can expect in aid.

What is the relative significance of agriculture in the German aid programs? A first observation is that whereas the donor countries that are members of the OECD's Development Assistance Committee (DAC), spend 12.8 percent of their commitments for cooperation to all developing countries in the fields of agriculture, forestry, and fisheries, Germany spends 13.1 percent of its aid in these areas in Africa alone.

Table 10-2. Distribution of German Development Aid to MADIA Countries among the Individual Countries, 1962–86

Country	*Percentage*
Cameroon	14.4
Kenya	23.9
Malawi	9.8
Nigeria	12.0
Senegal	9.5
Tanzania	30.4
Total	100.0

Source: Internal government documents.

Table 10-3. German Per Capita Aid to the MADIA *Countries, 1962–86*

Country	*Population 1985 (thousands)*	*Aid disbursements (millions of deutsche marks)*	*Per capita aid (deutsche marks)*
Cameroon	10,191	731	71.69
Kenya	20,375	1,213	59.55
Malawi	7,044	496	70.47
Nigeria	99,669	607	6.09
Senegal	6,558	480	73.24
Tanzania	22,242	1,543	69.35

Source: Internal government documents.

Tables 10-4 and 10-5 show that there are three leading sectors in German development aid to the MADIA countries: basic infrastructure (including transport); agriculture (including the regional and integrated projects); and education, training, and research. All other aid is spread over a wide range of targets. Note, too, that German aid covers a broad range of activities. Third, it must be emphasized that aid to the rural sector is much larger than expressed in the figures for agriculture. Many of the other items include rural aid components; for example, rural literacy programs are included under education, and agricultural development banks are included under banking. Thus aid to the rural sector may be considered one focal point of German assistance to the MADIA countries.

To assess whether German aid to the MADIA countries has special characteristics or whether it conforms to the aid profile of all developing countries, the percentage distribution of aid to the various aid sectors of the MADIA countries over the period 1962–86 is compared with overall German aid in 1986.

In 1986 the share of agriculture, forestry, and fisheries in German aid worldwide was higher than that for the MADIA countries over a quarter of a century. This was particularly so in multicomponent projects, the worldwide importance of which was almost double the quarter-century average for the MADIA countries. This pattern reflects German aid philosophy, which accords the highest priority to agricultural and rural development and advocates an integrated treatment of the components of development.

Investment for basic infrastructure and transport represents the most important item of all aid categories, but it is much larger in the MADIA countries (more than a third of all aid disbursements) than it is

Table 10-4. German Development Aid (Technical and Financial Cooperation) by MADIA Countries and Sectors, 1962–86
(millions of deutsche marks)

Sectors	*Cameroon*	*Kenya*	*Malawi*	*Nigeria*	*Senegal*	*Tanzania*	*Total*
Agriculture, forestry, fisheries	81	167	42	50	79	164	583
Multicomponent projects (integrated, regional projects)	7	34	94	4	3	29	171
Economic planning, public administration	44	65	19	7	14	12	161
Basic infrastructure including transport	367	367	189	224	142	470	1,759
Industries, mining, construction	25	78	—	1	45	123	272
Commerce, banking, tourism, services	31	98	12	6	9	51	207
Education, training, research	100	194	17	145	47	339	842
Public health	15	27	20	31	20	85	198
Social infrastructure, social care	7	20	28	77	10	52	194
Food aid	—	26	—	2	50	46	124
Other measures, including commodity aid	54	138	76	61	61	172	562
Total	731	1,214	497	608	480	1,543	5,073

— = Not available.

Note: Totals differ from corresponding figures in tables 10-1 and 10-3 because of rounding.

Source: Internal government documents.

worldwide. The emphasis on this category of aid in the MADIA countries is a reflection of the desire to overcome the severe infrastructure constraints in Africa.

Aid disbursements to education, training, and research are larger than those to agriculture (if one excludes multicomponent projects). The worldwide figure for 1986 makes evident the importance given to

Table 10-5. German Development Aid (Technical and Financial Cooperation), 1962–86
(percent)

Aid sectors	MADIA countries	All developing countries, 1986
Agriculture, forestry, fisheries	11.5	13.0
Multicomponent projects (integrated, regional projects)	3.4	6.5
Economy, planning, public administration	3.2	5.2
Basic infrastructure including transport	34.7	27.6
Industries, mining, construction	5.3	7.4
Commerce, banking, tourism, services	4.0	7.1
Education, training, research	16.6	26.0
Public health	3.9	2.6
Social infrastructure, social care	3.8	2.6
Food aid	2.5	—
Other measures, including commodity aid	11.1	1.7
Total	100.0	100.0

— = Not available.
Source: Internal government documents.

this sector in German aid and shows that the African countries are lagging somewhat behind in that respect. In recent years, the level of German aid for research has increased, since it is now widely recognized that research and training are the most productive investments.

Thus it can be said that there is substantial correspondence between the MADIA profile of aid and 1986 aid to the developing world as a whole. Consequently, many of the generalizations about German aid to the MADIA countries also hold true for all developing countries.

Table 10-6 shows that German aid to agriculture covers a wide spectrum of measures and includes almost all categories of this kind of aid. It is clear that agriculture in the narrow sense plays the dominant role and that forestry (including afforestation) and fisheries are insignificant in the German aid pattern for the MADIA countries. Agricultural extension receives 20 percent, or the largest share of

Table 10-6. Composition of German Development Aid for the Agricultural Sector in the MADIA Countries, 1962–86
(millions of deutsche marks)

Agricultural sector	*Cameroon*	*Kenya*	*Malawi*	*Nigeria*	*Senegal*	*Tanzania*	*Total*	*Percent*
Agricultural production	0.4	42.5	—	—	4.9	45.5	93.3	16.0
Irrigation	6.0	9.8	—	—	13.9	—	29.7	5.1
Plant and harvest protection	—	2.7	—	8.4	0.1	—	11.2	1.9
Plant production	3.1	5.5	2.1	—	17.9	27.6	56.2	9.7
Fertilizer	—	2.7	5.1	6.4	0.9	1.8	16.9	2.9
Agricultural tools and machinery	0.2	1.0	4.5	10.4	0.9	1.1	18.1	3.1
Animal production	1.7	2.7	10.1	10.9	7.1	0.1	32.6	5.9
Veterinarian measures	17.7	4.3	—	9.5	0.9	16.6	49.0	8.4
Agricultural services (e.g., cooperatives)	—	16.6	—	0.2	7.7	0.8	25.3	4.3

Agricultural extension	19.7	44.0	—	2.9	0.2	52.0	118.8	20.4
Agricultural research	—	0.2	—	—	0.9	—	1.1	0.2
Forestry, afforestation	—	4.9	8.3	0.1	23.1	0.6	37.0	6.4
Fisheries	—	—	—	—	0.1	6.0	6.1	1.1
Home economics, nutrition	—	—	—	—	0.2	—	0.2	—
Agricultural technology	26.0	2.3	—	—	—	1.3	29.6	5.1
Miscellaneous	5.9	27.5	11.6	0.6	—	10.5	56.1	9.5
Total	80.7	166.5	41.7	49.4	78.8	164.1	581.2	100.0
Multicomponent project (regional, integrated)[a]	6.8	34.0	93.9	4.2	2.9	28.8	170.6	

— = Not available.

a. Multicomponent projects generally have a heavy agricultural component. For this reason, multicomponent projects should be mentioned in the context of agricultural development, but they cannot simply be classified as agricultural projects.

Source: Internal government documents.

German aid to agriculture. This concentration is a consequence of the concept that smallholders should be the main target group of aid. The effectiveness of this strategy may, however, be challenged, given the fact that almost no agricultural research is supported by German aid in the MADIA countries. But agricultural extension can only be productive if there are attractive innovation messages—a task that must be shouldered by research programs prior to extension.

Kenya and Tanzania, with 28 percent each, receive the lion's share of aid to agriculture. Of particular interest is the relevance of multicomponent (regional and integrated) projects in German aid (table 10-4). These projects, which amount to about 30 percent of the sum spent on agriculture, contain a sizable agricultural component. These integrated projects are unimportant in the three West African countries, but they play a major role in the East African cases, as can be seen in the German aid to Malawi.

A comparison of the volume of aid to agriculture disbursed between 1981 and 1985 to the corresponding figures for 1973–80 shows that the share of agriculture increased by 8 percent of the total flows including regional projects and agricultural credit banks. The volume of aid to agriculture grew much faster than total disbursements per year, or remained stable as in the case of Cameroon.

Aid to agriculture grew at a very fast rate in two of the countries: Malawi and Senegal. Two countries, Kenya and Tanzania, received more than twice as much per year in 1981–85 as they did in the 1973–80 period. In only one country, Cameroon, did average disbursements remain stable.

A final word may be said about the development of personnel cooperation. Development experts for projects are provided by the German Agency for Technical Cooperation (GTZ). The number of experts in the MADIA countries has been rather stable over the years (table 10-7), and has even been expanding in recent years. The widely assumed attrition of the knowledge base in tropical agriculture thus is not a characteristic of German development aid.

Historical Background and Institutionalization of Aid

German development aid dates back to 1952, when the first contribution was made to an expanded United Nations aid program. In the 1950s, aid activities were institutionally handled either by the Foreign Ministry (AA) or by the Ministry of Economic Affairs (BMWi). The German Federal Ministry for Economic Cooperation (BMZ) was formed in November 1961 following a decision by the newly formed government coalition. Initially the ministry had only a coordinating function, but it was subsequently given full responsibility for implementing

Table 10-7. GTZ *Experts in* MADIA *Countries, Selected Years*

Country	*1970*	*1980*	*1988*
Cameroon	20	33	32
Kenya	43	46	61
Malawi	23	6	26
Nigeria	23	—	8
Senegal	8	13	21
Tanzania	45	55	54
Total	162	153	202

Source: Internal government documents.

technical cooperation. In December 1972 the BMZ was made responsible for capital aid (financial cooperation), which previously had come under the Ministry of Economic Affairs. Although now politically responsible for German development aid, the ministry only bears an indirect responsibility for implementation. The departments in the ministry restrict themselves to basic policy decisions, program control, and evaluation—entrusting the detailed implementation to subordinate institutions. In the case of technical cooperation, the relevant institution since 1975 has been the Deutsche Gesellschaft fur Technische Zusammenarbeit, GTZ (German Agency for Technical Cooperation), which was created following a merger between a German federal agency for development aid and an internationally active institution dating back to the period between the two world wars.

To implement capital aid (financial cooperation), the administrative structure chosen was the Kreditanstalt fur Wiederaufbau (KfW), formerly the Reconstruction Loan Cooperation, set up to administer aid funds under the Marshall Plan.

Still another important event in the evolution of German development aid was the foundation of the European Economic Community. The signing of the Treaty of Rome marked the birth of the European Development Fund (EDF).

German development policy is founded on a mix of philanthropic motives as well as political and economic interests. Germany is, however, committed to the principles elaborated by the United Nations. The first full-blown development policy concept elaborated by BMZ in 1971 and adopted by the cabinet states: "The German Federal Government is seeking in accordance with the UN strategy document to promote economic and social progress in developing countries within a system of international partnership as the objective of the Second Development Decade, in order to improve living conditions for the populations in these countries."

The integration into internationally agreed objectives was not seen as conflicting with the economic interests of Germany "Economically, this will create the conditions for greater trade in commodities and services in the mutual interest. An effective development policy strengthens the international position of Germany. It improves the long-term chances for securing peace."

For a long time, the Federal Republic sought to prevent developing countries from recognizing the other German state. After both German states were admitted to the United Nations as full members, development aid was not considered an appropriate means of restraining recognition of the German Democratic Republic.

Over the years, a tendency emerged to concentrate aid where it was most needed and in vulnerable countries, mainly in Africa and Asia. As these countries generally are unimportant trade partners for Germany, it cannot be maintained that there is a close link between economic interests and aid. A certain correction of the liberal aid policy was only made after the installation of the conservative-liberal government coalition in 1982; since then, German aid has had to take into account the employment effects of aid on the domestic front, with the consequence that policies on aid tying have become more restricted, especially under the instrument of mixed financing.

As for the institutional structure of German development aid, it is important to underscore the role of private organizations, of volunteer groups, and, above all, of the Protestant and Catholic churches. Since the beginning of organized development efforts, these societal aid groups, relying on long-established contacts, run their own aid programs subsidized by governmental funds. Moreover, in recent years, public support for private organizations has even increased—since they enjoy the reputation of higher efficiency in program execution, better performance in small projects, easier access to poverty groups, and more flexible work in politically troublesome areas. The bulk of commitments to the MADIA countries, however, emanate from financial and technical cooperation.

Financial cooperation. Financial cooperation, or capital aid, is channeled to the recipient countries by the KfW and comprises project-bound loans, sectoral programs, maintenance and support supplies, contributions to structural adjustment loans such as those paid under the Special African Facility, and a fund for specific studies and experts (project preparation and implementation assistance). Financial cooperation accounted for only 13.5 percent of total disbursements in agriculture to the MADIA countries during the 1973–85 period. However, the picture changed considerably in the 1981–85 period. Whereas financial cooperation disbursements represented only 5.6 percent of aid to agriculture in 1973–80, they accounted for 18.4 percent in 1981–85. This increase reflects the view of the BMZ that within financial cooperation, higher priority should be accorded to agriculture.

Because of the growing foreign exchange and budget problems in the recipient countries, more emphasis is being put on new forms of program aid (sectoral loans and maintenance support) in agriculture too (machinery and equipment, fertilizers), which is creating interesting export opportunities with guaranteed exchange transfer for German firms in countries traditionally belonging to the British or French preserve. Other cooperation instruments—foreign trade and investment considerations such as mixed financing—are not of great importance in the countries under analysis.

The conditions of financial cooperation vary considerably among the MADIA countries: Malawi and Tanzania, which belong to the least-developed category, are given aid entirely in the form of grants. Cameroon is considered a "most seriously affected country" and therefore qualifies for IDA soft loan conditions. Kenya and Senegal have to pay standard conditions (2 percent interest, thirty years, with ten years free). The assistance financed by BMZ via KfW in agriculture consists mainly of investments in rural infrastructure (roads, irrigation, settlement, marketing, and processing) or refinancing of rural credit schemes.

Technical cooperation. Technical cooperation is the most important instrument of German aid to Africa in the agricultural sector. It is by definition expert-intensive. However, within technical cooperation, supplies in kind and financial contributions have grown to almost 50 percent of disbursements.

Technical cooperation projects are even more difficult to categorize than those that fall under financial cooperation. They range from single-message projects carried out in a few months by highly specialized short-term experts to comprehensive rural development programs in which up to DM 100 million may be spent over a period of fifteen years or more; there are advisers fully integrated into the national civil service, and others working in almost independent project units. As far as the subsectoral allocation is concerned, most technical cooperation projects aim at improving small farming by promoting food production.

In summary, technical cooperation comprises the promotion of students, experts, and volunteers; the supply of equipment and material for research; training and demonstration; technical aid; and extension agencies.

In recent years, the two aid forms have come to resemble each other both in substance and in methodology. Financial cooperation is developing a technical cooperation component, and some technical funds can be spent as a kind of financial cooperation element within technical cooperation. In the MADIA countries, there are also more and more projects in which the two work closely together.

Food security. Food aid and food security programs (see table 10-1) were started in the three countries belonging to the drought-menaced Sudano-Sahelian region (Kenya, Senegal, Tanzania) after the drought of the 1970s and the mid-1980s. Food security programs began as something of an ad hoc program (construction of storehouses, security reserves)—which is why this aid form was not included in the technical cooperation category. Projects either supply food aid (the counterpart funds of which are often used to refinance "normal" projects such as rural development programs and the like) or contributions to food security programs, including stockholding, grain marketing, and the maintenance of security reserves (as in Senegal). This study does not cover multilateral aid to agriculture. However, it should be mentioned that German contributions to multilateral institutions and programs—for example, in the field of international agricultural research, as part of the Consultative Group on International Agricultural Research (CGIAR) system—are considerable.

The Conceptual Framework of German Agricultural Assistance

The broad range of aid activities in support of agriculture makes it difficult to distill a clear-cut set of principles and concepts from this kind of aid. However, aid to agriculture can be better understood if it is seen in the framework of Germany's general development policy.

Orientation of German development policy. The general goal of German development policy is to ensure that the basic life needs of the people in the developing world are met and to help these people become capable of helping themselves. The overall purpose of German aid is to contribute to the construction of a viable economy while maintaining societal pluralism as a prerequisite for self-reliant development. Developing countries that favor democratic structures and respect human rights are the preferred partners. To alleviate poverty, the development process should be founded on a broad economic, social, and political base. This broad base can be achieved by concentrating on the populations of rural areas and the urban informal sector.

Before the principle of self-help can be put into practice, favorable framework conditions are necessary, beginning with the freedom of private initiatives. It is also important for governmental institutions to provide their services for the poorer segments of the society. Experience has shown that the spread of the market economy in developing countries works best when people can develop according to their capabilities. In particular, societal structures in which an independent livelihood can be made in handicraft, industry, commerce, and services, and in which small and intermediate businesses can emerge contributes to development. Public aid cannot replace the dynamics of the private sector, which also has to provide capital and entrepreneurial and technological knowledge. In addition to improving the coordination of aid, the German government conducts a policy dialogue with the developing countries to achieve economic and social reforms, to ensure nutrition, and to promote administrative efficiency.

Between 1984 and 1986, the policy dialogue with the African countries focused on the question of how to resume economic growth. It had become evident that the growing food crisis, induced in part by climatic conditions, was also a product of distorted prices in agricultural markets and the lack of attention to the rural regions in development efforts. African governments therefore were encouraged to liberalize prices on agricultural commodities; it was also recommended that the state retreat from industrial enterprises, cut back on subsidies, and implement realistic exchange rates. Because of frequent project failures, German aid is particularly concerned that sociocultural aspects are respected in project areas and that target groups legitimize project work. The Seventh Development Policy Report of 1988 outlined another German concern: that more recognition should be given to the important role women play in agriculture, especially in rural Africa, and that income-generating development opportunities should be created for them.

The evolution of the German concept of agricultural promotion. The German concept of agricultural promotion in African countries has evolved slowly over time and has seen some drastic changes. Like other Western donor countries, Germany at first shared the assumption that development is largely synonymous with industrialization—and that the role of agriculture is to facilitate this industrialization. Although it was recognized that agricultural production should increase and provide a cash income for farmers, it was thought that in Africa, mostly cash crop production should be fostered—since Germany needed imports of tropical agricultural products (coffee, tea, citrus fruits, sisal, tropical woods, and bananas). Germany, in turn, was thought to be ideally equipped to supply industrial products. It was only later that problems of rural poverty and famine became prominent in policy thinking. Even in 1971 there was widespread optimism that nutritional problems could be solved by applying the green revolution techniques that had succeeded in Asia. The emerging problems of inequality of income distribution and the lack of purchasing power among the poorer segments of the population in rural areas were seen primarily as questions of agricultural reform.

There has been a continuing debate over what lessons can be learned from German agriculture and transferred to project work in Africa. Since agriculture in Germany was characterized by small family farms, it was thought that the institutional setup for this type of farming contained elements (for example, cooperatives) that could be transferred to small farms in a culturally different environment. This, for instance, is also the reason why German aid to African countries relies so much on extension.

The problems of the nutrition gap were clearly presented in the development policy report of 1973, which stated that agricultural production in developing countries was lagging behind the worldwide goal of 4 percent set for the Second Development Decade, and, moreover, was barely keeping pace with population growth. At that time the German federal government supported measures that would help increase the diversification of agricultural production, but it also provided assistance for measures that were expected to improve the structure of agriculture and help create additional employment. Special emphasis has been put on agricultural research and cooperation with the World Bank since 1972 through the World Bank Consultative Group on International Agricultural Research.

Modern thinking on agricultural promotion dates back to the middle of the 1970s, when the two predominant concerns were that development aid should help create and preserve employment and that food production should be the main function of agriculture.

The twenty-five development policy points issued by the cabinet in June 1975 were a landmark in German development thinking. Here the growing divergences that had emerged within and between developing countries were recognized, and priority was given to cooperation with the poorest developing countries, mainly those in Africa. Point 16 stated: "In view of the precarious situation in regard to food supplies in developing countries, the Government of the Federal Republic of Germany will as far as possible concentrate its resources available for cooperation on rural development in partner countries." The development policy reports of 1975, 1977, and 1980 clearly show how the problem of rural poverty became a priority. Global strategies, including multicomponent projects to promote rural development rather than just agricultural production, became increasingly important. The idea of fulfilling basic needs was described as productivity-oriented and was followed in project work, in addition to the target group approach by which aid is concentrated on smallholders.

In July 1980 the German federal government presented its development policy guidelines, taking into account the recommendations of the Brandt Commission—the Independent Commission on International Development Issues. Here again, combating absolute poverty was accorded top priority in German development policy. Although the policy also advocated integrating the developing countries into the world economy, it recognized that developing countries need to achieve self-sufficiency in food production. In a resolution in March 1982, all parties in the German Bundestag supported this philosophy. The policy statements after the coalition realignment in October 1982 show continuity in the area of rural development policy. The main stated goal of rural development is that areas concerned achieve a large measure of self-sufficiency in food supplies. The small farmer has top priority in bilateral cooperation designed to increase agricultural production. This emphasis is, however, subject to one qualification: It must not neglect "the rest of the rural population and other complementary areas important for the development of agriculture" (Sixth Development Policy Report, 1985). This qualification expresses a growing concern with the poorest of the poor (the landless laborers in rural areas)—a social category that tended to be neglected in conventional project work, but that is becoming more and more important even in Africa (among the MADIA countries, land pressure is a problem in Kenya, for instance).

The sectoral papers of the BMZ on rural development consider the following to be the main features of German aid to agriculture: a target group orientation, priority given to the rural poor and the smallholders; emphasis on food production; recognition given to the importance of environmental and gender issues; a farm-level approach; and explicit consideration of equity concerns.

Although there are obviously many other factors to consider when projects are being identified, these basic principles give a sense of the overall goals of the aid program.

The Determinants of Policy Choices

The final decision to cofinance a particular project in an African country is made after a continuous and complex process of dialogue between Germany and the respective recipient country. Basic policy choices with regard to the regional and sectoral allocation of aid are made at the minister's level of BMZ on the basis of the latter's budget as approved by Parliament—in close cooperation with the Ministry of

Economic Affairs, the Foreign Office, and other competent units, such as the Economic Cooperation Committee and the Budget Committee of the Bundestag. Several considerations may influence the decision: foreign policy criteria; Germany's foreign trade interests; the need to coordinate German aid with that of the European Communities (EC), the World Bank, and bilateral donors; and the concerns of internal constituencies.

The most important criterion, however, is the volume of aid that the country under review has received in previous years. The "don't change too much, for this may cause trouble" rule seems to be the leading one at that level—and for good reasons. The majority of commitments made during bilateral negotiations are usually accorded for replenishment and amplification of existing projects. A sharp reduction of overall commitments would cause problems for current programs. And a sharp increase could prove difficult to absorb for the receiving country. Decisions about the division of a global commitment for a specific country into projects are made during bilateral negotiations.

The negotiations are preceded by consultations with the recipient country on the basis of the previous agreement among the different desks within BMZ and between the latter and other competent ministries (such as the Foreign Office and the implementing agencies, that is, KfW and GTZ). The project identification procedure itself starts much earlier, however—long before the bilateral consultations. German aid is permanently present in African countries. There are experts working in staff units of ministries or the president's office. In some recipient countries, officials from the BMZ are permanently attached to the German embassy. If necessary, the administration may send out a particular project identification mission or ask an evaluation team to include proposals for new activities in connection with the project under review in their reports. This approach guarantees a permanent dialogue with the recipient country at all levels of decisionmaking and acts as a filter, so that projects that would not have a chance of being seriously considered do not appear on the official shopping list later on.

Projects in agriculture are usually long-term affairs. They need careful preparation during and even before the identification and planning stages if difficult-to-correct mistakes are to be avoided. The competition among donors for feasible and bankable projects requires their early and permanent presence, and the limited capability of recipient countries to work out project proposals drives the system in the same direction.

The donors' budgets compete for projects and counterpart resources—not the other way around. This in some cases leads to an involuntary softening of efficiency criteria, to an unjustified precedence of the disbursement ease argument, and, again involuntarily, to overoptimistic assumptions about development potential and capabilities on both the recipient and the donor side.

There are two conclusions to be drawn here. First, in contrast to the 1960s and 1970s, when projects were submitted by the recipient country to Germany, which reacted to the respective proposals, funding projects is now an interactive procedure, with both partners cooperating closely from the very beginning to work out more or less agreed proposals for the negotiations. The selection criteria laid down in the general and sectoral strategy papers are guidelines to keep this interactive procedure on course, but they are not used as a checklist to determine whether a recipient country's application should be accepted or refused.

Second, the complex project identification procedures described above make it difficult to attribute particular projects to clear-cut policy choices. The decisionmaking process has quite a number of determinants. However, over time, a number of standardized procedures have been developed—largely to help speed up the identification and negotiation process. In agriculture, nine key programs have emerged that can be offered as individual programs or as packages:

- Promotion of institutions: research promotion, extension services, training of extension officers and government advisers
- Rural development: rural regional development, self-help organizations, promotion of agricultural marketing, agricultural credit, data collection
- Plant production: production and distribution of high-quality tested seed
- Plant protection: protection services, pesticides, residues and formulation control, vertebrate pest control
- Forestry and forest industries: forest production and conservation, forest administration, training advisory service and planning, forest industries and timber processing
- Livestock production and animal health: cattle breeding and farming, tropical forage procurement and pasture management, feedstuff testing and control, veterinary services, veterinary laboratories and animal health services, trypanosomiasis control
- Marine and freshwater fisheries: offshore fisheries, freshwater fisheries
- Agricultural mechanization, soil conservation, and irrigation: agricultural engineering, development centers, training and extension work in agricultural engineering, irrigated farming

- Processing and manufacturing, agribusiness: food technology, postharvest and storage protection.

Country Profiles and Project Examples

This section presents country profiles of German aid and provides one project example for each country. Although the examples represent different types of projects, the main criterion for their selection is their proven effect on target populations, and regions, or at the national level.

Cameroon

In Cameroon, Germany ranks fourth as a donor (after France, the World Bank, and the EC) in ODA commitments. The main focus of German aid is infrastructure (railways, roads, harbors), rural development, and small industry. Because of its oil reserves, Cameroon alone among the MADIA countries has no problems financing local currency and running costs out of its own budget.

Country profile. Coordination with other donors is a particular feature of German aid in Cameroon. It has cofinanced projects in cooperation with the World Bank, the EC, and IFAD. However, the need to coordinate several donors within single projects has caused severe pipeline problems. This is the main reason for the rather slow growth of aid disbursements in Cameroon in comparison with the other countries.

The most important projects are those in the category of financial cooperation: a rural credit scheme for cattle production in the framework of the Plan Viande cofinanced by the World Bank (DM 6.5 million); a credit line for agricultural development in Northwest Province in cooperation with the EC and IFAD (DM 45 million); and a contribution to the construction of cereal storehouses (DM 12.1 million). In technical cooperation, there are seven major projects, including the agricultural utilization of the Benue Valley—which consists mainly of studies and a master plan (DM 9.2 million); the extension of appropriate cultivation systems by draught animal utilization (DM 5.2 million); advisers to FONADER to transform this authority into a rural development bank (DM 14.6 million); and training of young veterinarians (DM 3.6 million). Three of the seven technical cooperation projects have been handed over to Cameroon in recent years: the Agricultural Training and Settlement Center in the Wum region (DM 18.5 million); the Agricultural Mechanization Center, or CENEEMA (DM 22.1 million); and control of the tse-tse fly in the Adamoua Highlands (DM 8.9 million).

Project example. Since it has already been handed over to Cameroon, the Agricultural Training and Settlement Center in the Wum region may serve as a project example that permits some conclusions. The center was founded in 1966 and handed over in 1980, after an implementation and a transition period. The target of WADA was to increase agricultural income through the growth of agricultural production, intensification of the extension service, improvement of housing conditions, and support of local milk processing. To increase income, it appeared to be necessary to improve the agricultural cultivation methods, introduce new crops, switch to permanent crop production, promote rural cooperatives, and develop the production of seed.

During the implementation phase, a large central farm was established to gain substantial financial surpluses by modern large-scale production. These surpluses were to be used for financing a training and settlement center for young people. The initial objectives turned out to be far too ambitious, and the central farm was subsequently reduced; in addition, the settlement program was slowed down and efforts concentrated on improving existing farms. Through the Block Extension Service was introduced a group farming program and the use of animal traction.

The results achieved with this project were mixed. During the first phase the results on the whole were not encouraging because of overemployment problems, lower agricultural yields than expected, losses in most activities, and doubts as to whether the project would serve to support the economic development of the region.

After a reorientation phase, some small successes were achieved. The concept of group farming was accepted, and the introduction of rice and maize cultivation proved to be successful; the spread of animal traction gained momentum as well. However, other problems persisted. The participation in the Block Extension Program declined because the men who participated were unaccustomed to hard farm work. The yield of permanent crops like coffee and plantains was disappointing because of the poor location and diseases. In the settlement program, severe problems arose with the repayment of credits.

The central farm also had management problems, as reflected in the fact that the capacity used was less than 40 percent, there was no exact cost-revenue calculation, and the storekeeping was far from satisfactory. Moreover, animal traction proved difficult to introduce because of the necessary investment at the farm level and the inexperience in raising cattle. Oxen were only used for plowing and harrowing—that is, for only a few months of the year. In the long run, positive results favored oxen techniques, since investment and maintenance costs for tractors grew faster than comparable costs for oxen; raising cattle will contribute to the development of a more modern form of mixed farming, so that crop cultivation with oxen will be done in areas that until now were reserved for women's shift cultivation.

In conclusion, project experience has shown that, despite the large subsidies made available for this purpose, many farmers are not convinced that modern crop farming serviced by tractors is profitable and that animal traction is the more adequate solution. The initial package proved to be too ambitious for local farmers. Thus it was learned that a project should be prepared with an orientation phase so that serious drawbacks can be identified in time. Eventually, German experts were replaced by Cameroonian senior officers, and replacement was completed without serious disturbances in project activities. The smooth handing over indicated that there were capable and engaged Cameroonian staff members who could continue the project.

Kenya

In Kenya, Germany ranks third (after the United States and the United Kingdom) among bilateral donors. The total commitments in financial cooperation did not grow after 1982–83, which raised some eyebrows in the Kenyan administration.

Country profile. Agriculture receives the highest priority in both financial and technical cooperation. Four important agricultural projects are being implemented through financial cooperation: the irrigation scheme in Muka Mukaa and Mitunga (DM 26.5 million), which is to be extended to the Nkondi region; rice production in the Mwea-Tebere region, the goal of which is to make the country self-sufficient (DM 12.9 million); the refinancing of the Agriculture Finance Corporation's credit scheme to improve smallholder farming in the Kisii and Kericho districts (DM 6.4 million); and the promotion of fruit and vegetable production and marketing (DM 11.8 million).

Germany contributes a further DM 25 million to the Sectoral Adjustment Program under the African Facility. In technical cooperation, the project list is rather long: the most important and interesting project is the German Agricultural Team, or GAT (DM 81 million). There are two additional integrated settlement schemes—one in the Lamu and Kilifi District (DM 12.4 million) and another in the coastal region (DM 13 million). Another rather large program is being carried out jointly by Giessen and Nairobi universities in the field of veterinarian research and training (DM 8.1 million). Within the food security category, Germany also cofinances the Food for Work/Cash for Work Project in the Samburu District (DM 5.2 million).

Project example. The German Agricultural Team has a special position in German technical cooperation by virtue of its long history. A German group of advisers has been working in Kenya since 1963, either directly with the Kenyan Ministry of Agriculture and Livestock Development or under it. At the end of 1984 there were twenty-one technical cooperation experts working in line functions, advising their Kenyan counterparts and preparing projects, including those to be financed by German aid. Thus the GAT is not a project in the narrower sense of the term, but rather a program. It even had some influence on macroeconomic decisions because a German staff member was able, as a member of the Kenyan Price Commission, to exert influence on setting adequate producer prices.

In an evaluation done in 1985, this project was credited with significant effects on food production in Kenya. The project has concentrated primarily on small farms producing for the market and less on subsistence farmers. There was no explicit promotion of agricultural exports.

Besides having a favorable effect on central activities in planning and policy formulation, the project is having an impact in a wide range of other activities, as can be seen from its subdivisions. The farm management subproject is credited with success in collecting and processing primary statistics and developing practical models for farm management. Staff of the horticulture project dealt with marketing issues and expedited the construction of the wholesale vegetable market in Mombasa. The small irrigation subproject is currently implemented in the East Province by two projects supported by technical cooperation. The subproject for establishing a national gene bank is said to be contributing toward effective plant breeding. The Transmara pre-extension project has a special political function, since the use of rangeland is bound to expand in Kenya—a country with one of the highest population growth rates in the world.

When reflecting on factors that positively influence the success of this project, it must be pointed out that in contrast to normal practice elsewhere, the experts of the GAT were generally employed on the project for long periods. Thus they are not only extremely familiar with the situation and policy environment, but also can better exert influence.

A recent evaluation suggested that the stay may have been too long for the experts to remain adaptable and objective in their work. Several other important questions were raised. It was suggested, for example, that the wide range of activities, while demonstrating the flexibility of GAT, also contributed to the danger of marginalization. Another question was whether the numerous functions assumed by the team leader left enough time for him to coordinate project preparation and implementation, and especially project follow-up. Most important, the critique complained that not enough priority was given to the training of Kenyans.

A problem area—not only for German cooperation—will be the question of the political consequences of the recently introduced Kenyan policy of replacing foreign experts in project cooperation with Kenyan administrators. The existence of the German Agricultural Team as well as that of a similar team from Harvard University could become an issue.

Malawi

Germany ranks third (after the World Bank and the United Kingdom) as a donor in Malawi. The country is sometimes regarded as a model case for German aid in Africa.

Country profile. The delegation of responsibilities to German-sponsored projects within the Malawian administration (Rural Growth Centers, National Rural Development Program) shows the exceptionally far-reaching integration of German aid into Malawian development policies. In financial cooperation, German aid focuses on infrastructure (road construction and maintenance). In technical cooperation, priority has been given to agriculture and rural development ever since the beginning of Malawian-German cooperation, after independence.

After the delivery of the Salima Lakeshore Project (DM 30 million) to the Malawian government, only three German-assisted agricultural projects remained in Malawi. Within financial cooperation, German contributions for rural infrastructure amounted to DM 11.5 million. In technical cooperation, there is the Rural Development Program in Liwonde, where Germany assists the management unit of the Liwonde Agricultural Development Division (ADD) (DM 24.6 million), and the nationwide Livestock Development Project (DM 13.4 million).

Project example. The management unit of the Rural Development Shire East Liwonde Agricultural Development Division (LWADD) provides an important project example. This is a complex project with different activities financed by German technical and financial aid and by contributions of the African Development Bank. In view of its integration into the National Rural Development Program (NRDP), its counterpart organization is the Ministry of Agriculture; the project is one of the eight ADDs by which the Malawian government is implementing its NRDP.

The objectives of the project are to establish and put into operation a management unit that will contribute to the improvement of the living conditions of smallholder farmers, with special attention to women and young people, by increasing agricultural production and intensifying agriculture; by improving marketing facilities; by promoting education, health conditions, and the supply of potable water in rural areas; and by educating local experts.

The project supports the implementation of the NRDP by increasing cash crop and food crop production of smallholders, by providing inputs and services to the local population, and by preserving the national resources (soil conservation, protection of key watershed areas, and maintenance of forests). A concept of decentralization of rural administration is followed within the LWADD.

Despite its multisectoral approach, the project is more a rural development program than a regional development project in the strict sense of this term. The focal point of the German assistance is the support of the Liwonde ADD management unit. The establishment of a functional management system for rural services in the Liwonde ADD can be considered the primary result. Second, the extension service has improved, and the number of farmer participants and users of the input package is quite satisfactory. Advice for individuals was stopped in favor of counseling groups of farmers. Third, an acceptable repayment rate of credit was achieved by having group members exert pressure on single borrowers. Fourth, the construction of a road from Liwonde to Nsaname had positive effects, as shown by the increase in users. And fifth, basic needs could be satisfied by supplying potable water and health services.

Although the external activities (mainly of the extension service) started only in 1982–83 and the impact of the project therefore cannot be fully assessed, a number of risks exist that should receive special attention. The supply of public services has boosted farmers' expectations, and they now expect more public support in favor of self-help activities. Support for farmers at present mainly means for farmers of middle-size and large farms—so that the disparity between the lower third and the larger two-thirds will grow; a formerly homogenous target group will be divided into different strata. Furthermore, the project environment will see a steady growth of estate ownership detrimental to the development of smallholder cultivation. Consequently, the target group in the project zone will become a minority.

In judging the project results, cost-effectiveness can be considered satisfactory, since costs for the credit program are recovered by high repayment rates and the effects of the extension service are considered to be adequate. However, there is the problem of how to cover the high recurrent costs of the project. The German aid group has agreed to take over the recurrent costs of the administration of the project; in the long run, however, the Malawian government will be unable to finance these costs, so that in the future the project must give priority to cost reduction. This represents a general problem of aid, as many

African governments not only have problems continuing a project after the handing over, but also are unable to provide adequate counterpart funds to cover recurrent costs during the aided period of a project. In the foreseeable future, the LWADD will be impossible to develop and maintain without the support of donor organizations. There is little chance that the counterparts will take over responsibility for the activities.

Despite these problems, the significance of the project is clear. Since 1983, thirty-four Malawian staff have been trained. A last gap within the system of a regional administration of agriculture was closed. Compared with other administration units on the ADD level, the Liwonde MU is well equipped, well organized, and—in the field of planning and evaluation—a most competent organization.

Senegal

In Senegal, Germany ranks fifth as a donor (after France, the United States, the EC, and the World Bank).

Country profile. Although physical infrastructure (water supply and transport) is the priority of Germany's financial assistance, agriculture is the priority of its technical assistance. Three projects in agriculture do, however, receive financial assistance. One is the Nianga Project in Senegal's Fleuve region, a small irrigation project, substituting pumping to individual holdings for *culture de décrue*, and costing DM 21.4 million. It is part of a project package in the Podor Department financed by the World Bank and the EC. The second is an irrigation project in the Casamance region (DM 3.5 million), and the third a government fund for financing small self-help projects (DM 4 million).

Germany's technical cooperation consists in part of cofinancing for a large afforestation project in northern Senegal (DM 24.9 million) that is trying to contain further desertification in the catchment areas of wells brought down by the French in the 1950s. Other important projects are the Maize Seed Production Project (DM 6.5 million), which is closely linked to the financial cooperation irrigation project in the same area; a project to improve the production of cashew nuts (DM 5.0 million); and the Food Security Program (about DM 15 million), which has financed storehouses for local cereals (with a capacity of 84,000 tons) and is now refinancing a market intervention scheme for local grains (millet).

Project example. The Maize Seed Production project is attempting to provide Senegal's rural population, as well as its urban population (which is accustomed to imported rice), with locally produced alternatives in the form of "maize rice." The propagation project has rather an ambitious objective. Recognizing that the government executing agencies have operated inefficiently, the Senegalese government has allowed a largely "German project" to be set up and to cooperate directly with the target group of small farmers. The project took on the role of a credit agency, and by 1986 had achieved repayment ratios of up to 95 percent.That year the project purchased approximately 500 tons of maize seed from the farmers and used maize that was unsuitable for seed to produce maize rice for sale.

Since the beginning of the project, maize production has risen significantly in Senegal, but it is currently hindered by the absence of an effective supply system. A de facto line of responsibility stretches from the German project to the Senegalese farmers. Structural solutions must be found. So far, no definitive agreements have been reached between the German and the Senegalese partners. In times of crisis in Africa it must be asked whether this kind of project should not be replicated more frequently—at least for a period of time.

If the project is to succeed in increasing production, a more direct line of responsibility between the donor institution and agricultural producers must be allowed—even though this formula is not in line with conventional aid philosophy. Of course there is a danger that aid agencies employing such a technique will be called interventionist. But in a study on this project, the interesting question was raised: "Is it conceivable that the donor might assume responsibility in areas of strategic agricultural importance until the producers themselves are in a position to organize themselves and possibly receive financial assistance directly without the intervention of government agencies?"

It should be noted that assistance to the two great dam projects, DIAMA and MANANTALI, will have a great effect on agricultural production in the Senegal Valley in the medium term—although it is not yet clear precisely how they will be used. Financing and implementation problems in dam construction have been in the foreground so far, and the settlement programs still need to be ironed out. The two countries mainly involved, Mauritania and Senegal, are considering using the water for intensive irrigated agriculture, particularly for rice, but detailed planning is still in the early stages. In the first phase of using the MANANTALI dam, a conflict of interest emerged: The dam could be used to produce an artificial flood to revive the traditional flood in agriculture, but this could compete with the use of MANANTALI water potential to generate electricity all year round. In the medium to long term, this conflict would be resolved, because irrigated agriculture using pumps to obtain two crops a year would also require a largely continuous release of water from the dam.

agriculture, but this could compete with the use of MANANTALI water potential to generate electricity all year round. In the medium to long term, this conflict would be resolved, because irrigated agriculture using pumps to obtain two crops a year would also require a largely continuous release of water from the dam.

Tanzania

Until 1984, Tanzania was one of the most important recipients of German aid in Africa.

Country profile. Between 1973 and 1985, Tanzania received almost DM 1,100 million in ODA. In addition, some DM 500 million were spent for programs carried out by nongovernmental organizations (NGOs). In 1984, commitments were heavily cut in order to support the recommendations of the IMF and the World Bank that the Tanzanian government reform the country's economic policies.

German financial assistance has no commitments to Tanzanian agriculture, but there are several technical cooperation projects in Tanzania: the Tanga Integrated Rural Development Project (TIRDEP, DM 100 million), the Coconut Development Program (DM 23.0 million), the Ministry of Agriculture's Training Institute at Nyegezi (DM 17.7 million), and the Food Security Program in the Rukwa region (DM 4.1 million).

Project example. TIRDEP is not only one of the biggest projects under German technical cooperation, but it is also regarded as a model for regional development projects by other donors. After the program started up in 1971, a comprehensive regional development plan was worked out for the Tanga region. The plan listed in detail the available national resources, reviewed and analyzed all economic and social sectors, and presented general ideas for a development strategy from which forty-five project proposals were derived.

When problems arose in attempting to coordinate individual projects, a BMZ evaluation of the situation found that individual projects were being coordinated and formally integrated into the administration without meeting the standards of an integrated regional program. It was said that TIRDEP is not actually an integrated project, but rather a loose bundle of individual measures in a single region. GTZ, as the executing agency, considered this critique to be too dogmatic and argued that loose coordination—combined with a high degree of autonomy on the part of individual projects—was what made it possible to work directly with the farmers, obviating bureaucratic inertia and deficiencies. Thus the project attempted to assist farmers with

The main components of TIRDEP are its village development programs, with a relatively broad self-help component; agricultural planning and extension work; an agroforestry project and erosion monitoring; a small irrigation project; improvements in the regional veterinary service; a water supply program; and an education program. Although TIRDEP cannot be described as resting on an overall concept and having clear objectives, it has improved the living conditions of the rural population, and the cumulative effects of the individual projects have been positive.

Performance, Impact, and Lessons

Judging the performance of an aid program means measuring its effects against criteria that reflect the objectives and targets pursued both by the donor and the recipient countries. Evaluators must assess how the inputs—programs, projects, and activities—may contribute to goal achievement. In principle, judging aid performance presupposes an understanding of agricultural development, a clear concept of how development can be advanced by aid inputs, and an ability to separate the effects of projects from what Uma Lele has called "numerous and immensely variable factors." Without in-depth knowledge about complex socioeconomic systems it is not only difficult to design complex programs, but also to judge their performance. Thus the discussion in this section should be read with caution. It should also be noted that the sample is rather small and that the projects are almost all examples of technical cooperation.

Problems in Measuring Aid Effectiveness

The evaluation reports of the BMZ provide few clues to the problems in financial cooperation projects, such as dam construction or the cofinancing of rural development banks. Furthermore, these reports show a strong bias on the part of the evaluators, which makes it almost impossible to rank the projects on the basis of their performance.

In view of these problems and the lack of a development theory from which clear criteria to judge aid performance can be deduced, the only alternative is to attempt to glean some general lessons from the evaluation studies that are available. The sections that follow are based on a 1986 BMZ report on nine years of project evaluations, a cross-sectional study on performance and impact of German projects in agriculture written in 1983, evaluations of projects in the MADIA countries, and a cross-country evaluation of German projects in Malawi that was prepared by the inspection unit of the BMZ in 1986 as a background document for the MADIA project.

Learning from Mistakes

In 1986, the BMZ published a cross-sectional analysis of the results of evaluations done on 6 percent of all German projects carried out between 1976 and 1984.[2] One important finding was that "about 30 percent of all projects examined were judged positively without reservations. Another third (33 percent) were assessed positively with reservations. About 25 percent of the projects were partly positive and partly negative. About 12 percent were assessed as being mainly negative in their effects." The effectiveness of development measures was found to be strongly related to the overall economic situation of the country. Thus positively rated projects were more numerous before the beginning of the world economic crisis in 1979–80.

About a third of the projects inspected were found to have the following weaknesses: insufficient knowledge of the general conditions; insufficient attention paid to ecological and sociocultural conditions; inadequate analysis of requirements and markets; lack of data and evaluations; insufficient participation of the target groups in planning and implementation and insufficient information provided for the population about the targets and advantages of the project and the significance of individual contribution; and a lack of coordination between individual aid instruments and other donor institutions. Weak projects usually had deficiencies right from the beginning—especially when the period of project planning was too short.

Agricultural and forestry projects have to deal with complex situations and therefore require more detailed preliminary studies. Otherwise, as demonstrated by the experiences in agricultural extension, the methods used may have to be changed quickly, and even then the changes themselves may not always be based on sound principles. In plant production projects, it was found that extension packages often were often poorly adapted to economic conditions and not designed to maintain the long-term yield capacity. Plant protection projects were "sometimes too ambitious in scope instead of concentrating on key activities" and could have benefited from an early warning service and a control threshold specific to the region. In addition, not enough attention was given to natural control methods. In animal production, an integrated approach was judged to be promising: "Upstream and downstream production areas and flanking services" should complement the sector of animal production.

In regional development projects, it was again found that the population did not often participate in planning and decisionmaking. This participation cannot be expected to take place smoothly unless ethnological and sociological problems are first resolved. In complex projects, a step-by-step procedure starting with an orientation phase is advocated, since integrated regional development projects tend to try to cover too many fields and to become overly complex. Many demands are made on the management capacity of these projects, and consequently the handing-over phase comes too late, if ever.

Another common problem identified in the reports is that the evaluation and inspection missions on agricultural projects seldom measure the efficiency (cost-benefit ratio) of the projects. Although the costs are evident, it is often difficult to express the benefits in monetary terms and on a short-term basis. Because of the many practical problems involved in collecting and evaluating data, assessments or general criticisms tend to consist of qualitative judgments. Thus the overall evaluation is based on a mix of quantitative and qualitative data, supplemented by personal inspections by which BMZ tries to gain an insight into the project reality.

The significance of projects and programs—that is, their "sustained effects on the economic, social and cultural development of a country, region or target group" must also be taken into consideration. The available evidence indicates that

> the greatest developmental impact (significance) has been achieved by projects that have participated in removing bottlenecks in the field of basic needs, which have included target groups in the planning and implementation phases, which were integrated into a larger regional and sectoral context and which have cooperated with qualified, reliable local project executing agencies.

However, the sustainability of quite a number of projects is doubtful, and effects once achieved can "evaporate" in the long run. Project discussions of recent years have been putting more and more emphasis on attaining sustainability of projects through the concentration of activities, follow-up work, and the stimulation of self-help work. Although the BMZ report "Learning from Mistakes" compiles firsthand empirical evidence from project work, it fails to relate the findings to the structural problems of development economies—such as growing ecological imbalances, the dissolution of a subsistence economy without a full realization of the market economy, or the structural deficits (if not the decay) of the state.

The Findings of the Schubert Study

Another important study of aid impact was the cross-sectional analysis of the effectiveness and sustainability of agricultural technical cooperation projects after handover carried out in 1983 by Schubert and his colleagues.[3] The study produced several significant findings:

- Project effects have been both positive and negative. The reasons for these effects have been highly mixed. In view of the great diversity of project types, of the numerous factors that determine project effects, and, last but not least, an unavoidable evaluator bias, it is difficult to come to clear-cut general conclusions about aid effectiveness on the basis of project evaluation studies.
- Failures or even negative consequences are "not as great as may have been feared"—that is, there are some good and a few poor projects according to analysis of the project evaluation reports.
- When measured against the projects' systems of objectives, "half of the projects exhibited a high level of effectiveness at the time of handover, but only a quarter could be rated high in significance. After handover, effectiveness of some of the projects declined but significance remained largely stable."
- The sustainability of projects with high effectiveness and significance is better than expected. The view often expressed by experts that "when we leave, everything will fall apart" is not confirmed as a general rule.
- Relatively small projects with sectorally limited activities and clear innovative messages have "more lasting effects than larger and more complex projects."

The Schubert report is the only study available that attempts to assess German aid in agriculture on a global scale. However, some methodological weaknesses reduce its relevance to German aid to Africa. First, the Schubert report deals exclusively with technical cooperation projects in the narrower sense—that is, expert-intensive projects executed by GTZ. Second, of the twenty-four projects analyzed, only six are located in Sub-Saharan Africa and only three in the MADIA countries. Furthermore, the effectiveness of projects is judged by goal achievement only, taking the goals and targets as they were formulated in the planning studies or the respective terms of reference as given. The question is never raised as to whether these project goals were consistent with the development needs of the country concerned or what the cost-benefit indicators reveal about efficiency.

Evaluation Reports on Projects in the MADIA Countries

Even if one takes into account that the "evaluator bias" probably has positive rather than negative aspects, it is evident that the aid results in the MADIA countries as a whole have been mixed—but not too disappointing. There have been many good and some very good projects, in the view of evaluation teams including, as a rule, staff from the recipient country itself. Only one project out of about twenty-five was rated a complete failure. All other projects were criticized for various reasons, but for more than half of them, the evaluation proved good or at least not bad. In all projects, even the ones with poor performance, the conclusion was that if solutions could be found to the problems identified, their respective impact could be improved. In some cases projects that were considered extremely difficult if not hopeless in the early stages—such as the German Assisted Settlement projects in Kenya—later on worked out quite well.

At least five main points seem to recur throughout the evaluation reports:

- The objectives of the projects under review were not entirely clear. This deficiency was, as a rule, traced back to the identification and planning phase of the project. For example, the evaluation study on the Food Security Program in Kenya's Samburu District, written by the evaluation unit of the BMZ, states that the objectives of the project had been ambitious and unrealistic and that the competent sectoral desk had started the project for political reasons in spite of its well-known risks and problems. As a consequence, some projects were dissipating their energies in numerous activities that were not as relevant as the main objective or in stated activities that were not covered by the project plan. For example, the CENEEMA project in Cameroon established regional stations for lending heavy machinery to farmers and started bush clearing with its own equipment to the detriment of its original tasks, namely training and applied research.
- Poor framework conditions hampered the work. Almost all reports call particular attention to the poor planning and implementation capability of the counterpart institution. At times this complaint pertains to budget constraints and bottlenecks (recurrent costs).
- According to some reports, marketing problems have been neglected. These reports also complain about other constraints, such as sociocultural factors (lack of acceptance of the project by farmers). Some also note that no effort has been made to formulate a general conceptual framework to help avoid the uncoordinated addition of single activities (as in TIRDEP in Tanzania and livestock projects in Cameroon and Kenya).
- Projects performed quite well on infrastructure, institution building, training, and the like but did not increase agricultural production, according to many reports. Considering the high priority accorded by German aid to the growth of food production, this criticism is rather serious. This point was also stressed in various

particular projects such as TIRDEP in Tanzania, the Draught Animal Project in Cameroon, and the Salima Project in Malawi.

- According to some studies, it was difficult not only to start and implement a project but also to evaluate it, for want of answers to some general questions about agricultural development. These answers are necessary for judging whether the respective project approach was significant or not. The cross-sectional analysis of settlement projects, including those financed by German aid in Kenya, states that serious attention should be given to the notion that "it would be more efficient to increase production in already settled areas than to establish new settlement schemes in remote areas."

The Case of Malawi

In Malawi, German aid to agriculture was evaluated in 1986 by the inspection section of the BMZ as a part of the preparatory activities of the MADIA program. In their report the evaluators search for the reasons behind the limited aid performance and try to draw from their findings some general conclusions about German aid in Malawi and other African countries. Four general messages are put forth by the inspection team.

First, the effects on smallholder production were "far less satisfactory than expected," and "the impact of the measures can in the main be assessed as disappointing." The reason given by the team was that the extension programs had little to offer to smallholders, that is, that the innovations German projects proposed (such as the introduction of hybrid maize) were not adapted to the needs and the potential of existing farming systems and the intrinsic logic of their development. Consequently, the team suggests that more be done in the area of applied agricultural research, but that particular attention be paid to the socioeconomic situation of the "low-acceptance smallholder" and that new concepts and methods of agricultural extension be formulated on this basis.

Second, the Malawian government needs assistance in cofinancing recurrent costs that occur as a consequence of sectoral adjustment and recurrent costs of projects cofinanced by foreign aid. The team believes that it is better to limit the amount of money spent on, for example, oversized RDPs; to concentrate the efforts on smaller projects having a better chance of performing successfully; and to spend more in financing recurrent counterpart costs, insofar as the costs are vital for the project concerned.

Third, the report suggests investing more in rural infrastructure, including resource-saving activities (fruit-tree growing).

Fourth, the team lists some general problems of rural smallholder development that have to be dealt with by socioeconomic research in order to work out new strategies of agricultural and rural development.

Major Problems

The available evidence has brought to light a number of general problems confronting German aid to African agriculture.

Overloading with goals. German projects and programs often are overloaded with sometimes hazy and overambitious goals. The multiplication of goals that aid programs and particular projects are required to pursue is born of the need to establish a consensus among constituencies with dissenting views on aid policy, which is arrived at by adding up their priorities in the aid program. Each new line of thinking in Bonn, every new concern about, say, women or the environment, means that a new set of goals must be tacked on to new and old projects alike and is often used to question projects that have shown good performance in helping to increase production and to generate income—or, conversely, to justify projects with poor results in terms that allude to intangibles such as social effects or institution building. As a result, scarce financial and human resources are at times frittered away and the "tangible content" of cooperation projects lost. At other times, this overburdening inflates the amount of counterpart resources (trained manpower, budget) used and generates follow-up costs.

Does Germany take it too easy? Agricultural development is a matter of trial and error. Development cooperation is challenged to find answers, to finance trials, and to learn from errors—thus shortening the costly detours that are unavoidable in a developing society. However, the correct answers that rural Africa must seek under the pressure of population growth, environmental degradation, and all the other elements of social stress are difficult to find. Agricultural development *is* difficult. More than that, wrong answers given by donors via projects (or policy dialogue) can make the situation worse—either if the donor pulls out after the mistakes made have become too evident or if the donor tries to solve the problem by a continuous financing of sunk costs.

German aid projects in the MADIA countries reflect a "tendency to charge ahead of our knowledge base."[4] A good example is the Food Security Project in Senegal, which comprises storage building and the refinancing of a market intervention scheme for local cereals (millet and sorghum). Do we really know what happens within the extremely sensitive system of subsistence production, on-farm storage, local consumption, and local trade (including barter) if producer prices paid for subsistence crops are subsidized?

German know-how in tropical agriculture originates and accumulates almost exclusively in the community of development experts. There is almost no (more) direct transfer of expertise from agriculture at home to agriculture abroad. This does not necessarily constitute a comparative disadvantage of German aid, since Germany has had time to catch up. Compared with other donors, including those with a long colonial past, the German project staff is fairly well-prepared professionally and has the incentive to do a good job abroad. The training of German experts is carried out by a rather elaborate system of institutions. However, the considerable efforts of these institutions to improve the professional training of German experts working in the tropics cannot yet fully balance the deficiency of specific know-how, particularly if an aid agency or a consulting firm gets a project tender and has to look for qualified staff afterward. In addition, there is pressure exerted on aid institutions to disburse the aid commitments made in bilateral negotiations. This leads in many cases to overoptimistic assumptions, for example, in quantifying the parameters for cost-benefit calculations.

The point here is not simply that there should be "more research," but that a more patient and comprehensive observation and analysis of the regional economy, the farming system, and the reasons for their stagnation, and, last but not least, the absorptive capacity of recipient countries in terms of budget and staff could lead to more caution in project identification and a considerable increase in aid efficiency.

Marginal locations and the rural poor as the main target group. German projects are often located in marginal regions, where it is easy to identify problems but extremely difficult to find a clear message or an innovative package promising short- or medium-term production and income effects. This tendency suggests that policy is being formulated under the strain of constituency concerns; that planning is guided by the methods used by the German Agency for Technical Cooperation, which is more problem-oriented than resource-oriented (goals are formulated as negative problems); and that Germany has relatively weak bargaining power in the international competition among donors for "good" projects. Of course, development cooperation is not for the rich and the privileged. But if poverty and income distribution concerns outweigh the developmental potential argument too much, there is a risk that the projects elaborated will not even reach the poor. Besides, there is sometimes a great deal of semantic confusion with regard to the target group and thus a mixing up of the "rural poor," the "poorest of the poor," and the smallholder. This confusion and the resulting effacement of a clear distinction between social welfare activities and the self-help principle could be avoided by defining the target group as those small and medium farmers who seek survival and growth by introducing innovations that can be provided by development cooperation. Given the enormous development potential of small farms in Africa, there are a great many poor and very poor people within this group.

The point here is simply that if one is too anxious to focus on the income differentiations inherent in rural development and if the definition of the "poor" is too exclusive, German aid risks punishing itself in being tangled up in projects that may be justified in advance with convincing intentions but that produce poor results in terms of production development. Aid programs consequently will be tempted into financing subsidies with questionable economic effects and high social opportunity costs in the long run and thus come into conflict with the basic principle of German aid—the self-help perception, or principle that eventually the donor should be worked out of the aid projects. Furthermore, an overly rigid poverty orientation leads directly to the claim that stronger local pressure in aid agencies and NGOs in the rural areas is needed to identify target groups, to motivate them, and to allow them to participate in a program conceived by donors.[5] Thus, defining the target group exclusively on the basis of criteria of poverty could lead to new forms of paternalism, which would be contradictory to all principles of development cooperation.

Framework conditions and consistency problems. Almost every person interviewed drew attention to the difficult framework conditions of bilateral projects. This observation took two different forms: (1) that too little attention was paid by the donor's agencies or consultants to the given socioeconomic environment of projects during identification and early planning stages, or (2) that the macroeconomic and sectoral policies or nonpolicies of the recipient country concerned provided too many constraints for a project to succeed.

In many cases, bottlenecks and difficulties labeled by donors as unsuitable or unacceptable framework conditions simply reflect the lack of attention to economic intra- and intersectoral consistency during the identification and planning stage of a project. This is an old problem. For instance, the maize project in Senegal has had excellent results in the area of seed production and multiplication, but there was no market for the maize produced through high-yielding varieties. Various similar examples could be quoted to show clearly how persistent and stubborn relatively banal and simple problems such as the neglect of market constraints can be.

The reason behind this is obviously not only the lack of feedback and the hazards of learning by doing, but also an overly simplistic view of a suitable sectoral allocation of aid. German aid shows a sort of agricultural bias that is not always helpful when it comes to aid efficiency. It may be true that recipient countries should consider agricultural development a priority for public attention and investment and should change the urban bias of their domestic policies.

But this does not mean that, from a donor's perspective, doing something in or for agriculture is always a good thing—irrespective of sectoral interdependencies, market or input constraints, higher marginal returns to capital in neighboring sectors and subsectors (for example, agroindustry), and, with regard to technical cooperation, the comparative advantage of a donor with specific know-how. As far as financial cooperation is concerned, one should keep in mind that an element that is obviously scarce in the view of a country and its economy—namely, capital—is not necessarily the most binding constraint on agricultural projects refinanced with foreign capital inflows. The fact that countries that urgently need fresh money for their macroeconomic rehabilitation have the greatest problems in prompt aid disbursement is proof of inappropriate allocation decisions, rather than a poor implementation capability on the part of the recipient country.

Institution building. In view of the well-known difficulties inherent in the traditional transfer of technology, it seems to be good advice for a donor country like Germany to focus on strengthening the institutional and human capabilities of an African country rather than to rely on technical cooperation in the narrow sense of the term. If framework conditions are detrimental for goal achievement, why not create better conditions by building up and improving the respective institutions? Indeed, the German approach to cooperation implies a strong public institution-building component. However, state bureaucracies and parastatals in African countries are, for several reasons, not always the most dynamic actors when it comes to improving agricultural development. In many cases, the German contribution is mainly to get this machinery moving, and only a small part of the funds is allocated to activities that create direct benefits in terms of income formation. This leads to an interesting contradiction: German aid aims, in principle, at improving the economic and social living conditions of individual farmers as small entrepreneurs, but, on the way to that goal, most of the funds are lost in building up or repairing a large state bureaucracy, which has little to offer farmers in the way of innovation messages. This does not mean that institution building as such is always a bad thing. There are several cases in which the institution-building component contributed a great deal to a good project performance, as in the GAT program in Kenya. In several projects, however, the strong institution-building component leads to difficulties in integrating foreign staff that would not be that prevalent in innovation-oriented projects. If German experts are acting in a purely advisory function in an African administration, they risk becoming isolated from decisionmaking—particularly if they have no right to allow budget aid components of the project to be disbursed. An evaluation report on the FONADER project in Cameroon explains that the main bottleneck of the project is the institutional structure and the behavior of the counterpart institution. The evaluators indicate that the German experts had been employed as "academic subordinates for erratic subjects rather than as authorized consultants for specific problem solutions."

Line functions of expatriates have been a good solution in some projects, as in the GAT project in Kenya. The central issue, however, was not the full integration of the experts into the Kenyan administration, but the matrix structure of the project: The German staff in the ministry was in a position to initiate and to coordinate many innovation-oriented subprojects cofinanced by Germany in a rather flexible way. However, line functions of expatriates are not, as a rule, consistent with the philosophy of strengthening the administrative capability of the recipient country. In addition, a recipient country may perceive a heavy presence of expatriates as unfair competition against their own personnel. In Kenya this has led to the absurd but understandable situation that the Kenyan government had to pursue a sort of containment policy in order to keep the number of expatriates consistent with the absorptive capacity of the administration, as well as with the high qualification standards of its own staff. The is not to challenge the need for institution building as such, but merely to point out that the institutions that foreign aid establishes, maintains, or repairs should not remain empty of innovation messages.

Methodological problems in project analysis and feedback. Since the late 1960s the German aid administration and research institutes such as the German Development Institute in Berlin have made continuous efforts to enlarge and refine the analytical toolbox of planning and evaluating aid programs and to adjust the methodology to both changing aid concepts and growing experience acquired during project implementation. There are, however, some problems.

First, it must be acknowledged that German aid is really trying to learn from earlier mistakes. But the error-embracing strategy works only if the institutions are ready and able to react to critical evaluation reports on projects or to cross-sectional studies. Individual evaluators and even the inspection unit of the BMZ are sometimes under the impression that their efforts in analyzing projects do not trigger the decisions that need to be taken in the operational units of the ministry and the executing agencies.

Second, evaluation and planning instruments cannot fill the gap left by a poor data base or deficiencies in understanding agricultural development. Today, the links between policy formulation and the project level are established by analytical instruments developed on the basis of the Little-Mireless version of cost-benefit analysis (CBA) and, in the late 1970s, the logical framework methodology. The latter provided the base of the goal-oriented project planning (ZOPP) that GTZ today uses for all technical cooperation projects. However, both instruments are weak in the sense that they design a future and compare it to the present without making explicit how a farming system or a rural society changes. Furthermore, ZOPP and CBA often are applied after the project decision already has been taken, so that ZOPP, in particular, is used as a training tool rather than as an instrument of decisionmaking. But ZOPP and CBA based on what lies ahead only make sense if the systems to which they are applied are not just black boxes, but if the projects under review are understood in terms of "what happens if." If applied to programs where it is not clear what happens within a socioeconomic system when one changes parameters such as prices, factor proportions, and technologies, or when the assumptions on project impacts are too optimistic, the outcomes of ZOPP or CBA will be necessarily misleading or, in the best case, meaningless.

These problems can only be resolved by putting more emphasis on empirical research and analysis as the way to understand how agriculture behaves and develops, in particular farming system analysis, in which Germany has a long tradition. German aid should make more use of this tool to avoid action without effects, institutions without messages, and planning without facts.

A Summary of Open Questions

After almost thirty years of cooperation with African countries in the agricultural sector, German aid has acquired reliable experience and learned lessons by observing, studying, and learning from mistakes made and successes achieved. However, it would be inappropriate to end this discussion with a list of simplified recommendations from these findings. It is one thing to summarize the problems analyzed, but another to transform the collected information into a program for future action. The problem is not only that each country and each project is, in a way, a world in itself, so that generalized recommendations would not fit into the particular characteristics of a specific country program or a project, but also that nobody knows exactly the right direction for African agriculture to follow in the next decade. Thus a concluding list of recommendations would be a risky exercise and an unfair one, inasmuch as there certainly are scholars, experts, administrators, and politicians who may not share the opinions expressed in this report or who might even hold the opposite view.

Are African Countries Overaided?

The numerous obstacles to the identification of "good" projects and the severe disbursement problems in the aid program of all donors have led many observers to conclude that African countries are "overaided" and that the absorptive capacity of the administration is exhausted or even overdrawn by donors. It is indeed difficult not to come to that conclusion if one knows the hard business of finding projects—and if one takes note of the amount of time spent by African administrators on receiving one aid mission after another. If, beyond the point of maximum absorptive capacity, there is a reverse relation between disbursement ease and aid efficiency, the conclusion would be, theoretically, to reduce aid commitments at the level of project- or program-bound financial transfers. There is, in principle, something to be said for this line of thinking and reason to believe that in some cases (Senegal, Kenya) it would be better to improve the quality of aid projects than to increase the disbursement speed—even if growing quality pretensions would lead to shrinking disbursement chances. However, there are competent people who support exactly the opposite view. It is argued that poverty in Africa will soon reach a dimension that will not allow a stagnation or even a reduction of aid commitments. In this view, the absorptive capacity problem reflects donor conditionalities and restrictions rather than management and administration bottlenecks at the recipient country's end. Consequently, donors should be ready to soften the conditionalities with particular reference to the recurrent costs that should be included in foreign aid contributions. In addition, donors could do more in the area of rural infrastructure, including investment in resource- and environment-protecting activities. Furthermore, in view of the population growth rates, the problems created by intra-African migration, the employment situation in the cities, the speed of desertification, and the threat of famine and malnutrition, donors should be less restrictive with regard to the social component of foreign aid. The absorptive capacity problem results partly from the tradition that donors channel their contributions to the target groups through the governments and their inefficient civil service instead of looking for NGOs, such as rural cooperatives, that are more efficient in ensuring aid quality and ease of disbursement. But is project- and program-bound cooperation the proper way to increase the volume of transfers? Or should one again take up the pros and cons of the massive transfer issue, as discussed some years ago in the context of the New International Economic Order?

More or Less Aid to Agriculture?

As already mentioned, German aid shows a growing agricultural bias. The need for giving a higher priority to agriculture by the governments of African countries does not, however, necessarily mean that a donor should concentrate its efforts too much on agriculture. Indeed, there are some arguments that urge rethinking of the sectoral allocation of German aid.

The first point is that almost all projects that are successful in increasing agricultural production are, sooner or later, confronted with marketing problems. Obviously, under the impression of immediate and increasing food shortages in a fast-growing population, the trivial truth of the importance of identifying need and demand is too often overlooked, tempting planners into overoptimistic assumptions about the markets for agricultural produce. Second, there are many projects, in particular the big rural development programs, that have little "hardware" to offer to farmers. This occurs when there are no tested innovations available that fit into the development logic of present farming systems and that are consistent with the various social constraints of agricultural development. Third, there is a particular problem with regard to financial cooperation. A lending institution such as the KfW has, as a rule, only one contribution to offer, namely capital, and in many cases capital is by no means the most binding constraint on rural development. All this leads to the question of whether a bilateral donor like Germany should shift the emphasis of its aid program of technological and institutional know-how to industry or to the service sector.

It must also be asked if the low world market prices, in particular for cereals such as wheat and rice, are a long-term reality that has to be accepted, and whether these prices are the result of surplus production and dumping practices of the United States and the EC. German aid is not aiming for full autarky of African countries in food production. However, the principle of "achieving food security on the basis of the country's own efforts" and the importance accorded to food self-sufficiency argue strongly for food production rather than export crops. In view of the realistic outlook for a continuous overproduction of cereals not only in traditional surplus countries in the OECD but also in Southeast Asia and Latin America, the optimum degree of food self-sufficiency in Africa needs further rethinking.

Focusing on Production Increase?

The evaluations of German aid have demonstrated that smaller technical cooperation projects that concentrated on a clear and tangible production-oriented message performed better than did large programs aiming at comprehensive and "soft" goals such as institution building. This has also been the experience of other donor projects. However, as pointed out above, it turned out to be difficult in many projects to identify such tangible innovations in agricultural production with a critical visible minimum effect. The report on the German aid program in Malawi goes so far as to call into question whether extension-oriented projects bear visible productivity effects at all. The conclusion then would be either to influence production by indirect measures, such as price policies, or to concentrate on infrastructure in the broader sense—including education, training, and research, which may have a long-term effect on productivity but are not measured against short-term production indicators.

A careful consideration of problems in a recipient country and of donors' capabilities could, for some countries, lead to a gradual shift from production-oriented extension projects to medium-term programs in infrastructure. In any case, the basic principle should be to ask and to answer the questions "what is the problem," and "what have we to offer to solve it" at the same time.

Should the Target Group Orientation of German Aid Be Modified?

This discussion has argued for a more precise definition of the target of German aid to agriculture. The suggestion was to define the target group as the African smallholder with his family, who seeks survival and growth by accepting and introducing innovations that could be offered by bilateral cooperation projects. Inasmuch as there are many poor people within that group, there would be no need to define the target group on the basis of absolute poverty. On the contrary, the inclusion of acceptance and potential criteria in the target group could improve project efficiency (and probably complicate project identification), particularly with reference to the aim of really reaching the rural poor.

Independent from official wording, the aid administration—that is, the BMZ and the two agencies GTZ and KfW—have shifted gradually toward a more pragmatic definition of the target group, so that this suggestion probably will not lead to a controversial discussion in the German aid system.

The real question is a methodological one: How and by what instrument can the target group, however defined, be reached? How far can it be proved that the "basic needs" strategy, which was designed in the late 1960s and has since been made one of the basic features of German aid, has indeed produced better results with respect to creating income and eliminating poverty than did the traditional methods that relied more on the market principle and "trickle-down" effects? German aid could again have more confidence in the market principle as the most important component of mixed economic systems, without leaving behind the basic needs principle as such. This could help to overcome some bewildering inconsistencies in German aid. Germany accepts the ideas of a free market when supporting the IMF and World Bank in adjustment issues, but its aid concepts show a curious timidity concerning market mechanisms (such as the role of private merchants in rural areas) and at least a verbal preponderance of social concerns such as equity or resorting to the poorest of the poor in the target group. It also sometimes follows purely mercantilistic lines of thinking in shaping and implementing its aid program (maintenance and repair of centralized parastatals and the undisputed priority of food self-sufficiency). This leads in some cases to strange contradictions, when, for example, Germany strongly supports Senegal's New Agricultural Policy, designed with the help of the World Bank and the Paris Club, but opposes with the same verve the policies pursued within this framework that trim organizations that are the counterpart institutions of a poverty-oriented German project. Here again it is obvious that the spectrum of opinions within the aid community is rather broad and controversial.

Does Germany Need a New Aid Concept?

In the absence of a widely accepted general theory of development, an aid concept cannot be developed by deduction but must grow from below on the basis of a heuristic and pluralistic learning-by-doing and error-embracing methodology. Thus the answer to the question often asked inside and outside the aid community as to whether Germany should change its aid concept on principle is a misleading one. It would be of little use to sit together in the upper floors of BMZ, GTZ, and KfW to design a new aid philosophy. However, it would be equally wrong to lean back and to continue development business as usual. The MADIA program has brought the core problems of cooperation in agriculture to the surface, and this chance should be used by all donors to rethink their aid programs on the basis of hard-won experience in their programs.

Notes

The views expressed herein are those of the authors and not necessarily those of the German Aid Administration, the World Bank, or other organizations affiliated with the MADIA study. To reduce their own biases and errors, the authors have consulted competent people inside and outside the administration. Furthermore, the dissenting or diverging views of others are quoted when authors had to accept the possibility that certain lines of their own thinking might be wrong. The authors express gratitude to those interviewed and to the ministry, which was tolerant enough to extend them full freedom in the preparation and writing of this study.

1. Although Nigeria is considered in this section, it is excluded from the remainder of the chapter. When Nigeria joined the Organization of Petroleum Exporting Countries (OPEC) in 1971, new commitments to this country were sharply reduced. The German decision not to continue bilateral aid programs with OPEC countries will not be discussed here.

2. Federal Ministry for Economic Cooperation, "Learning from Mistakes—Nine Years of Evaluating Project Reality" (Bonn, 1986).

3. B. Schubert, "Sustainability of the Effects of Agricultural Projects in German Technical Cooperation: Methodology and Selected Findings of a Cross-Sectional Analysis of 24 Agricultural Projects after Handover to Partner Countries," *Quarterly Journal of International Agriculture* 24 (July-September 1985):212–41.

4. Bruce F. Johnston, Allan Hoben, Dirk W. Dijkerman, and William K. Jaeger, "An Assessment of AID Activities to Promote Agricultural and Rural Development in Sub-Saharan Africa," MADIA Working Paper (Africa—Technical Department, Agriculture Divison, Washington, D.C., 1987).

5. Deutsches Institut für Entwicklungspolitik (DIE), "Strukturverzerrungen und Anspassungsprogramme in den armen Ländern Afrikas" (Berlin, 1985), 273ff.

11 *Food Aid and Development in the* MADIA *Countries*

John W. Mellor and Rajul Pandya-Lorch

FOOD AID is an unusually controversial form of foreign assistance.[1] In developed and developing countries alike, the politics of food—encompassing all of the policy issues influencing production and consumption, as well as trade—are important and complex. The effective use of food aid, particularly for rural infrastructural development and the alleviation of poverty, requires more complex projects and policies by donor institutions and recipient countries than do other forms of aid and consequently is more susceptible to management imperfections. Moreover, rural development and poverty alleviation are themselves politically controversial activities that further complicate and obfuscate food aid policy.

In developing countries, the politics of food and food aid are crucial to human well-being and even survival. A large proportion of the population spends 50–80 percent of its income on food. In such circumstances, temporary shortages of food—due to unanticipated bad weather, poor stock policy, inadequate planning with respect to commercial or food aid imports, or purposive actions by foreign assistance donors—all bear heavily on a large mass of the poor. Governments wish to avoid food shortages and to shift the blame if they do arise.

Furthermore, if the reliability of food aid is in question, it may be politically prudent not to use it for long-term poverty alleviation or rural development projects for fear of the economic and social repercussions resulting from sudden stoppages.[2]

In addition, there are fears that extensive reliance on food aid would have negative disincentive effects on recipient countries' food production and would lead to extended dependence on donor countries. Yet the record of countries that were recipients of large amounts of food aid two decades ago refutes these fears: These countries now no longer rely on food aid but meet their consumption needs through accelerated rates of domestic production growth and commercial imports.[3] The experience of these countries shows that in the past food aid filled a domestic food gap during the time that complex technological changes were being worked out in agriculture.

The politics of food and food aid are different in developed countries—but no less complex and important. On the one hand, food aid can reduce both the cost and the visibility of farm support by providing an outlet for surplus stocks arising from price support policies. This feature makes a dollar of food aid cheaper in political cost than a dollar of financial aid.[4] On the other hand, precisely because food aid may relieve the political pressure to reduce agricultural production by shifting the cost of building food stocks or subsidizing exports from the agricultural budget to the foreign assistance budget, it is opposed by those who seek to force extensive structural adjustment in the agricultural sector of developed countries.

There is also a perception that food aid, when used to forward rural development in recipient developing countries, fosters competition with the farmers of donor countries. However, this tends not to be the case. In fact, high growth rates in food and agricultural production are associated with large food imports in Kenya, for instance—as pointed out in the introduction to this book.[5] The fact that food aid can directly reduce poverty by providing the principal consumption good of the poor should in principle gain it a lobby among humanitarians. However, that lobby seems generally to be missing—in part because of inadequate understanding of the mechanisms and policies by which food aid helps the poor, and in part because of unrealistic expectations of perfection in the administration of food aid.

The conceptualization for the effective use of food aid is based on the developmental effectiveness of increasing employment and hence the consumption of food. From the point of view of attaining optimal development results, employment (and hence returns to labor and food consumption) in the MADIA countries is too low. On the order of one-third to two-thirds of the rural population in the MADIA countries is sufficiently poor to have a nutritionally inadequate diet.[6] Rising real food prices over the past decade have added to that poverty, particularly in the context of increasing landlessness. Most of the rural poor rely on nonfarm sources for a third or more of their income and are often net purchasers of food.[7] Evidence from the work of the International Food Policy Research Institute (IFPRI) in Burkina Faso shows that during the period 1981–85, which included good as well as bad crop years, more than half of total income of a subset of rural households in areas of both low and high potential came from noncropping sources.[8] Purchases comprised 25–50 percent of food consumption, depending on whether it was a good or a bad year.[9]

Large rural development expenditures are needed on infrastructure, education, agricultural improvements (such as contour bunding), irrigation, and reforestation—improvements that at their most efficient require sizable increases in employment and the incomes of the poor. The role of food aid should be to move development expenditure toward an optimal level. Thus food aid can be used both to back higher employment policies that increase demand for food, on the one hand, and to decrease the cost of production by labor-intensive investment, on the other.

Even though food aid should work to reduce poverty primarily by creating assets and growth, it should also be viewed as a means of directly alleviating poverty, especially in the short term. It is unconscionable that any food output should be considered "surplus" and that production capacity should be underutilized in the world's rich countries while vast numbers of people go hungry in the poorer countries. The problem is a lack of imagination as to how to get that food from the rich to the poor without reducing incentives to produce. Food security programs, including stocking and import policies, targeted distribution to the poor, and early famine warning and response programs are all means of meeting this need.

The favorable consumption and production aspects of food aid operate best in the context of small enterprises and local governments.[10] Developing countries, however, tend to be administratively and politically centralized, to have ineffective local governmental structures (especially in rural areas), and to favor relatively large industries.[11] As the introduction to this book shows, it is not an accident that, among the MADIA countries, Kenya—the country most oriented politically and administratively to the rural areas and the country that has done best in agriculture—is the one to have put substantial quantities of food aid to use.

For food aid to be effective, four sets of policy issues must be addressed. First, macroeconomic policies of balanced budgets and market-related pricing policies are as important to the effective use of food aid as they are to other aspects of development. Public specification of domestic food price ranges is essential to ensure that the quantity of food aid received will not depress prices below incentive levels. While setting such prices is conceptually simple, in practice it requires complex administrative and analytic structures.[12] It is now widely recognized that the adjustment programs of the past decade have given inadequate attention to the severity of the short-term effects of higher food prices and lower employment on the poor.

Second, the choice of development strategy, particularly the weight given to the rural areas and to poverty reduction, is particularly important to the use of food aid. Food aid is most effective when combined with a high-employment strategy with the main emphasis on rural development and rural infrastructure. An agriculture-based strategy offers opportunity for accelerated overall growth, broad participation in that growth by low-income people, and accelerated diversification of the economy into nonagricultural sectors.[13] In that context, food aid can provide effective support to employment-oriented investment—stimulating increased employment and incomes to the poor ahead of the increased food production that arises from such a strategy. Indeed, preserving stability in food prices is a difficult to achieve but essential part of such a strategy.

Third, a high-employment, high-food-consumption strategy is dependent on administrative decentralization, as discussed above.

Fourth, the subsectoral issues of agricultural technology and rural infrastructure provision must receive close attention if there are to be high returns to development projects that receive food aid. Without effective policies in these areas, agricultural production and employment growth will lag, and food aid will appear to be responsible. The MADIA study in particular gives special attention to this myriad of complex sectoral and subsectoral issues.

As the comparison of Kenya's and Tanzania's experiences presented later in this chapter will illustrate, food aid is a two-edged sword that may be used in support of policies that foster agricultural and employment growth or in support of those that do not. The real issues relate to macroeconomic, strategic, and sectoral policies, not to the form of aid flows.

Cereal Food Aid in the MADIA Countries

Levels of Food Aid and Production Disincentives

In recent years, food aid to Sub-Saharan Africa—particularly to Ethiopia, Somalia, Sudan, and the Sahelian countries—has been heavily weighted toward emergency "famine" relief.[14] Since none of the MADIA countries have recently experienced widespread famine conditions, the share of Sub-Saharan African food aid received by the MADIA countries is low relative to population. Although the MADIA countries include 40 percent of Sub-Saharan Africa's population and received 25 percent of the region's food aid a decade ago, they now receive only 10 percent.

During the 1970s food aid receipts grew rapidly in the MADIA countries, but they slowed or even turned negative in the 1980s, in contrast to the rest of Sub-Saharan Africa (table 11-1). Nigeria, comprising one-quarter of Sub-Saharan Africa's population, no longer receives food aid because of its oil revenues and perceived foreign exchange availability. This substantially reduces the relative share of food aid to the MADIA countries as a group. Nevertheless, for three of the MADIA

Table 11-1. Growth in Cereal Imports and Food Aid, MADIA and Sub-Saharan Africa, 1971–87
(percent)

	Cereal food aid			Cereal imports		
Country	*1971–80*	*1980–87*	*1971–87*	*1971–80*	*1980–87*	*1971–87*
Cameroon	4.06	4.14	5.12	6.00	10.17	5.89
Kenya	45.28	3.69	44.72	6.02	0.13	15.92
Malawi	39.58	3.57	29.75	−3.76	−16.74	−1.99
Nigeria	−26.67[a]	—	—	23.93	−11.31	9.18
Senegal	12.05	3.03	10.96	3.92	1.46	3.45
Tanzania	40.15	13.96	17.23	6.63	−6.57	6.32
All MADIA countries	15.87	−2.31	13.41	14.58	−6.18	6.99
All MADIA countries, except Nigeria	23.06	−2.13	13.41	5.17	−0.20	5.10
Sub-Saharan Africa	12.95	12.13	15.12	9.73	0.57	7.57
Sub-Saharan Africa, except MADIA	12.42	14.70	15.32	7.22	3.87	7.79

— = Not available.
a. Growth rate for 1971–76 only.
Source: See table 11-2.

countries, Kenya, Senegal, and Tanzania, food aid is a significant form of foreign assistance (figure 11-1).

The MADIA countries illustrate four notable features of food aid practice: substantial support of favorable development policies (Kenya); substantial support of unfavorable development policies (Tanzania); support of food supplies in the face of unfavorable weather and a difficult environment (Senegal); and grossly inadequate use of food aid to redress extreme poverty (Malawi).

Nigeria has received essentially no food aid since the mid-1970s. Food aid has also been insignificant in Cameroon, where it accounted for about 5 percent of cereal imports in 1985–87 and about 1 percent of net disbursements of official development assistance (ODA) (table 11-2). Food aid has been more or less inconsequential in Malawi, where it accounted for less than 1 percent of cereal food consumption over the same period.

Even for the larger recipients, food aid can hardly be said to have significantly depressed agricultural prices. In Kenya, food aid comprised nearly 80 percent of cereal imports averaged over 1985–87 and

Figure 11-1. Volume of Food Aid to the MADIA Countries: Comparison of Totals for 1970/71–1979/80 and 1980/81–1986/87

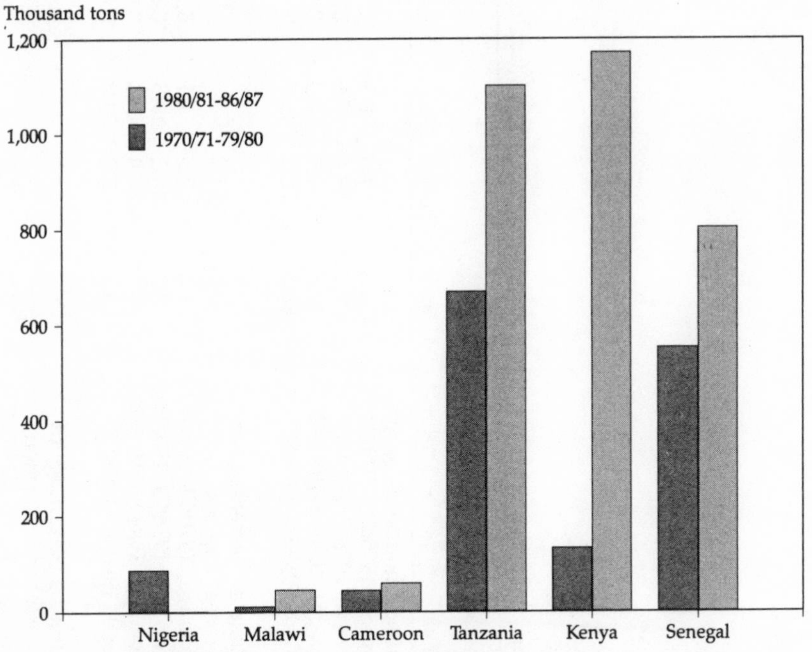

Source: FAO, *Food Aid in Figures*, (Rome, 1983 and 1989).

Table 11-2. Comparison of Food Aid among the MADIA Countries and Sub-Saharan Africa, 1970–87

Food aid	*Cameroon*	*Kenya*	*Malawi*	*Nigeria*	*Senegal*	*Tanzania*	*All MADIA countries*	*All MADIA except Nigeria*	*Sub-Saharan Africa*	*Sub-Saharan Africa, except MADIA*
Volume (thousands of tons)										
Average, 1970/71–1972/73	4.3	1.8	0.3	21.7	30.3	8.0	66.6	44.8	490.2	423.6
Average, 1978/79–1980/81	7.2	89.6	7.9	0.0	91.1	126.2	321.9	321.9	1,723.9	1,402.0
Average, 1984/85–1986/87	10.5	195.3	7.0	0.0	109.5	82.0	404.2	404.2	4,038.4	3,634.2
Total, 1980/81–1986/87	58.8	1,172.2	46.0	1.4	805.3	1,102.1	3,185.7	3,184.3	22,211.2	19,025.5
Volume as percentage of cereal imports										
Average, 1970/71–1972/73	4.5	2.5	1.1	5.0	8.2	8.5	6.1	6.8	13.3	16.3
Average, 1978/79–1980/81	5.3	48.2	19.3	0.0	19.7	51.0	10.3	10.0	21.6	29.0
Average, 1984/85–1986/87	5.1	78.8	42.4	0.0	22.3	30.3	15.8	33.1	44.2	55.3
Total, 1980/81–1986/87	5.1	62.2	20.7	0.0	22.1	58.0	15.7	36.3	35.5	45.0
Volume as percentage of cereal consumption										
Average, 1970/71–1972/73	0.7	0.1	0.0	0.4	4.8	0.7	0.6	0.9	1.8	2.6

Average, 1980/81–1982/83	1.0	7.2	0.6	0.0	13.1	9.7	3.4	4.3	6.7	9.2
Value as percentage of net disbursement of ODA, 1985–87	1.3	10.1	0.9	0.0	5.5	3.0	4.6	4.9	10.4	12.0
Value as percentage of government revenue, 1984–86	0.1[a]	4.0	0.5	0.0	7.7	3.1[b]	0.95	2.7	—	—
ODA as percentage of government revenue, 1984–86	9.2[a]	32.8	65.9	0.5	87.2	48.0[b]	14.5	39.8	—	—

— = Not available.

Note: Cereal food aid data are based on the crop year (July/June), whereas cereal import data are based on the calendar year. Food aid data have been made compatible with data on a calendar-year basis by assuming that the crop year corresponds with the second half of its year. Therefore, crop year 1980/81 is compatible with calendar year 1981. Discrepancies were observed in cereal import figures for any one year in various issues of the *Trade Yearbook*. Therefore, the figure in the yearbook with the most opportunity for revision was taken. For example, if the 1983 figure was available in the 1983, 1984, and 1985 yearbooks, the figure in the 1985 yearbook was accepted.

a. Calculated only for 1984 because data are limited.

b. Calculated only for 1985 because data are limited.

Source: Volume of food aid from FAO, *Food Aid in Figures*, (Rome, various years); value of food aid calculated from information contained in FAO, *Food Aid in Figures*, (Rome various years); cereal imports from FAO, *Trade Yearbook*, (from various years); food consumption from FAO, Supply Utilization Accounts Tape (Rome 1984); net disbursements of ODA from all sources from World Bank, *World Development Report*, (New York: Oxford University Press, various years); and government revenue from IMF, *Government Finance Statistics* (Washington, D.C., 1987).

about 7 percent of cereal consumption over 1981–83 (although the proportion was higher later, because food aid deliveries increased in the mid-1980s). For the period 1981–83 the maximal price depressing effect of food aid in Kenya was at most 3.5 percent.[15] This in turn may have depressed production once and for all by at most 1 percent.[16] Food aid was large enough to have raised total aid flows and total government expenditure. It was a substantial 10 percent of net disbursements of ODA over 1985–87 and 4 percent of government revenue over 1984–86.

Since 1980/81, Tanzania's volume of food aid deliveries has been similar to Kenya's. However, because Tanzania was a larger recipient of financial assistance than Kenya, its food aid made up a much smaller proportion of net disbursement of ODA—3 percent compared with Kenya's 10 percent over 1985–87. In both Kenya and Tanzania, food aid constituted two-thirds of food imports over the period from 1980/81 to 1986/87 (figure 11-2)—a share so large that it might be thought of as offering political leverage in food policy. But at such a small percentage of total aid, especially in the case of Tanzania, the fungibility of resources can easily neutralize such an effort. Note that Tanza-

Figure 11-2. Volume of Food Aid as Percentage of Cereal Imports: Comparison of Totals for 1970/71–1979/80 and 1980/81–1986/87

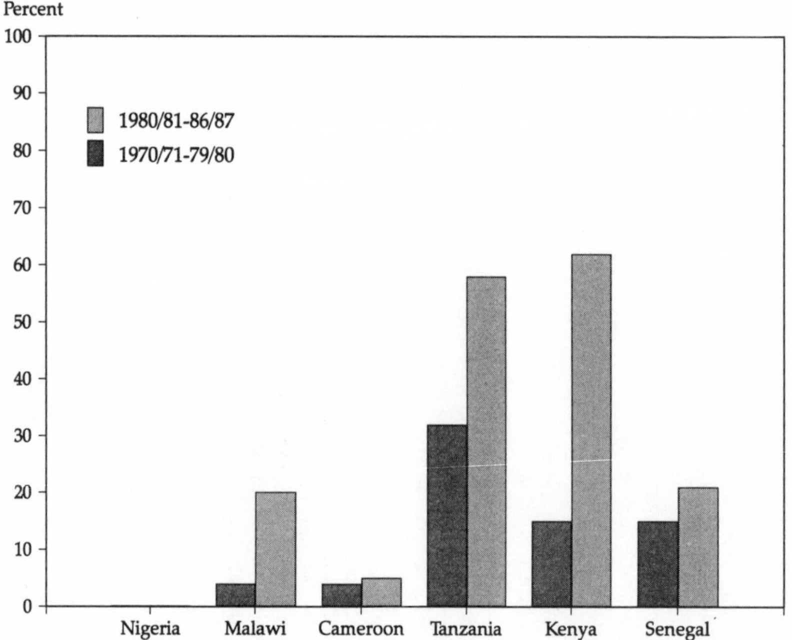

Note: See note to table 11-2.
Source: See figure 11-1.

nia's commercial cereal imports did not decline in the face of sharp declines in food aid in the mid-1980s. The fungibility of foreign exchange and of aid generally allowed maintenance of food imports.

Senegal has been such a large recipient of foreign aid as well as a large cereal importer that it is not surprising that food aid represents a much higher percentage of cereal consumption over 1981–83 (but still only 13 percent) than in the other MADIA countries or in Sub-Saharan Africa as a whole. Consequently, the maximum price-depressing effect of food aid would be higher than for the other countries, but still no more than 6 percent, which in turn would depress production by at most 2 percent. Studies show Senegalese food production to be quite inelastic with respect to price, in large part because of the high fixed costs of developing irrigated rice, a severe shortage of suitable land for rice cultivation, and an inadequate input distribution system.[17] Of course, total cereal imports affected prices greatly—contributing from more than one-half to three-quarters of food consumption. With food aid at about 8 percent of government revenue and 5 percent of net disbursements of ODA, fungibility was high and the food aid leverage low. The introduction to this book emphasizes how large per capita foreign assistance is in Sub-Saharan Africa. The sheer magnitude of the total aid flows ensures that the food aid proportion is at best modest.

As the introductory chapter also shows, during the 1970s, food producer prices were rising in real terms as well as in relation to export crop prices in the MADIA countries (except in Kenya). In the 1980s, structural adjustment and associated policy changes raised export crop prices relative to food prices even as food prices continued their rise relative to nontradables. These price relations appear to have held throughout Sub-Saharan Africa, where real cereal prices were on balance rising throughout the 1970s.[18]

Disincentive effects are widely debated in the food aid literature, but the overall conclusion from a recent review of the literature is that "the debate on the past macroeconomic and agricultural impact of food aid remains inconclusive [and] massive disincentive effects do not seem to have occurred."[19] The price disincentive debate is too closely associated with the argument that getting prices right is the only significant factor in agricultural development. Such a view is particularly unrealistic in the African context. The basic results of the MADIA study presented in this volume and elsewhere emphasize the fundamental importance of nonprice factors in determining production decisions.

Commodity Composition of Food Aid and Distortion of Consumption Patterns

Particularly in Africa, food aid is thought to shift consumer tastes from traditional foods, such as coarse grains and roots, toward wheat and rice, which are thought to be too expensive or unsuitable to produce domestically. Such effects are a function of the commodity composition of food aid, the underlying income and demographic forces influencing taste, and the fungibility of foreign exchange.

There is large variation across the MADIA countries in the commodity composition of food aid—with traditional coarse grains dominant in Malawi, rice in Cameroon, and wheat in Kenya (table 11-3 and figure 11-3). Since the early 1970s, rice food aid to the MADIA countries has grown from insignificant to one-fifth of all cereal food aid. With the concurrent increases in wheat food aid, the share of coarse grains in the MADIA food aid package has declined by half.

Malawi, an insignificant food aid recipient, is the only country whose food aid commodity composition has remained unaltered, with coarse grains continuing to form the bulk of food aid. In contrast, Cameroon, a minor recipient, received no rice food aid in the early 1970s, but by the mid-1980s, more than four-fifths of its food aid consisted of rice. In Kenya, wheat was already dominant in the food aid package in the early 1970s and continues to be so even though the shares of rice and coarse grains have both increased. In Senegal and Tanzania, food aid has been diversified away from coarse grains toward rice and wheat, so that all three commodities are now received in sizable proportions.

Food aid composition reflects the overall shift in cereal consumption toward wheat and rice and away from coarse grains. In the early 1970s, wheat and rice each made up about 5 percent of total cereal consumption in the MADIA countries, but ten years later, the proportions had risen to 10 percent for wheat and 14 percent for rice.[20] The share of maize in cereal consumption has remained constant, and hence the declines that have occurred in coarse grains consumption have been in millet and sorghum. The patterns of cereal consumption differ from country to country, but in all countries rice consumption has risen sharply (from a small initial base).

These shifts in consumption have been going on for a long time. In the case of Senegal, both rice and wheat imports originated in the French colonial era.[21] The principal reason for the shift of food consumption toward rice and wheat has been rapid urbanization, as a result of which consumer demand has shifted toward more convenient foods.

The shift to rice consumption has been at least as evident among low-income as among high-income urban consumers. For instance, low-income urban consumers in Ouagadougou, Burkina Faso, spend a somewhat higher proportion of their income on rice than do high-income urban consumers.[22] Similarly, although a decline in relative rice prices at the international level has no doubt favored a shift in

Table 11-3. Commodity Composition of Cereal Food Aid, MADIA *Countries and Sub-Saharan Africa, 1970–87*
(percent)

Country	*Average share in total cereal aid, 1970/71–1972/73*			*Average share in total cereal aid, 1984/85–1986/87*		
	Wheat	*Rice*	*Coarse grains*	*Wheat*	*Rice*	*Coarse grains*
Cameroon	46.2	0.0	53.8	0.0	87.2	12.7
Kenya	83.6	0.0	16.4	65.8	7.2	27.0
Malawi	10.0	0.0	90.0	6.7	1.9	91.8
Nigeria	24.9	0.0	75.1	—	—	—
Senegal	10.6	0.0	89.4	23.9	28.7	47.4
Tanzania	23.3	0.0	76.7	43.9	26.5	29.6
All MADIA countries	21.1	0.0	78.9	47.3	18.9	33.8
All MADIA countries, except Nigeria	19.3	0.0	80.74	47.3	18.9	33.8
Sub-Saharan Africa	55.8	3.72	40.5	53.2	14.4	32.3
Sub-Saharan Africa, except MADIA countries	61.3	4.31	34.4	53.9	13.9	32.2

— = Not available.
Source: Calculated from FAO, *Food Aid in Figures,* (Rome, various years).

Figure 11-3. Commodity Composition of Cereal Food Aid: Comparison of Totals for 1970/71–1979/80 and 1980/81–1986/87
(percentage shares in total cereal aid)

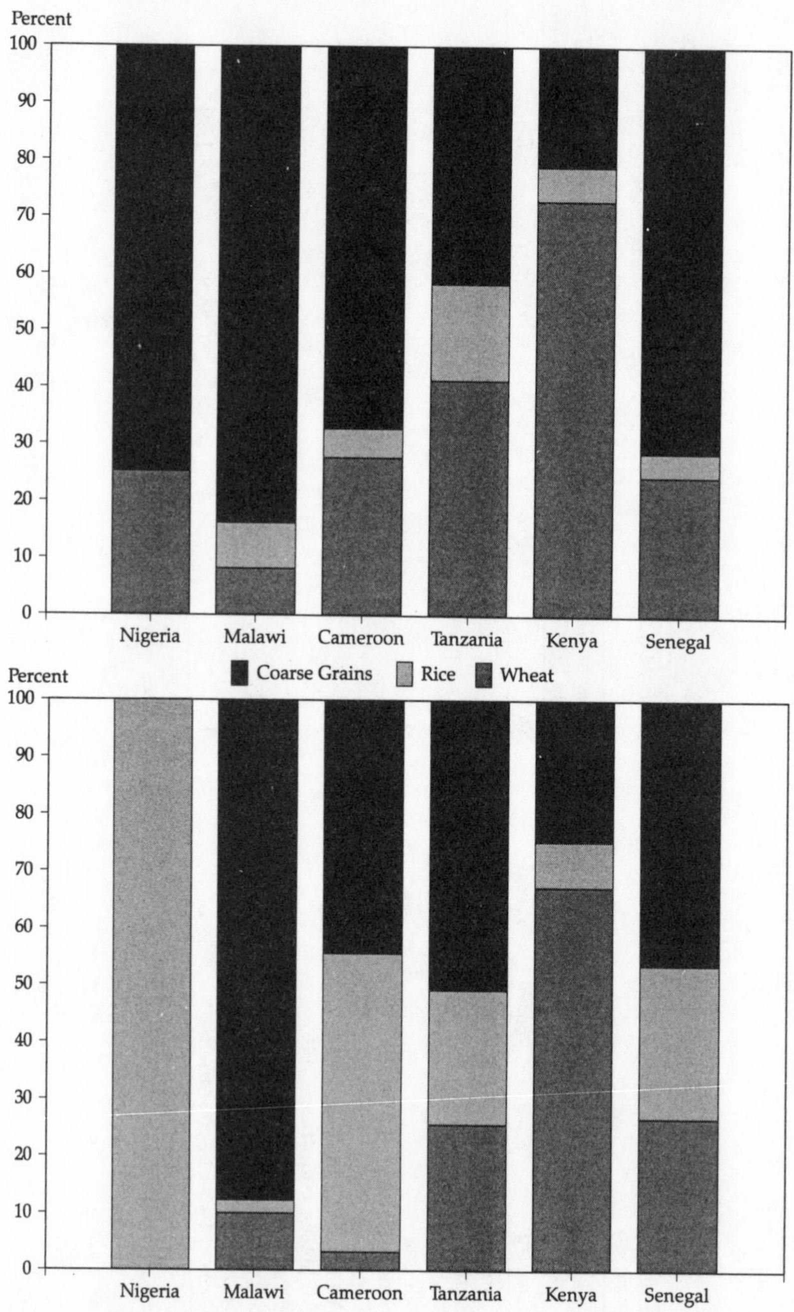

Source: See figure 11-1.

consumption toward rice, there is little evidence that food aid has pushed those relations in African countries further in that direction.[23]

IFPRI research in West Africa suggests that nonprice factors such as income distribution, the need to eat away from home, and occupation may be more important in driving the rice and wheat consumption at both household and national levels.[24] Evidence from consumer surveys also suggests that it is the increasing value of time, especially women's time, that is driving the increased consumption of wheat and rice. Studies from Sri Lanka show that the increasing value of women's time is the most important explanation of increased wheat consumption.[25] It is the fungibility of overall foreign exchange availability that is facilitating these underlying taste changes.

Food aid can be adapted by innovations such as triangular transactions and local purchases to address lingering issues of commodity composition.[26] Triangular transactions in particular have several advantages: They provide commodities indigenous to the region, such as white maize; they encourage food production in the region by providing a market; they help overcome some of the hurdles of transportation and distribution, and thus lower costs; and they encourage intraregional trade. Triangular transactions in Sub-Saharan Africa have averaged about 375,000 tons annually in recent years and have been rising steadily each year.[27] The somewhat different timing of fluctuations in production—even among adjacent countries—further increases the benefits from such arrangements.[28]

Fluctuations in Food Aid, Cereal Import Flows, and Production Instability

Year-to-year fluctuations in food production are particularly large in Sub-Saharan Africa. A thirty-country study found that a third of these countries have a 25 percent probability of a 5 percent decline in food consumption, that is, once every four years.[29] Furthermore, variability in cereal production has increased over time.[30] The poor are hit particularly hard by production shortfalls; typically, the reduction in consumption that they make in response to a given reduction in supplies is ten times that of the rich (when the bottom 20 percent is compared with the top 5 percent in income distribution).[31]

Cereal production fluctuates considerably in all MADIA countries, although to a lesser extent in Cameroon (see figure 11-4, which illustrates deviations from trend cereal production plotted against food aid receipts). Food aid has an obvious natural role in reducing fluctuations in food supplies and consequent privation for the poor by arriving at a time countercyclical to deviations from trend cereal production; that is, when deviations from trend production are negative—which

Figure 11-4. Cereal Food Aid and Fluctuations in Cereal Production, 1971–87

Countries with Insignificant Food Aid Receipts

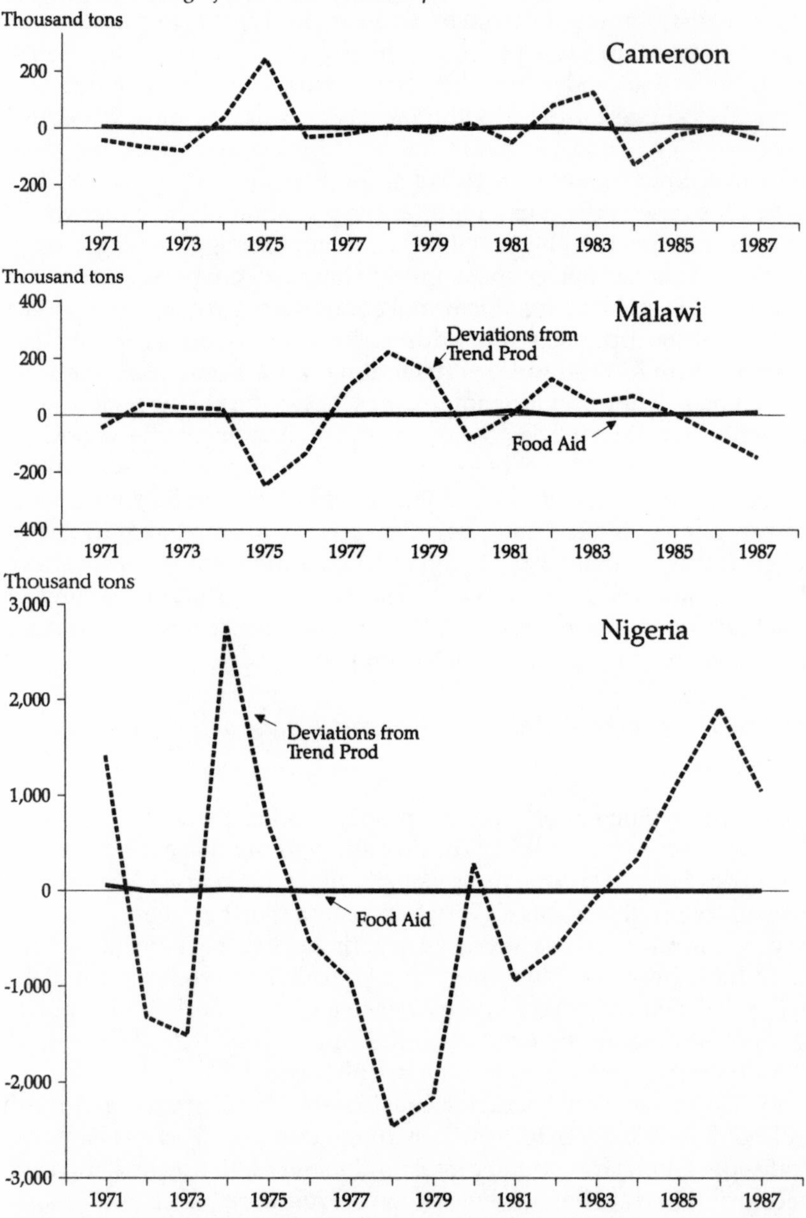

Note: Food aid data is on a crop year (July/June) basis, and is plotted at the conclusion of its period. For example, food aid in crop year 1970–71 is plotted in mid–1971. Production is on a calendar year basis. Trend production is obtained for 1971–87 and deviations calculated by subtracting trend from actual production.

Countries with Significant Food Aid Receipts

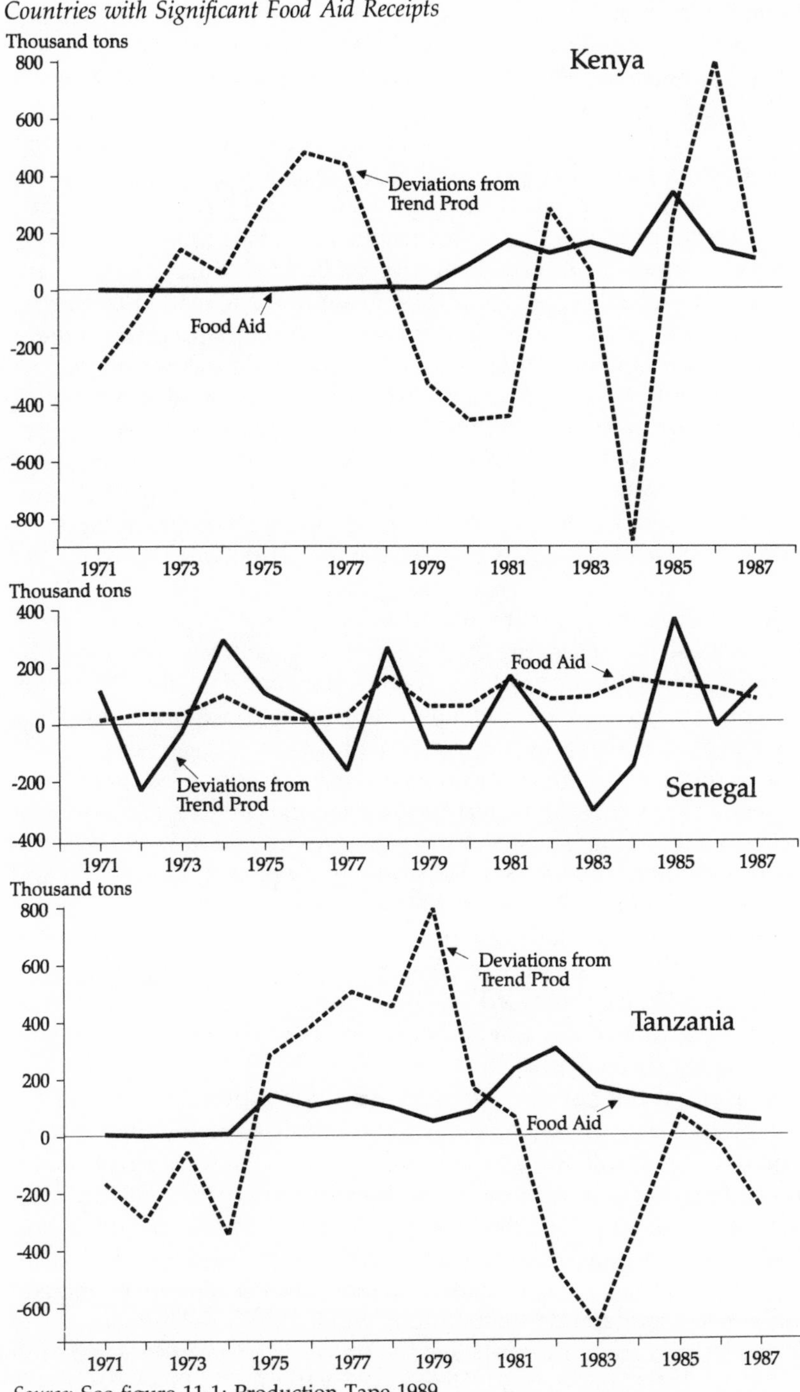

Source: See figure 11-1; Production Tape 1989.

implies actual production is below trend levels—food aid receipts should increase to stabilize cereal supplies, and vice versa.

Food aid has not played that stabilizing role in Cameroon, Malawi, and Nigeria, since it has been received in insignificant quantities.

In Senegal, cereal food aid receipts appear to be on the whole destabilizing to total cereal availability—increasing when cereal production rises above the trend and decreasing or remaining steady when cereal production is below trend. In Kenya, food aid made an inconsequential contribution toward stabilization during most of the 1970s, since actual cereal production exceeded longer-term trend production for most of the decade. Since then, as cereal production registered below trend levels for several years, food aid has been stabilizing. The exception was an aberrant two years in the mid-1980s, when food aid was quite destabilizing; increasing during years of positive production growth and declining in years of negative growth, it moved out of sync with production. It is plausible that the Kenyan government has played a role in steering food aid in a stabilizing direction in the context of its stated food policy.[32] In Tanzania, food aid has been stabilizing in most years, except in the most recent period.

Several factors contribute to food aid's poor performance as a stabilizer in these countries. On the recipient side, although several of the countries have food price and stabilization policies, they have not brought management of food aid explicitly into those strategies. Food aid is in many cases still perceived as a resource of last resort instead of as a regular stabilizing mechanism. On the donor side, although the Food Aid Convention has promoted some degree of stability in food aid shipments, since donor obligations are laid down in terms of tonnage (which is not affected by rising grain prices), donors can and do vary the volume of program food aid from year to year in response to variations in their own food production, and in response to political factors, which are unlikely to mesh with recipient needs. Moreover, donors have hardly focused on the issues of food supply and price instability and its onerous effects on the poor. The latter may in part be a failure to recognize the extent to which a large and growing proportion of the poor in rural Africa are net purchasers of food.

Timing of delivery is obviously important in determining whether food aid is a stabilizing or destabilizing factor. Kenya, which had a record food harvest in 1985, was in the same year still receiving food aid in response to the 1984 drought.[33] Slow domestic handling and distribution of food aid is another source of destabilization. The situation is one of some concern in Africa—not least because an inadequate and poorly maintained transportation and institutional infrastructure, particularly in rural areas, delays the transportation and distribution of food aid. In Sudan, only 64 percent of the food aid pledged was distributed in 1984–85, even though 91 percent was delivered to the ports. In Ethiopia during the same period, only three-fourths of the food aid delivered was actually distributed.[34] All the MADIA countries are deficient in rural infrastructure.[35] Hence the use of food aid to build rural infrastructure will indirectly also address the problem of food aid distribution itself. Thus, although food aid in the MADIA countries has had few deleterious effects on food production and consumption, it has had little favorable effect on food supply stability.

It is particularly harmful, in the contemporary context of privatization and appeals to market pricing systems, for food prices to fluctuate widely in response to internal and external supply and demand shifts. Since food trade is an important means of reducing food price fluctuations, it is important that food aid donors reform their policies so as to use food aid to stabilize rather than to destabilize domestic food prices. Even with effective trade policies, however, domestic stock policies are needed.[36] Thus food aid should also be used to help build and stock necessary storage.

Another feature of stabilization neglected by food aid donors is the potential for poor people to follow income-stabilizing strategies. IFPRI research shows that ten times the amount of food aid went to Sahelian households compared with Sudanian households in the 1984–85 drought in Burkina Faso—despite the fact that Sahelian zone households earned 25 percent more income and were much less likely to be hungry.[37] Food aid was targeted to areas that were thought to be suffering more in terms of crop output—but the purchasing power of households was not taken into account. It would be better if the short-run emergency food aid were targeted to areas with the lowest purchasing power and the greatest dependence on cropping outcomes and hence with the least diversification of incomes.

It should be noted that since food aid sales are a significant source of public sector revenue for recipient governments, they may also press for deliveries in good crop years. The lack of stabilization in the use of food aid is not entirely the fault of donors—all the more reason then for recipient governments to understand the need for stability and to develop the necessary analytical capacity.

Sources of Food Aid and Donor Leverage

Food aid to the MADIA countries is characterized, on the one hand, by the presence of a dominant donor (the United States) and, on the other hand, by a multiplicity of donors who intermittently enter and exit the food aid arena, usually responding in times of crises. Such donors have included Norway, Sweden, and the Netherlands. Even India and China have provided food aid in some years. The fact that the weight of various donors varies among the recipients (figure 11-5) is potentially advantageous for the quantity and quality of aid flows, as donors pursue their respective comparative advantages (a point underlined by many components of the MADIA study).

In general, the United States is the only donor with sufficient food aid weight to influence policy—and even in that case, only for a portion of the MADIA countries. However, the scope for individual donors to influence policy is illustrated by the consistent efforts of the European Communities (EC) in Kenya to help build food security in the context of market liberalization by using its food aid in support of those policies.

The United States is the source of two-fifths of the cereal food aid delivered to the MADIA group (see table 11-4). The EC (European Economic Communities Action), plus European bilateral donors, are, in sum, the next largest category of donors. The contributions of Australia and Canada together are nearly half as large as those of the European Economic Communities Action and European bilateral donors combined.

Food aid is also received through multilateral channels. Shipments through the World Food Program (WFP), the premier multilateral food aid agency, make up 10 percent of cereal aid shipments to the MADIA countries.[38] Malawi is the exception, in that more than 90 percent of its cereal food aid deliveries are channeled through WFP. Clearly, bilateral sources of cereal food aid on a government-to-government basis or through nongovernmental organizations predominate.

In Cameroon, Kenya, and Senegal, the United States has been the source of half or more of the cereal food aid receipts in recent years. However, there was no one dominant donor to Tanzania, and no one donor has provided more than one-fifth of Tanzania's cereal aid receipts since 1981–82. Tanzania has received cereal aid from almost two dozen donors, with Japan, followed closely by Australia, being the country's largest source of cereal aid.

Despite the dominance of the United States, the very existence of a multiplicity of donors offers scope for policy innovation as well as stabilization—provided that effective policy frameworks exist in the recipient country. Note how the use of food aid for development in India followed a consistent and reliable pattern in the context of clear policy and dynamic leadership from the recipient.

From the donors' perspective, none of the MADIA countries is currently an important recipient of food aid. Except for Australia, less than 10 percent of any individual donor's food aid was targeted toward the MADIA group; and even in Australia's case it never exceeded 15 percent. The United States, the largest source of food aid to the region,

Figure 11-5. Sources of Cereal Food Aid, 1981/82–1986/87

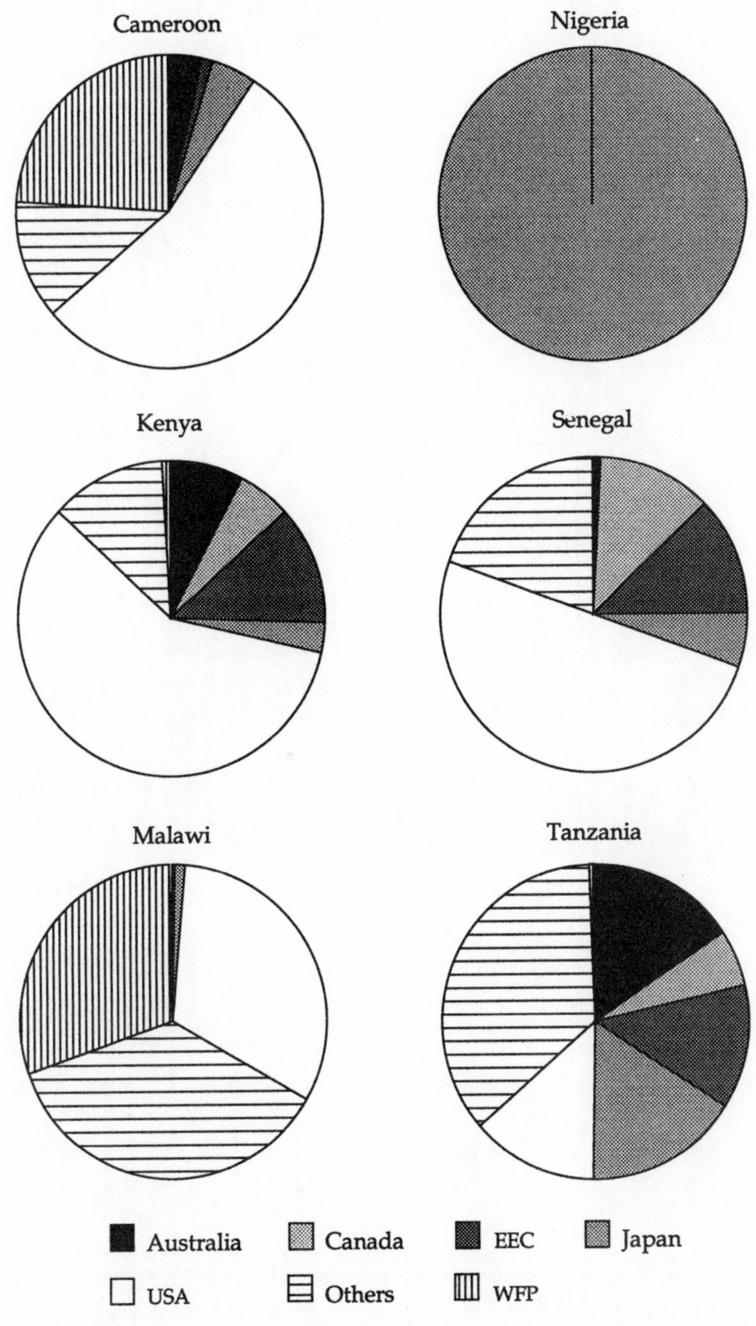

Source: See figure 11-1.

Table 11-4. Sources of Cereal Aid, MADIA *Countries, 1981/82–1986/87*
(thousand tons)

Donor	Cameroon	Kenya	Malawi	Nigeria	Senegal	Tanzania	MADIA	Cameroon	Kenya	Malawi	Nigeria	Senegal	Tanzania	MADIA
	Total volume of cereal aid received from donors[a]							*Percentage of donors in cereal aid receipts*[a]						
Australia	1.7	80.0	0.1	—	5.8	137.2	224.8	3.7	8.0	0.4	—	0.9	15.8	8.7
Canada	0.6	54.5	—	—	78.5	48.7	182.3	1.3	5.5	—	—	12.1	5.6	7.0
EEC (European Economic Community Action)	—	120.8	—	—	78.8	110.7	310.3	—	12.1	—	—	12.2	12.8	12.0
Japan	2.2	32.1	0.3	1.4	35.7	139.1	210.8	4.7	3.2	1.2	100.0	5.5	16.1	8.1
United States	25.3	582.2	9.0	—	323.2	115.2	1,054.9	54.4	58.4	31.9	—	49.9	13.3	40.8
Other MADIA donors[b]	—	32.5	3.8	—	42.8	80.8	159.9	—	3.3	13.5	—	6.6	9.3	6.2
Other European[c]	5.7	71.4	6.4	—	42.8	120.8	247.1	12.3	7.2	22.7	—	6.6	13.9	9.6
WFP purchases	11.0	7.4	8.5	—	0.4	2.7	30.0	23.7	0.7	30.1	—	0.1	0.3	1.2
Others	—	16.0	0.1	—	39.6	111.3	167.0	—	1.6	0.4	—	6.1	12.8	6.5
Total	46.5	996.9	28.2	1.4	647.6	866.5	2,587.1	100.0	100.0	100.0	100.0	100.0	100.0	100.0
WFP shipments[d]	(15.9)	(90.1)	(26.2)	(0.0)	(61.4)	(47.5)	(241.1)	34.2	9.0	92.9	0.0	9.5	5.5	9.3

— = Not available.

a. Multilateral shipments of food aid, particularly those channeled through the WFP, are already included under individual donors. No breakdown is available on what proportion of an individual donor's aid to a specific recipient country was channeled through WFP. Total WFP shipments to the recipient country are presented separately.

b. Includes Denmark, France, Germany, Sweden, and the United Kingdom.

c. Includes Belgium, Italy, Luxembourg, the Netherlands, Norway, Spain, and Switzerland.

d. WFP cereal food aid shipments (project and emergency) are on a calendar-year basis. The sum for the years 1982–87 is presented here. Any proportions in the second half of the table should only be treated as indicative.

Source: FAO, *Food Aid in Figures* (various years); World Food Program, personal communication from J. M. Boucher, chief, Policy and Data Analysis Branch, 23 June 1989.

at no stage allocated more than 4 percent of its worldwide food aid shipments to the MADIA countries.[39]

Types of Cereal Food Aid and Development Effect

The distribution of cereal food aid in its three conventional categories of nonproject (program), project, and emergency aid varies widely among the MADIA countries (table 11-5).[40] Cameroon and Malawi have received virtually no nonproject cereal food aid. The bulk of Cameroon's cereal food aid receipts have consisted of project aid—except in the drought year of 1984/85, when emergency aid made up more than 85 percent of cereal food aid receipts. Until very recently, Malawi has received only project cereal food aid; since 1987, however, emergency cereal food aid, provided largely in response to the sudden inflow of Mozambiqan refugees, has become important.

Kenya, in contrast, has a clear predominance of nonproject aid in its cereal food aid receipts, with significant volumes of project and emergency cereal food aid received in crisis years. In the crisis year of 1984/85 almost half of all cereal food aid receipts consisted of project aid; otherwise, it made up about one-tenth. Nonproject cereal food aid also predominates in Senegal, but emergency cereal food aid plays an important role. In 1983/84, for instance, about three-fifths of cereal food aid was directed toward emergency relief, compared with just 4 percent the year before. In Tanzania, there has been no clear pattern; in some years project aid has dominated cereal food aid receipts, whereas in other years nonproject aid has been dominant. In both Kenya and Tanzania, however, emergency cereal food aid did not even at its height exceed one-fifth of all cereal food aid receipts, whereas in Senegal it did so in most years.

The share of project aid in total cereal food aid has been quite small in the first place, and in most countries it has declined in recent years. In Sub-Saharan Africa as a whole, the share of total cereal food aid allocated for project purposes declined by half in five years—from 35 percent in 1982/83 to 16 percent in 1987/88—whereas the share of cereal food aid for emergency purposes more than doubled.[41] In the MADIA countries, the volume of project cereal food aid receipts has been on a declining trend in Cameroon, Senegal, and Tanzania since 1980, and it shows a positive but insignificant trend in Kenya and Malawi. The positive trend in Malawi is in fact quite deceptive, given recent refugee inflows; the share of project aid in total cereal food aid receipts dropped from 100 percent to 2 percent from 1985/86 to 1987/88, or to just one-third their previous volume. The positive trend in project cereal food aid receipts is also quite deceptive in Kenya, since it is influenced by the drought year of 1984/85, when project food aid

Table 11-5. Shares of Project, Emergency, and Nonproject Food Aid in Total Cereal Food Aid Receipts, MADIA *Countries, 1979/80–1987/88*
(percent)

Country	*1979/80*	*1980/81*	*1981/82*	*1982/83*	*1983/84*	*1984/85*	*1985/86*	*1986/87*	*1987/88*
Cameroon									
Project	100	64	100	100	100	14	75	90	80
Emergency	0	36	0	0	0	86	25	10	20
Nonproject	0	0	0	0	0	0	0	0	0
Kenya									
Project	17	5	6	9	15	47	3	3	11
Emergency	8	13	19	0	0	16	0	1	16
Nonproject	75	82	75	91	85	37	97	96	73
Malawi									
Project	60	32	100	100	100	100	100	54	2
Emergency	40	0	0	0	0	0	0	46	95

Nonproject	0	68	0	0	0	0	0	0	3
Nigeria									
Project	0	0	0	0	0	0	0	0	0
Emergency	0	0	0	0	0	0	0	0	0
Nonproject	0	0	0	0	0	100	100	0	0
Senegal									
Project	50	43	77	32	9	20	21	38	24
Emergency	42	52	23	4	62	40	28	3	25
Nonproject	8	5	0	64	29	40	50	59	50
Tanzania									
Project	75	63	19	20	93	4	99	76	12
Emergency	0	4	16	8	7	18	1	2	23
Nonproject	25	32	65	73	0	79	0	22	65

Note: Percentages may not add up to 100 because of rounding.
Source: World Food Program, personal communication from J. M. Boucher, chief, Policy and Data Analysis Branch, (December 1, 1989).

receipts shot up, as did other cereal food aid receipts; since then, project food aid receipts have declined to about 5 percent of 1984/85 levels.

In summary, two points stand out in examining project cereal food aid receipts in the MADIA countries: first, project cereal food aid receipts have been declining, a trend that has unfortunate consequences from the point of view of project development in the recipient countries; and second, project cereal food aid receipts have fluctuated significantly from year to year, which also has unfortunate consequences from the point of view of building institutional capacities in both donor agencies and recipient countries.

The decline in project cereal food aid is a reflection of food emergencies and the need for general foreign exchange and budget support. It probably also reflects disenchantment with projects arising from the poor performance documented throughout the MADIA study. Food aid projects do not stand out as exceptions to this finding. However, the appropriate way to deal with project implementation problems is not by avoiding them. The kinds of projects most appropriate to food aid—for example, rural roads, school feeding, soil conservation, and reforestation—are important, and the capacity to do such projects needs to be increased. Well-conceived food aid projects could play a large role in building that capacity. The failure to do so is a serious deficiency of food aid in the MADIA countries.

The Development Context of Food Aid

Food aid is in principle a resource transfer not particularly different from any other resource transfer. It can be sold in the market in place of commercial food imports and thus be converted into any other imported or domestically produced goods and services, with the same effects as financial aid; or it can be sold on the market as an increment to domestic food supplies, with the same effects as financial aid used to finance increased food imports; or it can be used to finance specific projects, by payment in kind or by sales and cash payments, and the projects so financed may or may not have a large employment and hence food content. The projects it helps finance may reduce the costs of agricultural production, for example, by rural roads construction; or they may not, for example, by direct feeding programs in urban areas. Food aid may be used to condition policy at the macroeconomic, sectoral, subsectoral, and project level, or it may not be used for those purposes. Thus the issue is not how food aid can be used, but rather how it is used and whether that usage differs from other forms of aid.

The MADIA countries illustrate four sharply different development contexts in which food aid has been received. Kenya illustrates the use of food aid in a context of substantial economic growth, which in turn has spurred growth in the demand for food beyond what can be produced domestically even with reasonably encouraging domestic results. In Tanzania, food aid has been used to maintain policies inimical to growth, which without food aid would have had a particularly harsh impact on the poor. Tanzania also demonstrates that fungibility of aid can prevent a reduction of food aid alone from having an effective policy conditioning role. Senegal demonstrates the use of food aid to combat food shortages arising from both poor weather and adverse policies. And Malawi illustrates lost opportunities in which food aid, if received in sufficient quantities, could have been particularly effective in alleviating poverty and contributing to growth.

The Kenyan economy experienced broadly based growth and development in both the agricultural and nonagricultural sectors as a result of well-designed and favorable development policies. That growth, combined with one of the highest population growth rates in the world and reinforced by the heavy weight of noncereal commodities in agricultural growth, generated a rate of growth in demand for food well beyond the capacity of even the most effective domestic food production policies. Increased food imports were vital to the pro-agriculture, pro-employment strategy. If the increased food demand had not been met by imports, food prices would have soared, with severe political and economic consequences. Food aid was a highly effective means of providing food. Paying for those food imports with food aid made unnecessary a reallocation of foreign exchange that would have slowed imports of capital goods and intermediate products, which are themselves essential to the development strategy. Having made this case, it is notable that not even Kenya has dealt with food aid explicitly in its food policy and regulated the flow with a clear domestic price policy objective. Nevertheless, the process has worked reasonably well.

A state of continuous crisis has characterized the Tanzanian economy for much of the period from the mid-1970s until recently.[42] The agricultural sector basically collapsed in the face of a development strategy that rhetorically favored the agricultural sector, rural investments, rural participation, and decentralization, but that in practice favored capital-intensive urban industrialization and inefficient parastatal growth. The poor performance of the agricultural sector in Tanzania is explained by a combination of factors: increased government expenditures on defense and industry at the expense of agriculture; frequent changes in institutional arrangements; a variety of experiments, such as Ujamaa in the agricultural sector; and implicit and explicit taxation of the agricultural sector, particularly export crops such as coffee.[43]

Policies toward the rural sector, including the lack of maintenance of rural infrastructure and lack of incentive goods for purchase, helped to reduce the commercialization of agriculture. At the same time, large foreign assistance flows allowed rapid growth in public employment and in urban growth generally—urbanization has been proceeding at growth rates exceeding 10 percent since 1965 (well beyond those of Kenya).[44] The result of these divergent forces in the rural and urban sectors was a large increase in food imports to meet the needs of the urban populace while food supplies for the rural population were maintained. In the period 1980–84, food imports were two-thirds greater than they had been during 1975–79. Food aid provided one-third of the marketed sales of the preferred cereals from 1975 to 1981.[45]

These are the very reasons why some argue that without food aid, the reform of agricultural and urban policies would have been forced at an early stage. However, this seems not to have been the case. Although food aid clearly facilitated these policies, they were so entrenched that the drop in food aid in 1982, following donor disenchantment, did not have the intended result of a significant decline in food imports and a forcing of higher food prices and more pro-agricultural development policies. It was foreign aid more generally and its fungibility that facilitated Tanzania's policies, its neglect of agriculture, its rapid urbanization, and the consequent rapid growth of food imports. Conversely, selected conditionality by the donor community as a whole with respect to its total resource transfers has played an important role in policy changes in Tanzania since 1986.

Senegal is another MADIA economy existing in a state of crisis since the late 1970s. In its case, the crisis is the result of a combination of poor financial and investment policies, declining terms of trade, and successive droughts.[46] For the period 1960–87, Senegal's agricultural growth rate of 1.2 percent was the lowest in the MADIA countries with the exception of Nigeria, and its per capita GNP growth rate of -0.9 percent was the lowest of all.[47] With its long-standing comparative advantage in groundnut production, Senegal has a consequent long history of food imports. About 90 percent of all marketed food is imported.[48] Senegal's problem is perhaps less one of food imports per se than one of failure to preserve vigorously its comparative advantage in groundnuts through continuous research and technological development—and, of course, a long period of historically low rainfall.[49] The result has been dependence on food aid rather than growth that could have eventually led to the self-reliance of commercially financed food imports.

As it was, without food imports, food prices would have increased greatly, causing marked privation among the poor; and without the food aid component, foreign assistance development expenditures no doubt would have been lower. Food aid makes up about a fifth to a quarter of all cereal imports. Senegal, aware of the difficulties it faces in attempting to meet its food deficits with local production, has well-developed institutional mechanisms in place for handling and distributing food aid internally. To improve donor coordination, a common counterpart fund to which most food aid donors contribute, and which is administered by the WFP, was established. Food aid has been important to Senegal in the face of natural disaster; but in contrast to Kenya, Senegal has not received food aid in the context of an effective national strategy of agricultural development.

Malawi epitomizes a country that could have benefited from food aid but that did not receive it in significant volumes until recently—and even then, not so much for its own population as for refugees from neighboring countries. Despite its exceptionally low income and nutritional status, Malawi in fact has been a net exporter of food, reflecting not so much excellence in food production as poor income distribution and hence slow growth in the demand for food.[50] Relative to the other MADIA countries, Malawi has the highest proportion of its rural population living in absolute poverty and nutritional deprivation. Nutrition surveys in particular have documented the extensive prevalence of child malnutrition and consequent wasting and stunting in Malawi for some time.[51]

How could food aid have been effectively used in larger quantities to increase food consumption by a large, malnourished population? The means is through a development strategy that raises incomes of smallholder farmers—presumably in part through a faster growth rate in food production, but probably also by accelerated growth in export crops and in the rural nonagricultural activities stimulated by rising agricultural incomes. The net effect of such forces, as in Kenya, undoubtedly would have been effective demand for food rising beyond the domestic capacity to produce—and hence food imports increasing and a full return to aid in the form of food. In addition, food aid should have filled the gap in low-production years, so that the poor would not have had to reduce consumption in those lean periods. It should have formed part of a carefully defined food security program.

The Future Role of Food Aid

Absorptive Capacity for Food Aid

The total amount of donor food aid is dependent on production trends in donor countries, which are driven by their domestic policies and technological development, as well as by global supply and demand balances and consequent prices. On the assumption that food aid may grow or be reallocated to the MADIA countries, one may ask how much they could absorb without depressing domestic prices or straining administrative capacity. An appropriate answer can be derived from inspecting past trends in food imports and by projecting future supply-demand balances. Inspection of those variables makes it clear that future absorptive capacity for food aid is immense. The problem is rather one of determining appropriate strategies and projects.

If one simply projects past trends for production and consumption for Sub-Saharan Africa, the future gap between food production and consumption widens immensely.[52] A recent IFPRI study projected the food gap of leading food crops (cereals and noncereals) would widen more than sixfold—from 8 million tons in the beginning of the 1980s to 50 million tons in the year 2000.[53] Another IFPRI study conducted specifically on food aid projected demand-based food aid requirements in the year 2000 by measuring the gap between (a) projected past trends in domestic supply and demand and (b) a formula-based estimate of commercial food imports.[54] The trend rate of growth of total imports represented by this gap is also one that has been managed by growth in the physical and institutional capacity of each country and thus represents a reasonable basis for projecting that absorptive capacity. The results for the MADIA countries are presented in table 11-6. In the case of Tanzania, they show a declining capability to absorb increased food supplies—a result that at first glance seems peculiar, but is not unreasonable, given a continuing decline in institutional capacity for a wide range of activities. All the other countries show rapid growth in the capacity to absorb food imports without a depressing effect on domestic relative food prices. Food aid requirements or absorptive capacity, by this calculation, are shown as largest in the case of Nigeria, but even in the other countries, the quantities projected are at least ten times the volume of food aid received during 1984–86.

The exercise of projecting past trends into the future magnifies, of course, nascent imbalances and should suggest corrective action to both aid donors and recipients. It is unlikely that imports of the magnitude shown will occur, although it should be noted that the same view about today's imports was widely expressed when the current level of imports was projected by IFPRI over a decade ago![55] But the point remains that how much food aid can be received is not likely to be restrained by inadequate secular growth in absorptive capacity or by inadequate effective demand.

More Attention for Project Use of Food Aid

It is clear throughout the MADIA studies that the necessary conditions for an improved macro environment must be accompanied by

Table 11-6. Projected Absorptive Capacity for Food Aid to the Year 2000
(thousands of metric tons)

Country	*Volume of food aid*		
	Actual average, 1984–86	*Established absorption, year 2000*	*Average annual increments*
Cameroon	8.9	1,910	126.7
Kenya	200.3	5,030	321.9
Malawi	4.8	1,260	83.7
Nigeria	0.0	12,190	812.7
Senegal	132.9	1,250	74.5
Tanzania	110.7	0	—
All MADIA countries	457.6	21,640	1,419.6

— = Not available.

Note: Average annual increments are derived by dividing the difference between year 2000 and of 1984–86 by 15, which is the number of years.

Source: Estimates for year 2000 are from Hannan Ezekiel, "Medium-Term Estimates of Demand-Based Food Aid Requirements and Their Variability" (update), December 1988. Estimate for Nigeria from additional work carried out later. Food aid requirements in this study are defined as "that part of the food import requirements of developing countries determined at a reasonable price level that are not filled by commercial food imports." The food import requirements themselves are defined as "the gap between total domestic use (TDU) and the total domestic production of food." Production is projected on the basis of past trends in growth of each staple food growth. Total domestic use is projected as the sum of its various components, which in turn have been projected as follows: (i) Per capita food consumption is projected on the basis of trend rates of growth of per capita GNP and FAO projections of relevant income elasticities of demand and applied to trend per capita consumption in 1983; population projections are then used to obtain the total *food use.* (ii) *Feed use* is estimated in a similar way to food use, but the income elasticity of the demand for meat is used as a proxy for the income elasticity of the demand for feed. (iii) *Seed use* is projected as a proportion of production (the proportion having been established in the base period. (iv) *Other uses* is projected as a proportion of the sum of food and feed uses (the proportion having been established in the base period). The sum of the projections of these four uses is the estimate for future total domestic use. Gross commercial imports are assumed to grow at the growth rate of per capita GNP; (v) exports are assumed to remain a constant proportion of production based on the period 1979–83. Actual figures from FAO, *Food Aid in Figures,* (Rome, various years).

improved projects if development is to occur. It is particularly important that attention be given to the project aspects of food aid. On the one hand, food is the key element in labor-intensive projects, which require technical assistance and subsectoral policy conditioning in particular if they are to succeed. On the other hand, there is much to be said for ensuring growth in effective demand for food aid by tying it to high-employment-content projects.

As noted earlier, there has been a recent diversion of food aid and foreign assistance attention away from projects during a short-run period marked by particularly inappropriate macroeconomic policies in developing countries. Once policies are reformed and broad macroeconomic and sectoral policies appropriate for growth are in place, the critical limitations to growth in most developing countries, and certainly in those of contemporary Africa, once again will be institutional, infrastructural, technical, and personnel inadequacies. The need for projects that build technical capacity and that help develop this and other requisite national capacities is increasing rapidly and is becoming indispensable.

The following section deals with the opportunity for a massive increase in rural infrastructural investment in the MADIA countries. A case is made for concentrating food aid and assistance in general on providing a complete grid of rural infrastructure, particularly roads, in these countries. There are three important reasons for doing this: (1) rural infrastructure is an underlying condition for all aspects of rural development; (2) economies of scale need to be established in particular kinds of projects to overcome present project problems that arise from excessive fragmentation of efforts in the face of poor administrative capacity; and (3) to illustrate simply that there is a massive nascent need to utilize food aid. The food and labor requirements for such an effort are immense. However, this is not to argue that food aid should not be provided for other projects—such as maternal and child-feeding projects or emergency assistance—but rather that food aid has a vital developmental and nutritional role in the African context and the need for it must be equated with its useful and productive long-term use. As infrastructure develops, the returns to, and the need for, a wide range of other labor-intensive activities, including conservation structures such as bunding and reforestation, will be enhanced.

Focus on Rural Infrastructure

The logic for a massive investment in rural infrastructure is clear. Agriculture is the main engine of growth in developing countries, given the share of the labor force that it employs and its contributions to the net domestic product. In the MADIA countries, more than three-quarters of the labor force is engaged in agriculture for at least a substantial proportion of its time and generates from one-quarter to one-half of the gross domestic product. Moreover, agriculture has strong links with the other sectors of the economy. Even though excellent performance in agriculture provides growth rates well below those of well-performing nonagricultural sectors (the 3–6 percent range as opposed to the 8–12 percent range), it would take truly extraordinary rates of growth in the nonagricultural sectors alone to achieve a high overall rate of growth in the economy. Indeed, the MADIA study shows consistently that countries that tried to grow on nonagriculture alone failed miserably.

Accelerated growth in the agricultural sector occurs through the application of productivity-increasing technology, including new crops, commercialization, increased input use, and increased output for sale. These activities are not profitable unless the transaction costs for buying and selling are maintained at a low level. This, in turn, requires good physical infrastructure. This commercialization and transaction cost argument for physical infrastructure is powerfully reinforced by the need for modern institutions—for example, for fertilizer distribution, extension education, and credit systems. All of these are operated by trained people who for professional and personal reasons require ready access to commercial markets through public and other means of transportation.[56] Improved infrastructure is instrumental in the successful integration of the small farms into the commercial development process.

An interesting corroboration is shown by the experience of Kenya in its successful introduction of horticultural products for export. Today, horticultural commodities are the third largest source of foreign exchange among Kenya's agricultural exports. The provision of a road that provided fast links to export outlets reduced marketing costs and facilitated access to markets and thus the adoption of these new crops, which in turn created additional employment—especially in the transportation and processing of the vegetables.[57] Good transportation links contributed to the success in the first place, but it is increasingly recognized that further expansion of this sector depends on the further improvement of the road network.

A recurrent theme in the MADIA studies is the importance of rural infrastructure to agricultural growth and the deficiency of that infrastructure in the MADIA countries.[58] Studies from Bangladesh show that areas that are otherwise similar, in terms of agroecological conditions and rural population density, but that differ in having relatively greater infrastructural development, have 35 percent more gross agricultural production, twice as much fertilizer use per hectare, more than twice as much employment of hired labor, and twice the wage income per capita relative to areas with underdeveloped infrastructure.[59] Moreover, the incomes of the landless and small owners increased proportionately more than for large owners, thus addressing the income-distribution issue. The Bangladesh study focuses on rural areas that have effective productivity-increasing technology available—but to have such technology potential is an objective for the policy improvements that come out of the MADIA study.

Availability of "hard" physical infrastructure also influences the availability of social infrastructure. In North Arcot district in India, the availability of social infrastructure such as health, education, and credit was positively and significantly linked with the availability of "hard" infrastructure such as roads and irrigation systems.[60]

The current coverage of basic physical infrastructure in the MADIA countries is poor—especially in comparison with South Asian countries, which even now have a grossly inadequate coverage. Rural road densities range from 50 meters per square kilometer in Cameroon to 90 meters in Nigeria and Kenya (table 11-7). All-weather rural road densities are much lower. Rural Nigeria has only about 3 percent of the all-weather rural road network in place to reach full coverage, whereas India is already about one-third of the way toward reaching full coverage.[61] Thus a significant opportunity exists for food aid to make an effective contribution to that critical element of development.

Optimally built labor-intensive rural roads have a high employment content and hence a high food content—on the order of 50 and 25 percent, respectively, of total construction cost. Labor-intensive rural roads cost much less than equipment-intensive rural roads. For instance, in Nigeria in 1987, the per-kilometer cost of an equipment-intensive road in Kaduna ADP was $16,200, whereas that of a labor-intensive pilot public works program UNDP-ILO road was only $6,350.[62] Effective rural road projects need policy conditioning if necessary decentralization is to occur, and they require technical inputs that make good use of technical assistance. All this makes them ideal subjects for food aid projects.

Perhaps most important, the broad need for infrastructure offers opportunities for economies of scale and learning by doing that particularly recommend them for a massive food aid concentration. The complexity of food aid projects causes them to suffer greatly from excess diversity and, because of that diversity, to lack of scale economies in design, execution, policy conditioning, and, most important, in learning by doing. Thus this recommendation to concentrate food aid on rural infrastructure so as to obtain scale economies is an important one. Within that concentration there may, at least initially, need to be further concentration by subregions, so as to take advantage of the free mobility of labor to further ease the burden on scarce administrative resources.

For this study, a simple illustrative exercise was carried out on four MADIA countries to estimate the construction costs (and their breakdown into labor and food costs) of a grid of all-weather rural roads that would provide full infrastructure coverage for the rural population of these countries. The definition of full coverage was taken from in-depth analyses of India, and "ideal" or "ultimate" rural road target densities were established in line with Indian state rural road target densities to achieve full rural road coverage.[63] The analysis is disaggregated to the MADIA regional and to the Indian state levels.

Table 11-7. Summary Statistics on Rural Road Construction in Four MADIA Countries

Allocation	*Cameroon*	*Kenya*	*Malawi*	*Nigeria*
Length of rural roads (kilometers)	23,492	48,083	5,608	84,429
Rural road density (kilometers/square kilometers)	0.050	0.085	0.059	0.090
Additional rural roads needed (kilometers)	113,532	228,621	51,202	592,633
"Ultimate" target density (kilometers/square kilometers)	0.24	0.49	0.60	0.73
Construction costs per kilometer (U.S. dollars)	34,000–56,000	18,000	8,000–10,500	15,000–25,000
Total construction costs (millions of U.S. dollars)	5,030	4,115	484	11,111
Labor share (millions of U.S. dollars)	2,520	2,058	242	5,556
Food component (millions of U.S. dollars)	1,260	1,029	121	2,778
Food tonnage required (millions of tons)	8.40	6.87	0.81	18.52

Note: Construction costs data were not available for Cameroon, Kenya, and Malawi. Hence they are assumed to be double the level of rehabilitation costs. Kenyan and Malawian costs have been brought up to 1989 levels by inflating with Consumer Price Index and converting to U.S. dollars at exchange rates prevailing in June 1989 for Kenya and February 1989 for Malawi. Nigerian and Cameroonian costs have already been estimated. There is great variation in all-weather rural road construction costs in the four countries arising from differences in labor and fixed costs, overvalued exchange rates, per capita incomes, road standards, and so on. Although the size of differences seems excessive, we nevertheless felt that we should observe these costs.

Source: Juan Gaviria, Vishva Bindlish, and Uma Lele, "The Rural Road Question and Nigeria's Agricultural Development," in Uma Lele, A. T. Oyjide, Vishva Bindlish, and Balu Bumb, eds., "Nigeria's Economic Development, Agriculture's Role, and World Bank Assistance, 1961–88: Lessons for the Future," MADIA Working Paper (Africa—Technical Department, Agriculture Division, World Bank, Washington, D.C.); Republic of India, Ministry of Shipping and Transport (roads wing), *Road Development Plan for India, 1981–2000* (New Delhi: Indian Road Congress, 1984); Juan Gaviria, "The Impact of Rural Roads on Regional Agricultural Performance in Cameroon," SSATP/MADIA Working Paper (Africa—Technical Department, Agriculture Division, World Bank, Washington, D.C., 1989); Uma Lele and Steven Stone, "Population Pressure, the Environment, and Agricultural Intensification in Sub-Saharan Africa: Variations on the Boserup Hypothesis," MADIA Working Paper (Africa—Technical Department, Agriculture Division, World Bank, Washington, D.C., 1989); Juan Gaviria, "Kenya's Rural Road Programs: Lessons from Project Planning and Implementation at the District Level," SSATP/MADIA Working Paper (Africa—Technical Department, Agriculture Division, World Bank, Washington, D.C., forthcoming); Republic of Malawi, Ministry of Works and Supplies, "District Roads Improvement and Maintenance Project, Phase IV," draft final report, vol. II (March 1988); Republic of Malawi, Ministry of Works and Supplies, *Inventory of Designated Roads in Malawi, 1985* (1986); *Malawi Statistical Yearbook, 1985;* International Monetary Fund, *International Financial Statistics Yearbook, 1989 (Washington, D.C.);* Juan Gaviria, "Malawi: Good Rural Road Infrastructure but Few Users; Its Implications on Agricultural Performance." SSATP/MADIA Working Paper (Africa—Technical Department, Agriculture Division, World Bank, Washington, D.C., forthcoming).

Initial comparisons are made on the basis of population densities to identify comparator regions and states.[64] Once the comparators are established, the relevant Indian state target rural road densities are adopted as MADIA regional target densities.

It is eye-opening to compare the existing rural road densities with target densities—for instance, Nigeria's existing rural road density of 0.09 kilometers per square kilometer compared with its target density of 0.73 kilometers per square kilometer means that Nigeria is trying to develop its agriculture with more than 85 percent of its area so inadequately served by infrastructure as to be largely left out of the commercialization process. No wonder the overall growth rate is so slow.

The difference between target and current road densities was calculated, along with the additional road length needed to reach full coverage. The additional rural road length needed ranged from 50,000 kilometers in Malawi to almost 600,000 kilometers in Nigeria and called for an increase of up to ten times the current coverage in (for instance) Malawi. Under varying regional costs of construction, the total cost of construction of an "ultimate" rural infrastructure grid ranges from $500 million in Malawi to over $11 billion in Nigeria. The costs for Kenya and Cameroon are $4 billion and $5 billion, respectively. These costs are immense, but when spread over twenty years they range from $25 million (for Malawi) to $550 million (for Nigeria) per year (in 1989 dollars) for the MADIA group of countries.

Only a full recognition that rural development requires commercialization and hence requires all villages to be close to a rural road can find these expenditures realistic. These rural road densities and coverage are ultimate targets—attainable in two decades at best, but useful now to guide policy decisions on expenditure allocations toward that goal.

The fundamental assumption underlying this exercise is that the additions to the rural road system will be constructed with labor-intensive methods as opposed to capital-intensive methods. Only in this way will the full benefits of rural road construction be dispersed broadly as workers' incomes are spent on goods and services in the rural areas and as other benefits of infrastructural development are tapped that help to initiate almost immediately stimulating effects on agricultural and nonagricultural activities. The vibrancy of rural market towns with rapidly growing service and small manufacturing activities in the smallholder tea-growing areas of Kenya illustrate the power of these connections.

The labor and food components of the total financing required for labor-intensive road construction were also estimated. Of the total cost, it was assumed that at least half would accrue directly to the laborers in the form of wage payments. Further assuming an average propensity of consuming cereals of 0.5 (on the low side), total expenditure on cereals would be half of the wage expenditure. Thus the construction of a full coverage of rural roads in Nigeria would require about 19 million tons of cereals and almost $6 billion paid out to laborers as wages. Spreading this massive rural infrastructure investment over a twenty-year period would involve an annual investment of $550 million, of which the wage payment would be $275 million per year (in 1989 dollars) and almost 1 million tons of incremental cereal consumption. In Cameroon, annual construction costs would be $250 million, of which wage payments would be $125 million and incremental cereal consumption would be 0.4 million tons of cereals per year over twenty years. Annual wage payments and incremental cereal consumption are lower for Kenya—about $100 million and 350,000 tons respectively. In Malawi, where construction costs are much lower, an annual wage payment of $12 million and about 40,000 tons of additional cereals would be called for. Thus it would cost an estimated $1 billion and 1.7 million tons of incremental cereal consumption per year for twenty years to construct a complete grid of all-weather roads in these four countries.

Extrapolating these cost estimates to all of Sub-Saharan Africa, it would cost an estimated $2.5 billion and 4 million tons of incremental cereal consumption per year for twenty years. Moreover, these estimated costs represent a substantial underestimation of the total costs because the rest of Sub-Saharan Africa averages out to have somewhat lower population densities than Nigeria, which could mean somewhat higher costs per family reached by rural infrastructure.

The current total volume of cereal food aid to Sub-Saharan Africa is nearly 4 million tons per year. In the short run, much of that food aid would continue to be used for famine relief, balance of payments support, and similar purposes, but as rural development gathers momentum, the need for these forms of food aid will gradually diminish. Nevertheless, for several years at least, phasing up to a doubling of food aid would probably be necessary to meet the needs of famine relief and balance of payments support and to construct rural infrastructure.

Rural road construction on such a massive geographic scale calls for extensive decentralization—preferably on the political side, but at least on the administrative side—to allow for more rural input into decisionmaking and operation. Centrally devised and executed infrastructure projects run into severe problems of coordination, overextended authority, and lack of touch with project site problems, as well as problems of illegitimacy as rural inhabitants feel little responsibility for something they did not construct. Reform sufficient to make such an effort feasible almost certainly requires decentralization to the rural communities. But there is no choice if broadly based rural development is to be pursued: The issue is whether agriculture is to be central to the growth strategy and the pace at which essential capital accumulation can proceed, not whether there can be a compromise on a full grid of rural infrastructure. Of the MADIA countries, Kenya has substantially decentralized administratively and politically to the provincial level, thus creating a favorable context for its rural development activities—but all the MADIA countries face large political problems in undertaking the required degree of decentralization.

Maintenance of the existing and future rural road infrastructure must be a priority. It is no use to build a road if no provision is made for its maintenance and the road is washed away or overgrown within a few months or years. Horror stories abound in Sub-Saharan Africa of roads disappearing into forests or being totally washed away because oversight or maintenance has been neglected, so that the cost of reclaiming these roads is as much as the cost of new construction. Projects supported by food aid, like any other road construction projects, must factor road maintenance into their estimates. A minimum of 10 percent of the initial cost must be devoted to annual maintenance, and 20 percent would be more reasonable. Labor-intensive road construction projects in Kenya have already developed successful mechanisms to ensure maintenance of newly built roads by hiring former road construction employees on a part-time basis to be responsible for the detection of problems. This is particularly effective because the persons who were employed on the road construction scheme already are familiar with the road and know how to take care of it.[65]

Rural workers are attracted to work on labor-intensive road construction projects if food aid is to be provided in kind at the site. Such payment in kind is additionally attractive if food markets work inadequately in rural areas. Of course, when such markets work well, food aid may be efficiently monetized by selling the food in urban areas and paying wages in cash. The amount of food that will be purchased is easily predicted from consumption studies. Monetizing food aid can provide financing for the complementary inputs, such as construction tools and increased surface material, that are essential to building a viable, longer-lasting road.

Strengths and Weaknesses of Food Aid Projects

The potential strengths of project food aid and projects supported by food aid, particularly food-for-work schemes, already have been identified. They include, among many others, the creation of employment opportunities, the construction of durable long-term rural assets that will contribute to agricultural and overall growth, the satisfaction of food security and nutrition needs of the poorest population, better targeting, the development of the technical capacity of recipient countries, and additionality to financial aid. The success of a food-for-work project (FFW) in Kenya can be noted in this regard:

> FFW in the study area augments own farm output by contributing to the minimum nutrient requirement, eases the capital constraint by the second year of participation, increases the marketable surplus from both own-crop and livestock production, increases hired labor in farm production, causes a shift from maize to millet production, and increases savings. As a result, the net income for the representative farm household with FFW is 55 percent higher than those without FFW.[66]

Furthermore, this program improved the pattern of income distribution in the study area, as the lowest income groups were the major beneficiaries.[67]

Despite such successes, the overall record of projects supported with food aid in Sub-Saharan Africa has been as dismal as that of much of the rest of aid projects and of agricultural development in general. A survey of food aid projects reveals a long list of endemic problems: poor project effectiveness; poor long-term impact of food-for-work schemes; limited quality and questionable viability and sustainability of assets; labor disincentives; high overhead costs of food aid transportation, storage and distribution; poor supervision and accountability; and inadequate forecasting of needs.[68] All of these factors hamper the efficiency, effectiveness, and target achievement of these projects. They are primarily the result of poor commodity and project management, institutional shortcomings of both donors and recipients, and infrastructural and resource constraints. Although these problems are neither unsolvable nor unique to Africa, they are certainly more endemic in Africa, and their alleviation will require a massive and concerted effort. The MADIA study addresses these problems broadly and in a manner that is fully relevant to food aid projects.

Poor commodity management creates and exacerbates some of the most common planning and distribution problems of food aid. Food supplies may arrive erratically at project sites. In Senegal, for example, because port procedures are slow and the institution responsible for handling food aid commodities has limited resources, these commodities often remain in Dakar for four to six months before being transferred to the project site.[69] In Tanzania, six original projects of a PL-480 Title III food for development project were delayed from eighteen months to two years.[70] Sometimes, a full ration may not be completed if commodities do not arrive in conjunction; for example, in a project in Kenya, one of the commodities to complete the ration did not arrive for eighteen months.[71] Another result of poor commodity management is that food may not be distributed on a regular basis, thereby reducing one of the incentives underlying the successful outcome of such projects. Little control may be exercised on whether the food aid has reached the intended beneficiaries, and thus the effectiveness of the project is likely to be diluted.

Poor project management is another commonly encountered problem. There is a serious shortage of trained national personnel, and projects experience competitive difficulties in hiring and holding on to trained personnel. Unremunerative salaries and limited promotion opportunities led to a loss of trained staff on a land development project in Tanzania.[72] Often project directors are seconded from other governmental positions. Moreover, project directors may be insufficiently involved with project administration, especially if they already hold other full-time responsibilities, reside in capital cities, and owing to a lack of time and funds, pay only a few supervisory visits to project sites. A review of a Catholic Relief Services (CRS) feeding program in Tanzania noted among various factors that few-and-far between visits by supervisors contributed to the program's lack of effectiveness in addressing food insecurity problems in the region.[73] If funds are not budgeted for field trips for the technical supervision of project implementation, little quality control is maintained, and asset quality is inadequate. Recordkeeping is poor, making it difficult to plan ahead, to monitor progress, or to carry out evaluations. Essentially, resource constraints—mainly of personnel, financial, and infrastructural capacities—are the root cause of many project management problems.

Institutional shortcomings of recipient countries are another fundamental factor influencing project performance and outcome. There are two aspects to the issue of institutional shortcomings. The first is poor institutional development, which results in inadequate institutional capacity and in institutions incapable of efficiently handling food aid or of overseeing and supporting food aid project administration. For instance, a WFP-assisted rural development project in Senegal was hampered by working with an institution that "does not seem well equipped to assist in the establishment of technical perimeters, which are the backbone of the project. [The institution] has not been able to provide the right conditions, either for the study of the project or for the conduct of the work."[74] Contributing to poor institutional capacity is the lack of trained national personnel and other resources as well as inadequate supporting systems of food and agricultural data. The second aspect of institutional shortcomings is inadequate support by recipient-country institutions of the requisite projects—owing to the lack of interest or commitment or just the sheer overburden of tasks allotted to them. Political support for food aid is minimal in many African countries because of their colonial experiences and strong food self-sufficiency rhetoric. "Food aid in Africa has a serious image problem which influences, to a large extent, its potential for effective use."[75] This is a serious problem, since it is highly unlikely that a project can be successful without domestic support. For instance, little institutional backing by the national body in charge of developing the Senegal River Valley contributed to farmers' lack of interest in a project on irrigation development in the Senegal River Valley assisted by the World Food Program.[76]

Project implementation is hindered by inadequate infrastructural capacities and transport resources, as well as by insufficient financial resources. The lack of transport, particularly of all-weather roads, and of storage facilities can make the delivery of commodities inefficient and expensive and can exacerbate commodity management problems. The cost of delivery to the project site, which is usually borne by the recipient country, is also jacked up. Third, project supervision is reduced since personnel are not able to move around project sites as often as they wish.

Inadequate financial resources are another frequently noted deficiency. For instance, in a previously mentioned PL-480 Title III food for development project in Tanzania, the implementation of projects was delayed because of slow rice sales, coupled with delays in the deposit of sales proceeds into a special account. On average, these projects received half of their planned budgets over the first two years of the projects; hence project directors were unable to program short-term budget expenditures because they were not sure how much money they would have in the near future.[77]

In other instances, project implementation was hindered when projects were unable to acquire complementary materials and equipment to increase the productivity of the labor engaged in labor-intensive work effort. The availability of vehicles, spares, and fuel was particularly crucial. Large schemes in a WFP-assisted project in Senegal came to a standstill for want of fuel, or for the want of other fairly small outlays required from the equipment budget.[78]

Inadequate coordination among donors, between donors and recipients, and between various institutions within the recipient country is becoming a serious problem for recipient countries as increasing volumes of food aid are received from a variety of donors. Institutional capacities, which are inadequate to begin with, are further strained by having to perform duplicate coordinating tasks with donors. Senegal has created a common counterpart fund for food aid sales to which most food aid donors now contribute, and of which WFP is the secretary, to address the problem of donor coordination. Senegal has also streamlined internal arrangements for food aid distribution by making various agencies responsible for handling specific types of food aid.[79] In contrast, Tanzania, to note an extreme case, has to coordinate with about two dozen donors and has different counterpart funds policies for different donors—for instance, the United States requires counterpart funds from its food aid to be deposited in special accounts in Tanzania's National Bank of Commerce and the Cooperative and Rural Development Bank; in the EC such funds are sent to a special account at the Treasury; and Canada requires 20 percent of the funds to be spent on projects agreed to beforehand by the two governments and 80 percent to be attributed to the development budget of the government.[80]

Projects supported by nonfood resources in MADIA countries have experienced much the same parochial problems that have hampered the efficiency and effectiveness of resource transfers and the long-term viability of the projects. This is demonstrated by virtually all the donor studies in this book. Many of these problems can be addressed by the food aid projects themselves. For instance, an infrastructure project can help reduce delays and costs in the delivery of food aid and other commodities to the region.

The lessons of past experience indicate that the following actions should be taken to make food aid projects more effective:

- Determine the total resources needed and ensure that adequate funding will be available for the nonfood complements (this may require coordination between food aid and financial assistance donors, such as the WFP and the World Bank).
- Decentralize administration to the local level to ensure that local expertise will be available for the project.
- Build into the project adequate training and financing of technical people.
- Rely on markets to move food and other supplies when administrative capabilities are low (recognizing that deficiencies in markets may limit the geographic areas in which projects may operate).
- Provide a high level of planning skills to ensure that all components of the project will be coordinated.

The more difficult it is to meet these requirements, the clearer must be the priority of projects and the greater the need to concentrate on a few kinds of projects to obtain scale economies.

Adjustments to the African Context

The wealth of experience with large food aid projects for rural employment in Asia provides useful lessons for Africa—provided that appropriate adjustments are made, particularly in response to African labor markets. The average productivity of labor tends to be lower in Africa than in Asia, whereas the marginal productivity tends to be higher.[81] Thus there is a greater probability that pulling labor out of agriculture will cause significant declines in agricultural production in Africa. Furthermore, a substantial proportion of the income of poor households in Africa already comes from activities carried out in the slack season.[82] The policy implications are twofold. First, a somewhat higher wage will have to be paid on food aid projects in Africa than in Asia. Second, great care will have to be taken to restrict project employment to carefully defined periods of seasonal labor surplus; or, perhaps frequently, food aid flows must take into account possible short-run declines in food production.

Since African population densities tend to be lower than for Asia, the totality of labor that would be attracted to a specific project site would often be smaller. Hence individual food-for-work projects would need to be smaller in Africa and would also need greater management resources. In view of the scarcity of indigenous management resources, donors and recipients alike should not hesitate to tap external sources until local management resources are developed.[83]

Impact on Poverty

There is large variation in rural absolute poverty in the MADIA countries—as well as in the poverty estimates themselves. Estimates from the *Social Indicators of Development* of the rural population living below an absolute poverty income level range from 40 percent in Cameroon to 55 percent in Kenya, 60 percent in Tanzania, and 85 percent in Malawi.[84] Estimates for Senegal and Nigeria were not available. The estimated absolute poverty income level was established as "the level below which a minimal nutritionally adequate diet plus essential nonfood requirements are not affordable." In 1975, the most recent year for which estimates were available, these rural poverty income levels were set at $105 in Cameroon, $112 in Kenya, $99 in Malawi, $82 in Senegal, and $109 in Tanzania. Applying these estimates of poverty incidence to the latest population estimates, the numbers of rural poor are 2.4 million in Cameroon, 5.6 million in Malawi, 9.7 million in Kenya, and 11.9 million in Tanzania. These surveys were, however, done more than a decade ago and seem to define high poverty lines and hence high estimates of the numbers of the poor when compared with the poverty line of Rs 672.72, or $84, in 1977–78 in India, where the poverty line stands at a calorie requirement of 2,250 calories per capita daily.[85] When the absolute poverty line is defined more narrowly, the number of poor people is, of course, lower. In Kenya in

1974–75, 39 percent of smallholder households fell below the food poverty line, defined as providing a recommended daily allowance of 2,250 calories per adult.[86]

Because the numbers from the World Bank's *Social Indicators of Development* seem so high, although the relations among the countries seems reasonable, it may be appropriate to reduce the poverty incidences reported there by 25 percent. This is roughly the difference between the values reported from work in Kenya by Greer and Thorbecke (see note 86) and the *Social Indicators of Development* estimates. This of course does not allow for differences in poverty reduction (or increases) among countries since 1975. In particular, Kenya—given its broadly based rural growth—is probably shown too high in relation to the others. The poverty incidences for Nigeria and Senegal are both arbitrarily set at 35 percent. Thus rural poverty incidences are estimated to be 30 percent in Cameroon, 35 percent in both Nigeria and Senegal, 41 percent in Kenya, 45 percent in Tanzania, and 64 percent in Malawi.[87] This translates into a total of 51.3 million absolute rural poor in the MADIA group of countries: 1.5 million in Senegal, 1.8 million in Cameroon, 4.2 million in Malawi, 7.2 million in Kenya, 8.2 million in Tanzania, and 28.4 million in Nigeria. If a much narrower definition of an absolute poverty line is employed—for instance, that defined by the Food and Agriculture Organization as sufficient energy to provide 1.4 times the energy required for the basic metabolic rate—the number of poor would be less than half these 51 million.[88]

Assuming that a supplement of 25 percent of the recommended daily allowance would be needed to pull the defined 51 million hungry poor above the poverty line, about 3 million tons of additional cereals would be required per year for these MADIA countries as a group.[89] Earlier, it was shown that about 1.7 million tons of cereals would be needed for the construction of rural infrastructure. Thus a rural works program of the magnitude delineated would take care of almost 60 percent of this defined poverty requirement. In theory, an additional 1.25 million tons of cereal food aid, properly distributed, could take care of the rest. Assuming that the incidence of poverty prevailing in the MADIA group also prevails for Sub-Saharan Africa as a whole, there would be about 125 million rural poor who would require about 7.2 million tons of additional cereals per year to pull them above the poverty line.[90] Previous calculations have shown that Sub-Saharan Africa would require about 4 million tons of incremental cereal consumption for rural infrastructure construction. Hence, a further 3.2 million tons, at a minimum, would be needed to take care of the rest of the rural poor.

It must be emphasized that although well-designed rural public works would greatly reduce rural poverty, the calculations here are based on assumptions of a high level of efficiency, which should form the objective but which may take some years to achieve. The presence of such initial inefficiency is, of course, not an argument against commencing this effort. The increase in employment and the reduction in poverty from rural public works themselves will gradually be replaced by production activities stimulated by increased agricultural incomes flowing to the rest of the rural population and stimulating the rural economy. Note that if there is overall growth in income in which the poor are participating but no increase in food supplies, the effect of the consequent price inflation of food will remove benefits from the poor and redistribute these benefits from them to other sections of the population.[91] Increasing employment and nominal incomes of the poor cannot improve their real incomes and food intake without a nearly commensurate increase in the supply of food. Therefore the provision of increased supplies of food is necessary to address this problem.

Rural public works programs operating at the level previously delineated for the MADIA countries would serve a number of poverty-oriented functions. First, they would lift 50 percent of the rural people falling below the poverty line up to that poverty line in the short run through the works themselves, as well as stimulate a growth process that would keep them above that line. For comparison, note that in Bangladesh, a 40 percent reduction in poverty was observed in areas with all-weather roads.[92] Second, they would provide a rural infrastructure grid that would allow the totality of the rural areas to participate in the growth process. Third, they would provide an early warning system of approaching hunger stress.[93] Fourth, they would ensure a continuing administrative structure for providing increased supplies of food in the rural areas in periods of stress. Note that the biggest problem in preventing famine is the need to rapidly develop structures for moving food into rural areas. The Maharashtra Employment Guarantee Scheme in India provides an example of how this can be done.[94]

Policy Conclusions

Food aid has not been a significant element in foreign assistance flows, government revenues, and food supplies in three of the MADIA countries: Cameroon, Malawi, and Nigeria. Even in the other three—Kenya, Senegal, and Tanzania—it has played little or no role in stabilizing food supplies or contributing to project development. It has, however, been an important addition to foreign aid and has contributed to the overall food security in those countries. At least in Kenya, it has also played a significant role in support of generally favorable rural development policies.

Food aid could productively and efficiently contribute much more to these functions, particularly through investment in rural infrastructure. The MADIA countries are grossly underinvesting in rural development in general, in rural infrastructure specifically, and particularly in labor-employing—and hence food-consuming—activities. There is a distortion in the MADIA economies away from employment and food consumption. That distortion is probably particularly marked in Malawi, which receives little development-oriented food aid. Food aid can help rectify those distortions.

For food aid to contribute significantly to long-term agricultural and overall development, donors would need to institute the following changes—affecting both donors and recipients:

- Condition aid on the subsectoral, political, and administrative changes needed to build and obtain returns from massive rural infrastructural investment.
- Provide greatly expanded project-oriented technical assistance to make food and labor-intensive projects work.
- Coordinate food aid and financial aid to ensure that nonfood components essential to productive projects will be provided.
- Manage food aid programs to ensure that they stabilize rather than destabilize food availability; alternatively, develop the International Monetary Fund cereal facility as a viable means of meeting developing country needs by stabilizing food supplies through international borrowing.

Several actions also need to be taken by the recipient countries:

- Provide a favorable macroeconomic environment for the growth of decentralized small farms and businesses, including substantial privatization and freeing of prices.
- Provide an explicit food price policy, related broadly to international prices, but with appropriate stabilization stocks to ensure that food aid is used to complement domestic production.
- Decentralize the political and administrative processes of revenue collection and expenditure into rural areas.
- Recognize that food aid can play an important role in the economic growth and development of the country if properly designed and managed.
- Commit expenditure and personnel to rural infrastructure, and to complementary central infrastructure on a massive scale.
- Recognize that rural infrastructure does not provide growth without a complex set of technologically oriented institutions and expen-

diture patterns that may have to be completely reoriented along the lines of the findings of the MADIA study.

With these fundamental changes, food aid at some substantial multiple of current levels could help to accelerate growth and to broaden participation in that growth.

Notes

We are grateful to Hannan Ezekiel for access to a number of as yet unpublished pieces dealing with food aid; to Juan Gaviria for access to his papers on rural infrastructure in the MADIA countries and for advice on cost estimates; to Charles Paolillo, John Shaw, and J. M. Boucher for comments and access to World Food Program data, analyses, and reports; to Owen Cylke for access to Agency for International Development (USAID) country documents on food aid; to Carole Theauvette for access to Canadian International Development Agency (CIDA) country reports on Senegal and Tanzania; and to Christopher Delgado, Rahul Jain, Valeriana Kallab, Thomas Reardon, and Joachim von Braun for carefully reading earlier drafts and providing suggestions for improvement.

1. Separate treatment of food aid assumes some degree of nonconvertibility into other commodities. In practice, a large proportion of food aid is converted by the displacement of commercial food imports and resulting conversion into local currency through market sales. In those circumstances, food aid is not different from other forms of aid. Throughout, this paper analyzes the circumstances in which food aid supplements food supplies and represents a net addition to foreign assistance. That implicitly assumes that the politics of aid in donor countries make food aid somewhat cheaper or more abundant than other forms of aid. See John W. Mellor, "The Utilization of Food Aid for Equitable Growth," in *Report of the World Food Program/Government of the Netherlands Seminar on Food Aid* (The Hague, Netherlands, 3-5 October 1983); and T. N. Srinivasan, "Food Aid: A Cause of Development Failure or an Instrument of Success?" *World Bank Economic Review* 3(1, 1989):39–66.

2. Between 1965 and 1978 twenty-seven recipients of food aid experienced a reduction in food aid from more than 15 percent of food imports (averaged over three years) to less than 3 percent of food imports in the next year. In none of these cases did the reductions occur in years of bumper harvests; on the contrary, they occurred in years of average or below-average domestic food production. Furthermore, situations of unexpected drastic reductions in food aid are not diminishing. See Joachim von Braun and Barbara Huddleston, "Implications of Food Aid for Price Policy in Recipient Countries," in John W. Mellor and Raisuddin Ahmed, eds., *Agricultural Price Policy for Developing Countries* (Baltimore, Md.: Johns Hopkins University Press, 1988). Such a record affects not only the willingness to receive food aid but also its allocation and efficiency.

3. See Barbara Huddleston, *Closing the Cereals Gap with Trade and Food Aid*, Research Report 43 (Washington, D.C.: International Food Policy Research Institute, January 1984); and Hans W. Singer, "Food Aid: Pros and Cons," *Intereconomics* 23(March-April 1988):79–83.

4. See Mellor, "The Utilization of Food Aid for Equitable Growth"; and Srinivasan, "Food Aid."

5. See Kenneth L. Bachman and Leonardo A. Paulino, *Rapid Food Production Growth in Selected Developing Countries: A Comparative Analysis of Underlying Trends, 1961–76*, Research Report 11 (Washington, D.C.: International Food Policy Research Institute, October 1979); E. D. Kellogg, "University Involvement in International Agricultural Development Activities: Important Issues for Public Education," in *Proceedings of the Association of U.S. University Directors of International Agricultural Programs* (1985): 121–36; J. E. Lee and M. Shane, *United States Agricultural Interests and Growth in the Developing Economies: The Critical Linkage* (Washington, D.C.: United States Department of Agriculture, Economic Research Service, 1985); J. P. Houck, "Foreign Agricultural Assistance: Ally or Adversary," Staff Paper P86-50 (Minneapolis: University of Minnesota, 1986); C. Peter Timmer, "Foreign Assistance and American Agriculture" (Harvard Institute for International Development, Cambridge, Mass., 1987); and John W. Mellor, "Agricultural Development in the Third World: The Food, Poverty, Aid, Trade Nexus," *Choices* (First Quarter 1989):4–8.

6. See World Bank, *Social Indicators of Development, 1988* (Baltimore, Md.: Johns Hopkins University Press, 1988).

7. See Steven Haggblade, Peter Hazell, and James Brown, "Farm-Nonfarm Linkages in Rural Sub-Saharan Africa," *World Development* 17 (August 1989): 1173–1202; and Dharam Ghai and Samir Radwan, eds., *Agrarian Policies and Rural Poverty in Africa* (Geneva: International Labour Office, 1983).

8. See Thomas Reardon and Christopher Delgado, "Income Diversification of Rural Households in Burkina Faso," paper submitted for inclusion in the working paper of the World Bank, Environment Department and Human Resources Development Division concerning the Proceedings of the Workshop on Dryland Management (International Food Policy Research Institute, Washington, D.C., December 1989).

9. See Thomas Reardon, Christopher Delgado, and Peter Matlon, "Farmer Marketing Behavior and the Composition of Cereals Consumption in Burkina Faso," paper prepared for the IFPRI-ISRA conference on the Dynamics of Cereals Consumption and Production Patterns in West Africa, Dakar, Senegal (International Food Policy Research Institute, Washington, D.C., July 1987).

10. See John W. Mellor, *The New Economics of Growth–A Strategy for India and the Developing World*, (Ithaca, N.Y.: Cornell University Press, 1976).

11. Ibid.

12. See Mellor and Ahmed, *Agricultural Price Policy for Developing Countries*.

13. See Mellor, *The New Economics of Growth*; and John W. Mellor, "Agriculture on the Road to Industrialization," in John P. Lewis and Valeriana Kallab, eds., *Development Strategies Reconsidered*, U.S.–Third World Policy Perspectives 5 (New Brunswick, N.J.: Transaction Books, 1986).

14. Unless otherwise noted, food aid in this paper refers to cereal food aid, which includes wheat, rice, and coarse grains.

15. Assumes: (1) the elasticity of consumption with respect to price is 0.5; (2) there are no positive production and consumption effects from the use of food aid; and (3) food aid is additional to domestic availability of cereals, that is, does not substitute for commercial imports.

16. Assumes: (1) the supply response coefficient is 0.3; and (2) food aid is not used to reduce the cost of agricultural production. In practice, the incentive-depressing effects of food aid should be markedly reduced by financing employment-oriented development and feeding programs and by reducing the cost of production through road construction.

17. See Frederic Martin, "Food Security and Comparative Advantage in Senegal: A Micro-Macro Approach," Ph.D. diss., Michigan State University, 1988.

18. See Dharam Ghai and Lawrence D. Smith, *Agricultural Prices, Policy and Equity in Sub-Saharan Africa* (Boulder, Colo.: Lynne Rienner, 1987).

19. See E. J. Clay and H. W. Singer, "Food Aid and Development: Issues and Evidence—A Survey of the Literature Since 1977 on the Role and Impact of Food in Developing Countries," World Food Program Occasional Paper 3 (Rome, 1985).

20. Food and Agriculture Organization of the United Nations, *Supply Utilization Accounts Tape* (Rome, 1984).

21. See Simon Maxwell, "Food Aid to Senegal: Disincentive Effects and Commercial Displacement," Institute of Development Studies Discussion Paper 225 (Brighton, England, 1986).

22. See Thomas Reardon, Christopher Delgado, and T. Thiombiano, "The Demand for Imported Cereals versus Coarse Grains in Ouagadougou: Implications for Cereal Price Policies," paper presented at the IFPRI-ISRA Conference on the Dynamics of Cereals Consumption and Production Patterns in West Africa, Dakar, Senegal (International Food Policy Research Institute, Washington, D.C., July 1987).

23. See Christopher Delgado, "The Role of Prices in the Shift to Rice and Wheat Consumption in Francophone West Africa," paper prepared for the IFPRI-ISRA Conference on the Dynamics of Cereals Consumption and Production Patterns in West Africa, Dakar, Senegal (International Food Policy Research Institute, Washington, D.C., July 1987).

24. See Christopher Delgado, "Why Is Rice and Wheat Consumption Increasing in West Africa?," paper prepared for presentation to the European Seminar of Agricultural Economists held May 29–June 2 at Montpellier, France (International Food Policy Research Institute, Washington, D.C., June 1989).

25. See Ben Senauer, David Sahn, and Harold Alderman, "The Effect of the Value of Time on Food Consumption Patterns in Developing Countries: Evidence from Sri Lanka," *American Journal of Agricultural Economics* 68 (November 1986): 920–27.

26. Triangular transactions take place when a donor country purchases food surpluses from a developing country and provides it as food aid to another developing country in the region. Local purchases take place when a donor country purchases food surpluses from a developing country and provides it as food aid to the same country, usually for project assistance.

27. Calculated from World Food Program, Committee on Food Aid Policies and Programs, "Review of Food Aid Policies and Programs," presented at Twenty-Seventh Session, 29 May–2 June, Agenda Item 4: Annual Report of the Executive Director (Rome, April 1989).

28. See Ulrich Koester, *Regional Cooperation to Improve Food Security in Southern and Eastern African Countries*, Research Report 53 (Washington, D.C.: International Food Policy Research Institute, July 1986).

29. See Colin Kirkpatrick and Dimitri Diakosavvas, "Food Insecurity and Foreign-Exchange Constraints in Sub-Saharan Africa," *Journal of Modern African Studies* 23, (2, 1985):239–50.

30. See Peter Hazell, "Sources of Increased Variability in World Cereal Production Since the 1960s," *Journal of Agricultural Economics* 36 (May 1985): 145–60; and Uma Lele and Wilfred Candler, "Food Security: Some East African Considerations," in Alberto Valdes, ed., *Food Security for Developing Countries* (Boulder, Colo.: Westview, 1981).

31. See John W. Mellor, "Food Price Policy and Income Distribution in Low-Income Countries," *Economic Development and Cultural Change* 27 (1, 1978):1–26.

32. See Republic of Kenya, *Sessional Paper No. 4 of 1981 on National Food Policy* (1981).

33. See World Bank, *World Development Report 1986* (New York: Oxford University Press, 1986).

34. Ibid.

35. See Juan Gaviria, "The Impact of Rural Roads on Regional Agricultural Performance in Cameroon," SSATP-MADIA Working Paper (Africa—Technical Department, Agricultural Division, World Bank, Washington, D.C., 1989); Juan Gaviria, "Kenya's Rural Road Programs: Lessons from Project Planning and Implementation at the District Level," SSATP-MADIA Working Paper (Africa—Technical Department, Agricultural Division, World Bank, Washington, D.C., 1989); Juan Gaviria, "Malawi: Good Rural Infrastructure but Few Users: Its Implications on Agricultural Performance," SSATP-MADIA Working Paper (Africa—Technical Department, Agricultural Division, World Bank, Washington, D.C., 1989); and Juan Gaviria, Vishva Bindlish, and Uma Lele, *The Rural Road Question and Nigeria's Agricultural Development*, MADIA Discussion Paper 10 (Washington, D.C.: World Bank, 1989).

36. See Thomas Pinckney, *Storage, Trade, and Price Policy under Production Instability: Maize in Kenya*, International Food Policy Research Institute Research Report 71 (Washington, D.C., December 1988); and John McIntire, *Food Security in the Sahel: Variable Import Levy, Grain Reserves, and Foreign Exchange Assistance*, Research Report 26 (Washington, D.C.: International Food Policy Research Institute, September 1983).

37. See Thomas Reardon and Peter Matlon, "Seasonal Food Insecurity and Vulnerability in Drought-Affected Regions of Burkina Faso," in *Seasonal Variability in Third World Agriculture: The Consequences for Food Security* (Baltimore, Md.: John Hopkins University Press, 1989); and Thomas Reardon, Peter Matlon, and Christopher Delgado, "Coping with Household-Level Food Insecurity in Drought-Affected Areas of Burkina Faso," in *World Development* 16 (9, 1988):1065–74.

38. Shipments through WFP already are included under shipments from individual donors. Because of the lack of information, it is not possible to distinguish in a consistent time-series what proportion of WFP food aid to a specific MADIA country came from which donor. Moreover, even if it were known, it would not necessarily be the case that the donor explicitly dictated that its food aid should be directed toward a specific recipient; instead it is quite likely that the multilateral agency, for cost and other considerations, opted to use aid from that donor.

39. See Food and Agriculture Organization, *Food Aid in Figures* (Rome, various years).

40. Program food aid is sold in the market and generates domestic currency counterpart funds; when it substitutes for commercial imports, it releases foreign exchange as well. Project food aid is provided in support of specific projects—for instance, feeding and food-for-work projects (which may cover an array of developmental projects). The financing is often through payment in kind, but it could conceivably come from the sale of food, with the proceeds used for specified projects. Emergency food aid is provided in times of emergency and specifically to increase consumption in those areas directly affected by the emergency. The statistical information in this section (unless otherwise stated) originates from the World Food Program (personal communications from J. M. Boucher, chief, Policy and Data Analysis Branch, 23 June 1989 and 1 December 1989); although it does not reconcile with the basic source of food

aid data used in this study—which is *Food Aid in Figures* from the FAO—it is the only source of such information that the authors have been able to locate. It is useful for showing trends and making country comparisons.

41. See World Food Program, Committee on Food Aid Policies and Programs, "Review of Food Aid Policies and Programs" (Rome, 1987).

42. See Frances Stewart, "Economic Policies and Agricultural Performance—The Case of Tanzania," Development Centre Paper (Organisation for Economic Co-operation and Development, Paris, 1986).

43. See Uma Lele, Pierre-Roche Seka, and Mathurin Gbetibouo, "Agricultural Performance in a Macroeconomic Context: The Relative Roles of 'Luck' and Policy," paper prepared for presentation at the Western Economic Association Meeting, June 19, Lake Tahoe, Nevada (1989); and Stewart, "Economic Policies and Agricultural Performance."

44. See World Bank, *World Development Report 1989* (New York: Oxford University Press, 1989).

45. See Stewart, "Economic Policies and Agricultural Performance."

46. See Maxwell, "Food Aid to Senegal."

47. See Lele and others, "Agricultural Performance in a Macroeconomic Context."

48. See Maxwell, "Food Aid to Senegal."

49. See John W. Mellor and Sarah Gavian, "Famine—Causes, Prevention and Relief," *Science* 236(January 1987):539–45.

50. See Lele and others, "Agricultural Performance in a Macroeconomic Context."

51. See Centre for Social Research, "The Characteristics of Nutritionally Vulnerable Sub-Groups within the Smallholder Sector of Malawi: A Report from the 1980–81 NSSA" (University of Malawi, Zomba, 1988); and Pauline E. Peters and M. Guillermo Herrera, "Cash Cropping, Food Security and Nutrition: The Effects of Agricultural Commercialization among Smallholders in Malawi" (Harvard Institute for International Development, Cambridge, Mass., 1989).

52. See International Food Policy Research Institute, *Food Needs of Developing Countries: Projections of Production and Consumption to 1990*, Research Report 3 (Washington, D.C., December 1977); Leonardo Paulino, *Food in the Third World: Past Trends and Projections to 2000*, Research Report 52 (Washington, D.C.: International Food Policy Research Institute, June 1986); Shahla Shapouri, Arthur J. Dommen, and Stacey Rosen, "Food Aid and the African Food Crisis," Foreign Agricultural Report 221 (United States Department of Agriculture, Economic Research Service, Washington, D.C., 1986); Hannan Ezekiel, "Medium-Term Estimates of Demand-Based Food Aid Requirements and Their Variability" (International Food Policy Research Institute, Washington, D.C., December 1988); Stacey Rosen, "Consumption Stability and the Potential Role of Food Aid in Africa," ERS Staff Report AGES 89-29 (USDA-ERS, Washington, D.C., 1989); and Joachim von Braun and Leonardo Paulino, "The Food Needs of African Countries and the Potential and Desirability of Meeting Them through Domestic Production and Intraregional Trade," Study for the U.N. Secretary-General's Expert Group on African Commodity Problems, Studies on National and Regional Issues (International Food Policy Research Institute, Washington, D.C., July 1989).

53. See von Braun and Paulino, "The Food Needs of African Countries."

54. See Ezekiel, "Medium-Term Estimates."

55. See International Food Policy Research Institute, *Food Needs of Developing Countries.*

56. See Raisuddin Ahmed and Mahabub Hossain, "Development Impact of Rural Infrastructure: Bangladesh," International Food Policy Research Institute Research Report (International Food Policy Research Institute in collaboration with Bangladesh Institute of Development Studies, Washington, D.C., 1990).

57. See Morton Owen Schapiro and Stephen Wainaina, "Kenya: A Case Study of the Production and Export of Horticultural Commodities," in *Successful Development in Africa—Case Studies of Projects, Programs, and Policies*, Economic Development Institute Development Policy Case Series, Analytical Case Studies 1 (Washington, D.C.: World Bank, 1989).

58. See Gaviria, "The Impact of Rural Roads," "Kenya's Rural Road Programs,"and "Malawi: Good Rural Infrastructure"; and Gaviria and others, *The Rural Road Question*.

59. See Raisuddin Ahmed, "Agricultural Production, Employment, and Income in Bangladesh," in *Infrastructure and Agricultural Development—Policy Issues and Research Priorities*, Policy Brief 3 (Washington, D.C.: International Food Policy Research Institute, 1988).

60. See Sudhir Wanmali, "Provision and Use of Rural Infrastructure in the Growth of the Regional Economy: A Case Study of North Arcot District, Tamil Nadu, India" (International Food Policy Research Institute, Washington, D.C., May 1989).

61. Calculated from Gaviria and others, *The Rural Road Question*; and Republic of India, Ministry of Shipping and Transport (Roads Wing), *Road Development Plan for India, 1981–2001* (New Delhi: Indian Road Congress, 1984).

62. See Gaviria and others, *The Rural Road Question*.

63. Full coverage is defined as all villages with more than 500 persons (at the time of the 1981 census) lying on an all-weather road and those with fewer than 500 persons within 3 kilometers of an all-weather road in plain areas and within 5 kilometers in hilly areas (Republic of India, *Road Development Plan*, op. cit.). India's plan is to have full coverage by the year 2001. It is currently about one-third of the way toward reaching full coverage. See Gaviria and others,*The Rural Road Question*. The Indian target densities are derived mainly by grid analyses to arrive at the total length of roads for the whole country, which is then allocated per state with respect to topographical features, patterns of habitation, degree of development, and so on. All villages are given road connections, and a uniform distribution of habitations is assumed. It is further assumed that there is a road grid in the shape of squares. See Republic of India, *Road Development Plan*.

64. This method picks up a similar one employed by Gaviria and others in *The Rural Road Question*, which noted that the Indian population density of approximately 135 persons per square kilometer in 1961 was equivalent to the population density expected in Nigeria in the year 2000. The study then ranked the Indian states by population densities in 1961 and correlated them with the expected population densities of Nigerian states in the year 2000. In such a manner, the group of northern Nigerian states was correlated to the Indian states of Assam, Gujurat, Orissa, Mysore, Maharashtra, and Andhra Pradesh; the group of southern Nigerian states with Punjab, Uttar Pradesh, Madras, Bihar, West Bengal, and Kerala; and the group of middle-belt Nigerian states with Jammu and Kashmir, Rajasthan, and Madhya Pradesh. For the other MADIA countries, it has been independently established, by comparing population densities in the year 2000, that in Cameroon, the north and tropical rainforest regions are comparable in population density with Jammu and

Kashmir State, and the Western Lowlands and the Western Highland regions with Rajasthan State. In Kenya, the Northeastern Province is considered comparable in population density with Jammu and Kashmir State; the Coast, Eastern, and Rift Valley provinces with Rajasthan; and Central, Nyanza, and Western provinces with Punjab. In Malawi, the Northern and Central regions are comparable in population density with Rajasthan, and the Southern region with Madhya Pradesh.

65. J. J. de Veen, *The Rural Access Roads Program, Appropriate Technology in Kenya* (Geneva: International Labour Office, 1980).

66. See Mesfin Bezuneh, Brady J. Deaton, and George W. Norton, "Farm Level Impacts of Food for Work in Rural Kenya" (Virginia Polytechnic Institute and State University, Blacksburg, 1985).

67. See Brady J. Deaton and Mesfin Bezuneh, "Food for Work and Income Distribution in a Semi-Arid Region of Rural Kenya: An Empirical Assessment" (Virginia Polytechnic Institute and State University, Blacksburg, 1985).

68. See Deloitte, Haskins, and Sells, "Final Monitoring Report on the Drought Emergency Relief Program for USAID Mission to Kenya," Contract 615-0000-C-00-4121 (March 1986); Jack Royer, Gary Robbins, and Joel Strauss, "Review of the Tanzania Food Aid Program," (U.S. Agency for International Development, Washington, D.C., 1987); John W. Thomas, *Food for Work, An Analysis of Current Experience and Recommendations for Future Performance*, Development Discussion Paper 213 (Cambridge, Mass.: Harvard Institute for International Development, January 1986); United States Agency for International Development, "Project Evaluation Summary (PES) of PL-480 Title III—Food for Development for USAID-Senegal"; WFP, Committee on Food Aid Policies and Programs, "Interim Evaluation Summary Report on Project Cameroon 773 (Exp. 1)—Assistance under the Fourth Five-Year Plan," WFP/CFA: 18/11 Add. C2 (Rome, September 1984); WFP, Committee on Food Aid Policies and Programs, "Interim Evaluation Summary Report on Project Senegal 2236 (Exp. 1)—Conservation and Development of Natural Vegetation," WFP/CFA: 18/11 Add. C5 (Rome, August 1984); WFP, Committee on Food Aid Policies and Programs, "Interim Evaluation and Summary Report on Project Tanzania 2583—Rehabilitation of Housing on Sisal Estates," WFP/CFA: 19/16 Add. 81 (Rome, 15 March 1985); WFP, Committee on Food Aid Policies and Programs, "Project Cameroon 773 (Exp. 2)—Assistance under the Fifth and Sixth Development Plans," WFP/CFA: 19/13-A (WFMA) Add. 1 (Rome, 16 April 1985); WFP, Committee on Food Aid Policies and Programs, "Interim Evaluation Summary Report on Project Kenya 2502—Feeding of Primary and Preschool Children," WFP/CFA: 22/11 Add. A4 (Rome, 24 July 1986); WFP, Committee on Food Aid Policies and Programs, "Progress Report on Project Senegal 2236 (Exp. 2)—Conservation and Development of the Natural Vegetation," WFP/CFA: 23/17 (ODW) Add. 3 (Rome, 3 March 1987); WFP, Committee on Food Aid Policies and Programs, "Project Kenya 2502 (Exp. 1)—Feeding of Primary and Preprimary School Children," WFP/CFA: 23/13-A (ODE) Add. 3 (Rome, 6 March 1987); WFP, Committee on Food Aid Policies and Programs, "Project Tanzania 2496 (Exp. 1)—Land Development for Rice Cultivation in Zanzibar,"WFP/CFA:24/9 (ODE) Add. 4 (Rome, 30 July 1987); WFP, Committee on Food Aid Policies and Programs, "Project Tanzania 2583 (Exp. 1)—Rehabilitation of Housing on Sisal Estates," WFP/CFA: 23/13-A (ODE) Add. 4 (Rome, 7 March 1987); WFP, Committee on Food Aid Policies and Programs, "Project Cameroon 773 (Exp. 2)—Assistance under the Fifth and Sixth Development Plans," WFP/CFA: 26/2-F (ODW) Add. 2 (Rome, 12 September 1988); WFP, Committee on Food

Aid Policies and Programs, "Interim Evaluation Summary Report on Project Senegal 2630—Irrigation Development in the Senegal River Valley," WFP/CFA: 27/SCP:2 (Rome, 4 April 1989); WFP, Committee on Food Aid Policies and Programs, "Interim Evaluation Summary Report on Project Senegal 2693—Rural Development in the Region of Podor and Matam," WFP/CFA: 27/SCP:2 (Rome, 21 March 1989); WFP, Committee on Food Aid Policies and Programs, "Project Kenya 2269 (Exp. 1)—Integrated Livestock Development Including Soil Conservation," WFP/CFA: 27/SCP:2 (Rome, 7 April 1989); WFP, Committee on Food Aid Policies and Programs, "Project Kenya 3935—Food Aid to Core Activities in Arid and Semi-Arid (ASAL) Areas," WFP/CFA: 27/SCP:2 (Rome, 7 April 1989); and WFP, Committee on Food Aid Policies and Programs, *Review of Food Aid Policies and Programs.*

69. See World Food Program, "Interim Evaluation Summary Report on Project Senegal 2630."

70. See Royer and others, "Review of the Tanzania Food Aid Program."

71. See World Food Program, "Project Kenya 2502 (Exp. 1)."

72. See World Food Program, "Project Tanzania 2496 (Exp. 1)."

73. See Royer and others, "Review of the Tanzania Food Aid Program."

74. See World Food Program, "Interim Evaluation Summary Report on Project Senegal 2693."

75. See Osei Owusu, "The Future of Food Aid in Sub-Saharan Africa," *Food Policy* 14(August 1989):207–17.

76. See World Food Program, "Interim Evaluation Summary Report on Project Senegal 2630."

77. See Royer and others, "Review of the Tanzania Food Aid Program."

78. See World Food Program, "Interim Evaluation Summary Report on Project Senegal 2236 (Exp. 1)."

79. See Maxwell, "Food Aid to Senegal."

80. See John W. Mellor and Hannan Ezekiel, "Food Aid in Sub-Saharan Africa. A Study of Four Donors: USAID, Canada, EEC, and WFP; and Four Recipients: Kenya, Tanzania, Senegal, and Cameroon" (International Food Policy Research Institute, Washington, D.C., March 1987).

81. See John W. Mellor and C. G. Ranade, "Technological Change in a Low-Labor Productivity, Land Surplus Economy: The African Development Problem" (International Food Policy Research Institute, Washington, D.C., 1988), mimeographed.

82. See Reardon and Delgado, "Income Diversification of Rural Households in Burkina Faso."

83. See Thomas, "Food for Work."

84. See World Bank, *Social Indicators of Development, 1988.*

85. See V. M. Dandekar, "Agriculture, Employment and Poverty," in Robert E. B. Lucas and Gustav F. Papanek, eds., *The Indian Economy—Recent Developments and Future Prospects* (Boulder, Colo.: Westview, 1988), pp. 93–120.

86. See Joel Greer and Erik Thorbecke, *Food Poverty and Consumption Patterns in Kenya* (Geneva: International Labour Office, 1986).

87. Although these estimates seem reasonably safe, it should be pointed out that the data is this area are particularly difficult to generalize. For example, recent International Food Policy Research Institute surveys in a rural area of The Gambia, which resembles parts of rural Senegal, shows that food energy consumption for 18.4 percent of the population was significantly below nutritionally adequate levels—less than 80 percent of RDA. See Joachim von Braun,

Detlev Puetz, and Patrick Webb, "Irrigation Technology and Commercialization of Rice in The Gambia: Effects on Income and Nutrition," Research Report 75 (International Food Policy Research Institute, Washington, D.C., 1989). However, other parts of Senegal are poorer and so one can reasonably argue for a higher standard. In western Kenya, a similar survey found 27.6 percent in this category. See Eileen Kennedy, "The Effects of Sugarcane Production on Food Security, Health, and Nutrition in Kenya: A Longitudinal Analysis," Research Report 78 (International Food Policy Research Institute, Washington, D.C., 1989). That result may be consistent with a reduction in poverty since 1975. Any way one reads the data suggests a considerable incidence of nutritionally deprived poverty in rural areas of the MADIA countries.

88. See Food and Agriculture Organization, *The Fifth World Food Survey* (Rome, 1985).

89. Assume each person needs a supplement of 550 calories per day (assuming that the recommended daily allowance is 2,250 calories), which works out to 550 × 365 × 51.3 million calories required per year. Further assume that one kilogram of cereal equivalence is 3,500 calories.

90. Such an incidence of poverty, 38 percent, may in fact lead to an underestimation of the extent of poverty in Sub-Saharan Africa, given that the MADIA countries have higher per capita incomes in general and are more economically developed than the rest of Sub-Saharan Africa. However, using the MADIA incidence of poverty provides a base-level estimate of Sub-Saharan African poverty.

91. Note that since the price elasticity of food demand of the poor is significantly higher than the price elasticity of the food demand of the entire population, the effects of rising prices should be a larger reduction in the food consumption of the poor. Assuming that the overall price elasticity of food demand is −0.4, the price elasticity of food demand of the poor is −0.8, the rate of population growth exceeds the rate of growth of food production by between 2 and 3 percent, the price elasticity of food production ranges from zero to 0.4, and the rate of growth of per capita income of the poor is 0.5 percent per annum—then the rate of growth of per capita food consumption of the poor ranges from −1.80 to −6.40 percent. If the rate of growth of nominal per capita income of the poor is assumed to be 1 percent per annum, then the rate of growth of food consumption of the poor ranges from −1.40 percent to −6.00 percent. The effect on overall per capita food consumption of rising prices, with the same assumption, is that the rate of growth of overall per capita food consumption will range from −0.8 percent to −3.0 percent. See Hannan Ezekiel, "Program Food Aid and Food Consumption of the Poor in Developing Countries: A Model" (International Food Policy Research Institute, Washington, D.C., August 1989); and Mellor, "Food Price Policy and Income Distribution in Low-Income Countries."

92. See Shubh K. Kumar, "Effects on Nutrition in Bangladesh and Zambia," in *Infrastructure and Agricultural Development—Policy Issues and Research Priorities*, Policy Brief 3 (Washington, D.C.: International Food Policy Research Institute, 1988).

93. See Hannan Ezekiel, "A Rural Employment Guarantee Scheme as an Early Warning System" (International Food Policy Research Institute, Washington, D.C., August 1986).

94. See Hannan Ezekiel and Johann Stuyt, "The Maharashtra Employment Guarantee Scheme" (International Food Policy Research Institute, Washington, D.C., February 1988).

12 *Aid to African Agriculture: Lessons from Two Decades of Donors' Experience*

Uma Lele and Rahul Jain

AS OUTLINED AT THE BEGINNING of this volume, some countries in the MADIA sample pursued more effective policies than others in achieving agricultural growth through a balanced accumulation of human, physical, institutional, and technological capital. Smallholder development, it was also shown, is necessary to spur growth in the rest of the economy. Without such broadly based growth in agriculture, import-substituting strategies such as those pursued by Nigeria, Tanzania, and Senegal come to a halt as the demand for food and other wage goods increases under the pressure of urbanization. Even a rapid increase in food imports cannot sustain such a strategy in most African countries if there are no exports to finance these imports. In these countries, agriculture constitutes the engine of export growth.

In recent years macroeconomic difficulties have made it difficult not only to muster the financial resources needed to accumulate these different kinds of capital but also to focus policy attention on establishing key priorities for long-term development. This makes it all the more important to search through the record of donor and government actions in the past to determine which costly and unproductive strategies are to be avoided and which strategies will put donor assistance to the best use.

Donor assistance to Africa rose rapidly during the 1970s and has supported a large share of government expenditures in all of the MADIA countries except Nigeria. Not surprisingly, donor influence has been crucial in shaping the rate of capital accumulation and balance in the MADIA countries and thus in determining the source and breadth of productivity growth.

Indeed, individual donors greatly influenced the strategic investment choices made by recipients beginning in the 1970s, although some played a more overt role than others. The World Bank, for example, has had a direct influence since it has provided policy analysis and advice for a considerable period. The bilateral agencies have played an indirect role through their influence on the relative allocations to agroprocessing, large-scale industry, transport, agriculture, or social service sectors. Within the agricultural and rural sectors, donor assistance has influenced the relative priority accorded to food crop and export crop production, regions of low and high potential, growth and equity objectives, support for parastatals and private initiatives, and, more generally, short-term physical results and long-term capacity building. The substantial expansion of the public sector in countries such as Tanzania and Senegal in the 1970s, for example, would not have been possible without the active and generous support of donors. These strategic choices have in turn determined the extent to which the large inflows of external assistance caused Dutch disease effects instead of contributing to the growth of the traded goods sectors.

Lacking the necessary institutions and human resources, the recipients were not able to formulate and implement development strategies and therefore depended on external assistance in determining development priorities. These were influenced in part by the different constituencies supporting the different donors as well as the institutions and resources of aid-giving agencies. The real value of the resources transferred to recipients has thus been greatly overstated. The external shocks of the 1970s and the early 1980s have finally brought home the realization that countries need to build an internal capacity for sound economic management and policymaking if they are to develop a successful long-term development strategy.

In this concluding chapter the overall experience of the donors in the MADIA countries—the successes and the failures—is analyzed with two basic questions in mind.[1] First, to what extent have donors helped recipients (a) develop balanced, long-term strategies for broadly based agricultural development within the context of political and institutional constraints peculiar to each country, and (b) choose and undertake the necessary strategic investments? Second, what constraints have donor constituencies, resource bases, and various institutional factors imposed on the nature and effectiveness of donor assistance?

The Role of Donors in Ensuring Balanced, Long-Term Agricultural Strategies

An important contribution of donors during the 1970s was that they by and large helped to enshrine the smallholder-based agricultural development strategy as a means for achieving overall economic growth—even in circumstances where the African commitment to this cause was weak at best and donors' own interventions had many shortcomings. Yet these efforts—however well-intentioned and individually successful in many cases—were not conceived in the framework of the broader vision of long-term development. With growing concerns about the environmental and health issues, attention to agriculture has waned. Moreover, the failure of the integrated agricultural development strategy and doubts about the ability of governments to perform their important role in smallholder agriculture have discredited the agriculture-led strategy, even though choice of poor means should not damn the ends.

Promoting a Smallholder, Agriculture-Led Strategy for Overall Growth

Ample examples exist of how donor assistance can act as both a catalyst and a protector of smallholder development: as it did when the United Kingdom promoted smallholder export agriculture with tea and coffee in Kenya and when France did the same in Cameroon and Senegal with cotton; when the World Bank helped to establish a smallholder-oriented agricultural development strategy in Nigeria; when Sweden and Denmark assisted with soil conservation and dairying, respectively, in Kenya; when Germany helped with the development of hybrid maize in Senegal; or when the STABEX assistance provided by the European Communities (EC) helped stabilize the revenues of groundnut producers in Senegal. Similarly, the contributions of the United States toward agricultural colleges and universities in these countries exemplify donor attempts to develop longer-term human and institutional capital in the agricultural sector.

Yet neither the donors' project-by-project approach of the 1970s nor their concern for policy reform in the 1980s has to date helped African governments face the inescapable hard work of constructing long-term, country-specific development strategies that can withstand the requirements of everyday macroeconomic management in the face of an ever-changing external environment.[2] The challenge for the 1990s is to balance the enabling macroeconomic environment with sound sectoral polices and the alleviation of microeconomic constraints. In this regard, donors have not devoted much attention to the sequencing and phasing of policies and investments or appreciated the need for selectivity. They have not given priority to the investments to develop human, institutional, and technological capital that are needed to modernize traditional agriculture. These imbalances have been reinforced by the the inability of African governments to effectively articulate their strategies and by their preference for maximizing financial resource flows rather than methodically pursuing the long-term development of internal absorptive capacity.

It is difficult, therefore, to find much connection between where donor assistance went and where growth occurred in the MADIA countries, as the following shows:

- In Malawi, for example, although donors concentrated on smallholders, growth occurred among the estates because of the policies pursued by the government (favoring the estates) and because of the fungibility of donor assistance, which the government channeled into large-scale agriculture.
- In Senegal, despite massive donor assistance, and in Nigeria, despite the oil boom and World Bank commitments of nearly $1.7 billion, there was little agricultural growth except in irrigated rice, maize, and horticultural crops—all of which constitute minor subsectors when the area planted, value added, or employment generated are taken into account.
- In Tanzania, although donors supported agroprocessing and food crop production (mainly via integrated rural development projects), food production both stagnated and moved increasingly into the parallel market, and the performance of export crops declined.
- Even in Cameroon and in Kenya—countries that performed relatively well—donor intervention in commodities that were successful constituted but a small part of the total assistance provided. In Cameroon, it is difficult to attribute the growth in the agricultural sector to donors except in the case of investments in cotton and rice in the north. In both Cameroon and Senegal, moreover, the economic viability of the irrigated rice schemes has been questioned by donors, yet this has not affected their financing.
- In Kenya, where a substantial proportion of donor assistance went to marginal areas, much of the growth achieved was accounted for by high-value activities such as tea and coffee production and dairying in areas of high agricultural potential. The Commonwealth Development Corporation and the World Bank played an important role in institutional strengthening in the case of the Kenya Tea Development Authority, and the World Bank also helped establish processing capacity for tea, as well as services for coffee. Yet the Bank's advice to Kenya and its lending policies toward the development of these crops reflected a continuing export pessimism and an inconsistency with the Bank's project activities and their subsequent outcomes. Kenya's strong internal political support (lacking in many other African countries) for export agriculture provided the impetus for the rapid growth of smallholder tea and coffee.

At the microlevel, the absence of a long-term framework for promoting smallholder agriculture and a declining appreciation within the donor community of the importance of technical know-how and expertise have contributed to the inadequate grasp of complex, location-specific factors. This problem has been accentuated by the inadequate internal capacity in Africa; governments have not made adequate use of the limited, but growing, supply of trained nationals, preferring instead to rely on large numbers of expatriate technical assistance personnel.

Several donor studies in this book have drawn attention to the lack of understanding among expatriate personnel of the complex farming systems evolved by African farmers and of the crop- and location-specific constraints on smallholder intensification and efficient use of the available (but rapidly declining) extensive margin. These problems appear to have been particularly critical in the widespread failure of extension projects. For example, the efforts of both Germany and the World Bank to spread innovations (for instance, hybrid maize) in Malawi stalled because of inadequate knowledge of producer preferences, problems of storability, and the limited risk-taking ability and access to credit of a large number of farmers operating below the subsistence level. Similarly, USAID's extension activities in Senegal, Cameroon, Tanzania, and Nigeria had a limited impact, as they were based on an imperfect knowledge of the socioeconomic constraints facing small farmers. In Cameroon, the Dutch disease effects of the oil boom, on the other hand, contributed to an increase in nonfarm labor demand and—through labor shortages in agriculture—led to the poor performance of virtually all World Bank projects in the forest areas of South and East Cameroon.[3] But the effects of such macroeconomic policies on agriculture, too, were poorly understood.

The recent emphasis on macroeconomic policy reforms and the correction of price signals is encouraging some labor to return to agriculture. Combined with the rise in export crop prices through exchange rate adjustments and the reduction of taxes, this is leading to supply response in agriculture in the short run. The ability to sustain this response, however, will remain constrained by the myriad policy, institutional, and microlevel constraints that only Africans can address.

Striking a Balance among Strategic Investment Choices

The absence of a long-term vision of agricultural development has also contributed, if inadvertently, to the perception that the different strategic choices available in recipient countries are "alternatives" rather than complementary elements of a balanced overall strategy. This is illustrated later in the chapter with examples of the shift donors have made from the earlier emphasis on shorter-term physical results to the long-term absorptive capacity, and, within agriculture, from food crops to export crops, from regions of high potential to regions of low agricultural potential, from growth to equity objectives, and from parastatals to private initiative.

Recent trends suggest that a donor consensus on some of these issues is beginning to be established. For example, Sweden and Denmark have reduced their tolerance of burgeoning and inefficient public operations. Similarly, the United States, which has been at the forefront of policy reform initiatives, may have begun to moderate its views about the speed with which privatization can proceed, given the outcomes of initial reform efforts. The United States may now be beginning to appreciate once again the critical role of the public sector in the provision of public goods.

Short-term gains and long-term capacity building. The emerging donor consensus is finally providing an opportunity to formulate successful long-term strategies on a country-by-country basis. Donor support could be mobilized around these strategies to undertake complex interventions in support of capital accumulation at the sectoral, subsectoral, and local level in countries that offer a conducive policy environment. But such strategies are impossible to conceive unless effective analytical and policymaking capacity is developed at the national and sectoral levels both inside and outside governments. This should go hand in hand with far more informed public debate within each country on the real causes and consequences of government actions and donor policies (although the situation has varied considerably among countries).[4]

That the development of recipient capacity can ensure the success of donor interventions has already been demonstrated in Latin America and Asia. Capacity building can resolve one of the biggest problems that donors currently face: On the one hand, they are held increasingly accountable by constituencies in aid-giving countries that demand quick, positive results in exchange for their continued support, and, on the other, they are viewed as threatening by recipients when they intervene to ensure that policy reforms are carried out (without which projects tend to perform poorly).

The experience of the MADIA countries shows that donors, instead of embracing a broad and long-term strategy for developing internal capacity, have leaned toward the achievement of visible and immediate results by investing large sums in physical and social infrastructure as an easy means of ensuring accountability to their internal constituencies. Chapter 11 has shown how, in the infrastructure-deficient MADIA countries, investment in rural works programs with a high employment and food content could reduce the proportion of the rural poor by enabling rural areas to participate in the growth process. Furthermore, such an infrastructure grid would provide both an early warning system for periodic hunger and an effective mechanism for famine relief. Donor experience in the MADIA countries, however, shows that investments in infrastructure have not been conceived in the context of a viable, long-term strategy. The lack of accompanying investments in human, institutional, technical, and informational capital has precluded the adequate maintenance of the infrastructure put in place. Most important, the institutional responsibility for operation and maintenance—a critical factor in successful infrastructure development—has not been delegated to the local governments and grass roots organizations that benefit from these services. National governments have time and again increased central control, and donors have inadvertently supported these actions.

The development of transport networks plays a crucial role in broadening factor and product markets, spreading new technologies, increasing input use, and in performing other such services. Investments in basic infrastructure, particularly in transportation networks, constituted nearly 35 percent of total German assistance to the six countries during the period 1962–86, more than 29 percent of total World Bank assistance to these countries during 1965–88, and 32 percent of total EC project aid to Tanzania, Cameroon, and Senegal during 1958–85.[5] But strategies of transport development have paid more attention to trunk routes than to rural feeder roads.[6] Moreover, the absence of institutional capacity at local levels and the shortages of recurrent funds plagued the maintenance of feeder roads—for example, in Tanzania and Nigeria. There has similarly been neglect of feeder roads in Senegal.

Sweden, Denmark, and the World Bank similarly provided substantial assistance to Tanzania and Kenya for social infrastructure. The shares of water supply, health, and education together accounted for 52 percent and 29 percent of the total assistance the Swedish International Development Agency (SIDA) gave to Kenya and Tanzania, respectively, until 1984; and for 27 percent of the total assistance that the Danish International Development Agency (DANIDA) gave to Tanzania over 1962–84. These investments helped shape the sectoral strategies of recipient countries—as, for instance, in the case of Tanzania, where the water supply program was expected to achieve universal coverage by 1990 with the help of SIDA and other donors. As pointed out in chapter 5, fiscal infeasibility, technological inappropriateness, and inadequate decentralization turned out to be the main barriers to the ambitious plans of Swedish assistance. By 1984, after thirteen years of implementation, only 12 percent of the rural population in Tanzania had access to reliable drinking water, and in all likelihood this proportion had declined by the end of the 1980s.

Furthermore, by inadvertently contributing to the growth of non-traded goods sectors in countries such as Tanzania and Senegal, excessive donor assistance during the latter half of the 1970s led to a Dutch disease syndrome. In Tanzania, for example, external assistance fueled large increases in public consumption (in part accounted for by the rapid rise in public sector employment associated with expenditures on social services) that had limited effect and exerted upward pressure on both inflation and the exchange rate. Collier has shown that the distributional consequence of this aid boom was to benefit the net consumers of tradable goods (the prices of which fell relative to nontradables) at the expense of net producers.[7] Since the rationed allocation of imported consumer goods favored urban areas (especially Dar es Salaam) and the only producers of tradables were farmers growing export crops, this amounted to a redistribution of resources from these farmers to urban households. The production of tradables suffered in the absence of efforts to rectify the policy biases against export agriculture. More generally, the large influx of donor assistance enabled the government to reembark on its costly and counterproductive Basic Industries Strategy, which had been briefly abandoned following the first oil crisis and which proved politically difficult to reverse.[8]

Donors preferred relatively short-term interventions for relieving the more visible shortages of physical and social capital. But the strategies that were successful in promoting smallholder development in the MADIA countries—for example, tea, coffee, hybrid maize, and dairying in Kenya and cotton in Francophone Africa—involved complex packages of public policy measures. These included, but were not limited to, the development of rural infrastructure and required long periods of gestation. In the development of tea and coffee in Kenya, field-level technical services had to be sustained for well over a decade and a half.[9] It has taken almost as long to develop cotton in Francophone West Africa, which has depended on long-term technical assistance of high quality.

In other notable examples of smallholder development, long periods of high-quality donor commitment have also been necessary (although not necessarily a large volume of assistance, as in the case of high-profile infrastructure projects), particularly to develop sustainable human, institutional, and technical capacity at the local level. The United Kingdom's Cotton Research Corporation (CRC) spent more than fifty years in Malawi and nearly forty years in Tanzania to develop research capabilities in this area (see chapter 9). The successful training of Malawians by the British helped preserve these capabilities after the withdrawal of the CRC. In contrast, the insufficient training of nationals and a combination of poor policies and weak government commitment in Tanzania in the 1970s led to the erosion of the substantial earlier gains. Short-term support in the case of the United Kingdom's maize agronomy projects in Kenya and Malawi, and its potato research project in Kenya, in turn failed to establish programs and institutions capable of sustaining themselves without external financial and technical support. Similarly, erratic funding and shifting priorities in USAID's maize-breeding activities reduced the effectiveness of the successful maize program at Kitale in Kenya.

It is clear, therefore, that the greatest impact has been made by the longest supported measures, with the help of on-site experts who, because of their long field presence, have developed a technical grasp of the contextual issues and, most important, have helped institutionalize these efforts. This experience underscores the importance of having detailed knowledge of the grass roots—rather than the sheer volume of assistance alone—as a source of well-planned and well-executed development programs. In addition to the commitment of such high-quality technical assistance, which helps develop local capacity for nurturing new technologies and institutions to maturity, these efforts have also involved a high degree of rapport with nationals.

Parenthetically, it needs to be mentioned that one important consequence of the association of long gestation with successful smallholder development has been the short-circuiting of this process by some governments—for example, those of Malawi and Nigeria—which have promoted large farms in their efforts to secure a quick, near-term payoff.[10] As stated earlier, although donor resources are targeted mostly at smallholders, they have, because of their fungibility, unwittingly furthered these aims.

On a broader level, long-term agricultural development is demanding of human and organizational capital and can be realistically deployed on the necessary scale only by developing the recipient's capacity for effective research, analysis, and policymaking. In Africa, however, the pressures to modernize and to cope with a rapid succession of domestic and external crises have been immense. As a result, the efforts of African governments to build national institutions that could provide a steady flow of highly qualified economic researchers, analysts, and managers have been few and far between. Nor have governments made active attempts to foster an intellectual climate conducive to the genesis of arms-length organizations that could provide objective policy research and advice. Furthermore, the governments of small African countries have been less vocal in demanding high-quality donor assistance for the long-term training of nationals and less successful in choosing from the array of donor assistance and advice of varying quality than, say, their larger Asian counterparts, such as India, China, or Indonesia. The weak technocracies in Africa have not adequately represented the larger governmental and political interests or articulated them in cohesive macroeconomic and sectoral policies that directly address developmental concerns.

Nor have donors done much either to strengthen the weak analytical and policymaking capabilities at the macroeconomic and sectoral level or to institutionalize macroeconomic and sectoral policy research. The United States, however, is an important outlier in this respect. United States assistance has been more unstable than that of other bilateral donors and reflects the dominance of strategic interests. It has nevertheless played a significant role in building policy planning and research capacity in Asia and Latin America.[11] In the MADIA countries, USAID has spent a quarter of all assistance to agriculture and rural development (which comprises some 60 percent of total USAID assistance) on agricultural education and training.[12] It has sought to strengthen indigenous capabilities over the long run by promoting institutions for higher education in Nigeria, Kenya, Malawi, and Tanzania. In addition, the Agricultural Management and Planning projects in Senegal and Cameroon are good examples of strengthening the local base for policy research and analysis. These activities constitute an important link in the sequence of public investments needed to modernize agriculture, but the direct impact of USAID's institution-building efforts on agricultural development is not easily assessed. For example, the sporadic nature of United States assistance to agricultural colleges in East Africa adversely affected its effectiveness, as pointed out in chapter 6. In Nigeria, however, inadequate governmental support (in addition to the civil war and the ensuing political instability) crippled the functioning of the various faculties of agriculture and veterinary medicine that USAID supported. Moreover, USAID's institution-building efforts were mainly confined to agriculture (instead of creating a policy planning capacity more generally, as the agency had done earlier in Asia and Latin America), and they were withdrawn in 1976, after the oil boom and Nigeria's accession to the Organization of Petroleum Exporting Countries.[13]

In contrast, until recently the World Bank has done little to support local research and analytical capabilities by promoting institutions of learning or the work of individual local researchers. This is in part a consequence of the weak internal demand for capacity building in Africa, but it also reflects an inadequate appreciation of this need within the World Bank itself. Thus, although the Bank recognized the weak analytical capacity for policy formulation in the Kenyan Ministry of Agriculture in the 1970s, its assistance did not address these concerns adequately. It chose to undertake its own projects through expatriate technical assistance rather than to persuade the Kenyan government to make better use of the substantial national expertise that was by then available.[14]

The World Bank has now undertaken a large new initiative for developing capacity in Africa through centers of excellence. These efforts are still focused on improving macroeconomic policy, which is only the tip of the iceberg. The Bank's efforts need to be complemented by similar efforts in all areas that contribute to the macroeconomic imbalance and that have become increasingly reliant on external technical assistance in recent years (see chapter 3).

Detailed sectoral and subsectoral data are essential for well-documented analytical work that is strongly grounded in the realities of smallholder agriculture. The MADIA study in general has highlighted, in addition to the shortage of trained African personnel at the macroeconomic level, the paucity of reliable and timely data on such essential microeconomic matters as the area, yields, and production of crops by region—a problem that has consistently plagued agricultural planning in Africa.

The number of educated and trained African nationals has increased significantly, albeit from a low initial base. In the face of the weak human and institutional capacity in recipient countries, the training of nationals has occurred mostly on the job. The high population growth rates and progressive degradation of the natural resource base will make it increasingly difficult to revive agriculture unless both governments and donors give the highest priority to achieving a balance in the deployment of human and physical capital and thereby to developing and sustaining long-term capacity.[15] Documents such as the Lagos Plan do emphasize this important need, but it has not yet been effectively articulated in the assistance sought by governments.[16]

Export crops and food crops. The attainment of food security is of fundamental importance in the farming decisions of small rural households.[17] Assured food crop production releases land and labor for diversification into other higher-value production for domestic use or export. Export crop production, however, helps raise and stabilize household and national income, thereby increasing food security. Because of their labor intensity, export crops tend to generate greater employment than food cropping. Moreover, the production of most export crops tends to be scale-neutral and therefore can be undertaken by small farmers. Indeed, where marginal productivity in export crop production is high and the returns assured—as in the case of tea and coffee in Kenya or cotton in Cameroon—farming households have relied on the market for food out of choice, unlike their poorer rural counterparts who have depended on the market out of necessity.

Donor attention, however, has swung between support for either food security or export crop development—instead of pursuing a consistent and balanced approach to both food and export crops. Beginning in the early 1970s, most donors who had promoted export crop agriculture in the 1960s shifted their investment emphasis and policy attention toward food crops. The reasons for this shift are more numerous, complex, and interactive than is usually recognized. First, concern about food security and poverty alleviation intensified sharply in the aftermath of the world food crisis. Second, the export pessimism led donors to support and encourage the taxation of export crops as a way of pressing diversification out of traditional export crops such as tea, coffee, groundnuts, and sisal, into new activities (see chapter 3). Third, donors faced a dilemma in balancing the interests of individual exporting countries with those of the primary commodity producers at large. In the case of tea, for example, the World Bank in 1973 adopted a policy of financing only the rehabilitation of existing productive capacity instead of the expansion of acreage (except when the tea-producing countries had no alternatives) on account of the perceived conflicts among its various borrowers (for example, Sri Lanka in relation to East African countries). Because demand is price and income inelastic and assumed to be concentrated in the industrial countries, increase in aggregate production was assumed to cause a fall in the incomes of individual producers without benefit to "deserving" consumers. Similar de facto guidelines applied to the financing of coffee production. Since 1982 more overt restrictions have applied to World Bank lending for coffee and cocoa. Similarly, there has been reluctance in the EC to finance crops whose fluctuations in export earnings have triggered STABEX assistance. Fourth, the competing interests of developing countries have been paralleled by those of donor countries in the case of several other primary commodities—making the argument apply more broadly. The United States, for example, has refrained from financing research in countries producing commodities whose export to third parties might compete with United States exports of the same commodities.[18] From time to time, producers in industrial countries have also put pressure on the World Bank to restrict lending to developing countries for commodities such as palm oil, soybean oil, tobacco, citrus fruits, and sugar, whose production competes with their own.

African governments in turn faced a paramount concern for food security—a concern that they felt had been ignored by the colonial powers earlier. Second, they hoped to diversify out of colonial modes of production and modernize through industrialization. Tanzania, for example, which shared and articulated these concerns most effectively, moved into the processing of its traditional agricultural exports and import-substituting industries. In a variety of ways, the government discouraged the involvement of individual farmers in high-value export crops and, as pointed out in chapter 9, rejected the Commonwealth Development Corporation's smallholder crop authority model, which had proved successful in Kenya.

The net result of these numerous factors was that the MADIA countries have lost world market shares in important export crops (with the exceptions of tea and coffee in Kenya and tobacco in Malawi) to other developing and developed countries. Senegal's share in world exports of groundnuts (oil equivalent), for example, fell from an average of 27.8 percent in 1969–71 to 12.1 percent by 1986, whereas the United States share increased from 5.7 percent to 21.0 percent over the same period. Nigeria's share in world palm oil exports fell from 22.9 percent over 1961–63 to 0.6 percent in 1971–73, whereas Malaysia's increased from 17.7 percent to 49.8 percent.

In the 1980s emphasis began to swing back toward export crop production, as was evident in the United Kingdom's program in Tanzania, where the government finally agreed to correct the policy distortions that afflicted export crops. Although World Bank support for food crops in Nigeria continued into the 1980s, there was also a renewed interest in promoting nonfood export crops such as cotton.

As noted at the outset of this volume, the distinction between area expansion and rehabilitation made in donor policy toward export crop farming has, in retrospect, turned out to be arbitrary since much of the actual increase in smallholder export crop production in Africa has come from area expansion, even though it was intended to come from productivity increases.[19] Labor availability and the lack of farm services have been obstacles to intensification, and it has been more profitable, at the margin, for farmers to increase acreage than to intensify existing production. Donor investments in processing facilities and in the rehabilitation of existing acreages have also served to encourage the expansion of acreage by providing a market stimulus that would not otherwise have existed. In such circumstances, therefore, it might be better to provide the poorest countries, which have few alternative sources of growth and lack access to nonofficial external capital, with the requisite assistance to increase production. Such increases are unlikely to have more than a marginal impact on the aggregate situation. Moreover, since the growth in world consumption of commodities such as tea, cotton, edible oil, and sugar derives largely from developing countries, it is no longer true that continued increases in the production of these commodities will only benefit consumers in developed countries. Consumers and producers of primary commodities are spread throughout the world. Thus, a policy that denies African producers the right to expand production because they depend on external aid for such expansion is inconsistent with the recently renewed donor emphasis on the concepts of competition, efficiency, and equal opportunity.

The experience with food crop production clearly shows that many African governments have neglected the production of their traditional food crops—for example, sorghum, millet, cassava, and yams—produced and consumed by a large majority of their citizens. Instead, they have favored the high-cost production of import-substituting rice and wheat to meet rapidly growing demand emanating from the urban population; indeed, rice has been the fastest growing crop in the MADIA countries. France and the EC, for example, assisted the Senegalese government in diversifying the economy out of groundnuts, the traditional export and mainstay of its economy, into the uneconomical production of irrigation-based rice (in addition to confectionery groundnuts, groundnut oil, cotton, and vegetables). The World Bank did the same in Cameroon in the 1970s, but later changed its position.

In general, the shift of donor investments in extension, input supply, and rural infrastructure toward food crops—often in areas of low productive potential and high transportation cost—was understandable on the grounds of improving regional income distribution. But investments in large rural development projects proved difficult to sustain in the absence of both an established research and technological base (with the notable exception of hybrid maize) and insufficient levels of human and institutional capacity. Moreover, their effectiveness was limited by their narrowly defined project objectives, short time horizons, ambitious project targets, inadequate understanding of the broad policy and sector issues and of their impact on project operation, and poor knowledge of the sociocultural environment. In the evaluations commissioned by the donors themselves, these factors had already been identified as important constraints on smallholder growth.[20] Yet this literature had little impact on donor behavior. Agricultural research, for example, accounted for a very small share of donor assistance to the MADIA countries in the 1970s, and much of it tended to be of a quick, adaptive nature in the context of rural development projects. In general, donor efforts have not addressed the need for a systematic buildup of local capacity for research and technology to solve the more fundamental farm constraints posed by soil degradation, the slow growth of fertilizer use, declining fallow periods, and the like. Furthermore, as discussed in chapter 2, donor efforts—including those of the Consultative Group on International Agricultural Research—have been largely supply-driven, given the weak internal demand in African countries for developing effective research capability.

The countries that relied on their comparative advantage and moved least rapidly to diversify their economies performed well—and, ironically, achieved rapid diversification. For example, despite donor warnings of poor export prospects in the 1970s, Kenya continued to expand its traditional tea and coffee exports (which together account for 50–60 percent of its total export earnings). Considerable strides were also made in the production of (improved) maize and horticultural crops. Moreover, Kenya further broadened employment opportunities by successfully developing decentralized, small-scale industries. In contrast, the costly and complex diversification strategies attempted by Tanzania and Senegal ignored the sequencing and phasing of the strategic investments necessary for broadly based growth by undermining agriculture in favor of capital-intensive, import-substituting industrialization. These countries performed poorly in *both* food and export crops.[21] Furthermore, the development of large public sector industries—such as Tanzania's fertilizer and pulp and paper industries, made possible by the active support of donors—created far fewer income-earning opportunities. Although food imports rose steeply in all three countries, in Kenya they served to meet the growing demand from broadly based growth in employment and incomes stimulated by an agriculture-led industrialization, whereas in Tanzania and Senegal they reflected the weakness of the chosen strategy.

At present, intellectual and political support for the role of export crops is inadequate both among African governments and among donor constituencies—despite the fact that Africa has become a major net importer of commodities such as cotton and edible oils, which it previously exported, because internal demand has burgeoned but capacity to finance these growing imports has declined. While food security, poverty alleviation, and environmental conservation concerns dominate the development agenda of donors, little attention is directed toward the issues of (a) export crop research and technological capacity; (b) the complex production, processing, and organizational requirements of these crops, which vary by commodities; and (c) the development of viable export strategies.[22]

In the case of food crops, expenditures on research have increased significantly in recent years—in part in response to the concerns outlined here. However, there has been excessive emphasis on technical assistance and the brick and mortar in donor assistance, and not enough on establishing long-term human and institutional capacity—or even on using the pool of human capital that has been developed—to address the substance of technological issues. The SPAAR initiative of 1989 should redress this shortcoming by supporting research that is more demand driven.

The current preoccupation with food security raises a question about the validity of concentrating resources and policy attention on food production programs, given the disappointing results of a similar, single-minded emphasis in the 1970s. One positive consequence of such a focus, however, has been a more conscious attempt by donors to integrate food aid with financial assistance as part of a concerted strategy (see chapter 11). Recipients are concerned, however, that this might lead to conditionality on the receipt of food aid.

Resource-rich regions and remote and resource-poor regions. To achieve rapid growth, agricultural investments need to be channeled into activities and regions that have the greatest technological potential for growth. A strong production policy in areas of high agricultural potential needs to be accompanied by strong consumption and welfare-oriented activities in areas of low potential (including policies to subsidize and stabilize food prices and to promote migration from such areas). In the MADIA countries, this picture is complicated by the incidence of human and animal diseases and historical patterns of settlement. Areas of highest potential are not always those where population densities are the greatest.[23] The desire on the part of governments to generate employment and income in marginal areas leads them to invest in areas where population densities and political support for governments are usually high. Employment and incomes in the marginal areas can only be generated by investment in the nonagricultural sectors.

In the 1970s donor emphasis shifted toward food crop production and poverty alleviation in marginal areas. The results were disappointing for DANIDA in the semiarid areas of Tanzania (for instance, in livestock, grain storage, and road-building activities) but encouraging in the relatively more productive temperate areas of Kenya (see chapter 4). In the case of German assistance, the resource-poor areas continued to have problems even when attempts were made to introduce the concept of self-help (chapter 10). The failure or near failure of most donor projects to increase food crop productivity in such areas is well illustrated by the disappointing performance of the numerous donor-financed integrated rural development projects—such as the World Bank's projects in Tanzania, northern Nigeria, and Senegal; and the United Kingdom's projects in Phalombe, Malawi, and Mtwara-Lindi, Tanzania.

These experiences suggest that the problems of resource-poor areas can only be addressed through the growth of nonagricultural employment that is based on a sound knowledge of location-specific, microlevel constraints and that emphasizes public sector investment in transportation, education, etc. This implies that the public sector will have to play a complex and sophisticated role in formulating development policy that combines agricultural with nonagricultural employment—one that most MADIA governments have not been able to articulate.

Growth and equity. Complex growth and equity objectives can only be reconciled through a sophisticated development strategy with a strong emphasis on macroeconomic management—especially in countries that have fluctuating external terms of trade and whose expenditures are supported by large and unstable flows of external assistance. As the experience of Kenya (and to a lesser extent Cameroon) demonstrates, a successful smallholder strategy carried out in the context of responsible macroeconomic management can achieve both growth and equity objectives. In an adverse policy environment, however, emphasis on poverty alleviation and the provision of education, health, and other welfare services in all regions and among all socioeconomic groups simultaneously with an import substitution strategy leads neither to equity nor growth. Most of the health centers established by SIDA, for example, suffered from a chronic shortage of essential supplies and equipment. In Tanzania, the heavy industry made inordinate demands on resources that Tanzania could not sustain once adverse external shocks ensued.

The World Bank took the lead in promoting integrated, multisectoral projects. Short-term physical targets were often achieved (for example, in building rural infrastructure and housing for staff), but it was more difficult to sustain farm revenue in resource-poor regions. The absence of suitable food crop technologies led to low or negative returns in production-oriented activities, and a weak local administrative capacity (as in Nigeria, Tanzania, and Senegal) made it impossible to maintain the established infrastructure.[25] The strong and sustained shift out of export crops caused the situation to grow worse—since export crop projects were generally more successful and usually boosted farm revenue, as the EC experience demonstrates (chapter 7). With little or no growth in food production in marginal areas, and without the foreign exchange earnings from an increased volume of those export crops in which Africa has a strong comparative advantage, the MADIA countries became increasingly reliant on food imports—particularly on food aid (despite the development of import-substituting crops such as rice production through irrigation).

The overall record of the 1970s shows that, no matter how worthy the underlying intentions, neither growth nor equity are likely to be advanced by a single-minded emphasis on food security and poverty alleviation that undermines growth of export crops, that neglects the technological factors affecting improvement in food crop productivity, and that diverts resources into the pursuit of rapid industrialization.

The structural adjustment efforts in the 1980s were intended to achieve precisely such a balance. However, the initial structural adjustment efforts in the 1980s led to a sharp and excessive swing of donor attention toward efficiency and away from equity concerns such as the consumption and welfare needs of the poor—as reflected in the indiscriminate abolition of fertilizer and food subsidies.[26] Restoring the balance between efficiency and equity objectives may entail, among other things, reinstating such subsidies in the short run as a way of protecting disadvantaged groups.

Macroeconomic adjustment, privatization, and a role for the public sector. It is evident from the preceding discussion that sound macroeconomic and sectoral policy management simply cannot be separated from a long-term development strategy. If donor assistance is to be efficiently applied to individual countries and the circumstances in specific locations and areas of the economy, not only must there be an effort to remove policy-induced distortions in the macroeconomy, there must also be sound subsectoral strategies working together as a "macroeconomic whole" to remove the myriad constraints at all levels of the economy. Therefore a balance needs to be struck between structural adjustment assistance (at the macroeconomic and sectoral levels) and project assistance (at the subsectoral level). In general, greater developmental substance is needed in the adjustment policies promoted by donors for these to engage the imagination of African policymakers.

In the 1970s donors failed to grasp the complex repercussions of the adverse policy environment in countries such as Tanzania, Senegal, and Nigeria—as well as the consequences of their own actions in contributing to these problems in circumstances of weak internal capacity—and their projects performed poorly. In the 1980s, given the deterioration in many developing countries' terms of trade, their rising public expenditures, and past patterns of inefficient use of resources, donors have correctly emphasized macroeconomic and sectoral policy reform as a precondition for sustainable, long-term development, but they have left the responsibility squarely with the recipients.

Despite the problems inherent in judging the impact of structural adjustment assistance, there is no doubt that sustained macroeconomic difficulties and pressure from donors have induced governments to undertake necessary macrostructural reform. A good example is the adjustment of the excessively overvalued exchange rates in Nigeria and Tanzania in 1986, which, in the case of the latter, led to a revival of donor support. Similarly, as chapter 6 has shown, structural adjustment aid to Kenya in 1983 may have been an important factor in trimming the country's budget and current account deficits, as well as its inflation rate.

Current programs for structural adjustment are a necessary condition for economic recovery in several African countries. However, it is clear from the evidence presented in this book that short-term stabilization measures and the related privatization and deregulation initiatives alone cannot stimulate sustained growth in the agricultural sector.

First, structural adjustment assistance can strain absorptive capacity while leaving intact longer-term structural problems. This is illustrated by the experience of the World Bank and USAID program grants to address complex land issues in Malawi and Kenya.[27]

Second, donors have found it difficult in practice to link adjustment assistance to agricultural aid in particular. The targeting of foreign exchange and other inputs on agricultural (particularly smallholder) production has often had limited impact. Furthermore, as illustrated by U.K. program aid to Kenya and Malawi, importers of agricultural inputs may already have preferential access to foreign exchange and may not procure as much as is anticipated from program aid sources.

Third, where privatization and deregulation initiatives are part of the adjustment effort, these may need to be coordinated with public sector efforts to relieve microlevel constraints, as well as to ensure market competitiveness. For example, in view of the nature of the agricultural services needed for export crops, the economies of scale in their processing, and the relatively long gestation lags, it may be essential to allow for public sector provision of transport, information, credit, and distribution networks as complementary but essential preconditions for decentralized, private sector agricultural activities. Unfortunately, in the 1970s the policies of some African governments deviated substantially from this perception of an important, but limited, public sector role.[28] As the data on growth in public expenditures presented in chapter 2 show, recent liberalization attempts have frequently overlooked the extent to which donors themselves contributed to this indiscriminate growth of the public sector—particularly in the latter half of the 1970s, when Africa was recovering from the drought, the prices of primary commodities were on the rise, and aid commitments soared. At the time, donors took little notice of the fundamental factors determining the efficiency of public sector operations—for example, the domestic political environment and the shortage of working capital and of technical and managerial expertise. By the same token, in the 1980s, when the climate for public sector growth was far less propitious, donors did not pay sufficient attention to the adverse effects of public sector withdrawal. The African private sector, operating in the same setting and experiencing similar problems, is not adequately compensating for these negative repercussions.

The challenge is thus again one of achieving a balance—in this case between appropriate emphasis on public and private sector roles. If the nature and sources of some of the current constraints on both sectors were better understood, inefficiencies in public sector performance could in some cases be corrected without dismantling existing structures. Several cases of donor experience illustrate these complex interrelationships. Donor experience with grain liberalization in Kenya and Malawi demonstrates that success depends on government support as well as on the timing, speed, and extent of privatization activities. The United Kingdom's insistence on private sector procurement under its second program grant to Malawi in 1984 meant that there was limited direct support for the supply of imported agricultural inputs to smallholder agriculture (which was primarily served by the public sector). In the same vein, the private sector response to donor attempts to liberalize fertilizer distribution has been swift, but it is likely to benefit mainly large farmers and the better organized smallholders in the relatively more accessible areas—as the demand for fertilizer among these groups is already well established. In Kenya, Malawi, and Senegal, poor and marginal farmers who received much donor attention in the 1970s are likely to be neglected in the period of adjustment unless public distribution and credit programs are devised to complement private activities.

Correcting—and avoiding—such imbalances will require well-conceived, long-term interventions that ensure foreign exchange availability, together with subsidies targeted to the needs of these groups, until improved technological packages are available and distribution costs are reduced.[29] Some African governments have clearly demonstrated a relatively stronger ability than others to implement such complex interventions; they should clearly receive primacy in donor assistance as a way of inducing others to get their houses in order.

Adjustment assistance has only partly reflected an understanding of the myriad microlevel constraints in Africa or distinguished between the differing abilities and commitments of the governments there. Cuts in government budgets in the process of structural adjustment and the declining importance of project assistance have intensified the resource shortage, thereby restricting opportunities to fill in the gaps in the private servicing of smallholder agriculture.

Overall, the discussion of donor experience in this section suggests that, despite the strong donor influence on capital accumulation, African governments have managed to pursue their own sociopolitical objectives in choosing and undertaking strategic investments. As the case of Kenya demonstrates, however, unless there is a strong political will for an agriculture-led strategy, and unless technocrats can successfully translate this commitment into a long-term framework for sequencing and phasing investments in an appropriate policy setting, growth and equity objectives will be difficult to achieve.

Donor Country Constraints on Aid Effectiveness

The institutionalization of donors' internal constituencies for aid, their political philosophies, their resource bases, and their developmental experiences in the programming process have all affected the design of their assistance programs. The mix of these parameters has often constrained aid effectiveness, diminishing the real value of the resource transfers to recipients.

Institutional Constraints

A great pitfall of donor assistance, as pointed out in chapters 3, 4, and 6, has been the weakness of its underlying analytical foundations. First, as the cases of USAID and DANIDA illustrate, most bilateral donors do not have the in-house capacity to engage in comprehensive macroeconomic or sectoral analysis that could provide sound economic justification for undertaking agricultural investments. Even in the World Bank, strategic thinking on long-term agricultural development issues has been limited, and the internal capacity for such thinking is rapidly diminishing through the attrition of experienced staff.[30] Second, the experiences of these donors reveal that actual commitments depend on a staff incentive structure that largely responds to top-down initiatives to meet political objectives set in donor capitals, and on the procedural pressure to transfer resources—rather than on donors' country or sector analyses, or even the grass roots articulation of African needs.

Furthermore, as chapter 5 has emphasized, donors have not placed much emphasis on broader and longer-term evaluative work to guide them in their efforts to improve assistance strategies. Project evaluations and, more recently, structural adjustment evaluations are proliferating (indeed, donor assistance is considered to be one of the most intensively evaluated industries). But little systematic attempt is being made to assess donor assistance in a wider conceptual framework—from the viewpoint of long-term macroeconomic or sectoral strategies or the effect of domestic aid lobbies in donor countries, discussed below, on resource allocation. The effectiveness of donor assistance often has been considered simply in terms of its volume rather than its quality. Moreover, the DANIDA and World Bank experiences indicate a weak learning process among donors and governments alike from the reviews and assessments of project activities—which explains why they tend to perpetuate operations with high risks of failure.

Constituency Pressures

Constituencies have proven to be extremely useful allies in enabling donors to generate public support for preserving or increasing their development budgets, as in the case of Denmark (see chapter 4). But their powerful impact on aid philosophy and practice has also given rise to various operational problems adversely affecting effectiveness of assistance.

The strategic interests of the United States have played a critical role in determining the content and stability of its assistance to developing countries.[31] For example, the lack of a clear political constituency for long-term United States assistance to African countries has contributed to erratic funding and policy shifts (chapter 6).[32] However, even unstable assistance, if deployed effectively, can have substantial positive effects—as the cases of countries in Asia demonstrate.[33] For this to occur, however, the domestic capacity of recipients to plan and implement policy and investments needs to be strong.

The development assistance policies of Denmark, Sweden, and Germany, in contrast to that of the United States, have been founded on a wide mix of philanthropic and economic interests that have contributed to the diversification and fragmentation of aid portfolios (albeit relative stability in aid levels). Structural economic problems within Germany and Sweden—for example, unemployment in Germany and external deficits in Sweden—have, over the past decade, led to a strengthening of the commercial constituency over the philanthropic interests, with the result that assistance from these countries has become increasingly tied.

Arising from the domestic policies and surpluses of donors, food aid is a prime example of constituency pressure determining the type of assistance. Although relatively unimportant in Nigeria, Cameroon, and Malawi, food aid comprised 10 percent of net official development assistance (ODA) to Kenya, 5.5 percent to Senegal, and 3.3 percent to Tanzania during 1970–87. Although food aid is heavily criticized, it does not seem to have performed any worse than other forms of aid.

Overextension of Comparative Advantage

Donors should ideally fund those activities that reflect a strong correspondence between their own internal strengths and interests arising from their resource bases and the recipient's interests. Yet in practice this is far from simple because of the sheer range and magnitude of activities that recipients have been keen to undertake (regardless of absorptive capacity) and that donors have been eager to finance for fear of alienating constituencies that currently or potentially support assistance programs. The overextension of donor involvement beyond their comparative advantage as well as their planning and implementation capabilities has contributed to the marginalization of their portfolios and to the misallocation of assistance and of the associated recipient country capital.

A positive example of donors putting their comparative advantage to good use is provided by USAID assistance to the MADIA countries, where the United States has put considerable emphasis on establishing institutions of higher learning and training programs for nationals. These efforts have been shaped by the replication of the successful land-grant college model in promoting agricultural development in the United States itself and elsewhere—notably in Asia.[34] Similarly, British and French assistance to the MADIA countries, with the help of strong technical assistance support, extended the colonial programs of agricultural research, technical services, and export crop production into the postindependence era.

As is evident from the assessments in this volume, however, the United States and United Kingdom assistance programs have experienced shifts in emphasis away from their chief areas of expertise. Although the USAID program was restarted and enlarged in Senegal it was redirected toward extension activities following the Sahel drought. The USAID program in Cameroon experienced a similar shift—albeit to a lesser extent—toward diversifying into irrigation, input supply, and livestock, in addition to providing assistance for education and training. In Tanzania, the USAID mission rejected the government's request for support for advanced training in agriculture on the grounds that Washington preferred projects that "benefit the poor directly in the shortest time possible." Similarly, U.K. assistance shifted away from budgetary support to East Africa in the late 1960s—and away from sustaining long-standing research programs and institutions—toward shorter-term projects in support of direct poverty alleviation in the 1970s.[35] This change was associated with a gradual attrition of British expertise in tropical agriculture.

Swings in donor policy are of course grounded in complex factors—as illustrated by the shift away from export crop production and toward food security in marginal areas in the 1970s or the emphasis on adjustment following the macroeconomic difficulties in the 1980s. However, these shifts have degenerated into fads that have made particular activities—whether integrated, multisectoral projects in the 1970s, policy reform in the 1980s, or (most recently) proenvironmental "sustainable" development—fashionable among all donors without definition of "sustainability" in the differing circumstances of recipient countries and regardless of their implications in terms of the technological, administrative, planning, and implementing capacity of recipient countries. The problem has really been one of too much top-down leadership on these issues. Although this has galvanized the relevant constituencies around these worthy objectives, the responses of donor agencies have focused more on the form of assistance rather than on the substance of the problem. Incentives provided to the staffs of donor agencies have ensured that assistance targets are met no matter what the theme (or the "fad" it may have degenerated into). Thus, fads in development assistance programming, while originating in genuine developmental concerns, have led to wholesale shifts in donor concerns and policies, overshadowing the need for stable, long-term assistance strategies.

When donor assistance has not suited their own objectives, recipient governments have resisted donor preferences as to projects, programs, and policies—and have often reacted by adopting intransigent postures. Cases in which influential donors can affect the views of other donors are especially problematic. In those involving conditionality, for example, such a situation can seriously curtail donor commitments—as happened in Tanzania in the 1980s.[36] Donors, for their part, have quite justifiably perceived recipient policies as playing off one donor against another to secure the desired types of assistance.

The principal factor underlying such recipient-donor conflicts has been the weak capacity of African governments. Countries such as Kenya and Cameroon, with their relatively better economic management infrastructure, have resisted donor pressures more successfully than others—but their recalcitrance has won them some notoriety among donors. Senegal, on the other hand, has accepted conditions but has often been slow on implementation.

Tied Assistance and Its Effects

Regardless of its particular underlying motivations, tied assistance can have a substantial positive impact on development. Food aid, for example, is by definition tied aid, but examples abound of the United States' disposal of food surpluses that served important humanitarian and fiscal objectives in India and elsewhere in Asia. Such assistance at the same time allowed experts to focus on the development of agricultural science and technology—thus fueling the green revolution—instead of diverting recipient time and resources by causing a proliferation of projects or structural adjustment operations. Indeed, as mentioned before, similar tied food aid can contribute significantly to employment, income generation, and food security in the MADIA countries by financing labor-intensive construction of rural infrastructure.

Nevertheless, the tying of donor assistance can be one of the more pernicious forms of constituency pressure. Donors generally operate on the assumption that it is easier to maintain public and parliamentary support for development assistance programs either if assistance is provided as emergency relief or if immediate, tangible benefits can be shown to accrue to the donors' own production, exports, and employment. In the aggregate, the effects of these tying arrangements on the balance of trade of donor countries are generally minuscule in the short run, but, through the misallocation of capital, can have serious consequences for a recipient's long-run growth and, in turn, for the export prospects of donors. Yet the untying of assistance poses a real dilemma for donors in that losing the support of constituencies that benefit from tied bilateral assistance can seriously curtail the aid program.

The most direct and obvious mechanisms of tying are (1) by source, which requires the recipient to use assistance to purchase goods and services in the donor country; and (2) by end-use, which requires the assistance to be directed to a specified project or sector.[37] Tying overstates the real value of donor assistance when it decreases the ability of recipients to obtain the most economic and efficient forms of assistance—that is, when the equipment costs more than it might have cost if purchased from an alternate source, or when it leads to the use of technologically inappropriate equipment.

In this book, only chapters 4 and 5 have addressed the issue of tied aid—focusing mainly on the incidence of tying by source and the consequences of allowing the donor's resource base to determine the choice of technology. SIDA and DANIDA are by no means the only agencies engaging in this practice. Perhaps because the issue is politically sensitive, some of the other donor studies in this book have been less candid about it, although it is pointed out in chapter 6 that the problem of maintaining donor-made equipment can undermine project success.

Statistics of the OECD's Development Assistance Committee (DAC) show that, during the period 1973–87, fully and partly tied assistance accounted for 60–80 percent of total bilateral assistance from the United States and the United Kingdom and for some 60 percent of French assistance to developing countries. In the 1980s the tied component of total bilateral ODA decreased relative to the 1970s in the United States and, to a lesser extent, in the United Kingdom. Only 20–40 percent of the assistance provided by Denmark, Sweden, and Germany has been formally tied. Nevertheless, the return flow of orders for goods and services to industry in Denmark and Sweden is about twice as high. Although part of this can be attributed to the competitiveness of these countries' industries, a substantial flow appears to result from the informal tying of assistance. Thus in the case of DANIDA, for example, much of the hardware (not to mention the required technical personnel), even for untied (that is, project) aid, is procured in Denmark, and it has been difficult to get projects approved if such items are not produced at reasonable cost in the country. In line with the observation in chapter 5 that Sweden's traditional altruistic constituency has weakened in favor of commercial interests, DAC statistics show an increase in the proportion of tied assistance in bilateral Swedish ODA—from 17 percent in 1980 to 35 percent in 1987. Similarly, the desire to take into account the employment effects of development assistance in Germany in the 1980s has been instrumental in raising this share from 18 percent to 42 percent over the same period.

In general, tied assistance has negative consequences when it leads to financing projects that are not strategically appropriate to undertake at an early stage of development. In the smaller bilateral agencies—which have fewer but concentrated areas of expertise—it is perhaps less surprising that the donor's resource base (which may not necessarily coincide with the recipient's real needs) should become an important determinant of the technological content of tied foreign assistance. The experience of DANIDA and SIDA illustrates an all too frequent outcome in many donor projects—namely that inappropriate technological choices (such as, for example, diffusion-based sugar extraction, mechanical grain storage, and diesel-powered water supply installations) can undermine the success of the project.[38] Moreover, as pointed out in chapter 4,"the spoils of tying have in practice been limited to an elite group of no more than fifty large export-oriented Danish firms, dealing mostly in state-of-the-art technology."

A step toward untying donor assistance—although it applies solely to bilateral adjustment operations, not to project assistance or project-related technical assistance—was made in 1988 in the context of the Special Program of Assistance for nineteen low-income, debt-ridden countries in Africa (including Kenya, Malawi, Tanzania, and Senegal). The United States, France, Sweden, Norway, Germany, Japan, Finland, and Switzerland have agreed to untie 50–100 percent of their (bilateral) cofinancing and coordinated financing in support of World Bank (IDA) adjustment operations in these countries—making this assistance available for procurement on a worldwide basis. Since the success of these adjustment programs depends on a timely flow of disbursements to finance essential imports of raw materials, spare parts, and basic consumption goods, this provision is expected to reduce the procedural constraints of tied procurement that not only tax recipient capacity but also slow down the rate of disbursement.

Technical Assistance and Its Effects

In view of the need to develop human and institutional capital for sustained growth, expatriate technical assistance must be committed to improving local capacity through the support of institutions that can train the kinds of personnel needed in the recipient country. To determine what donors can do to help build such capacity it is necessary to look at both the quantity and quality of their technical assistance. If there is no process for transferring donor technical and managerial expertise to nationals, technical assistance simply means a corresponding reduction in the real financial resources accruing to recipients. This raises questions about the real value of the resources being transferred to Africa through external assistance—and the deceptiveness of numbers on aggregate assistance. Since most technical assistance takes the form of grants, it does not impose any apparent financial costs on the recipient, but its adverse effects nevertheless may be substantial.

The donor studies in this book indicate that technical assistance has constituted a substantial input of donor projects and programs in the MADIA countries. It is important to exercise caution, however, in interpreting the technical assistance figures here. Although some chapters have provided the share of technical assistance in the donors' agricultural assistance, others have only indicated its share in donors' total assistance to these countries.

Chapters 7 and 10 have indicated the share of technical assistance expenditures in donor assistance to agriculture in the MADIA countries. In the case of Germany, although technical "cooperation" expenditures during the period 1973–85 accounted for about 45 percent of total assistance to the six countries, they accounted for more than 85 percent of agricultural assistance. In the case of the EC, however, technical assistance accounted for only 10–15 percent of assistance for agriculture and rural development to Cameroon, Senegal, and Tanzania (although their share rose to 20 percent in the fifth European Development Fund—covering 1981–85).

The other donor studies have only indicated the share of technical assistance in total assistance to the MADIA countries. In the case of French assistance to Cameroon, expenditures on technical assistance as a percentage of total Ministry of Cooperation assistance rose more or less steadily from 33 percent in 1961 to 81 percent in 1985 (whereas total assistance actually declined in real terms); the share of technical assistance in total Ministry of Cooperation assistance to Senegal, on the other hand, has fluctuated between 46 percent and 76 percent during 1960–85 (while total assistance increased by barely a quarter in real terms). The United Kingdom's expenditures on technical assistance have accounted for up to 35 percent of total bilateral flows to Malawi, Tanzania, and Kenya. SIDA's and DANIDA's technical assistance represented some 20–30 percent of their total assistance to Kenya and Tanzania. Meanwhile, the World Bank's technical assistance has accounted for a very small share of its total assistance to the six MADIA countries—ranging, during the period 1965–88, from 0.3 percent of total assistance in the case of Malawi to 5 percent in Senegal—and most of it was provided in the 1980s. The differences between the World Bank and the French assistance show the extent to which financial transfers were emphasized by the Bank, other objectives by the French. According to DAC statistics, the share of technical assistance in United States assistance has ranged from 15 to 30 percent of total ODA disbursed by the United States to all developing countries.[39]

The effect of these large shares of technical assistance on the development of local human and institutional capital are difficult to estimate. Substantial qualitative scrutiny of technical assistance in the sample countries leads to the conclusion that, despite the scale of this external involvement, technical assistance has made little lasting impact either on agricultural performance or on the development of long-term local capabilities. The successful experiences with tea and coffee in Kenya and with cotton in Francophone West Africa clearly reveal that it is the quality rather than the volume of technical assistance that determines its effectiveness.

Particularly critical among the quality considerations are (1) the duration of technical assistance programs and the real and relevant expertise that so-called technical experts bring to bear; and (2) the effectiveness of such programs in developing long-term human and institutional capabilities through training and in generating local confidence rather than creating a sense of psychological dependency on outsiders.

As argued earlier, the experience of the former colonial donors illustrates that donor efforts cannot succeed unless they help build up a long-term presence as well as expertise in particular areas that can only be supplied by personnel based in Africa who are knowledgeable about local circumstances. As the example of cotton development by the Compagnie Française de Développement des Fibres Textiles (CFDT) shows, high-quality technical assistance that leads to substantial positive externalities over time may be desirable even if it entails relatively high costs.[40] But in view of the decline in Senegal's per capita GNP during 1960–87, the presence of very large numbers of French technical assistance personnel suggests that this large French investment has had little developmental impact on Senegal.

Over time, however, a large attrition of high-quality donor expertise has occurred, not only in the staffing of donor agencies but also in their field-based personnel—as shown in the substantial reduction of U.K. contributions to research programs in East Africa. Between the 1970s and the 1980s, the number of British personnel in the field fell sharply. This decrease may imply increased local technical capabilities in Africa. It may also signal a decline in the familiarity of bilateral donors with African issues, as well as greater reliance on shorter-term consultants, whose field experience is limited to a few visits.[41] The contractual nature of these newer forms of technical assistance has not been conducive to the creation of a cadre of high-quality field staff willing and able to help with long-term development at the project, subsectoral, sectoral, or macroeconomic level.

The training and development of local scientific and technical personnel depends on the quality of the relations between donor and recipient personnel—in addition to the long-term association of the former with local circumstances. The extended involvement of the colonial donors has contributed to the development of smallholder agriculture, but it has not been effective in creating sustainable human capacity. Deficient training and institutional development inhibited the consolidation of research gains after the reduction of U.K. commitments in East Africa. The newer technical assistance programs, while not contributing much to the growth of smallholder productivity, have had even less influence on the creation of long-term capacity (unlike, for example, the earlier experience with the Kenya Tea Development Authority). The experiences of the German Agricultural Team in Kenya, the World Bank's ADPs in Nigeria, or SIDA's technical assistance to the ministries of water in Tanzania and Kenya all indicate that the training components of projects have been consistently overshadowed by more pressing, shorter-term objectives—such as procedural pressures to transfer resources and demonstrate physical results. Considering the large proportions of donor assistance going to the MADIA countries in the form of technical assistance, it is disturbing that its contribution to the long-term accumulation of human and institutional capital and thus to the growth process has been so limited.

The implications of these large shares of technical assistance are even more serious in the light of the relative importance of the different donors in the respective recipient countries. Multilateral institutions such as the World Bank, which rely little on technical assistance, have played a smaller role than the bilateral agencies in official capital flows to the MADIA countries. Thus the World Bank, although it has been among the top three donors in Malawi, Kenya, and Tanzania, has accounted for a large share (22 percent of total ODA receipts during 1970–84) only in Malawi. It has had a 10 percent share in Kenya, Tanzania, and Cameroon. There has been an important role for the EC mainly in Senegal (17 percent) and to a lesser extent in Cameroon

(11 percent). In contrast, among bilateral donors that have provided large amounts of technical assistance, France—the leading donor in Senegal and Cameroon—has accounted for a third of all ODA receipts in both countries. Similarly, the United Kingdom has had a 28 percent share in Malawi and a 15 percent share in Kenya. Although the multilateral component of U.K. assistance has continuously increased as a share of total assistance—reaching 42 percent of the total program by 1987—it is less clear how much the share of French and German bilateral assistance in the 1980s has been reduced. Thus the relative ineffectiveness of large technical assistance components is likely to persist to the extent that the trend toward multilateralization of donor assistance still constitutes a small amount of the total assistance to African countries. Yet the growing trend at the same time poses a dilemma for donors as concern intensifies about what are perceived to be incursions of multilateral institutions into the sovereignty of African countries.

Awareness of these issues among bilateral agencies is gradually leading them to put more emphasis on training and capacity building. If these are not to become another set of clichés to be replaced by still others, African governments and elites need to focus on effectively articulating their demands.

The Problem of Financing Recurrent Costs

Donor policy on the financing of recurrent costs has not been explicitly treated in this book. Donors have shied away from providing recurrent resources mainly because these entail, in principle, a never-ending commitment likely to create adverse dependency effects for the recipient. However, the importance of fully ascertaining the implications of recurrent costs at the project preparation stage is now generally recognized. Financial participation for longer periods of time and sustainability—with its implications for sectoral concentration and long-term commitment—are being gradually internalized in aid programming.[42]

Although the recurrent costs of agricultural and rural development activities vary greatly, on the whole they are high. Smallholder agriculture in particular puts a constant drain on recurrent funds, which are needed to maintain a supportive physical and service infrastructure.

Tanzania, Nigeria, and Senegal have suffered from large budget deficits in comparison with Cameroon, Malawi, and Kenya, but since 1985–87 the situation has worsened even in Malawi and Kenya. The experience of the MADIA countries in general illustrates that their governments have tended to plan larger investment portfolios than their resources permit. Moreover, both governments and donors placed too much emphasis on physical structures and on protecting their pet projects from the budgets of finance ministries—but too little on providing for their operation and maintenance.

In general, there are three main reasons for the shortage of recurrent finance in developing countries.[43] First, donors and recipients alike have tended to equate development expenditure with investment, and the overarching need to generate funds for this purpose has put arbitrary ceilings on the recurrent budget. Second, the recurrent expenditure requirements depend on the sectoral mix of development projects; thus development programs placing heavy emphasis on projects in health, education, and agriculture will require higher recurrent outlays per unit of investment than investments in physical infrastructure such as roads and dams. Third, excessive expenditures on high-profile nondevelopmental activities such as defense and public administration (for example, in Tanzania and Senegal) compete with the recurrent expenditure needs of development projects and programs and add to the political difficulties of allocating resources.

The investment bias of public expenditures—and of the large inflows of donor assistance supporting them in countries such as Kenya and Tanzania—accelerated the rate of growth of the aid-financed capital stock (and of the funds needed to keep it operational) well beyond the government's revenue-earning capabilities (chapters 3 and 5). Experience with SIDA's water supply and health programs in Tanzania and Kenya, and with the World Bank's feeder road development (via agricultural development projects) in Nigeria, shows that donor programs, while contributing significantly to the formation of physical capital in Africa, have been beset by shortages of recurrent resources that have led to low rates of utilization and, in many instances, to the decay of the accumulated stock.

In the early 1970s, the mix of investments in the MADIA countries shifted from a heavy emphasis on the development of physical infrastructure toward a variety of agricultural and rural development projects promoting food production and welfare services in poorer areas—that is, toward activities requiring larger recurrent cost commitments. The sharp increase in donor commitments to agriculture and the diversification of donor activities led to a multiplicity of projects that were poorly integrated into the overall budget process. The recurrent costs of a wide array of separately devised projects proved unsustainable because of the overall resource constraint, and all too often it led to low, nil, or negative returns. For example, projects cofinanced by the World Bank and other donors—all of which generated low economic returns—in just four subsectors accounted for at least half of the entire development expenditure budget of the Kenyan Ministry of Agriculture during 1977–82. The World Bank's IRDPs in Kigoma,

Tabora, and Mwanza/Shinyanga in Tanzania; the Agricultural Research Project in Senegal; and the large irrigation schemes by the EC in Cameroon and Senegal—all exemplify the problem of recurrent expenditures in poorly conceived agricultural and rural development investments. One consequence of the growth of these investments has been an excessive increase in wage and salary costs and few resources available for maintenance and operations. Such projects fail to consider whether the aggregate investment programs are feasible, and—for lack of effective sequencing and phasing—overextend available resources, do not generate adequate returns, and thus remain dependent on government or donor support. These experiences underscore the importance of conceiving rural development projects in the framework of an appropriately managed and funded long-term development strategy.

Within agriculture, the shift away from export crops toward food crops also has had important negative budgetary implications. Export crop production generally brought in higher economic rates of return and contributed substantially to fiscal revenues. In contrast, food crop production demanded more recurrent resources, particularly in the form of extension services, and, together with price stabilization, usually has been subsidized by governments. In Malawi, for example, the Agricultural Development and Marketing Corporation cross-subsidized the production of maize from tobacco revenues. Moreover, grain marketing parastatals have run up huge losses. The accumulated overdrafts of the National Milling Corporation of Tanzania, for example, had risen to T Sh 2.8 billion (about $250 million) by 1983. In the case of Kenya, a recent EC-funded study of the National Cereals and Produce Board estimated the accumulated losses at nearly K Sh 5 billion (about $300 million).[44] These losses compare with total central government expenditures on agriculture of T Sh 545.1 million in Tanzania in 1983 and K Sh 131 million in Kenya in 1986. This should not be interpreted to mean that food subsidies are either unnecessary or undesirable, but that growth in exports and in government revenues is essential to pay for them. Nor does this imply that projects for increasing food crop production should not be undertaken—rather, they must be conceived as part of a balanced, long-term strategy.

Lessons from Donors' Experience

This book has not dealt with every kind of external assistance accruing to agriculture and rural development programs in the MADIA countries. By definition, a study of official development assistance will ignore the increasingly vital role played by voluntary agencies in the development process.[45] Admittedly, this is a serious omission in view of the number of such organizations involved in African countries, the attendant problem of coordination, and, most important, the concerns expressed in this book about the tendency of governments to centralize power and discourage the development of genuine grass roots institutions. Nevertheless, in view of the large amounts of donor assistance going to most MADIA countries, it is clear that the lessons drawn here are both valid and useful.

In general, donor involvement in the MADIA countries has been wide and varied and has laid some important foundations of physical and social capital—which are necessary, if not sufficient, conditions for long-term growth. Although these capital stocks have grown steadily since independence, the contribution of donors to the development of human and institutional capacity to effectively manage these resources for the purposes of broadly based, sustainable growth has been far from satisfactory—a deficiency that has in many cases led to decay of the physical stock.

Several broad lessons for MADIA donors and governments emerge from this study:

- A flexible, balanced, long-term agricultural strategy, set in a favorable macroeconomic and sectoral policy framework that is feasible on a day-to-day basis, is essential for broadly based growth. The MADIA study findings in this connection are instructive. The countries whose agricultural sectors have grown the fastest have also been the best performers when it comes to GDP growth. Moreover, their macroeconomic and sectoral policies in general have been more important than their endowments—or the impact of exogenous shocks—in explaining their performance. In Kenya and Cameroon, where a relatively sound macroeconomic and sectoral policy framework was in place, the performance of agriculture and the overall economy was characterized by growth with equity. In Malawi, where macroeconomic policies were sound but sectoral policies weak, the benefits of the growth achieved went largely to the estates. In Tanzania, Nigeria, and Senegal, where policies were adverse at both the macroeconomic and sectoral levels, there was little growth.
- Building human and institutional capacity is crucial for planning and implementing strategies for long-term growth and for maintaining a supportive policy environment. The World Bank's shift toward a consensus approach and a long-term commitment by both national governments and donors to capacity building is a step in the right direction. If such efforts are to be successful, African governments should develop and use their own personnel and institutions; donors must assist in enhancing African capabilities for sound macroeconomic and sectoral policy research and analysis in support of

the effective articulation of African development goals and needs; centers of excellence on African issues should be established in both donor and African countries; donors must provide high-quality technical expertise that explicitly ensures the gradual transfer of technical and managerial skills to African nationals on a long-term basis; and donors should help African governments set up viable national systems for collecting and analyzing data over the long term. African governments, in turn, must improve the flow of this information to both African and donor nationals in order to generate public debate on the causes and consequences of government and donor actions.

• A strategy for long-term growth must ensure that a balance is struck between the production of export crops and food crops. The pessimism that led African countries to shift out of export crop production continues, on account of the concern about how to dispose of surplus commodities, the serious deterioration in productive capacity for all important export crops (for example, tea, coffee, and cocoa, as well as cotton, groundnuts, and palm oil) in many African countries, and the resulting inability to compete in world markets. Donors must help African countries revive the production of traditional export and food crops in which they still have a clear comparative advantage.

• Raising factor productivity is essential, in view of rapidly increasing population pressure, the deterioration of the natural resource base, and low rates of agricultural intensification. Although expenditures on agricultural research have increased significantly, much more effort needs to be put into the *substance* of research. More research is needed on export crops as a complement to, for instance, the currently exclusive focus on food crops of the Consultative Group on International Agricultural Research. Moreover, research and extension efforts need to be broadened beyond plant breeding to soil management techniques that (as SIDA and DANIDA projects in this area demonstrate) could help farmers conserve and enhance soil potential and integrate cropping with livestock and forestry.

• Programs for increasing agricultural production should focus on areas of high potential. Policies to address the employment and consumption needs of populations in remote and resource-poor regions must be conceived in the context of a long-term overall development strategy.

• Donors should address microeconomic constraints in conjunction with macroeconomic structural reform and privatization. A positive effect of the crisis in Africa has been to force African governments to closely examine domestic policy failures and to bring issues such as privatization—that were overlooked in the 1970s—out into the open. It is clear, however, that the adjustment approach of the 1980s, which relied mainly on policy reform, cannot alone put African agriculture back on a growth path.

If reform and investment packages are to have sustainable positive effects, they must be tailored to the diverse circumstances, specific endowments, and long-term development needs of each country. More attention must be given to easing microlevel constraints—such as weak research, transport, credit, marketing, and information networks—that persist even while structural adjustment programs are being completed. Traditional crops will be difficult to revive in Africa unless such nonprice constraints are alleviated at the same time that price incentives are being restructured. In many cases, this requires public sector efforts to complement privatization by providing a regulatory but sustaining environment. An active role for the public sector must not, however, be allowed to deter or suppress the political representation of private producer interests. It will also be necessary to reinstate assistance at the subsector and project level as a development catalyst and guarantor of macropolicy reform within a framework of appropriately funded and targeted macroeconomic and sectoral policies.

- Donors should establish and emphasize their own comparative advantage in developing assistance strategies. The broader donor record in the MADIA countries suggests that, for a number of reasons, including the nature of their own resource bases and constituencies, donors possess distinctive strengths and weaknesses that directly affect the effectiveness of their assistance. Donors need to carefully select the particular area or areas in which they can provide consistent, high-quality expertise to African countries.

The multilateral agencies may have a comparative advantage in assisting recipients with economic and policy research and analysis for developing tailor-made, country-specific strategies in addition to large financial transfers for ensuring macroeconomic and sectoral policy reforms. In contrast, smaller, bilateral agencies are likely to be better at promoting the development of local human and institutional capacity, which requires fewer financial resources but much more intensive nurturing over a long period. Building on its earlier experience in establishing agricultural universities in Asia and Africa with the help of various United States land-grant universities, USAID is particularly well placed to encourage long-term twinning arrangements between African and home-based institutions. Similarly, the United Kingdom and France, given their long experience with tropical agriculture in Africa, need to develop mechanisms to ensure that the critical expertise and knowledge base developed over time is transferred to African nationals before it erodes any further. Bilateral donors also possess important specialized expertise in certain areas that have been successfully developed in their own economies. Two such examples are DANIDA's expertise in livestock and SIDA's in forestry and soil conservation. Yet experience with these activities in Tanzania demonstrates that a supportive macroeconomic and sectoral policy environment must also exist and that donors must be sufficiently familiar with local conditions.

In general, donors need to coordinate their assistance around the substance of long-term strategies. But they must also concentrate their resources in their areas of expertise rather than attempt to undertake tasks for which they are not well equipped. Thus donors need not all be involved in the currently fashionable trend of giving assistance for securing structural adjustment. They must, however, ensure that their assistance programs in individual countries successfully combine a long-term development strategy with the more pragmatic considerations of day-to-day economic management.

Notes

1. The agricultural performance and policies in the six countries—outlined in the introduction—provide the context for objectively assessing the evidence contained in the donor studies.

2. Robert Cassen recognizes this to be more generally true for Africa relative to the more positive experience with donor assistance in Asia. See Robert Cassen and Associates, *Does Aid Work? Report to an Intergovernmental Task Force* (Oxford: Clarendon, 1986). In a more longitudinal study of donor assistance and development involving the experience of countries in Latin America as well as Asia, Lele and Nabi arrive at similar conclusions. See Uma Lele and Ijaz Nabi, eds., *Transitions in Development: The Role of Aid and Commercial Flows* (San Francisco: Institute for Contemporary Studies, 1990). See also World Bank, *Rural Development: World Bank Experience, 1965–1986* (Washington, D.C., 1988).

3. See Christine Jones, "A Review of World Bank Agricultural Assistance to Six African Countries," MADIA Working Paper (Africa—Technical Department, Agricultural Division, World Bank, Washington, D.C., 1985).

4. Kenya, Malawi, and Senegal, for example, have better information bases than Tanzania, Cameroon, or Nigeria. Yet even in periods of military dictatorships, Nigeria has perhaps had the most open debate on public policy and its consequences of any of the MADIA countries to date.

5. The differences in time periods reflect the differences in data availability between the aid studies.

6. Uma Lele and Juan Gaviria have elsewhere documented the contribution of these to linking production with markets in some cases—as in Nigeria, linking the north with the south. See Juan Gaviria, Vishva Bindlish, and Uma Lele, *The Rural Road Question and Nigeria's Agricultural Development*, MADIA Discussion Paper 10 (Washington, D.C.: World Bank, 1989).

7. See Paul Collier, "Aid and Economic Performance in Tanzania," in Uma Lele and Ijaz Nabi, eds., *Transitions in Development*.

8. As Paul Collier has discussed, the Basic Industries Strategy preempted public resources, was foreign exchange intensive, and allocated resources to investments that generated little output.

9. See Uma Lele, "Sources of Growth in East African Agriculture," *World Bank Economic Review* 3(January 1989):119–44.

10. The costs of procuring, transporting, and marketing smallholder output and of providing services and inputs for smallholders can be greater than those for large farmers (as the experience with tea and coffee in Kenya demonstrates). There has been a poor understanding of the impact of these factors on increasing public expenditure commitments to smallholder agriculture in the absence of commensurate growth in factor productivity. See Uma Lele and Manmohan Agarwal, *Smallholder and Large-Scale Agriculture in Africa: Are There Trade-Offs in Growth and Equity?* MADIA Discussion Paper 6 (Washington, D.C.: World Bank, 1989).

11. For a discussion of the role of the United States in India, see Uma Lele and Arthur Goldsmith, "The Development of National Agricultural Research Capacity: India's Experience with the Rockefeller Foundation and Its Significance for Africa," *Economic Development and Cultural Change* 37(January 1989).

12. It should be noted, however, that the USAID study includes various sizable investments in transport infrastructure (such as the Trans-Cameroon Railway and Tanzam Highway) under this rubric. If the category "rural infrastructure" is excluded from aid to "agriculture and rural development," then the share of the latter in total USAID aid to the MADIA countries falls to about 47 percent, which is still high in comparison with the other donors.

13. See Lele and Nabi, eds., *Transitions in Development*. See also Lele and Goldsmith, "The Development of National Agricultural Research Capacity."

14. The Kenyan government, in turn, has not used the substantial numbers of trained Kenyan personnel that are now available. See Uma Lele and L. Richard Meyers, "Kenya's Agricultural Development and the World Bank's Role in It" (Africa—Technical Department, Agriculture Division, World Bank, Washington, D.C.).

15. See Uma Lele and Steven Stone, *Population Pressure, the Environment, and Agricultural Intensification: Variations on the Boserup Hypothesis*, MADIA Discussion Paper 4 (Washington, D.C.: World Bank, 1989); and Uma Lele, Robert Christiansen, and Kundhavi Kadiresan, *Issues in Fertilizer Policy in Africa: Lessons from Development Programs and Adjustment Lending, 1970–87*, MADIA Discussion Paper 5 (Washington, D.C.: World Bank, 1989).

16. See Organization of African Unity, *Lagos Plan of Action for the Economic Development of Africa, 1980–2000* (Geneva: International Institute for Labor Studies, 1981).

17. See Uma Lele, Mathurin Gbetibouo, and Paul Fishstein, "Planning for Food Security in Africa: Lessons and Policy Implications, 1960–88," MADIA Discussion Paper 13 (Washington, D.C.: World Bank, in preparation).

18. As pointed out in chapter 6, for a donor trying to grapple with periodic problems of surplus production at home, the development of agricultural colleges in Africa was less controversial than directly productive research. Since the effects of the former on agricultural production would only be felt after long lags, it would be less threatening to United States interest groups.

19. See Lele and Meyers, "Kenya's Agricultural Development"; and Lele and Agarwal, *Smallholder and Large-Scale Agriculture*.

20. See J. C. de Wilde, *Experiences with Agricultural Development in Tropical Africa* (Baltimore, Md.: Johns Hopkins University Press, 1967); and Uma Lele, *The Design of Rural Development: Lessons from Africa* (Baltimore, Md.: Johns Hopkins University Press, 1975).

21. An important exogenous factor underlying agricultural stagnation in Senegal has been the declining and variable rainfall.

22. See Uma Lele, Nicolas van de Walle, and Mathurin Gbetibouo, *Cotton in Africa: An Analysis of Differences in Performance*, MADIA Discussion Paper 7 (Washington, D.C.: World Bank, 1989).

23. See Lele and Stone, *Population Pressure, the Environment, and Agricultural Intensification*.

24. As pointed out by virtually all the authors in this volume, the adverse policy environment in Tanzania in the 1970s was a principal cause of the poor performance of donor projects.

25. Seventy-five percent of the World Bank's rural development projects in East Africa implemented over 1974–79 failed (the corresponding figure for West Africa was 40 percent). These were mostly integrated projects focused on poorer areas and populations, and on average generated a weighted rate of return of less than 2 percent. See World Bank, *Rural Development*.

26. See Uma Lele, *Structural Adjustment, Agricultural Development, and the Poor: Lessons from the Malawian Experience*, MADIA Discussion Paper 9 (Washington, D.C.: World Bank, 1989).

27. Ibid.

28. Marketing parastatals, for example, have been one of the most important forms of public intervention in both East and West Africa. They have been the means for distributing scarce resources and services such as agricultural credit, fertilizers, consumer goods, food aid, food supplies, and employment patronage. See Uma Lele and Robert Christiansen, *Markets, Marketing Boards, and Cooperatives: Issues in Adjustment Policy*, MADIA Discussion Paper 11 (Washington, D.C.: World Bank, 1989).

29. See Uma Lele, Robert Christiansen, and Kundhavi Kadiresan, *Issues in Fertilizer Policy in Africa: Lessons from Development Programs and Adjustment Lending, 1970–87*, MADIA Discussion Paper 5 (Washington, D.C.: World Bank, 1989).

30. See Uma Lele and L. Richard Meyers, *Growth and Structural Change in East Africa: Domestic Policies, Agricultural Policies, and World Bank Assistance, 1963–86*, MADIA Discussion Paper 3 (Washington, D.C.: World Bank, 1989). See also Uma Lele, A. T. Oyejide, Balu Bumb, and Vishva Bindlish, "Nigeria's Economic Development, Agriculture's Role, and World Bank Assistance: Lessons for the Future" MADIA Working Paper (Africa—Technical Department, Agriculture Division, World Bank, Washington, D.C.).

31. See Committee on Foreign Affairs, *Background Materials on Foreign Assistance: Report of the Task Force on Foreign Assistance to the Committee on Foreign Affairs* (Washington, D.C.: U.S. Government Printing Office, February 1989).

32. See Lele and Nabi, *Transitions in Development*. The country case studies of Egypt and Pakistan, for example, document how United States assistance, more than that of other donors, has been determined by the superpower status of the United States and bilateral political considerations in Asia and Latin America. John Mellor and William Masters further discuss the instability of USAID's assistance in their paper, "The Changing Roles of Multilateral and Bilaterial Foreign Assistance" in Lele and Nabi, *Transitions in Development*.

33. See Uma Lele and Manmohan Agarwal, "Four Decades of Economic Development in India and the Role of External Assistance," in Lele and Nabi, *Transitions in Development*.

34. See Lele and Goldsmith, "The Development of National Agricultural Research Capacity."

35. By contrast, the discussion of Senegal in chapter 8 makes clear that French assistance has continued to be more intimately linked to the entire gamut of agricultural and rural development policies and institutions in its former colonies (despite a declining share in their total aid receipts as well as their trade) and that its impact has been pervasive and longer-lasting. French training of African nationals, however, has been inadequate and not commensurate with the high levels of technical personnel supplied.

36. Some have argued that a shock treatment was necessary to get the government to focus on the need to adjust. It was equally necessary, however, to get the donors to focus on Tanzania's weaknesses, which they had continued to overlook.

37. See Jagdish Bhagwati, "The Tying of Aid," and Hans W. Singer, "External Aid: For Plans or Projects?" in Jagdish Bhagwati and Richard Eckaus, eds., *Foreign Aid* (Harmondsworth, Middlesex, England: Penguin Books, 1970).

38. Even without tying, donor assistance sometimes provides levels of technology inappropriate for recipient country circumstances. This was the case in the World Bank's (cofinanced) large Bura irrigation project in Kenya, agroprocessing projects in Tanzania, and feeder roads in Nigeria.

39. In general, DAC statistics on technical assistance support the data provided in the other aid studies as well—over 1970–86, for example, the share of technical assistance has ranged from 45 to 50 percent of total French ODA, from 40 to 50 percent of total German ODA, and from 30 to 50 percent of total UKODA. In the case of Denmark, DAC statistics indicate a somewhat higher share—from 30 to 55 percent—than that suggested in chapter 4.

40. See Lele and others, *Cotton in Africa*.

41. Although the French have been involved in West African agriculture considerably longer, chapter 8 indicates a similar fall in the number of French technical personnel in Senegal. His study, however, refers to total technical assistance personnel, that is, in all sectors (including teachers) and not just agriculture.

42. In chapter 10, for example, it is argued that Germany has recognized the necessity of assisting the Malawian government in financing the recurrent costs arising from sectoral adjustment and project aid. On the other hand, DANIDA's assumption of the recurrent costs of its health and education programs in Tanzania during the recent economic crisis highlights the need for the long-term nurturing of sectors in which benefits accrue only after substantial lags.

43. See Peter Heller and Joan Aghevli, "The Recurrent Cost Problem: An International Overview," in John Howell, ed., *Recurrent Costs and Agricultural Development* (London: Overseas Development Institute, 1985).

44. See Lele, "Sources of Growth in East African Agriculture."

45. Kennes has briefly discussed the emerging role of nongovernmental organizations in EC development cooperation and the usefulness of small projects based on direct local participation.

Index